# Mad as Hell

# *Mad as Hell*

## The Crisis of the 1970s and the Rise of the Populist Right

# Dominic Sandbrook

ALFRED A. KNOPF  NEW YORK  2011

This Is a Borzoi Book
Published by Alfred A. Knopf

Copyright © 2011 by Dominic Sandbrook

All rights reserved. Published in the United States by Alfred A. Knopf,
a division of Random House, Inc., New York, and in Canada by
Random House of Canada Limited, Toronto.
www.aaknopf.com

Knopf, Borzoi Books, and the colophon are registered trademarks of
Random House, Inc.

Library of Congress Cataloging-in-Publication Data
Sandbrook, Dominic.
Mad as hell : the crisis of the 1970s and the rise of the populist Right /
by Dominic Sandbrook
p.   cm.
"This is a Borzoi book" — T.p. verso.
Includes bibliographical references.
ISBN 978-1-4000-4262-3
1.  United States — Politics and government — 1974–1977.
2.  United States — Politics and government — 1977–1981.
3.  Populism — United States — History — 20th century.
4.  Conservatism — United States — History — 20th century.
5.  Politicians — United States — History — 20th century.
6.  Political culture — United States — History — 20th century.
7.  Social change — United States — History — 20th century.
8.  United States — Social conditions — 1960–1980.   I.  Title.
E865.S26.2010
973.92 — dc22      2010037726

Jacket art: Associated Press
Jacket design by Barbara de Wilde

Manufactured in the United States of America
First Edition

For Catherine,
grá mo chroí

# Contents

# *Preface*

> I have to make my witness.
>
> —**HOWARD BEALE,** in *Network* (1976)

It is evening in New York City. Lightning flashes overhead, and rain thunders down onto the shabby streets. Far above the crowds, in the tense quiet of a network news studio, a man is staring into a camera. Beneath his shabby beige raincoat, you can just make out the collar of his pajamas. His eyes are blazing, his face is haggard, his gray hair is plastered to his brow. "I don't have to tell you things are bad," he says. "Everybody knows things are bad. It's a depression. Everybody's out of work or scared of losing their job. The dollar buys a nickel's worth, banks are going bust, shopkeepers keep a gun under the counter. Punks are running wild in the street and there's nobody anywhere who seems to know what to do, and there's no end to it."

In the control room, the producers are looking nervously at one another; in the studio, the man is still talking. The air is unfit to breathe, he says; the food is unfit to eat; on television, they tell you that fifteen people were murdered today, "as if that's the way it's supposed to be." So, he says, you don't go out anymore. You stay at home with your toaster and your TV, and you ask only to be left alone. "Well, I'm not going to leave you alone," he says, raising his voice, his eyes searing now. "I want you to get mad."

> I don't want you to protest. I don't want you to riot. I don't want you to write to your congressman, because I wouldn't know what to tell you

to write. I don't know what to do about the depression and the inflation and the Russians and the crime in the street. All I know is that first
you've got to get mad. You've got to say, *"I'm a human being, goddam-
nit! My life has value!"* So I want you to get up now. I want all of you to
get up out of your chairs. I want you to get up right now and go to the
window, open it, and stick your head out, and yell: *"I'm as mad as hell,
and I'm not going to take this anymore!"*

He *is* mad, of course: not in the sense of being angry, but in the sense
of being demented, deranged, mentally disintegrated. But people are listening. In the studio, word comes that people are yelling in Atlanta, then
that "they're yelling in Baton Rouge." In his New York apartment, the
president of the news division, an old friend, is watching the anchorman's
tirade in speechless horror. But his daughter goes to the window and
sticks her head out into the darkness and the pouring rain. And she hears
first one voice, then another, raised in a swelling public chorus: "I'm mad
as hell, and I'm not going to take it anymore!" "I'm mad as hell, and I'm
not going to take it anymore!" *"I'm mad as hell, and I'm not going to take
it anymore!"*

**Howard Beale never existed;** he was merely a character in the satire *Network*, one of the hit films of 1976. But he might as well have done, for
many Americans *were* mad as hell in the 1970s, and every now and again,
from quiet residential streets and spanking-new shopping malls, there
were reports of people shouting, "I'm mad as hell, and I'm not going to
take it anymore!" On college campuses, visitors sometimes saw leaflets
being handed around: "IMAHAINGTTIAM Midnight." And then, at the
appointed hour, they would hear the clatter of windows being opened,
and hundreds of youngsters would stick their heads out into the night and
scream at the tops of their voices: "I'm mad as hell, and I'm not going to
take it anymore!"[1]

This book tells the story of why Americans became so mad, and why
it mattered. It is the story of an extraordinary time in the nation's history,
a period of economic depression, political corruption, military defeat,
and cultural introspection, but also one of unexpected popular protest
and artistic vitality. It is the story of Richard Nixon, Gerald Ford, Jimmy
Carter, and Ronald Reagan, of stagflation, gas lines, and conspiracy theories. It is the story of the fall of Saigon, the collapse of détente, and the
revolution in Iran; of the Sunbelt, the Me Decade, and the Third Great
Awakening; of Archie Bunker, Farrah Fawcett, and Bruce Springsteen; of

Milton Friedman, Roger Staubach, and Phyllis Schlafly; of *Roots, Hotel California,* and *The Deer Hunter.*

At the time, many Americans did not know what to make of the 1970s. For one influential columnist, Joseph Alsop, they were "the very worst years since the history of life began on earth"; for another, Russell Baker, they were simply tiresome, their legacy "an engulfing swamp of boredom." It was a decade that remained "elusive, unfocused, a patchwork of dramatics awaiting a drama," wrote *Time*'s essayist Frank Trippett in December 1978. In the end, he decided that the 1970s would be remembered as "a confused time, neither here nor there, neither the best nor worst of times, as free of a predominant theme as of a singular direction."[2]

**Parceling up history** into ten-year chunks is merely a journalistic trick borrowed from the calendar, and it often obscures as much as it illuminates the past. There was more continuity between the 1960s and the 1970s, or the 1970s and the 1980s, than we often remember. The great historical trends, from the rise of the suburbs and the Sunbelt to the decline of racism and the changing role of women, did not stop and start with the changing of the seasons. When conservatives rail against the legacy of the 1960s, complaining about the collapse of discipline and the family, the rise of crime, and the spread of pornography, they are often talking about things that peaked in the 1970s. And the continuities run even deeper than that, for, as this book shows, many things that we imagine started in the 1970s—women's liberation, the New Right, the "culture wars"—actually had their roots in earlier decades. Every generation likes to think itself unique; in fact, the arguments people were having during the presidency of Jimmy Carter were often strikingly similar to those people had when Calvin Coolidge was in the White House.

And yet there was a palpable difference between 1976 and 1966, a difference that explains why so many ordinary Americans empathized with Howard Beale when he yelled that he was mad as hell. There was an indefinable change of flavor, of atmosphere, which meant that life often felt tougher, grittier, more heavily weighed down by gloom and disappointment. Once Americans had talked of possibilities; now they talked of limits. Once they had talked of growth and prosperity; now they talked of inflation and unemployment. Once they had marched and campaigned, confident that moral fervor could move mountains; now the civil rights movement seemed fragmented, the peace movement had faded away, and even university campuses had fallen silent. By the end of Richard Nixon's first term, the passions of the 1960s seemed to have given way to the cold, hard realities of retreat abroad and retrenchment at home.

Even the president himself seemed unable to escape the shadow of the past. The Watergate scandal exploded into the headlines just as American involvement in Vietnam was ending, but its origins stretched back to 1960, when Nixon felt that the eastern establishment had robbed him of the presidency. The transcripts of his conversations show that he was obsessed with the events of the previous two decades, from the Alger Hiss case to the Cuban missile crisis. Nixon told the nation to move on from the 1960s, but he never did so himself. It was as though his psychological clock had stopped in 1968.

This book begins where the story of Watergate ends, with the resignation of a president whose career encapsulated the political passions of the 1950s and 1960s. In August 1974, when Nixon finally disappeared into internal exile, the nation was still struggling to come to terms with the effects of the global oil shock the previous October. More than any other event, in fact, it was this moment that marked the end of optimism and the onset of gloom, the point when Americans, whatever they thought of Vietnam or abortion or women's liberation, really started to get mad. For it was then that ordinary Americans, staring in horror at the price of gasoline in their local service stations, or reading headlines that warned of shortages and rationing, realized that they were living in the "age of limits." Indeed, the idea of limits, which reached its apotheosis in Jimmy Carter's notorious crisis-of-confidence speech, is one of the central themes of this book. One of the things that made the 1970s different from both the 1960s and the 1980s was that for the first time in more than a generation, ordinary Americans genuinely doubted that tomorrow would be better than today. They were not used to feeling so pessimistic—which is one reason why people who lived through the 1970s often shudder to recall them.

In their shock and disappointment at the apparent overthrow of their ambitions, many Americans turned inward, to introspection and self-doubt. Although Tom Wolfe's famous line about the 1970s being the "Me Decade" has become a cliché, it does have the ring of truth. To be sure, plenty of people still marched for causes much bigger than themselves, from the ERA to the Moral Majority. But when Carter talked of a "growing doubt about the meaning of our own lives and in the loss of a unity of purpose for our nation," he was expressing anxieties that dominated much of the popular culture of the time, from the music of Bruce Springsteen to the films of Martin Scorsese.

This was a world in which traditional narratives were undermined by feminism, multiculturalism, and postmodernism, in which cherished notions of American virtue were challenged by Vietnam and Watergate, in which the boundless possibilities of the American Dream were denied by inflation, pollution, and unemployment. This was the world of war films in which Americans lost; of moody, tortured heroes; of murky ambiguity instead of moral clarity. And just as Americans were not used to feeling pessimistic about the future, so they were not used to feeling uneasy about their place in the world—which is why, in the end, they returned to the comforting nostalgia of Steven Spielberg, George Lucas, and Ronald Reagan.

But the defining theme of this book, and the one that gives it its title, is the rise of a new kind of populism. Of course the politics of the people was deeply rooted in American history, from Jacksonian democracy to the Omaha Platform, from Tom Watson to Huey Long. But as populism reawakened in the 1970s—partly as a reaction to Vietnam and Watergate, partly as a result of the growth of individualism, the decline of institutions, and the conflict between liberalism and traditionalism—it became the most powerful political and cultural force in the nation. The notion of the virtuous citizen locked in battle against big government, big business, and a decadent elite was the single most compelling theme of the 1970s. It drew on the pessimism of stagflation and the shock of defeat; it united liberals from Massachusetts who thought the military-industrial complex had killed President Kennedy and conservatives from Dallas who thought that the country was sliding into godless debauchery. It was there in George Wallace's attacks on pointy-heads and in Richard Nixon's farewell remarks; in the Boston busing protests and the Kanawha County textbook war; in the backlash against détente, the campaign to pass Proposition 13, and the rise of the Moral Majority. And it was there, above all, in Jimmy Carter's promise of a government as good as its people—and in the patriotic, small-government, anti-establishment appeal of the man who beat him.

And while this is the story of Nixon, Ford, Carter, and Reagan, it is also the story of millions of unsung people to whom Howard Beale's tirade about being mad as hell made a great deal of sense—that vast majority who did not join protest marches or political groups, who never bought Eagles records or apocalyptic best sellers, who did not visit swingers' clubs or New Age retreats, but who went to college, got a job, fell in love, got married, bought a house, had children, and did all those other things that made up the texture of everyday life and individual memory. It is the story of Bill and Pat Loud, the first stars of reality television; of Lorraine Faith, whose teenage son was stabbed during the Boston busing protests; of Dorothy Waldvogel, who left her Illinois farm to fight against the ERA; of

Penne Laingen, who tied a yellow ribbon round the tree in her yard while she waited for her husband to come home from Iran.

Many of them belonged to that group Richard Nixon had memorably called "the great silent majority," the "forgotten Americans, the non-shouters, the non-demonstrators." But in the 1970s, with the nation apparently under siege from without and within, they were silent no longer. They were mad as hell, and they were not going to take it anymore.

# A Note on Money

Comparing monetary values from different periods is enormously complicated: the invaluable Web site www.measuringworth.com, run by a group of academic economists from the United States and Britain, gives six different ways of doing it. If we use a combination of the consumer price index and the so-called consumer bundle, a reasonable estimate is that a dollar in 1970 was worth between five and six times what it is today. During the following decade, however, inflation made rapid inroads into the dollar's value. In 1970, $100 was worth about $550 in today's money. Five years later, however, $100 was worth only $400 or so, and by 1980 it was worth just $260 in today's money. As these figures suggest, inflation was no laughing matter, especially for savers.

# Part One

On his last night as president of the United States, Richard Nixon slept badly. As so often during his embattled presidency, he sat up into the small hours of the morning, the telephone clutched to his ear, asking old friends and allies for their reactions to the resignation announcement he had made just a few hours before. At almost two in the morning the thirty-seventh president made his last call, and then he sat alone, brooding in the shadows. When Manolo, his loyal valet, came to ask if he wanted anything, Nixon asked merely that he turn out all the lights in the Residence. It was, he said, "a time for darkness."[1]

The next morning, Nixon got up at six. Dressed in his pajamas and robe, he went into the little second-floor kitchen and asked the chef to prepare his favorite meal, corned beef hash and poached eggs—the same meal he had eaten on the famous occasion, after the invasion of Cambodia four years earlier, when he had paid an unexpected predawn visit to the young peace demonstrators camped at the Lincoln Memorial. Now he ate it on his own in his beloved Lincoln Sitting Room, scribbling on a yellow pad and staring into the fire's dying embers. The desk, like those in the Oval Office and Executive Office Building, had already been emptied, its contents packed into boxes for the trip to California. After breakfast there was a knock on the door: Alexander Haig, bringing the ceremonial letter to Henry Kissinger. Beneath the words "I hereby resign the Office of President of the United States," Nixon scrawled his name.[2]

Shortly after nine, Nixon strode in his familiar awkward gait across to the West Sitting Hall, where the second-floor staff had assembled to say goodbye. He walked down the line, shaking hands, and then led his family downstairs for the last farewell. For the first time since she became First Lady, Pat Nixon had not bothered to do her hair and was wearing dark glasses to hide her tears, but at the last moment she decided to take them off. It was "not a moment to be ashamed of tears," said her son-in-law Ed Cox. Through the double doors they could hear the Marine band, playing a tune from *Oklahoma!* while their guests waited. In the last moments, an aide began to brief the president about the television cameras. "Television?" exclaimed Mrs. Nixon. "Who authorized television?" "I did," her husband said curtly. Then he nodded to the others. "We'll go out there and do it."

As the doors swung open and the band struck up "Hail to the Chief," Nixon led his family into the East Room and onto the platform, where they looked down at ranks of applauding staff members. Even on this last, emotionally searing occasion, everything had been planned with television in mind, and little pieces of tape indicated where each of them should stand. For Pat Nixon it was one last humiliation: her raw, reddened face, wrote Bob Woodward and Carl Bernstein, "seemed to convey her whole life." And for Nixon's elder daughter, Tricia, the ordeal was equally dreadful. "Platform ahead," she recorded in her diary, remembering the scene. "Step up onto platform. Find name marker. Do not trip over wires. Stand on name marker. Reach for Mama's hand. Hold it. Applause. Daddy is speaking. People are letting tears roll down their cheeks. Must not look. Must not think of it now."

Exhausted from lack of sleep, emotionally shattered after eighteen months of unrelenting pressure, her father stood perspiring beneath the television lights. After everything that he had fought for, after all his hard work to drag himself from the parched earth of California to the elegant rooms of the White House, he was leaving in the deepest disgrace. The self-consciousness, the shame, must have been overwhelming. He stood there before the world, red eyed, half-smiling, "fighting back a flood tide of emotions." As so often at times of stress, he retreated to the self-pity of the self-made man. "I had come so far from the little house in Yorba Linda to this great house in Washington," he reflected. "I thought about my parents, and I tried to tell these people about them."[3]

"I remember my old man," Nixon said thoughtfully. "I think that they would have called him sort of a little man, common man. He didn't consider himself that way. You know what he was? He was a streetcar motorman first, and then he was a farmer, and then he had a lemon ranch. It was the poorest lemon ranch in California, I can assure you. He sold it before they found oil on it." By now a deep hush had descended on the room, but on the platform the president's mind was elsewhere:

Nobody will ever write a book, probably, about my mother. Well, I guess all of you would say this about your mother—my mother was a saint. And I think of her, two boys dying of tuberculosis, nursing four others in order that she could take care of my older brother for three years in Arizona, and seeing each of them die, and when they died, it was like one of her own.

Yes, she will have no books written about her. But she was a saint.

For a moment, there was total silence. Then, blinking away tears, Nixon pulled himself back. He took a book from Ed Cox, put on his glasses for the first time in public, and in a trembling voice read the moving words written by Theodore Roosevelt after the death of his first wife. At the last line—"And when my heart's dearest died, the light went from my life forever"—his voice almost broke with the strain, and there were muffled sobs from the chairs before him. Yet Nixon went on, as he always had. Even the deepest anguish, he told his listeners, was "only a beginning, always."

The young must know it; the old must know it. It must always sustain us, because the greatness comes not when things go always good for you, but the greatness comes and you are really tested, when you take some knocks, some disappointments, when sadness comes, because only if you have been in the deepest valley can you ever know how magnificent it is to be on the highest mountain.

On the last words, Nixon's eyes briefly closed, as though he were lost in memory. Then, abruptly, he dragged himself back into the present. He had some last advice for his audience. "Always give your best," he said seriously, "never get discouraged, never be petty; always remember, others may hate you, but those who hate you don't win unless you hate them, and then you destroy yourself."

And then it was over, and the suffocating tension was broken. "You will be in our hearts and you will be in our prayers," he said, and turned to leave. Many, perhaps most of his listeners were in tears or holding hands; even hardened cabinet members were wiping their eyes. "At last the 'real' Nixon was being revealed," thought Tricia, so that "people could finally know Daddy." Alexander Haig thought Nixon's performance had been "unabashedly old-fashioned and American." But Henry Kissinger, who had endured a similar routine two nights before, had lost patience with his master's appetite for self-flagellation. "It was horrifying and heartbreaking," he wrote later. "I was at the same time moved to tears and outraged at being put through the wringer once again."[4]

There was just one goodbye left. With the applause ringing in his ears, Nixon led his family downstairs, where Vice President Gerald Ford and his wife, Betty, were waiting for them. "Good luck, Mr. President," Nixon said coldly, staring his successor full in the face. They stepped out onto the South Portico and walked slowly along the red carpet, past the honor guard, toward the Army helicopter. Pat and Betty clung to each other as they walked, in an endearing gesture of solidarity. Walking on the left of the foursome, Nixon had an odd, slightly deranged smile, as though he knew something nobody else did. Pat, her daughter Tricia, and her son-in-law Ed climbed up into the helicopter. At the foot of the stairs, the outgoing president paused, and Ford said nervously and incongruously: "Drop us a line if you get the chance. Let us know how you are doing."

They shook hands again. Nixon mounted the steps and then suddenly turned to face the White House. Glaring furiously, he waved his right arm across in a clumsy farewell and then, in the final bizarre moment of his presidency, thrust both arms into the air in his trademark V-for-victory salute. He held the gesture for a moment, defying the world, his face cracked by an enormous grin. And then at last the helicopter lifted off the lawn, and he was gone.[5]

**Gerald Ford lingered** a moment on the lawn, his hand raised in farewell. He leaned toward his wife and whispered, "We can do it," then he took her arm and walked back toward the South Portico. It had just turned ten o'clock, and he had a long day before him. Even as he walked toward his vice presidential office, aides were removing every trace of the outgoing president, whipping the Nixon family pictures off the walls of the West Wing and replacing them with images of the Fords. In the Oval Office, a removal team was swiftly working its way through the shelves, wrapping Nixon's possessions in plastic and packing them into cardboard cartons for the journey to California.[6]

An hour later, Gerald and Betty Ford walked into the East Room, where the chairs from Nixon's farewell were still in place and the Marine band was now playing gentle, soothing music. On the platform waited the chief justice of the Supreme Court, Warren Burger, a man Nixon had appointed. "Mr. Vice President," Burger asked, "are you prepared to take the oath of office of President of the United States?" "I am, sir," said Ford, and his wife passed him the family Bible.

Ford was obviously nervous, but as he turned to face the crowd, there could be no mistaking the lighter mood. There were smiles this time, not sobs. And if Ford's voice sounded thin and shaky after Nixon's familiar baritone, there was a reassuring sincerity to his words. This was "just a little straight talk among friends," he said. "I am acutely aware that you have not elected me as your President by your ballots, and so I ask you to confirm me as your President with your prayers . . . I am indebted to no man, and only to one woman—my dear wife—as I begin this very difficult job." And then came the line that Ford thought was too strong but that his speechwriter, Robert Hartmann, had insisted remain. "My fellow Americans," the new president intoned gravely, "our long national nightmare is over. Our Constitution works; our great Republic is a government of laws and not of men."[7]

While Ford was speaking, his predecessor was picking mournfully at his lunch on board the *Spirit of '76*. Richard Nixon paid no attention to the new president's remarks. Later, Nixon wandered along the gangway, trying to joke with his aides. "Well," he said nervously, rubbing his hands, "is everybody enjoying the trip?" He had a few words for everyone. "I see you remembered to bring along the good-looking girls," he said as he passed his press aide Diane Sawyer. When he reached the back, where his bodyguards were sitting in the places normally reserved for the press, Nixon said: "Well, it certainly smells better back here!" They laughed, and then he walked back alone to his cabin and closed the door.

A few hours later, the *Spirit of '76* landed in El Toro, California. It was a crystal clear summer's day, and a crowd of five thousand people cheered as the plane reached a standstill. Grinning wildly at the top of the steps, Nixon threw up his arms in another V-for-victory salute, strode down to the tarmac, and immediately plunged into the sea of hands. He might have been returning from Beijing in unimaginable triumph, rather than fleeing the White House in disgrace. The crowd broke into "God Bless America," and some of Nixon's aides started crying. At the microphones, the former president promised his listeners that he would "continue to work for peace among all the world." There were more cheers, and then he took his wife and daughter across the tarmac to the helicopter that would take them to San Clemente.

The first thing Nixon did when he got home was to pick up the phone to call Alexander Haig, ordering him to send his White House tapes and papers as soon as possible. Then he went out to the cliffs overlooking the Pacific, staring into the waves. Once again he found it hard to sleep, and the next morning his friends found him tired and listless. On Sunday he walked alone on his private beach, lost in thought, and the next day he picked up the telephone and called his old associates, chatting vaguely about nothing. But by Tuesday, he was ready to get back to work. At seven in the morning he was in his office, dressed in his blue suit, wondering what had happened to his staff. Half an hour later he started calling to get them out of bed. Nothing had changed, he said; they must go on as they always had. A week later, he asked them to assemble in the conference room he had used for National Security Council meetings. They turned up, slightly bewildered; one was even wearing Bermuda shorts. Nixon glared around the room. "I've called you here to discuss an important topic," he said. "And that is, what are we going to do about the economy in the coming year?"[8]

**Gerald Ford spent** his first afternoon as president in a flurry of energy, whisked from meeting to meeting: the congressional leaders, the press, the Nixon loyalists, the economic team, and finally fifty-eight foreign ambassadors, all of whom wanted photographs. Just before six, he met with his transition team, headed by the NATO ambassador, Donald Rumsfeld, before holding a brief session with Nixon's cabinet. And then, at last, it was all over. The guests had long since gone home, and the press had packed away their notebooks. Outside the White House, the streets were empty for the first time in weeks. Lafayette Park, where the anti-Nixon demonstrators had huddled with their signs, was deserted. A few placards still lay on the ground, turning damp in the cloudy weather. Dusk fell slowly over Washington. The White House stood silent and bare, a few lights still burning in the windows. And Gerald Ford, thirty-eighth president of the United States, sat in his office, his desk piled high with papers and folders and memos, and worked on alone into the evening.[9]

# Chapter One    *Conspiracy Theory*

Forget it, Jake. It's Chinatown.

—**LAWRENCE WALSH,** in *Chinatown* (1974)

T his just doesn't feel as good as I thought it would," one Delaware
man said sadly after Nixon's resignation. Like most people, he was
relieved that Nixon had finally gone, but the long months of revelation and scandal, of Senate committees and Supreme Court rulings, of
Haldeman, Ehrlichman, Mitchell, and Dean, had left him emotionally
exhausted. Another man, a forester from New Hampshire who had voted
for tickets carrying Nixon's name in eleven elections, thought that the
resignation was like an inoculation: "You hate to get it because you know
it's going to hurt. But when it's over, you're glad you got it."

In the Houston Astrodome, where twelve thousand people were watching a baseball game, the news of Nixon's departure was announced to
a long silence and scattered, desultory applause. In Jacksonville, where
thousands of people were watching a game in the new World Football
League, cheerleaders burst into tears. And in Lawrence, Kansas, the telephone company put extra long-distance operators on duty to cope with
the expected flood of calls, but found that there was nothing for them to
do. People seemed numb, even sad.

Watergate, said *Time* magazine after Nixon's departure, had been
"America's most traumatic political experience of this century." For two
years the scandal had been a national obsession, and as one revelation

followed another, the public recoiled from the petty meanness of their political leaders. Breaking into the Democratic national headquarters, after all, had been only one detail in a wider story of dirty tricks, political espionage, and financial misconduct. If the newspapers were to be believed, President Nixon had spied on his opponents, fiddled his taxes, used public money to improve his homes, abused the intelligence services for political gain, and smeared the reputations of good and honest men. And he had bugged even himself, providing his detractors with all the evidence they needed. When the tape transcripts were finally released, the conservative *Chicago Tribune* called him "devious," "profane," and "humorless to the point of being inhumane." Walter Cronkite remarked that he wanted to "take Lysol and scrub out the Oval Office."[1]

But what the journalist Theodore White called Nixon's "breach of faith" with the American people went beyond the crimes of one man. For many people, the president's misdemeanors had been part of a wider culture of deceit and corruption. "It is a classic idea that a whole community may be infected by the sickness of its leadership, by a failure of ideals at the top," wrote the columnist Anthony Lewis. "We are infected by corruption at the top, and most of us know it."

Corruption was the story of the year. In April 1973, the most sensational month of the Watergate investigation, Nixon had lost his chief of staff, his chief domestic policy adviser, and his counsel John Dean. But the same month also saw the indictment or sentencing, for quite different reasons, of a whole host of public officials: the mayor of Miami, the former governor of Illinois, the district attorney for Queens, New York, two Dade County judges, two Maryland state legislators, and two Chicago aldermen. Before Nixon's presidency was out, they had been joined by two attorneys general, a congressman from New York, the mayor of Camden, New Jersey, the lieutenant governor of California, the former chief judge of the U.S. Customs Court, and the chairman of the Securities and Exchange Commission.[2]

And as Nixon's fall demonstrated, even those entrusted with enforcing the law were not immune. "Who can trust a cop who don't take money?" asks a character in the hit film *Serpico* (1973), which tells the true story of a New York cop who went undercover to expose the corruption of his comrades. In Indianapolis, newspapers alleged that the police and county judges were up to their necks in bribery, prostitution, and drug rackets. In Philadelphia, a crime commission found that corruption was "widespread, systematic and occurring at all levels of the police department" and suggested that no fewer than four hundred officers were lining their pockets. Even at West Point, the hallowed military academy famous for its motto, "Duty, Honor, Country," the bacillus was spreading. In August 1976, ninety-four cadets were expelled for cheating on a take-home exam, and another forty-four resigned. By the following summer, more than four hundred students had been implicated in an elaborate cheating ring. "The social incentives to deceit are at present very powerful," wrote the Harvard philosopher Sissela Bok in 1978 in her timely book *Lying*, blaming the pressures of the modern world for the fact that individuals felt "caught up in practices they cannot change."[3]

"After Watergate, it's crazy to have trust in politicians," one New Yorker told an interviewer after Nixon's fall. "I'm totally cynical, skeptical. Whether it's a question of power or influence, it's who you know at all levels." Indeed, trust in government—and in public life more broadly, too—had never been more fragile. Seven out of ten people, according to a survey in 1975, agreed that "over the last ten years, this country's leaders have consistently lied to the people." A year later, just two out of ten said that they trusted the government, while for the first time an outright majority agreed that public officials did not "care much what people like [us] think." A decade previously, the answers had been very different. But as the pollster Daniel Yankelovich reported, "The changes move in only one direction, from trust to mistrust. They are massive in scale and impressive in their cumulative message."[4]

Yet the steady decline of trust actually predated Watergate, and even though the culture of suspicion reached its peak in the 1970s, it was really a product of the years beforehand. The shock of the Kennedy and King assassinations, the tumult over civil rights and urban unrest, and the corrosive effects of the Vietnam War had all played crucial parts in destroying popular faith in politicians. It was not just trust in the government that was in steep decline; it was trust in authority, in the collective, in public life itself. "The energy shortage is the least important of the shortages in our life," Harold Enarson, president of Ohio State University, remarked in 1974. "American society is now short of those attributes that, mattering the most, undergird all else: integrity, high purpose, confidence in one another, faith in a brighter future."[5]

Across the board, institutions were in retreat. Between 1966 and 1975, confidence in Congress, corporations, colleges, and medicine suffered a severe drop. Of course this was not a uniquely American phenomenon, but in the United States, where individualism and suspicion of the state were so deeply rooted, the turn against public life was more striking than anywhere else in the Western world. Buoyed by affluence and educational opportunities, many people clearly felt that they no longer needed the solace of the institutions—family, church, school—that had supported their parents and grandparents. And as Vietnam and Watergate eroded their faith in the moral superiority of their leaders, an entire generation—the baby boomers—refused to give their generals, doctors, and lawyers the respect once taken for granted. The success of Garry Trudeau's irreverent comic strip, *Doonesbury*, first syndicated in 1970 and rewarded with a Pulitzer Prize five years later, was only one illustration of this new skepticism. Medical malpractice suits, for example, became so common that in 1975 the major insurance companies tripled their doctors' premiums. "All authority in our society is being challenged," concluded a report by the Department of Health, Education, and Welfare. "Professional athletes challenge owners, journalists challenge editors, consumers challenge manufacturers."[6]

From skepticism and suspicion it was only a short step to paranoia. Thanks to Vietnam, Watergate, and the assassinations of the 1960s, what Richard Hofstadter called the "paranoid style"—"heated exaggeration, suspiciousness, and conspiratorial fantasy"—had seeped deep into American popular culture by the time Nixon gave way to Ford. In January 1973, for example, Lyndon Johnson gave a last interview in which he hinted that his predecessor had been murdered by a conspiracy. In March, reviewers scratched their heads over Thomas Pynchon's conspiracy-theory masterpiece *Gravity's Rainbow*, a bewildering journey through the twentieth century that ends with the mysterious 00000 rocket heading for a Los Angeles cinema managed by one "Richard M. Zhlubb." In May, *The New York Review of Books* printed an essay by the radical activist Kirkpatrick Sale arguing that the country was run by a hidden "nexus of power" and that Watergate was really a secret struggle for power between the old eastern interests and the new money of the South. And in November, the Burt Lancaster movie *Executive Action* told how an unholy alliance of Texas oilmen, industrial magnates, and CIA-trained professionals had plotted to kill President Kennedy. At the end of the film, the screen shows a collage of eighteen witnesses to the murder, sixteen of whom had allegedly died of unnatural causes by 1965. The odds of them all doing so, a voice-over grimly intones, were 1,000 trillion to one.[7]

At the center of the whirlwind of suspicion was an institution once synonymous with the struggle against Communism, but now a byword for conspiracy and corruption. On December 22, 1974, *The New York Times* ran a front-page article by the muckraking reporter Seymour Hersh charging that "the Central Intelligence Agency, directly violating its charter, conducted a massive, illegal domestic intelligence operation during the Nixon Administration against the antiwar movement and other dissident groups." Some of Hersh's details were wrong, but the shocking thing was that his story merely scratched the surface. Just a year before, the CIA had commissioned an internal report which revealed that the agency had wiretapped and followed a number of reporters and columnists, broken into the apartments of former employees, kidnapped and locked up Russian defectors, opened ordinary citizens' letters, and collected thousands of files on members of the antiwar movement. On top of all that, the CIA had conducted mind-control experiments on unwitting members of the public, using LSD, heroin, mescaline, and marijuana, and had also organized unsuccessful assassination plots against Fidel Castro, Patrice Lumumba, Rafael Trujillo, and the Chilean general René Schneider. That the Castro plot had been devised in collaboration with the Mafia boss Sam Giancana, using Kennedy's mistress Judith Campbell Exner as a go-between, only added to the impression of lurid fantasy.[8]

Hersh's revelations set the scene for what was later called the "Year of Intelligence." A presidential commission under Nelson Rockefeller failed to mollify the agency's critics; instead, attention focused on Senator Frank Church of Idaho, who called the CIA a "rogue elephant" and began holding public hearings in September 1975. It was a disaster for the administration and, above all, for the CIA. Day after day, under the gaze of the television cameras, agency chiefs admitted spending millions on poisons and biological weapons. With an eye firmly on the coming presidential race, Church even posed for the cameras holding a silent electric gun that fired poisoned darts, hilariously described by the CIA as a "Nondiscernible Microbioinoculator." Wiretaps, assassinations, exploding seashells, Mafia bosses, poisoned darts: it was the stuff of a James Bond film, yet even the most daring Hollywood screenwriter would have struggled to make it up.[9]

As it happened, just ten days after the Church hearings began, Hollywood gave it its best shot. Few films capture the mood of the Ford years better than Sydney Pollack's thriller *Three Days of the Condor*, the story of a junior CIA officer (played by Robert Redford) who spends his days studying books and newspapers from around the world, but who returns after lunch one day to find that a hit man has killed everyone in his office. After going on the run, the Redford character soon realizes that he cannot trust anyone, not even his own colleagues: even the postman turns out to be a hired killer. In the end, he tracks down the conspirators, a CIA cabal with a plan to invade the Middle East in the event of another oil crisis. "As a serious exposé of misdeeds within the CIA," remarked the critic Vincent Canby, "the film is no match for stories that have appeared in your local newspaper."[10]

In many ways, though, the impact of films like *Three Days of the Condor* was to make the small-print revelations of the newspapers seem terrifyingly real. The very intensity of the moviegoing experience—the enveloping darkness of the auditorium, the enormity of the images, the sheer power of the sound—seemed perfectly suited to the new populist nightmares. Even before Nixon resigned, a black vein of paranoia ran through the most successful films of the era, from the police brutality in *Dirty Harry* and *The French Connection* (both 1971) to the corporate irresponsibility in *The Poseidon Adventure* (1972), the demonic possession in *The Exorcist* (1973), and even the negligent skyscraper construction in *The Towering Inferno* (1974). Of course there was more optimistic fare, too. But not for nothing were the two most critically lauded films of 1974, Roman Polanski's *Chinatown* and Francis Ford Coppola's *The Godfather Part II*, both unrelentingly cynical revisions of the American Dream. At once a commentary on contemporary political corruption and a revisionist interpretation of the nation's recent past, *Chinatown* is set in 1937 and tells the story of Jake Gittes (Jack Nicholson), a Los Angeles private eye who uncovers a conspiracy to steal water from the city supply, creating a drought that will enable the corrupt developer Noah Cross to buy up the San Fernando Valley. Unlike the classic private eyes of the 1930s and 1940s, Gittes is powerless to stop him: he even spends much of the film with his wounded nose wrapped in a bandage, like a badge of impotence. And *The Godfather Part II*, too, rewrites recent history to show the villains as the winners. In the previous *Godfather* film, Michael Corleone (Al Pacino) had been a fresh-faced war hero; now he broods in the shadows like Nixon in his final days, his vampiric face glimmering in the darkness. But Michael's crimes do not place him outside the American mainstream; instead, they put him at its very heart, blackmailing senators, infiltrating the FBI, running casinos in Havana and Las Vegas. As he tells the senator who dares to challenge him: "We're both part of the same hypocrisy."[11]

But the most paranoid film of all—its effect all the greater because it was set in the present—was Alan J. Pakula's thriller *The Parallax View* (1974), inspired by the Kennedy assassinations as well as the disillusionment of the Nixon years. Reluctantly drawn into investigating a senator's murder, the film's endearingly scruffy hero, Joseph Frady (Warren Beatty), discovers that the mysterious Parallax Corporation is recruiting assassins to eliminate troublesome presidential candidates. Slowly, he, too, is sucked into the conspiracy, and in the film's shocking denouement he is framed for the murder of another senator and gunned down by the real assassin. In this supremely suspicious vision of contemporary life, conspiracy is everywhere. Even modern architecture is implicated: as Frady penetrates deeper into the conspiracy, he wanders through an alienated, unconventionally framed landscape of clean lines, wide spaces, and white surfaces, from a gleaming West Coast office complex to a new Atlanta hotel and a cavernous conference center. But in the very last scene we return to the shadows: just as at the beginning, an investigating panel, barely visible in the darkness, announces that the "assassin" acted alone. "Although I'm certain that this will do nothing to discourage the conspiracy peddlers," says the chairman flatly, his face imperceptible in the gloom, "there is no evidence of a conspiracy . . . There will be no questions."[12]

**If Hollywood's casting directors** had been asked to pick one man in Washington to banish the paranoid suspicions of the Nixon years, they might well have chosen Gerald Ford. When the new president addressed both houses of Congress on the evening of Monday, August 12, struggling to contain his emotions as applause rolled down from the galleries, the contrast with Nixon could hardly have been greater. Where Nixon had appeared a dark, unhealthy figure, hunched and introverted, Ford came across as open and trustworthy, every inch of six feet tall, fair-haired, square jawed, and broad shouldered. He seemed an American Everyman, a simple man who said his prayers and loved his football, whose favorite meal was steak, baked potato, and butter pecan ice cream. *Time* likened him to "the furniture that used to be produced in such abundance in his Michigan home town, Grand Rapids: durable, dependable and easy to live with."[13]

Months before he assumed the presidency, Ford told an audience that it was "the quality of the ordinary, the straight, the square that accounts for the great stability and success of our nation." And it was the sheer ordinariness of the Ford family that impressed observers during his first days in the White House. While Pat Nixon had always maintained an icy reserve and her daughters had been stereotyped as robotic political props, Betty Ford and her children, Mike, Jack, Steve, and Susan, were manifestly flesh and blood. Lonely and unhappy as a congressional wife, Betty had started drinking, taking tranquilizers, and seeing psychiatrists during the mid-1960s. In interviews she freely admitted that she had experienced mental problems, although she played down the fact that she was still swallowing more booze and pills than were good for her. Yet her problems made her seem human. The Fords might be "a bunch of squares," as one reporter put it, but at least they were an ordinary family with ordinary problems. And to the delight of the press, the new First Couple made no secret of their mutual affection, moving their king-sized bed into Pat

Nixon's old room so that they could be the first presidential couple since the Eisenhowers to sleep together. "We've been doing it for 25 years and we're not going to stop now," said Betty defiantly.[14]

Richard Nixon inevitably cast a long shadow over Ford's first days in the White House. Yet for a time this worked in the new man's favor. *Time's* front-page appeal for "a time for healing" had struck a chord across the nation. In his first days in his new job Ford struck all the right notes, reaching out to friends and foes alike, inviting reporters to White House parties, repeatedly proclaiming his modesty and humility, commuting from his Alexandria home rather than moving in straightaway. The new chief executive liked his comforts, but he could hardly have been less at ease with the grandiose trappings of the imperial presidency. Out went "Hail to the Chief," with the White House band instructed to play the Michigan fight song, "The Victors," instead. The White House living quarters reverted from "the Executive Mansion" to simply "the Residence." Press conferences, organized by Ford's new press secretary, Jerry terHorst, were held in front of the long White House hall, the doors thrown symbolically open, while even the presidential aircraft, which Nixon had renamed the *Spirit of '76*, returned to plain Air Force One. And when Betty Ford described their private sitting room to CBS, with "Jerry's favorite blue leather chair and footstool, and his exercise bike, and all of his pipes and his pipe rack, and our old television set," it sounded like the sitting room of any middle-aged businessman.[15]

If there was one president whom Ford tried to emulate in his early months, it was Harry Truman. Ironically, as a young man Ford had been a fierce critic of his Democratic predecessor, but Truman's forthright, small-town style had never been more fashionable. Merle Miller's book *Plain Speaking*, a collection of Truman memories, sold more than two million copies, while James Whitmore's one-man show *Give 'Em Hell, Harry!* was a hit across the nation. In antiques stores, Truman buttons fetched as much as $150; walking down the streets of major cities in 1974 and 1975, visitors could see Truman T-shirts and bumper stickers; and the rock group Chicago even recorded a song called simply "Harry Truman." "America needs you, / Harry Truman, / Harry, could you please come home?" the lyrics begin. And as a self-consciously ordinary man who had worked his way up from small-town obscurity to the vice presidency and was unexpectedly catapulted into the Oval Office, Truman made an obvious role model for the new president. In the Cabinet Room, Ford hung a portrait of Truman alongside Lincoln and Eisenhower. And when reporters came to see him in the Oval Office, he ostentatiously left a copy of Merle Miller's book on his desk. Truman, he explained, "had guts, he was plain-talking, he had no illusions about being a great intellectual, but he seemed to make the right decisions."[16]

While Ford undoubtedly had much in common with his pugnacious predecessor, he was taking over in an altogether different institutional context. When Truman had succeeded to the presidency in 1945, it had been the most respected office in the land. But Vietnam and Watergate seemed to have put paid to that. In 1973 the War Powers Act reined in the president's power to send troops into combat without congressional approval, while in 1974 the Budget and Impoundment Control Act challenged his power over the nation's finances. To many observers, it was not the White House but Congress, with its new General Accounting Office and research service and hordes of eager young staffers, that set the national agenda. One Maryland voter spoke for many when he told an interviewer in 1976 that "what happens in our country is not really controlled by the President. It's controlled by Congress."[17]

As Ford well knew, however, Congress was in the throes of radical change, reflecting deeper shifts in the way Americans thought and voted. For ordinary voters and elected politicians alike, loyalty to the party machine was no longer the binding force it had been in Truman's day. Many of the new arrivals on Capitol Hill in the early 1970s, especially Democrats such as Gary Hart (Colorado) and John Glenn (Ohio) in the Senate, and Tom Harkin (Iowa) and Paul Tsongas (Massachusetts) in the House, had cut their teeth on the civil rights and antiwar struggles of the late 1960s and were impatient with the conventions and rituals of the past. The Democratic majority leader in the House, Tip O'Neill, reflected that many "never came through the organization, never rang a doorbell in their life, never were a precinct worker, never stayed late at the polls, never brought people to an election, weren't brought up in the realm of party discipline." Instead, they wanted "to come down to Washington and change the establishment. They wanted to open it up. They wanted to take the power out of the hands of the committee chairmen." They wanted, in other words, to blow away the cobwebs.[18]

If there was one moment that captured the changing mood, it was what happened to Wilbur Mills in the fall of 1974. The elderly Arkansan had chaired the pivotal Ways and Means Committee for almost twenty years. Often considered the most powerful man on Capitol Hill, he was the classic southern party baron, exercising a virtual veto over great swaths of domestic legislation. On the night of October 7, however, his car was pulled over by the Washington police for speeding. Closer examination revealed Mills behind the wheel, clearly drunk and covered in bruises, while his companion, a stripper called Fanne Foxe, "the Argentine Firecracker," threw herself into the Tidal Basin in an attempt to escape. Both were arrested, yet in November Mills disgraced himself again, staggering drunkenly onto the stage while Foxe was performing in a Boston night-club. Of course congressmen had drunk too much, cavorted with cour-tesans, and behaved badly in the past; what had changed, however, was the attitude of the media. Mills woke to find his picture on the front page of every newspaper in the nation. Not only was he forced to give up the chairmanship of his committee, but Ways and Means was stripped of its crucial power to make committee assignments for other Democrats.[19]

Change would undoubtedly have come even if Wilbur Mills had kept off the bottle; yet there was no better symbol of the new era than the humiliation of the man who had once dominated the House. When other elderly chairmen followed him onto the scrap heap, it was as though a moldering, darkened old building suddenly found itself bathed in daz-zling sunlight. By the end of 1976, some 150 different subcommittees were competing for attention, each with its own budget, staff, and indepen-dent momentum. There were now so many, joked the Democrat Mor-ris Udall, that he greeted any unfamiliar congressman by saying: "Good morning, Mr. Chairman." Staffs swelled accordingly: between 1972 and 1978 the House committee staff more than doubled, while the Senate staff increased by more than a third. Almost overnight, the echoing corridors of Congress had come alive with activity and enthusiasm. It is no exaggera-tion to say that it had become a different institution: the place that Wilbur Mills had entered in 1939, and in which he had spent most of his adult life, simply no longer existed.[20]

And yet there was a serious downside to the reforms of the early 1970s. With the hierarchies broken up, there was no real sense of organization or leadership in Congress, making it harder to secure working majorities and sometimes almost impossible for the president to get his bills passed. With a proliferation of subcommittees, single-issue politics became the norm, replacing the broad coalitions of old. Every conceivable issue or social group now had its swarm of lobbyists, from women and homosexu-als to ethnic minorities and gun owners. And by the end of the decade, more than five hundred corporations had lobbying offices in Washington, with the K Street area, the "Great Gulch," overflowing with law firms, trade associations, and interest groups. Hardly the cleaner government, it turned out, that had been promised.[21]

The fall of Wilbur Mills also illustrated another crucial development of the mid-1970s: the emergence in the media of a new skepticism toward politics and politicians. Just over a decade before, John F. Kennedy had enjoyed his extramarital adventures in the knowledge that no newspaper would dare to report them. Yet in the aftermath of Watergate, it seemed that every reporter dreamed of emulating Bob Woodward and Carl Bernstein, and the front pages were full of sleaze and scandals. Mills was only one of many victims who failed to realize that times had changed. In May 1976, for example, the front page of *The Washington Post* broke the story that Representative Wayne Hays of Ohio, chairman of the House Administration Committee, was paying his mistress $14,000 a year in public money. "I can't type, I can't file, I can't even answer the phone," the so-called secretary, Elizabeth Ray, admitted. In a delicious irony, Hays had recently advised her to start coming into the office for two hours a day because he was worried that the *Post's* Bob Woodward might find out about them. Like Mills before him, he was forced to relinquish his chairmanship and eventually his congressional seat, ending his career as a figure of ridicule.[22]

But the media did not confine their investigations to the sins of the present. In December 1975, William Safire broke the news that President Kennedy had enjoyed the charms of Judith Campbell Exner, "a beautiful girl who divided her time between the Chicago underworld leadership and the President of the United States." *Time* followed suit a week later, reporting his dalliances with two more non-typing secretaries, "Fiddle" and "Faddle," as well as tales of Jackie Kennedy finding mysterious pairs of panties lying around the White House. By the time that Ford faced the electorate in 1976, few people were unaware of the stories about Kennedy's sexual exploits or Johnson's financial peccadilloes, not to mention Nixon's own well-attributed misdemeanors. Once the presidents had seemed glamorous, admirable figures. Now they looked sordid and seedy: appropriate figureheads, perhaps, for a people whose illusions had been shattered by Vietnam and Watergate, and for a nation that seemed to have fallen out of love with heroism itself.[23]

**On Sunday, September 8,** the nation's attention was focused on the small town of Twin Falls, Idaho, where the daredevil motorcyclist Evel Knievel, the bourbon-swilling, cane-twirling darling of the southern and western white working classes, was preparing to leap across the Snake River Canyon on his death-defying, patriotically painted Skycycle X-2. In the event, the Skycycle failed even to make it off the ramp properly, and as the chastened Knievel was whisked away in a limousine, the crowd turned ugly, smashing the television crews' equipment, gutting the concession stands, and setting cars on fire. With his flared white jumpsuit and patriotic trimmings, Knievel had been billed as an American hero. Now he stood exposed as just one more failure, one more icon who had let down his admirers.

But the next day's headlines would belong not to Knievel but to another fallen star, another all-American hero who had turned out to have feet of clay. Even as the daredevil was preparing for his abortive jump, Gerald Ford was putting the finishing touches to an extraordinary decision. And at five minutes past eleven in the Oval Office, the camera lights blinked on and the president began to read a stunning statement.[24]

"Ladies and gentlemen," Ford began flatly, "I have taken a decision which I felt I should tell you and all my fellow American citizens as soon as I was certain in my own mind and in my conscience that it is the right thing to do." His predecessor's fall, he said, was "an American tragedy in which we have all played a part," but it was time "to write an end to it." He had been advised that Nixon's trial could drag on for at least a year, in which case "the credibility of our free institutions of government would again be challenged at home and abroad." But Ford had to ensure "the greatest good of all the people of the United States whose servant I am." And so he had made up his mind. Nixon's family had suffered enough. He looked down and read a brief proclamation issuing a "full, free and absolute" pardon for any offenses that Nixon "has committed or may have committed," and then, taking out his pen, he signed it.[25]

Even as Ford was signing the pardon, Richard Nixon was arriving at the California estate of Walter Annenberg, the billionaire he had appointed ambassador to Britain. Nixon and his wife were looking forward to an extended break on their friend's desert estate, with its pool, nine-hole golf course, and twenty-seven lakes. But that day, despite the heat, Nixon stayed indoors, a glowering presence nursing a leg swollen with phlebitis. He had got what he wanted, but he was not happy. To his wife, Pat, he said simply: "This is the most humiliating day of my life."[26]

By contrast, walking out of the White House after the broadcast had ended, Ford felt "an unbelievable lifting of the burden from my shoulders." He spent the afternoon at the Burning Tree club in Bethesda, where he and his partner, Nixon's old defense secretary Melvin Laird, were leading the congressional golf tournament. As they crossed the course, Ford cheerfully asked Laird what he thought of his decision. "We're still in this tournament and we have a pretty good chance of doing well," Laird said grimly. "I don't want to talk to you about the pardon now. We'll play golf, and then we'll talk about it later." They walked on in silence. That afternoon, Ford played dreadfully.[27]

With one stroke of a pen, Ford had transformed his image. "Jesus, don't you think it's kind of early?" his friend Tip O'Neill, the Democratic

House leader, had burst out on hearing his plans earlier that day, while another old friend, the president's press secretary, Jerry terHorst, was so appalled by the pardon that he handed in his resignation just moments before Ford went on the air. In the next few days, almost 200,000 letters poured into Washington denouncing Ford's decision, demonstrators gathered outside the White House, and at a conference in Pittsburgh he was heckled by protesters chanting, "Jail Ford! Jail Ford!" In just a week, his Gallup approval rating tumbled to 49 percent, the steepest fall in the poll's history. Never again would he enjoy the confidence and respect of the press. For *The New York Times*, the pardon had been "profoundly unwise, divisive and unjust." *Time* thought that Ford had "needlessly, even recklessly, squandered some of that precious public trust that is so vital to every President." He had "embraced the demon of Watergate," agreed *Newsweek*, while for the *Chicago Tribune* "a sour smell" had returned to the White House.[28]

To many people there was an obvious explanation for Ford's decision: before becoming president, he had clearly done a deal with Nixon, exchanging a pardon for the presidency. It was a charge that Ford angrily refuted: testifying to a House subcommittee a month later, he pounded the table as he insisted, "There was no deal, period, under any circumstances." And yet Ford himself admitted that the subject had been raised even before he assumed the presidency. On August 1, in a meeting with Nixon's consigliere Alexander Haig, Ford had discussed six possible options for Nixon's future, one of which involved resigning "in return for an agreement that the new president—Gerald Ford—would pardon him." In his memoirs, Ford denied that he had approved this option; indeed, his speechwriter Bob Hartmann later made him call Haig back, in front of witnesses, to distance himself from it. But as the pardon's most meticulous historian, John Robert Greene, points out, the subject had been "unquestionably on the table."[29]

The obvious drawback with this explanation was that there was nothing in the deal for Ford himself. Since Nixon was doomed, his ascent to the presidency was only a matter of time, and he would have been exceptionally foolish to compromise it by striking a deal. What is true, though, is that he found himself under immense pressure to settle the Nixon issue as quickly as possible. Haig constantly urged him to make up his mind, while David Eisenhower called from California warning that his father-in-law "might go off the deep end" unless he was reprieved. Even allies like the Republican Senate leader, Hugh Scott, and Ford's vice presidential nominee, Nelson Rockefeller, alarmed that the interminable uncertainty was destroying the party's credibility, publicly appealed for clemency. The pressure peaked on August 28, when Ford received a three-page memo from Nixon's old friend Len Garment, summarizing the case for a pardon. According to Garment, Nixon was being "hounded, perhaps literally, to death." For Ford to pardon him "would be strong and admirable," and after the initial press furor there "would be a national sigh of relief."[30]

Other factors also played their part. Just hours after Garment handed him the memo, Ford's first presidential press conference rapidly degenerated into a "question-and-answer session on the fate of Richard Nixon." This clearly would not do, and Ford realized that he had to "get the monkey off my back." Meanwhile, the Watergate special prosecutor Leon Jaworski reported that although Nixon faced charges in ten areas, the evidence was not clear enough to guarantee a conviction. With public opinion inflamed against him, it was unclear whether Nixon could get a fair trial: there might not even be enough people to make up a jury. And while jury selection could take two years, the trial was bound to be a long one, and if Nixon was found guilty, he was bound to appeal. Unless Ford pardoned his predecessor, therefore, the legal process would drag on for years, embarrassing the nation in the eyes of the world. Jaworski himself had no stomach for such a spectacle. For the rest of his life he defended Ford's decision: the pardon, he thought, was as good a symbol of Nixon's guilt as any courtroom verdict.[31]

On August 30, Ford made up his mind, telling his senior advisers that he was "very much inclined" to grant Nixon immunity from prosecution as soon as possible. Asked whether this was the right time, he snapped back wearily: "Will there *ever* be a right time?" Bob Hartmann put up a fight, arguing that Ford should wait until Nixon enjoyed more public sympathy, but the president's decision was final. In many ways it made excellent political sense: Ford was sick of the press asking him about Nixon, sick of the arguments about Nixon's papers, sick of dealing with the legacy of Watergate, and keen to move on to the country's economic problems. And since Nixon's trial was likely to overshadow the rest of his term, pardoning him seemed the obvious solution. As Stanley Kutler, the definitive chronicler of Watergate, puts it, the pardon "may have been necessary if Ford was to get on with the business of running the government" and may also have "spared the legal process from mockery and embarrassment," especially since Nixon stood a good chance of being acquitted. Indeed, Ford had a strong case that Nixon's acceptance of the pardon was tacit admission of wrongdoing. In 1915, the Supreme Court had ruled that the gift of a pardon "carries an imputation of guilt; acceptance a confession of it." For the rest of his days, Ford kept in his wallet a yellowing clipping of the Court's ruling.[32]

Whether Ford could have handled it differently, though, is another matter. There was always likely to be a fierce reaction, but the solitary, secretive way he took the decision made it far worse. And he had only himself to blame, having rejected plans to raise the issue with a few close allies on Capitol Hill or to ask a friendly Democrat to "float the idea as a trial balloon." He later explained that he wanted to emulate Abraham Lincoln's lonely courage in issuing the Emancipation Proclamation. This was an understandable spasm of vanity on Ford's part: after weeks of being told what a nice, modest fellow he was, he wanted to show the world that he could take tough decisions. But it was a bad mistake. If he had taken his time, reaching out to Congress, building a consensus, allowing the arguments to seep into the public consciousness, the reaction would surely have been less ferocious. "What's the rush?" Hartmann had asked. It was a good question.[33]

However clumsily Ford took the decision, though, it was indisputably the right one in the long term. Publicly humiliated, depressed, suffering from severe phlebitis, and brooding in exile on the West Coast, Nixon had surely suffered enough. His trial would have been a grotesque circus, overshadowing American politics for years. And it is striking that prominent critics of the pardon, notably the journalists Richard Reeves and Bob Woodward, later changed their minds. In 2001, Ford was even awarded the John F. Kennedy Profile in Courage Award, a reward "for doing the right thing—the courageous thing—even though he knew it would be so harmful to him politically," wrote the veteran political correspondent Godfrey Sperling. "Here's to you, Jerry Ford, a real nice guy who's finally getting his due."[34]

But in September 1974 few people would have guessed that history's verdict would be so generous. Just a month into his presidency, Ford's credibility was in tatters, and he never managed to lift the albatross of the pardon from around his neck. What was worse, he now received a piece of devastating news on the domestic front. On September 26, a Navy doctor found a lump in Betty Ford's right breast and recommended immediate surgery to determine whether it was malignant. The following evening, she left for Bethesda Naval Hospital. Ford was preparing a major address on the fight against inflation, but his thoughts were with his wife. "That night was the loneliest of my life," he wrote. "The thought that the woman I loved might be taken away from me was almost too much to endure." The following morning, rain poured down from slate gray skies. In the

Oval Office, Ford was reviewing his speech with Bob Hartmann when the phone rang. It was the White House doctor. The lump was malignant. Betty would have to undergo a full mastectomy, but even then he could not be sure whether the cancer had spread. Ford excused himself, went to the bathroom, and stood alone for a minute, struggling to master his feelings. When he returned to his desk, Hartmann said simply: "Go ahead and cry. Only strong men aren't ashamed to cry. You're among friends."[35]

Although Betty Ford fought and eventually won her battle against breast cancer, her husband's political fortunes showed no sign of improving. The immediate fallout came in the November midterm elections, when the Republicans were expecting heavy losses. Polls found that voters ranked the three major problems facing the country as the "high cost of living," "corruption in government," and the continuing energy crisis, a desperately unpromising combination. None of these was Ford's fault, but he still had to deal with them. His new press secretary, Ron Nessen, remembered that during a family dinner in Colorado, one of the Ford family dogs disgraced himself on the floor. A White House steward went to wipe up the mess, but Ford waved him away and cleaned it up himself. In Nessen's words, "Ford's role in history was to clean up other people's messes."[36]

Unfortunately, Ford was a terrible campaigner, and the midterm results could hardly have been worse for the White House. Barely one in three people bothered to cast a ballot, a depressing vote of no confidence in the political process. But the Democrats were not complaining: after capturing forty-nine Republican seats in the House, they had a comfortable two-thirds majority, allowing them to ignore the threat of presidential vetoes as long as they kept their discipline. Indeed, with their party looking remarkably strong even in the Republican Midwest, the country seemed more heavily Democratic than ever. As for the Republicans, not only did they lose a further three seats in the Senate and five governorships, they claimed the allegiance of just 18 percent of the American electorate. Not since the Depression had the Grand Old Party been in such dreadful disarray. At a bleak postelection meeting, the pollster Robert Teeter reported that it was generally regarded as "the party of big business" and seen as "wealthy," "untrustworthy," and "incompetent." Two out of three people could think of nothing good at all to say about it. If the trend continued, he warned, "in 20–30 years the party will be extinct."[37]

The biggest loser, of course, was Ford himself, whose reputation never recovered from those rocky first weeks of his presidency. NBC's young reporter Tom Brokaw, who asked Ford at the beginning of 1975 whether he was "intellectually up to the job of being President," was merely voicing what many of his colleagues privately suspected. In fact, Ford's intellectual credentials, including a law degree from Yale, were perfectly in order. But he could never shake the pervasive sense that he was an amiable idiot who had been at the right place at the right time. Reporters loved to quote Lyndon Johnson's quip that Ford had played too much football without a helmet, or his much-repeated line that "Jerry Ford is so dumb he can't walk and chew gum at the same time."* And cartoonists had enormous fun with his bumbling image. One cartoon, originally published in *The Dayton Daily News*, showed a middle-aged couple hidden behind their morning newspapers. "That does it," the husband is saying. "Look at this month's cost of living increase . . . Somebody better tell the President to get off his duff and start giving us some answers." His wife replies: "But you're the President, dear."[38]

Ford was the most athletic president in history, a superb football player who could easily have played professionally. Even in office he enjoyed skiing, tennis, swimming, and golf, and loved to pepper his speeches with sporting metaphors. Yet reporters delighted in portraying him as a clumsy oaf who could barely walk down a corridor without falling over. In November 1974, the cover of *National Lampoon* depicted Ford as a slack-jawed Neanderthal who, missing his mouth, had stuck an ice-cream cone onto the middle of his forehead. And when, in June 1975, Ford slipped on the rain-drenched steps of Air Force One, the image stuck. Whenever he bumped his head while swimming, or fell over while skiing, or stumbled while working a crowd, the newspapers pounced. One joke ran that toy manufacturers were planning a "Jerry Ford doll" that, when wound up, would immediately lurch into the nearest furniture; another held that the Secret Service had banned him from throwing out the first pitch of the baseball season for fear that he would hit himself with the ball. In the hands of *Saturday Night Live*'s Chevy Chase, poor Ford became a pitiable caricature. He even turned up in the Inspector Clouseau comedy *The Pink Panther Strikes Again* (1976), obsessively watching football games on an Oval Office television and tripping every time he left the room.[39]

Like many politicians, Ford was surprisingly thin-skinned. What really annoyed him were the quips about his skiing: it infuriated him that many of the reporters laughing at him were half his age, could not ski themselves, and "would sit in the bar all day long" waiting for a picture of him falling down. But pride was not the only thing at stake. The more the

---

*This was the most common version of the joke. Some people claimed that Johnson had really said that Ford "can't fart and chew gum at the same time"; another version had "can't walk and fart at the same time."

image of the clumsy oaf took hold, the harder it became to build confidence in his political and economic competence. As *The New Republic's* John Osborne put it, Ford looked like "a loser, a bumbler, a misfit President . . . prone to slip on airplane ramps, bump his head on helicopter entrances, entangle himself in the leashes of his family dogs, and fall from skis in front of television cameras that showed him asprawl in snow." And as 1975 began, Osborne issued a judgment that was coming to be shared by millions. "Gerald Ford," he wrote, "is an awfully nice man who isn't up to the presidency."[40]

## Chapter Two   *If He's So Dumb, How Come He's President?*

The more I think about the Ford Administration,
the more it seems I remember nothing.

**—JOHN UPDIKE,** *Memories of the Ford Administration* (1992)

By the end of 1974, the dreary, damp grayness of the weather seemed to have seeped into the souls of the American people. Even Manhattan's ritual celebrations of the New Year were tinged with gloom, as a strike by twenty thousand porters and cleaners was averted only at the last moment. And New Year's Eve itself was cold, bitterly cold. In Times Square, freezing rain pounded down upon the revelers who had gathered to cheer the arrival of 1975. Beneath the gloomy, boarded-up shop-windows of central Manhattan, balloons, party hats, and ribbons bobbed sadly down a river of filthy slush.

The weather was not the only thing keeping New Yorkers at home. "The economic scars of the last year were evident," wrote one reporter. "People who usually go out on the town said they had drinks at home before midnight." Seasonal goodwill was in short supply: in Central Park, the Queens Symphony Orchestra was forced off the stage by a drunken mob of snowball-throwing teenagers. "Times Square is packed with people pretending they're animals," muttered one cabdriver bitterly. "They throw bottles, and drop fire-crackers on the street without looking who might be standing there." On Forty-third Street, a man selling party horns gazed down miserably at his soggy box of unsold toys. "I'm too old," he said glumly, "and it's too cold."[1]

In the nation's capital the atmosphere was not much cheerier. For the new president, the outlook could hardly have been worse. His popularity had been shattered after the Nixon pardon, and his party had been humiliated in the midterm elections. The headlines were full of collapsing firms and jobless workers, of decrepit Rust Belt cities ravaged by crime and unemployment. Polls suggested that three out of four Americans felt that the country was on the wrong track, while almost nine out of ten had no confidence in Gerald Ford's economic leadership. It was as though Nixon's removal had been only a brief respite from the storm, a temporary break in the narrative of national despair. "We live in a time of collapse," wrote Colman McCarthy in *The Washington Post* on the last day of 1974, "with expressions of hope able to take no brighter form than Albert Camus' belief: 'The important thing is not to be cured but to live with one's ailments.' "[2]

Living with one's ailments, however, was not good enough for Gerald Ford. Two weeks into the New Year he was due to give the annual State of the Union address for the first time. If he was to rebuild his political credibility, he needed to give a convincing impersonation of someone who could cure the nation's sicknesses. And yet it was a telling indication of the mess in which Ford found himself—as well as the disorganized, faction-ridden nature of his administration—that at nine o'clock the evening before he was due to give the speech, he was still sitting at his desk with two rival drafts, one by Bob Hartmann and one by Donald Rumsfeld. It took hours for his speechwriters to weave the two together, and not until four in the morning did a weary Ford approve the final text and haul himself off to bed.[3]

Just after one on the afternoon of January 16, Ford walked into his beloved House Chamber to address his old congressional colleagues. Much of his speech was the usual combination of lofty presidential clichés and mind-numbing policy detail, but what made it distinctive—and memorable—was the unprecedented frankness and pessimism of his tone. In his opening remarks he remembered the first State of the Union speech he ever attended, Truman's address to the Eighty-first Congress in 1949, when the feisty Democrat had proudly proclaimed that "the state of the Union is good." Twenty-six years on, Ford's message was very different. "Today," he said bluntly, "I must say to you that the state of the Union is not good . . . I've got bad news and I don't expect much, if any, applause."

He did not get much: only nine times did clapping interrupt his words.

His energy plan, he admitted, meant "sacrifices": with new duties on imported oil, there would be no return to the oil-rich paradise of the 1960s. And to keep inflationary pressures in check, Ford also announced a one-year moratorium on all federal spending except on energy, a far cry from the largesse of the Great Society and the Nixon years. His message, said one reporter, had been "the gloomiest delivered by a President since the Depression of the nineteen thirties." Yet even liberal critics admitted that he had struck an appropriate tone for the age of limits. "President Ford met the first test of leadership, which is candor," said *The New York Times*. It was not, agreed *The Washington Post*, "a pulse-quickening performance, and that perhaps was the best thing about it. After the war and disorders of the 1960s and the scandals and constitutional stresses of the early 70s, what this country may be in need of is straight talk and realistic ambitions. And that is basically what it got."[4]

**For most of his adult life,** Gerald Ford had known nothing but American affluence. When he had returned to his hometown of Grand Rapids after serving in the Pacific during World War II, the Depression he remembered from his childhood was already fading into history. And when, in 1948, he won his first election to represent Michigan's Fifth District in Congress, history's biggest boom was already under way, launching two decades of unprecedented prosperity and economic optimism. With his wife, Betty, and their young family, Ford basked in the sunshine of the affluent society, a brave new world of spreading suburbs and overflowing supermarkets, of televisions and computers, photocopiers and lasers, credit cards and communication satellites. Horizons were broader, opportunities greater, waistlines wider. *Life* magazine imagined Americans as shoppers in a gleaming new grocery store, "picking from the thousands of items on the high-piled shelves until their carts became cornucopias filled with an abundance that no other country in the world has ever known."[5]

For those who shared in the extraordinary prosperity of the postwar decades, there seemed no reason why it should ever end. The columnist Robert Samuelson, who grew up during the 1950s, when Ford was steadily climbing the congressional ladder, recalled being a "daily witness to the marvels of affluence," surrounded by "a seemingly endless array of new gadgets and machines." Televisions, jet engines, air-conditioning, long-distance telephone calls, interstate highways, automatic washing machines, antibiotics: the list went on and on. Even poor families could reasonably expect to own a car, to watch television, to take an annual vacation, luxuries that most people around the world could scarcely imagine. Polls showed a growing sense of material entitlement, reflecting public optimism in the possibilities of prosperity. And despite bitter public wrangling about the civil rights movement, the Great Society, and the war in Vietnam, there still seemed reasons to be cheerful as the 1960s neared their close. "Progress had triumphed," reflected Samuelson; "ever broadening affluence would continue indefinitely."[6]

Yet as Ford contemplated his domestic inheritance in the dying months of 1974, the outlook could hardly have been gloomier. The passions that had torn cities and campuses apart in the late 1960s might be spent, but the bitterness remained. "Pessimism is the mood of the nation," declared *The Washington Post*. It was almost two years since American troops had left Vietnam, but the scars of the nation's longest war had yet to heal. The campuses had fallen quiet, but a generation of students had left college angry or disillusioned. Chanting crowds no longer marched through the nation's capital, but in the forgotten byways of the rural South and the crumbling ghettos of the nation's cities the fight for racial justice went on. And in every town in the nation, history unfolded every day in millions of tiny, unheralded revolutions, as teenagers grew their hair long and smoked their first joints, as marriages collapsed and couples divorced, as married women applied for their first jobs, as white girls brought home black boyfriends, as all-American boys came out of the closet, as supposedly strong men lost their jobs and buried their heads in their hands and wept.[7]

Underpinning it all, though, was the cold, hard economic reality that the good times were over. President Ford, said *The New York Times*, was inheriting "the worst inflation in the country's peacetime history, the highest interest rates in a century, the consequent severe slump in housing, sinking and utterly demoralized securities markets, a stagnant economy with large-scale unemployment in prospect, and a worsening international trade and payments position." That August the nation's trade deficit had reached a record $1.1 billion, inflation was running at more than 12 percent, and more than five million people were out of work. Wall Street's confidence was ravaged by soaring prices, energy shortages, and stringent interest rates. The Dow Jones Industrial Average was in free fall, the market had lost half its value since 1972, and brokers, it was said, were "happy only that the windows can't be opened in these fancy new buildings." No president since Franklin D. Roosevelt had faced more desperate economic challenges, and according to an opinion poll taken the week after Ford's inauguration, almost half of all Americans thought that the country was heading for the worst depression since the 1930s.[8]

Of all the economic ills that confronted the new president, the most frightening was inflation. Thanks to rising consumer demand, high wage increases, and, above all, the cost of the Vietnam War, inflation had been mounting ominously since the late 1960s, and the federal government seemed powerless to stop it. Richard Nixon had made matters even worse by recklessly pushing for growth before the 1972 election, hoping that wage and price controls would allow him to clean up the damage afterward. But Nixon's controls merely stoked up the inevitable inflationary pressures; when they were relaxed in 1973, it was as though the dam had burst. The brief boom had created an unsustainable demand, workers claimed higher wages to make up for the months of enforced restraint, and soaring global commodity prices pushed inflation still higher. By the end of 1973, the consumer price index had risen by almost 9 percent and wholesale prices by 18 percent. To make matters worse, unemployment was steadily rising, too.[9]

During the quarter century of glorious, heedless affluence, most Americans had gone about their daily lives in blissful ignorance of the perils of inflation. But now food prices were rising so quickly that, as the conservative commentator David Frum recalled, "steakhouse menus arrived with stacks of little white handwritten stickers over their printed prices," so that he could scrape off "a little mountain of superimposed surcharges to gaze at the primordial price at the bottom." In April 1973, infuriated consumers announced a nationwide meat boycott, forming spontaneous groups like Operation Pocketbook, Fight Inflation Together, and Housewives Expect Lower Prices (HELP). Their members, reported *The New York Times*, were simply ordinary citizens outraged at rising prices: "groups of tenants in apartment buildings, neighbors who shop at the same markets in small towns, block associations, and—perhaps most typical—groups of women who meet every morning over coffee."[10]

There had been food-price protests before, but none as potent as this. Inflation made no allowances for creed or color, wealth or status; it allowed nobody to escape. According to the polls, one in four shoppers supported the boycott, while a New York congressman who visited a supermarket in Queens told reporters: "I've seen rent petitions and antiwar petitions and all sorts of petitions. But I've never seen a petition like this where not one single person refused to sign." Yet Nixon remained unimpressed, condemning the boycott as counterproductive and pointedly serving beef at a White House dinner for South Vietnam's President Thieu. One Brooklyn shopper called him "the Marie Antoinette of American politics," while half a million consumers from New York, New Jersey, Connecticut, and Pennsylvania sent him cash register tapes in protest.[11]

Although the boycott left a permanent institutional legacy in the

National Consumers Congress, it gradually lost momentum. For as the months went on and inflation continued to bite, the economic downturn acquired a numbing sense of inevitability. For the first time in decades, real take-home pay was dropping, with hourly earnings falling by 2.8 percent in 1974 and still further a year later. "There's nothing left after the rent and food," one Boston woman told *Newsweek* in March 1974. "Sometimes I just want to give up." Another woman, this time from San Francisco, admitted that she had given up keeping a budget because "it got so discouraging . . . The whole economic picture scares me. It's so unreal." And a Chicago housewife summed up the general gloom. "You always used to think in this country that there would be bad times followed by good times," she said grimly. "Now, maybe it's bad times followed by hard times followed by harder times."[12]

As so often, the people who suffered most were those near the bottom of the ladder. In 1974, an engineer made around $18,000 a year, a skilled construction worker $12,000, a male schoolteacher $12,000 (but a female teacher only $9,000), a secretary $7,000, and a farm laborer $5,000. With both partners working, most American families took home a total annual income between $10,000 and $25,000. Yet in an age of high consumer expectations and rampant inflation, many struggled to make ends meet. According to the Bureau of the Census, the cost of living for an "average" family, consisting of a thirty-eight-year-old employed husband, his homemaker wife, thirteen-year-old son, and eight-year-old daughter, living on a moderate budget in a metropolitan suburb, was more than $14,000 a year. And even on the bureau's proposed "lower" budget, they could expect to spend more than $9,000—which meant precious little room for maneuver but plenty of scope for anxiety.[13]

Far from getting steadily richer, as they had done during the 1950s and 1960s, many families felt compelled to tighten their belts. By the end of the 1970s, the typical blue-collar worker commanded less spending power than at any point since the end of the 1950s, making a mockery of politicians' promises of growth and prosperity. When the sociologist Jonathan Rieder visited Brooklyn's Canarsie neighborhood in 1975, residents told him again and again that they felt "squeezed," "screwed," or "fucked up the ass" by food prices, utility rates, and the financial demands of government. Against this background of economic anxiety, other resentments, from busing to obscenity, took on a sharper edge. "Someone is coming in and squeezing us and taking it all away," one Canarsie merchant said. "First, they squeeze my pocketbook, so I can't do anything. Then they come in with busing and squeeze my kids." This sense of impending loss, this dread of forfeiting everything, of being sucked back under the poverty line, was a common feeling in working-class areas. "It's all in danger," one resident remarked: "The house you always wanted is in danger, the kids are in danger, the neighborhood is in danger. It's all slipping away."[14]

For many workers, the pain was all the more acute because the jobs they took for granted were threatened as never before. The national economy was in the process of deep structural change, with manufacturing fleeing the cities, car plants and steelworks losing money, and automation causing millions of layoffs. In this new era of computers, services, and specialized office jobs, older workers found that their skills were no longer needed. In the steel industry, 100,000 people were thrown out of work between the summer of 1974 and the spring of 1975, and many were unable to find new jobs. And plant closures and job cuts had a devastating impact on local communities. At the Sparrows Point steel complex outside Baltimore, residents were appalled when Bethlehem Steel, crippled by a nationwide coal strike, began to lay off thousands of workers in November 1974. The largest tidewater steel plant in the nation, Sparrows Point employed twenty-two thousand people and was vital to the local economy. Most men took home around $240 a week: if furloughed, they were reduced to a mere $89 in unemployment benefits. "It was a real shock," one twenty-nine-year-old plate-mill worker, Leon Green, told reporters. Christmas, he said miserably, would "just have to be another day." Although he had planned to buy watches for his two children, "we'll just have to do with having a nice meal."[15]

By the spring of 1975, Bethlehem Steel had laid off at least two thousand workers at Sparrows Point—the exact figure was disputed by the company and the union—and by May, with the economy limping out of recession, some seven thousand steelworkers were still out of work. Since Sparrows Point was the biggest single private employer in the state of Maryland, the cuts had a powerful effect. By February 1977, the lines at the Baltimore unemployment office were often fifteen deep, crowded with waitresses, shipyard workers, mechanics, and carpenters. "The snow is gone, the stores are open, the traffic moves along the streets," wrote one reporter, but "in the city, you look for the winter in the faces . . . in the faces of the workmen without jobs."[16]

Yet many workers were not prepared to give in without a fight, and the 1970s saw more strikes than any other period since World War II. The first year of the decade saw national strikes by the Teamsters, the United Automobile Workers, and General Electric employees, as well as walkouts by New York postal workers, grave diggers, and tugboat crewmen, Cincinnati and Atlanta city workers, and rubber workers in Akron. But this was only the beginning. New York City spent much of the early 1970s utterly beset

by public-sector strikes, with 4.2 million working days lost in 1971 alone.
A year later, striking autoworkers shut down the GM factory in Lord-
stown, Ohio, hailed as the "plant of the future" when it had opened in
1966. Furious at a new efficiency drive and program of layoffs, the workers did not merely put down their tools; they deliberately produced cars
with "slit upholstery, scratched paint, dented bodies, bent gearshift levers,
cut ignition wires, and loose or missing bolts." These were not hardened
union men who remembered the clashes of the 1930s and 1940s. They
were the youngest GM workforce in the country, "long-haired, pigtailed
and bell-bottomed," with an average age of twenty-four—a not-so-silent
majority.[17]

The ordeal of the unions, which were rapidly shedding members as
corporations moved to the business-friendly suburbs of the South and the
West, was matched by the woes of bosses and managers themselves. As
many Americans were only just coming to realize, their twenty-five-year
global swagger was over. Complacent about their domestic position and
seduced by cheap labor markets, American firms had invested billions
in overseas manufacturing capacity, allowing domestic investment to
stagnate. Meanwhile, foreign competitors like Japan and West Germany,
whose infrastructures had been ravaged by wartime destruction, were
catching up much more quickly than anyone had foreseen. By the 1970s,
American productivity growth and capital investment rates had fallen
badly behind those in Japan and West Germany. While the three biggest American automobile companies produced an average of ten cars
per worker per year, Toyota produced fifty. In 1948 the United States had
enjoyed a quarter of all world trade; by 1970 this had fallen to barely 10
percent. In 1950 it had produced almost half of the world's steel; now it
produced a fifth. As late as 1965 it had produced half the world's automobiles; now it produced less than a third.[18]

What really brought home the shifting balance of power, however, was
the flood of imports. For the first time, many American manufacturers
found themselves competing in a genuinely globalized marketplace—
which meant that the domestic customers they had once taken for granted
were now shopping elsewhere. The value of overseas imports, from Italian purses and British raincoats to Swedish furniture and Japanese televisions, doubled in just ten years. By the end of the 1970s almost every
household in the nation boasted a foreign appliance, and a quarter of all
manufactured goods bought in the United States had been made abroad.
Even the typical car, once the supreme symbol of American affluence,
was now likely to be an imported foreign model: by the late 1970s, American drivers were buying more than two million Japanese cars a year. Not

for nothing is Rabbit Angstrom, John Updike's dissatisfied Everyman, a Toyota salesman. Indeed, Toyota, Nissan, and Honda were more than car brands; the very names were symbols of global competition and national decline. To domestic manufacturers left high and dry by the tide of globalization, talk of open markets and international exchange seemed scant consolation for their falling profits. "What is happening to the middle classes?" one New York garment merchant demanded. "The coats which Alexander's sells are foreign-made—I resent that. Burlington Mills buys from the Japanese. The small man like me can't market his product in a fair, equitable exchange. People on this block are losing their jobs. It's a tragedy."[19]

**As a native of Michigan,** a state dominated by the leviathans of the car industry, Ford was well placed to grasp the anguish of the Rust Belt in an age of economic contraction. But like any other American of his generation, he had only gradually come to realize that the great postwar boom had been entirely dependent on one cheap commodity above all: oil. It was oil that heated homes and drove generators; it was oil that fueled cars, trains, ships, and airplanes. The factories that built the consumer goods of the 1950s and 1960s were powered by oil; the plastics that typified the affluent society were transformed from it. Oil was cheap, reliable, easily transportable, and endlessly adaptable, and far more popular than natural gas, coal, or nuclear power.

Between 1948 and 1972, American oil consumption had increased threefold. "Oil emerged triumphant," writes Daniel Yergin, the great historian of the oil industry, "the undisputed King, a monarch garbed in a dazzling array of plastics. He was generous to his loyal subjects, sharing his wealth to, and even beyond, the point of waste. His reign was a time of confidence, of growth, of expansion, of astonishing economic performance." Every street corner boasted an emblem of his authority: gasoline stations, big and small, where you could have your tires and oil checked and your windows washed, where you could even pick up fast food, groceries, sweepstakes forms, and free gifts. They were temples not merely to the car but also to the creed of conspicuous consumption.[20]

But signs of trouble were already on the horizon. With consumption soaring, domestic oil production peaked in 1970. And then, slowly but surely, it began to decline. By 1974, one in three barrels of oil came from abroad. Just like their overseas counterparts, American consumers, almost unnoticed, were coming to depend on the gigantic oil fields of the Middle East. And with international demand mounting, the phrase "energy crisis" was becoming disturbingly familiar to anyone who read a newspaper. During the summer of 1971, capacity restrictions on the East Coast had led to brownouts and blackouts, and over the next couple of years power cuts were an unhappily frequent occurrence in many eastern households. When 1973 opened with yet another great freeze, schools and factories in the Midwest were forced to shut down. By the spring, more than a hundred independent gas stations had closed down in Minnesota alone, and there were genuine fears that nationwide supplies would run out over the summer. In April 1973, Nixon delivered the first presidential address on energy, scrapping quotas on oil imports, liberalizing natural gas prices, and urging support for an Alaskan oil pipeline. Two months later he unveiled a new Department of Energy, a $10 billion research and development program, and a conservation drive to cut federal energy use. "Unless we act swiftly and effectively," Nixon said ominously, "we could face a genuine energy crisis in the foreseeable future."[21]

It was the outbreak of war in the Middle East in October 1973, when Egypt and Syria launched a stunning surprise attack on Israel, that really marked the turning point. For months Arab leaders had been warning that unless the United States reassessed its relationship with its Israeli client, they would unsheathe their "oil weapon"; indeed, Saudi Arabia's King Faisal even told viewers of NBC that "America's continued support of Zionism against the Arabs makes it extremely difficult for us to continue to supply the United States with oil." "Can the Arabs really blackmail us?" asked a gloomy essay in The New York Times Magazine later that month. Three weeks later, after Nixon and Kissinger had organized a massive military airlift to Israel, Americans learned the answer. By Saturday, October 20—by coincidence, the day that Nixon fired the Watergate special prosecutor in the so-called Saturday Night Massacre—the Gulf states had announced a 5 percent overall cutback in oil production and a total embargo on shipments to the United States. Within two weeks, total Arab oil output was down by an estimated 4.4 billion barrels, and with rumors of more cutbacks to come, the oil companies scrambled to get their hands on whatever supplies they could find. By the end of the year, the posted price of oil had reached $11.65, four times the price six months earlier—and ten times the price in 1970.[22]

The reverberations of the oil shock—rampant inflation, recession, unemployment, and a general sense of depression and decline—were felt around the industrialized world. At the time, Nixon announced a range of measures, from year-round daylight saving time and lower state speed limits to the disappearance of every other lightbulb in long federal office corridors, the removal of the lights from the White House

Christmas tree, and a drive for national self-sufficiency under the title Project Independence, that characteristically combined grandiose rhetoric with attention-seeking gimmickry. Others followed his lead: several New England states shut down the evening lights on their capitol domes for the first time since World War II, Pittsburgh and Detroit canceled their Christmas lights, and Georgia's governor, Jimmy Carter, called for cutbacks in the use of state aircraft and ordered building temperatures reduced to sixty-eight degrees.[23]

But although Nixon's new "energy czar," the abrasive William Simon, tried to introduce a mandatory allocation system to ensure there was enough oil to go around, the result was panic. With the newspapers full of price hikes, shortages, and even the prospect of gas rationing, motorists besieged their gas stations. Terrified that the oil might run out at any moment, drivers pulled in even when their tanks were virtually full, sometimes waiting in line for three hours with their engines running. In eight states, stations tried to control the lines by allocating days of the week to motorists with odd- or even-numbered license plates. Responding to a request from the White House, more than nine out of ten stations closed on Sundays, so that, as one reporter put it, "the country's major superhighways and parkways were barren stretches of asphalt and concrete, their service islands bare, their toll-takers inactive." But it was no good. SORRY, NO GAS TODAY signs went up in front of stations across the nation, replacing the confident promises of discounts that had blossomed during the years of abundance.[24]

Most drivers eventually found the gasoline they needed. But the shortages and lines were monumentally inconvenient, and some communities did run dry. Thanks to Simon's allocation system, there were bizarre regional disparities, so that while New Jersey's gas stations ran out, those just miles away in eastern Pennsylvania had all the supplies they needed. Not surprisingly, tempers flared. The nation's truckers launched a two-day strike, and in the Midwest, strikers opened fire on truckers still on the roads. In Indiana, a pump attendant was shot dead by a furious motorist. In Connecticut, staff in one station had to barricade themselves in with their own cars. In New Jersey, the lines were so long that the last cars backed onto a railroad line and were crushed by a train. And, equally unsurprisingly, some people became hoarders. One Ohio motorist stored sixty-five gallons of gasoline in his home; another man in Pennsylvania rashly kept emergency supplies in the trunk of his car and met an unhappy end when they ignited and blew him up.[25]

By the time Ford moved into the White House, the oil embargo had been over for almost six months. But the damage had been done, for as the price of crude oil went up, so did the costs of related commodities like plastics, chemicals, and synthetic textiles, and so too did the prices of manufactures like stockings, cosmetics, and records. In the first quarter of 1974, gross national product fell by the biggest margin in sixteen years—while at the same time, defying conventional economic wisdom, inflation reached an annual rate of almost 15 percent. And for ordinary Americans, the great inflation meant a radical redrawing of their expectations. Unable to pay their bills, students dropped out of college; young couples abandoned their dreams of owning their first home; pensioners, having watched the value of their savings disappear, were reported to be scavenging in the garbage dumps of Miami and Milwaukee. Even the chairman of Chrysler, reflecting on a terrible year for the car industry, admitted that Americans could not "continue piling luxury upon luxury. There has to be an end."[26]

**During most of** Ford's political career, the idea that there had to be an end would have been virtually unthinkable. But at a time when thousands of Americans had watched postapocalyptic fantasies such as the films *Logan's Run* and *Silent Running* and had read antitechnological jeremiads such as Barry Commoner's *The Closing Circle* and Paul Ehrlich's *The Population Bomb* ("too many cars, too many factories, too much detergent, too much pesticide . . . hundreds of millions of people are going to starve to death"), the rhetoric of limits had enormous resonance. Since the 1960s, predictions of ecological disaster and an antitechnological future had become ever more popular, inspired by the environmental movement and the counterculture's distaste for big business. Appalling pollution scandals such as the Santa Barbara oil spill of 1969 had torn holes in the complacent narrative of economic progress, and a year later a staggering twenty million Americans participated in the first Earth Day, listening to worthy speeches, signing petitions, picking up litter, and planting trees. By 1972 the membership rolls of the Sierra Club had lengthened to include some 136,000 names—up almost tenfold in twelve years—while the Audubon Society boasted almost 232,000 members. Even General William Westmoreland, whose record in Vietnam had made him a figure of hatred on college campuses, had become an unlikely convert to the new green orthodoxy. "We have become literally and figuratively fat," he announced in December 1973. "Perhaps the crisis will bring us back to some of the virtues that made this country great, like thrift and the belief that waste is sinful."[27]

Not everybody was convinced, of course. "People don't give a shit about the environment," Richard Nixon told his staff, dismissing it as "crap" for "clowns." But other evidence tells a different story. A survey of more than twenty thousand newspaper editorials in 1970 and 1971 found that it was easily the most commonly discussed domestic issue, while one in four Americans named it as the nation's most pressing problem. And Nixon's own record was a testament to environmentalism's appeal: although some scoffed at his promise to leave the nation "a little cleaner, a little better," he signed the Clean Air Act amendments, two Endangered Species acts, and the Safe Drinking Water Act, established the Environmental Protection Agency, and helped to create an entire industry devoted to waste disposal, environmental review, and pollution control. He was not the only politician to trumpet his born-again green credentials: when the British economist E. F. Schumacher published his manifesto *Small Is Beautiful* in 1973, calling for "Buddhist economics" and a greater emphasis on "health, beauty and permanence," his vociferous admirers included public figures such as Elliot Richardson, Jerry Brown, and Ralph Nader—as well as, most famously, Georgia's ambitious governor, Jimmy Carter.[28]

Of course not all Americans shared the new green sensitivity, which often owed as much to fashion as to genuine conviction. On the left there were complaints that environmentalism meant a retreat from growth, liberalism, and the amelioration of social ills: the National Urban League's president, Whitney Young, condemned middle-class elites for inventing "new causes whose main appeal seems to be in their potential for copping out," while a black activist in Chicago told *Time:* "Ecology? I don't give a good goddamn about ecology!" Yet the "greening of America" had gone further than anyone could have expected. Even the governor of California, one Ronald Reagan, devoted much of his 1970 State of the State address to the need for "all-out war against the debauching of the environment." And popular culture, fashion, and the media were in full retreat from technological utopianism, preferring instead to emphasize all things natural. Fashionable women wore their hair loose and disheveled, rejected heavy makeup, and wore cosmetics like Revlon's Charlie, which promised "the natural look." Vegetarianism was the latest thing, while brown rice, granola, tofu, and yogurt had never been more popular. And these were not just passing fads; they were the first tremors of what were to become seismic shifts in American tastes, not merely in the cultural laboratory of California, but in ordinary households in South Dakota and South Carolina, in Mississippi and Maine.[29]

It was *The New York Times*, so often a barometer of fashionable opinion, that best captured the new mood. "With 1973, an era died, an era of profligacy unprecedented in human experience," declared the paper's editorial at the end of the year. The next few years, it hoped, would see "the rebirth of an ancient virtue, thrift, and the development of a new national ethic dedicated to the conservation of rapidly vanishing resources." The nation had entered a "new era of scarcity" in which "the independence [we] cherish can only be preserved by maintaining a substantial measure of self-sufficiency."

If readers had not yet donned their hair shirts and started growing their own lentils, then William D. Smith's op-ed column five days later would surely have convinced them. "American children growing up in the next several years are likely to have fewer material comforts than their parents enjoyed during their childhoods," he predicted, almost relishing the prospect of "sharply higher gasoline prices . . . quite possibly some form of rationing . . . more discomfort and less convenience, as more sweaters in the winter and less air conditioning during the summer become standard." As if that were not enough, car sales would fall, "the hotel and travel business will likely suffer," "there will likely be a number of bankruptcies in the highway shopping centers," and to crown it all, "convenience items, such as electric combs, tie racks and can openers, will fade from the market as the price of electricity increases." Even garbage bags would become scarce, but since few people would have anything to throw away, it hardly mattered. If Smith were to be believed, the age of affluence was over. A new era of austerity had begun.[30]

**On Gerald Ford's** first morning in the White House, *The Washington Post* announced that his "first and most urgent concern" must be inflation, a problem that was "affecting every family and diminishing the nation's general standard of living." A few days later, two presidential advisers warned that "a prolonged period of unchecked, double-digit inflation poses a severe threat to the economic and social structure of the United States." And at his first press conference three weeks later, Ford bluntly told reporters that inflation was "public enemy number one."[31]

But what on earth was he to do? Even to many economists, the great inflation of the early 1970s was a mystery. For decades, the conventional wisdom had been that there was a trade-off between inflation and unemployment, the so-called Phillips curve. Yet when Ford took office, both were rising simultaneously. And while liberals and conservatives alike, spearheaded by John Kenneth Galbraith and Milton Friedman, agreed that tackling inflation must be the priority, they had very different ideas about what to do. Some blamed the unions, others the employers. Some argued for a tax cut to help the struggling poor; others—including, surprisingly, Galbraith—urged austerity. And while Ford organized fourteen inflation "summits" across the nation in the fall of 1974, they achieved nothing. The central dilemma was this: if Ford increased taxes or cut spending to tackle inflation, he would almost certainly send the economy further into recession, throwing hundreds of thousands out of work. He was damned whatever he did.[32]

Despite his bumbling image, Ford knew more about economic policy than most modern presidents, having spent years working on the House Appropriations Committee. He even gave the press briefing for the 1977 fiscal year budget himself, the first president to do so since Truman, drawing rave reviews. But despite his moderate reputation, his instincts were solidly conservative: he always favored low taxes and lean budgets, although with none of the stridency of some other Republicans. Despite the gulf in style, he was much closer to Ronald Reagan than many conservatives realized.[33]

Ford never concealed his belief that Americans would have to "tighten their belts and get rid of the fat and excesses." He was keen for the First Family to set an example, and Betty pledged to give up expensive clothes and ban sugar from their breakfast table. But he knew that the public wanted something rather more uplifting than thin gruel and frugal living. Inspiration came from a financial columnist, Sylvia Porter, who suggested that ordinary citizens ought to be "enlisted" in the battle against inflation. Ford loved the idea and asked his officials to devise a voluntary program, like the New Deal's Blue Eagle initiative. The result was "Whip Inflation Now," which the president enthusiastically unveiled in a national broadcast on October 8, 1974. Responsible Americans, he said, must spend and waste less, hunt for bargains, trim their food budgets, and shop at stores that kept their prices down. And at the end, he produced a WIN button from his pocket and pinned it ostentatiously on his lapel.[34]

At first the initiative appeared a roaring success. Over the next few weeks, more than 200,000 people sent enlistment forms to the White House, major corporations canceled planned price rises, and stores competed to display the WIN logo in their windows. A national citizens' WIN committee came up with a series of inflation-fighting pledges for businessmen and consumers alike, while thousands of people sent suggestions to the White House, from digging up school playgrounds for vegetables to giving children haircuts at home. Banks and businesses raced to jump aboard the WIN bandwagon, the Marine band recorded a special WIN marching song, and McDonald's even tried to market its new Egg McMuffin as a cheap, inflation-fighting breakfast.[35]

To Ford's economic team, however, it was a ridiculous gimmick. His

Treasury secretary, William Simon, thought it was "ludicrous," recalling that every time it was mentioned, "we at the Economic Policy Board would hide our heads in embarrassment." And since it was always short of funds, direction, and institutional weight, it never went beyond a public-relations stunt. Democratic critics lined up to mock Ford's appearance with the WIN button, while cartoons habitually portrayed the president wearing an outsized button long after the campaign had faded from view. By the beginning of 1975, WIN had become a painful embarrassment, and Ron Nessen recommended that it "be allowed to die a quiet and unlamented death."[36]

But WIN's ignominious failure was the least of Ford's troubles. At the beginning of December 1974, the White House finally confirmed what many analysts already suspected: with consumer confidence at rock bottom, investment stuttering, and businesses struggling, the United States had gone into recession. Ford's Economic Policy Board warned him that the recession was "likely to be the most severe since at least 1958, and probably the worst since the 1930s." As 1975 began, real growth stood at a terrifying minus 5 percent. In the auto industry, more than 200,000 people had been laid off; in the housing industry, tens of thousands of apartment buildings stood empty, waiting for buyers. In Miami–Fort Lauderdale alone, eighteen thousand units stood bare and lifeless. Some architects' firms laid off more than half of their workers, while a spokesman for the National Association of Home Builders described the slump as "by far and away the worst since the Depression."[37]

This was stagflation with a vengeance, an unprecedented combination of soaring inflation and soaring unemployment. "Out of Work," blared a *Newsweek* cover story in January 1975. That month, industrial production suffered the steepest drop since the 1930s, while dozens of major companies, including Goodyear, Westinghouse, and General Electric, laid off thousands of workers. By April, unemployment was almost 9 percent. When interviews for public-sector jobs were advertised in Atlanta, a crowd of more than three thousand fought for places in the line. And in the White House, Ford and his advisers seemed powerless to respond. Meetings were "somber, even frightened," recalled Ron Nessen. When the president asked one aide for the good news, he replied: "That will take about four seconds."[38]

Yet despite the appalling headlines, Ford refused to contemplate government intervention. It would be easy to "spend a lot of money," he told the press, but the resulting inflation would be "infinitely more severe." A surprisingly high proportion of the electorate agreed with him: even in the gloom of January 1975, almost five out of ten voters said they wanted him to concentrate on fighting inflation. Still, the president's critics had a field day. He was a "seventeenth-century physician bleeding his patients in an attempt to cure them," insisted Hubert Humphrey, while Ralph Nader called him "a smiling man who makes cruel decisions." The Indiana senator Birch Bayh, preparing a bid for the presidency, claimed that "high unemployment was deliberately brought about" by Nixon and Ford "as their short-sighted, callous and ultimately unproductive response to the problems of inflation." And the liberal economist Robert Nathan, parodying the WIN program, handed out buttons with the legend BATH— "Back Again to Hoover."[39]

What really infuriated Ford's critics, though, was not so much that he refused to spend money himself as the fact that he insisted on stopping Congress from doing so. In just over two years he vetoed sixty-six congressional bills, many of them spending measures for housing subsidies and public-sector jobs. Keeping inflation down, he maintained, was more important than winning a short-term respite from unemployment. Borrowing from the playbook of his new hero, Harry Truman, he presented himself as the scourge of an irresponsible and wasteful Congress. "What did Congress do in March?" he asked during one national address on energy, melodramatically tearing off the pages of a calendar. "What did Congress do in April in energy? Congress did nothing."[40]

Against a backdrop of rising unemployment, empty factories, and shattering dreams, however, Ford's fiscal conservatism won him few friends. In the press he was habitually portrayed as a hapless clown way out of his depth. Even when he narrowly avoided death in two shocking assassination attempts—both in September 1975, both in California, and both by lonely women (Lynette Fromme and Sara Jane Moore) who had been washed up amid the detritus of the late-1960s counterculture—he still struggled to win public sympathy. If Harry Truman had survived two shootings in three weeks, there would have been an anguished national debate as well as a boost in sympathy for the president. But the depressing reality was that by now assassination attempts were neither exceptional nor shocking. Even the basic elements of the story—the lone gunman with a history of disaffection, the politician working the crowds, the cheerful banter turning to screams of horror—had become clichés. To make matters worse, Ford's reactions—awkwardly throwing up his arm the first time, flinching and blinking the second—seemed cruel confirmation of jokes about his ungainliness. Woody Allen even quipped that Ford had asked him to "follow him around the country and take a shot at him now and then, being careful to miss. He said it would give him a chance to act bravely and could serve as a distraction from genuine issues, which he felt unequipped to deal with."[41]

Allen was on safe ground mocking Ford in the fall of 1975: after all, everyone else was doing it. On October 11, just weeks after the second assassination attempt, NBC launched a new late-night sketch show designed to appeal to young viewers. Skeptical, irreverent, and anti-establishment, NBC's *Saturday Night* (later *Saturday Night Live*) was aimed at college-educated baby boomers who distrusted authority and liked to laugh at their elders. And it was never funnier than in its first year, when its outstanding star was a thirty-two-year-old unknown called Chevy Chase. His trademark was his ability to fall over amusingly, and in Gerald Ford he found the perfect pretext. In the very first episode, Chase even claimed that Ford's new slogan was "If he's so dumb, how come he's president?"* As Ford, Chase tripped over his own lectern, stuck pencils into his hands, tried to play golf with a tennis racket, and stapled his ear to his head. On one occasion, he fell over so violently that he bruised one of his testicles and had to record sketches for the next two weeks from a hospital bed.[42]

But Chevy Chase was the least of Ford's concerns as 1975 slunk toward its end. Inflation showed little sign of easing, and interest rates remained prohibitively high. "The Ford Administration's economic policies are failing," *The New York Times* declared bluntly that fall. Even when he took to the airwaves with a pledge to slash taxes and spending by $28 billion, the biggest tax cut in American history, the reaction was lukewarm. His conservative rhetoric, promising to end "the momentous growth of government," went down badly on Capitol Hill, and in the end Congress forced him to settle for a mere $9 million in tax cuts, accompanied by a vague commitment to limit spending a year later. He seemed a lame-duck president, out of his depth in the choppy waters of the mid-1970s.[43]

The last months of 1975 ended on a distinctly downbeat note: the two attempts on Ford's life, a fiscal crisis in New York City, an unexplained bomb atrocity in LaGuardia Airport, and the continuing fallout from the humiliating collapse of Cambodia and South Vietnam. For Gerald Ford, as for many Americans, it had been a year of disappointments, and in his second State of the Union address in the New Year he struck a markedly conservative note. Government had become "overconfident," he said, trying "to be a policeman abroad and the indulgent parent here at home."

---

*Chase despised Ford, calling him a "terrible president" and "a totally compassionless man." But Ford was not a man who held grudges; later, extraordinarily, they became unlikely friends.

It was time for a "new realism": the government "must stop spending so much and stop borrowing so much of our money." Taxes must be slashed, billions of dollars should be handed back to the states, and welfare programs should be severely cut back. Above all, he called for "a new balance in the relationship between the individual and the government—a balance that favors greater individual freedom and self-reliance." As the *New York Post* put it, this was not Fordism so much as "the new Reaganism."[44]

In the next few weeks a thin shaft of sunlight broke through the economic gloom. The latest inflation and unemployment figures were down, car sales had picked up, and the Dow Jones index showed signs of recovery. And yet it was not all good news: in the Midwest and the Northeast, where the next election would surely be decided, thousands were still out of work. Unemployment was a gift to the Democrats, who brandished their so-called Humphrey-Hawkins bill, proclaiming the right of all Americans to a paying job and committing the federal government to work toward an unemployment rate of 3 percent. In an era when liberalism seemed to have run out of gas, Humphrey-Hawkins offered a welcome rallying point. But it was an exercise in public relations rather than sensible economic management. In an age of rampant inflation, even many Keynesians doubted whether the federal government should be spending millions on new public-sector jobs. Humphrey-Hawkins would "greatly accelerate the inflationary spiral," warned the impartial Congressional Research Service, and even liberal economists such as John Kenneth Galbraith and Paul Samuelson joined the chorus against it.[45]

As 1975 turned into 1976, some of Ford's aides suggested that a little economic pump priming might be in order, so that, like Nixon, he might ride a rising tide to victory. But since Ford was still cleaning up the results of Nixon's preelection spree, he had no desire to repeat his mistakes. In February he vetoed a $6 billion public works program, and when Congress sent it back, he promptly vetoed it again. Even when the recovery faltered, he refused to act. He knew that if he increased spending or cut interest rates, he would win praise in the press and probably more votes in November. But his advisers had already explained that this was merely a "pause": if they intervened, they risked overheating the economy and pushing up inflation. Ford's reaction was both politically insensitive and admirably responsible. "I'm not going to gun the economy for short-term benefits," he told his aides. "It just isn't right."[46]

Even at the time, though, he knew it was a gamble. He would go down in history either as the accidental president whose responsibility won him the acclaim of his compatriots or as the blundering caretaker who, in the name of price stability, had sacrificed the election, the presidency, and his political career. As if his burden were not heavy enough already, he now faced the real prospect that he would not even be able to put his case to the people. On the afternoon of November 19, 1975, Ford was conferring with his senior officials in the Oval Office when an aide quietly placed a message on his desk. "Governor Reagan is on the telephone," it read. "Would you like to speak to him?"

Ford picked up the phone. "Hello, Mr. President," said the familiar mellifluous voice. "I am going to make an announcement, and I want to tell you about it ahead of time. I am going to run for President. I trust we can have a good contest, and I hope it won't be divisive." Ford was not impressed. "I'm sorry you're getting into this," he said grimly. "I believe I've done a good job, and that I can be elected. Regardless of your good intentions, your bid is bound to be divisive." "I don't think it will harm the party," Reagan repeated. "Well, I think it will," Ford said coldly, and then he hung up.[47]

# Chapter Three  Archie's Guys

ARCHIE: If your spics and your spades want their rightful share of the
American dream, let 'em get out there and hustle for it like I done . . .
I didn't have no million people marchin' and protestin' to get me my job.

EDITH: No, his uncle got it for him.

                    —*All in the Family* (1971)

One morning in May 1971, Richard Nixon told his aides about a new
show he had caught on television. "A panel show?" asked his domestic policy chief, John Ehrlichman. "No," said Bob Haldeman, the
White House chief of staff, "it's a regular show. It's on every week. It's
usually just done in the guy's home. It's usually just that guy, who's a
hard-hat." "Looks like Jackie Gleason," Nixon added, explaining that the
series was called *Archie's Guys*.

What really bothered Nixon about the show was the fact that it glorified homosexuality. "Archie is sitting here with his hippie son-in-law, married to the screwball daughter," he explained. "The son-in-law apparently
goes both ways. This guy. He's obviously queer—wears an ascot—but not
offensively so. Very clever. Uses nice language." Nixon sighed. "I don't
mind the homosexuality. I understand it. Nevertheless, goddamn, I don't
think you glorify it on public television, homosexuality, even more than
you glorify whores. We all know we have weaknesses. But, goddammit,
what do you think that does to kids? You know what happened to the

Greeks! Homosexuality destroyed them. Sure, Aristotle was a homo. We all know that. So was Socrates." Yes, Ehrlichman said solemnly, but Socrates "never had the influence that television had."[1]

The show that had outraged Richard Nixon was actually called *All in the Family*, and it was easily the most popular and controversial sitcom of the 1970s. Effectively a remake of a British show written by a socialist playwright, it smashed television taboos from the very beginning. ABC was so disturbed by its content that it turned the show down after a pilot, and the producer Norman Lear eventually took it to CBS, which was desperate to banish its old-fashioned image. Even there, executives were so worried that they broadcast a warning before the first episode in January 1971, explaining that the show "seeks to throw a humorous spotlight on our frailties, prejudices, and concerns. By making them a source of laughter we hope to show, in a mature fashion, just how absurd they are."

Archie Bunker is an American Everyman, a middle-aged dock foreman from Queens, New York, who feels left behind by the cultural changes of the 1960s and worries that his livelihood, his masculinity, and his family are besieged by an unholy alliance of bureaucrats, liberals, blacks, Jews, and Catholics. He struggles against enemies within, too, especially his daughter, Gloria, and son-in-law, Mike "Meathead" Stivic, a permanently unemployed graduate student of radical opinions. In short, Archie is an antihero, an ordinary blue-collar patriot who adores Richard Nixon and despises the "pinkos," "fags," "dagos," "spades," and "jungle bunnies" who threaten his way of life. "Archie Bunker ain't bigoted!" he exclaims at one point. "I'm always the first to say, 'It ain't your fault you're colored!' " But bigoted, of course, is exactly what he is. "Ever since you were little, people kept asking me what kind of man should marry my daughter," he tells Gloria. "I always said that it doesn't matter, so long as he loves her . . . and he's white."[2]

Many black leaders were deeply troubled by the show: Whitney Young, for example, condemned the "creative liberals who find racism a fit subject for television comedy," while the Anti-Defamation League insisted that Archie made "bigotry tolerable." But it was an extraordinary success, topping the ratings and picking up four consecutive Emmy awards. By the time its popularity peaked in 1976, Archie Bunker had become a household name, his face supposedly the most recognized in the country. To millions of viewers, he was the archetypal ordinary guy. And while many watched the show purely for the jokes, there is no doubt that for others Archie's outspoken irascibility reflected their own half-buried fears. The actor Carroll O'Connor, himself staunchly liberal, complained that strangers congratulated him on "telling the truth for a change." "I wish there were more Archie Bunkers," one Oregon storekeeper remarked. "What's great about that show," said a railroad switchman, "is that . . . it's just like you feel inside yourself. You think it, but ole Archie, he *says* it, by damn."[3]

*All in the Family* transcended divisions of generation, gender, class, and political affiliation, making it the nation's favorite mirror onto its own changing values. "The only thing I was hoping," Jimmy Carter told the press after concluding the historic Camp David Accords in 1978, "is that we didn't interrupt *All in the Family*." But Archie was no fan of Jimmy Carter. Always a loyal supporter of "Richard E. Nixon," he had written Ronald Reagan's name on the ballot in 1976, and predicted that Reagan would win in 1980. For once, he was right.[4]


**All in the Family** would never have been so popular had it not tapped a rich vein of working-class discontent. Historians have often written of a white "backlash," especially in neighborhoods teetering between poverty and comfort, against black militants, long-haired hippies, radical protesters, women's libbers, and other groups that Archie Bunker regards with horror. Actually, the roots of the backlash went back even further: in the 1940s it was already apparent in cities like Detroit, where white working-class families felt threatened by black migration and industrial decline. But thanks to the impact of the civil rights movement and the Vietnam War, as well as the shock of violent crime, pornography, and feminism, it was in the second half of the 1960s that backlash first dominated the headlines.[5]

In April 1968 a reporter for *The Saturday Evening Post* found some superbly revealing examples of the new climate in the small town of Millersburg, Pennsylvania. Although residents were generally protected from crime, permissiveness, and protest, they had watched with horror as the Kennedy and King assassinations, urban riots, and the slaughter in Vietnam had unfolded on their television screens. "Everything seems so prosperous and secure now," one woman said, "but I have never felt more insecure in my life." A factory foreman wished that the government "would crack down hard a few times" to "straighten out" the "punk kids, draft-card burners [and] all those Rap Browns." And a third resident worried about "crime, the streets being unsafe, strikes, the trouble with the colored, all this dope-taking, people leaving the churches. It's a breakdown of our standards, the American way of life."[6]

The voters of Millersburg were precisely the kinds of people whom, later that year, Richard Nixon would describe as "the great majority of Americans, the forgotten Americans, the non-shouters, the non-demonstrators."

According to the political strategists Richard Scammon and Ben Wat-tenberg, they were "unyoung, unpoor and unblack," the kinds of people supposedly overlooked by liberal Democrats amid the tumult of the late 1960s. As *The Washington Post*'s Joseph Kraft saw it, they included mil-lions of Americans who had worked their way up to the brink of affluence, owned their own homes, and were terrified of being dragged back under by inflation and unemployment. They wanted better schools, better hous-ing, and cleaner air, but they hated high taxes, interfering bureaucrats, and creeping inflation. For Nixon, they were the "silent majority"; for Kraft, they were the "Middle Americans."[7]

Kraft was only one of dozens of writers who latched onto the idea of the forgotten white majority during the first years of the Nixon presidency. *Harper's* devoted a long piece to "the forgotten American," arguing that some eighty million white citizens, marooned between the ghettos and the affluent suburbs, were in revolt against both liberalism and establishment conservatism. A few weeks later, *Newsweek* called them "the troubled Americans," citing their fury at the rise of crime, busing, obscenity, and street unrest. And in *New York* magazine, Pete Hamill warned that "the working-class white man is actually in revolt against taxes, joyless work, the double standards and short memories of professional politicians, hypocrisy and what he considers the debasement of the American Dream."[8]

When *Time* crowned the Middle Americans as the Man and Woman of the Year for 1969, it was a sign that journalistic attention had definitively shifted from black protest to white backlash. The Middle Americans, said *Time*, were a "vast, unorganized fraternity bound together by a roughly similar way of seeing things": perhaps 100 million people, including the entire blue-collar workforce, much of the elderly population, and "a sub-stantial portion" of the white-collar population. "They live in Queens, N.Y., and Van Nuys, Calif., as well as in Skokie and Chillicothe," the magazine explained. "They tend toward the middle-aged and the middle-brow. They are defined as much by what they are not as by what they are. As a rule, they are not the poor or the rich . . . Few blacks march in the ranks of Middle America. Nor do the nation's intellectuals, its liberals, its professors, its surgeons. Many general practitioners, though, are Middle Americans."[9]

Of course the "silent majority" and "forgotten Americans" were cari-catures, but they were caricatures grounded in fact. And if there was one thing that genuinely united the millions of people who supposedly belonged to these categories, it was their outrage at rising crime. Since the early 1960s, the shift in public attitudes had been extraordinary. In

1965 only a minority of Americans thought that the courts were not harsh enough, but by 1969 three out of four thought they were too lax. In 1966 a plurality of Americans opposed the death penalty, but by 1970 a growing majority supported it. Even in small towns where crime was relatively rare, the impact of television meant that fear still ran high. One reporter visited the quiet little town of Webster City, Iowa, which billed itself as the original "Main Street, U.S.A." The worst Webster could expect, the city manager admitted, was underage drinking and "kids going around breaking windows." And yet even though anarchy in the streets was about as likely as visitors from Venus, the issue that most worried residents was violent crime. "We see it," one resident explained. "We see it two or three times a day in television coverage."[10]

Although fears of crime are sometimes dismissed as a kind of disguised racism, the Iowans' fears were perfectly understandable. It was hardly racist to point out that the national crime figures were genuinely appalling. Between 1965 and 1970, the number of reported crimes jumped from 4.7 million to 8 million, while the number of *violent* crimes (murders, robberies, assaults, and rapes) almost doubled, from 387,000 to 738,000. And if people thought that a new decade would bring a new spirit of law and order, they were greatly mistaken. By 1980, more than a million violent crimes were being reported every year. In twenty years following the election of President Kennedy, the murder rate had doubled, the assault rate had more than trebled, and the rates for robbery and rape had quadrupled. These were, by an enormous margin, the most frightening figures in the Western world.[11]

"Wicked people exist. Nothing avails except to set them apart from innocent people," wrote the conservative sociologist James Q. Wilson in *Thinking About Crime,* an immensely influential tract published in 1975. But while many criminals were undeniably wicked, this hardly explained why there had been such a stunning boom in crime since World War II. Liberal commentators sometimes blamed poverty, but since most Americans were richer than ever, it was hard to see why. Others, on both left and right, blamed drugs. But although drugs clearly played an enormous role in urban street crime during the 1970s and 1980s, the crime boom began before hard drugs were really a factor. The nation's gun culture was another favorite culprit. But while this was certainly a factor in the appalling murder rate, it did not explain why the rates for other crimes—burglaries, stabbings, rapes—were so high. Some conservative critics blamed television and films. Yet it is hard to believe that the relatively tame popular culture of the early 1960s was sufficiently subversive to launch a nationwide crime wave—and if the fault lay with entertainment, then why were Europeans who watched even more explicit films not similarly corrupted?[12]

One obvious factor was that there were simply a lot more potential criminals than ever before. In 1950, some twenty-four million Americans had been young men between fourteen and twenty-four, the most likely group to commit criminal acts; by the mid-1970s, there were more than forty-four million. They lived in a more fluid, mobile, and uncertain society than ever, in which politicians and advertisers urged the virtues of individualism and self-reliance and in which it was normal for families to be fragmented and the bonds of community to be frayed. Those people who committed most crimes, notably young black men, often grew up in crumbling urban tenements, in an atmosphere of neglect and alienation where parental authority was weak or absent. In cities like New York and Detroit, crime was both a temptation and a cancer—simultaneously a ladder to wealth and respect and a social disease eating at the sinews of decency and civility. Although it was an issue that liberals feared to address in case they were labeled racist or authoritarian, it blighted the lives of some of the poorest and most vulnerable members of society. "I am locked up like in the ghettos of Eastern Europe," one elderly Jewish woman told a Brooklyn meeting. "I am afraid of people knocking down my door. I am still not free."[13]

For many Americans, the worst thing about the crime wave was that instead of cracking down hard on offenders, the courts seemed determined to protect them. Since the late 1950s the Supreme Court had guaranteed defendants the rights to counsel, silence, due process, and a quick trial. To those who cared little about the niceties of constitutional law, this was simply mind-boggling. The Supreme Court judges, Archie Bunker used to say, were pampered liberals who were protected from crime and did not understand ordinary people. By 1972, three out of four Americans thought that the courts were not tough enough. Two years later another poll found that an overwhelming 85 percent thought the courts were too soft, while confidence in the Supreme Court had fallen to just 28 percent. "Too much is given away to the criminal," a New York building contractor complained. "They felt sorry for them. It makes me very bitter that people do something wrong and get away with it."[14]

These sentiments would have gone down well with Harry Callahan of the San Francisco Police Department, the hero of Don Siegel's thriller *Dirty Harry* (1971). A huge commercial success, the film was one of many that tapped ordinary Americans' fear of crime and fury at the courts. In his pursuit of wrongdoers, Harry pays no heed to rules and regulations: as played by Clint Eastwood, he is simultaneously a throwback to the cow-boys of the Old West and a spokesman for the silent majority. "When an adult male is chasing a female with intent to commit rape, I shoot the bastard," he tells his appalled superiors. "Where the hell does it say you've got a right to kick down doors, torture suspects, deny medical atten-tion and legal counsel?" asks the district attorney. "Where have you been? Does *Escobedo* ring a bell? *Miranda*? I mean, you must have heard of the Fourth Amendment. What I'm saying is, that man had rights." "Well, I'm all broken up about that man's rights," Harry replies sarcastically. Moments later, he asks in frustration: "And Ann Mary Deacon, what about her rights? I mean, she's raped and left in a hole to die. Who speaks for her?"[15]

While Richard Nixon loved *Dirty Harry*, liberal critics hated it. What troubled them most about the vigilante films of the early 1970s was that they invited white audiences to cheer a white man shooting down crimi-nals who were often black. According to Justice Department figures for 1974, victims of crime blamed black men in three out of ten cases of aggravated assault, four out of ten rapes, and six out of ten robberies, while black men were six times more likely to commit murders than their white counterparts. In fact, most violent crimes were actually committed against other black men, often in connection with the drug trade. There were 223 murders in Boston in 1973–74, for example, yet only two dozen of them involved black men killing whites. But this did not prevent white politi-cians from whipping up fear of black criminals. The antibusing activist Louise Day Hicks claimed that "there are at least one hundred black peo-ple walking around in the black community who have killed white people during the last two years." And Lisa McGoff, a high-school student from working-class Charlestown, was not alone in her belief "that most black boys were out to molest and rape white girls, that black girls would attack white girls in the ladies' room, and that blacks of both sexes carried knives, razors, scissors, stickpins, and other weapons."[16]

In other cities, too, passions ran high. A white trucker from Brooklyn's Canarsie neighborhood soiled himself with fear when five black youths cornered him in an elevator, put a knife to his throat, and took $200 and a gold watch. "Listen you white motherfucker, you ain't calling the law," they said. But he did, and the police caught one of the boys. "The judge gave them a fucking two-year probation," the trucker recalled in disbe-lief. "My next door neighbor was mugged," said another man. "She's a schoolteacher, she used to be real pro-black before, but she hates them now." A third Canarsie man was even blunter: "It's because these people don't know how to live. They steal, they got no values. They say it's history, but that's bullshit. It's not history, it's the way they live. They live like animals."[17]

In Canarsie, fears of black crime were mixed up with all sorts of other anxieties, not least because the neighborhood's character had been radically reshaped by the influx of black families in the 1950s and 1960s. Racism unquestionably played its part in this, but so too, as the neoconservative sociologist Nathan Glazer pointed out in 1975, did hard-edged facts. As black families became more prosperous and moved into formerly lily-white neighborhoods, working-class whites—many the children or grandchildren of immigrants—found themselves competing with the newcomers for jobs and housing. "The blacks want my job, they want to take my little box of a house, they won't leave me alone!" exclaimed one Jewish salesman. "All over Canarsie, people feel others are eroding what they have gained," agreed a local politician. "Today, with the economy so bad . . . people are saying, 'Blacks are coming in and taking our jobs.' "[18]

Racial polarization in the cities of the North was to have a deeply corrosive effect on the fortunes of political liberalism. Places like Brooklyn and Boston had once been reliable Democratic strongholds, but residents' support for welfare programs and tolerance of black activism were wearing very thin indeed. Thanks to the largesse of Lyndon Johnson's Great Society, welfare rolls had more than doubled between 1965 and 1975, yet for white working-class residents frightened by busing and crime, the fact that many of their neighbors were on welfare was the ultimate slap in the face. "These welfare people get as much as I do and I work my ass off and come home dead tired," said one. "They get up late and they can shack up all day long and watch the tube. With their welfare and food stamps, they come out better than me."[19]

Hubert Humphrey, the battle-scarred warhorse of liberalism, later claimed that people who attacked Washington—meaning Jimmy Carter and Ronald Reagan—were "making an attack on government programs, on blacks, on minorities, on the cities. It's a disguised new form of racism, a disguised new form of conservatism." But he was only half-right. Ordinary people who blamed Washington for their plight were indeed often attacking welfare, blacks, and minorities, but they did not think of themselves as racists. No doubt some were still prejudiced, but many insisted that they were personally tolerant. Rightly or wrongly, they felt that they were being punished by inflation and unemployment while others were rewarded for idleness and vice. That Humphrey simply did not understand boded ill for liberalism's prospects in the years ahead.[20]

But Humphrey was not alone in having something of a tin ear where crime and welfare were concerned. Many other liberals either tried to avoid the subject for fear of being considered racist or dismissed white residents' anxieties as mindless bigotry. When New York City's electricity went out on July 13, 1977, the ensuing chaos saw more than sixteen hundred shops ransacked amid apocalyptic scenes of plunder and devastation, with police officers overwhelmed by crowds of predominantly black looters. Yet it was extraordinarily revealing that when store owners denounced the looters as "animals," liberal commentators instinctively jumped to their defense. The looters were merely "victims of economic forces that they sense but do not understand," said *The New York Times*, while the former civil rights activist Andrew Young, now ambassador to the United Nations, insisted that they had been protesting against poverty and unemployment. "If you turn the lights out," he explained, "people will steal"—conveniently ignoring the fact that there had been almost no looting when the power had failed twelve years before.[21]

While liberals wrung their hands, the black store owners who had suffered most were rather less indulgent. The Harlem-born owner of Fedco Foods denounced liberalism's "vicious double standard" by which "whites are expected to obey the law, but blacks are allowed to defy it—so long as they confine their depredations to other blacks." The Brooklyn assemblyman Woodrow Lewis agreed: "When you see a black florist on Nostrand Avenue wiped out, and a supermarket on the same street suffer the same fate, both black-owned, how can I buy excuses that no jobs and poverty motivated this mob action?" And talking to *The Washington Post*, one black police sergeant from Bedford-Stuyvesant was admirably blunt: "The lights went out. A bunch of greedy people took advantage. Plain and simple. Don't go with all that sociological bullshit."[22]

Meanwhile, many readers were outraged that *The New York Times* would even try to excuse the looters' depredations. Among hundreds of furious letters came one from Edward Cherney of Long Island, condemning the "decrepit clichés" spouted by "professional liberals and your editorial board." It was clearly "bad form," he wrote sarcastically, "to tell these parasites that looting, vandalism, arson and other violent crimes are no-nos. It is so much more elegant, so much more profound, so much more chic to blather on about the debt which our society owes to its destroyers." Another Long Island man was "stunned and aghast" to be told that "we do not spend enough of our ingenuity and our affluence to solve the problems of the poor; or that since the rules of society do not work for these people, they do not have to play by the rules." And a third reader, from Manhattan, was appalled that "you still try to justify their behavior. They live on welfare and rip off the Federal Government on all the anti-poverty programs. We either cut them off completely, or we will have to face a drastic evaluation of the situation. The Puerto Ricans can go back to P.R. They belong there anyway and if the blacks do not shape up they can go back to the South."[23]

What the row revealed was not just the link between crime and race but also the gulf between people who wrote editorials for *The New York Times* and people for whom crime was the stuff of everyday nightmares. It was hardly surprising that to many ordinary readers, the very word "liberalism" was beginning to acquire a host of extremely undesirable connotations: "profligacy, spinelessness, malevolence, masochism, elitism, fantasy, anarchy, idealism, softness, irresponsibility and sanctimoniousness." Ironically, it was a populist Democrat, Mario Procaccino, who first coined the damning term "limousine liberal" to describe his patrician opponent, John Lindsay, in New York's mayoral election in 1969. But with Lindsay's brand of moderate Republicanism in deep decline, most limousine liberals were Democrats. A tiny but revealing example came during Sargent Shriver's stint as George McGovern's running mate in 1972. Educated at boarding school and Yale, Shriver was hardly a man of the people, but on a campaign trip to Youngstown, Ohio, he gamely agreed to go into a bar near the steel mill and buy a round of drinks. At first it went perfectly: everybody seemed to be having a good time, and another round was called for. Up went the cries—"Schlitz! Budweiser! Pabst!"— and in his enthusiasm, Shriver momentarily forgot himself. "Make mine a Courvoisier!" he yelled. It is hard to imagine Mario Procaccino making the same mistake.[24]

Of course crime was not the only threat to the relationship between liberals and their blue-collar constituents: the Vietnam War and the emerging feminist movement also left many working-class Democrats bewildered and angry. But the nexus of race and crime posed the biggest threat to the liberal order because it was so emotive. A Brooklyn carpenter who had bought his own home for the first time told Jonathan Rieder: "The rich liberals, they look down on my little piece of the American dream, my little back yard with the barbecue here . . . The liberals and the press look down on hardhats like me, but we've invested everything we have in this house and neighborhood. I can be a good father and a nice guy and still say, 'Fuck those niggers.' "[25]

Some historians, such as George Wallace's distinguished biographer Dan Carter, argue that "fears of blackness" lay at the root of the antiliberal backlash. But this seems far too reductive. The targets of the backlash were not just blue-collar blacks but also affluent white students, well-educated white liberals, and cosseted white judges. Barbara Mikulski, the daughter of a Baltimore grocer and a passionate champion of her fellow Polish

Catholics, wrote that the Middle American was "sick of being stereotyped as a racist and a dullard by phony white liberals, pseudo black militants, and patronizing bureaucrats." As she saw it, the real issue was class, not race: "He pays the bill for every major government program and gets nothing or little in the way of return. Tricked by the political rhetoric of illusionary funding for black-oriented social programs, he turns his anger to race—when he himself is the victim of class prejudice."

"Now people say we're only out for ourselves and we're against the Negroes an' all that," one welder remarked. "Well I don't know. I've never been asked. If they did come around and talk with us at work and ask us their question, I'll bet we confuse them. One minute we'd sound like George Wallace, and the next we'd probably be called radicals or something."[26]

**Although George Wallace** never came close to winning the presidency, he is rightly remembered as one of the most important politicians of the postwar decades. The Alabama governor's determination to defend segregation—and not to be "outniggered" by his rivals, as he charmingly put it—made him the champion of the Old South. But his appeal transcended regional boundaries. During his independent presidential campaign in 1968, he attracted so much support from northern workers that labor bosses feared he would cost the Democrats the election. In working towns like Gary, Indiana, one reporter noted, union members supported him as "a kind of surly class assertion," a vote of confidence in a politician who "talked like them, angered like them, even dressed like them." Indeed, researchers into the Wallace vote in blue-collar Gary found that the more "working-class" voters considered themselves, the more likely they were to give him their vote.[27]

Racism was not the only element in Wallace's appeal. Running to regain the governorship of Alabama in 1970, he reminded audiences of the "rich folks" in the country clubs and "big old houses," sipping "those martinis with their little fingers up in the air" and calling for school integration. "And guess where their children go to school?" he sneered. "They go to a lily-white private school. They've bought above it all!" During his presidential campaign two years later, which was eventually cut short by an assassin's bullet, some of his biggest laughs came when he poured scorn on the "hypocrites who send your kids half-way across town while they have their chauffeurs drop their kids off at private schools." Liberal intellectuals, he said, had "looked down their nose at the average man in the street too long. They look down at the bus driver, the truck driver, the fireman, the policeman, and the steelworker, the plumber, and the communications worker, and the oil worker and the little businessman, and they say, 'We've gotta write a guideline. We've gotta tell you when to get up in the morning. We've gotta tell you when to go to bed at night.' "[28]

Wallace's itineraries represented a comprehensive tour of Middle America in the early 1970s: shopping malls in white working-class suburbs, county fairgrounds, a stock-car racetrack, a drag strip, a high-school football stadium, a string of highway motel-restaurants. Polls suggested that, contrary to myth, his supporters were not much more racist or conservative than other voters. What set them apart was their keen sense of frustration and powerlessness against the tides of liberalism, permissiveness, and modernity. "They feel the established system has not been sympathetic to them in their problems of everyday life," Ted Kennedy remarked, "and in a large measure they are right."[29]

A common misapprehension about Wallace is that he served as a "bridge" for Democratic voters on their way to the Republican Party. In fact, most of his voters later returned to the Democratic fold, and even in 1980 most of Wallace's old districts stayed loyal to the Democrats. His real historical importance was that he brought to the national stage a rhetorical style drawn from the long history of southern populism. He was the first national figure to capitalize on the growing backlash against crime, permissiveness, and welfare; he was also the first to focus white working-class anger on Democrats, intellectuals, bureaucrats, and the federal government. The vocabulary and themes of populism had long existed, but Wallace's achievement was to weld them into a "new symbolic language," identifying an evil establishment of liberal politicians, intellectuals, and bureaucrats, the sworn enemies of the ordinary workingman. Even at his peak he was too strident to reach out beyond his southern and blue-collar base. But other conservative politicians would learn from his example.[30]

For much of his presidency, Richard Nixon was obsessed by the need to woo Wallace's supporters. His vice president Spiro Agnew spent much of his time as a kind of Wallace tribute act, furiously denouncing "permissivists," "thieves, traitors and perverts," and "radical liberals." Meanwhile, Nixon's aides did their best to borrow Wallace's political vocabulary. "We should increasingly portray [George] McGovern as the pet radical of Eastern Liberalism, the darling of the *New York Times*, the hero of the Berkeley Hill Jet Set; Mr. Radical Chic," Patrick Buchanan suggested in 1972. "By November, he should be postured as the Establishment's fair-haired boy, and RN postured as the Candidate of the Common Man, the working man." And of course it worked. For the first time in its history the AFL-CIO refused to endorse the Democratic candidate, and in November 1972 Nixon picked up more than half of the labor and manual worker votes, both records for a Republican. In *Newsweek*'s words, he was "the champion of the good, God-fearing burghers of Heartland U.S.A."[31]

But God had changed a great deal since the days when the driving spirit of the Republican Party was old-fashioned Anglo-Saxon Protestant-ism. Although tradition held that the Catholic Church was the Demo-cratic Party at prayer, more and more Italians, Poles, and Slavs were voting for the Grand Old Party. In office, Nixon worked hard to appease tra-ditional Catholic Democrats appalled by pornography, black militancy, and antiwar protest. One White House aide, a former garbageman with a doctorate called Michael Balzano, secured funds for Radio Free Europe, a National Heritage Day, and the Ethnic Heritage Studies Act, which provided grants for research in "ethnic studies." And although Nixon's Quaker upbringing and general air of Anglo-Saxon repression made him seem one of the least "ethnic" men in the nation, he did his best. "Every time I'm at an Italian-American picnic," he told an audience in Mary-land, "I think I have some Italian blood." In private, however, he had other ideas. "Italians, they're not like us, they smell different, they act dif-ferent," he muttered one day to John Ehrlichman. "The trouble is, you can't find one who is honest."[32]

Nixon's drive to win over so-called ethnic Americans made perfect electoral sense. Just under fifty million people identified themselves as "ethnic" at the start of the decade, the majority having just a high-school education and earning less than $10,000 a year. During the early postwar years there had been little sense that they wanted to be seen as anything other than ordinary Americans. But during the 1960s, ideas of group iden-tity began to gain ground, influenced by the black civil rights movement and Black Power. Beleaguered by everything from stagnant wages and surging prices to student militancy and the spread of pornography, Ital-ians, Poles, and Slavs began to turn inward, taking solace from their trou-bles in the values of their fathers. If there was such a thing as Black Power, asked the *Ukrainian Weekly* in 1970, then why not "Ukrainian Power"?[33]

If the cult of ethnicity had a high priest, it was Michael Novak, the Catholic sociologist who transformed himself from radical leftist to neo-conservative hard-liner. Protestant politicians, he wrote in 1971, had stig-matized American Catholics as "unenlightened, stupid, immoral, and backward" and tried to dissolve them in the melting pot of modernity. But now the very idea of assimilation was history: hence the title of his bestselling tract, *The Rise of the Unmeltable Ethnics*. Others took a simi-lar line. White ethnics had had enough of hiding their "warmth, charm, and zesty communal spirit," claimed Barbara Mikulski, and were in open revolt against the "phony liberals" whose welfare programs supposedly favored lazy, greedy blacks over their hardworking white neighbors. "The lid is coming off America's 'melting pot,' and a bitter residue is being discovered inside," agreed *The New York Times*. "For many ethnic groups, the American Dream has dissolved into a fearful reality as the communities they fashioned have begun to cave in."[34]

In hindsight, all this was wildly overblown. Ethnic Americans did not turn their backs on the patriotic ideal, and the United States continued to be the world's most effective melting pot, assimilating thousands of new citizens from countries as diverse as Mexico, South Korea, India, and Lebanon. At the time, however, the ethnic revival was becoming an industry in its own right. Fleeting best sellers like Peter Schrag's lament *The Decline of the WASP* (1970), think tanks like the National Center for Urban Ethnic Affairs, pressure groups like the Italian American Civil Rights League, even ethnic political champions like Novak and Mikulski, all testified to an explosion of self-consciousness among so-called hyphenated Americans. Half-forgotten immigrant sagas found new audiences, while Chaim Potok and Philip Roth attracted critical praise with novels steeped in the second- or third-generation experience. Ethnicity made it onto Broadway in *Fiddler on the Roof,* onto television in *Bridget Loves Bernie,* and into the kitchen in cookbooks like *Czech Your Cooking*. In schools and colleges, history primers gave unprecedented space to immigrant stories. "We are inundated by a virtual flood of books, articles, and dissertations dealing with the roles of race, nationality, and religion in American history," concluded a survey of the field in 1979.[35]

But it was in Hollywood that the ethnic revival made the greatest cultural inroads. Hyphenated Americans had always played a crucial role in the film industry, and during the 1970s they moved to center stage. The surnames of the decade's biggest male stars tell the story—Marlon Brando, Al Pacino, Robert De Niro, Sylvester Stallone, John Travolta—while directors such as Francis Ford Coppola, Martin Scorsese, and Woody Allen made no secret of their ethnic sensibilities. Scorsese even remarked that his great breakthrough, *Mean Streets* (1973), was "an attempt to put myself and my old friends on the screen, to show how we lived, what life was like in Little Italy. It was really an anthropological or sociological tract." A year later he made the documentary *Italianamerican,* including interviews with his parents, memories of the journey from Sicily to New York, and, inevitably, footage of his mother stirring a rich meatball sauce, with the recipe revealed in the credits. It was not quite the territory of "Mamma mia, that's-a some spicy meatball," the slogan of a controversial

Alka-Seltzer commercial dropped after pressure from Italian American groups. But it was not far off.[36]

The supreme cinematic expressions of the ethnic revival, though, were the work of another Italian American director. Released in 1972 and 1974, Francis Ford Coppola's two *Godfather* films were based on Mario Puzo's gangster thriller, which had stormed to the top of the best seller lists. What appealed to audiences, though, was arguably not that they were films about crime but that they were films about *family*. The first film, for example, opens not with a gangland shoot-out but with a wedding party, immersing us in the ritualized world of the Corleones' extended household. One of the guests, an Italian immigrant called Amerigo Bonasera, has come to Don Corleone with a request for justice. It is classic silent-majority stuff. His daughter has been badly beaten by two boys who tried to rape her (not Italians, he adds). So he went to the police, "like a good American." But the judge handed down only a three-year suspended sentence. "I stood in the courtroom like a fool," he moans. "And those two bastards, they smiled at me."

The Godfather's response is initially chilly. "Why did you go to the police?" he asks. "Why didn't you come to me?" He mocks Bonasera's attempt to assimilate: "You found paradise in America, you had a good trade, you made a good living. The police protected you and there were courts of law. And you didn't need a friend like me." But as Bonasera has come to realize, family and ethnicity are stronger than the institutions of law and order. "Be my friend, Godfather," Bonasera begs, kissing the Don's hand, and at last the Don accepts: "Someday, and that day may never come, I'll call upon you to do a service for me. But, until that day, accept this justice as a gift on my daughter's wedding day." Tellingly, they part in Italian: "*Grazie*, Godfather"; "*Prego.*"

The real hero of the film is the Don's youngest son, Michael, played by the handsome and unmistakably Mediterranean Al Pacino. As a Dartmouth graduate who has served in World War II and first appears in a Marine's uniform, he wants nothing more than to be an assimilated American: hence the good Protestant girlfriend with the patriotic surname, Kay Adams. Discussing the Don's criminal activities, Michael assures her: "That's my family, Kay, that's not me." But by the end of the film he has become his father's true heir, a cold-blooded murderer who shoots a crooked police captain, flees to his ancestral home in Sicily, and returns as the new Godfather. In the last scene, Kay watches from a distance as Michael's Italian underlings pay their respects, and then the door closes firmly in her face. Assimilation has been decisively rejected: Michael's wartime service, his Marine uniform, and even his frank relationship with his Protestant wife have all been banished to the past.

Like so many aspects of the ethnic revival, *The Godfather* offered a taste of Old World "authenticity" in a suburban, rootless world. At a time when modernity itself was coming into question, it looked back to the unchanging virtues of family and faith; in an increasingly individualistic society, it held out the virtues of collective loyalty. Its vision was nostalgic, even comforting: it looked back to an age of solid matriarchs, wise fathers, and faithful sons, an age of what Francis Ford Coppola called "benevolent authority." And while Archie Bunker might inveigh against "wops" and "dagos," the values of the Corleone family were not a million miles from his own. They were not so far, either, from the values of his favorite president, who requested a private screening just nine days after *The Godfather* opened.[37]

**By the late 1970s,** ethnic self-assertion had become such a familiar feature of American life that it was in danger of becoming a cliché. What the sociologist Herbert Gans called "symbolic ethnicity" was now a familiar feature of American life, giving working-class white Americans a sense of tradition in an increasingly homogeneous suburban world. The Census Bureau found that in just a few years the number of people identifying themselves as Polish Americans had leaped by a million, while the Italian American Civil Rights League boasted twenty-five chapters from coast to coast. No community lacked its champions and boosters; none was without its "bootstrap mythology" of sacrifice and struggle.[38]

All this had two effects. First, it perpetuated a new sense of identity based on suffering, hard work, and achievement, allowing blue-collar whites to draw an implicit contrast with the supposed laziness and criminality of their black neighbors. It encouraged not interracial sympathy but ethnic exclusivity; it allowed almost anyone, except for the wealthiest Anglo-Saxon Protestants, to console themselves that once upon a time, they too had been harshly treated. Ethnic Americans, wrote Michael Novak, had achieved "moderate success" through "loyalty, hard work, family discipline, and gradual self-improvement." Why could blacks not do the same, instead of marching and looting? Why did they "want to jump, via revolutionary militance, from a largely rural base of skills and habit over the heads of lower class whites?" As for the charge of racism, he dismissed it outright: "Racists? Our ancestors owned no slaves."[39]

But the second result was perhaps even more profound. Although Novak would later become a fierce critic of multiculturalism, nobody would have predicted this in 1971, when he called for "'the American way of life' [to] be broken open like a cocoon giving way to the burgeoning wings of a butterfly." Yet with his insistence on roots and his cherished sense of grievance, he was a prophet of the introspection and fragmentation that was to come. As early as 1974, the Supreme Court ordained that school districts must allow pupils who spoke little English to study math, science, and social studies in their native tongues. Five years later the new Department of Education came up with a bilingual education plan to set up hundreds of new programs and employ some fifty thousand new bilingual teachers. And that same year, a federal judge ordered the Ann Arbor school district to offer "black English" teaching for its black children.[40]

Of course the American people had never been ethnically or culturally homogeneous, and the nation's great cities had long rung with dozens of different tongues. But this was something new: the veneration of the individual at the expense of the collective, the little group at the expense of the wider body, rights at the expense of duties, past grievances at the expense of optimistic ambitions. Some observers celebrated a new climate of diversity befitting a postmodern age of multiple identities and individual rights. But it took a tired old liberal, the man whom Archie Bunker had rejected in favor of "Richard E. Nixon," to see that what would be lost would be a sense of solidarity, common effort, and public good, and that the victims would be society's weakest members. Only a sense of "mutual needs, mutual wants, common hopes, the same fears," Hubert Humphrey insisted, could banish the prejudices and inequalities that still haunted millions of Americans, black and white.[41]

But nobody was listening. Humphrey, after all, was yesterday's man. And if anybody doubted that his brand of social-democratic liberalism was in deep trouble, then he needed only to look to New York City in the last months of 1977, when the former vice president was fighting his final battle against cancer. Once a paragon of big-government liberalism, the city seemed to be turning its back on the creed Humphrey had made his own. In the spectacularly vicious Democratic mayoral primary, the incumbent, Abraham Beame, an old-fashioned machine politician who had worked his way up from Lower East Side poverty, could finish no better than third. His tears of disappointment on September 8 seemed more than a lament for his own defeat; they were a lament for "a vanishing New York, a New York in which the sons of socialists overcame poverty and then quietly devoted themselves to making the city a better place to live." The days of party hacks and urban machines, of civic trust and social solidarity, had gone.[42]

And revealingly, the issue that dominated the campaign was the one thing Hubert Humphrey least liked to discuss: crime. Even Manhattan's black borough president, Percy Sutton, had jumped aboard the law-and-order bandwagon, his radio spots describing New York as "a city turned sick with the fear of crime" and lambasting the criminals "cheating, stealing, and driving away our families and our jobs." Sutton's lurch to the right horrified his supporters, but he had divined which way the wind was blowing. Year by year, public attitudes were hardening. Even in supposedly liberal New York, opposition to the death penalty was now an electoral handicap, and during the Democratic runoff New York's secretary of state, Mario Cuomo, was bombarded with questions about his position on capital punishment. As he patiently recited his answer—that it would not deter hardened criminals, that it would fall disproportionately on the poor, that it would do nothing to alleviate the conditions from which crime sprang—audiences shook their heads. In the Bronx, one man shouted, "Kill them!" before Cuomo had finished; in Brooklyn, an elderly woman spat at him. "The city was scared to death, angry and frightened," he said later, "angry at the police and angry at me for not supporting the death penalty."[43]

It was not Cuomo but the man who beat him to the mayoralty, Ed Koch, who represented the future. Once a loyal liberal Democrat, Koch ran in 1977 as the incarnation of the ordinary New Yorker, a plain-talking white ethnic who promised to crack down on crime and clean up the streets. By cultivating a sassy, wisecracking persona, he harked back to the legendary Fiorello La Guardia, but in his populist conservatism he represented something new, a Reagan Democrat before the term had been invented. Unlike Cuomo, he strongly affirmed his belief in the death penalty; had he been running city hall during the blackout, Koch said, he would have asked for the National Guard and taken no prisoners.

As mayor, he slashed New York's budget, raised subway fares and tuition fees, and allowed private developers a virtual free hand in rebuilding the city. Under Koch's cocky stewardship, the "laboratory of American liberalism" was to become a very different kind of place, reborn in the furnace of unfettered capitalism—a city of ruthless extremes, a city of the superrich and the hopeless poor, a city in which homeless beggars lived and died just yards from the high-rise windows of Wall Street and the gleaming excesses of Trump Tower. In Ed Koch's New York, Hubert Humphrey's common hopes would become a very distant memory indeed.[44]

# Chapter Four    *The Porno Plague*

The American family is in trouble. I have campaigned all over
America, and everywhere I go, I find people deeply concerned
about the loss of stability and the loss of values in our lives.

**—GOVERNOR JIMMY CARTER, 1976**

Labor Day 1974, and in Kanawha County, West Virginia, tempers were
running high. Eight thousand people gathered to hear the fundamentalist preacher Marvin Horan urging them to boycott the new school
year. When schools opened the next morning, more than nine thousand
children stayed at home. The next day, more than three thousand coal
miners in the remote Upper Valley walked out, ignoring orders from their
union officials. A week later, thousands more had joined them in seven
neighboring West Virginia counties. Every morning huge crowds gathered outside the school district headquarters in Charleston, the state capital. And at schools, bus garages, and businesses serving the county education system, hundreds of protesters blocked roads and entrances, erecting
makeshift barricades along the picket lines.

Day after day, school buses ran the gauntlet of stones, shots, and Molo-
tov cocktails, while parents who ignored the boycott risked being stoned in
their homes or having their cars set on fire. Two schools were firebombed,
another was dynamited, and more were vandalized in the night. Someone
opened fire on the car of the Classroom Teachers Association president.
Protesters beat up a CBS news crew; a UPS driver was shot trying to cross

the picket line; a demonstrator was shot in the heart by a terrified truck terminal janitor. And despite all the school board's efforts to find a settlement, fifteen sticks of dynamite, hidden beneath the gas meter in their main office building, went off just minutes after the end of a board meeting. Only by sheer good luck was nobody killed.[1]

The most populous county in West Virginia, Kanawha was a rural backwater, a place where change came slowly, if at all. Most people were white Protestants, but there was a deep cultural divide between the Charleston middle class and the rural Appalachian majority, many of them miners in the Upper and Lower Valleys. Since the 1950s, dozens of small valley schools had been closed down, forcing Appalachian children to take the bus to urban schools, where they were exposed to ideas that clashed with their parents' old-fashioned morality. What happened in 1974 was a collision between the traditional values of the Appalachian valleys, with their emphasis on faith and family, and the secular values of liberal modernity—a collision that would soon become familiar across the nation.[2]

The seeds of the controversy were sown in 1970, when Alice Moore, a mother of four schoolchildren, was elected to the county board of education. Like those other populist heroines of the decade, Louise Day Hicks, Phyllis Schlafly, and Anita Bryant, "Sweet Alice" presented herself as an ordinary housewife. In fact, she was married to a fundamentalist pastor and had extremely conservative convictions. Her initial target was sex education, which she described as a "humanistic, atheistic attack on God," winning her great popularity with West Virginia's poor rural "creekers." But what really infuriated her was the board's decision in March 1974 to adopt more than three hundred new titles for its K–12 language-arts curriculum. After leafing through the books, Moore was horrified. She put a selection on display at the St. Albans library, delivered talks at churches and parents' groups, and reached out for allies among the dozens of self-ordained preachers with rural followings. She also made contact with the veteran campaigners Mel and Norma Gabler, who had spent more than ten years scouring textbooks over their kitchen table in Longview, Texas, looking for anything that questioned the free market, the American way of life, or the "morals, values, and standards as given to us by God through his Word written in the Ten Commandments and the Bible."[3]

There had been textbook controversies before: in Anaheim, California, conservative parents had thrown out a sex education program in the late 1960s. But the striking thing about the Kanawha County controversy was that the books were so inoffensive. While the textbooks were standard D. C. Heath material, the literary texts included such titles as *The Iliad, Paradise Lost, Crime and Punishment, Animal Farm, Lord of the Flies,* and *The Crucible*. The most widely criticized were titles by black authors such as James Baldwin and Alice Walker: some contained words like "tits" and "piss," but none was likely to turn local children into deranged radicals. To their critics, though, they were insufficiently patriotic. Mike Edds, a youth pastor who joined the campaign, told the historian William Martin that the books "challenged the sacredness of everything that we believed about America." "They said the flag was just a piece of cloth," he explained. "Well, that's not what we believe. We have a lot of relatives who died under that banner."

Other common complaints were that the books were "socialist" or "communist-inspired" or, if they addressed contemporary social problems, that they were "morbid" and "negative." Bizarrely, one of these was a book called *Monologue and Dialogue*, which included poems by Browning, Blake, Arnold, and Eliot but was too depressing for the young minds of West Virginia. Finally, anything that encouraged symbolism, irony, or role-playing was deeply suspicious, for multiple and playful interpretations of a text might undermine the notion of biblical truth. Alice Moore was particularly aggrieved by the fable of Androcles and the lion, because it might encourage children to question the story of Daniel in the lions' den. "That kind of thing doesn't happen by accident," she said. "Their intent was obvious."[4]

By the summer of 1974 the battle lines had been drawn. The West Virginia Human Rights Commission, the local NAACP, and the YWCA all backed the books, as did Charleston's major newspapers and most mainstream Episcopalian, Catholic, Methodist, and Presbyterian churches. On the opposite side was ranged a loose coalition of rural parent-teacher groups and conservative white evangelical churches: a people's army, or so it seemed. In fact, Moore's group boasted powerful sponsors, from local businessmen who wanted to strike back against liberal government to conservative champions from outside the state. Above all, she benefited from the financial support of the Coors-backed Heritage Foundation, which sent the lawyer James McKenna to defend fundamentalist preachers arrested in the course of the campaign.[5]

What followed came close to anarchy, with passions whipped up by fundamentalist pastors who saw themselves as warriors for Christianity. The Reverend Charles Quigley, for instance, asked "Christian people to pray that God will kill" the board members who had "mocked and made fun of dumb fundamentalism." On December 1, the Reverend Avis Hill led two thousand people through Charleston carrying placards that read "No Peaceful Co-existence with Satanic Communism." Eleven days later, protesters broke into a televised school-board meeting and attacked the superintendent and board members. The New Year brought more violence. On January 17 a grand jury indicted the Reverend Marvin Horan and five accomplices for "conspiracy to blow up two elementary schools and other School Board property." The next day, Horan's supporters gathered outside the state capitol to welcome a delegation from the Ku Klux Klan. "The Communist, socialist, nigger race is going to dominate this nation," warned Imperial Wizard James Venable to applause from the crowd.[6]

The Klan's appearance was a turning point. Even die-hard textbook protesters were shocked by their intervention, and with the conviction of Marvin Horan, who served three years in a federal prison, the public confrontations lost their edge. As for the textbooks, most remained on the list and were sent to classrooms throughout the county. But it was a Pyrrhic victory. The more controversial titles were never used, especially in schools where teachers were frightened of parental opposition. And the conflict proved a model for hundreds of textbook battles across the nation, usually launched by Christian parents objecting to such authors as John Steinbeck and Mark Twain. By 1981, one in five school districts had experienced challenges to its textbooks. And while no district suffered the agonies of Kanawha County, the obvious explanation was that many school boards had lost the will to fight a battle they suspected they could never win.[7]

**The Kanawha County** controversy was more than a squabble about new textbooks. As the Reverend James Lewis, the liberal rector of Charleston's major Episcopal church, explained in a nationally syndicated article, the "anti-textbook people of Kanawha County" were "confused and angry about everything from marijuana to Watergate. Feeling helpless and left out, they are looking for a scapegoat. They are eager to exorcise all that is evil and foul, cleanse or burn all that is strange and foreign." It was a battle, said Alice Moore, against "the administrators, the people from other places who have been trying to tell us what is best for our children." It was a struggle against "elitism," agreed Mike Edds, "that saw the majority of the county's population as ignorant, uneducated folks." The people of Kanawha County, he went on, were "very pro-American, very patriotic—it's apple pie, Mom, the flag, and the church. These textbooks struck at every area of that belief system."[8]

In many ways the Kanawha County affair was merely the latest episode in a long-running conflict between conservatism and change, taking its turn in the headlines as the temperance movement and the issue of evolution had before it. For moral conservatives, however, there seemed something uniquely alarming about the pace of change in the age of Watergate and Vietnam. Once, committed Christians could virtually escape the sinful secular world, especially if they lived in remote rural communities little touched by modernity. But with the arrival of air travel and mass communications, it was almost impossible to build a sealed "city on a hill," free from vice and corruption. Cities and suburbs threw together millions of people with entirely different values, while television beamed threatening images, from hippies and peaceniks to gays and feminists, directly into their living rooms. For many moral conservatives, television was the decisive provocation; as one writer puts it, it brought "pornography into Baptist living rooms," penetrating their "walls of separation." "An Alabama farmer can flick a dial and there's Allen Ginsberg on a talk show," remarked another observer. "Or Archie Bunker fraternizing with a black or homosexual . . . Some very provocative ideas slide through that tube into homes that never would have been reached before."[9]

At the heart of the new culture wars was a growing sense that the institution at the center of the national moral order—the American family—was under unprecedented threat. From the 1940s to the 1960s, the family had played a central role in Americans' images of their own society. The *Time-Life* vision of the happy family was an idealized picture of middle-class affluence: children contentedly playing in suburban yards, mothers gliding effortlessly around their gleaming new kitchens, square-jawed fathers behind the wheels of their shiny new cars. The nuclear family, writes the historian Natasha Zaretsky, was the cornerstone of the national effort in the Cold War, preparing "children for the duties of liberal citizenship," instilling "a healthy work ethic and a sense of military honor into boys," and socializing girls "for the demands that would one day be required of them as wives, mothers, and homemakers." As one conservative activist put it in 1980, the family was "the core institution that decisively determines the nature of society itself."[10]

Yet by January 1973, when PBS broadcast the first installment of its pseudo-anthropological documentary series, *An American Family*, it was impossible to pretend that everything in the garden was rosy. Hailed in advertisements as "television's first 'real family,' " the aptly named Louds of Santa Barbara, California, seemed a long way from Alice Moore's vision of the traditional Christian household. The producers had picked them precisely because they seemed to have been shaped "by the national myths and promises, the American dream and experiences that affect all of us." Yet despite their ostentatious affluence, their hillside home, swimming pool, stable, and four cars, Bill and Pat Loud presided over a family that was gradually ripping itself apart.[11]

It became an almost archetypal pattern: the handsome, career-driven husband with an eye for the ladies; the bored, lonely housewife experiencing an emotional awakening; the household torn apart by the sexual, economic, and cultural pressures of the early 1970s. The Louds' eldest son, Lance, for example, occasionally wore lipstick and women's clothes and came out as gay during the filming of the show, becoming television's first openly gay icon. Meanwhile, not only was Bill's company in financial trouble, but his repeated infidelities had brought his marriage to the breaking point. "Bill and I have never been able to have a relationship where we could honest-to-God talk to each other," Pat Loud admits on camera. "If we had any sex life, that would be nice. But it's kind of like a courtesy 'Thank you, ma'am.' " In the climactic episode, she greets him from a business trip with the words: "I've seen a lawyer. I want you to move out." Bill does not argue. "Fair deal," he says wearily. "I won't have to pack."[12]

What made *An American Family* so powerful was that the Louds' experience resonated with thousands of other ordinary families in the early 1970s. Where the collapse of a marriage would once have been seen as shameful, it was now becoming almost routine. Beginning with California in 1969, all but three states introduced no-fault divorce provisions, and by 1975 more than a million couples were divorcing every year, one for every two that got married. There had always been deeply unhappy unions, of course, but with people working longer hours, the economic downturn biting into family incomes, and millions of wives choosing to forge their own distinctive careers, the pressures were arguably greater than ever. Feminism played its part, too: like Pat Loud, millions of women who had married young now believed that a formerly romantic union could no longer satisfy their changing desires. The result was easily the highest divorce rate in the developed world. If the trend continued, observed *Newsweek*'s review of *An American Family*, four out of ten couples that married in 1973 would soon be divorced. Not for nothing did Tom Wolfe call it "the Great Divorce Epidemic."[13]

For some commentators, the rise of divorce represented freedom from the shackles of a dying moral order. Divorcées "almost without exception look and feel better than ever before," claimed Susan Gettleman and Janet Markowitz's preposterous manifesto *The Courage to Divorce* (1974). "They act warmer and more related to others emotionally, tap sources of strength they never knew they had, enjoy their careers and their children more, and begin to explore new vocations and hobbies." Divorce was a modern *"rite de passage,"* agreed Gail Sheehy in her pop-psychological best-seller *Passages* (1976), "a ritual necessary before anyone, above all herself, will take a woman's need for expansion seriously." But while feminist writers were often quick to applaud a woman's need for "self-realization," they were far slower to appreciate the terrible damage that divorce could wreak on her children. Gettleman and Markowitz even had the gall to claim that divorce was "liberating" for children. It would give them "greater insight and freedom as adults," they claimed, "in deciding whether and when to marry."[14]

And when *New York* magazine ran the story of a thirty-one-year-old mother of four who had left her family after ten years of marriage, moved to New York, and divorced her husband, the label of the Me Decade had never seemed more appropriate. Some might call her "spoiled," the woman admitted, because she was taking "so many other people—like my husband and children, just to pick some at random—over the hill with me in my decisions." But she thought she was "moral in the deepest sense because I would no longer in the name of sacrifice to others—like my husband and children, just to pick some at random—let slip away the one life I was given as wholly mine to do something with."[15]

All of this unfolded against an intellectual backdrop that was less sympathetic to the traditional family than at any time in living memory. One crucial influence was the Scottish radical psychologist R. D. Laing, who emphasized the destructive role of the "family nexus" in the formation of mental illness. Another was radical feminism, which blamed the nuclear family for denying female self-realization and condemning millions of housewives to loneliness and drudgery. In feminist consciousness-raising groups, "marriage" and "pregnancy" were reviled as dirty words. Women needed to escape "the psychological penalties of the biological family . . . by every means available," claimed the radical feminist Shulamith Firestone, while even the feminist historian and single mother Alice Kessler-Harris was told that she needed to be "separated" from her daughter for her own good.[16]

Even outside radical circles, there was a growing consensus that the American family was in deep trouble. In September 1973 a Senate subcommittee heard three days of testimony from psychologists, anthropologists, and clergymen about the unprecedented pressures on the family. Four years later, the eminent child psychologist Urie Bronfenbrenner declared in *The Washington Post* that "the American family as we know it is falling apart," citing the decline of traditional marriage, the collapse of families' communal eating and leisure time, the rise in child abuse, infanticide, juvenile crime and drug abuse, and even falling SAT scores. The family, Bronfenbrenner said, was "a critically important institution in shaping our children's minds, values and behavior. But it's equally clear that the American family is disintegrating."[17]

In many ways, of course, this was a wild exaggeration. Even in the 1970s it was obvious that the ideal of marriage still appealed to millions of people who had never heard of Urie Bronfenbrenner or R. D. Laing. In 1970 a nationwide poll found that 96 percent of Americans believed that the ideal arrangement was for two people to spend their lives together; in 1980, exactly the same proportion believed the same thing. Surveys found that they wanted a different, more egalitarian union, but they had not lost faith in marriage itself: it was revealing that four out of five divorcées chose to remarry within three years. And although some conservative commentators interpreted the rise of cohabitation—living together outside marriage—as a sign of moral breakdown, it could easily be seen as a commitment to the ideals of marriage without the associated religious rituals. Common-law marriage, after all, had been legal in England until 1753; to a certain extent, therefore, cohabitation, which accounted for more than a million American households in 1979, was simply a return to the traditions of the past.[18]

Even so, more people were living alone than ever before. In the early 1950s, the unmarried had been regarded as at best unlucky or at worst depraved. But where the idealized bachelors of *Playboy* magazine led, millions followed. Between 1970 and 1979 the number of people living on their own rose by 60 percent, and by the end of the decade one in four households consisted of just one person. "Meals for one" became a familiar sight in supermarkets, while newspapers reported on the emergence of singles bars, singles spas, singles vacation clubs, singles condominiums, and even specialist singles therapists. Singlehood was "newly respectable," announced *Newsweek* in 1973, adding rather patronizingly that it was "finally becoming possible to be both single and whole." And single women had a compelling role model in Mary Richards, the heroine of the Emmy-garlanded sitcom *The Mary Tyler Moore Show*, which made its debut in September 1970 and ran for seven years. Mary is no strident, bra-burning feminist, but an independent career woman, living alone and pursuing her own interests, a female equivalent of the *Playboy* bachelor. Although she has plenty of dates, she never meets Mr. Right and appears in no great hurry to do so. In the staid world of network television this made her a genuinely revolutionary figure, as well as the personification of one of the most significant social trends of the age.[19]

**Although it was** never spelled out, Mary Richards was not a virgin; indeed, she often spent the night with the men she dated. Ten years before, it would have been unimaginable for a prime-time heroine to behave in this way. Public attitudes toward sex, however, were in flux. In 1969, according to Gallup, 68 percent of Americans believed that sex before marriage was wrong; by 1973, this proportion had tumbled to just 48 percent, and it carried on falling. Among college students, meanwhile, 76 percent of women said that they had lost their virginity by their junior year, while 40 percent thought that couples should live together before they were married. And by this time, more than one in three American women thought that premarital sex was "not wrong at all." In the words of one of 1980's more unlikely best sellers, "Nice Girls Do—and Now You Can Too!"[20]

That more and more nice girls did was beyond dispute. Of the generation that came of age during the 1950s, only one in three women admitted to sleeping with more than one man before they were thirty. But of the women who came of age between the elections of Richard Nixon and Ronald Reagan, more than nine out of ten had done so, while two out of ten claimed to have slept with five men or more. They were also losing their virginity earlier: whereas their parents claimed to have waited until marriage, sixteen was now the average age. More than four-fifths of boys and two-thirds of girls were having sex by the time they were nineteen. Unsurprisingly, teenage pregnancies soared, increasing by 10 percent in the five years from 1973 to 1978. And illegitimacy, too, was rising. In 1970, 11 percent of all births had been to unmarried mothers; by 1980, it was 18 percent; and by 1990, 28 percent, with rates particularly high among black women.[21]

To conservatives like Alice Moore and her friends in Kanawha County, the surging premarital sex and illegitimacy rates, just like the rise of sex education, the soaring figures for abortions since *Roe v. Wade,* and the increasing openness of homosexual life in New York and San Francisco, were part of a broad sexual revolution that was sweeping away traditional Christian values. Yet the idea of a sexual "revolution" is probably exaggerated. According to Paul Gebhard, who ran the Kinsey Institute at Indiana University from 1956 to 1982, people certainly talked more freely about sex, and young people were "far more tolerant and permissive." But he doubted that "there have been changes that we could truly call revolutionary. Our studies indicate that there has just been a continuation of pre-existing trends, rather than any sudden revolutionary changes."[22]

As so often, however, what mattered was not the nuanced, halting nature of real change but the media's exaggerated, often lurid picture of an unprecedented revolution, dwelling on sensational images of sex clubs and swingers. In May 1971, group sex made its mainstream press debut in *The New York Times*, which claimed that between one and two million Americans were regular swingers. The *Times* seems to have invented this figure out of thin air, and the piece managed to identify only three self-described swingers. One, perhaps unsurprisingly, was a divorced artist of "erotic paintings" who described group sex as "a little bowling league kind of thing." The others were John and Mimi Lobell, a couple of architectural designers, who saw group sex as "life art" and claimed that it helped them achieve "spiritual growth." In fact the Lobells were the poster children of swinging, posing for explicit photographs in avant-garde magazines, giving interviews about their favorite techniques, and even writing a memoir about their career highlights. Yet despite its prominence in John Updike's meticulously explicit novel *Couples* (1968) or John Irving's equally frank *The 158-Pound Marriage* (1974), there is little evidence that group sex appealed to anything more than a minuscule minority. A hobby that attracted just 368 people to its first "national convention," which was held in Chicago in 1970, was not necessarily insignificant. But it was still a long way behind plane spotting or watching reruns of *Star Trek*.[23]

As for the fabled sex clubs of the decade, most were conspicuously unsuccessful. The short-lived Sandstone Retreat in the Santa Monica Mountains claimed high-profile clients such as the journalist Max Lerner, the NFL star turned actor Bernie Casey, and the Pentagon Papers informant Daniel Ellsberg, but its crippling annual dues of $740 meant that it did not last long. In New York, meanwhile, Steve Ostrow's Continental Baths briefly attracted enormous publicity, thanks partly to celebrated cabaret performances by the young Bette Midler and Barry Manilow, yet it lasted for just six years before the business dried up. In September 1977, it reopened as Plato's Retreat, a dedicated sex club run by a chubby divorcé called Larry Levenson who had once managed a branch of McDonald's and now fancied himself an impresario of the sexual revolution. But although Plato's Retreat claimed to be attracting six thousand clients a month in its early days, its history was ultimately the same old story. When the state authorities cracked down by withdrawing its liquor license, the club began to make heavy losses. Like Studio 54, the notorious nightclub with a very similar life span, Plato's Retreat ended the decade in deep trouble, and in 1981 Levenson was charged with fraud and tax evasion. The club staggered on without him, but successive sexual health panics had long since destroyed its appeal, and four years later its doors closed for good.[24]

While Plato's Retreat floundered, other entrepreneurs were making serious money from sexual permissiveness. The pornography boom owed a great deal to rising living standards, lower printing costs, and the ease of producing cheap hard-core films. But it also owed a lot to the Supreme Court, which had gradually dismantled the laws censoring obscene material. By 1970, an estimated forty-five million pieces of sexually explicit material were being sent through the mail every year, while two hundred theaters across the land showed silent hard-core stag films, 830 adults-only bookstores sold erotic literature, and another 425 bookstores boasted adults-only sections. Surveys found that eight out of ten boys and seven out of ten girls had seen or read depictions of sexual intercourse by the time they were eighteen. Even outside the industry, standards were becoming more liberal: more explicit articles in magazines like *Cosmopolitan*, more suggestive lyrics by rock bands, more profanity on the silver screen after the MPAA revised its ratings. In 1970, the X-rated *Midnight Cowboy* won the Oscar for Best Picture, even though it included scenes of straight and gay prostitution and glimpses of naked breasts and buttocks. It was just four years since *The Sound of Music* had succeeded *My Fair Lady* as Best Picture, but it seemed longer.[25]

Pornography had always existed, of course; what was different was that it seemed to be seeping into the fabric of urban life. By the early 1970s, newsstands in almost every major city in the nation sold not only *Playboy* and *Penthouse* but more extreme material too, in full view of customers of all ages. In Woody Allen's early comedy *Bananas* (1971), his character wanders into a Manhattan newsstand and casts his lascivious eyes over a selection of dirty magazines, including *Screw, Big Boobs, Hustler, Orgasm*, and *National Review*. Finally, he picks up a bundle of news magazines ("I'll get a copy of *Time* magazine, and I think I'll take *Commentary*, and the *Saturday Review*, and, let's see, *Newsweek*"), quietly sliding a pornographic magazine into the pack ("I'll just grab one of these"). The vendor sorts through them and loudly asks a colleague: "Hey, Ralph, how much is a copy of *Orgasm*?" "Just put 'em in a bag, will you?" Allen exclaims hurriedly. "I'm doing a sociological study on perversion," he explains to his fellow shoppers. "I'm up to advanced child molesting."

In fact, most consumers were a long way from the seedy, raincoat-clad tramps of urban legend. A presidential commission on pornography reported that of five hundred visitors to a Boston sex shop, nine out of ten were white, most wore wedding rings, and five out of ten were in business suits. And far from being embarrassing, pornography suddenly seemed fashionable, even almost respectable. *Playboy's* monthly sales, for example, hit an all-time peak of seven million in November 1972, partly thanks to the editors' decision to show their girls with pubic hair, thereby recapturing the low ground from *Penthouse* and *Hustler*. The spread of erotica, the film scholar Foster Hirsch told the readers of *The New York Times*, was "a sign of health rather than of sickness, of hope rather than despair." And watching pornography in a public theater was "a purgative social event, a means of easing inhibitions, of alleviating hypocrisy and fear, of freely acknowledging that we are all sexual beings."[26]

Clearly, an awful lot of people agreed with him. When the former hairdresser Gerard Damiano's film *Deep Throat* reached the city's theaters a year later, it found an extraordinarily enthusiastic reception, attracting admirers such as Truman Capote, Johnny Carson, Jack Nicholson, and Warren Beatty. By January 1973 the *Times* was reporting that *Deep Throat* had made more than $3.2 million, and was attracting "celebrities, diplomats, critics, businessmen, women alone and dating couples." When charges were brought against one New York theater for showing it, a parade of experts assembled to proclaim its merits. *Deep Throat* was a great social breakthrough, claimed Arthur Knight, professor of film at the University of Southern California and film critic for the *Saturday Review*. Audiences would find it "cleansing," agreed John Money, professor of medical psychology at Johns Hopkins, to watch its depiction of oral, vaginal, and anal sex.[27]

The appeal of *Deep Throat* and other pornographic films is often exaggerated: they were generally shown only in big-city theaters, and in more than half the country they were banned by local jurisdictions. But in New York, *Deep Throat* was a sign of things to come. For by the early 1970s, parts of the city were already "effectively closed off to families." As mainstream businesses fled to the suburbs, the sex trade moved in, taking advantage of liberal licensing requirements. In 1965 there had been just nine pornographic establishments in Manhattan; by 1977, there were more than ninety around Times Square alone, where not even the most innocent visitor could help noticing the seedy adult bookstores, the grubby pornographic theaters, the hookers soliciting on every corner. There were periodic attempts to clean up the neighborhood, but in August 1973 the state supreme court threw out a law that would have outlawed much of the porn trade on grounds of obscenity. It was impossible and illiberal, said the judge, to define arbitrary "community standards" and impose them on the city.[28]

The climate of liberalism, as well as the insistence on civil liberties, left New York City defenseless against the inroads of the sex industry—the profits of which generally went to organized crime. In 1976 the Show World Center, a multistory sex arcade with live acts, video booths, and private rooms, opened on the corner of Forty-second Street and Eighth Avenue. Horrified residents staged a demonstration one Sunday afternoon, joined by more than a thousand marchers from the Church of the Holy Cross and two hundred schoolchildren carrying placards reading, WE WANT OUR CITY BACK! The smut merchants, however, were unimpressed: in the straitened economic climate of the day, one of them argued, the trade "keeps Eighth Avenue going." And it was extremely difficult to drive them away, since anti-loitering laws and strict zoning plans were regularly struck down by the courts for infringing on First Amendment rights. When Mayor Abraham Beame led a series of police raids on the area's strip clubs a year later, the state supreme court ordered them reopened within hours.[29]

Across the nation, officials seemed incapable of stemming the tide. When federal authorities in Kansas pursued *Screw*'s editor Al Goldstein, his conviction was overturned on appeal. Even when the government successfully prosecuted *Hustler*'s publisher, Larry Flynt, in 1976, the conviction was overturned on a technicality. With the Supreme Court insisting that local obscenity laws be determined by "community standards," prosecutors from Seattle to San Francisco complained that they were unable to secure a single conviction. In Chicago, the sex industry had taken over Wells Street; in Minneapolis, Hennepin Avenue. And as it snaked through West Hollywood, Santa Monica Boulevard became what *Time* called "a garish, grubby, milelong gauntlet of sex-book stalls, theaters and 8-mm. peep shows . . . a zone of temptation and humiliation, harshly lit by neon signs that crackle their messages: ADULT, ENTER and OVER 18."

Santa Monica Boulevard was merely one symptom of what *Time*, in its inimitable sententious style, called the "porno plague," an "open, aggressive $2 billion-a-year, crime-ridden growth enterprise." Pornography's age-old foes in the churches were in retreat, and "most of the traditional barriers to porn are now down." The laws were full of loopholes, officials hamstrung by lack of will, juries paralyzed by uncertainty. Few would mourn "the old narrow Puritanism," *Time* conceded, yet it wondered "if the mounting taste for porn is a symptom of decay, of corrosive boredom, of withdrawal from social concern for obsessive personal pleasures." But the man it called "Raunch King Al Goldstein," publisher of *Screw* magazine, came to a different and perhaps more prophetic verdict. Porn, he said triumphantly, was becoming "part of the mainstream of American life."[30]

**Not everyone was ready** to give in to the pornographers without a fight. While some early feminists hesitated to speak out for fear of seeming puritanical, there was a growing sense in the women's movement that pornography degraded women and encouraged sexual violence. "Pornography is the theory, and rape the practice," ran Robin Morgan's formulation. In Seattle, women attacked bookstores with stink bombs; in New York, three adult theaters were firebombed; in San Francisco, activists organized the first "Take Back the Night" march in 1978, demonstrating outside adult bookstores and massage parlors. A year later, activists in New York founded their own group, Women Against Pornography, leading a well-publicized march on Times Square. And with angry feminist writers like Andrea Dworkin and Catharine MacKinnon producing well-reviewed books on the dangers of pornography, the antipornography lobby had become one of the most dynamic elements of the feminist movement by the end of the 1970s.[31]

To millions of other Americans, however, the "porno plague" was a sign of a society that had lost its moral bearings and was sliding relentlessly into godless decadence. Even *Playboy* readers were often troubled by the extremely public nature of sexual liberalization in the 1970s: the storefronts on Times Square, the magazines in the neighborhood store, the bouncing breasts on prime-time television. "We were strict and we respected our parents, but now?" lamented an Italian worker from Brooklyn. "This sexual permissiveness is disgraceful, it's like dogs in the street." Another Italian union member took a similar view. "If they want to live together and not be married, that's fine," he explained. "If they want to read pornographic books and see pornographic movies, that's okay. I believe you should not infringe on people's rights." But showing promiscuity on television was another matter: "Because I really believe that the business of people living together is fine as long as they don't *broadcast* it to the point of making it an outright thing on television or in the newspapers. They talk about these things as though they were nothing!"[32]

Interviewing Middle Americans in Brooklyn, Jonathan Rieder found that the same words—"shame, animals, strictness, permissiveness, looseness"—came up again and again. "The kids have no shame," said a Jewish housewife. "They have no respect." And like the fundamentalist Christians of Kanawha County, working-class New Yorkers lined up to express their fears about the state of the American family. "The family is the solid rock of social values," one Italian parent said, "but now the mother and the father are looking for sexual satisfaction, and they won't devote the time to instilling values and ideals. The family is the center of our community, and if you don't keep it solid and together, you will have educated animals."[33]

It was not surprising, then, that by the mid-1970s, few politicians passed up the opportunity to proclaim their own support for family values and to promise to do all they could to stem the tide of "filth." And yet in the second half of the decade the trends continued: more divorce, more premarital sex, more illegitimacy, more pornography. And with the family apparently under greater pressure than ever, millions of Americans, like the textbook protesters of Kanawha County, began to look outside mainstream politics for a response.

**In 1976 a conservative** child psychologist called James Dobson, who had already written two best-selling books about Christian approaches to parenting and marriage, left his job at the University of Southern California to write and lecture full-time. He was so successful that in March 1977 he was presenting his first weekly radio show, and three months later he set up a small pressure group to fight for old-fashioned Christian moral values, the same values that had inspired Alice Moore's campaign in Kanawha County, three years before.

Dobson's organization began life with just one staff member. By 1980, his radio show was being carried by a hundred different stations, and his group employed more than thirty people. By its thirtieth anniversary his radio programs were carried by five thousand stations in fifty-five different countries, while the group had more than two thousand employees and brought in more than $140 million in revenue. Its name was Focus on the Family. It never managed to stem the tide of permissiveness. Yet long after *Deep Throat* had been forgotten, long after *Playboy* and *Hustler* had seen their sales plummet, Focus on the Family was bigger than ever, playing a key role in the new politics of the religious right. And that, of course, is another story.[34]

It was just an ordinary Friday night at Kenny's Castaways in Greenwich Village: no great sense of anticipation, just thirty people sipping beers and waiting for the show. Few of them knew who the headline act was; outside, on the hand-scribbled marquee, the manager had spelled his name wrong. "He arrived onstage in jeans and a beat-up hooded sweat-shirt," remembered one listener, "adjusted the mike to his acoustic guitar, dropped a flat pick, bent to retrieve it, stood up, strummed a bit, and asked out over the audience's head to one friend at the back, 'How long have I been up here?' " But when he began to sing, his raucous voice growling out the lyrics, "it was like the ocean had calmed out and you knew a storm was coming by the way it prickled your skin."[1]

The singer's name was Bruce Springsteen, and in December 1972 he was almost entirely unknown. Although his first two albums, *Greetings from Asbury Park, N.J.* and *The Wild, the Innocent, and the E Street Shuffle*, were well reviewed, sales were slow. The market was already swollen with introspective singer-songwriters, and to many people Springsteen seemed just another folk-turned-rock artist in the mold of Bob Dylan. And yet slowly but surely the critical acclaim began to pay dividends. In April 1974, *Rolling Stone*'s critic Jon Landau saw Springsteen play at the Harvard Square Theatre. "I saw rock and roll['s] future," he wrote afterward, "and its name is Bruce Springsteen. And on a night when I needed to feel young, he made me feel like I was hearing music for the very first time." Indeed, Landau was so enthusiastic that he took over as co-producer on Springsteen's next album, persuading him to switch studios to the famous Record Plant on West Forty-fourth Street.[2]

Still the great breakthrough eluded him. Springsteen "has it all," mused *The New York Times*'s John Rockwell in August 1975. "He is a great lyricist and songwriter, he is a wonderful singer, guitarist and piano player, he has one of the best rock bands anybody has ever heard, and he is as charismatic a stage figure as rock has produced." But why had he not "become an internationally known superstar long since, if he's as good as everybody who sees him knows him to be"? Perhaps he was too intense, too wrapped up in his music to pander to commercial imperatives. "His songs are about the street life of the New Jersey coast towns and New York City," Rockwell noted. "But just as he owes his authority to his roots, so is he bound by a suspicious, nervous, provincial mentality that makes him indecisive in the glittering world of rock careerdom."[3]

Yet the very things that appeared to hold Springsteen back—the obsession with his provincial New Jersey roots, the unfashionable torn T-shirts, scruffy caps, and black leather jacket, the songs about working-class losers—would become his greatest strengths. Born and bred in suburban Freehold, New Jersey, the son of a bus driver and a legal secretary, he had spent his teenage years as a typical disaffected blue-collar kid, drifting through the down-at-heel malls and boardwalks of the Jersey shore. It was in these shabby, faded surroundings that he found his voice, playing regularly at little clubs and gathering a cult following. It was classic run-down white-flight territory, lashed by the wind and rain of the Atlantic, a world of empty streets and boarded-up storefronts, of scruffy dives and greasy cafés, of hopeless lives and broken dreams.

Springsteen's achievement was to take this dreary world and to turn it into the stuff of poetry. In songs like "4th of July, Asbury Park (Sandy)," he captured the "dusty arcades" and the "factory girls," the "switchblade lovers" and the "stoned-out faces" who made up the texture of life on the Jersey shore. His songs told of dead-end workers and lovesick teenagers, of penny arcades and circuses, of hustlers and pimps, of lonely streets and "cheap little seashore bars." They mourned a disappearing world, but they also celebrated the intensity with which blue-collar Americans struggled to find beauty in their shabby urban surroundings. Looking back decades later, the rock writer Robert Santelli likened them to Edward Hopper paintings: "stark and austere and romantic and hot-blooded all at the same time."[4]

In August 1975, Columbia released Springsteen's third album, *Born to Run,* and this time they left nothing to chance. Like *Jaws,* that other great blockbuster of the summer of 1975, *Born to Run* benefited from enormous hype. Columbia spent far more money promoting the new album than it had ever done on anything by Bob Dylan. It booked a record number of radio commercials and trade press advertisements, reserved a thouand promotional tickets for Springsteen's five nights at the Bottom Line club in New York, and persuaded both *Time* and *Newsweek* to grant him the honor of a cover story. And as with *Jaws,* the hype paid off. Within two months, Springsteen had been awarded a gold disc to mark half a million sales, and in the end *Born to Run* sold more than six million copies. "1976 is the year of Bruce Springsteen," ran a full-page *Rolling Stone* ad at the end of November. "Why wait?"[5]

No album of the decade earned more ecstatic praise. It was "urban folk poetry at its best," said John Rockwell in *The New York Times*, "overflowing with pungent detail and evocative metaphors." For *Rolling Stone's* Dave Marsh, it was "the definitive American rock LP"; for the famously highbrow Greil Marcus, it was "a magnificent album that pays off on every bet ever placed on Bruce Springsteen." And yet the hype inevitably generated its own backlash. *Born to Run* was hardly a great breakthrough, objected the rock writer Henry Edwards, since its "kid-as-loser" ethos was so familiar as to be a cliché. "Springsteen [is] a collagist who does not form his collage into something fresh," Edwards wrote; his songs were merely "copies of some of rock 'n' roll's finest moments." *Born to Run* was "the complete monument to rock and roll orthodoxy," agreed Langdon Winner in *The Real Paper*, and Springsteen was "the consummate bore."[6]

And yet the album's nostalgic sound was the key to its appeal. The early to mid-1970s, after all, was a deeply nostalgic moment in American cultural history: in *Time*'s words, "the most popular pastime of the year is looking back." This was an era of genealogical research and architectural renovation, gentrifying nineteenth-century neighborhoods and Victorian nostalgia parties, SoHo warehouses and Boston brownstones, Leon Uris sagas and James A. Michener blockbusters. In fashion, designers talked of re-creating the "Gatsby look"; at the movies, audiences flocked to *The Godfather, Badlands*, and *The Last Picture Show*. On the best-seller lists, nothing matched the appeal of John Jakes's Kent Family Chronicles, which interwove fact and fiction to tell the story of the nation since the 1770s; on television, the sensation of the season was ABC's *Happy Days*, a nostalgic comedy about middle-class teenagers in the 1950s wallowing in what the network called "the relatively carefree life and lifestyles of young people in those bygone, happy, innocent days." The critics tore it apart; the viewers loved it.[7]

In an era of introverted ballads and pretentious "adult-oriented" rock, many listeners yearned for something more visceral, more in keeping with the harsh texture of everyday life. The president had resigned, the nation had lost a war, the gas was running out, and the economy was stuck in recession. Millions of ordinary Americans lived in exactly the kind of dismal, dilapidated neighborhoods that Springsteen evoked in "Thunder Road" and "Backstreets." His studied populism, his grimly affected ordinariness, his stories of alienated youngsters with dead-end jobs in crumbling towns made perfect sense to millions across the nation. "He is a glorified gutter rat from a dying New Jersey resort town," remarked *Time* magazine. And that, in the late summer of 1975, in the decaying factories and dingy backstreets of blue-collar America, was exactly what many people wanted. If Bruce Springsteen had not existed, they would have had to invent him.[8]

# Chapter Five  *Let's Look Ferocious*

> We have no national memory. Maybe it's a good thing.
> Maybe it's a mark of a young and vigorous people . . .
> I think we've already forgotten Vietnam.

**—LILLIAN HELLMAN,** in Gloria Emerson, *Winners and Losers* (1976)

In the end there were just eleven Marines left in South Vietnam, huddling on the roof of the American embassy, waiting nervously for the last helicopter. Dawn was breaking over Saigon, flickers of gray and blue and pink and gold lighting up the night sky far to the east, where the Seventh Fleet waited offshore. In the gathering daylight, the last Americans could see fires still burning below, could taste the smoke billowing over the city, could hear the muffled sounds of the mob smashing its way through the floors of the embassy below them. They sat there quietly, eleven tiny figures waiting on the roof while history unfolded beneath them, wondering anxiously whether they had been forgotten, half planning an alternative escape to the sea. And then, in the blue of the morning sky, the exhausted Marines saw specks to the southeast, growing larger every minute: one last Chinook helicopter, escorted by six Cobra gunships.

It was 7:53 a.m. on Wednesday, April 30, 1975, the last day of the Vietnam War. And after all the effort, all the money, all the bloodshed, all the lives lost, there was no poignant farewell, no grand leaving ceremony. There was just the spectacle of eleven ordinary Marines gathered on the roof, ducking gratefully beneath the whirl of the blades, heaving their tired limbs aboard the battered helicopter. In a final gesture that said so much about the American enterprise in Vietnam, they tossed their tear-gas grenades over the side of the embassy in a final effort to deter the advancing looters. Then the helicopter lifted into the sky, and they were gone.[1]

For the Americans who had fled Saigon in those desperate hours, there were no words to describe the grief and shame they felt that morning. In two weeks, they had supervised the evacuation of six thousand Americans and more than fifty thousand Vietnamese: a heroic effort under any circumstances, but one that fell horribly short of an honorable exit. "The rest of our lives we will be haunted by how we betrayed those people," one diplomat said on the USS *Okinawa*. "It made me cry when I got here. There were lots of people who were crying when they got here."

"They lied to us at the very end. They promised. They promised," Captain Stuart Herrington, sitting tearful and shirtless at the edge of his bunk, told a reporter. "I have never received an order in my life to do something I was ashamed of. If I had known how it was going to end, I would have refused the order." Herrington had been in charge of organizing Vietnamese evacuees for transfer to the fleet; he had even arranged for Vietnamese firemen to stand by in case there was an accident with one of the helicopters. In the end even the firemen had been abandoned. "They listened to us and believed us," Herrington said softly. "They waited confidently in those rows, believing their friends would not let them down." From the next bunk, a barrel-chested lieutenant colonel cut in. "Do you know what you saw? Do you really know what you saw?" he asked. "You saw deceit. You saw how we let this country down to the very end."[2]

**On May 11, 1975,** fifty thousand people gathered in New York's Central Park to celebrate the end of the Vietnam War. The atmosphere, wrote one reporter, was that of "a joyous all-day carnival of songs and speeches in the perfect sunshine." As the singer Peter Yarrow rolled back the years with a selection of protest ballads, the crowd chanted along in unison, many of them linking arms or hugging old friends, a sea of denim, hair, and emotional self-indulgence. Two local Democratic congresswomen, Elizabeth Holtzman of Brooklyn and Bella Abzug of Manhattan, were on hand to deliver rousing speeches, and there were songs from Pete Seeger, Joan Baez, Paul Simon, and other veterans of the good old days. "There's a lot of lumps in a lot of throats," one tearful demonstrator told reporters. "It's unbelievable. Today is the first day I really realize the war is over."[3]

Yet for many people who had watched the pictures of despairing refugees, of terrified women and children, of black smoke rising over the American embassy, the overwhelming feelings were shame and guilt. Guilt at the arrogance that had sent thousands of Americans to their deaths, guilt at the appalling human costs for the people of Vietnam and Cambodia, guilt at the miscalculations and the mistakes, guilt at the brutality and the bloodshed, guilt at the final, heartbreaking betrayal. Immediately after the evacuation, recalled Frank Snepp, the CIA's chief analyst of North Vietnamese strategy in Saigon, he felt "horror and a terrific revulsion." "A terrible feeling of guilt remains with me to this day," he wrote on the tenth anniversary of the airlift. "I suffer still from the memory of some Vietnamese who didn't escape. I am still trying to get them out." The people of Vietnam, reflected Thomas Polgar, the CIA chief in Saigon, "would have been much better off if we had never gone there in the first place."[4]

A few weeks after the fall of Saigon, the radical journalist Andrew Kopkind paid a visit to what he called "the ultimate strategic hamlet." It was a military strategist's dream, a safe, well-guarded city of some twenty-five thousand South Vietnamese men, women, and children, united in their faith in the American way of life and their hatred of Communism. But this settlement was not in Vietnam: it was in Fort Chaffee, Arkansas, and its inhabitants were refugees, crowded into the wooden barracks of the reservist base. They had fled the wreckage of a country that had now disappeared, taking their hopes and ambitions with it.[5]

And yet despite all they had suffered, Fort Chaffee's refugees were hardly welcomed with open arms; indeed, local reporters claimed they were riddled with leprosy and venereal disease. Meanwhile, local residents, pointing out that unemployment in the area stood at almost 10 percent, complained that so many homeless foreigners were bound to create problems. "I don't like it at all," one Arkansas veteran told the press. "Somebody's going to have to take care of them. I have no idea where they'll learn a trade and there's no knowing what kind of diseases they'll bring. I don't like the people personally. I didn't see anything worth saving [during the war] and I don't now."

Hostility to the Vietnamese refugees was not confined to Fort Chaffee. According to Gallup, 54 percent of the American public disliked the idea of their settling permanently in the United States, with only 36 percent supporting them. In the inaptly named town of Niceville, Florida, where more than ten thousand refugees were quarantined at Eglin Air Force Base, residents circulated a petition demanding that the Vietnamese be moved somewhere else. In a poll taken by the local radio station, eight out of ten people deplored the refugees' arrival in Niceville, while schoolchildren joked about shooting them. And in a nearby barbershop, a reporter heard two men discussing the refugees' arrival. "We got enough of our own problems to take care of," insisted the barber. "I don't see why I ought to work and pay taxes for those folks who wouldn't work over there. They ought to have stayed on over there." "Right," his friend agreed. "Who the hell's going to feed them when they get here?" "We are," said the barber. "We are."

Since times were hard, it was not surprising that some people dreaded the thought of competition for their jobs. "People are losing their cars, houses, jobs," a black Detroit autoworker told *The New York Times*. "Let them stay there until we do something for people here." "It's a hard world everywhere," agreed a Polish American cashier. "Charity begins at home. Keep the Vietnamese in Vietnam. Send funds to help them in their own country." But there was more to the public reaction than fears of job competition. GOOKS GO HOME, placards read in Arkansas. Hundreds of Vietnamese women who had married American personnel already lived near Eglin Air Force Base: many confided that they had never been accepted. In neighboring Fort Walton Beach High School, students talked of organizing a "Gook Klux Klan," while members of a twelfth-grade psychology class worried that the refugees would "attempt to convert them to Communism." "How do you know we're not getting the bad guys?" wondered a Valparaiso salesman. "You can't say for sure. Nobody can, and Lord knows we've got enough Communist infiltration now."[6]

Of course, millions of Americans felt genuine sympathy for the refugees: some Niceville residents hung WELCOME banners to greet the Vietnamese, while *The New York Times* found plenty of people who thought they should be given a warm welcome, since "we are all the descendants of refugees." Yet the widespread hostility to the Vietnamese made for a stark contrast with the warm reception for the Eastern European and Cuban refugees who had arrived in the hundreds of thousands in the 1950s and 1960s. No doubt the transformed economic context, which meant that immigrants were treated as unwelcome competitors, played a key part. But the South Vietnamese also suffered because they were associated with a humiliating episode that most people would rather forget. Many people saw them as yellow devils who had taken thousands of American lives, while liberals treated them as the children of a corrupt regime or associated them with a war they had spent years marching to stop. Seattle's city council voted by 7 to 1 to reject a resolution that would have welcomed the refugees to the United States, while California's governor, Jerry Brown, always keen to jump aboard the nearest bandwagon, demanded that Congress amend a refugee aid bill with a pledge to provide "jobs for Americans first." People were "full of self-pity," remarked Harvard's David Riesman. "We are all justifying our grievances by striking out at others. The national mood is poisonous and dangerous and this is one symptom—striking out at helpless refugees whose number is infinitesimal."[7]

The one man who emerged with credit was Gerald Ford, who ignored the polls and badgered Congress to provide funds for the refugees' resettlement. When the House rejected a $327 million aid package two days after the fall of Saigon, Ford was furious, privately denouncing "those sons of bitches." It was the first time his press secretary, Ron Nessen, had heard him curse in the Oval Office. It would have been easy to abandon the fight. But Ford stood firm, insisting that the United States had an obligation to support its wartime comrades and that "to ignore the refugees in their hour of need would be to repudiate the values we cherish as a nation of immigrants." He applied more pressure, recruiting the AFL-CIO and various state governors, and eventually Congress approved the aid. It was a moment that reflected well on Ford's instinctive decency. But it was yet more proof that the wounds of the Vietnam War would take a long time to heal.[8]

In Washington there was remarkably little political fallout from the collapse of Saigon. As national security adviser and then secretary of state, Henry Kissinger had been intimately associated with the war for more than six years, yet he insisted that the blame lay with the peace movement and, especially, the liberals in Congress for losing their nerve and cutting aid to Saigon when it mattered most. When Ford asked him to draft some thoughts on "the lessons of Vietnam," Kissinger's verdict was extraordinarily sanguine. It was "remarkable," he thought, "considering how long the war lasted and how intensely it was reported and commented, that there are not really very many lessons from our experience in Vietnam that can usefully be applied elsewhere." Thousands of Americans had not died "in vain," because they had "prevented Indonesia from falling to Communism and probably preserved the American presence in Asia." It had been a "high price," Kissinger admitted, "but we gained ten years of time and we changed what then appeared to be an overwhelming momentum. I do not believe our soldiers or our people need to be ashamed."[9]

It was testimony to Kissinger's colossal self-belief that even after the collapse of Cambodia and Vietnam, he refused to draw more sweeping lessons. What he called a "high price"—$140 billion in American money, fifty-eight thousand American lives, and at least two million Vietnamese lives—struck most observers as downright obscene. At the very least he had been guilty of serious mistakes, notably his failure to adapt American strategy to reflect events on the ground and his insistence on subordinating Indo-Chinese affairs to superpower diplomacy. And contrary to everything he had ever said, Indochina had never really mattered to American security. Vietnam and Cambodia both fell to Communism, but instead of the dominoes tumbling in rapid sequence, the two promptly turned on each other. The key American allies in the region were never seriously imperiled by the loss of Vietnam. It had all been for nothing, after all.[10]

That Kissinger had learned nothing from the debacle of Vietnam was aptly demonstrated by his performance a few days later. In the early hours of May 12, Cambodian sailors boarded an American merchant ship, the *Mayaguez*, which had been carrying supplies from Hong Kong to Thailand and had strayed into disputed waters. According to the first reports, thirty-nine American crewmen had been taken hostage, but the mysterious, unreachable isolation of Cambodia's new Khmer Rouge government meant that the news was sketchy and negotiations were difficult. Still, these kinds of situations were hardly unknown and rarely made the headlines. Ecuador, for example, had seized American crews in disputed waters twenty-three times in as many years, and previous administrations had simply paid a fine to release them.[11]

Coming so soon after the fall of South Vietnam, however, the *Mayaguez* incident represented the perfect opportunity for Kissinger and Ford to flex their muscles and restore American credibility. And while they claimed that the fate of the crew was their first priority, this was simply not true. "We should not just think of what is the right thing to do, but of what the public perceives," Bob Hartmann bluntly told Ford in front of the National Security Council (NSC). It was a chance for the United States to "draw the line," Kissinger agreed. "We should do it on a large scale," he said enthusiastically. "We should not look as though we want to pop somebody, but we should give the impression that we are not to be trifled with."[12]

By the following evening, Kissinger's bellicosity had swollen to even greater levels. It was still unclear whether the *Mayaguez* crewmen were still on the boat, or had been moved to the remote little island of Koh Tang, or were being transferred to the Cambodian mainland. But Kissinger did not really care. Getting the crew back was "not just enough," he said. "I think we should seize the island, seize the ship, and hit the mainland. I am thinking not of Cambodia, but of Korea and of the Soviet Union and of others." Perhaps consciously emulating Nixon's beloved "madman" theory, he suggested that "people should have the impression that we are potentially trigger-happy," and urged Ford to order B-52 bombing raids on the Cambodian coast. When one of Ford's advisers gingerly mentioned the War Powers Act, the secretary of state brushed it aside: "I would hit, and then deal with the legal implications."[13]

On the afternoon of the fourteenth, with the crew's whereabouts still shrouded in confusion, Ford finally approved military action, including air strikes on the Cambodian mainland. But the result was a fiasco. On Koh Tang, a Marine landing party ran into heavy fire from Cambodian troops and lost fifteen men and eight helicopters within the first hour. When they boarded the *Mayaguez*, the captured crewmen were nowhere to be seen; meanwhile, American fighters had begun pounding nearby Cambodian gunboats. Eventually, a Navy pilot spotted thirty men waving white flags from a little fishing boat, and a great cheer went up in the Oval Office. But Henry Kissinger was not done just yet. "Tell them to bomb the mainland," he insisted. "Let's look ferocious!"[14]

"All's well that ends well," Ron Nessen told the press after the *Mayaguez* rescue was over. But this was a remarkably generous verdict on what had been, in military and intelligence terms, an utter shambles. Eighteen Marines had been killed and fifty wounded in action, while another twenty-three died when their helicopter crashed during preparations— a disturbing portent of another hostage rescue attempt five years later. Sacrificing forty-one lives in order to save thirty-nine men hardly counted as a happy ending. What is more, reports indicated that the Cambodians had been preparing to release the captives anyway. And bizarrely, it turned out that some had rather enjoyed their unexpected stay in Cambodia. "They were so nice, really kind," one seaman remarked of his captors. "They fed us first and everything. I hope everybody gets hijacked by them."[15]

In many ways the *Mayaguez* fiasco, which was supposed to banish the bad taste of Vietnam, was like an action replay in miniature. As the NSC minutes show, the fate of the American crewmen was almost entirely overshadowed by the desire to "look ferocious," to "draw the line," to show "strength" and "credibility"—precisely what had cost so many American lives in Vietnam. And yet one of the lessons of Vietnam was that military and political success could be entirely different things, for in purely political terms the *Mayaguez* episode was probably the single greatest success of Gerald Ford's presidency. In the aftermath of Vietnam, many Americans were itching to see their country reassert its strength, especially if its antagonists were yellow-skinned Communists, and within days Ford's approval rating had leaped eleven points. "Ford Draws the Line," roared *Time*'s cover headline, while *Newsweek* hailed "a daring show of nerve and courage." "It was wonderful," enthused Barry Goldwater, in a supremely revealing exclamation of joy. "It shows we've still got balls in this country."[16]

**Although the *Mayaguez*** operation gave Gerald Ford's popularity a temporary boost, it did little to assuage the bitterness and shame of those Americans who had fought and bled in the paddy fields of Vietnam. Unlike veterans of previous conflicts, Vietnam vets were symbols not of glorious victory but of disgraceful defeat, returning to a country that apparently regarded the very notion of heroism as deeply suspicious. When veterans appeared in the newspapers or in fiction, it was as haunted killers, traumatized victims, or violent rejects, not as the square-jawed supermen of old. They had become unwelcome reminders of a war that had transformed Americans "from victors into, at best, victims; from heroes into, at worst, killers; their leader, a self-proclaimed madman; their soldiers, torturers; their democratic public, a mob of rioters and burners; their army, in a state of near collapse; their legislative bodies, impotent." More than six out of ten people told a Harris poll that they associated veterans with "a war that went bad." And half agreed that they were "suckers" who had risked their lives "in the wrong war, in the wrong place, in the wrong time."[17]

For those tortured at the hands of the Vietnamese, their frosty reception seemed unbearably unjust. "The pain and the loneliness," remarked the future vice admiral James Stockdale, who was shot down over North Vietnam and horrifically abused by his captors, "were shallow complaints compared to finding yourself stripped of all entitlement to reputation, love or honor at home." Veterans' hospitals were often poorly funded, inadequately equipped, and overrun by vermin. Patients were left for hours with dirty bedclothes, hooked up to overflowing urine bags, unnoticed by nurses too busy to cope. Bobby Muller, a former Marine paralyzed by a Vietcong bullet, described his hospital in the Bronx as a dumping ground for "lunatics, drunks, and convicted criminals," while in *Born on the Fourth of July* (1976) the similarly paralyzed Ron Kovic wondered how the government could "keep asking for money for weapons and leave us lying in our own filth." A shocking exposé of hospital conditions in *Life* magazine drew national outrage, especially pictures of a helpless quadriplegic veteran abandoned in the shower. "It's like you got put in jail," he told the magazine, "and you're being punished for something."[18]

Even veterans who returned with their bodies intact testified to the same sense of abandonment and punishment. The conflict had taken a dreadful psychological toll: two years after the fall of Saigon, a study at Cleveland State University estimated that half a million veterans were suffering from post-traumatic stress disorder, while more than six out of ten men at veterans' hospitals were diagnosed with psychiatric problems. "Post-Vietnam syndrome," a combination of "guilt, depression, anger, self-deprecation, and persistent distrust of authority," drove many veterans to drink or drugs to blot out the memories. Families and marriages buckled under the strain: a staggering 38 percent of married veterans separated from their wives within six months of coming home, while the suicide rate was 24 percent higher among Vietnam veterans than for the rest of their age-group. The American people, Bobby Muller complained, had put "the onus of responsibility on the backs of 18- and 19-year-olds who got suckered into fighting the war . . . Instead of being seen as heroic, you are perceived as a psycho. You're the son of a bitch that killed those women and children."[19]

To traumatized young men like the three friends in the film *The Deer Hunter* (1978), for whom the war once seemed a chance to prove their virility, public rejection was the ultimate insult. Like other public institutions, the military struggled to ride out accusations of corruption, brutality, and obscene indifference to suffering. Even war itself, once celebrated as the high point of manhood, now seemed less noble, glamorous, and heroic than at any time in living memory. School textbooks dwelled not on the glories of American arms but on the massacred Indians and slaughtered Japanese. In an extraordinary reversal, Sears cut all military toys from its catalog, while Hasbro dropped military-looking pieces from its G.I. Joe special sets and even—horror of horrors—gave Joe a distinctly left-wing beard. By 1974, Joe had taken on a kind of Bruce Lee persona thanks to his "oriental grip," and two years later he disappeared completely. Poor Joe "was typical of the rest of the war story in child culture in those years," writes Tom Engelhardt in his history of national mythology in the Cold War. "So many years of Vietnamese resistance had transformed the pleasures of war-play culture into atrocities, embarrassments to look at . . . The very word *war* had been stripped out of children's culture and childhood transformed into something like an un-American event."[20]

Even masculinity itself seemed to be changing beyond recognition. When the last POWs were released from captivity in February 1973, the Pentagon arranged special classes on cultural change since the late 1960s. According to an investigation for *The New York Times*, the POWs' biggest challenge was to adjust to the new sexual landscape, in which their wives' and daughters' horizons had broadened dramatically. Barely four months after their return, 39 out of 420 married POWs were involved in divorce proceedings. And after what they had already suffered in Vietnam, it was sometimes all too much. In June 1973, the press reported the tragic fate of the Air Force captain Edward Brudno, who had been a prisoner for seven years. Married only two months before he was shot down, Brudno idolized his wife and had written an epic poem about her during his captivity. When he returned to upstate New York, however, he found that his innocent young bride had grown into a "very strong woman." The day before his thirty-third birthday, he wrote a two-line suicide note, tied a plastic bag around his head, and killed himself.[21]

What disconcerted many veterans was not just the new assertiveness of their wives, or even the spectacle of sons and brothers with shaggy, flowing hair, floral shirts, and high-heeled shoes, but the fact that strength, stoicism, and sacrifice no longer elicited widespread admiration. John Wayne no longer seemed the ultimate role model, and most movie heroes of the mid-1970s were tortured, sensitive souls—although few were quite as weedy as the balding, bespectacled Alvy Singer, Woody Allen's alter ego in *Annie Hall* (1977), with his kooky girlfriend in male attire, his mysterious "sexual problem," and the 4-P draft classification that means that "in the event of war, I'm a hostage." This put him in the same league as Philip Roth's alter ego Nathan Zuckerman, who comments in the novel *My Life as a Man* (1974) that he would be so useless in battle that "he might just as well be carrying a parasol and wearing a bustle." In the same book, another of Roth's alter egos, Peter Tarnopol, wonders: "How do I ever get to be what is described in the literature as a *man*?" The answer, surely, is not by dressing up in his wife's underwear, which Tarnopol does to make the point that, as a man, he has "surrendered."[22]

But if Warren Farrell was to be believed, Tarnopol was on the right lines. In *The Liberated Man* (1974), Farrell insisted that men had allowed themselves to be tyrannized by their own masculinity; what they should do, therefore, is take a leaf out of feminism's book, cast off their old self-image, and surrender themselves to "vulnerability" and "empathy." A healthy, well-adjusted man, agreed Marc Fasteau in *The Male Machine*, published in the same year, was gentle, sensitive, slightly androgynous, even a bit feminine. In future, Fasteau predicted, "girls will be allowed to play baseball, and boys will be allowed to play with dolls." But there was no need to look to the future. The New Man was already at large, in the persons of lank-haired singer-songwriters like James Taylor, Jackson Browne, and Neil Young, with their miserable ballads about lonely men wandering dejectedly along the seashore.[23]

**To the small band** of commentators who still believed that Vietnam had been a "noble cause," as Ronald Reagan later put it, the decline of the all-American hero seemed a disturbing symptom of a wider loss of courage and conviction. Since the advent of Nixon and Kissinger in 1969, the principle of détente—meaning the relative rapprochement between the Western and the Communist worlds—had governed American foreign policy. As Kissinger described it, this marked a return to the principles of the nineteenth-century balance of power, with hardheaded realism taking precedence over misguided idealism. The United States had "no permanent enemies," he declared, and would "judge other countries, including Communist countries . . . on the basis of their actions and not on the basis of their domestic ideology."[24]

To the horror of their critics, Nixon and Kissinger were as good as their word, making groundbreaking trips to Beijing and Moscow, signing an Anti-Ballistic Missile Treaty with the Kremlin, and agreeing to sell the Soviet Union a million bushels of American wheat. And when Gerald Ford replaced Nixon in the White House, he showed little sign of wanting to revive the spirit of the Cold War. His first major presidential trip abroad, in November 1974, took him to Vladivostok, where in the freezing weather he agreed to a new arms control deal, nicknamed SALT II, with Leonid Brezhnev. By now, however, détente was losing its luster. When Ford and Kissinger returned in triumph, they were astonished to find themselves accused of craven appeasement. SALT II, said the Democratic senator Henry Jackson, sanctioned "the massive continuation of Soviet arms expenditures" and a huge Soviet "advantage in strategic warheads." Even newspapers formerly sympathetic to détente echoed his criticisms. The Senate should reject the treaty, argued *The New York Times*, and tell Ford "to return to the conference table to seek more meaningful arms control." As Kissinger grimly remarked, anyone who thought that the Soviet leaders would happily start all over again was out of his mind.[25]

Despite the publicity surrounding Nixon's expeditions to Moscow and Beijing, détente had never been especially popular on Capitol Hill. Many liberals refused to give the Republicans any credit for policies they would otherwise have applauded; others complained that Kissinger made no allowance for morality. On the right, a common criticism was that Ford and Kissinger were sacrificing American ideals and appeasing an evil empire. Since the late 1960s, military spending had declined from more than 40 percent to almost 23 percent of the federal budget, and the anti-Soviet hard-liner Paul Nitze, who had worked for Roosevelt, Truman, and Kennedy, told friends that Kissinger was a "traitor to his country."[26]

Indeed, for all his popularity with the gossip columnists, Kissinger could never shake the allegation that as a Bavarian-born Jew with a thick Germanic accent, he had no sense of America's global mission. Admiral

Elmo Zumwalt claimed that Kissinger had told him that since the United States was "on the downhill," his job was "to persuade the Russians to give us the best deal we can get, recognizing that the historical forces favor them." Although Kissinger furiously denied it, other associates reported hearing similar remarks. The West German newspaper *Der Spiegel* quoted him telling journalists that Europe would be "Marxist-dominated" within ten years. "Every civilization that has ever existed," he once told *The New York Times,* "has ultimately collapsed."[27]

By the time that Saigon fell to the Communists, Kissinger was already under ferocious attack from an odd coalition of Cold War liberals, right-wing hawks, and neoconservative intellectuals, led by the Democratic senator Henry Jackson. Nicknamed the "Senator from Boeing" after the aerospace corporation that provided so many jobs in his native Washington state, Jackson was popular with the labor movement for his fidelity to New Deal liberalism, but was also respected by conservatives for his support for the Vietnam War. Few prominent politicians were more spectacularly uninspiring: Sidney Blumenthal called him a "black hole of charisma," while Garry Wills wrote that the more Jackson talked, "the more he fades, leaving nothing but a Cheshire frown." But somehow this stolid blandness worked in his favor. While Kissinger plotted for advantage, Jackson would not yield an inch. And while Kissinger drew elaborate comparisons with Metternich and Bismarck, Jackson repeated that the Soviet Union was a vicious totalitarian empire, that defense spending should be going up, that the Cold War must be won, and that the United States had a God-given mission to bring democracy to the world—a message that found an increasingly receptive audience as détente ran aground.[28]

To Jackson and his neoconservative allies, such as Irving Kristol, Norman Podhoretz, and Nathan Glazer, the fall of South Vietnam seemed conclusive evidence that American power was in desperate decline. More proof followed a month later, when Ford refused to attend an AFL-CIO banquet in honor of the exiled Nobel laureate Aleksandr Solzhenitsyn, whose books *One Day in the Life of Ivan Denisovich* and *The Gulag Archipelago* had exposed the horror of the Soviet labor camps. Détente was not the only factor: always a stubborn man, Ford hated being forced into a corner, and in any case he thought that the Russian writer was a "goddamned horse's ass." Given Solzhenitsyn's well-chronicled egotism, anti-Semitism, and wild attacks on Western civilization, perhaps he was not far wrong.[29]

Although Ford had spared himself an awkward hour making small talk into Solzhenitsyn's beard, he had set off another public uproar. *The New*

*York Times* wondered whether Ford knew "the difference between détente and appeasement," while George Will claimed that "not even Watergate was as *fundamentally* degrading to the presidency as this act of deference to the master of the Gulag Archipelago," a ludicrous thing to say even by his standards. And of course one solid figure pushed his way to the front of the crowd. A real leader would have "met with Solzhenitsyn," said Henry Jackson, "rather than cowering with fear of the Soviet reaction."[30]

In the meantime, Solzhenitsyn could hardly have been a better champion for the neoconservatives' case that détente meant appeasement of an evil empire. At the AFL-CIO banquet he devoted most of his speech to a withering indictment of American policy, even hinting that his hosts should still be fighting in Vietnam. A few weeks later, he told *National Review* that the administration ought to cut off all talks with the Soviet leadership, since "the Communist ideology is to destroy your society." To the argument that détente was the best way to stop a nuclear war, Solzhenitsyn's reply was scathing. "Why should there be a nuclear war," he asked, "if for the last 30 years they have been breaking off as much of the West as they wanted—piece after piece, country after country, and the process keeps going on?"[31]

Solzhenitsyn's greatest ire was reserved for Ford's next meeting with the Soviet leaders, scheduled for the end of July in Helsinki. According to the Russian writer, this would be the final "betrayal of Eastern Europe," where "an amicable agreement of diplomatic shovels will bury and pack down corpses still breathing in a common grave." This was an extraordinarily melodramatic way to describe a mundane exercise in diplomatic housekeeping, for Helsinki was effectively a meeting to tidy up the legacy of World War II, covering such banalities as borders, science, tourism, and trade. In fact the treaty eventually became a touchstone for Eastern European dissidents such as Václav Havel and Lech Wałesa, who pounced on the Soviet leaders' promise to respect the "universal significance of human rights."[32]

At the time, however, Ford's critics were more exercised by the fact that he had apparently acquiesced in the Soviet military occupation of Eastern Europe, especially in the Baltic states, Lithuania, Latvia, and Estonia. Before Ford had even set foot in Helsinki, ethnic groups bombarded the White House with letters accusing him of accepting a "second Yalta." It was a "miserable and un-American treaty," declared the vice president of the Latvian Press Society, "a treaty which buries the hopes of millions of Eastern European peoples." Even *The New York Times* warned that Helsinki condemned to Soviet tyranny "all three independent Baltic states plus large chunks of Poland, Czechoslovakia and Rumania." And the usual suspects sharpened their knives. "At Kissinger's insistence," Ronald Reagan said witheringly, "Mr. Ford flew halfway around the world to sign an agreement at Helsinki that placed the American seal of approval on the Soviet empire in Eastern Europe ." "I think we lost in Helsinki," agreed Governor Jimmy Carter. "We ratified the takeover of Eastern Europe. We got practically nothing in return."[33]

By this stage détente was already in tatters. The Soviet leadership had long since lost interest, especially as their goal of winning most-favored-nation trade status had been torpedoed when Jackson and the neoconservatives kicked up a fuss about their treatment of Jewish emigrants. On Capitol Hill and in the press, meanwhile, détente had become "a fancy French word for appeasement," as one critic put it. Détente meant "ultimate Soviet military superiority over the West," George Meany explained to the Senate Foreign Relations Committee. "Appeasement was built into détente," Theodore Draper told the readers of Commentary, although its "moral flaccidity" would never succeed, because "appeasement cannot appease the unappeasable."[34]

But Kissinger's critics in the press were now the least of his problems. By now, Ford's aides felt that the secretary of state attracted too much negative publicity and conjured up unhappy memories of Nixon, Vietnam, and Watergate. By June 1975, The New Republic was reporting the "fairly widespread belief among some of the President's closest associates that Mr. Ford ought to diminish his reliance upon and identification with Henry Kissinger." Chief among these voices was the ruthlessly ambitious chief of staff, Donald Rumsfeld, who argued that Kissinger should be stripped of at least his position as national security adviser. Of course Kissinger had faced bureaucratic rivals before, but few had been as wily or ambitious as Rumsfeld. And Kissinger knew a worthy opponent when he saw one. "Don," he casually remarked during one cabinet meeting to muffled laughter, "your wife was over measuring my office today."[35]

On Saturday, October 25, 1975, Ford called Kissinger and Rumsfeld into the Oval Office. Kissinger's unchecked control of foreign policy was over; although he stayed on as secretary of state, he surrendered the position of national security adviser to Brent Scowcroft. Meanwhile, Rumsfeld took over as secretary of defense, replacing the hawkish, arrogant, and perennially insubordinate James Schlesinger, whom Ford had inherited from Nixon. Rumsfeld's old job, meanwhile, passed to his deputy, a laconic Westerner called Dick Cheney, whom the Secret Service had aptly code-named "Backseat." Cheney's rise through the ranks would eventually make him one of the most powerful men on the planet, but at the time his promotion was virtually overlooked in all the fuss about Ford's most controversial change—his decision to drop Nelson Rockefeller as his running mate in 1976. Ford had hoped that this would show the smack of firm government; instead, the press saw it as a sign of indecision and weakness. Instead of satisfying both wings of the Republican Party, Ford had alienated everybody at once. Moderates howled with rage at the dropping of Rockefeller, while Jackson and Reagan led the outcry at the dismissal of James Schlesinger. Among Republican voters, polls put Reagan twelve points ahead.[36]

The so-called Halloween Massacre marked not just the end of Kissinger's dominance over American foreign policy but also the last rites for détente itself. "Détente is a particularly unpopular idea with most Republican voters, and the word is worse. We ought to stop using the word wherever possible," the president's pollster Bob Teeter told Dick Cheney two weeks later. A month later, Teeter warned that "in foreign affairs, the country has become more hard-nosed towards our adversaries," adding that any "actions or statements that would put the President in the position of taking tough stands with our adversaries would be helpful." By the time the Republican primaries kicked off in the New Year, détente was effectively dead. Not only did Ford promise to stop using the word, but Kissinger even stayed away from the Republican convention until the last possible moment. His presence, Ford's aides warned, would only inflame the party faithful.[37]

**Kissinger's fall from grace** meant that foreign policy shifted to the right. For many observers, Communism was on the march. While Vietnam and Cambodia had been lost, Nixon and Ford had cut defense spending, and the CIA had been humiliated by the Church Committee. Britain, West Germany, and Italy were haunted by terrorism, while Spain and Portugal were tottering toward revolution. In the developing world, Communism seemed the wave of the future. The mineral-rich country of Angola, for example, had thrown off Portuguese rule at the beginning of 1975, yet within months it was on the brink of falling to a Soviet-backed insurgency. To the neoconservatives, it seemed that the United States had lost the will to fight. *Commentary* warned that Soviet victory in Angola, giving it access to vital raw materials and shipping lanes, would weaken "the security of the West." And according to Daniel Patrick Moynihan, who had just resigned from a tumultuous stint as Ford's UN ambassador to run for the Senate in New York, Moscow was "the new colonial imperialist power in Africa."[38]

We know now that the apparent Soviet expansion in the mid-1970s was much exaggerated. At the time, however, the American military advantage seemed to be disappearing. In early 1975, James Schlesinger had predicted that the Soviet Union would soon enjoy military "preponderance." Two years later, Robert Tucker, a hawkish political scientist at Johns Hopkins, wrote of the "impressive and persistent growth of Soviet military power," while the military historian Edward Luttwak told *Commentary*'s readers that "the Russians are building missiles, bombers, and warships to acquire a worldwide strategic reach," reflecting their "expansionist intent." At the Pentagon, the new secretary of defense was "absolutely convinced that the United States was falling behind the Soviet Union." There had been a "tremendous shift" in Moscow's favor, Donald Rumsfeld told the House Armed Services Committee—which was why he wanted a $14.4 billion hike in the defense budget.[39]

Barely eighteen months after the fall of Saigon, the mood in Washington was becoming more hawkish than at any time since the Kennedy years. And when an independent panel set up under the aegis of the President's Foreign Intelligence Advisory Board, nicknamed Team B, prepared a report on Soviet weapons capabilities, its tone was predictably bleak. Wherever Team B looked, one scholar writes, "it saw the worst case," from bomber production and ABM capacity to antisubmarine systems and even laser-beam potential. Perhaps that was hardly surprising: chaired by the passionately anti-Communist historian Richard Pipes, Team B relied on the expertise of hawks such as Paul Nitze, as well as a brilliant young neoconservative analyst called Paul Wolfowitz. Later, scholars mocked it as a "kangaroo court," driven by exaggerated fears of national decline and Communist expansionism. As Anne Hessing Cahn, a former intelligence officer who worked on arms control for President Carter, remarked, "If you go through most of Team B's specific allegations about weapons systems, and you just examine them one by one, they were all wrong."[40]

Yet at a time when the headlines were full of doom and gloom about the Soviet advance and American appeasement, Team B's rhetoric seemed terrifyingly compelling. According to Pipes and company, Leonid Brezhnev was bent on world conquest through nuclear war. "All the evidence," they wrote, "points to an undeviating Soviet commitment to what is euphemistically called the 'worldwide triumph of socialism,' but in fact connotes global Soviet hegemony." Indeed, the report went on, "while hoping to crush the 'capitalist' realm by other than military means, the Soviet Union is nevertheless preparing for a Third World War as if it were unavoidable." If military spending continued at current levels, within ten years *the Soviets may well expect to achieve a degree of military superiority which would permit a dramatically more aggressive pursuit of their hegemonic objectives.*[41]

Team B was not the only sign of the new mood. In March 1976, just days after Gerald Ford had promised to "forget the use of the word détente," Paul Nitze had lunch with a group of friends at the Metropolitan Club in Washington. There they agreed to set up the Committee on the Present Danger to warn the American people of the "growing Soviet threat."* Its members included an extraordinary selection of the great and the good, including veterans of administrations from Truman to Ford. Many were former allies of Henry Jackson's; others had been sympathetic to the neoconservatives' abortive Coalition for a Democratic Majority back in the Nixon years. And although the new organization purported to be nonpartisan, its founding statement, published just after the presidential election, was pure neoconservatism. "The principal threat to our nation, to world peace, and to the cause of human freedom," it warned, "is the Soviet drive for dominance based upon an unparalleled military buildup . . . The Soviet Union has not altered its long-held goal of a world dominated from a single center—Moscow."[42]

**In the immediate aftermath** of defeat in Vietnam, many commentators had predicted that the American people would turn inward. In 1974 one in four Americans described themselves as "isolationist," and a remarkable Harris poll after the fall of Saigon found that only 39 percent would support military intervention to defend Western Europe from Soviet attack. Not surprisingly, the European press described the fall of Saigon as an unparalleled calamity for the Western alliance: London's *Daily Telegraph* called it "utterly shocking and disastrous . . . world communism's biggest victory, the free world's biggest defeat." As many European commentators saw it, American power—military, economic, even cultural—seemed in drastic decline. Gerald Ford was shocked to see a front-page editorial in the *Frankfurter Allgemeine Zeitung* with the headline "America—a Helpless Giant," while *The Economist* ran a cover story titled "The Fading of America," predicting that "the Indochina rout will now make every ally of the United States doubt whether it can believe in promises of American support."[43]

Yet for all the predictions of American retreat, all the columns about the loss of national faith and the end of military heroism, popular patriotism was much more resilient than many had expected. "The sense of guilt created by the Vietnam War in the minds of many Americans is not warranted," wrote Guenter Lewy in *America in Vietnam* (1978), a groundbreaking revisionist account of the war that proved hugely popular with

---

*The name was borrowed from an earlier Committee on the Present Danger, which had been set up in 1950 to make the case for a Cold War military buildup.

conservative readers. But perhaps the sense of guilt had been exaggerated all along. In almost all the Vietnam retrospectives of the late 1970s, from literary best sellers such as Michael Herr's *Dispatches* (1977) and Tim O'Brien's prizewinning *Going After Cacciato* (1978) to Hollywood blockbusters such as *The Deer Hunter* (1978) and *Apocalypse Now* (1979), sympathy is reserved for the ordinary American boys plunged into the inferno of the Asian battlefield, not for their victims or adversaries. Vietnam, said *The Deer Hunter*'s young writer-director, Michael Cimino, was "not the only war in the history of the world where there have been terrible atrocities," and his film was a tribute to "the ordinary people of this country who journeyed from their homes to the heart of darkness . . . They were disparaged by the press. But they were common people who had an uncommon amount of courage."[44]

To its critics, *The Deer Hunter*'s treatment of the war seemed shockingly one-sided. On the one hand, we have three handsome young Ruthenian-American steelworkers from Clairton, Pennsylvania, their home life a lovingly detailed tapestry of patriotic banners and bowling trophies, hunting trips and pool tables, the Orthodox church and the Pittsburgh Steelers. "These are ordinary people whom I honestly cared about," a New Jersey man wrote in a letter praising the film. Yet on the other hand the Vietnamese emerge as uniformly greedy and sadistic, a race of pimps and torturers, "sadistic subhuman caricatures, their untranslated speech akin to animalistic grunts." Even Pauline Kael, who admired the film's sensitive portrayal of masculine camaraderie, condemned Cimino's "xenophobic yellow-peril imagination." In *Film Quarterly* a panel of critics slammed his "reactionary jingoism"; in *The New York Times*, the Australian journalist John Pilger called the film an "insult [to] the memory of every American who died in Vietnam." Cimino had "cheapened and degraded the memory of the war as no one else," agreed Gloria Emerson, who had just won the National Book Award for *Winners and Losers*, a fierce meditation on the legacy of the war. *The Deer Hunter* was "the most racist film I have ever seen."[45]

At the Academy Awards in April 1979, protesters from the Hell No, We Won't Go Away Committee handed out pamphlets denouncing *The Deer Hunter* as "a racist attack on the Vietnamese people." But a few hours later, as Cimino celebrated winning five Oscars, including the awards for Best Picture and Best Director, the protests were forgotten. The American people, it turned out, had only a very limited appetite for introspection and self-flagellation. They were sick of films like Robert Altman's *Nashville* and Martin Scorsese's *Taxi Driver*, awash with satire and self-loathing; after more than ten years of bad news and terrible headlines, they wanted to feel good about themselves and their country. That was why *The Deer Hunter*'s final scene, in which the characters reunite in a neighborhood bar to toast the fallen and sing "God Bless America," struck such a chord. Some critics thought it was meant to be ironic, but *Time*'s thoughtful essayist Lance Morrow saw it as "an absolution, a subtle exoneration of the American role in Viet Nam." It was "not irony," Cimino confirmed, "but a sincere expression of faith in America."[46]

**It was another** young film director who really exploited the public thirst for heroism in an age of defeat and disappointment. In February 1973, a bespectacled movie geek from Modesto, California, had started writing what he called "a fantasy in the Buck Rogers, Flash Gordon tradition." George Lucas dreamed of a "real Errol Flynn, John Wayne kind of adventure" that would "introduce a kind of basic morality," a fairy tale that would begin not with "Once upon a time" but with "A long time ago, in a galaxy far, far away." The screenplay went through draft after draft, and although Fox gave him a multimillion-dollar deal, the shoot was crippled by rewrites, bickering, and budget problems. Yet Lucas never lost sight of his film's basic optimism. "We all know, as every movie in the last ten years has pointed out, how terrible we are," he told an interviewer after it came out in the spring of 1977, "how wrong we were in Vietnam, how we have ruined the world, what schmucks we are and how rotten everything is. It had become depressing to go to the movies. I decided it was time to make a movie where people felt better going out of the theater than when they went in."[47]

For all its thrills, *Star Wars* was hardly *Citizen Kane*. The plot is clearly cobbled together from adventure serials, swashbucklers, and Westerns, the dialogue is often laughable, and even the film's splendid composer, John Williams, called it a "Saturday morning space movie." And that, of course, is precisely why it was so successful. *Star Wars* opened in May 1977; by the beginning of July it had made a record $32 million, by the end of the year $193 million, and by its first anniversary it had taken in $215 million, not including the sales of merchandise and action figures. It was the ideal post-Vietnam entertainment: a new version of the founding myth, a story of plucky rebels taking arms against a bloated imperial superpower, a chance to wave an imaginary flag and enjoy the retelling of an old American story. In *Star Wars*, Lucas recaptured the crusading spirit of the early Cold War, evoking a world in which there is no moral doubt, no self-hatred, in which faith trumps technology, duty gets its reward, and the heroine even wears a dress. He once admitted that he was "inherently conservative." And after seeing *Star Wars*, nobody could have doubted it.[48]

# Chapter Six   Southie Won't Go

I was one of a few people my age who made it out of Spanish Harlem
alive. And I ended up in Boston, with someone trying to kill me
with the American flag.

—THEODORE LANDSMARK, April 1976

Theodore Landsmark's day started badly and got worse. Due at city hall
at ten o'clock, the smart young executive director of the Boston Contractors Association realized he was going to be late when he failed to
find a parking space and had to abandon his car a quarter of a mile away.
On foot, he hurried through the spring air toward City Hall Plaza, quick-
ened his pace around the New England Merchants National Bank, and
moved swiftly toward the center of the square, a picture of respectability
in his gray three-piece suit. As he did so, he caught sight of several dozen
young white men coming around the corner toward him. And before he
could reach the steps of city hall, he heard one of them shout, "There's a
nigger!" and they were on him.

The first man hit him from behind, sending Landsmark's glasses flying,
and as he tried to recover his balance, a second man knocked him to the
ground. Before he could get up, he sensed the others moving in: kicks
rained down on his ribs, his shoulders, his head. His glasses shattered
under him; he got up, but one of the men grabbed him round the neck
and dragged him back down. "Kill the nigger," he heard them breath-
lessly repeating. He got up again. Then, through the haze of panic, he saw

one of them waving, of all things, an American flag at the end of a long pole. The man leveled the flag, the Stars and Stripes waving gently in the breeze, and thrust it like a javelin, catching Landsmark on the head. Dazed, he staggered back and broke toward the steps. He saw a policeman coming toward him, and then a minute later the anxious face of the deputy mayor. His assailants seemed to melt away. His face was throbbing; when he wiped it with a handkerchief, it came away red with blood.

Ted Landsmark was the last person anyone would have expected to see in a fight outside city hall. In many ways he was a poster boy for black progress. The son of a New York subway conductor, he had been one of only 16 black students out of 1,090 in his Yale class, had joined a prestigious Boston law firm, and now ran the Contractors Association, a group of black builders working to win public contracts. At the very least, he had been horribly unlucky. If he had been able to find a parking space, he might never have run into the South Boston High and Charlestown High students outside the federal courthouse, where they had been chanting slogans against the forced integration of Boston's schools. And now, through no fault of his own, he had a broken nose, eight stitches, and a face covered in bandages. He was going to keep the bloody handkerchiefs, he told reporters. "It's my blood. Some people in this town who thought so little of me spilled my blood because of my race."[1]

Stanley Forman's Pulitzer Prize–winning photo of the attack on Ted Landsmark became a symbol of the bitter struggle over busing in the 1970s. That it was also the world's abiding image of Boston during the bicentennial year only added to the city's shame. It was a "tragic irony," wrote *The Boston Globe*'s Jeremiah Murphy, "that the American flag and all it symbolizes would be used to distort and dishonor the image of South Boston, [whence] came so many thousands of young men who have fought and too often died for that same flag." It was impossible to imagine a "scenario with more poisonous consequences for American influence and, yes, national security," agreed another columnist, David Wilson, "than the repulsive and nauseating spectacle of white hoodlums ganging up on a black man and beating on him with the national emblem of the 'land of the free and the home of the brave.' "[2]

But not all Bostonians were so quick to join the chorus of contempt for Landsmark's attackers. James M. Kelly, president of the South Boston High Home and School Association, told the *Globe* that the attack had merely been "retaliation" for "black crime"; it was "unfortunate" because it allowed the "liberal media" to "ignore the peaceful aspect of the demonstration." And while dozens of readers wrote to express their horror, others took a rather different line. "To say I was disgusted and incensed by your front page article showing a black man being beaten 'without provocation' by primarily South Boston youths is putting it mildly," wrote Mary Rudenko of Arlington. "You insult the intelligence of the reading public. If your newspaper cited the rapes, muggings, arson and murders performed by the 'blacks' you would have enough sensationalist material for years. My sympathies lie with the courageous people of South Boston, who are constantly maligned by your newspaper."[3]

**In 1954 the Supreme Court's** decision in *Brown v. Board of Education* had apparently outlawed overt school segregation forever. Yet many schools remained defiantly lily-white: even fifteen years later, almost seven out of ten black children in the South went to all-black schools. By this stage the judicial process had developed a momentum of its own, and in two more landmark decisions—*Green v. County School Board of New Kent County* (1968) and *Swann v. Charlotte-Mecklenburg Board of Education* (1971)— the Supreme Court ruled that local authorities had an "affirmative duty" to make sure children went to integrated schools. If parents refused to make the right educational choices, then that was too bad. Schools should reflect the racial balance of the community as a whole: if necessary, the authorities would have to put thousands of children on buses and drive them across town.[4]

Given the legacy of racial segregation, the *Green* and *Swann* decisions were entirely understandable. Yet the tragedy was that they were also dangerously insensitive. Busing would have to overcome massive popular resentment, often among black and white alike. Some polls put white support in the mid-1970s as low as 2 percent, while even black support was barely more than 50 percent. "If we follow popular wishes," wrote the sociologist Jennifer Hochschild, "we will not desegregate successfully." So the authorities "must find the will to ignore (temporarily, one hopes) popular opposition," leaving the public with no hope of turning back the clock and forcing them to "learn to accept and even support what they cannot change." It was a staggeringly high-handed prescription for social transformation, but it made sense in the common rooms of Princeton. Whether it would work quite as well on the streets of Boston was another matter.[5]

School segregation was not just a southern problem. In cities such as Los Angeles and Detroit, the vast majority of black students went to all-black schools—not just because of bad luck, or housing and employment patterns, but because of deliberate zoning decisions, real estate selling policies, and the political choices of individual school boards. The case of Boston, once the capital city of abolitionism, was particularly striking. Its black population had grown enormously since World War II, as southern blacks streamed north to find work in New England's factories and military installations. At the same time, thousands of white Bostonians were moving out of the city in search of better housing and bigger salaries. So by the beginning of the 1970s, Boston's 104,000 black residents, concentrated in inner-city enclaves like Roxbury and the South End, accounted for a sixth of the city's population, encircled by a suburban ring of more than a million people, almost all of them white.[6]

"Like many cities," wrote Andrew Kopkind in 1976, "Boston is dying without much dignity." He was only slightly exaggerating: as another reporter put it, Boston in the 1970s felt like a "hidebound, distrustful, turf-conscious, class-conscious, parochial city." At barely $9,000, median income was among the lowest in any major city in the nation, yet the average weekly "market basket" cost $72, the steepest price in the country. Meanwhile, as industry fled to the suburbs, the urban fabric was visibly crumbling. The subway, the second oldest in the United States, was in desperate need of repair, its trains broken down and battered, its tunnels infested with rats. The old Victorian lead water mains, which badly needed replacing, had already poisoned parts of the city. As for the schools, Kopkind remarked with grim understatement that they had "a Dickensian character that is quaint for the tourists but not terribly conducive to good education."[7]

Boston's school system had been controlled for years by the heavily Irish Democratic Party, which treated the city as a gigantic machine for jobs, patronage, and self-promotion. Meanwhile, black children were channeled into all-black schools, so that Boston had precisely the kind of "dual system" outlawed by the *Brown* decision. Yet when the local NAACP demanded reform, the School Committee obdurately refused. Even when Massachusetts passed the Racial Imbalance Act requiring School Committees to dismantle segregation, Boston dragged its feet, buying time with a Byzantine array of optional attendance zones, gerrymandered district lines, differential grade structures, and even portable school classrooms. Although the state punished the city by withholding $52 million in funds, school segregation in Boston actually got worse during the civil rights era. By 1973, almost two-thirds of the city's black pupils attended schools where seven out of ten students were black. Their buildings were old and ramshackle, their teaching materials hopelessly antiquated: one textbook recommended the song "Ten Little Niggers Sitting on a Fence" as an arithmetic tool.[8]

In March 1972 a group of frustrated black parents filed a class action suit against the Boston School Committee, which became known as *Morgan v.*

*Hennigan.* If central casting had been asked to provide a Boston Brahmin to decide the *Morgan* case, they could have done a lot worse than send Wendell Arthur Garrity Jr. The son of a middle-class Irish lawyer, Garrity had five battle stars from the Normandy landings and impeccable connections in the Kennedy Democratic machine. Bald, bespectacled, unfailingly polite, he seemed the model of high-minded judicial activism. He took his time over the *Morgan* decision: every morning, sitting beneath his signed photographs of the Kennedys, he pored through hundreds of depositions, as well as dozens of legal precedents. And at last, on June 21, 1974, the final day of school, Garrity handed down his opinion. The Boston School Committee had "knowingly carried out a systematic program of segregation" and "intentionally brought about and maintained a dual school system." And so the city must put into immediate effect the only integration plan on the table, an uncompromising blueprint prepared by the state board of education.[9]

There was never any doubt about the legal virtues of Garrity's decision. The problem was what he proposed to do about it. The state's busing plan had been drawn up in early 1973 by Charles Glenn, a civil rights veteran and Episcopalian minister who simply took a map and divided the city from northwest to southeast into school districts, each with the right mixture of black and white children. At the end he was left with two neighborhoods: white working-class South Boston, and poor black Roxbury. Glenn was in a hurry, so he simply decided to send the entire South Boston High junior class to Roxbury, while black sophomores would be bused to "Southie." Seniors would be allowed to choose whichever school they wanted. South Boston High's principal likened it to "the hostage system of the Middle Ages, whereby the princes of opposing crowns were kept in rival kings' courts as a preventive against war."[10]

This was a recipe for disaster. Between them, Roxbury and South Boston contained six housing projects and had some of the worst educational records in the city. Roxbury was classic ghetto territory: thousands of southern blacks had moved in, jobs had dried up, and the area was now a desolate stretch of vacant lots and burned-out buildings, of dirt and trash and graffiti. South Boston, however, was almost entirely white. With its small wood-framed houses, family-run grocery stores, and sports-mad corner bars, it was a self-consciously nostalgic, even reactionary kind of place. Like Roxbury, it suffered from unemployment, petty crime, and a dreadful high-school dropout rate. But South Boston also had an intense local spirit. As a local teacher put it, "Southie meant strong community pride, a fierce loyalty to one another, a distrust of any change, and—among some—a suspicion of those who might be different."[11]

South Boston was not a welcoming place for African Americans in the early 1970s. Many white families felt threatened by the black influx into surrounding areas, while hundreds of South Boston men worked for the police or fire departments and were frightened of losing promotions to affirmative action. Their lurid stories of crime and arson intensified fears that Roxbury was a place of drug addicts, murderers, and rapists. Many South Bostonians equated blackness with welfare and crime: the walls of South Boston High were painted with racist graffiti, black visitors were abused, and immigrant families were harassed into leaving. As so often, there was a strong sexual theme. "We do not expect you to fight blacks," read a flyer at South Boston High, "but we *demand* that white girls keep away from black students and aides. *We will seek revenge on anyone who violates this rule.*"[12]

Even at the time, observers thought that Glenn's busing plan was dangerously tactless. During hearings on the plan, the Harvard law professor Louis Jaffe suggested that since South Boston was "intensely hostile to blacks," Glenn should consider pairing it with another district. But his warning fell on deaf ears. Glenn had run out of sympathy for South Boston; he later described its high school as "an ugly institution" and insisted that it "deserved to be changed." One colleague told the journalist Anthony Lukas: "I think he said to himself, 'We've had enough of you racists in South Boston; you're going to Roxbury; let's see how you like that.'"[13]

The real blame for the disorder of the mid-1970s, however, lay not with the judge or the planners but with a group of self-appointed demagogues who were whipping up public anger even before Garrity's verdict. The School Committee had been stoking the flames for years, warning parents that their children would be bused to inferior, black-dominated schools and organizing demonstrations on Beacon Hill and at city hall. In April 1974, months before Garrity's decision, twenty-five thousand demonstrators crowded onto Boston Common to call for the repeal of the state's Racial Imbalance Act, their wrists bright with color-coded bands: brown for Charlestown, purple for Hyde Park, red for Dorchester, green for South Boston. In a conscious parody of the protesters of the 1960s, they chanted, "Hell no, we won't go!" while their placards read: "No Forced Busing! Suburban Meddlers Go Home! Southie Won't Go!"[14]

The demagogues riding the wave of antibusing sentiment were a colorful but unattractive lot. Some were openly racist, such as Pixie Palladino, an East Boston housewife who broke up meetings by screaming abuse at her adversaries and condemned blacks as "jungle bunnies." A more substantial figure was the School Committee chairman, John Kerrigan, who sported a bowling jacket with the legend "Bigga" (supposedly a reference to his physical endowment) and boasted: "I may be a prick, but at least I'm a consistent prick." For Kerrigan, liberals were the friends of "convicted felons, homosexuals [and] abortionists," while blacks were "savages" and journalists "motherfucking maggots." During a break at Garrity's courtroom, Kerrigan spotted an ABC reporter who happened to be black. "He's one generation from swinging in the trees," Kerrigan remarked, crouching and scratching his armpits in imitation. "I bet he loves bananas."[15]

By far the most prominent antibusing champion, however, was Louise Day Hicks, a former schoolteacher from South Boston. The daughter of a local judge, Mrs. Hicks was part of the neighborhood's "Irish aristocracy," a model of lace-curtain respectability. With her "round, outsized baby-doll face, her high-pitched, singsong voice and elocution-school manners, and her orchid-corsage style of dress," she initially seemed a typical middle-class reformer. When the NAACP began its campaign against school segregation, however, she became an unexpected champion of white resistance, calling busing "undemocratic, un-American, absurdly expensive and diametrically opposed to the wishes of the parents of this city." As for the School Committee's critics—who included senior politicians, college presidents, and, before his death in 1970, Cardinal Cushing—they were "a small band of racial agitators, non-native to Boston, and a few college radicals who have joined in the conspiracy to tell the people of Boston how to run their schools, their city, and their lives."

Since Mrs. Hicks had black friends, it was probably political ambition rather than personal prejudice that propelled her into defending segregated education. Her stance made her a folk heroine, and by the early 1970s she had perfected the art of racism by indirection. "You know where I stand," ran her favorite slogan. Like so many populists, she also took aim at the "radical agitators" and "pseudo-liberals" of the antiwar movement and the counterculture. But there was almost always a racist undertone as, her pearl-draped frame heaving with emotion, she lamented that white women "can no longer walk the streets in safety," or that justice "means special privileges for the black man and the criminal," or that "black militants . . . tyrannize our schools, creating chaos and disruption."[16]

Mrs. Hicks's enemies could not contain their loathing. One civil rights leader likened her to Adolf Hitler, another called her the "Bull Connor of Boston," and the liberal commentator Joseph Alsop thought she was "Joe McCarthy dressed up as Pollyanna." But a profile in *Newsweek*, dripping with social snobbery, nevertheless captured her potent appeal in the bars of South Boston:

> They looked like characters out of Moon Mullins, and she was their homegrown Mamie-made-good. Sloshing beer at the long tables in

the unadorned room of the South Boston Social and Athletic Club sat
a comic-strip gallery of tipplers and brawlers and their tinseled over-
dressed dolls . . . After Mrs. Hicks had finished reading off her familiar
recitation of civic wrongs the other night . . . the men queued up to
give Louise their best, unscrewing cigar butts from their chins to buss
her noisily on the cheek, or pumping her arm as if it were a jack handle
under a trailer truck.

Never one to miss a trick, Hicks took out full-page advertisements in
the Boston press to attack the article. "I deeply resent your insults to Boston and its residents," she wrote. "I am proud of my heritage. No article of
yours can lessen that pride."[17]

Louise Day Hicks gave the antibusing movement a figurehead of
unexpected respectability whose femininity played well on television and
allowed her to reach out to wives and husbands alike. She was also a crucial organizing figure, putting together the antibusing alliance Restore
Our Alienated Rights (ROAR), named after a toy lion she had spotted in
a friend's car. ROAR drew more support in blue-collar areas than in more
affluent or diverse ones, but it was easily the most popular channel for antibusing resentment. The very night that Garrity announced his decision,
it agreed to sponsor a two-week boycott of Boston's schools—ironically, a
tactic Hicks had condemned as illegal when used by black activists ten
years before.[18]

If a time traveler had found himself in Boston in late 1974, surrounded
by long-haired teenagers with flags and placards, he might easily have
imagined himself in the middle of a civil rights march. Indeed, ROAR's
techniques, from buttons and banners to sit-ins and prayer vigils, came
directly from the civil rights playbook. The difference, as Ronald Formisano remarks, was that "the housewives, blue-collar ethnics, and middle
Americans shouting slogans, marching and chanting in the 1970s [were]
the wrong people," while their objectives were diametrically opposed to
the integrationist spirit of the civil rights movement. But one of the lessons
of the 1970s—as the Kanawha textbook protesters in West Virginia, the
campaign for Proposition 13 in California, and Anita Bryant's "Save Our
Children" campaign against gay rights were to prove—was that there was
nothing automatically progressive about grassroots activism. Indeed, with
their contempt for authority, their insistence on their rights, their sense of
victimhood, and their appetite for confrontation, Louise Day Hicks and
her confederates were genuine heirs to the marchers of the 1960s.[19]

. . .

**As the beginning** of the school year drew closer, Boston seethed with apprehension. City officials held meetings to persuade parents that busing would go ahead smoothly, while local sports stars like the Red Sox legend Carl Yastrzemski and the Bruins' legendary defenseman Bobby Orr recorded television ads urging viewers to put the safety of Boston's children first. Yet not only white parents but also many liberal politicians, NAACP officials, and even black parents thought that busing between South Boston and Roxbury was unnecessarily inflammatory. Eight out of ten residents with school-age children opposed the plan; so too did most policemen, firemen, and labor officials, as well as much of Boston's influential Catholic clergy. Meanwhile, the tribunes of resistance stoked public anger, as John Kerrigan asked the people of Boston "to join me and the School Committee in non-violent activity." With a note of grim sarcasm, he added: "I hope we will be so non-violent that we will win the Nobel Peace Prize."[20]

If anyone believed that Boston could avoid violence, those illusions were shattered on Monday, September 9, three days before classes began. In beautiful sunny weather, ten thousand protesters assembled on Boston Common and marched down to City Hall Plaza, where they had challenged the state's senior senator, Ted Kennedy, to meet them face-to-face. For Kennedy the busing controversy presented a tricky challenge. On the one hand, he was the city's favorite son, the voice of the Boston Irish, and supposedly the only man capable of rallying blacks and working-class whites behind the Democratic banner. But he was also the standard-bearer for old-fashioned liberalism, a Washington insider who believed in racial integration. Just the day before, *The Boston Globe*'s Mike Barnicle had urged Kennedy to speak out. "You have the one voice that can help keep this city calm, leaving the clear ring of justice and common sense in homes and streets where people sit, uncertain," Barnicle wrote. "To you, Senator Kennedy, they would listen."[21]

All three Kennedy brothers liked to boast that unlike other liberals, they had "guts" or "balls," and so, when the marchers arrived at city hall, Ted Kennedy decided to meet them. It was not a wise decision. The mood was ugly, the demonstrators had already hung Garrity in effigy, and one of Kennedy's aides begged him to leave immediately, telling him they were "wacko." Ignoring him, Kennedy walked through the crowd and up to the microphones. His very presence seemed to inflame the crowd; the jeering grew louder, and through the din his aides made out individual insults: "Why don't you put your one-legged son on a bus for Roxbury?" "Yeah, let your daughter get bused, so she can get raped!" "Why don't you let them shoot you, like they did your brother?" Kennedy's jaw tightened, and the noise redoubled. The crowd sang "God Bless America" and then, as one, symbolically turned their backs on their senator so that they were facing—ironically—the John F. Kennedy Federal Building.

Kennedy stepped down from the platform and began to walk toward his office, and then, suddenly, it was as though the crowd had snapped. First one ripe tomato, then another, smacked into Kennedy's pin-striped suit; then came the eggs. A wailing woman with an American flag pinned into her hair ran at him, punching him on the shoulder. As he stumbled, another demonstrator elbowed him, and then a man kicked at his shins. Somehow Kennedy made it to the Federal Building, but as security guards struggled to hold the crowd back, the mob hammered their fists against the tinted glass windows so hard that one gigantic pane shattered inward. Inside, Kennedy's hands were shaking. Mike Barnicle, who had seen it all, broke the tension: "I think you really had them, Teddy."[22]

Pictures of Kennedy's ordeal were flashed all over the country. So too were pictures from the first day of classes, three days later. And the media focused not on Jamaica Plain or Dorchester, where integrated schools opened with little fuss, but on South Boston High, where racist graffiti covered the walls, protesters scuffled with policemen, and school buses were pelted with rocks and bottles. On Friday, the mayor sent the police into South Boston; on Monday, South Boston youths sacked the Andrew Square subway station, ripping out phones and beating up black commuters. On September 29, thousands marched through South Boston, chanting, "Southie won't go!" A week later, hundreds gathered outside Garrity's home in the affluent suburb of Wellesley, chanting slogans before a thin black line of helmeted policemen. It was like Little Rock, Birmingham, or Selma all over again, but with the roles reversed. And when a Haitian maintenance man stopped his car at the wrong place at the wrong time, he was nearly lynched by a South Boston mob screaming "Get the nigger!" and hacking at him with a hammer and sawed-off hockey stick. One foreign reporter thought that South Boston was "like Belfast. The women look the same, talk the same . . . Anytime there's trouble, you see them egging the kids on."[23]

What was it like to be at South Boston High, the dilapidated brick schoolhouse at the center of the violence? Every day, demonstrators gathered outside, chanting and throwing stones at the buses bringing black students from Roxbury. For parents and children alike, whether black or white, it was a terrifying experience. Many parents told of teenage children sobbing and vomiting with fear as they prepared to run the gauntlet. One South Boston High teaching aide wrote to Judge Garrity about her daughter, a senior, who cried and screamed at the thought of school.

On one occasion, the aide came across a crying fifteen-year-old white girl who had not eaten lunch all year because she was afraid to go into the cafeteria, a bear pit of insults and violence. Every day, fights broke out in the corridors; once, in early October, state troopers had to be called into the cafeteria after a white boy kicked over a black boy's tray and lunch degenerated into a mass brawl.[24]

On December 11, the violence reached a climax. At ten that morning, as students were waiting for their second class, a black pupil called James White stabbed a seventeen-year-old white boy, Michael Faith, puncturing his lung and liver. The news spread, and a vengeful mob assembled outside the school, many of them men with buttons reading, "Southie Is My Home Town." A chorus of mothers, reported one onlooker, "kept up a stream of racial invective and jibes at the police," leading the crowd in chants of "Niggers eat shit." By now all the white students had been evacuated, leaving about 130 black teenagers from Roxbury. Louise Day Hicks pleaded with the crowd to let the children go home; but, for the first time in her career, they howled her down. At last, as a lone bus struggled toward the schoolhouse door, mounted riot policemen charged the crowd. But it was a trick; while this was going on, the black students were being spirited out of a side entrance to safety.[25]

By the beginning of 1975 it had become clear that the trouble was not going to end anytime soon. The city's total school enrollment was eighty thousand, but ROAR boycotts and fear of violence meant that tens of thousands of students regularly stayed away. Some integrated schools were genuine success stories, but by May 1975 six out of ten white adults agreed that the Garrity plan had caused an "almost complete breakdown" of the Boston education system. At demonstrations, Garrity was burned in effigy, while all over the city graffiti proclaimed "Fuck Garrity" or "Kill Garrity." Yet he knew that he was doing the right thing: there could be no compromise with the law. In May 1975, he rejected a compromise plan for the next school year and ordered that a uniform racial ratio be imposed on the entire city. Again, South Boston was paired with Roxbury, and this time busing would involve twenty-five thousand children—among them the students of Charlestown High.[26]

With fifteen thousand Irish and Italian Catholics packed into a small peninsula north of central Boston, Charlestown was famously rough, tough, and crime-ridden. "Townies" nursed a historic sense of grievance: older people remembered how the city barons had driven an elevated railway through the heart of Main Street, how hundreds of houses had been torn down to make way for the Bunker Hill housing project, and how the Port Authority had demolished dozens of homes to build ramps onto

I-93. Run-down, short of jobs, many families moving out as fast as they could, it was a terribly unpromising venue for the second phase of Garrity's experiment. "Charlestown's resistance to busing this fall," one Townie remarked, "will make South Boston look as peaceful as the Vatican."[27]

True to predictions, the beginning of classes at Charlestown High in September 1975 was the cue for a familiar succession of images: protesters battling with policemen, mobs of screaming mothers, buses struggling through a hail of stones. When black parents were invited to visit the school a few days before classes opened, they arrived to find a mob waiting outside, chanting, "Niggers, go home! Niggers, go home!" Inside, half-erased slogans were still visible on the crumbling walls: "Welcome Niggers," "Bus is for Zulu," and "Be illiterate. Fight forced busing." When they left, after listening to reassuring platitudes from the teachers, the mob was bigger than ever. And as the parents' buses pulled away, they had a taste of what their children would hear every day: "Go home, niggers! Keep going all the way to Africa!"[28]

At South Boston High, meanwhile, there was little improvement. In December 1975, after months of boycotts and brawls, Garrity placed the school in federal receivership and brought in a new principal from Minnesota. Grants poured in, but by the third year South Boston High was actually *less* integrated than in 1974–75. When classes opened in September 1976, violent clashes put five people in the hospital, and in the first three weeks almost two hundred students were suspended. And so it went on. Even when classes opened in the fall of 1979, mobs stoned buses of black children outside South Boston High, a black football player was attacked and paralyzed at Charlestown High, and a white East Boston student was stabbed with a hunting knife. It was little wonder that fourteen thousand children stayed at home. By 1982, black support for the Garrity plan had fallen to a pitiful 14 percent. And in the most tragic irony of all, not one of the original plaintiffs in *Morgan v. Hennigan* with children in school still supported compulsory busing—a terrible indictment of integration in Boston, eight years on.[29]

**What happened in Boston** in the mid-1970s was both a national embarrassment and a reminder that the legacy of racism would not easily go away. There was plenty of blame to go around, the chief culprits being the School Committee and Louise Day Hicks and her fellow rabble-rousers, who deliberately exploited voters' fears and prejudices. But Judge Garrity was not entirely blameless. Of course he had to find the School Committee guilty, but it was surely a mistake to endorse the state's controversial busing plan. Few people would have criticized him for taking a more cautious, pragmatic approach; in the long run, a less comprehensive blueprint might have converted more Bostonians to the virtues of integration. Instead, the Garrity plan brought out their worst instincts and made thousands of children's lives a misery.[30]

Racism clearly played a major role in the antibusing movement, and of course discrimination lay at the heart of the entire education issue. And yet the struggle against busing was not simply a matter of naked prejudice. Revealingly, Louise Day Hicks was not happy when George Wallace publicly applauded her. He was a "segregationist," she said: "I don't want to be connected with him." In another interview, she admitted that while "a large part of my vote probably does come from bigoted people . . . I know I'm not bigoted. To me that word means all the dreadful Southern, segregationist, Jim Crow business that's always shocked and revolted me."[31]

In her apparent distaste for segregationist prejudice, Hicks was not alone. When a Charlestown antibusing group screened a propaganda film praising the Ku Klux Klan, several people walked out, and the executive committee later issued a public apology. Polls consistently found that most people had complicated, even contradictory attitudes to race and education. As early as 1965, almost no white Bostonians said that they would object to their children being educated alongside a black minority, while only 22 percent would object to them attending a school that was half black. Even at the height of the protests, almost nine out of ten white Bostonians disapproved of violence to stop forced busing, while 63 percent disliked demonstrations outside schools and 57 percent opposed school boycotts.[32]

The majority of white Bostonians might have hated busing, but they were horrified by violence, and they did not hate blacks. One city employee from Brighton lied about his address so that he could send his son to school in Quincy, a long bus ride away, rather than to the ghetto school mandated in the Garrity plan. Yet he was no racist; previously, he had sent his son to an integrated school. Then there was his neighbor, who had sat on biracial parents' councils to ease the integration process. Once the Garrity plan began, however, she removed two of her children from Boston Technical High School for fear that they were turning into racists. Another son attended Boston Latin but was beaten up by black youths on his way home from school, leaving one side of his face heavily bruised. Now, she wrote to Judge Garrity, he "has different racial feelings from myself, that I have not been able to change"—while she had become "a consciencious [sic] objector against forced busing."[33]

Even Lorraine Faith, the mother of the white boy stabbed at South Boston High in December 1974, had ambiguous attitudes to race and busing. Immediately after the attack, she told a rally on Boston Common that Judge Garrity had "more power than any dictator who ever crawled the face of the earth." "We will breathe long after he is dead," she proclaimed. "With our last breath, we say to you—Never!" But when her anger had cooled, she made it clear that she was not a thoughtless bigot. "I myself am filled with prejudices," she admitted to *The Boston Globe,* "and I think we all are." Asked if she was a racist, she replied: "Probably not, like a lot of people, I have gone through periods when maybe I have been and didn't know it." Her attitudes defied simple stereotypes: "I don't love all black people. I haven't known too many. Any time I've come across [them] in a similar situation to my own, they've been terrific."[34]

There were plenty of reasons to dislike busing that had nothing to do with race. Parents who had worked hard to live in a particular neighborhood and send their children to the local school were furious that they had to put them on a bus across town. They naturally assumed that they, not the courts, had the right to decide where their children went to school; the loss of that right, even in the name of the greater good, hit them hard. And to families in working-class areas like South Boston, busing struck at their cherished community identity. "When I was a kid, every kid I knew had one real dream in life. Every kid wanted to go to South Boston High and play football," one protester explained. "Now, it's not possible anymore . . . Kids from Southie have to be bused out of the neighborhood and go somewhere else. That's heartbreaking. Something very special has been taken out of their lives."[35]

Busing was also a clash of white against white, pitting blue-collar neighborhoods like South Boston against middle-class suburbs like Arthur Garrity's Wellesley. The city's public school population was notably poor: in 1976, six out of ten pupils grew up below the federal poverty level. It was these children, not those from wealthy families, who bore the burden of busing. In 1974, the Supreme Court had ruled in *Milliken v. Bradley* that busing should not generally cross suburban district lines, ensuring that lily-white suburban schools were preserved intact. Louise Day Hicks was not alone in believing that this gave the nod to suburban hypocrisy. It was a "scandal," the pro-integration psychologist Robert Coles wrote in *The Boston Globe,* that busing was "imposed like this on working-class people exclusively." "If there is to be busing," agreed the priest and writer Andrew Greeley, "let it be imposed on all social classes, not on those who are most ill-equipped to bear its burden."[36]

What often drove the busing protests, therefore, was not race but class. For although blue-collar protesters picked on black children, sometimes with horrifically violent results, they also targeted middle-class liberals, from the well-heeled ERA activists whose Faneuil Hall rally they disrupted in 1975 to the staff of *The Boston Globe*, whose delivery trucks they persistently attacked. "You lead your life perfect as a pane of glass, go to church, work 40 hours a week at the same job—year in, year out—keep your complaints to yourself, and they still do it to you," one South Boston father told the *Globe*. "Someone's got to tell me how this Garrity guy, this big-deal judge gets all this power to push people around, right the hell out of their neighborhood, while everybody else in the world comes out of it free and equal."[37]

"Reactionary populism," Ronald Formisano calls it: an inchoate attempt by blue-collar Americans to regain control over their own lives and to punish the affluent progressives they blamed for their alienation. This kind of populism was to play a central role in the conservative politics of the future, discrediting the ambitions of big-government liberalism and inculcating a powerful sense of injustice among ordinary working-class Americans. "We're the poor sunavabees who pay our taxes and sweat tuitions, sweat mortgages and car payments and the cost of groceries and fuel, get no hand outs, give our blood, take our turn in line, volunteer for charities, and work two jobs, sometimes three," wrote the columnist Dick Sinnott in a piece reprinted across the city in the summer of 1974. All he heard from the liberals was "Praise Angela Davis! Hurrah for Ellsberg! Feel sorry for poor Patricia Hearst! But the poor, battered, bruised Bostonians? Forget them."[38]

**Boston was not unique.** As late as 1979, more than fifteen hundred school districts across the nation, educating more than twelve million young Americans, were still subject to court-ordered busing. And although local circumstances gave Boston's school crisis a distinctive flavor, the pattern of busing, boycotts, and violence was repeated in other cities across the nation, from Pasadena, San Francisco, and San Diego in California to Minneapolis, Chicago, and Cleveland in the Midwest.

A good example was Louisville, Kentucky, another industrial city struggling in the stagflation of the 1970s. There a federal judge ordered massive busing across municipal lines, with twenty-five thousand students shuttled across the city every day beginning in September 1975. As in Boston, the first week was greeted by huge protests, with thousands of working-class whites chanting racist slogans and throwing rocks at the police. On the first evening of school, a mob smashed up forty buses outside Southern High before the police arrested two hundred people. Eventually, the governor sent in the National Guard and stationed armed guards on every school bus. Even two years later, there were violent demonstrations when schools opened, with police firing tear gas at rioting protesters.[39]

Yet busing in Louisville was actually a long-term success. Its public school system experienced much less white flight than those in most other cities: by the late 1980s, seven out of ten children were white, and almost no black children went to majority-black schools. The reason was that in Louisville the judge had specifically ordered the consolidation of the city and the suburbs. Busing affected all children equally, whether rich or poor, and since families could not escape by fleeing to the suburbs, they had a stake in making integration work. And Louisville was not the only success story. In other cases where judges ordered metropolitan solutions, such as Indianapolis, Wilmington, Greenville, and Tampa, there was little white flight and almost total integration. And busing was not always controversial: in Denver, Seattle, and Austin, court-ordered integration went ahead with very little violence.[40]

Even in the South, busing could work. In the hi-tech Sunbelt boomtown of Charlotte, North Carolina, blacks and blue-collar whites worked together on a "fairer" busing plan that involved the affluent southeastern suburbs, ensuring that the burden did not fall on the poorest families alone. Despite howls of protest from wealthy families, it proved a great success. By 1983, *The New York Times* was hailing Charlotte as proof that busing worked. A year later, when President Reagan visited the city and delivered a formulaic denunciation of busing, his Republican audience responded with an embarrassed silence. "You were wrong, Mr. President," explained an editorial in *The Charlotte Observer*. "Charlotte-Mecklenburg's proudest achievement of the past 20 years is not the city's impressive new skyline or its strong, growing economy. Its proudest achievement is its fully-integrated school system . . . shaped by citizens who refused to see their schools and their community torn apart by racial conflict."[41]

But Charlotte, like Louisville, was relatively unusual. Most busing plans were much more limited, cutting city school systems off from their wealthy white suburbs. In Detroit, for example, a district judge ordered the most ambitious busing program in history, covering three counties, fifty-four separate school districts, and almost 800,000 students, to ensure that every school had the same four-to-one white-black ratio. But two years later, in *Milliken v. Bradley*, the Supreme Court struck down his plan by a narrow majority of 5 to 4, ruling that local authorities were only obliged to create a unitary, fully integrated system covering the entire metropolitan area if there was evidence that multiple districts had connived at a segregated system. "No single tradition in public education," wrote Chief

Justice Warren Burger, a Nixon appointee, "is more deeply rooted than local control over the operation of schools."[42]

*Milliken v. Bradley* marked a turning point in the history of school integration, effectively giving the authorities a perfect excuse to avoid cross-district busing. After 1974, most suburban areas (with a handful of exceptions, such as Louisville) were protected from forced busing, and the color lines between city and suburb became starker than ever. As the dissenting justice Thurgood Marshall put it, the Court had taken "a giant step backwards," allowing "our great metropolitan areas to be divided up each into two cities—one white, the other black." Of course white flight was not just about education: many people simply wanted to escape the crime, dirt, and noise of the city for the greater space and new jobs of the suburbs. But the Court's decision threw up an iron wall around the inner cities, turning suburbia into a haven for affluent white parents desperate to escape busing. Meanwhile, private school enrollment, which had been falling for decades, abruptly reversed: between 1970 and 1980, the proportion of elementary-school-age children in private schools rose from one in nine to one in seven.[43]

As a result, many public school systems were blacker and poorer than ever. By 1980, fewer than one in three Los Angeles public school students were white; in St. Louis and Detroit, fewer than one in five. And in the South, white flight was particularly glaring. In Memphis, the tenth-largest school district in the nation, court-ordered busing provoked thousands of white students to abandon the system. By the late 1970s, thirty-seven thousand white students attended 125 private schools across the Memphis area, while the public school population was "75 percent black and substantially poor." In Houston, white enrollment fell to 17 percent in 1986, in Dallas it fell to 21 percent, in New Orleans just 8 percent. "Official, legal segregation indeed was dead," the legal scholar Lawrence Friedman wrote in 2002, "but what replaced it was a deeper, more profound segregation. Tens of thousands of black children attend schools that are all black, schools where they never see a white face; and they live massed in ghettos which are also entirely black."[44]

**By May 1990,** when Arthur Garrity formally closed *Morgan v. Hennigan,* Boston had spent hundreds of thousands of dollars on school buses, planners, consultants, and policemen. Although the antibusing movement had long since collapsed, the scars remained. In blue-collar and middle-class districts alike, the Democratic vote had suffered a severe drop. And although busing was not the only factor, there is little doubt that many voters wanted to punish the liberals they blamed for the school crisis.[45]

It would be very hard to argue that busing improved the Boston school system. Between 1972 and 1976, school enrollment dropped from ninety thousand students to just seventy-one thousand, and almost all of the missing twenty thousand were white, now attending parochial, private, and suburban schools outside the Garrity plan. As more white parents turned their backs on the system, the trend continued. In 1973, about 60 percent of Boston's public school students had been white. By 1980, the proportion had fallen to just 35 percent, and by the early twenty-first century it was just 14 percent, concentrated in a few elementary schools. Ten years after Garrity's decision, Boston's schools were in a worse state than ever. An astonishing 93 percent of students were so poor that they were entitled to free or discounted school lunches, half could barely read their textbooks, and almost 40 percent dropped out before graduating from ninth grade. "The effects of massive segregation by class," writes Formisano, "were all too obvious."[46]

Three decades after his horrifying ordeal in City Hall Plaza, Theodore Landsmark was one of the most distinguished men in Boston. To his credit, he had refused to let the famous photograph define him: as president of the Boston Architectural College, he had left City Hall Plaza long behind. "It's not easy to be thought of as a symbol for most of one's life," he mused three decades on. "My life has been a lot more interesting than the twenty second moment captured in that picture." He was even asked to lead a sixteen-man task force to advise the city on how to assign children to public schools—another of the many ironies in Boston's history of busing.[47]

At the end of 2006, Landsmark was among many supporters who applauded as Massachusetts elected its first black governor, Deval Patrick. On the day Patrick was sworn in, the *Globe* later remarked, "Bostonians noted the powerful symbolism of the giant American flag suspended over Beacon Street, contrasting starkly with the searing photo of thugs using an American flag to attack another black man, Theodore Landsmark, on City Hall Plaza in 1976."[48]

But Patrick, like Landsmark, had been exceptionally fortunate. Born into a family living on welfare, he had benefited from inspirational teaching, a scholarship to a prestigious Massachusetts boarding school, and a Harvard education. Like Landsmark, he had led a charmed life. But for the thousands of black Bostonians caught up in the busing crisis of the mid-1970s, there were no such opportunities. Ted Landsmark might have been the most famous victim of the decade's antibusing passions. The real tragedy, though, was that in the long run, he was one of the tiny minority of lucky winners.

# Chapter Seven    *Redneck Chic*

See, the thing with these country people is
they have a real grassroots appeal.

—**JOHN TRIPLETTE,** in *Nashville* (1975)

In May 1971, *Time* magazine did something that would have been unthinkable just a few years before. It devoted its cover story to an enthusiastic portrait of the South. "Dixie Whistles a Different Tune," proclaimed the cover, above a lurid image of Georgia's new Democratic governor. Inside, the magazine quoted his groundbreaking words at his inauguration five months before, which had captured the new mood of southern politics. "I say to you quite frankly that the time for racial discrimination is over," Jimmy Carter had told his audience. "Our people have already made this major and difficult decision. No poor, rural, weak or black person should ever have to bear the additional burden of being deprived of the opportunity of an education, a job or simple justice." It was "a promise so long coming," wrote *Time*'s correspondents, but now "spoken at last." It marked the end of the long night of racial segregation; it was a harbinger of "new images, new goals" for the American South.[1]

*Time*'s glowing picture of the New South—a booming region of new industries, enthusiastic suburban newcomers, progressive politicians, and integrated schools, "a region of investment, both human and economic"— marked an extraordinary contrast with Dixie's popular image ten years before. Well into the 1960s, many Americans regarded the South with condescension, pity, and revulsion. To outsiders, it seemed a land permanently scarred by slavery and civil war, its politics dominated by sweating demagogues, its culture an unattractive blend of "moonshine and fiddle music, racism and possum stew." Even after he reached the White House, Lyndon Johnson could never quite shake the feeling that others looked down on him because he hailed from the old Confederacy. "I was not thinking just of the derisive articles about my style, my clothes, my manner, my accent and my family," he said later, but "a disdain for the South that seems to be woven into the fabric of Northern experience."[2]

Yet by the early 1970s the image of the South had radically changed. According to Richard Nixon's young political consultant Kevin Phillips, the old Confederacy was at the heart of something called the Sunbelt, a great crescent of political and economic opportunity stretching from Virginia, the Carolinas, and Georgia through the sweltering orange groves of Florida, the oil fields of Texas, and the new suburbs of Arizona and New Mexico, and into the small towns of Southern California. The white middle classes of the "Florida-California sun country," said Phillips, would create a coalition of "the pleasure-seekers, the bored, the ambitious, the space-age technicians and the retired"—a new Republican majority.[3]

Nixon loved Phillips's thesis. More than half of his cabinet hailed from the states of the Sunbelt, as well as a third of his agency chiefs, half of his Supreme Court nominees, and two-thirds of his senior staffers. His two homes in Key Biscayne and San Clemente were visible demonstrations of the president's interest in the sun country. And in May 1970, in a powerful symbol of his enthusiasm for all things southern, Nixon sent his vice president to Stone Mountain, Georgia, where three granite memorials to Robert E. Lee, Stonewall Jackson, and Jefferson Davis were being dedicated. "The South that will make its greatest contribution to the American Dream is the New South," declared Spiro Agnew. "The New South embraces the future and presses forward with a robust economy fueled by industrial development . . . Just as the South cannot afford to discriminate against any of its own people, the rest of the nation cannot afford to discriminate against the South."[4]

**When outsiders read** or heard about the South during the 1960s, it was almost always in the context of the civil rights movement. But behind all the sound and fury, a quiet economic revolution had begun to transform the nation's poorest region. In the place of farms and fields was rising an unrecognizable new world of gleaming skyscrapers and sprawling suburbs, populated by millions of ambitious newcomers from the North and

the Midwest, a Great Migration in reverse. Poverty was yielding to affluence, and since the South had been so backward for so long, the change
was all the more impressive. "Growth, Not Grits, Symbolizes the New
South," announced *The New York Times* in 1977. In a quarter of a century,
the region's population had increased by 50 percent, per capita income
had grown fivefold, bank assets had swollen by seven times, and industrial
output had risen sixfold. "The South's time has come," declared Florida's
governor, Reubin Askew. "Our region is the new economic frontier."[5]

Given the South's reputation as a hotbed of conservatism, it is one of
the great ironies of postwar history that its transformation from backwater
to powerhouse owed an enormous amount to New Deal liberalism. From
the 1930s onward, federal agriculture programs nurtured the rise of corporate agribusiness, while energy programs, tax breaks, and the controversial depletion allowance sponsored the expansion of the oil industry. The
National Interstate and Defense Highways Act of 1956, the largest public
works program in history, not only drove up demand for southern gasoline
but also enabled millions to move to the booming Sunbelt suburbs. Even
the vast new retirement complexes of Florida and Arizona, with their golf
courses, swimming pools, and condominiums, could trace their origins
to Roosevelt's Social Security legislation. And across the region, a vast
network of military bases, aerospace factories, and NASA research centers
testified to the impact of Cold War defense spending. "Our economy is
no longer agricultural," wrote William Faulkner. "Our economy is the
Federal Government."[6]

A key factor in this flood of largesse was the shrewd pork-barrel politics of the region's congressmen, who used their years of seniority to good
effect. By the time Mendel Rivers, chairman of the House Armed Services Committee, died in 1970, his Charleston, South Carolina, district
boasted an Air Force base, a naval base, a naval shipyard, a naval hospital, a submarine training station, a Polaris missile maintenance center,
a mine warfare center, and the headquarters of the Sixth Naval District.
But other southern districts were no less fortunate. In Georgia, Louisiana,
Mississippi, Tennessee, and New Mexico, the defense industry was the
single largest employer. Fifty percent of the Pentagon's research budget
went into the Sunbelt, and some towns were utterly transformed.

In 1950, Huntsville, Alabama, was a quiet cotton town of 16,000 people.
By 1976, its population had boomed to an estimated 143,000. More than
four thousand people worked at the George C. Marshall Space Flight Center, the original headquarters of NASA. Thousands more were employed
by Army Missile Command, the Ballistic Missile Defense Systems Command, or one of seventeen other military commands in the area; others

worked for Chrysler, IBM, Rockwell International, General Electric, and Lockheed, all of which had plants nearby. The defense and space industries accounted for more than half of Huntsville's total employment; as the local information officer put it, the relationship between the Army and the community was "one of mutual admiration and love."[7]

But federal spending was not the only thing driving southern economic growth. Businesses were drawn south because of the region's low labor costs and "right-to-work" laws outlawing the closed shop and union shop. State governments also offered an impressive range of tax breaks and subsidies for new investors, from free real estate to publicly funded training programs. By 1970 half of all foreign investment in the United States came to the old Confederacy. And five years later, the Fantus Factory Locating Service, which had moved thousands of companies from north to south, announced that six of the nation's most business-friendly states were in the South, with Texas, Alabama, and Virginia in the top three. As *Fortune* magazine put it in 1977, "Business loves the Sunbelt."[8]

And there was another factor in the rise of the Sunbelt. For centuries its economic development had been held back by the oppressive semitropical weather, which fostered staple crops, plantations, slavery, and segregation. What changed all this, as the historian Raymond Arsenault famously argued, was one of the most underrated inventions of the century. The world's first air conditioner had been built in Brooklyn in 1902, but as late as 1960 fewer than one in five homes were air-conditioned. By the mid-1970s, however, nine out of ten high-rise office buildings, banks, apartments, and railroad passenger coaches in the South were air-conditioned, as well as eight out of ten hotels and government buildings, six out of ten private homes, and even three out of ten tractors. Without air-conditioning, the South's economic miracle—the factories and malls, the vast new domed stadiums and sprawling convention centers—would have been unthinkable. "Can you conceive a Walt Disney World over in the 95-degree summers of central Florida without its air-conditioned hotels?" asked one southern columnist in 1978. "Can you see a Honeywell or a Sperry or anyone else opening a big plant where their workers would have to spend much of their time mopping brows and cursing mosquitoes?"[9]

**The growth of** the Sunbelt was easily the most striking demographic story of the decade. Between 1970 and 1980, the population of Georgia grew by 19 percent, Texas by 27 percent, Florida by 44 percent, Arizona by 53 percent, and Nevada by 64 percent. During the last four years of the 1970s alone, three million people chose to move south of the Mason-Dixon

Line, many of them young, affluent, and well educated, tempted by new jobs in the defense, aerospace, plastics, and electronics industries.

Al Massey moved from Detroit to Atlanta with his wife and two young children in 1976, after being appointed general manager of the new southeastern division of Clayton Manufacturing, which made steam generators and automobile test equipment. He had no regrets about leaving the decaying, crime-torn Motor City. In Detroit, he confided, the people were "harsh and cold"; in Atlanta, "you have neighbors." His family did not miss the snow at Christmas, because "there's artificial ice all over," and his daughter could skate all year round. And like so many middle-class migrants, he shuddered at the thought of the North's soaring crime rate. "Detroit, it was almost like taking your life in your hands," he reflected. "You couldn't even go to the theaters, the concert. On the freeways, they were even running into you, to rob you, rape your wife. They warn you not to go downtown. Cultural advantages are all there, but you couldn't take advantage of it. Here, you could send your daughter downtown."[10]

Given what had happened in Detroit just a few months earlier, not even its keenest defenders could have blamed him. By the mid-1970s, gangs operated almost unchecked in some parts of the city: on the dilapidated East Side, for example, the Black Killers, the Errol Flynns, and the Sheridan Strips roamed with impunity, boarding buses and robbing the passengers, dragging female motorists from their cars and raping them, smashing their way through house after house. Yet in July 1976 the city's mayor, Coleman Young, had laid off a thousand policemen because the city no longer had the money to pay for them. Disaster swiftly followed. A month later, more than a hundred gang members invaded a rock concert at downtown Cobo Hall, beating members of the audience and subjecting one terrified woman to a horrific gang rape. Outside the hall, a handful of policemen did nothing, refusing to intervene because the hall had promised to handle its own security.[11]

With its appalling levels of crime, family breakdown, urban decay, and drug addiction, as well as its overloaded services and heavy taxes, Detroit seemed a long way from the confident Motor City that had once embodied American enterprise. Yet the most celebrated example of urban decline was the city that had once been a byword for everything that was best about American life, the city of the Yankees and the Giants, *The New Yorker* and *The New York Times*, *Breakfast at Tiffany's* and *Barefoot in the Park*. By the middle of the 1970s, New York seemed to have become a terrifying urban Hades, infested with crooks and corruption, where child prostitutes touted for business on street corners, racism simmered close to the surface of every conversation, and violence was only a moment away—its atmosphere captured in films such as *The French Connection* (1971), *Serpico* (1973), *Dog Day Afternoon* (1975), and *Taxi Driver* (1976). An "open sewer," *Taxi Driver*'s deranged antihero, Travis Bickle, calls it, "full of filth and scum." A few months later his words found an unsettling echo in those of a genuine serial killer who called himself Son of Sam. "Hello from the gutters of N.Y.C. which are filled with dog manure, vomit, stale wine, urine and blood," began David Berkowitz's letter to Jimmy Breslin of New York's *Daily News* in May 1977. "Hello from the sewers of N.Y.C. . . . . Hello from the cracks in the sidewalks of N.Y.C. and from the ants that dwell in these cracks and feed on the dried blood of the dead that has settled into the cracks."[12]

Given the publicity surrounding Berkowitz's crimes, perhaps it was hardly surprising that just 6 percent of Americans told a national poll that New York City was "a good place to live." But the city's problems went deeper than the crimes of a sick loner. New York had become "a metaphor for what looks like the last days of American civilization," wrote the film critic Vincent Canby. "It's run by fools. Its citizens are at the mercy of its criminals who, often as not, are protected by an unholy alliance of civil libertarians and crooked cops. The air is foul. The traffic is impossible. Services are diminishing and the morale is such that ordering a cup of coffee in a diner can turn into a request for a fat lip." Even *The New York Times*, usually so supportive of the city's image, wondered whether it might be "a failed ultra-urban experiment in which people eventually crack, social order eventually collapses, and reason ultimately yields to despair."[13]

What happened to New York City was a depressingly familiar story. While Sunbelt cities were booming, the old leviathans of the North seemed terminally diseased. By the mid-1970s, almost every week brought news of more New York factory closures, with Pepsi and Shell moving out and hundreds of thousands of jobs disappearing every year. Even NBC's *Tonight Show*, once a symbol of the city's hold on the popular imagination, disappeared: in May 1972, Johnny Carson and the team headed west to California and never came back. And while more than half a million newcomers from the Caribbean and Central America moved in, there were simply not enough jobs to go around. Unskilled, uneducated, these new immigrants not only faced the usual problems of prejudice and housing discrimination but now shouldered the burden of stagflation: no work, little money, rising prices, no hope. By July 1977, when the notorious blackout brought the city's problems to the world's attention, just three out of ten black New Yorkers and just two out of ten Hispanics had regular jobs.[14]

With the white middle classes fleeing to the suburbs and the Sunbelt, the mayors who ran the big cities of the North found that their tax base was becoming dangerously narrow. By the time Gerald Ford moved into the White House, barely a week went by without another city—Boston, Chicago, Cleveland, Detroit, Pittsburgh—finding itself in desperate financial straits. In the spring of 1975 it was New York's turn. Although the city's residents had long paid some of the highest taxes in the nation, the lengthening welfare rolls meant that it stood on the brink of bankruptcy. In May, the city's new mayor, the diminutive Abraham Beame, appealed directly to the federal government for aid. At first Ford seemed reluctant to help: hence the *New York Post*'s typically sensationalist headline: "Ford to City: Drop Dead." In the end, with the city facing a winter of wage freezes, job cuts, and soaring taxes, the administration stepped in with a $2 billion short-term bailout.[15]

But in the meantime, Beame's desperate efforts to save money had provoked outrage. Under pressure from the state, he closed libraries, hospitals, and firehouses, hiked the subway fare from thirty-five cents to fifty, and scrapped the tradition of free classes at the city's public colleges— a source of particular sorrow to the mayor, who had personally benefited from free tuition. What caused most anger, however, was the firing of sixty-three thousand city employees, including thousands of teachers, hospital staff, firemen, and policemen. When public employees walked out, mounds of garbage piled up on the city's streets, filth seeping out of bags and trash cans, openly rotting in the summer heat. On Brooklyn Bridge, disgruntled cops blocked rush-hour traffic, chanting obscenities and throwing beer bottles at the stationary cars. And at the airports and stations, members of the police union handed out an apocalyptic brochure warning tourists not to use the subways or leave their hotels after dark because there would no longer be enough cops to protect them. "Welcome to Fear City," read the message on the front.[16]

Fear City was not an inaccurate label for New York in the mid- to late 1970s. The NYPD itself had become a byword for corruption: as the whistle-blower Frank Serpico and the subsequent Knapp Commission had made clear, officers had taken bribes from gangsters and porn merchants, had traded heroin and cocaine, had betrayed their own informants to the Mob, and had even provided armed bodyguards for drug barons. Meanwhile, crime in the city had risen to astronomical levels, driven by rising drug use, persistent unemployment, and the steady deterioration of the urban environment. Between 1966 and 1973 the murder rate went up by a horrifying 173 percent and rape by 112 percent. By 1976, then the worst year for crime in the city's history, there were not only some fifteen hundred murders a year but also a staggering seventy-five felonies *every hour,* increasing the burden on the distrusted, underfunded, and demoralized police department.[17]

Like so many Rust Belt cities, New York had become transfixed by fear. In surveys, crime easily outstripped inflation and unemployment as residents' chief concern. Visitors from out of town were no less nervous: as a small boy from California, the writer Jonathan Mahler noticed his parents anxiously locking the doors of their taxis, looking quickly around them as they rode the filthy, graffiti-smeared subway, and tightly gripping his arm as they walked through the litter-strewn streets. Fear was everywhere, wrote *The New York Times*'s David Burnham, eating away at the bonds of decency that bound the city together: "It can be seen in clusters of stores that close early because the streets are sinister and customers no longer stroll after supper for newspapers and pints of ice cream. It can be seen in the faces of women opening elevator doors, in the hurried step of the man walking home late at night from the subway . . . And finally it becomes habit."[18]

If there was one neighborhood that became a symbol for the fall of the American city, it was the South Bronx. Once a thriving Jewish lower-middle-class area, it had been ravaged by white flight, high taxes, and the lunacy of the Cross Bronx Expressway, which turned middle-class communities into cowering slums. Beneath the concrete fastness of Yankee Stadium, supposedly every American boy's theater of dreams, extended miles of abandoned buildings and smoldering ruins. Wild dogs roamed the streets, stores conducted their business through panes of bulletproof glass, and pushers openly sold drugs on the corners. One reporter watched a twelve-year-old mother playing with her two-year-old son; later, he saw a seven-year-old alcoholic helping his adolescent brother to inject heroin in a ruined basement. Drug addiction consumed the lives of twenty thousand local people; infant mortality was more than double the national average; and the South Bronx accounted for one in four of New York's malnutrition cases and almost one in five of its venereal disease cases. The NYPD had virtually conceded control of the streets to Puerto Rican gangs, and when the city spent almost $3 million to renovate nine tenements as low-cost housing, the buildings were taken over by drug addicts and stripped of anything of value.

By the mid-1970s the Bronx had become a byword for urban decay. "The South Bronx is a necropolis—a city of the dead," said the founder of the local Martin Luther King Jr. Health Center, a valiant but futile effort to stem the tide of disease and despair. Even Robert Moses, the controversial urban planner whose Cross Bronx Expressway had helped to destroy the neighborhood, agreed that it was "beyond rebuilding" and "must be leveled to the ground." In October 1977 the neighborhood's woes even found their way into the World Series. During the second game between the Yankees and the Dodgers, an abandoned elementary-school building caught fire, the leaping flames lighting up the sky above Yankee Stadium. "There it is, ladies and gentlemen," Howard Cosell said sententiously, "the Bronx is burning."[19]

But while the Bronx burned, southern observers felt little sympathy. When New York's governor, Hugh Carey, called for economic aid to rebuild the cities of the Northeast, his pleas fell on stony ground, even though the Empire State remained one of the nation's biggest net taxpayers. "Now that the South and the Southwest are making economic progress," asked *The Birmingham News*, "why should Sunbelt taxpayers bail out the Northeast?" And after the devastating blackout and looting in the summer of 1977, the general consensus was that, as *The New Yorker* mournfully put it, the city "had just got what it deserved, considering the kind of place it was." In Washington, one reporter wrote, it had the reputation of being full of "welfare cheats (read that 'lazy niggers')" and "arrogant smart-asses who don't give a damn about the rest of the country." Even the liberal *Washington Post* thought the looting was "a terrible indictment of the state of the city, its government and its people." The executive vice president of Miami's Chamber of Commerce went further. "It's just about what you would expect from New York," he remarked. "Most of us expected the worst and [they] didn't let us down."[20]

Meanwhile, the cities of the Sunbelt seemed a study in self-confidence, hailed as a gleaming landscape of sleek skyscrapers, roaring highways, and well-fed businessmen in overflowing suits. The old agrarian South seemed to be dying, its hallowed folkways, babbling streams, and humid hunting grounds disappearing beneath the office buildings where air-conditioning and piped music held the heat and mosquitoes at bay. Once, Charlotte, North Carolina, had been a sweltering cotton town; now it was a middle-class city of glinting towers, golf courses, and shopping malls, at the heart of one of the nation's fastest-growing metropolitan areas. As one San Diego newspaper put it, this was "America II emerging from the diminished promise of America I."[21]

Perhaps the most striking example of Sunbelt growth was Houston, which would soon overtake Philadelphia to become the fourth-largest city in the nation. For decades, explained a *New York Times* series on the city in 1976, it had been "a steamy little southeast Texas swamp town commanding little attention and less respect." Now, thanks to the oil industry, it boasted the nation's third-busiest port, the world's largest petrochemical complex, and an internationally renowned space center and medical center. It was the "newest, most prosperous, fastest-growing urban industrial center in America . . . the sassy new Pittsburgh of the Southern rim." And for those hoping to make a killing from plastics or petrochemicals, or simply those who hoped for a more affluent lifestyle, it could hardly be better. John and Heidi Lewis, a young couple from Peoria who moved in the winter of 1977, found good-paying jobs as a loan officer and a bank secretary within just two weeks. The city was "new and clean," they thought, and they loved being able to play golf at Christmas. There were downsides, of course: not everyone liked the featureless expanse of downtown skyscrapers looming above vast freeways choked with traffic. But by the end of the 1970s, Houston was attracting six thousand newcomers a month, and even *The New York Times* grudgingly admitted that by most standards it was "an attractive place to live and do business."[22]

Like so many Sunbelt cities, Houston partly owed its extraordinary growth to the efforts of its country-club establishment, made up of the leaders of the banking, construction, and real estate industries. Across the South, city elites encouraged what the historian Matthew Lassiter calls the "Sunbelt Synthesis," a business-friendly blueprint based on economic development and racial compromise. Atlanta, for instance, branded itself "the city too busy to hate," the perfect slogan for a city that was growing enormously thanks to the presence of Dobbins Air Force Base and the Lockheed factories in the northern suburbs. As the home of Coca-Cola, Atlanta could ill afford to alienate northern businessmen, and so its municipal elites fostered a corporate consensus that dismantled overt segregation and tried to sweep the past under the carpet. Atlanta, said Mayor Ivan Allen in 1969, had become a truly "national city . . . known for gleaming skyscrapers, expressways, the Atlanta Braves and—the price you have to pay—traffic jams."[23]

By the 1970s, Atlanta had become the universally recognized symbol of regional progress. *Time* called it "the South's showcase, the Southern city of the future." This was music to the ears of its business lobby, which had been working for a decade to encourage developments like Atlanta Stadium and the enormous Peachtree Center, with its atrium hotels, offices, and restaurants. As elsewhere in the Sunbelt, Atlanta's new landscape reflected its corporate ethos. By the beginning of the 1970s seventeen buildings of more than fifteen floors had gone up in the center, and from downtown a bewildering network of highways snaked out toward the suburbs. By 1975, the city boasted four million square feet of office space and three thousand new hotel rooms, many in the seventy-eight-floor silver cylinder of the Peachtree Plaza, the world's tallest hotel. Stagflation had little effect on such a boomtown: as the decade ended, the skyline was crowded with cranes, with work under way on huge new headquarters for Coca-Cola, Georgia-Pacific, Georgia Power, and Southern Bell. And when Hartsfield International Airport opened in September 1980, it seemed proof that Atlanta had become a truly global powerhouse—although an even more auspicious development, barely noticed at the time, was Ted Turner's establishment of the Cable News Network. As a spokesman for the Central Atlanta Progress development group proudly told the press, the city's "momentum was unstoppable."[24]

Yet Atlanta's apparently inexorable rise did not come without a cost. As one resident wrote to *Time*, many locals took no pleasure in the "polluted air," "clogged freeways," and "transient population that causes more problems than it cares about solving." In 1975, *The Atlanta Constitution* ran a gloomy series of articles proclaiming Atlanta to be a "city in crisis," citing rising unemployment and welfare rates, a surge in crime, and a stalemate in the political establishment. Of course any city expanding so quickly was bound to run into problems. Houston suffered from exactly the same ills—horrendous smog, fires, floods, water shortages, and rising crime—and critics called it "tarnished, congested, polluted and esthetically depressing." Like Atlanta, it was a victim of its own success: its freeways choked with too much traffic, its planning policies encouraging breakneck, sprawling development, its low-tax regime ensuring weak, toothless government.[25]

Most Sunbelt cities suffered the same problems, exacerbated by feeble zoning regulations, flagrant indifference to the dangers of pollution, and callous disregard for their poorest citizens. The overall picture, therefore, was more complicated than the New South boosters claimed: while at one level cities like Houston and Atlanta were beacons of hope, they also exemplified the drawbacks of pursuing economic growth no matter what the environmental cost. In Charlotte, homeowners complained that their city had become a sprawling commercial wasteland suffocating in traffic fumes. In Phoenix, smog sent hundreds of people to their doctors with lung infections. And in Fort Lauderdale, complained one visitor, a three-mile drive from the interstate to the sea "now lasts an infuriating hour of stops and starts, much of it past block after gaudy block of neon-lit hamburger stands and banner-bedecked service stations," with apartment buildings "stacked so high that the afternoon sun cannot reach the narrow strip of beach that remains."[26]

For the critics, one of the Sunbelt's least attractive features was its addiction to suburban sprawl. Most people who moved to cities like Houston and Atlanta lived in suburban developments, where they could be assured of spacious housing, decent schools, welcoming churches, and brand-new shopping malls. More than half of the southern population lived in metropolitan areas by the early 1970s, especially in wealthier states like Florida and Virginia. Even in poor rural states like Alabama and Louisiana, almost one in two people had a metropolitan address.[27]

Despite their popularity, suburbs never had a good press. The suburban myth, as *Time* remarked in 1971, was of "an affluent, WASPish, Republican hotbed of wife-swappers," the men overworked, the women frustrated, the children spoiled and arrogant. Yet this bore little resemblance to reality: a detailed survey of a hundred communities the same year produced "a picture of unexpected diversity, some contradiction and occasional surprise." Suburbanites were not all Republicans, nor were they inevitably affluent, commuters, or wife swappers. What they had in common, though, was that they generally enjoyed suburban life. The majority had moved so that they could own their own homes, with a better atmosphere for their children, and most were pleased with the results. Four out of ten said they had no reservations at all about their neighborhood, while seven out of ten thought that there was "a strong sense of neighborliness." They complained about crime and taxes and schools and morals, just like city dwellers, but they seemed distinctly contented. "Most, in other words, have found what they were looking for," concluded the report. "Once they have arrived, they do not look back."[28]

**While the South's** booming economy and changing skylines were enjoying unprecedented national attention in the mid-1970s, political commentators were fascinated by a dramatic transformation in the region's balance of power. Until the Voting Rights Act changed the game in the mid-1960s, the South had been governed by a motley collection of octogenarian conservatives, populist demagogues, ardent segregationists, and a few New Dealers—all of them white, and almost all of them Democrats. Only in the Appalachian highlands did the Republicans have much support; outside these unusual districts the Democratic dominance was astounding. Out of 2,434 congressional elections in the first half of the century, the Republicans won just 7. And as late as 1950 there were just 2 Republicans in the South's 105-man delegation to the House of Representatives, and no southern Republicans at all in the Senate.[29]

In many accounts of southern political history, the man who changed all this was George Wallace, who laid the foundations for the new populist conservatism and led millions of voters away from the Democratic Party. But this is not really true. Wallace won most support among poor white voters in the Deep South, not the affluent suburban whites who became the bedrock of southern Republicanism. And his supporters did not march into the Republican fold, as is often thought. Of Wallace's forty-eight districts in 1968, all but ten reverted to the Democrats in 1976. Even in the landslide of 1980, twenty-eight of the old Wallace districts stayed loyal to the Democrats. In fact, blue-collar Wallace fans were much more likely to remain loyal to the Democrats than were their affluent neighbors.[30]

While many people imagine that it was low-income rednecks who first moved to the right, spitting tobacco and brandishing their rifles as they drove their pickups toward the Republican Party, the opposite is true. To cut a long story short, the real reason the Republicans became the majority party in the South is that the region became more affluent. And the key figure was not Wallace but Dwight D. Eisenhower, who won five southern states in 1952 and added four more in 1956. His supporters were wealthy businessmen and professionals in areas with few black residents who liked the Republican message of low taxes and a smaller state. And the richer the South became, the more of them there were. In the 1970s they voted for Nixon, in the 1980s they supported Reagan, and by the 1990s they had been joined by enough middle-income white Southerners to give the Republicans a clear congressional majority. Meanwhile, despite the stereotypes, poor whites remained loyal to the Democrats. As one analysis puts it, working-class white Southerners were "no more Republican in the 1990s than they had been in the 1950s."[31]

Of course racism was still a factor in southern politics, often disguised in coded rhetoric about crime or the cities. The career of Jesse Helms, who won his Senate seat in North Carolina in 1972 after a campaign of raw racial conservatism, demonstrated that old prejudices died hard. And court-ordered school busing played a central role in driving suburban parents away from liberalism and the federal government. Yet many were already voting for Republican presidential and congressional candidates before the issue blew up. Even if busing had never happened, the middle-class families it alienated would probably have drifted toward the Republicans anyway—but for economic reasons, not racial ones.[32]

In general, despite the coded rhetoric of politicians such as Helms, race played a much less visceral role than it had done in the past. Public attitudes had undergone an extraordinary change over a very short space of time, and surveys suggested that overt prejudice was in deep decline. In 1963, Gallup had found that 78 percent of white southern parents would refuse to send their children to schools where half the students were black, while 61 percent would not send their children to a school with even a few black students. But in 1970, Gallup announced "one of the most pronounced shifts in the history of opinion polling" as these numbers fell to 43 percent and 16 percent, respectively. Even if this reflected merely what people felt they *ought* to think, it marked a profound change. Nationwide polls found similar results: eight out of ten whites in the early 1970s thought that blacks were just as intelligent as whites, more than eight out of ten favored integrated schools, and a similar proportion said they would welcome a black neighbor of the same social class.[33]

It is also telling that race-baiting in the old style had disappeared by the mid-1970s. Even Strom Thurmond, once the poster boy for segregation, moderated his language and adopted more nuanced positions. By the middle of the decade he had become the first southern senator to hire black aides and recommend black constituents for federal judgeships, and he even enrolled his daughter in an integrated school. George Wallace, meanwhile, ran for the presidency in 1976 boasting of his record appointing blacks to high-level positions and insisting that he was one of the founders of the New South. Two years earlier, he had reached out to Alabama's black community by asking the members of the Progressive Baptist State Convention for their forgiveness, and in the late 1970s he made a point of calling black clergymen to apologize for his record. In Wallace's case, this was more than political grandstanding: he seems to have been genuinely penitent, having become a born-again Christian after he was paralyzed by the would-be assassin Arthur Bremer in 1972. But he was only the most notorious of many southern politicians who changed their tune, reflecting the new racial consensus.[34]

By the end of the 1970s, then, southern politics was marked by what David Broder called a "pattern of intense competition," with the Democrats trying to hold together a coalition of blacks and poor whites and the Republicans relying on younger, more affluent suburban whites. But the Republicans did not have it all their own way: the huge, reliable black vote meant that the Democrats were still competitive. The success of Dale Bumpers, who won the governorship of Arkansas in 1970 and a Senate seat four years later, offered a classic template for victory as a New Democrat. After running as a folksy "country lawyer" in 1970, Bumpers built a reputation for racial moderation, economic populism, and Sunbelt development that protected him against Republican attacks for almost thirty years.

Other ambitious Democrats took note. Among them was a fellow Arkansan called Bill Clinton who won the governorship in 1978 with a similarly broad-based coalition. As Clinton explained a year later, Democrats could still win in the South "if you can persuade people you've got a center core they can understand and relate to and trust." Politics is a fickle business, however. In 1980, Clinton was thrown out by the voters of Arkansas as punishment for trying to introduce an unpopular car registration tax. But he had learned his lesson; he would be back.[35]

**In many forgotten** corners of the South, life in the 1970s went on much as before, rural traditions and time-honored folkways barely touched by modernity. And yet the economic changes that rebuilt the urban landscape, the political changes that destroyed the old one-party system, and the social changes that eroded the legacy of segregation were real enough. For years, historians had insisted that the South was different, set apart by its unique record of slavery and discrimination. Now the tide had turned: the region's "racial and economic and urban and political characteristics," argued the liberal Atlanta journalist John Egerton in 1974, "are very nearly the same as the dominant characteristics of the nation." "For good and ill," he concluded, "the South is just about over as a separate and distinct place."[36]

But was the South falling under the sway of the rest of the nation, or was the rest of the nation falling under the sway of the South? In his book *Power Shift* (1975), the radical activist Kirkpatrick Sale argued that power was already moving to a new establishment, based in the "Southern Rim" and made up of an unholy alliance of the defense, aerospace, oil, and agribusiness corporations. He even thought that Richard Nixon had fallen victim to a power struggle between the old eastern elite and the new southern-rim conservatives, an argument that reflected the conspiracy-theory vogue of the day. But his portrait of Sunbelt political appointees, southern millionaire donors, and oil industry money in conservative coffers told a compelling story. "The entrenched position of the Southern Rim in the American economy," Sale concluded, "is not likely to diminish—indeed, seems most likely to increase—in the decades to come."[37]

In many ways, the most revealing sign of the South's newfound self-confidence was not the success of its politicians or the profits of its businessmen but the astonishing rise of its popular culture. "I believe the South is gonna rise again," sang the crooner Tanya Tucker—and she was right. In an age of disco and hip-hop, the appeal of long-haired, Levi's-clad rock bands like Lynyrd Skynyrd, the Allman Brothers, and ZZ Top was obvious: with their beards, cowboy hats, jeans, and boots, they presented a defiantly old-fashioned vision of beer-swilling masculinity. The most extraordinary phenomenon, though, was the rise of country music, once lampooned as "the doleful maunderings of illiterate hillbillies," but one of the most unexpected success stories of the mid-1970s.[38]

Country music had always been out there, of course, overlooked by the record companies and underestimated by the *Billboard* charts. But by the early 1970s its rise was extraordinary. In 1961 a mere eighty-one stations around the nation had been dedicated to country, but by 1974 there were more than a thousand. More radio stations played country music, in fact, than played rock. Even New York City's resistance collapsed: when the ailing WHN switched to an all-country format, it doubled its audience and became the biggest country station in the nation, with more than one million listeners. In 1973, the Country Music Association symbolically held its annual convention in Manhattan. "Country-music fans can be found everywhere in the U.S. today," reported a *Time* cover story the following May. "After half a century of condescension, neglect and even ridicule, country in all its guises—bluegrass, heart songs, western ballads, rural blues, delta white soul, Memphis honky-tonk and of course the familiar pop hybrid known as the Nashville Sound—is in the midst of an astronomic growth and gives no signs of stopping."[39]

Country benefited from a broader vogue for southern culture, from stock-car racing and evangelical Protestantism to cowboy boots and the Confederate flag. But by the 1970s it had come to stand for something more than southern regionalism; from Nashville to New York, it stood for class and, increasingly, conservatism. "Country music celebrates the goodness in America, faith in America, patriotism," explained one convert. Singers conjured up a lost world of honest workingmen, simple homesteads, and loving families, light-years away from the limousine liberals, welfare scroungers, and bra-burning feminists who were driving the country into the ground. To millions of working-class Americans, the narratives of country ballads—"love unfulfilled or gone wrong, faithless women, bad whiskey, and the ultimate triumph of traditional morality"—struck a powerful chord. Even the fatalism of the lyrics, the numbing sense of failure, the cruelty of divine judgment, resonated with blue-collar audiences threatened by recession.[40]

It was the "king of country," Merle Haggard, who best embodied its populist appeal. The son of an Oklahoma railroad worker who had fled to California during the Depression, he fulfilled every stereotype: rugged and handsome, he had grown up in grinding poverty and had served time for robbing a bar. This only added to his air of authenticity, and by 1974 he had sold eight million albums and almost four million singles in just ten years. His trademark ballad, "Okie from Muskogee," was the supreme statement of silent-majority values, a patriotic anthem for all those Americans who did not smoke marijuana, did not burn their draft cards, and took pride in "livin' right and bein' free." It made Haggard a millionaire; to his discomfort, it also made him a spokesman for grassroots conservatism. But he saw himself as a spokesman for the little man: a populist, not an ideologue. In 1970 he turned down George Wallace's request for an endorsement in Alabama, although he accepted Nixon's invitation to sing at the White House in 1973. But only two months later Haggard publicly turned against the president, appalled, like so many others, by the revelations of Watergate.[41]

For populist politicians, country was the perfect sound track. When George Wallace campaigned outside the South, his rallies typically began with country bands playing patriotic songs to warm up the crowds. Nixon, meanwhile, hired country singers to record ballads for radio spots and told his chief of staff to recruit country stars for White House galas. As he undoubtedly realized, country had patriotic, homespun associations even north of the Mason-Dixon Line. It helped him appeal to working-class Democrats in the so-called Rust Belt, the kinds of people who might never have visited the South but felt drawn to Merle Haggard and Lynyrd Skynyrd, to Evel Knievel and Roger Staubach, and to old-fashioned values in an age of uncertainty.[42]

By the end of the 1970s, "Southernization" was everywhere, implicit in everything from the popularity of the Dallas Cowboys to the success of CBS's new show *The Dukes of Hazzard*, the tale of two simple good old boys tearing around in their souped-up Dodge Charger, flirting with their curvaceous cousin Daisy, and evading the corrupt Boss Hogg. Yet it often had very little to do with the contemporary South; instead, it was both a way for suburbanites to cling to an imagined "authentic" past and a way for working-class Americans to assert their patriotism and their pride. Songs like Vernon Oxford's "Redneck! (The Redneck National Anthem)," released in 1976, sold thousands of copies outside the South to people who were not really rednecks at all. The historian Bruce Schulman calls it "redneck chic," adopted by millions of Americans as "a gesture of resistance against high taxes, liberals, racial integration, women's liberation, and hippies." Even the Confederate flag was a way of extending a middle finger to the establishment, to the East Coast, to authority figures of all kinds. As one girl explained to the sociologist John Shelton Reed: "When I see the Confederate flag I think of a pickup truck with a gun rack and a bumper sticker that says 'I Don't Brake for Small Animals.' "[43]

For all this, however, anyone who doubted that real change had come to the South needed only to look to the Georgia state capitol one mild

Sunday afternoon in February 1974, where the unimaginable was happening. As a small knot of Ku Klux Klansmen demonstrated outside, Governor Jimmy Carter proudly unveiled portraits of three eminent black Georgians: the Victorian educator Lucy Craft Laney, the African Methodist Episcopal bishop Henry McNeal Turner, and Martin Luther King Jr. Only a few years before, it would have been unthinkable for the governor of Georgia to lead a racially mixed audience in singing "We Shall Overcome." But Carter had done it.[44]

Perhaps even then, on a day of harmony and reconciliation, Carter was already pondering what he might do when his term expired in January. Appropriately enough for a man who had been hailed as the poster boy for the buoyant New South, he was fiercely ambitious, but he was also maddeningly hard to pin down, at once peanut farmer and nuclear submariner, racial progressive and fiscal conservative, Reinhold Niebuhr devotee and Allman Brothers fan. There was no knowing what he might do next. "Whatcha gonna do when you're not Governor?" his mother asked him one day. And Jimmy Carter gave that big, toothy smile that Georgians had come to know so well, and said: "I'm going to run for President."[45]

# Chapter Eight   The Man of a Thousand Faces

A good man with some one-syllable answers
could do a lot for this country.

—**HAL PHILLIP WALKER,** in *Nashville* (1975)

On December 13, 1973, a slight, sandy-haired man strode onto the garish set of *What's My Line?* Grinning awkwardly, he signed in as "X" and took his seat beside the host, Larry Blyden, while the four panelists tried to work out who he was. Arlene Francis guessed that he provided a service of some kind, and wondered whether he might provide it specifically for women, at which the mystery man's grin spread even wider. Soupy Sales guessed that he worked in fashion, while the singer Dana Valery suggested that he was a recruiter of nuns, which made everybody laugh. Somebody suggested that Mr. X might work in government, and at last Gene Shalit, looking splendid in his handlebar mustache and clown's bow tie, asked: "Are you a state official? Are you a governor?" "That's it!" exclaimed Larry Blyden. "He is Governor Jimmy Carter of the state of Georgia!"[1]

Jimmy Carter was born in Plains, Georgia, in October 1924, the son of James Earl Carter, a farmer and small-business man, and Lillian Gordy, a trained nurse. Plains was poor and backward, a sleepy place whose clay streets baked in the summer and turned to mud in the winter. Although the Carters lived comfortably by comparison with their neighbors, they had no electricity or running water. For miles around, black farmhands tilled the fields, while their wives washed laundry by hand and cooked their meals on wood-burning stoves. Visitors were rare; most people spoke with a thick rural accent that strangers could not understand. When one journalist visited Plains in 1976, she felt she had stepped back into a past of ramshackle huts and desolate storefronts, "a strand of dilapidation and decay, and souls steeped in cheap alcohol, loitering in late afternoons on tiled wooden porches."[2]

Jimmy Carter's mother, "Miz Lillian," was an extraordinarily freethinking woman who later threw herself into social work, even going to India with the Peace Corps when she was sixty-eight. But his father, Earl, who died twenty years before his son became famous, was arguably far more influential. "My daddy was the dominant person in our family and in my life," Carter said later. In some ways Earl was very unlike his son; he loved drinking, smoking, and the company of local prostitutes. But there were also striking similarities. Earl was a stern disciplinarian, as was Jimmy. He strongly believed in hard work and entrepreneurship; he despised Franklin Roosevelt and the New Deal; and he was an ardent admirer of Eugene Talmadge, the Georgia populist who, behind the rhetoric, was a great friend to the rich Atlanta establishment. These views Earl bequeathed to his son, along with his business sense, his habit of exaggeration, and his toothy grin.

As a child, Jimmy Carter was an exceptionally bright and diligent student, a great reader conscious of his own cleverness who never liked to play in the yard and get his clothes dirty. There was in him a priggish streak that never quite disappeared. Although he later romanticized Plains, he left as soon as he was old enough for the U.S. Naval Academy in Annapolis, a tough, regimented world of hazing and flagellation in which boys needed great emotional resilience to survive. Carter came through successfully, graduating 59th out of 890, but he remained a loner with few close friends. Years later, none of his classmates could remember a single conversation with him about girls, politics, or religion, or anything personal or revealing. Then, as later, he was an extraordinarily self-willed and self-sufficient character.[3]

Immediately after graduating in the summer of 1946, Carter married his sister's pretty friend Rosalynn Smith, another native of Plains. They had started dating a year earlier, and after their very first date Carter announced to his family: "She's the girl I want to marry." Although they had only seventeen dates before he proposed, it was a very successful match. And although Carter was a "domineering and demanding" husband, Rosalynn was no shrinking violet. Like her husband, she had Spartan tastes, no close friends, a strict sense of morality, and no time for frivolity. In later years, reporters were struck by her shyness, intensity, and obvious love for her husband. But while polite and soft-spoken, she was an extremely tough and ambitious woman. Her campaign nickname, "the Steel Magnolia," was well deserved.[4]

After leaving the U.S. Naval Academy, Carter landed a position working under the formidable Hyman Rickover on the nuclear submarine program. Even at this stage, the traits that would mark his political career were already apparent. He had a strong sense of right and wrong, nurtured in the moralistic atmosphere of his Baptist church, and regarded compromise as a weakness. Highly competitive, he was an obsessive self-improver, whether teaching himself Spanish or forcing himself to keep fit. He was proud of his southern heritage: at the U.S. Naval Academy he refused to sing "Marching Through Georgia," even when threatened with a hazing. Finally, he was not one for small talk and parties; a sympathetic reporter later called him "serious and solitary." His nephew Willie, who stayed with him as a boy, claimed that he ran his household like a "barracks." Playfulness was totally frowned on, each meal began with a long grace, and the family gathered for prayers every evening. "He smiles outwardly," Willie said of his uncle, "but at heart he's a cold motherfucker."[5]

When Carter's father died in the summer of 1953, he returned to Plains and took over the family peanut farm, turning it into an extremely profitable enterprise. At the same time he became a pillar of the community, teaching Sunday school at the local Baptist church, running the Scout troop, and serving on the county library, school, and hospital boards. Entering politics seemed a natural step: in 1961 he became school-board chairman, and a year later he was elected to the Georgia Senate. There he worked exceptionally hard, taking speed-reading classes to study the hundreds of bills that came across his desk and toiling in his office on Fridays after his colleagues had gone home. On economic issues he was markedly conservative, while on civil rights, by far the most controversial issue of the day, he generally avoided comment. Personally he held fairly liberal racial opinions, refusing to join the local White Citizens' Council, but he was no firebrand. As a member of the county school board, he avoided visiting black schools and made no effort to encourage integration. Like many moderate businessmen of his generation, he was not averse to change, but had no desire to rock the boat.[6]

In the summer of 1966, Carter ran for governor only to finish a poor third in the Democratic primary. Still, his campaign was an illuminating preview of some long-running themes. He avoided specifics, preferring to talk about himself and his personality, and when reporters asked if he was a conservative or a liberal, he claimed that he was "a more complicated person than that." His campaign literature played on his record as a Baptist churchgoer and family man, and he told audiences: "We need in the state a competent, compassionate, caring government that is as good as its people," a formula that was to become very familiar. So too was his emphasis on honesty and trust. "If I ever let you down in my actions, I want you to let me know about it and I'll correct it," he said. "I promise never to betray your trust in me."[7]

Defeat took a heavy toll on a proud man used to winning, and afterward Carter lost a worrying amount of weight and seemed deeply depressed. This was the moment of his great spiritual crisis, triggered when he was walking in the woods with his younger sister Ruth. Having suffered severe depression, Ruth had found solace in evangelical Christianity, leavened with a considerable dose of therapeutic psychobabble. She was always looking for opportunities to bring others to God, and when her brother admitted his misery, she saw her chance. "A fresh, intimate, personal, loving, caring relationship with Jesus Christ," she said, was the only remedy. "You've got to be willing to accept God's will, Jimmy, no matter what he should want you to do."[8]

Soon after this, Carter's pastor asked his flock to consider whether, if they were arrested and charged with being Christians, there would be any evidence to convict them. Even though he was a Sunday-school teacher and deacon, Carter's answer was no. "I had never really committed myself totally to God," he said later. "My Christian beliefs were superficial, based primarily on pride, and I'd never done much for other people. I was always thinking about myself." It was at this point that he decided to become "born again." "It wasn't a voice of God from heaven," he said later. "It wasn't mysterious." But it was an "inner conviction and assurance that transformed my life for the better."[9]

Buoyed by this renewed sense of purpose, Carter prepared for a second tilt at the governorship in 1970. By now he was already surrounded by the tight-knit group of aides who would accompany him to Washington six years later, among them the gregarious, bearlike banker Bert Lance, the seasoned lawyer Charles Kirbo, and the irreverent advertising man (and self-styled "media masturbator") Jerry Rafshoon. Perhaps the most colorful members of Carter's inner circle, though, were the hard-drinking Hamilton Jordan and Jody Powell. Only twenty-two when he joined the Carter team, Jordan was affable and popular, with an eye for the ladies. He had served for six months in Vietnam and worked in a bank before finding his vocation as a ruthless political operative. Powell, meanwhile, was a rural Georgia farm boy who had been the most promising student in town until he was kicked out of the Air Force Academy for cheating on his finals. Good-looking, cheerful, and funny, he was often described as Carter's political son; on the campaign trail, it was Powell who traveled with him, shared meals with him, kept him company in the lonely evenings.

The revealing thing about Jordan and Powell, who served as Carter's closest aides for the rest of his political career, was that although they were very young, neither was particularly idealistic. They wore jeans and open-necked shirts, grew their hair over their ears, and ostentatiously enjoyed female company, but they never marched for civil rights or against the Vietnam War. Like Carter, they were proud of their southern heritage and military service, seeing themselves as outsiders defying the liberal establishment. In college, Jordan had been an ardent segregationist, while Powell was a great Civil War buff who admired the traditions of southern populism. He bitterly disliked external interference in southern affairs and respected George Wallace for standing up to Washington. "I never resented the blacks, because you knew who they were," he said. "It was the Northern white politicians who were the outsiders."[10]

This populism was the essence of Carter's second campaign for the governorship in 1970, when in the Democratic primary he faced the moderate Carl Sanders, who had run the state for four years in the mid-1960s. By most criteria, Sanders was the more appealing candidate, a combat veteran who had worked hard to improve Georgia's schools and coaxed the state toward racial desegregation. But Carter's campaign was a masterpiece of character demolition, designed to paint Sanders as a stuck-up, northern-loving liberal and playing on rural voters' resentment of city slickers telling them what to do. If you peeled off the stickers from Sanders's campaign buttons, Carter claimed, you found that beneath were slogans from Hubert Humphrey's presidential campaign—perfectly true, because the makers were recycling leftover buttons, but in Carter's hands a sinister sign of liberal influence.[11]

Carter declined to place himself on the ideological spectrum, telling journalists that he preferred to present "the issues" to the people. Instead, he tried to make the election a referendum on character, bragging that he was "basically a redneck" and painting Sanders as "Cuff Links Carl," a wealthy stooge of the Atlanta establishment. One particular ad stuck in people's minds. It opened with a shot of a tightly closed door, while a voice intoned: "This is the door to an exclusive country club, where big-money boys play cards, drink cocktails, and raise money for their candidate, Carl Sanders." The doors swung open, the camera focused on an elegant hand in French cuffs writing a check, and the voice said: "People like us aren't invited. We're too busy working for a living." Then the picture changed to show Jimmy Carter talking earnestly to a workingman. "Vote for Jimmy Carter," the narrator concluded, "our kind of man, our kind of governor."[12]

There was more to this than class populism. The slogan "Our kind of man" had already been used in George Wallace's campaign for the governorship of Alabama earlier that year, which was virtually a blueprint for Carter's campaign against Sanders. And although Carter vehemently denied it, there was an obvious racist element to his candidacy. He promised to "return control of our schools to local people," praised private schools that had been set up to resist integration, and actively sought the endorsement of segregationists like Lester Maddox. Toward the end of the campaign, he even denounced Sanders for barring George Wallace from speaking on state property. When elected, Carter promised, he would definitely invite Wallace to Georgia. Meanwhile, his campaign distributed thousands of pictures showing Sanders celebrating a play-off victory with black members of the Atlanta Hawks basketball team. As one of Carter's key strategists, Bill Pope, later boasted, it was a classic "nigger campaign."[13]

And it worked. In January 1971, Carter was sworn in as Georgia's seventy-sixth governor, stunning observers with his groundbreaking declaration that "the time for racial discrimination is over." Sympathetic writers always claim that this, rather than the campaign hatchet man, was the "real" Carter. But as his later campaigns would prove, both were "real": neither could exist without the other. In any case, his progressive rhetoric caught the attention of the media and set the tone for a very successful governorship. Carter worked hard to improve education, welfare, and environmental protection, established community mental health centers and services for the handicapped, and, above all, reorganized the entire state government, cutting a lot of waste in the process. He had his faults: legislators complained that he was self-righteous and moralistic, disdained compromise, and did not do enough to soothe opponents. But he was not very experienced; perhaps he would learn from his mistakes.[14]

**By the fall of 1972,** after an abortive bid to get Carter picked as the Democrats' vice presidential candidate, his inner circle was already working on the genesis of a presidential campaign. Even at this early stage, they had an impressively clear sense of how things would unfold in 1976. They agreed that George Wallace and Ted Kennedy were the two major threats, dismissing Hubert Humphrey as too old, Walter Mondale as too liberal, and Scoop Jackson as too dull. By November, Jordan had put together an extraordinarily prescient blueprint identifying New Hampshire and Florida as the crucial battlegrounds in which Carter's "farmer-businessman-military-religious-conservative background would be well received." As Jordan also recognized, new rules would make a huge difference in 1976. There were no winner-takes-all primaries; any candidate who got more than 15 percent of the vote would get a share of the delegates. To win, Carter would have to declare early, run everywhere, and do well in the first primaries. If he survived the opening rounds, beating Wallace and Kennedy was a real possibility.[15]

Throughout the next two years Carter worked hard to establish his reputation outside the South, using his position as the Democrats' honorary campaign chairman in 1974 to make contacts across the nation. He made more friends by joining the Trilateral Commission, a forum for political and business leaders from North America, Japan, and Europe, and he hired George McGovern's fund-raiser to bring in money by direct mail, although most donations came from Georgia businessmen. None of this guaranteed a good performance at the polls. But it gave him a head start over his rivals, most of whom started months later. Nobody would ever beat him for hard work and advance planning.[16]

Even at this stage, Carter had identified the themes that would dominate his campaign. Right from the start he made faith the cornerstone of his campaign, exploiting the public thirst for a change after thirteen years of Johnson, Nixon, and Ford. He was the only Democratic candidate who realized how much the public distrusted politicians and how much they wanted an outsider. In many ways he was always running against Nixon; indeed, he once described himself as a "longtime Nixon-hater from way back." The irony, however, was that Nixon and Carter had an enormous amount in common. Both were provincial outsiders, Navy veterans, and obsessive workers; both were deeply pragmatic and suspicious of ideological labels; both were prickly, proud, ambitious men. And when Carter talked about providing new moral leadership for the nation, or dwelled on his religious convictions, or hit at the corrupt establishment who had led the country astray, he did not sound like Kennedy or Truman or Roosevelt. The man he sounded most like was Nixon.[17]

**Carter had two** great strokes of luck before the campaign had even started. In September 1974, Edward Kennedy, the overwhelming favorite for the nomination, announced that he would not be a contender, citing the trauma of his brothers' assassinations and his teenage son's battle against bone cancer. Many people thought that voters might switch to Walter Mondale, who was relatively young but had an impeccable Senate record, strong ties to the labor movement, and a powerful patron in Hubert Humphrey. But just as Mondale's momentum was starting to build, he too pulled out. He had no desire to spend the next two years "sleeping in Holiday Inns," he told a press conference in November 1974—not a remark that impressed Carter's staff.[18]

With Kennedy and Mondale out, most commentators identified Henry Jackson as the front-runner for the nomination. Although the Washington senator had run a pretty turgid campaign in 1972, he was the obvious national security candidate, a relentlessly effective fund-raiser, and a solid party stalwart who appealed to labor leaders, veterans' groups, and blue-collar workers. But Jackson was also a painfully boring speaker whose hawkish views did not endear him to high-minded liberal activists. Thanks to Vietnam and Watergate, what many voters wanted was an outsider with a strong personal narrative and a sense of crusading idealism. But Jackson shrank from making attacks on big government; one of his guiding principles was that government programs were a force for good. The rhetoric of limits, too, left him cold. Only economic growth, he said, could end poverty, guarantee equal education, and give every worker a decent wage. To give up on growth would be "a cruel betrayal of the hopes of millions of Americans for a better life."[19]

Jackson's plight reflected the dilemmas of liberalism in the mid-1970s. Once so rich and vibrant, the liberal tradition seemed to be in headlong retreat, its optimistic assumptions eroded by the war in Vietnam, white backlash, and the shock of inflation. In 1972, *The Wall Street Journal* commented on the "dearth of creative new ideas coming from the entire liberal intellectual community," and indeed it is hard to think of any new economic ideas that liberalism produced in the 1970s. Institutions such as the AFL-CIO, Americans for Democratic Action (ADA), and the ACLU were absorbed in their own factional struggles, while the new breed of congressional Democrats were much more conservative on broad socioeconomic questions than were their predecessors. "The New Deal has run its course," declared George McGovern's old campaign manager Gary Hart, now Democratic senator from Colorado. "The party is over. The pie cannot continue to expand forever."[20]

This did not stop at least six Democrats who could reasonably claim to be liberals from throwing their hats in the ring, although most of them would have baffled the panel on *What's My Line?* Terry Sanford, the former governor of North Carolina, and Milton Shapp, the governor of Pennsylvania, were barely recognized outside their own homes. Sargent

Shriver never emerged from the shadow of his Kennedy in-laws, while Fred Harris, an ultra-ambitious former senator from Oklahoma turned radical tub-thumping Jeremiah, was much too unconventional to attract mass support. Perhaps the most attractive contender, meanwhile, was tarred by his Washington associations. Handsome, articulate, and experienced, Birch Bayh was many experts' pick for the nomination. But the Indiana senator made the disastrous decision to run as a Capitol Hill insider and failed to win a single primary.[21]

That left Morris Udall, a former basketball player and attorney who had represented Arizona in the House since 1961. A wry, thoughtful, stooping man, Udall was a reporter's delight, like a more amiable version of Eugene McCarthy. Reporters called him "the liberal's liberal," and his chief cheerleader was the former Watergate prosecutor Archibald Cox. Revealingly, though, Udall preferred to be known as a "progressive," claiming that the L-word had become a "barrier to communication." This did him no harm with the voters: in April 1975, a New Hampshire poll rated him as the most popular of all the contenders. But his campaign was a mess, short of both money and leadership. "We've got a reputation, frankly, as the sloppiest campaign in memory," his campaign manager wrote in December 1975. "No one knows who is in charge."[22]

Meanwhile, almost unnoticed by the media, Carter was making friends in Iowa, the first caucus state. Accompanied only by Jody Powell, he would drive from one farm, one labor hall, one mall to another, giving the same ten-minute stump speech and taking questions from a tiny handful of Democratic activists. Yet his disarming talk of "truth and honesty and decency" made an excellent impression on ordinary Iowans horrified by Watergate. "I wouldn't tell a lie," he would say. "I wouldn't make a misleading statement. I wouldn't betray a trust. I wouldn't avoid a controversial issue." And in place of the Ford administration he promised "a government that is as good, and honest, and decent, and truthful, and fair, and competent, and idealistic, and compassionate, and as filled with love as are the American people." It seemed to work: in October 1975, he won *The Des Moines Register*'s straw poll of Democratic activists at the Jefferson-Jackson Day dinner in Ames. His rivals laughed it off as an irrelevance; many had not even bothered to turn up. But two days later *The New York Times* ran the first major story on Carter's campaign, describing him as holding a "surprising but solid lead" in Iowa and praising his "courtesy" and "personal charm." As if from nowhere, he had become a serious contender.[23]

On the evening of January 19, thousands of Democrats trudged through the cold to libraries, sports halls, schoolrooms, and basements across Iowa.

In his last appeal, Carter had reminded Iowans how he had learned "love of country, love of land, love of God" back home in Plains. Perhaps they remembered his words as they gathered in 2,530 caucuses across the state. Either way, Carter had struck a chord. As Walter Cronkite told television viewers the next day, the voters had spoken, and "what they said was 'Jimmy Carter.'"[24]

Actually, that was not really true. Although Carter ran strongest with 28 percent of the vote, "uncommitted" won 37 percent. In any case, the numbers were so small as to be almost insignificant. Fewer than fifty thousand Iowans went to the caucuses, and fewer than fourteen thousand voted for Carter. As one reporter pointed out, that would not even get him onto the town council in Oyster Bay, Long Island. But it was enough to get him onto the covers of *Time* and *Newsweek*, and onto the *CBS Morning News*, *Good Morning America*, and the *Today* show the next morning, where television crowned him the victor. "No amount of badmouthing by others," Roger Mudd announced on CBS, "can lessen the importance of Jimmy Carter's finish. He was a clear winner in this psychologically important test."[25]

The Iowa caucus was a study in miniature for Carter's 1976 campaign. Reporters were struck by his success as a personal campaigner, his brilliant grassroots organization, and the self-destructive complacency of his opponents, but they also noted his extraordinary ability to be all things to all men and his knack of shifting his position (while still claiming that he would never tell a lie) to tell his listeners what they wanted to hear. In Iowa, observers were amazed by the breadth of his constituency, which included blacks, small towns, rural voters, blue-collar workers, and middle-class professionals. But there was also an undercurrent of unease at the way he had fudged his position on issues like abortion, telling some audiences that he disagreed with a constitutional amendment to ban it, and telling others that he backed an undefined "national statute." Was he quite what he seemed? The comedian Pat Paulsen joked that officials were already planning to put Carter on Mount Rushmore, "but they didn't have room for two faces."[26]

Meanwhile, the campaign moved on to New Hampshire, where everything continued to go right for Carter. Jackson sat out the primary, Udall's campaign was a shambles, and Bayh got bogged down in a list of his own legislative achievements. While his rivals squabbled about vetoes and welfare plans, Carter talked about the decency and compassion of the American people, about faith and love and trust. And all the time hundreds of middle-aged volunteers from Georgia, the self-styled Peanut Brigade, trudged through the snow with lists of every registered Democrat in the state's major towns. "If that many people thought that much about him to come all the way up here," said one Exeter voter, "then he must be a good man."[27]

Just before midnight on February 24, with his family pressing around him, flashbulbs popping, and his workers cheering so hard they could barely speak for days afterward, Carter came down to the ballroom of Manchester's Carpenter Hotel to claim victory. He had taken just over 29 percent of the vote, five points clear of Udall and well ahead of the rest. Once again it was hardly a resounding victory; if the liberal candidates' votes were combined, their total was more than double his. But as Carter celebrated, the fact that his opponents had allowed him to stroll through with the moderate and conservative votes hardly mattered.[28]

**In Iowa and New Hampshire,** Carter had won partly because he was the only non-liberal candidate in the race. "I was never a liberal," he had told the voters of Georgia in 1970. "I am and have always been a conservative." Indeed, as a small-business man, a rural Southerner, a Navy veteran, and a devout Christian, he did have relatively conservative opinions about many issues. Even Carter's chief domestic adviser, Stuart Eizenstat, thought that "he was clearly the most conservative of the Democratic candidates . . . the only one talking about balanced budgets and less bureaucracy and less red tape."[29]

But if Carter had run merely as a conservative, he would not have done half as well. Throughout the campaign, he introduced himself as follows:

> I am a Southerner and an American. I am a farmer, an engineer, a father and a husband, a Christian, a politician and a former governor, a planner, a businessman, a nuclear physicist, a naval officer, a canoeist, and, among other things, a lover of Bob Dylan's songs and Dylan Thomas's poetry.

It was revealing that he did not call himself a Democrat, that he buried his political experience deep within the second sentence, and that he opened by calling himself a Southerner, a patriot, and a farmer. Carter always made a great deal of his rural background, even though he had spent much of his adult life in the Navy or in Atlanta. His family was presented as a real-life equivalent of the Waltons, while southern rock bands like the Allman Brothers played at his fund-raisers. Television ads showed him strolling through cornfields in a farmer's checked shirt, running his hands through the crops. His aides encouraged journalists to make the pilgrimage to Plains; his plane was even nicknamed Peanut One.[30]

All of this sent a message that Carter was an outsider, a man of the soil, harking back to Jefferson's yeoman farmer and Jackson's common man. He welcomed visitors to Plains in faded jeans and tattered sneakers, inviting them to sit back with a beer and chatting about the iniquity of "Washington" and the "political elites." Though commentators scoffed, his invocations of "the people" were perfectly calibrated to take advantage of the distrust of politicians after Watergate. Like any good populist, he spoke the words "government" and "Washington" with ostentatious contempt. And when he promised to "take a new broom to Washington and do everything possible to sweep the house of government clean," it could easily have been Wallace or Reagan speaking.[31]

But there was another side to Carter's southern heritage. Some commentators argued that he was more New South than Old, less a tribune of the people than a technocrat who wanted to bring much-needed efficiency into American government. The progressive Carter was not the denim-wearing Plains farmer but the self-proclaimed "nuclear physicist," the technician obsessed with charts and statistics, the do-gooder who wanted to reconcile social justice and balanced budgets. This was the Carter who wrote in his autobiography that he was "a fiscal conservative, but quite liberal on such issues as civil rights, environmental quality, and helping people overcome handicaps to lead fruitful lives." This was the man *Time*'s James Wooten called a "pure pragmatist who had raised utilitarian politics to a new American art form." This was Carter the New Democrat, Bill Clinton's political godfather.[32]

Like Clinton, Carter struck a contradictory balance between conservatism, populism, and southern progressivism. And more than anything else, it was his deliberate ambiguity that defined him. He consistently underplayed ideology and made his character, not his politics, the center of the argument. Extraordinarily for a presidential candidate, he even suggested that talking about issues was irrelevant. People had concentrated on issues "in 1968 and in 1972," he said, "but I don't believe that's the case in 1976 at all. I think our people have been hurt and scarred so badly by Vietnam, Cambodia, Watergate, the CIA revelations, that they're simply looking for somebody they can trust."[33]

Instead of giving audiences a laundry list, therefore, Carter gave them love and compassion and honesty—things nobody could disagree with. And when questioners tried to pin him down—on abortion, for example— he talked about the "complexity" of the issues and added so many disclaimers that it was impossible to work out what he meant. This did not necessarily make him a hypocrite, just a calculating career politician. And yet there was a great danger in all this. After a while, journalists noticed that he never mentioned Martin Luther King's name when he was addressing white audiences. James Wooten called him "the Lon Chaney of 1976, the man of a thousand faces," while another writer quipped that he had "more positions than the Karma Sutra." Unless he was careful, warned his young pollster Patrick Caddell, people would start to call him "untrustworthy" and "dishonest." And if that happened, he would be in deep trouble.[34]

**Carter's next big test** came in Florida, where his accent, style, and moralistic message were expected to resonate with local Democratic voters. He had already suffered his first defeat, losing Massachusetts to Henry Jackson, and knew that only a win would keep his momentum going. This time, however, the threat was a fellow Southerner: the controversial figure of George Wallace. If the Alabama governor won, the Old South would have beaten the New South, and Carter might as well fly home to Plains. "If we blew it in the last few days and lost Florida," one of Carter's strategists said later, "it might all be over."[35]

At first glance, Wallace's campaign looked like his previous efforts: rallies at stock-car racetracks; sing-alongs with crooners from the Grand Ole Opry; shirtsleeve supporters clapping and hollering; the air "thick and bitter with the smell of perspiration." But in some ways his campaign was remarkably modern. More than any other candidate, he relied on computer-generated fund-raising, hiring the direct-mail guru Richard Viguerie to raise almost $7 million. And overt racism had now almost completely disappeared from his speeches. He presented himself as the tribune of the "working people," telling audiences that he was the true architect of the New South. He thundered against busing, but he also talked about inflation and unemployment, blaming the "liberals" and the "bureaucrats" for vanishing jobs and high taxes. As one reporter put it, his message "sounded at times like a translation of vintage Jimmy Carter into the vulgar."[36]

Yet that was Wallace's biggest problem. In previous campaigns he had been the only Democrat to run against big government and welfare cheats, but now, wrote the reporter Elizabeth Drew, his issues had been "picked up by other candidates and made a standard part of our politics: big government; regressive taxes; the bureaucracy." When he talked about red tape and welfare, she thought, the startling thing was that he had "nothing fresh to say now. They've all stolen his lines." And since voters could choose more respectable candidates who said the same things, why would they consider the feisty little fighter with the segregationist past, tired, ill, and deaf after a lifetime fighting the odds?[37]

Carter, meanwhile, was in ruthlessly canny form. He outflanked Jackson on the left by accusing him of running an antibusing campaign with "connotations of racism." Characteristically, when reporters asked if he was calling Jackson a racist, Carter said piously: "I didn't say Senator Jackson was a racist. I didn't say he wasn't, but I don't *think* he is a racist." He undermined Wallace, meanwhile, by picking up his old slogan "Send them a message" and suggesting that Southerners should "send them a president" instead. Above all, though, he reached out to Florida's black voters, henceforth a crucial part of his coalition. Carter had never been a great campaigner for civil rights, but he had grown up alongside black children, was comfortable with black audiences, and used his piety as a pulpit to reach black congregations. In almost every primary, he won the black vote by a huge margin; without it, he would never have been nominated. "Why, every Negro I ever met's goin' for Jimmy Carter," said an elderly Mississippi activist. "We just think he's the man. One reason, he seems to be a Christian man . . . He gonna get all the black votes."[38]

At eight o'clock on Tuesday, March 9, Jimmy and Rosalynn Carter settled down in front of the television in their Orlando hotel, eating hamburgers and drinking chocolate milkshakes. Outside, oblivious to the press attention, their daughter, Amy, skipped barefoot toward the swimming pool, a pretty little girl without a care in the world. Twenty minutes later her parents, too, were grinning from ear to ear. Carter had taken Florida with 34 percent to Wallace's 31 percent and Jackson's 24 percent. He had carried almost every social group and won more than three out of four black votes. Many supporters had never seen him so happy; he seemed almost giddy with delight. When he came down to the ballroom, his family mobbed by screaming supporters, the scene was pandemonium. "We're number one!" the crowd chanted, again and again.[39]

As Carter flew north, senior Democrats were struggling to make sense of this strangest of campaign seasons. Wallace was effectively out, even though he limped on to another defeat in North Carolina. Bayh and Shriver had given up, Harris was staggering on for reasons best known to himself, and Udall was becoming a specialist in second-place finishes. "Where are the liberals?" wondered *Time*, concluding that they were "in retreat . . . unmoored and fragmented." Only Udall remained a serious liberal contender, but as the former ADA head Joseph Rauh put it, "We have our second team on the field." Younger liberals who remembered

Vietnam were already arguing that at least Carter would be better than Jackson. "The liberals are an easy pickup for Carter," one Democratic strategist claimed. "A few key words and he's got them."[40]

Meanwhile, Carter continued to benefit from the most extraordinary good luck. In New York, which was perfect Jackson country, the Washington senator shot himself in the foot by predicting a landslide—which meant that even though he won with 38 percent to Udall's 25 percent and Carter's feeble 13 percent, the press interpreted it as a disappointment. On the same night in Wisconsin, Carter limped to an agonizingly narrow victory over Udall—who had canceled extra television spending in the state because he was sure he was going to lose. Even better for Carter, Udall prematurely celebrated an upset victory when it seemed he was going to win, which gave the Georgian the chance to pose with an erroneous headline in classic "Dewey Defeats Truman" fashion.[41]

As if that were not enough, the wheels then fell off Jackson's bandwagon completely in Pennsylvania, a heavily unionized state he really should have won. First, Hubert Humphrey undermined Jackson's bid by publicly flirting with entering the race himself. In the end, Humphrey decided discretion was the better part of valor, although not until after Carter had publicly mocked him as "too old" and "a loser." More important, however, Carter outflanked Jackson on the right by defending "people who are Polish, Czechoslovakians, French Canadians, or blacks who are trying to maintain the ethnic purity of their neighborhoods." The newspapers immediately pounced, forcing Carter into a belated apology—but only after his words had become front-page news across Pennsylvania. Some people said it was a gaffe, but, as Udall remarked, Carter's timing was "remarkable" given that "Wallace is leaving the race and Pennsylvania and Michigan are both coming up." There were even rumors that the "gaffe" had been planned to appeal to blue-collar voters. "I never do anything unintentionally," Carter said later, "even if it looks unintentional."[42]

The day after Carter won the Pennsylvania primary, his speechwriter, Bob Shrum, quietly resigned from the campaign. (It is a nice irony that although Shrum worked on eight different presidential campaigns, he never tasted victory: if only he had stuck with Carter until Election Day, he would not have to endure jokes about the "Curse of Shrum.") A week later, he went public with his reasons. He listed the issues on which he thought Carter had trimmed and lied, from defense spending and economic policy to compensation for diseased miners and funds for mass transit. "It would be bad for this person to be President," he said bluntly, for Carter was "the opposite of what [he] appeared to be," a "dangerous man" running a campaign of "manipulation and deception." He stood for nothing but his own ambition. Even his smile went "on and off like a lightbulb."[43]

Remarkably, the man who replaced Shrum as chief speechwriter, Patrick Anderson, became equally disillusioned with his candidate, although not until many years later did he write a memoir flaying Carter for his "endless, ill-concealed, eye-popping sanctimony." The significance of Shrum's attack was not that it robbed Carter of a speechwriter but that it confirmed what many commentators already suspected. Behind the talk of love and compassion, some said, was a ruthless politician, a Dickensian hypocrite. Elizabeth Drew found Carter "cold and hard. No smiles, no warmth." Even the sympathetic Kandy Stroud wrote of his "icy eyes and snide remarks." She recalled an incident in Boston when a small boy ran up to the candidate and squeaked, "What's your position on welfare?" just as he had seen people do on television. Carter did not laugh. "Get out of my way, will you?" he snapped, physically pushing the tearful little boy away.[44]

With stories like these circulating around Washington, as well as dark mutterings about Carter's inexperience, conservatism, and hostility to government, it was hardly surprising that there was one last effort to deny him the nomination. "Anyone but Carter" was the slogan as in the last primaries Democrats clustered around two new candidates, California's unorthodox governor, Jerry Brown, and the liberal senator Frank Church of Idaho. It was a strange final act to the campaign, with Carter cast as the front-runner against two fresh faces. And at first he struggled, losing four western states to the boyish Church, and then losing Maryland to the charismatic Brown. That meant it would all come down to the "Big Casino" on June 8, when more than five hundred delegates were up for grabs in three states. Brown was predicted to win California and New Jersey, so all the attention focused on Ohio. If Church could deny Carter victory there, then the race would go all the way to the convention in New York.

"Give me lucky generals," Napoleon famously remarked, and he would have loved Jimmy Carter in 1976. With just days to go, Church's schedulers sent him to California on a fool's errand to "boost the morale" of his skeleton campaign, only for the candidate to succumb to a nasty infection that left him bedridden in Los Angeles. When Church finally surfaced in Ohio, groggy and ashen, news broke that the vast Teton Dam in his native Idaho had burst. So on the last Saturday, back he went to Idaho, although only after a baggage truck had crashed into his plane and he had scrabbled around for funds for a new one. The next day Church flew back to Cleveland, secluded himself in a hotel to prepare a nationwide television address, and then discovered that the networks could not clear time for him. While his rival was enduring this catalog of disasters, Carter was out in shopping malls and church halls, always smiling, clearly confident, a winner in waiting.[45]

Of course victory did not just fall into Carter's lap; he had worked for it. He had run harder and longer than anyone else, sticking to a brilliant strategic blueprint, playing on his religious faith and southern background, and showing self-discipline and stamina that left his competitors in the shade. He understood the rules better than any other candidate, he gauged the mood of the electorate better than anyone, and on the campaign trail he often came across as a clever, self-effacing, decent, and honest man, even though his enemies claimed that he was none of those things.

And yet he was also incredibly lucky. One of the ironies of the campaign was that it was seen as a repudiation of old-fashioned liberalism, although more people voted for liberal candidates in the early primaries than for Carter. If Kennedy or Humphrey had run, Carter would surely have been crushed beneath the weight of sentimental support. If Mondale had run, Carter might have struggled to match him in the Midwest and the Northeast. If Brown had run from the start, his greater glamour and prestige as governor of California would surely have left Carter in the shade; similarly, if Church had not waited so long, he too might have gathered momentum.

Carter was also enormously lucky that so many weak candidates entered the race in the early stages, taking votes from one another and allowing him to sneak through. He was extraordinarily lucky that Jackson did not run in New Hampshire, and lucky that Udall and Bayh took votes from each other. He was lucky that Jackson sabotaged his own victory in New York, that Udall ran out of money, and that the Humphrey boom undermined Jackson in Pennsylvania. "Skill and luck," his pollster Pat Caddell said, "they're both key parts of the political process. And in 1976 we had the best of both."[46]

**In July 1976** the Democrats assembled at Madison Square Garden for their national convention. Pragmatism, not idealism, seemed to be the guiding spirit. "Every Convention seems to have a buzzword," Elizabeth Drew remarked, "and the buzzword for this year's Democratic Convention is 'dull' . . . The war is over and the passions are dead, and many of the delegates to this convention look, as a friend of mine remarked, like 'modified Republicans.' " In 1972 the Massachusetts delegation had been made up of antiwar activists and university professors; now it consisted of solid blue-collar Jackson delegates. Even the Californians had left their beads, bangles, and caftans at home, and seemed to have been on a group outing to one of the fustier Manhattan department stores.[47]

In many ways it was the first modern Democratic convention, tightly scripted from start to finish, and as the galleries filled up with actors, models, and socialites, the spirit of Harry Truman seemed a long way away. It was somehow symbolic that the hottest ticket of the week was for *Rolling Stone*'s party on the Upper East Side, where the guests included Jane Fonda, Warren Beatty, and John Belushi. Amusingly, the party degenerated into a gigantic open-air brawl between celebrities, gate-crashers, and the New York police. At one point Ron Kovic, the crippled Vietnam veteran who had been invited to address the convention, was left outside in his wheelchair surrounded by jostling partygoers. As Carter's staff hurried past him up the steps, he shouted after them: "That's right, you sons of bitches, throw me down the stairs! I'll bite you on your fucking ankles!"[48]

Yet Kovic's very presence told a heartening story. For all its slick efficiency, the Democratic convention was a chance to reconcile the divisions of the 1960s. Barbara Jordan, the charismatic black congresswoman from Houston, gave the opening address. Tom Bradley, the black mayor of Los Angeles, and Jerry Apodaca, the Hispanic governor of New Mexico, were named as convention co-chairs. César Chávez gave the nominating speech for Jerry Brown, whose California delegation also included the former SDS radical Tom Hayden, then Mr. Jane Fonda. Eight years after the bitterness of Vietnam had torn the Democratic Party apart, it seemed at last that the war was over.[49]

Oddly, the one man who seemed slightly out of place in Madison Square Garden was the nominee. Even now, Jimmy Carter felt like a stranger at his own party. He had done himself a great favor by picking as his running mate Walter Mondale, a man whose sober Protestantism and small-town background matched his own. But there was still a sense of disbelief that Carter, even now such an unknown quantity, was going to be the nominee. "I guess I'll get to like him" seemed to be the most common refrain. "How can he be nominated?" asked the bewildered party grandee Averell Harriman. "I don't know him, and neither do any of my friends."[50]

Late on Wednesday night, the convention formally nominated Carter as its candidate for president, the first time the party had chosen a non-incumbent Southerner since before the Civil War. Just after eleven, as his aides gathered in the suffocating heat of the Georgia delegation's pit, Ohio cast its votes for Jimmy Carter, sending him over the top. "Suddenly a convulsion of ecstasy rocked the entire Georgia delegation," wrote Kandy Stroud. "The Carter staff burst into a swaying, stomping, hollering, back-slapping, hair-mussing, kissing, hugging, weeping mass. The South had risen again. The Civil War was over." His face red with heat and emotion, Hamilton Jordan raised a clenched fist to the skies and let out a bloodcurdling rebel yell. "Four long, wonderful years!" he shouted.[51]

On Thursday, the final night of the convention, Carter spoke to the biggest audience of his life. On each side of the rostrum, banners read, "For America's Third Century, Why Not the Best?" American flags and giant photographs of the two nominees were everywhere, and every delegate was armed with a green and white Carter/Mondale placard. From the galleries, cards spelled out "Texas Loves New York City"; below, delegates bounced a gigantic bicentennial ball from one side of the hall to another. On the podium, Mondale walked out to a hero's welcome. "We have just lived through the worst political scandal in our history," he thundered, "and are now led by a President who pardoned the person who did it!"[52]

Then, as the party chairman introduced the "next President of the United States," Carter walked in from the side of the hall, making his way through a sea of smiles and outstretched hands, the man of the people coming from within their midst to the brink of the nation's highest office. He made his way up to the rostrum, a slight figure in a blue suit, and then, just as he had done in hundreds of little towns and shopping malls and churches and living rooms from coast to coast, he grinned and said, "My name is Jimmy Carter, and I'm running for president," and the audience roared.

It had taken endless drafts to get the speech right. Carter said later that he had "shifted back and forth between liberal and conservative" and wanted above all to be "populist in tone." And while another man might have paid tribute to the Great Society, or promised to cross new frontiers of action and activism, Carter's was the voice of an outsider. "It is time for the people to run the government," he said, "and not the other way around." It was time to kick out "a political [and] economic elite who have shaped decisions and never had to account for mistakes or to suffer from injustice . . . It is time for us to take a new look at our own government, to strip away the secrecy, to expose the unwarranted pressure of lobbyists, to eliminate waste."[53]

And after all the cheers and the applause, as his beaten rivals joined Carter and his wife on the rostrum, Martin Luther King Sr., "Daddy King," gave the benediction, and a wonderful stillness descended on the hall. "Surely," the preacher said, in his deep booming voice, "surely the Lord sent Jimmy Carter to come on out and bring America back where she belongs." As his words died away, the orchestra played "We Shall Overcome," and the delegates sang along, ever so softly. Watching from the floor, Elizabeth Drew looked across; beside her, two white women from Washington state, Jackson delegates, were crying.[54]

It had been a glorious convention, the most successful Democratic meeting since 1960. Pat Caddell's polls showed that almost eight out of ten people had been impressed by Carter's speech; even better, he had soared to a sensational lead over the two Republican candidates, ahead of Ford by thirty-nine points and Reagan by forty-two. As the Democrats packed their bags and said goodbye to New York, they all agreed there was no stopping him. "If he had packed up that night and flown home to Plains and gone fishing until election day," recalled his speechwriter Patrick Anderson, "he might have won by a landslide. Unfortunately, he campaigned."[55]

# Interlude: TV's Super Women

Traditionally the junior brother among the three television networks, ABC ruled the airwaves during the middle of the 1970s. But the success of *Happy Days* and *Laverne & Shirley* was not enough for the network's executives, and in the fall of 1976 they unveiled their latest attempt to win over the hearts and minds of the average American family. At 10:00 p.m. on September 22, Americans first laid their eyes on Aaron Spelling's new ratings winner, the story of three beautiful private investigators, played by Kate Jackson, Jaclyn Smith, and Farrah Fawcett-Majors, whose boss, the unseen Charlie Townsend, gives them their missions by telephone—hence the title of the show, *Charlie's Angels*.

Like so many shows during the 1970s, *Charlie's Angels* followed a formula that never altered. Typically, the girls have to go undercover in some sexually charged environment, with the situation demanding that they dress as beauty pageant contestants, roller-derby girls, and the like, thereby showing off their splendid figures. In the fourth episode, "Angels in Chains," they are commissioned to investigate a rural prison farm, and therefore have to get themselves sentenced to long stretches for speeding. Once inside, they are confronted by a fascistic prison matron, clearly a lesbian and therefore thoroughly evil, who tells them to "strip down to your birthday suits." After quick showers, the Angels have to open their towels and submit to the matron's inspection while she sprays them with disinfectant. "That's only the beginning," noted one amused reviewer. "Beatings, threats of rape and enforced prostitution follow, not to mention an imminent triple murder when they find out too much."[1]

Despite atrocious reviews, the show was an immediate hit, winning 59 percent of the audience share, drawing a weekly mailbag of eighteen thousand letters, and allowing ABC to sell commercial spots for $100,000 a minute. It was "not just a winner but a certifiable phenomenon," said one report on "TV's Super Women," noting that while most shows took half a season to break into the top ten, *Charlie's Angels* had done it straightaway. Indeed, its audience figures were "truly astonishing": not only was a 59 percent share usually reserved for national events like the World Series or the Super Bowl, but *Charlie's Angels* ranked fourth among all programs in metropolitan areas, seventh among college graduates, seventh among viewers with incomes above $20,000, and first with all adult viewers whatever their age or status. The show even inspired a haircut: by the spring of 1977, women across the nation were reportedly demanding a "Farrah flip," copying the pneumatic Angel's streaky-blond mane. Soon there were Farrah T-shirts, dolls, lunch pails, shampoos, and a pinup poster that sold two million copies in less than four months. In a 1977 poll, more than fourteen thousand high-school students nominated her as their "number one personal hero"—fifteen places ahead of the president of the United States.[2]

It is a sign of how deeply ideas of female liberation had percolated into the media that ABC executives claimed, however disingenuously, that *Charlie's Angels* was a study in "the evolution of women in society." Since women made up 60 percent of the audience after nine o'clock, they claimed, they had deliberately created the show to tap that market. And yet, although the production team expended a lot of effort on what they called "fashions and hairstyles"—far more, indeed, than on scripts or acting—the series remained a male fantasy. Lindsay Wagner in *The Bionic Woman* and Lynda Carter in *Wonder Woman* had already shown that sexy female leads could attract millions of male viewers, but Spelling and his colleagues took this a step further. "What we're talking about is a B exploitation movie, not even a B," one told *Time* magazine. "We understood that we needed to exploit the sexuality of the three girls." So almost every episode contrived to show at least one Angel in a bikini within the first ten minutes, while Fawcett's refusal to wear a bra went down very well with male viewers and network officials alike. "We love to get them wet," another producer said gleefully, "because they look so good in clinging clothes."

But while Farrah Fawcett's breasts are fondly remembered, what is often forgotten is how controversial *Charlie's Angels'* first season was. Critics lined up to denounce the epitome of "tits and ass" or "jiggle" television: one thought it merely "sixty minutes of suggestive poses by walking, talking pinup girls," while the CBS newsman Morley Safer called it "a massage parlor in the living room." Even *Time* thought that the show "offers very little to please a woman whose consciousness has been raised even a degree or two by the [women's] movement," and described it as "family-style porn, a mild erotic fantasy that appeals about equally to men and women."

Not all women, though: the feminist writer Judith Coburn called it "one of the most misogynist shows" on television and complained that "it perpetuates the myth most damaging to women's struggle to gain professional equality: that women always use sex to get what they want, even on the job." The story, she thought, was "a version of the pimp and his girls. Charlie dispatches his streetwise girls to use their sexual wiles on the world while he reaps the profits." And not all men were entirely comfortable with it, either. The critic John J. O'Connor admitted enjoying the "splendidly revealing costumes," but still wondered whether such "blatant exploitation" was really justifiable in the name of "ratings and profit." *Charlie's Angels*, he thought, was basically "a girlie show" and close to "soft-core pornography."

But Aaron Spelling was having none of it. "The people out there love it," he said defiantly, "and we have the numbers to prove it." And at least one prominent intellectual agreed with him. *Charlie's Angels* was "the only romantic television show today," the libertarian writer Ayn Rand told an incredulous Phil Donahue in May 1979. "It's not about the gutter. It's not about half-wit retarded children and all the other kind of shows today. It's about three attractive girls doing impossible things. And because they're impossible, that's what makes it interesting."[3]

# Chapter Nine    *The Weirdo Factor*

> Ten years ago, if anyone of wealth, power, or renown had publicly
> "announced for Christ," people would have looked at him as if his nose
> had been eaten away by weevils. Today it happens regularly.
>
> **—TOM WOLFE,** "The 'Me' Decade and the
> Third Great Awakening" (1976)

The weekend after he had been nominated as the Democratic candidate for president, Jimmy Carter taught Sunday school in a tiny wooden room at the Plains Baptist church. For the first time in the church's history, half the class were outsiders, and there were so many reporters that they spilled into the central hall. But Carter seemed unperturbed. With a Bible in his hand, he waited for the class to fall quiet and then, in his soft Georgia twang, he began to talk of Saint John's Gospel and the importance of faith.

When a man had true faith, Carter said, he could show "compassion, emotion, love, concern, equality, and even better than equality, the attitude of a servant." A true Christian, he said, would tell others: "I'm not only not better than you, you're better than I am"—not, admittedly, something he was planning to say to Gerald Ford. But what he said next gave a clue to something that had long intrigued reporters. What made Carter tick, and how would he react to the challenges of the presidency? "When we want to know how to deal with an unforeseen circumstance or how to orient our lives toward a proper decision," he said, "if we ask ourselves a simple question, 'What would Christ do?' then we have a very simple answer to a very difficult question."[1]

In later years, such sentiments became clichés of the quadrennial presidential circus. But in 1976, the general reaction in the media was utter incredulity. To the hard-bitten reporters who had been covering presidential campaigns for years, remarked Jules Witcover, it seemed frankly incredible to find a candidate who was "influenced in his conduct of public office by God's word and guidance." Many reporters did not know what it meant to be "born again," and The New York Times's chief religious writer noted that his colleagues associated Carter's faith with "a kind of backwoods yahoo-ism that they found very distasteful." At first some reassured themselves that Carter's faith was all a matter of political calculation. But they soon realized that he was worse than a hypocrite. He was a true believer.[2]

At first, Carter had made little of his Baptist faith. If he had been running ten years later, his religion would have been one of the first items in his official biography. But in 1976 most of his advisers believed that his evangelical piety risked alienating millions of voters outside the South. "The weirdo factor," Hamilton Jordan called it. So when Carter was asked about his faith in the first primaries, he gave brief answers, invoking the example of John Kennedy and pledging that he would not allow his church to dictate his policies. If reporters probed more deeply, he became uneasy: one described him "lapsing into embarrassed smiles, blushing, even looking away to avoid a cynical gaze."[3]

Carter first talked about the experience of being born again in North Carolina, a southern state with a Baptist majority, and the ideal place to broach such a sensitive subject. Although some commentators disapproved of his frank admission of faith, it rapidly became clear that what Newsweek called the "God issue" was no threat to his campaign. Even secular voters told pollsters that the country needed a moral, God-fearing man in the Oval Office. As Carter piled up Democratic delegates, he became more confident, openly talking about his religious background, recognizing that it was a powerful political asset. Not only did he invite reporters to watch him teach Sunday school, he boasted of praying "ten or twenty times a day" and reading a chapter of the Bible in Spanish every night. In typical fashion, he added that he could have done it in English "in three minutes" but "it wasn't a challenge."[4]

**In many ways,** the United States in the mid-1970s was becoming a godless society. Among the college educated, church attendance, prayer, and even faith in God were in manifest decline, while the rise of divorce, abortion, and pornography suggested that Americans were not immune to the secular changes that were transforming Western Europe. Fewer adults went to church every week, and fewer claimed membership in religious organizations. The most respectable Protestant denominations—the Episcopalians, the United Presbyterians, the United Methodists—were all losing members, funds, and school enrollments. And while the Catholic Church did a better job of holding on to its members, it was deeply divided over birth control and the Second Vatican Council. Thousands of priests rejected papal teachings on divorce, contraception, and the ordination of women, while the Church hierarchy found it hard to attract young recruits. Attendance fell sharply: by the mid-1970s, barely half of all American Catholics went to Mass every week. Even in Boston, the heartland of Irish and Italian Catholicism, weekly attendance fell by a third between 1970 and 1978, and during the city's busing crisis many ordinary Catholics openly displayed their contempt for the Church.[5]

And yet the American people remained by far the most religious in the Western world. Their politics and culture were steeped in religious assumptions that would have seemed extraordinary in most European countries, and the motto "one nation, under God" was more than just patriotic boilerplate. In the late 1970s, more than half of all Americans said they prayed every day. Around 75 percent said they believed in the divinity of Christ, 80 percent in life after death, and 90 percent in God, far higher than the proportions in Europe. For a serious politician publicly to question life after death or the existence of God would have been almost unthinkable.[6]

Although fewer Americans were attending mainstream services, society and culture were arguably more overtly spiritual in the 1970s than ever. One major influence was the counterculture of the late 1960s, with its emphasis on conscience and personal discovery. While hippies borrowed their language of "alienation" and "authenticity" from Christian existentialism, thousands of idealistic college students were drawn to religious themes. In 1971, *Time* reported that many Christian students were "afire with a Pentecostal passion for sharing their new vision with others." At Daytona Beach, the Campus Crusade for Christ organized a "Revolution for Jesus Christ" event. At the University of Illinois, 12,000 students turned up to a Campus Crusade convention; at Notre Dame, 20,000 came to a Catholic charismatic event. And in Dallas a "fundamentalist Woodstock" in June 1972 attracted 150,000 people to hear Johnny Cash, Rita Coolidge, and Kris Kristofferson, with a further 75,000 packing into the Cotton Bowl to hear Billy Graham, Florida's governor, Reubin Askew, and the Cowboys' quarterback Roger Staubach.[7]

Even on the wilder shores of the counterculture there were plenty of militant Christians, nicknamed Jesus People or Jesus Freaks. With their long hair, beards, and sandals, the Jesus People picked up plenty of members who had fallen out of love with the hedonism of the 1960s. According to one estimate, they had organizations on 450 campuses, where they printed T-shirts and bumper stickers with the legend "Smile, God Loves You," published underground newspapers, and devised a Jesus Power salute with a clenched fist and the index finger pointing toward heaven. They even had their own Martin Luther, the Reverend Chuck Smith, a California pastor whose Calvary Chapel services mixed charismatic hallelujahs with lilting guitars. On the beach at Corona del Mar he held gigantic ocean baptisms, where thousands of hippie converts, in bare feet and tie-dyed shirts, plunged into the Pacific to be received into the brotherhood of Christ. It was a formula that worked: thirty years later, Calvary Chapel had eight hundred franchises across the country, all with the same blend of slightly scary West Coast informality, fundamentalist teachings, and lashings of folk music.[8]

But Calvary Chapel was not the only destination for young people hungry for spiritual inspiration. The early 1970s was a period of extraordinary growth for sects, cults, and supernatural interests of all kinds, fueled by the loss of faith in traditional institutions, the shocks of Vietnam and Watergate, and a thirst for meaning in a world of suburban alienation. These were boom years for astrology (whose admirers famously included Nancy Reagan), for the occult, for stories of demonic possession like *The Exorcist* and *The Omen*, and for best sellers by authors as diverse as J. R. R. Tolkien, Carlos Castaneda, and Erich von Däniken. In the bookstores of Harvard Square, reported *The New York Times*, shelves were "crowded with Indian medicine men, magic, drug eaters, political writings fastened exclusively to the apocalyptic vision and a catalogue on how to flee the modern world."[9]

All of this was harmless enough. What disturbed many people, however, was the spread of unorthodox "cults," among them the Unification Church of Sun Myung Moon, the Love Family, and the Church of Scientology. Their importance was often exaggerated: while some estimates claimed that three million Americans had joined cults by the late 1970s, the real figure was probably in the tens of thousands. Yet hundreds of tiny sects proliferated in the 1970s, especially in California, where they attracted the dispirited detritus of the counterculture. Many were more like Christian communes than cults, though others were genuinely sinister, and groups like the Children of God and Synanon turned out to be fronts for organized prostitution and sexual abuse. Most famously, Jim Jones's People's Temple fled from California, where he was facing tax evasion charges, to Guyana, where in November 1978 almost a thousand men, women, and children died in an appalling cross between a mass suicide and a massacre.[10]

With so many competing religions to choose from, some people saw no reason to limit themselves to one. The sociologist Wade Clark Roof came across one woman, Linda, who had grown up in a small rural community in Ohio, which might have been expected to give her a sense of tradition and obligation. Instead, she left behind her family's Methodist faith and "checked out several different congregations," working on the assumption that "denomination is not important; all that really counts is if Christ is present." Finally, she settled on a huge Baptist megachurch offering music, stage productions, prayer and activity groups, a school, a gigantic library of books and tapes, and even a singles group, where she met her husband.

This ethos of "shopping around" was just as common at the more eclectic end of the spectrum. Another of Roof's subjects, Mollie, an upper-middle-class Jewish woman from New York who took handfuls of drugs in the 1960s and participated in love-ins and be-ins in Central Park, adopted a similar approach. She tried "holistic health, macrobiotics, Zen Buddhism, Native American rituals, [and] New Age in its many versions"; she joined a commune; she read books on reincarnation; she tried the controversial Erhard Seminars Training, or *est*. For a time, she was "into" Jesus because she apparently found "his teachings and writings very non-denominational, very spiritual." By the time Roof caught up with her, she was regularly going to Native American medicine wheel gatherings and also, rather incongruously, Quaker prayer meetings. As he understatedly put it, she was "an explorer down many religious paths."[11]

Despite their differences, both Linda and Mollie believed in putting their own instincts first. What mattered was the individual expression of spirituality, not loyalty to tradition, and they felt no shame about trying different alternatives. They were spiritual consumers, choosing between different brands as though picking cereals in the supermarket. And what emerged in the 1970s was a kind of "privatized religion," a commodity to be weighed, paid for, and discarded once it had served its purpose. Complicated theological doctrines were reduced to "simple steps, easy procedures, and formulas for psychological rewards," buttressed by a vast industry selling everything from crystals and crosses to books of Native

American wisdom. In this respect, religion was no different from any other aspect of life. At a time when Americans were retreating from collective idealism and labor unions were losing members, religion too was dominated by the iron rules of market forces and individual choice.[12]

Almost every successful spiritual brand in the 1970s emphasized self-expression and self-discovery. Communal obligations were not important; what mattered was to be "authentic." This was the ethos, for example, of Richard Bach's supremely self-righteous fable *Jonathan Livingston Seagull*, which topped the best-seller lists in 1972 and stayed there for a mind-numbing thirty-eight weeks. Life with the other gulls is not good enough for Jonathan, who insists on flying off on his own. After they kick him out, he finds a saintly teacher who advises him to "keep working on love." At last Jonathan returns to share his ideals, explaining that "it is right for a gull to fly, that freedom is the very nature of his being, that whatever stands against that freedom must be set aside, be it ritual or superstition or limitation in any form." "Set aside?" queries one of his pupils. "The only true law," says Jonathan solemnly, "is that which leads to freedom."[13]

Many critics were appalled that this horrific mishmash of Christian Science, Buddhism, anarchism, Hermann Hesse, Saint-Exupéry, and Horatio Alger had proved such a hit. But with its themes of spiritual perfection, independence, and self-improvement, *Jonathan Livingston Seagull* was the perfect fable for the times. Astonishingly, even Nixon's acting FBI director, Pat Gray, was a fan, urging his officials to read it and to allow "their spirits to soar"—although in his case, thanks to Watergate, they did not soar for long.[14]

Self-improvement was a central element in almost all the major cultural movements of the 1970s. When feminists came together for consciousness-raising sessions, or black nationalists tried to discover their African roots, or evangelical Christians felt the Holy Spirit working through them, they were hoping to become happier and more complete people. Self-fulfillment was a constant theme for singer-songwriters like James Taylor, Jackson Browne, and Joni Mitchell, while literary culture seemed steeped in self-consciousness. In Philip Roth's novel *The Professor of Desire* (1977), the protagonist thinks about nothing but his own emotional self-discovery, spending a fortune on psychotherapy and using his university literature classes to explore his desires. Even populist entertainment was not immune: in *Star Wars*, a naive farm boy finds himself through leaving his family and his home, "letting go" of his feelings, and surrendering to "the Force"—a classic piece of New Age waffle if ever there was one.[15]

Although this theme of personal discovery is always associated with the

Me Decade, it had much deeper roots. As the critic Catherine Morley points out, the search for self-realization has always been a major preoccupation of American writers; indeed, the title of Walt Whitman's poem "Song of Myself" would work nicely as a motto for the 1970s. Still, this kind of introspection became far more intense in the 1970s, thanks in part to the boom in "therapy culture." For as Americans became more materially comfortable, they developed a sense of entitlement, taking success for granted and reacting angrily when happiness was not forthcoming. Their parents, argued the pollster Daniel Yankelovich, had asked themselves, "Will I be able to make a good living?" But the generation that came of age in the 1970s asked rather different questions: "How can I find self-fulfillment?" "What does personal success really mean?" "How can I grow?"[16]

This was excellent news for the nation's therapists, who must have been rubbing their hands with glee. In 1970, about one million Americans were thought to be receiving psychiatric treatment; by 1975, the figure had increased sixfold. Mental health coverage was now included in Blue Cross, Medicaid, and employer health plans; psychology and psychiatry courses boomed; newspaper articles were full of pseudo-Freudian explanations for everything from blue-collar racism to the constitutional misdeeds of Richard Nixon. Bookshelves creaked under the weight of self-help best sellers: *I'm OK, You're OK, How to Be Your Own Best Friend, Looking Out for Number One.* And in the comedies of Woody Allen, such as *Annie Hall* and *Manhattan,* barely a moment goes by without another allusion to therapy or a joke about self-discovery.[17]

Meanwhile, overlooking the Pacific coast at Big Sur, California, the Esalen Institute attracted ten thousand people a year to seminars covering everything from Gestalt therapy and Eastern philosophy to yoga and deep massage. Some of Esalen's activities were less than wholesome: at one stage it provided a home for the psychoanalyst Fritz Perls, whose sessions invited patients to explore the darker recesses of their sexuality, with the secondary function of acting as pickup sessions for the aged therapist himself. "A lube job for the personality," Tom Wolfe sardonically called it. But by the standards of the time Esalen was actually pretty respectable. Its gorgeous location and outdoor pools attracted an impressive range of guest musicians, including Bob Dylan, Bruce Springsteen, and George Harrison, while Arnold Toynbee, Buckminster Fuller, and Linus Pauling came to deliver talks. It was certainly a long way from the enterprise that symbolized the least attractive side of the human potential movement, Werner Erhard's "awareness training" racket, Erhard Seminars Training, known as *est.*[18]

*Est* was like some terrible caricature of everything that was wrong with 1970s self-improvement. Even the slick "Werner Erhard," who sounded like an eminent Viennese professor, was actually a failed car dealer from Norristown, Pennsylvania. After abandoning his wife for a younger woman and dabbling in Scientology, Buddhism, and encounter-group therapy, he supposedly had a revelation while driving across the Golden Gate Bridge in 1971. On this rather tenuous basis he set up a series of workshops, usually lasting two consecutive weekends. Customers paid hundreds of dollars to subject themselves to relentless interrogation, including being locked in a stuffy room for hours without access to a bathroom, apparently designed to strip away the "layers" of personality and reveal the essential nothingness within. "You are an asshole!" trainers would yell. Once victims had shed their personality, or said they had, they were invited to "take responsibility" for their failures. Then came the reward. "You are omnipotent," Erhard would say. "You are a god in your universe."

Astonishingly—or rather, in a tribute to human gullibility—celebrities waxed lyrical about the effects of this foolishness on their lives. John Denver, Mike Oldfield, and Valerie Harper all claimed it had given them new confidence and a sense of possibility. Even a skeptical reporter for *The New York Times* in 1976 said that the routine of abuse and inspirational jargon had given him "a revelation of sorts." However, not all customers emerged satisfied, and psychiatric journals reported that several people, some already vulnerable, had been driven to near madness. Depressingly, Erhard pocketed fees from hundreds of thousands of customers before the seminars were wound up amid lurid allegations of cultism and sexual abuse. And even if these allegations were false—for Erhard's apologists blamed disinformation by his Scientologist rivals—the former car dealer had taken his place among the great American con artists.[19]

**It was a journalist** called Peter Marin, in a cover piece for *Harper's* in October 1975, who hit on the term that came to represent a decade of spiritual self-exploration. "The new narcissism," Marin called it, arguing that for all the talk of "psychic health," what really lay behind it was "selfishness and moral blindness." At Esalen, he had been horrified to hear two women therapists explaining "how the Jews must have wanted to be burned by the Germans, and that those who starve in the Sahel must want it to happen." When Marin asked what they would say to a child starving in the desert, one woman snapped back: "What can I do if a child is determined to starve?"

The exchange weighed heavily on his mind. At its root, he thought, was "the growing solipsism and desperation of a beleaguered class . . . a retreat from the worlds of morality and history, an unembarrassed denial of human reciprocity and community." It was a middle-class flight from a world of uncertainty, leaving millions of "neglected others" behind in the obsession with self and sex.[20]

Narcissism was a fashionable idea in the early 1970s. A few years before, scholars such as Otto Kernberg and Herbert Hendin had suggested that growing numbers of people, filled with grandiose fantasies of their own importance and demanding excessive admiration from their peers, were suffering from pathological narcissism. The fault, they argued, lay with a generation of overprotective mothers (already "blamed" for homosexuality in the mid-1950s), at once cold and smothering, demanding that their children fulfill certain goals and punishing them when they failed. Narcissism, they concluded, was the defining pathology of the times. Hendin suggested that "probably two-thirds to three-quarters of psychoanalytic patients have narcissistic problems." Kernberg thought that even many certified psychoanalysts had narcissistic traits. But not to worry, he added: "They usually stop practicing because narcissists hate to hear about other people's problems."[21]

But it was Tom Wolfe, pioneer of New Journalism, scourge of radical chic, self-invented southern gentleman, and wearer of the second-most-celebrated white suit in American literature, who became the most influential critic of the "new narcissism." The very title of his essay, which appeared in *New York* magazine in August 1976, bequeathed two phrases to the language, the "Me Decade" and the "Third Great Awakening." It began, incongruously enough, with hemorrhoids: specifically, the hemorrhoids of a female Los Angeles executive, who had come to an *est* meeting to rid herself of her anxiety, just as other clients had come to void their "self-hatred, self-destructiveness, craven fears, puling weaknesses, primordial horrors, premature ejaculation, impotence, frigidity, rigidity, subservience, laziness, alcoholism, major vices, minor vices, grim habits, twisted psyches, tortured souls."

What these people had in common, Wolfe argued, was their obsession with "remaking, remodeling, elevating, and polishing one's very self." This, he said, was something entirely new, since most people in history had lived for others—friends, family, ancestors—rather than for themselves alone. But the Americans who had reached maturity in the late 1960s and early 1970s were entirely self-absorbed. Cosseted by affluence, they had done "something only aristocrats (and intellectuals and artists) were supposed to do—they discovered and started doting on Me!" And this Third Great Awakening, as he called it, was nothing less than the "greatest age of individualism in American history."[22]

Wolfe's essay on the Me Decade, the cultural historian Christopher Lasch wrote a few weeks later in *The New York Review of Books*, was "very much to the point." Lasch himself drew even more sweeping conclusions. A former socialist who had adopted an unusual blend of Freudianism, conservatism, and populist radicalism, he saw narcissism as a social, not a personal, phenomenon, the "best way of coping with a dangerous world." Self-discovery, Lasch wrote, was an escape from "objective conditions of economic warfare, rising rates of crime, and social chaos." And so narcissism was not mere self-indulgence; it was the product of a social and economic "cult of consumption" that had left Americans bored, lonely, and unsatisfied.[23]

Wolfe and Lasch left a lasting impression on the historical image of the decade: even today, almost all accounts of the 1970s pay homage to the Me Decade and the culture of narcissism. The reputation of the 1970s as a period of unbridled selfishness is obviously an exaggeration: millions of Americans, from environmentalists, trade union organizers, and civil rights workers to Stop ERA campaigners and fundamentalist members of the Moral Majority, still worked for a better society. But while the Me Decade was a caricature, a good caricature, as any illustrator knows, must have a core of truth. There *was* a genuine sense of individualism and self-absorption, evident in everything from religious affiliation and neighborhood politics to folk songs and psychotherapy. Collective institutions were in retreat; individualism was on the rise. In this respect, as in so many others, the rightward shift of the 1980s was under way long before its greatest architect came to Washington.[24]

**Toward the end** of September 1976, as the presidential contest was entering its final stretch, George Gallup gave a speech that sent shock waves through the national media. Whether Jimmy Carter won or lost, Gallup said, the last twelve months had been the "Year of the Evangelical." In a new survey, his pollsters had found that one in three adult Americans—more than fifty million people—described themselves as "born again." Four out of ten, meanwhile, agreed that the Bible "is to be taken literally," and half said they had personally evangelized on Christ's behalf, urging their friends to accept him as their savior. "Isn't it time," asked Gallup, "to bring our religious feelings out of the closet?"[25]

Although American evangelicalism dates back to the first colonists' dreams of self-governing godly communities, it had long been dismissed as deeply unfashionable. To many of the reporters who followed Carter's campaign, belief in the literal truth in the Bible, in the imminence of the end-time, or even in personal salvation through Jesus Christ seemed not merely an incongruous element of a modern presidential campaign but an embarrassing relic of a vanished past. Yet as the historian William Martin notes, religious culture in the South and the West, where evangelicalism had been a central element of frontier identity, was still marked by "its absolute and unquestioning confidence in the Bible, its emphasis on piety and purity, and its unswerving dedication to the primary task of the revivals: the winnings of lost souls." Nowhere else in the world was there a Protestant population more committed to the literal truth of the Scriptures and the importance of personal salvation. One woman, born again in 1976, later recalled the excitement of her exchange with the pastor: "Do you believe you are a sinner?" "Yes!" "Do you believe God sent Jesus to die for your sins?" "Yes, I believe that!" "Would you like to turn toward him and repent?" "Yes, I want to turn, I believe, and please save me because I am lost!"[26]

Ever since the fiasco of the Scopes trial in 1925, most outsiders had assumed that evangelicalism and fundamentalism had effectively crawled under a rock to die. In fact, by the middle of the century fundamentalist churches were quietly picking up thousands of new members. The Pentecostal movement in particular—characterized by its belief that God was still at work in the world, communicating through the Holy Spirit and supernatural miracles—made astonishing strides after World War II, offering an emotionally spectacular experience that worked brilliantly on television. Almost unnoticed by northern commentators, evangelical preachers poured out books and publications, trained thousands of teachers, ran radio stations, and delivered thundering sermons to listeners across the country. Buoyed by their faith in the truth of the Scriptures and their personal experience of Christ, they saw themselves as soldiers in a war against Satan—a war they dare not lose.[27]

Evangelicalism benefited from two seismic demographic changes. First, its heartland was enjoying the biggest economic boom in its history. As Dixie became the Sunbelt, thousands of southern Christians, richer than their parents had ever dreamed, donated millions to evangelical preachers, building the schools, hospitals, and universities that became a crucial part of the evangelical empire. The evangelical surge was particularly noticeable in places that became emblematic of the middle-class Sunbelt—places like Virginia Beach, home to Pat Robertson's Christian Broadcasting Network; or Colorado Springs, the "Evangelical Vatican," home to the International Bible Society, the Association of Christian Schools International, and Focus on the Family.[28]

Not only were migrants flocking to the newly affluent South, Southerners were themselves on the move, taking new jobs in Yankee territory and bringing their values with them. "Not too long ago," one minister remarked in 1974, "the Gospel according to Billy Graham was strictly a southern product. Now, that gospel of individual salvation . . . appeals to persons throughout the land." As *Time* magazine put it three years later, discussing an Episcopalian church in Connecticut that had fallen under evangelical influence, "the Bible Belt is in fact bursting the bonds of geography and seems on the verge of becoming a national state of mind."[29]

By the mid-1970s, evangelical churches were booming. Between 1965 and 1980, the Southern Baptist Convention saw its membership increase from 10.8 million people to 13.6 million, while the Assemblies of God saw theirs almost double from 570,000 to 1.1 million. Meanwhile, polls suggested that evangelical attitudes were shared by millions of people — young and old, rich and poor, black and white—who rarely set foot in conservative churches. Half of all Americans believed the Bible to be the literal word of God, half genuinely expected Christ to return to earth, and eight out of ten expected to appear before God on Judgment Day. By 1978, almost 40 percent said they had been born again. Probably many were following the spiritual fashion, but the majority, surely, were quite serious.[30]

Secular liberals often explained evangelicalism and fundamentalism as a combination of "economic backwardness and a kind of cultural irrationality." But the people who joined evangelical churches in the 1970s were not superstitious failures but successful small-business men, managers, and clerical workers. Wade Clark Roof's interviewee Linda, for example, was a typical baby boomer, wearing beads in the 1960s and enjoying rock music. She married at nineteen, got divorced, went to business school, and worked outside the home, juggling work and motherhood. She tried several different churches and found that an evangelical Baptist megachurch suited her best, helping her to raise her children in a Christian framework. So did another baby boomer, Barry, who worked as a well-paid engineer in North Carolina's Research Triangle. Again, he was typical of his generation, opposing the Vietnam War and voting for McGovern, yet he regularly attended a Southern Baptist church. These people were not backward; they were ordinary Americans who proved that, in Alan Brinkley's words, "it is possible to be a stable, affluent, middle-class person" and still believe in the literal truth of the Bible and the presence of the Holy Spirit.[31]

The journalist Frances FitzGerald once wrote that evangelicalism offered "old certainties dressed up in glossy packages." But in an age of economic change, rising crime, and disintegrating marriages, old certainties were what many people wanted. And in the booming Sunbelt suburbs, where newcomers from the countryside could feel daunted or lonely, evangelical churches attracted plenty of recruits. With their innumerable groups and activities, they offered a warm welcome, a sense of stability, and a place to meet like-minded people. "People are concerned about you as a person," said Linda of her Baptist megachurch, "and they become like a family to you." On top of that, the evangelical emphasis on hard work and personal salvation was perfectly suited to people who already lived highly individualistic, entrepreneurial lives—which was why they had moved to the suburbs in the first place.[32]

But the "glossy packages" were also crucial. Evangelicalism was competing in a crowded market, and preachers needed to meet the expectations of their consumers. Like West Coast therapists, they emphasized the individual, offered a psychological makeover, and promised salvation in this world as well as the next. And their product was the perfect blend of tradition and modernity. Services took place in gleaming buildings with air-conditioning, overhead monitors, carpeted floors, and facilities for children. At the colossal First Baptist Church in Dallas, there were twin gymnasiums for men and women, as well as an ice rink, a sauna, bowling alleys, racquetball courts, and a dedicated radio station. Many of its twenty-seven thousand members worked in hi-tech industries, lived in gated communities, drove the latest cars, and watched huge televisions. They wanted their faith to match their own relationship with the postwar social and cultural landscape. The paradox, therefore, was that evangelical churches were at once refuges from modernity and temples to it. No less a figure than the Reverend Jerry Falwell, after all, had originally trained as an engineer.[33]

Falwell was one of the rising stars of American public life in the mid-1970s, a bullish, ebullient figure whose *Old-Time Gospel Hour*, taped in his studio in Lynchburg, Virginia, was shown on more than three hundred television stations to an audience of more than 1.5 million people. In some ways televangelism was nothing new; in the 1920s, after all, millions had tuned in to hear preachers on the radio, while the Arkansas revivalist Rex Humbard first began weekly television broadcasts as early as 1952. But it was only in the Nixon years that it became clear that with its emphasis on compelling speakers, tearful confessions, and uplifting rhetoric, evangelicalism was superbly suited to what a broadcasting executive called "the electric church." On *The 700 Club*, as FitzGerald observed, "sleek, good-looking Pat Robertson would interview a celebrity guest, such as Charles Colson of Watergate fame, then, minutes later, fall to his knees, lift his hands to heaven, and say, 'There's a woman in Philadelphia who has cancer—cancer of the lymph nodes. It hasn't been diagnosed yet, but God has just cured her of it!' " It was a lot better than watching reruns of *Bonanza*.[34]

Of all the "video vicars," Robertson was easily the most impressive: slick, erudite, and able to recall biblical quotations and lecture at will on all kinds of topics. The son of a conservative Democratic senator from Virginia, he served in the Korean War and attended Yale Law School and the New York Theological Seminary. Although he was an ordained Baptist minister, he was never part of the mainstream. As a charismatic preacher, Robertson believed that he could speak in tongues, prophesy the future, heal the sick, and be granted sudden revelations about others and their lives. These gifts attracted the suspicion of other Baptists, but they made for excellent television. As Robertson frankly admitted, "programming a simple person, Jesus, as showbiz" was the best way "to get people to listen to his message." And it clearly worked. Modeled on *The Tonight Show*, with a house band, a desk-and-sofa set, and segments on lifestyle and leisure, *The 700 Club* was the perfect entertainment for people who thought there was too much sex, swearing, and violence on the networks, and by 1975 Robertson's electric empire was bringing in a reported $10.7 million a year. Five years later, his network occupied a $50 million headquarters and had an annual budget of some $55 million—not bad for somebody who had failed the New York bar exam.[35]

Yet politicized preachers such as Robertson and Falwell were much less popular than they usually claimed. The four most popular televangelists in February 1980 were Oral Roberts, with 2.7 million viewers; Rex Humbard, with 2.4 million, Robert Schuller, with 2 million; and Jimmy Swaggart, with just under 2 million. By comparison, Robertson's audience of just 380,000 looked pretty pitiful. Revealingly, none of the top four was involved in public affairs, and research showed that their audiences were overwhelmingly southern or Midwestern, with the vast majority being elderly women. What the top four had in common was that they offered a potent mixture of evangelicalism, therapy, and unashamed commercialism, the perfect blend for the so-called Me Decade. As Robert Schuller told his affluent worshippers in Garden Grove, California, "God wants you to succeed."[36]

But it was the most popular televangelist of all, Oral Roberts, who best captured the new ethos of middle-class respectability. Originally an old-style Oklahoma tent preacher, Roberts realized that the rise of the Sunbelt demanded a new style, steeped in what Alan Brinkley calls "relentless and unembarrassed commercialism." Every broadcast began with the words "Something good is going to happen to you!" while huge chunks of airtime were devoted to selling books, tapes, and trinkets. According to Roberts, Christ wanted his followers to be financially successful, and he often quoted a verse from Saint John's Gospel: "I wish above all things that thou mayest prosper and be in health, even as thy soul prospereth." Christ certainly looked after Roberts: by the end of the 1970s, his Tulsa empire included a $100 million medical center, a $150 million university campus, and the gigantic two-hundred-foot Prayer Tower, the ultimate symbol of his worldly success and heavenly ambitions.[37]

Where Roberts led, others followed. On Sunday, September 14, 1980, in the sparkling sunshine of a California morning, Robert Schuller invited his congregation into their new home, the Crystal Cathedral, a gleaming steel-framed monument in the shape of a four-pointed star. After flirting with anti-Communism, he had become the best-known exponent of Christian positive thinking, promising his affluent congregation that prosperity was part of God's plan for the world. "You are a beautiful person," he would tell them. Like the therapists up the coast at Esalen, he believed there was no such thing as bad luck. "You fail because you deliberately, knowingly, and willingly choose to fail," he said. But once people had accepted Christ, success was inevitable. "God loves you, and so do I."[38]

For Schuller, that Sunday morning represented the climax of four years' hard work. He had employed professional fund-raisers, secured a $1 million donation from the Orange County mobile-home tycoons John and Donna Crean, and hired the nation's best-known modernist architect, Philip Johnson. As the congregation filed into their new church, the sunlight shimmered on more than ten thousand panes of glass, a glittering tribute to the glory of God and the ambition of man. From the outside, the glass panes worked as mirrors, reflecting God's suburban creation; from within, they were windows, letting light stream in from the heavens. It was an architectural triumph, a personal triumph: a triumph for God, evangelicalism, and the power of positive thinking. Once, even Schuller had suffered from low self-esteem. But not anymore. "God is my Father," he exclaimed. "I am somebody!"[39]

**Although reporters sometimes** treated Jimmy Carter as though he were the first God-fearing presidential candidate in history, evangelicalism and politics had always been tightly intertwined. "The great business of the church is to reform the world—to put away every kind of sin," said the evangelist Charles Grandison Finney in 1846, exhorting Christians to "secure a legislation that is in accordance with the law of God." Since then, evangelical Christians had always played an active role in national politics, from the antislavery activists of the 1850s to fundamentalist preachers like Billy Sunday, who claimed that World War I was a religious crusade.[40]

Even during the 1940s and 1950s, when they were supposed to have gone underground, evangelical preachers remained keenly interested in public affairs. The anti-Communist fundamentalist Billy James Hargis, for instance, denounced federal officials as devil worshippers, accused the Beatles of spreading Communism, and toured rural states in a customized bus on his "Christian Crusade." When Hargis denounced the "anti-God Liberal Establishment," or sent out computer-generated letters asking readers to send money to fight "moral decay," he sounded like a rudimentary version of Jerry Falwell, only two decades too early. Alas, the wheels fell off his bus when it emerged that he had been sexually molesting members of his youth choir—another precedent for more than a few televangelists of the future.

One of Hargis's biggest admirers was George Wallace, whose rallies were saturated with religion, patriotism, and country music. "We come to Thee tonight, our Lord and Savior Jesus Christ, thanking Thee and praising Thee for this great turnout" was a typical opening line, while speakers would urge audiences to take up "the sword of righteousness," for "the battle of Armageddon is approaching." And despite his unchristian private language, Wallace took his faith seriously. Having grown up listening to his parents read the Bible before bedtime, he made a celebrated visit to Jerry Falwell's Thomas Road Baptist Church in 1974, where he accepted Christ as his personal savior and became the most famous of thousands born again under Falwell's tutelage.[41]

Although Wallace was unusually quick to recognize the political potential of evangelicalism, self-consciously respectable politicians also shared his interest in religion. Dwight Eisenhower, for example, had been instrumental in adding the words "under God" to the Pledge of Allegiance and enthusiastically supported the adoption of "In God We Trust" as the national motto. Richard Nixon made even greater efforts to turn piety into a political asset, hosting regular prayer breakfasts and Sunday services. Charles Colson, the Nixon hatchet man turned evangelical preacher, later admitted that these were designed for purely "political ends." One memo even ordered him to "develop a list of rich people with strong religious interest to be invited to the White House church services."[42]

Nixon's most famous religious association was his friendship with Billy

Graham, then the most admired man in the nation. In fact, the preacher from North Carolina was originally a much more abrasive figure than is often remembered. During the early 1950s his sermons had more than a dash of anti-Communist spice, condemning socialism as "filthy, corrupt, ungodly [and] unholy" and demanding investigations into "the pinks, the lavenders and the Reds who have sought refuge beneath the wings of the American Eagle." As he became more successful, Graham tried to put himself above politics, but few people were fooled. By the Nixon years, he had become a regular visitor to the White House, where he would engage the gloomy president in anti-Semitic banter. Yet this high profile had its drawbacks, for by now Graham had become rather too moderate for listeners who had thrilled to his anti-Communist invective. Many Southern Baptists, reported *The Charlotte Observer* in 1971, thought he was "too close to the powerful and too fond of the things of the world, [and] likened him to the prophets of old who told the kings of Israel what they wanted to hear."[43]

Nixon's successor was much less comfortable with public displays of faith. As House minority leader, Gerald Ford had become close friends with the preacher Billy Zeoli, who ran a ministry for professional athletes and used to conduct locker-room services for the NFL. When Zeoli came to Washington to hold a "football chapel" for the visiting Dallas Cowboys, Ford went to hear him talk about "God's game plan." It was then, Zeoli said, that Ford first really "knew Christ." When Ford became president, the two men met every month for private prayers in the Oval Office. Zeoli even sent Ford a devotional memorandum every week, always beginning with the title "God's Got a Better Idea" and including a passage from the King James Bible.

Yet public piety was not to Ford's taste. He discontinued the ostentatious White House services and went instead to his familiar Alexandria church. It was not "appropriate," he said, "to advertise my religious beliefs." These admirable scruples were challenged, however, as the presidential election approached. In September 1975, one of Ford's strategists suggested that he try to mobilize the "silent majority" on the grounds of "neighborhood, community and family." Ford should put more effort, the thinking ran, into attacking "strange or offensive textbooks," "sex education," and the "liberal chic, women's lib content" imposed on "traditional educational programs."

No doubt a family-values platform would have gone down extremely well with evangelical voters in 1976. But Ford was uncomfortable campaigning on cultural issues, not least because it would mean coming out against his own wife. Perhaps if he had deployed Zeoli, a great favorite with southern football fans, it might have helped. But when Zeoli offered to put together a book about their spiritual relationship, Ford turned him down. He had no wish, he said, "to take advantage of our faith to get elected" and no desire "to name Jesus as his running mate." His rivals would not make the same mistake.[44]

# Chapter Ten    Reagan Country

Someday, when things are tough, maybe you can ask the boys
to go in there and win just one for the Gipper.

**—GEORGE GIPP (RONALD REAGAN),**
in *Knute Rockne, All American* (1940)

The biggest party in the nation's history began at 4:31 a.m. on Sunday, July 4, 1976, on Mars Hill in northeastern Maine. As the first rays of the rising sun struck American soil, National Guardsmen fired a fifty-gun salute and raised the Stars and Stripes. Across the nation, the American people woke to a gorgeously warm, sunny morning. "The sun always shines in Pennsylvania," Gerald Ford said to laughter from the huge crowd at Valley Forge, where at nine o'clock he greeted the Bicentennial Wagon Train.

Two hours later he was in Philadelphia, standing alongside Charlton Heston and the nation's guest of honor, Queen Elizabeth II, before the great bronze Liberty Bell outside Independence Hall. He reflected on the struggles of the Republic's early years, the injustice and prejudice that had blighted the American experiment, and he looked forward to the nation's third century. "The world may or may not follow," he said, "but we lead because our whole history says we must." He asked for a moment of silent prayer, and in the streets and squares around Liberty Hall a million people bowed their heads.[1]

By early afternoon, Ford was in lower Manhattan for the main event of the day, the arrival of the tall ships in New York Harbor. Along the shore, on Brooklyn's Belt Parkway and on the crumbling West Side Highway, an estimated seven million people watched as more than two hundred sailing ships, clippers and schooners and some of the grandest windjammers in the world, slipped under the Verrazano-Narrows Bridge and headed north toward the Hudson. In the skies, helicopters circled the towers of Manhattan; on the water, bobbing in the sunlight, thousands of little boats jostled for a better view. Ninety feet above them, on the flight deck of USS *Forrestal*, thousands of guests waved and cheered, among them Prince Rainier and Princess Grace of Monaco, seventy ambassadors, fifty congressmen, and most of the cabinet. At two o'clock precisely, Ford solemnly rang the ship's bell thirteen times, once for each of the original colonies. At exactly the same moment, in Philadelphia, the cracked Liberty Bell was softly struck with a rubber mallet, and across the nation, in every church and school, every city and town, bells rang out, a chorus of patriotism and pride.

That night, as the crowds lingered along the shores of the Hudson, chatting and laughing and eating ice cream, the biggest fireworks display in New York's history lit up the skies above them, rockets streaming up from Liberty Island, Ellis Island, and Governors Island. After the last burst of color had died away, the crowds turned toward the Statue of Liberty and sang "The Star-Spangled Banner," while overhead a helicopter towed a gigantic flag made from thousands of red, white, and blue lightbulbs. There were fireworks, too, along the Charles River in Boston, where 400,000 people crowded the Esplanade to hear the Boston Pops, with thousands more watching from sailboats on the river. As the orchestra reached the climax of Tchaikovsky's 1812 *Overture*, the church bells pealed, howitzers thundered, fireworks sent shards of color wheeling through the sky, and red, white, and blue geysers burst from a fireboat behind the Hatch Shell. On television, pictures showed girls applauding on their boyfriends' shoulders, fathers lifting their children in the air, a South Boston priest waving an enormous American flag. "In a day marked by crescendos," Walter Cronkite told a nationwide audience, "this is perhaps the high point."[2]

The bicentennial celebrations spoke of a zest for life and a sense of fun too often overlooked in all the gloom about inflation and energy crises. With official programs approved in more than twelve thousand communities, there was barely a street untouched by the birthday spirit. And despite the flood of commercial kitsch—the red, white, and blue bicentennial toilet seat, the bicentennial coffins and grave markers, the patriotic fifteen-hundred-gallon septic tanks, or even the $150 red, white, and blue dentures sold by a Miami firm promising to "set dentistry back two hundred years"—it was hard to find anyone with a bad word for what *The Washington Post* called "the birthday party of the century," a moment "of deep and moving reconciliation." "It was better, glory be, than anyone expected," agreed the *Chicago Tribune*, calling it "a great, spontaneous, do-it-ourselves celebration of neighbors, communities, churches, fellow countrymen" that made it possible "to feel a historic sense of good, of right, of mission about our country again."[3]

For one man in particular, the bicentennial was a moment he would never forget. As he left Monticello after an emotional naturalization ceremony on July 5, Gerald Ford asked his helicopter to circle Mount Vernon so that he could savor the mood. And as he looked down on the church where George Washington had prayed, he asked his companions: "Did you get the same feeling as I got this weekend? It was the feeling of people together." When the president went to bed that night, his mind's eye full of "seas of smiling faces with thousands of flags waving friendly greetings," he said to himself: "Well, Jerry, I guess we've healed America. We haven't done so badly, whatever the verdict in November."[4]

**From the very beginning,** Ford had struggled to win over the conservative movement. In an age when Eisenhower's "Modern Republicanism" seemed to be dying out—between 1969 and 1976, the number of progressive Republicans in the House of Representatives fell by two-thirds—many activists were deeply suspicious of a president who boasted of his "moderate Republican philosophy." A stiff, old-fashioned Midwesterner, an insider who had rarely ventured outside the confines of the House and was uncomfortable talking about his religious faith, Ford seemed the wrong man to lead a party swelled by Texas oilmen, Orange County housewives, and Bible Belt preachers. He had "consistently favored a policy of compromise with the premises of the liberal establishment," claimed *Conservative Digest*, especially "big government, big business and big labor." Absurdly, the director of the Hoover Institution even called him a "leftist." And by June 1975, 91 percent of *Conservative Digest* readers thought the Republicans should nominate somebody else to fight the election.[5]

Unfortunately for Ford, conservative activists were even less impressed with those closest to him. While millions of Americans had warmed to his outspoken wife, Betty, especially after her public battle with breast cancer, many conservatives were horrified by her uninhibited views on abortion, sex, and the Equal Rights Amendment. Describing herself as a "liberated woman," Betty appeared at pro-ERA rallies and fund-raisers, called wavering legislators, and cheerfully admitted to badgering her own husband, whom she jokingly called a "male chauvinist." Letters to the White House ran three to one against her, conservative protesters waved placards reading, "Betty Ford Get Off the Phone!" and critics claimed that she was using "taxpayers' dollars" to wage an "anti-family" campaign. But the criticism only egged Betty on to even greater disclosures. Interviewed on 60 *Minutes* in August 1975, she remarked that if her teenage daughter had an affair, she would not be surprised. "I think there's a complete freedom among the young people now," she mused. It was likely, she thought, that "all" her children had "tried marijuana." If it had been around when she was young, she added, she probably would have tried it herself.[6]

Watching that evening, Gerald Ford exclaimed, "You just lost me ten million votes!" and stormed out of the room. Next day the papers were full of the news that the First Lady had endorsed premarital sex and taking drugs. The rock star Grace Slick expressed her delight that Betty Ford was "gonna start steppin' out on the old man. Smoke a little dope. Have some parties." By October, Betty had received more than twenty-three thousand letters of complaint. "You are, because of the position your husband has assumed, expected and officially required to be PERFECT!" one correspondent told her. And in New Hampshire's *Manchester Union Leader*, the conservative publisher William Loeb printed a scorching page-one editorial calling her "a disgrace to the White House." Ford, he said, had shown his "lack of guts" by failing to control his wife: "What kind of husband is that? As President of the United States, he should be the moral leader of the nation. He is not in the position of an ordinary husband making the best of his wife's foolish and stupid remarks."[7]

While conservatives were appalled by the First Lady's apparent permissiveness, they reserved their greatest anger for Vice President Nelson Rockefeller, the billionaire and former governor of New York. At sixty-seven, the gregarious Rockefeller had more charisma than most men half his age, as well as a lot more money. Unfortunately for Ford, he was also intensely unpopular with grassroots conservatives, who had never forgiven him for his liberal social views, for leaving his wife for a divorced mother of young children, or for his biting criticisms of their beloved Barry Goldwater.

Merely by picking Rockefeller, Ford had proved that he could not be trusted. And even though Ford kicked him off the ticket in the Halloween Massacre, he won no credit from the conservatives, for whom it merely confirmed his lily-livered weakness. In later years, with typically disarming frankness, Ford admitted that it was "the biggest political mistake of my life," as well as "one of the few cowardly things I did." The irony, though, was that it was a waste of time. For by that stage, many conservatives were already looking to Sacramento—and to Reagan.[8]

**It is often** said of Ronald Reagan that, to borrow Winston Churchill's famous description of Russia, he was "a riddle, wrapped in a mystery, inside an enigma." Never afraid to show emotion in public, often kind to strangers and subordinates, he was also a distant father who barely noticed as his children grew apart from him. He had a brilliant memory for anecdotes, but he struggled to recall the most basic details of his own policies. He denounced appeasement abroad, but he shied away from personal confrontation. He was fascinated by stories about the Second Coming, but he had no time for conventional religion. He was a strict moral conservative, but he married twice at a time when divorce was still taboo, told dirty jokes, and never apologized for his Hollywood carousing. He denounced government spending, but he ran up the biggest deficit in the nation's history. He sometimes seemed like the biggest idiot in the country, but the next moment he was capable of devastating, moving eloquence.[9]

Reagan's extraordinary success was largely a matter not of luck but of skill and hard work. Like many modern presidents, he came from a rural small town—Tampico, Illinois—and had a difficult upbringing. But while another man might have honed a moving sob story about an alcoholic father and a saintly mother, Reagan turned his boyhood into a sepia-tinted all-American idyll, a past to match his apparently unquenchable optimism. Facing up to the ugly misfortunes of life was never part of his makeup. In high school, he wrote a revealing motto to accompany his yearbook entry: "Life is just one grand sweet song, so start the music."[10]

And yet like many children of alcoholics, he was wary of getting too close to anyone. Lyn Nofziger, his friend and press secretary, thought "there was a kind of veil between him and the rest of the world." His son Michael, whom Reagan notoriously failed to recognize at his graduation ceremony, commented that he was often "completely oblivious to others," while his daughter Patti "never knew who he was." Even Nancy wrote that he was "remote, and he doesn't let anybody get too close . . . There are times when even I feel that barrier."[11]

In a sense, Reagan was performing even as a child, constructing a world of make-believe to cope with his father's alcoholism, before becoming a successful Iowa sports announcer and then a solid Hollywood leading man. In later years, critics dismissed him as a mere "actor," as though only a complete fool could get on in Hollywood. But his film career gave him a superb political training, as well as instant name recognition and an indefinable star quality. As a film star, he became used to learning speeches, performing for the cameras, and being the front man for a backstage crew, as well as being recognized and meeting the public. Garry Wills once observed that Reagan was always playing himself, but the same is true of almost all public figures. "An actor knows two important things—to be honest in what he's doing and to be in touch with the audience," Reagan once said. "That's not bad advice for a politician either."[12]

Reagan grew up an enthusiastic Democrat, and even in later life he freely confessed his admiration for Franklin D. Roosevelt. When historians interviewed the nation's surviving presidents for the FDR centenary in 1982, Reagan was by far the most animated, telling anecdotes long after the meeting should have ended. He later described himself as a "New Dealer to the core" and remained a loyal Democrat even after he had become a committed anti-Communist as head of the Screen Actors Guild. In 1948 he campaigned for Harry Truman, sitting on the platform with the president when he visited Los Angeles. He recorded radio spots for the labor unions and even lent his voice to commercials supporting Hubert Humphrey's first Senate campaign in Minnesota. And two years later, he voted for Helen Gahagan Douglas, the "Pink Lady," in her losing Senate contest with Richard Nixon.[13]

Some of Reagan's biographers argue that it was his experience as president of the Screen Actors Guild that pushed him to the right. It certainly gave him a deep abhorrence of Communism. But Reagan was pretty consistent throughout his life: always a patriotic populist, always suspicious of the "establishment," always someone who saw himself as reflecting the commonsense values of the ordinary man. Still, he was never a man of extremes. Even as an anti-Communist, he was relatively restrained and criticized "witch-hunters" who whipped up public hysteria. When he switched to the Republicans in 1952, it was no damascene conversion. To Reagan, voting for General Eisenhower was simply the sensible, patriotic thing to do.[14]

During the early 1950s, Reagan found a new role as a corporate spokesman for General Electric. Not only did GE's free-market ethos reinforce his populist conservatism, but his seemingly endless speaking tours— he visited every plant in the country, spoke to every single one of the company's 250,000 employees, and sometimes gave fourteen speeches a day—were terrific training for a future presidential candidate. All the time he was honing "the Speech," a heady blend of traditional morality, free-market economics, and patriotic anti-Communism, a formula he produced at almost every public appearance for the rest of his career. And when he was asked to speak for Barry Goldwater in October 1964, what he delivered was basically an emotive version of the Speech, ending with a climax inspired by his two heroes, Abraham Lincoln and Franklin Roosevelt: "You and I have a rendezvous with destiny. We will preserve for our children this, the last best hope of man on earth, or we will sentence them to take the first step into a thousand years of darkness." It was an overnight success, "the most successful national political debut," according to David Broder and Stephen Hess, "since William Jennings Bryan electrified the 1896 Democratic convention with the 'Cross of Gold' speech."[15]

Reagan's speech for Goldwater brought him into the orbit of a group of rich California businessmen—Henry Salvatori, Holmes Tuttle, Ed Mills—most of whom had grown up poor, moved to the Golden State, and saw success as proof of the virtues of free enterprise. They abhorred liberalism, socialism, and Communism, worried that the nation was slipping into decadent collectivism, and saw themselves as plucky insurgents taking on the entrenched elites. In many ways they were similar to thousands of suburban Southern California activists who had stuffed envelopes for Barry Goldwater. But they had deeper pockets, and when they asked Reagan to run for governor in 1966, he listened.[16]

As a mere "actor," Reagan was hugely underestimated. Even the Democratic incumbent, Pat Brown, never took him seriously until it was far too late. He was written off as an empty-headed buffoon with unacceptable far-right instincts: *The New Republic* called him "anti-labor, anti-Negro, anti-intellectual, anti-planning, anti-20th century." But he was always much more pragmatic than his opponents realized, a measured populist rather than merely George Wallace with a smiling face. Although hardly the intellectual giant of conservative hagiography, he loved to read conservative periodicals, wrote long letters to correspondents, drafted many of his own speeches, and wrote his own radio scripts. Crucially, he presented himself as an ordinary man of the people, a citizen-politician tapping a rich vein of California populism. "I am not a politician," he said. "I am an ordinary citizen with a deep-seated belief that much of what troubles us has been brought about by politicians; and it's high time that more ordinary citizens brought the fresh air of common-sense thinking to bear on these problems."[17]

As early as May 1967, James Q. Wilson wrote the prophetic "Guide to Reagan Country," suggesting that Reagan's blend of libertarian and moralistic conservatism "will be with us for a long time under one guise or another." Even Wilson, though, could hardly have guessed that Reagan would be making almost exactly the same speeches two decades later. Critics saw this as a sign of simplistic inflexibility. But one of Reagan's favorite devices was to question the liberal belief that "there are no simple answers." "The truth is," he would say, "there *are* simple answers; there are just not easy ones." He genuinely believed that patriotism, positive thinking, and the pursuit of wealth could solve any problems, and he sold a vision of a "city on a hill" built on the timeless foundations of American exceptionalism. It was a shallow vision, perhaps; but it was also an extremely powerful one.[18]

The one thing for which Hollywood had not prepared Reagan was how to run anything; there was a serious point in his joke that he had "never played a governor." But once he had settled in, he proved a surprisingly disciplined and efficient executive. Like Roosevelt, he was secure enough to surround himself with aides who knew more than he did, and happily delegated as much as possible to the experts, a striking contrast with insecure micromanagers like Nixon and Carter. Even Garry Wills, one of his most incisive critics, notes that Reagan's team was "extraordinarily efficient" and that he governed "competently, popularly, routinely."[19]

What was really striking about Reagan's governorship, though, was its moderation. For all his attacks on government insiders, compromise came as easily to him as it did to any Capitol Hill veteran. Inheriting a budget deficit, he signed the biggest tax increase in the history of any state. He increased spending on state universities and student grants; he approved stricter regulations for home insurance, real estate, retailing, doctors, dentists, and auto repairs; he signed the nation's toughest water pollution controls; he agreed to a welfare deal that gave higher payments to eight out of ten recipients; he blocked the Dos Rios dam and trans-Sierra highway projects, saving vast tracts of wilderness from development. Most remarkably, he signed the nation's most progressive abortion law, permitting more legal abortions than in any other state before *Roe v. Wade*, a fact that most conservatives liked to forget. He might not have been one of the nation's greatest governors, but all in all he was a pretty good one. "Reagan had committed the very sin he inveighed against," writes Garry Wills—"government."[20]

**Since Reagan had** already toyed with a presidential bid in 1968, he was always likely to run eight years later. Even before Nixon resigned, Reagan's inner circle had made contact with one of the best consultants in the business, a thirty-four-year-old lawyer and former Nixon aide named John Sears. Imperturbable, calculating, ruthlessly ambitious, Sears thought Reagan a "great piece of horseflesh," provided he was "properly trained." By the late spring of 1974, Sears was quietly planning a nationwide primary campaign. Meanwhile, Reagan himself kept active, giving ten speeches a month, writing a column that appeared in 174 newspapers, and delivering talks on more than two hundred radio stations, cementing his reputation as the conscience of the conservative grass roots.[21]

The only question was whether he should run as a Republican. Some conservatives, such as *National Review*'s publisher, William Rusher, argued that he should break with the Republican Party altogether, citing poll findings that one in four voters would consider backing a new right-wing party. At a conservative conference in February 1975, some Republican officeholders, such as North Carolina's Jesse Helms, encouraged activists to build a new party. Reagan was certainly tempted, but he was a realist—not least because his California backers were not prepared to finance a third party. What he would stand for, he said, was "a new and revitalized second party, raising a banner of no pale pastels but bold colors which make it unmistakably clear where we stand on all the issues troubling the people."[22]

That Reagan would be carrying a banner of bold colors was evident from his campaign launch on November 19, 1975. He attacked government under Ford as "more intrusive, more coercive, more meddlesome and less effective," charged that the United States was "in danger of being surpassed" by the Soviet Union, and argued that "the root of these problems lies right here in Washington, D.C." And at every stop that fall, he hammered away on the same populist themes. Sometimes he borrowed from George Wallace's joke book, telling the story of the pencil pusher at the Bureau of Indian Affairs who burst into tears after his Indian died, or quipping that the only busing plan he liked involved "busing the Federal bureaucrats out into the countryside where they can meet the people." Sometimes he spoke of moral issues, promising a "spiritual revival" that would banish abortion, sexual decadence, and drug abuse.[23]

But his abiding theme was government itself. "Government is the problem," he told a meeting in Illinois, relating his favorite story of the Chicago welfare queen with "eighty names, thirty addresses, and twelve Social Security cards, [who] is collecting veterans' benefits on four nonexistent deceased husbands." Actually, the woman, whose name was Linda Taylor, had used two aliases, not eighty, and amassed $8,000, not $150,000 as Reagan claimed. As always with Reagan, though, the facts were not really the point. What mattered was that his audience loved it.[24]

To the press corps, Reagan appeared an outlandish, reactionary figure. "Here comes Barry Goldwater again," said the *Chicago Daily News*, calling his positions "cunningly phrased nonsense, irrationally conceived and hair-raising in their potential mischief." For *Time*, he was "another Barry

Goldwater calling on the party to mount a hopeless crusade against the twentieth century." For *The New Republic*'s veteran commentator John Osborne, he was "still the posturing, essentially mindless and totally unconvincing candy man" that he had been since the 1960s. "That he should be regarded as a serious candidate for President," agreed *Harper's*, "is a shame and an embarrassment for the country."[25]

If Reagan was to compete seriously with Ford, he needed to banish the Goldwater comparisons. But with one speech in Chicago in September 1975, he appeared to confirm them, making the reckless promise that he would slash federal spending by a gigantic $90 billion, balance the budget, and cut the average income tax burden by 23 percent. The critics pounced: when Reagan next appeared on *Issues and Answers*, all the questions were about his $90 billion plan, and whether, say, New Hampshire would have to raise taxes to cover its welfare costs. It was the worst possible start, exposing his inexperience as a national campaigner, his propensity to shoot himself in the foot, and the problem of his extremist image. "The American people don't want elderly people thrown out in the snow," Ford's campaign chief said with mock sorrow a few days later. And "they are not going to put up with a program that cuts back on Social Security."[26]

Ford, meanwhile, was looking forward to his first election outside Michigan. On the advice of his troika of advisers—his chief of staff, Dick Cheney, the pollster Robert Teeter, and the campaign strategist Stuart Spencer—he had agreed to play on the prestige of his office. "The best strategy for the President," Spencer told Elizabeth Drew, "is to be President." At a lunchtime meeting in a Concord high school, she watched him arrive surrounded by all the panoply of power: an American flag, the presidential flag, rows of officials, a gaggle of Secret Service men. Volunteers handed out leaflets showing him looking stern and presidential, while, from the platform, Ford reeled off the benefits that New Hampshire could expect under his new revenue-sharing scheme. "He is the President," Drew wrote, "bringing them their boodle."[27]

As Election Day approached, the Republican rivals pumped hands, kissed babies, and slapped backs, framed against the quadrennial backdrop of mountains and smokestacks, mill towns and farms, churches and bowling alleys, shivering under a blanket of snow. Despite his $90 billion gaffe, Reagan's team was confident of victory. After making more than two hundred appearances in the state, he had "outorganized and outdazzled Ford," reported *Time*, and with two weeks to go, his pollster Richard Wirthlin had him eleven points ahead. With six days to go, he was still

four points ahead. Now even *The New Republic* predicted that the challenger would win. Reagan himself certainly believed it; so did the state's
governor, who told the press that he would win by 5 percent.[28]

But Wirthlin was not so sure. The undecided voters, he feared, would
probably break for Ford, so it was imperative that Reagan not leave the
Granite State until after polling day. But John Sears, flushed with overconfidence, arranged for Reagan to spend some time in Illinois before
New Hampshire had even voted. Only as they flew on to New Hampshire
on election eve did Wirthlin tell Reagan that the race was now too close
to call. Reagan listened in silence. As the plane made its final descent, he
stared down at the lights twinkling in the night. "I hope someone down
there lights a candle for me," he said softly.[29]

The next morning, Reagan woke with a winning feeling, and as his
team gathered at Concord's Highway Hotel, the first returns seemed to
prove him right. In the ballroom, his volunteers were already giddy with
excitement; upstairs, a grinning Reagan posed with an early newspaper
edition showing him in the lead. But then the votes started to pour in from
small towns, and his lead narrowed. At eleven thirty the polls were too
close to call. At midnight, Reagan led by only fifteen hundred votes, and
as the candidate came down to thank his supporters, he already looked
"craggy and beaten, his smile pasted on like a felt-board cutout." Half an
hour later, Sears told a friend that "things are closing." At 12:49, Ford took
a five-vote lead. In Reagan's suite, two champagne bottles sat forlornly
next to his little green radio, the ice around them long since melted. No
one moved to uncork them.[30]

**As dawn was breaking** over the mountains of New Hampshire, John
Sears and Richard Wirthlin sat weary and red eyed amid the wreckage of
their campaign. They had lost by the tightest of margins, just 1,317 votes
out of more than 108,000, but even the narrowest defeat was still a defeat.
"We've got to go after Ford on foreign policy," Sears said bluntly. Wirthlin
agreed, not because he thought that voters cared about foreign policy, but
because he was desperate to get away from the $90 billion gaffe. A few
hours later, Sears went to see Reagan. "We didn't quite make it last night,"
he said. "We're going to have to start talking about foreign policy." Reagan
nodded. Then his face lightened. "How come you guys look so bad?" he
asked.[31]

The next primary, in Florida, did not go well for Reagan. Ford descended on the Sunshine State like Santa Claus on Christmas Day, bring-

ing a $33 million missile contract for an Orlando factory, an $18 million mass-transit project in Miami, a pledge to naturalize Cuban immigrants, and a Congressional Medal of Honor for a former POW from Eglin Air Force Base. There was the news that Orlando would host the 1978 International Chamber of Commerce convention; there was talk of a new veterans' hospital in Bay Pines; and of course there were Oval Office interviews for all the local journalists. "When you've got it," exclaimed one of his aides, "use it!" And it did the trick. On March 9, Ford beat Reagan by 6 percent, his second straight victory. Some party officials now said Reagan should pull out in the interests of unity. Even the challenger himself was reported—wrongly—to be losing enthusiasm.[32]

And yet in defeat, Reagan had at last found a line that worked. Five days before the primary, at a press conference in Orlando, he ripped into the administration's foreign policy, which had failed to "halt and reverse the diplomatic and military decline of the United States." Under Ford and Kissinger, the nation had become "number two in the world," for "Henry Kissinger's stewardship of United States foreign policy has coincided precisely with the loss of United States military superiority." And all Reagan could see when he opened the newspaper was "what other nations the world over see: collapse of the American will and retreat of American power."[33]

Reagan also pointed to a concrete case of what, to many conservatives, looked like appeasement: Ford's plan to hand over the Panama Canal to the local strongman General Omar Torrijos. "When it comes to the canal," Reagan said, "we built it, we paid for it, it's ours, and we should tell Torrijos and company that we are going to keep it!" At first this line got only a tepid response, but when Reagan used it a few days later at the Sun City retirement community, the reaction was pandemonium. Most of his listeners had probably never thought about the canal until he brought it up. But the issue became a metaphor for the nation's retreat in the wake of Vietnam. "The Panama Canal issue had nothing to do with the canal," his aide David Keene explained. "It said more about the American people's feelings about where the country was, and what it was powerless to do, and their frustration about the incomprehensibility of foreign policy over the last couple of decades."[34]

His campaign short of funds, his volunteers demoralized, his campaign manager contemplating withdrawal, and even his wife urging him to pull out, Reagan now took the Panama Canal message to the voters of North Carolina. With only a few days left in a state with strong military ties, he slashed into Ford and Kissinger at every stop. Radio spots funded by the American Conservative Union promised that he "would fire Henry Kissinger . . . would not cave in to Castro, and says American sovereignty in Panama must be maintained." All the same, defeat seemed inevitable. "Reagan Virtually Concedes Defeat in North Carolina," read a headline in *The New York Times* the day before the primary. Even Lou Cannon, the California reporter who knew Reagan best, asked when he intended to quit. "You too, Lou?" Reagan asked, his lips tightening with anger.[35]

Reagan was in La Crosse, Wisconsin, speaking to a sportsmen's group, when ABC's Frank Reynolds approached two aides and asked if they had heard the news from North Carolina. No, they said miserably. "Well I have," Reynolds said, grinning, "and your man is winning." By the time Reagan flew home to Los Angeles, they had uncorked the champagne at last. He had won North Carolina by six points. It was a turning point not merely in the campaign but in modern American history. If Reagan had lost in North Carolina, or if he had thrown in the towel, then his challenge for the presidency would have been over, and his cause would have been condemned as mere extremism. After a string of embarrassing defeats, he would have been very poorly placed to run four years later. There would have been no Reagan presidency, and perhaps no Reagan revolution either.[36]

North Carolina changed everything. Elizabeth Drew wrote that Reagan even looked younger, with rosy cheeks and a spring in his step. With more than a month until Texas voted on May 1, he now enjoyed his first real momentum, and his team paid for a full half-hour slot at prime time on NBC. President Ford, Reagan told viewers, had been "part of the Washington establishment" for most of his adult life. Under his leadership the United States was viewed across the world as "weak and unsure," which was why Ford had "traveled halfway around the world to sign the Helsinki Pact, putting our stamp of approval on Russia's enslavement of the captive nations." Reagan had been saying this kind of thing for a long time. But this was his first chance to reach a national audience, and it brought in $1.5 million overnight.[37]

Suddenly Texas, where Ford's strategists had hoped to deliver the knockout blow, had turned into Reagan country. In a state of near panic, Ford's men reported that the challenger's every appearance was greeted by raucous crowds, whipped up by "extreme right-wing political groups" like the National Conservative PAC, the Heritage Foundation, and Right to Life, "operating almost invisibly through direct mail." Reagan's supporters were "unknown," they complained, and had "not been involved in the Republican political system before." With George Wallace out of the Democratic race, his voters were flocking to Reagan: *The Wash-*

*ington Post* observed that one crowd "seemed much more like a typical Wallace rally—women in housedresses, sport-shirted men, lots of small American flags." As though punch-drunk, Ford's aides seemed at a loss how to respond. "We are in real danger," their report concluded, "of being out-organized by a small number of highly motivated right-wing nuts."[38]

The first of May, when workers worldwide traditionally march to celebrate the achievements of socialism, was a day to remember for Ronald Reagan. He not only beat the president in Texas; he won every congressional district in the state, picking up all 96 delegates. Stunned by the impact of 100,000 Democrats crossing over to vote for Reagan, Ford's men did not know what hit them. Days later, Reagan took three more states, picking up all of Georgia's 85 delegates, all 37 from Alabama, and 45 of Indiana's 54 delegates. As if from nowhere, he was suddenly out front: the *Washington Star* estimated that he had 381 delegates to Ford's 372. "We're in a state of shock," one of Ford's aides told *The New Republic.*[39]

Following the next few weeks of the campaign was like watching a prize fight between two evenly matched boxers, each round more grueling than the last, each fighter landing heavy punches, but neither able to deliver the killer blow. Ford kept his campaign alive by winning his home state of Michigan, but by the end of May Reagan had picked up Arkansas, Idaho, and Nevada. And although Ford responded with excruciatingly narrow victories in Oregon, Tennessee, and Kentucky, the race was still too close to call. Even the supposed showdown on June 8 failed to produce a winner, for while Reagan took California's 167 delegates by a massive margin, Ford picked up almost all the delegates in Ohio and New Jersey. That left the president about 170 delegates short of the nomination, with Reagan 100 behind. "They're So Close," read *Time*'s headline. The most exciting primary season in Republican history was over, but the identity of the winner was still anybody's guess.[40]

**In August 1976,** Kansas City welcomed the Republican National Convention with a display of patriotic razzmatazz that would have excited even the most jaded delegate. Thirty thousand delegates, reporters, and sightseers were expected in town; every street was decked out in red, white, and blue, every hotel was booked solid, every steak house and bar crowded with delegates. Even Ray's Playpen, Kansas City's leading sex shop, had redecorated its windows with an elephant and a donkey. Sadly, however, plans to float a fifty-foot-long inflatable elephant over the arena had to be abandoned when it failed to get off the ground.[41]

As usual, wrote the reporter Jules Witcover, the mood was "as if a strict parochial school has decided to hold its annual picnic in Las Vegas." "Who Says Republicans Don't Have Fun?" the badges defiantly read. But it was "country-club fun, Kiwanis fun; well-heeled and antiseptic, heavy on the posh cocktail party and the cold shrimp." The delegates were a mixture of Wall Street and Yale, Miami Beach and Ole Miss, the men bursting out of their sleek suits, the women apparently fresh from the beauty parlor. Yet there was also a sense of simmering emotion, of ardent feeling held in check. For all their conservatism, Republicans were deeply passionate people. And now they had a genuine decision to make.[42]

In the weeks before the convention, both candidates had done their best to woo the delegates still up for grabs, their scalp hunters using every trick in the book to beg, threaten, cajole, and implore. What none of them knew, however, was exactly how many scalps they had. *The New York Times* had Ford just thirty-nine delegates ahead; *The Washington Post* put his lead at sixty-one. If Reagan had made a better start, things might have been different. But even in the middle of July, there was a faint pessimism among the Californians that they could not compete with Ford's delegate-hunting machine. "Reagan's Camp: Air of Resignation," read one *Post* headline, as Lou Cannon called the governor "a supposedly defeated candidate who was going back to his ranch content, believing that he had done his best even if that best proved to be not quite enough for victory."[43]

It was this growing sense of inevitability that lay behind one of the most astonishing gambles of Reagan's career. Asked about possible running mates during the primaries, he had specifically ruled out "someone with an opposite philosophy." But as July crept on, John Sears concluded that only something extraordinary could prolong the voting to a second ballot. In collaboration with Reagan's campaign chairman, Paul Laxalt, he persuaded Reagan to announce the selection of Senator Richard Schweiker of Pennsylvania, a Navy veteran, a staunch anti-Communist, and a devout Christian, but also a good friend to organized labor, a critic of the Vietnam War, and a co-sponsor of the Democrats' Humphrey-Hawkins full employment bill. The AFL-CIO had given him the Senate's only 100 percent rating in 1975, while the liberal Americans for Democratic Action (ADA) had given him an 89 percent rating, the same as George McGovern. Indeed, McGovern quipped that if Schweiker failed to make it to the White House, he would recommend him as the next president of the ADA.[44]

On Monday, July 26, Gerald Ford was working on some papers in the Oval Office when Dick Cheney appeared in the doorway, grinning from ear to ear. "We've just got the best news we've had in months," Cheney said. Reagan had just announced Schweiker's selection, and most conservatives had reacted as though he had named Jane Fonda as his top tip for the Pentagon. It was "the dumbest thing I ever heard," said Congressman John Ashbrook of Ohio, who told one of Reagan's aides that the governor could "go plumb fuck himself." It was a "sad day in American history," said New Hampshire's governor, Mel Thomson, "when a public leader of Reagan's stature would abandon all that he stood for." The New Right activist Richard Viguerie told reporters that the Reagan ticket was a "coalition built on expediency and hypocrisy"; another pillar of the New Right, Howard Phillips, said that Reagan had "betrayed the trust of those who look to him for leadership."[45]

Sears had always seen Schweiker's selection as a gamble, but since he thought Reagan was going to lose, he saw it as a gamble worth taking. Indeed, more informed observers recognized that it at least kept the race alive until Kansas City. There, amid the claustrophobic pressure of the campaign trailers, Sears came up with one last gambit, trying to make Ford name his own running mate before the roll call. It was not a bad idea: Ford's choice was bound to alienate someone, and it might just make a difference. But it never came off. After ten months on the road, millions of dollars, thousands of speeches, and every last drop of effort, Reagan simply did not have the votes. On Tuesday, August 17, in an atmosphere of suffocating tension and thick cigarette smoke, the delegates voted on the rule change, and Ford won by 111 votes. Everyone knew now that Reagan was finished.

On Wednesday night Reagan's supporters mounted a raucous, desperate demonstration, a forty-five-minute surge of pride in their beaten candidate. It was "the emotion of people with something in their hearts," wrote Elizabeth Drew: people who believed not merely in a man but in a cause, people who had never been to a Republican convention before, people from towns and suburbs across the South and the West. As the band played "California, Here I Come," they waved placards that read, "Send Ford to Helsinki, Send Reagan to Washington," defying attempts to keep them quiet. But at last their passions died down, and the roll call began. It was midnight, well past television's prime time. But Ford did not care when, at long last, West Virginia gave him 20 of its 28 votes and put him over the top. As his advisers slapped him on the back, the screen showed the final tally: 1,187 to Ford, 1,070 to Reagan.[46]

At one thirty that morning, Ford paid a courtesy call to Reagan's suite, where they talked alone for half an hour. Ford asked Reagan to help him during the fall campaign, and added that he had six names for a new running mate. His personal favorite was William Ruckelshaus, formerly head of the Environmental Protection Agency, acting director of the FBI, and deputy attorney general, from which post he had famously resigned during the Saturday Night Massacre. But Reagan preferred Bob Dole, the acerbic World War II veteran from Kansas who would appeal to voters in the farm states and whose slashing wit might work well on the campaign trail. Ford made no promises and continued to discuss the issue with his aides until it was almost dawn. But in the end he went for Dole, calling the senator the next morning with the good news.[47]

To many commentators, Ford had been humiliated; for Garry Wills, he had "crawled through to the nomination on his knees." The Republican platform, with its promises of "less government, less spending, less inflation," was pure Reagan. Its "Morality in Foreign Policy" plank even saluted "that great beacon of human courage and morality, Alexander Solzhenitsyn," and repudiated agreements "such as the one signed in Helsinki," so it was probably just as well that Ford's advisers had banned Henry Kissinger from attending until the last night. The few remaining liberal Republicans were appalled. Charles Mathias, senator from Maryland, thought that the party had "lost its bearings," while Congressman John Anderson of Illinois said simply: "We have to stop appeasing the ultra-conservatives. We'll never convince them. They'll always say we weren't conservative enough."[48]

Four years later Anderson would take his discontent to the people, but now nobody was listening. In 1964, Barry Goldwater's insurgency had been dismissed as an emotional aberration. But twelve years on, Goldwater's heir had proved that the future lay with the conservative grass roots of the South and the West. True, Reagan had lost. But in an age of retreat abroad, austerity at home, and doom and decadence in the headlines, his patriotic populism had never looked more appealing. Whether he would be around in four years' time was anyone's guess; most observers suspected he would be too old. But nobody doubted that the future of the Republican Party belonged to the men and women who had supported him.

**The morning after his defeat,** Ronald Reagan bade farewell to his staff in the ballroom of the Alameda Plaza. The room was packed, and the air crackled with sadness as Reagan reassured his distraught young supporters that "the cause goes on." "Don't get cynical," he said hoarsely, his voice almost breaking as his listeners began to weep, "because, look at what you were willing to do and recognize that there are millions and millions of Americans out there who want what you want, that want it to be that way, that want it to be a shining city on a hill." It was a familiar line, but he had never delivered it with such feeling. At his side, Nancy turned her back on the cameras to hide her tears. Then Reagan himself turned aside, his eyes glistening, and abruptly walked away.[49]

Thursday evening, though, belonged to Gerald Ford. A biographical film showed him taking the oath of office after Nixon's departure, then cut to shots of the lonely man in the Oval Office, making crucial decisions of state. Over photographs of the young man from Michigan, the narrator explained that Ford had won an Eagle Scout badge, that he had been captain of his high-school football team, that he had always been a team player and a leader, a man of decency and character. Then the picture faded, the band struck up the Michigan fight song, and the president walked onto the stage, smiling and waving in his trademark dark blue suit.

Ford was no great orator, but his address that night was steeped in the simple patriotism with which most Americans associated him. He began with a kind word for his defeated rival: "Let me say this from the bottom of my heart: after the scrimmages of the past few months, it really feels good to have Ron Reagan on the same side of the line." He reserved his fire for the "vote-hungry, free-spending" Democratic Congress, which had refused to follow his advice on crime, drugs, busing, and tax cuts. "I am against the big tax spender," he said, "and for the little taxpayer." He was behind in the polls, he admitted. But "the only polls that count are the polls the American people go to on November 2. And right now, I predict that the American people are going to say that night, 'Jerry, you have done a good job, keep right on doing it.' "[50]

It was Ford's most forceful speech since the day he succeeded Nixon, and his audience responded with full-throated cheers. But as he acknowledged the applause, Rockefeller and Dole by his side, there was one surprise left.* As they waved at the sea of blue Ford/Dole signs, Ford turned toward the south end of the arena, where Ronald and Nancy Reagan were watching in their skybox, and ostentatiously beckoned them down. "Every eye in the arena turned up to Reagan," recalled one of his aides, "and some delegates began to rise from their chairs." Then everybody was

---

*With nothing to lose, Rockefeller had enjoyed an unusual convention. A few days earlier, he had started a fight with members of the North Carolina delegation when he wrestled away their Reagan banner. And during Ford's speech he had to be restrained from attacking Dick Cheney, who had planned for him to walk out onstage *after* Bob Dole. Sensibly, Cheney conceded the point.

standing, and the pressure was irresistible. Caught unawares, Reagan got up, and the delegates roared. He ran a hand through his hair—nerves, perhaps, or an actor's final touch before going onstage—and headed for the door. In the box, one of his advisers murmured: "Ford has just given the future of the party to Reagan."

By the time Reagan reached the platform, it seemed that every man and woman in the hall was standing, their balloons bobbing in the air, the applause deafening. As he and Nancy walked out under the lights to shake hands with a beaming Gerald Ford, the noise broke like a great wave over the stage and then subsided to nothing as the governor began to speak. He opened with a touch of chivalry, thanking the delegates for their warmth toward his wife and assuring Ford that his "kindness and generosity in honoring us by bringing us down here will give us a memory that will live in our hearts forever."

And then came the lines that no listener would ever forget. "I had an assignment the other day," Reagan said. He had been invited to write a letter for a tricentennial time capsule, to be opened in 2076: "And I said I could do so, riding down the coast in an automobile, looking at the blue Pacific out on one side and the Santa Ynez Mountains on the other, and I couldn't help but wonder if it was going to be that beautiful a hundred years from now as it was on that summer day."

He had thought hard about what to write, and one thing in particular struck him: that the great powers had "aimed at each other horrible missiles of destruction, nuclear weapons that can in a matter of minutes arrive in each other's country and destroy virtually the civilized world we live in.

> And suddenly it dawned on me: those who would read this letter a hundred years from now will know whether those missiles were fired. They will know whether we met our challenge.
>
> Whether they have the freedoms that we have known up until now will depend on what we do here. Will they look back with appreciation and say, "Thank God for those people in 1976 who headed off that loss of freedom, who kept us now a hundred years later free, who kept our world from nuclear destruction"?
>
> And if we failed, they probably won't get to read the letter at all because it spoke of individual freedom, and they won't be allowed to talk of that or read of it.

"This is our challenge," Reagan said, the atmosphere still with emotion, the cameras panning across the tearful faces. "And this is why here in this hall tonight . . . we must go forth from here united, determined that what a great general said a few years ago is true. There is no substitute for victory, Mr. President."

And then he fell silent, and the crowd roared their appreciation and regret, and it was all over.[51]

# Chapter Eleven    The Jimmy and Jerry Show

Some people considered that silent stretch the intellectual high point of the campaign. For 27 minutes, neither man was misleading the nation.

—**GEORGE WILL**, speaking on NBC's *Viewpoint*, March 27, 1979

The motorcade left Plains before dawn, its lights piercing the September darkness, but it was already getting hot when Jimmy Carter's car turned down the bumpy track to Warm Springs, the little cottage where Franklin D. Roosevelt had taken the waters, dallied with his mistress, and learned the full extent of southern poverty. Even at this early hour the track was lined with thousands of supporters, many waving placards that said, "The Grin Will Win" or "Let's Send Mizz Lilly's Boy to Washington." Among them, waiting in the early morning sunshine, were FDR's sons James and Franklin junior, standing beside a small group of patients in wheelchairs, their presence a reminder of Roosevelt's struggle against disability and of his party's commitment to fight for the afflicted.

By launching his general election campaign in Warm Springs, rather than the traditional Democratic choice of Cadillac Square, Detroit, Carter was sending a signal not only that he was a Southerner but that he was Roosevelt's unlikely heir. "This year, as in 1932, our nation is divided," he told the crowd. "Our people are out of work and our leaders do not lead." His opponent was another Herbert Hoover, a "decent and well-intentioned man who sincerely believed that there was nothing our government could or should do to attack the terrible economic and social ills of our nation." But the most memorable line was classic Carter. "I owe the special interests nothing," he said grandly. "I owe the people everything." Then the crowd cheered, the band played "Happy Days Are Here Again," and it was on to the Southern 500 stock-car classic in Darlington, South Carolina.[1]

With less than two months to go and a 29 percent lead in the polls, Jimmy Carter could hardly have been in a better position. Yet there was always a pervasive sense that things were too good to be true. Over the summer, his pollster Pat Caddell had repeatedly warned that many voters saw him as "vague, two-faced, too political": even many of Carter's supporters agreed that he "always seems to be changing his positions on the issues." Above all, Caddell worried that his support was desperately soft. Among women, Catholics, and young voters, Carter held only a narrow lead. And when researchers carried out interviews, they would often find voters defecting before their very eyes, starting out as Carter supporters and gradually talking themselves out of it. "That's frightening," Caddell said later. "That is the classic example of a soft vote."[2]

Carter's general election campaign was run from Atlanta by the triumvirate of Jody Powell, Jerry Rafshoon, and Hamilton Jordan, whose battle plan identified New York, Pennsylvania, New Jersey, and Ohio as the key battlegrounds. Revealingly, Jordan's blueprint envisaged little help from major party figures such as Edward Kennedy, Hubert Humphrey, and Henry Jackson. Indeed, one reporter noted that as Carter crossed the country, "old-time Democratic politicians greet him more often than not like a naturalized Martian rather than as a fellow soldier." But this was hardly surprising, for Carter's antigovernment rhetoric sat oddly with his party's liberal commitments. As he denounced "Washington" and promised a balanced budget and more robust foreign policy, he sometimes sounded closer to Ronald Reagan than to Hubert Humphrey.[3]

Meanwhile, having already seen off one anti-Washington challenger, Gerald Ford was ready to take on another. He had always expected to face a more traditional Democrat, and disliked Carter as "an outsider with little more going for him than a winning smile." Unlike Carter, however, he had not had the luxury of weeks to prepare for the general election, and when Stuart Spencer and Dick Cheney finally sat down with him to discuss strategy, they began with some harsh facts. Ford was behind in the polls, his party was unpopular, and wherever he had personally campaigned in the primaries, he had actually lost ground. "Mr. President," Spencer said bluntly, "as a campaigner, you're no fucking good."[4]

With this in mind, Spencer and Cheney had devised a campaign that relied on two things: television and incumbency. They had set aside millions of dollars for a last-minute media blitz, and in the meantime they wanted Ford to remain a "working president" dealing with the nation's business. So when Carter was in Warm Springs, Ford stayed in the Oval Office. The next day, when Carter visited New York, Philadelphia, and Scranton, Ford signed a child day-care bill in the Rose Garden. And the day after that, when Carter went to Carbondale, Springfield, Peoria, Chicago, and Milwaukee, Ford gave a White House briefing on the death of Mao Tse-tung, signed an interstate sewage bill, and received the ambassador of Guinea. "We would go out in the Rose Garden and say nothing," Dick Cheney recalled with satisfaction, "just sign a bill, and we'd get the coverage."[5]

At the time, many commentators complained that neither candidate seemed interested in issues. That was not quite true: on the economy, for example, Ford talked about tackling inflation and cutting spending, while Carter talked about bringing unemployment down through job programs. But on other issues the candidates were remarkably similar, partly because they were competing for the votes of the same floating voters but also because both had moderate instincts. Both disapproved of court-ordered busing, both were personally opposed to abortion, both supported equality for women. Whatever else it was, the election was not a culture war.[6]

What this meant was that the campaign was all about character. Ford's pollster Bob Teeter told his advertising firm to emphasize "love of God," "love of country," and "love of family," and his television spots typically included gushing tributes from his children. This was a good way of competing for the Christian vote, since Mike Ford was training to be an evangelical pastor and talked glowingly of his "very devout" parents. Although Ford himself always looked stiff on television, even when strolling across the White House lawn with his dog, audience reaction was very favorable. The ads certainly worked a lot better than Carter's commercials, which featured him talking earnestly to the camera in a dark suit.[7]

Carter's difficulties did not end there. Cast in the unfamiliar role of the front-runner, he was suffering from deteriorating press relations. Even veteran journalists were shocked by his young aides' cocky style; the reporter Kandy Stroud, who covered the Carter campaign from start to finish, called them "irreligious, undisciplined, arrogant, disorganized, rowdy and nonideological." And most reporters still could not understand what made Carter himself tick. By the late summer they had started calling him "Weirdo" or "Crater," distorting his name to denote someone "a bit *off*, a bit *miswired*." When he boasted of reading *War and Peace* when he was twelve, they had to stifle their laughter. Above all, there was much talk of his "mean" streak. "Many people have begun to see a rather cold, mean-spirited side to him," recorded Elizabeth Drew, adding that Rosalynn was so humorless, her face seemed "molded, perhaps of metal." Even Hamilton Jordan warned his candidate not to make any more "personal attacks on Gerald Ford"—a sign of how far Carter had traveled since the days when he talked about peace and love.[8]

Two weeks after Labor Day, things were not going well for Carter. He still held a double-digit lead, but it was falling all the time. While Ford was strolling cheerfully around the Rose Garden with his dog, Carter was shaking hands at factory gates and looking increasingly tired, irritable, and shrill. And on Monday, September 20, he was making an old-fashioned whistle-stop journey through Pennsylvania when news broke that *Playboy* was about to run a sensational new interview. According to the story, Carter had not only used the words "screw" and "shack up" to describe sexual relations but also admitted to committing adultery in his imagination. "What in hell is going on?" demanded one of his aides. "Has this whole thing gone mad?"[9]

That Carter had given an interview to *Playboy* was not especially disturbing: in recent months, it had run interviews with Walter Cronkite, William Simon, and the retired naval chief Elmo Zumwalt. The problem was what he had said. After nine unexceptional pages in which he came across as thoroughly sensible, he had answered one final question about his religious beliefs. He talked most of his determination not to be proud. Then he said:

> The Bible says, "Thou shalt not commit adultery." Christ said, "I tell you that anyone who looks on a woman with lust has in his heart already committed adultery."
>
> I've looked on a lot of women with lust. I've committed adultery in my heart many times. This is something that God recognizes that I will do—and I have done it—and God forgives me for it. But that doesn't mean that I condemn someone who not only looks on a woman with lust but who leaves his wife and shacks up with somebody out of wedlock. Christ says, "Don't consider yourself better than someone else because one guy screws a whole bunch of women while the other guy is loyal to his wife."

Clenching his fist, Carter added: "But I don't think I would *ever* take on the same frame of mind that Nixon or Johnson did—lying, cheating and distorting the truth . . . I think my religious beliefs alone would prevent that from happening to me."[10]

Carter's speechwriter Patrick Anderson later called this "one of the most self-serving pronouncements I can imagine." But that was not really the problem. The immediate reaction in evangelical circles was utter horror: some of the nation's best-known preachers took to the airwaves to express their shock that a good Baptist would grant an interview to *Playboy* at all, let alone talk of lust and screwing. Republican strategists, however, were delighted. They immediately mailed two million copies of a newspaper titled *Heartland* to rural households, its cover quoting reactions from religious leaders to the *Playboy* interview. In 350 small-town newspapers, they ran full-page print advertisements asking people to read the cover story of *Playboy* to learn about Carter, and the cover story of *Newsweek* to learn about Ford.[11]

But the damage from the *Playboy* interview went deeper. For both Jimmy and Rosalynn Carter, the embarrassment must have been excruciating. Hamilton Jordan admitted that the interview reopened the issue of the "weirdo factor," while Boston's Democratic mayor, Kevin White, observed that Carter was a "very strange guy." Hecklers, on the other hand, loved it. At Boston College, Carter was greeted by a banner that read: JIMMY CARTER FOR PLAYMATE OF THE YEAR. In Nashville, a sign said simply: SMILE IF YOU'RE HORNY.[12]

"*Playboy* killed us," Pat Caddell said later. Within days Carter's poll ratings were in free fall, and *National Review* gleefully compared his campaign to a football team that had thrown away its playbook after a brilliant preseason and was now paying the price. Meanwhile, he faced a chorus of disapproval from Texas, where Lady Bird Johnson and her friends were furious at his attack on her late husband for "lying, cheating and distorting the truth." Carter claimed that his remarks had been misquoted—but this turned out to be a downright lie. There was an air of disintegration about him now; Patrick Anderson thought that he was "close to the edge." "God only knows what inner torment he was suffering then," he remembered. "This proud, self-righteous man had somehow used his religion to make himself a laughingstock and perhaps to lose the election."[13]

**At this moment,** the calendar furnished Carter with the perfect distraction. For the first time since the legendary Nixon-Kennedy debates in 1960, the candidates had agreed to three live televised debates, sponsored by the League of Women Voters. Both campaigns saw the debates as crucial. For Ford's advisers, they were the ideal opportunity to assert his experience and narrow the poll gap; for Carter's team, they were a chance to prove his superior brainpower, debating skills, and leadership mettle.

The way the two men prepared spoke volumes about their differences. Carter buried himself away with his briefing books, refusing to rehearse. He was confident, even cocky; when Jody Powell came to find him after a revision session, he found the candidate reading comic books with his daughter, the briefing books unopened. Ford, by contrast, took advice from the only man who really knew about presidential debates. "Prepare, prepare, prepare," advised Richard Nixon. "Take the amount of time you plan for preparation and double it." So Ford had his men build a mock set in the White House theater, and there he stood for hours, taking questions from Alan Greenspan, Dick Cheney, and Brent Scowcroft. As Jules Witcover put it, he was like "a boxer training for the big championship fight."[14]

The first debate in Philadelphia on September 23, however, was sensationally dull. Seventy million people watched as the two men—Carter looking slight and nervous, with a clearly forced smile; Ford taller and more confident, but stiff and wooden in his delivery—talked earnestly about tax relief, job creation schemes, and budget deficits, without either landing a decent blow. Given the low expectations, Ford had at least put in a solid performance. But Carter's mumbled answers were so full of statistics that they sounded like a computer printout, which was hardly going to appeal to viewers watching in their pajamas after a long day at work, or propped up at their local bar with their fourth beer, or slumped in their armchairs after a heavy meal. Indeed, the highlight for most people was when the sound suddenly went off while Carter was complaining about "a breakdown in trust," leaving the two men to stand there for half an hour in bewildered silence while the technicians rushed about. The sound came back on eventually, but it might as well not have.[15]

Afterward, polls gave Ford a clear edge. Among independent voters and in the West, he had now recaptured the lead, and in Carter's campaign concern was turning into real fear. Furious at her husband's lax preparation, Rosalynn Carter told him he needed to change his style. Campaign workers whispered that the big chiefs in Atlanta had become complacent. Carter himself complained that the press was treating the president with kid gloves. On October 1, Gallup reported that his lead was down to eight points; three days later, a Yankelovich poll showed Carter and Ford in a tie for the first time.[16]

Ford, meanwhile, was in his best form of the campaign, visibly enjoying himself as he sailed down the Mississippi in an old-fashioned steamboat. But now, in one of those subtle momentum shifts that happen in all campaigns, it was his turn for some bad news. At the end of September, John Dean, the former White House counsel whose Watergate testimony had helped to destroy Richard Nixon, claimed that Earl Butz, the secretary of agriculture, had told him black voters wanted only three things, "a tight pussy, loose shoes, and a warm place to shit." Ford heard the story on September 30, but he hesitated to act. Dean, he thought, was a "sniveling bastard," while Butz was extremely popular in the farm states. Senior Republicans, however, made it clear that if Ford wanted to win any black votes at all, Butz had to go. Racist jokes, even off the record, were simply no longer acceptable, and Ford knew it. On October 4, ashen with embarrassment, Butz announced his resignation.[17]

To recapture the momentum lost in the Butz fiasco, Ford needed a strong showing in the next presidential debate, scheduled for San Francisco on October 6. This time the subject was foreign policy, about which Carter had said little except that it should reflect the "honesty and morality" of the American people. Ford's aides expected the challenger to echo Reagan's criticisms of Henry Kissinger, and in particular to bring up Helsinki. Only a few months before, Kissinger's aide Helmut Sonnenfeldt had controversially remarked that Eastern Europe was in the Soviet Union's "area of natural interest" and should have a more "organic" relationship with the Kremlin. Carter was bound to bring that up, too.[18]

In Ford's briefing book, therefore, was a riposte prepared by the NSC staff. "I have visited Poland, Romania and Yugoslavia as president," Ford was supposed to say. "Our relations with and support for the countries has never been stronger. I don't see how you can talk about conceding Soviet domination in light of this record." This was a bit weak, so Ford tried a stronger version during his last rehearsal, insisting that he was committed to "the independence, the sovereignty and the autonomy of all Eastern European countries" and that "we do not recognize any sphere of influence by any power in Europe." His aides liked it, so Ford tucked a handwritten note into his briefing book: "No Soviet sphere of influence in Eastern Europe."[19]

At first, the debate went as expected. Carter was in better form, speaking slowly and calmly, using the words "strong" and "strength" thirty times and referring to Kissinger's "secrecy" and "secret" diplomacy eleven times. His opening statement was pure Ronald Reagan, complaining that "our country is not strong anymore; we're not respected anymore . . . We've lost in our foreign policy the character of the American people." Détente, Carter said, had given the Soviet leaders exactly what they wanted: "We've been out-traded in almost every instance." Even the Republican platform had "criticized the foreign policy of this administration. This is one

For millions of Americans, Richard Nixon's resignation in August 1974 set the seal on an age of moral decadence and institutional corruption. By contrast, Gerald and Betty Ford (pictured here less than two weeks after they had entered the White House) seemed normal, dependable, and ostentatiously affectionate, Middle America incarnate.

As an unelected president, Ford struggled to impose himself on his bickering officials. Pictured above, watching the president's address to the nation on the economy in October 1975, are (left to right) Jack Marsh, Dick Cheney, Ford, Alan Greenspan, Ron Nessen, Donald Rumsfeld, and Robert Hartmann. Meanwhile, his outspoken First Lady, shown below arriving in Phoenix, Arizona, in March 1976, inspired admiration and outrage in equal measure.

With détente unraveling, Ford came under fierce criticism for his supposed appeasement of the Soviet Union. Above, Ford and Henry Kissinger hold talks with Leonid Brezhnev on a train near Vladivostok, November 1974. Meanwhile, the fall of South Vietnam seemed further proof that the Communists were winning the Cold War. Below, Betty Ford meets Vietnamese refugees at Camp Pendleton, California, May 1975.

*All in the Family*'s Archie Bunker (Carroll O'Connor), shown here locking horns with his neighbor Henry Jefferson (Mel Stewart), captured perfectly the anxieties of Middle America in the early 1970s. But in *The Godfather* (1972), the Corleone organization offered an even more compelling vision of the American family, tapping growing antigovernment sentiment and enthusiasm for the "ethnic revival."

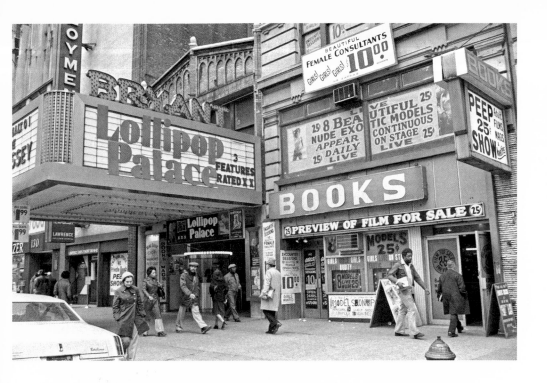

By the mid-1970s, with the area around Times Square a seedy wilderness of peep shows and massage parlors, many New Yorkers were embarrassed by what had become of their city. "Someday a real rain will come," predicts Robert De Niro's deranged Vietnam veteran Travis Bickle in *Taxi Driver* (1976), "and wash all this scum off the streets."

One of the defining characteristics of the mid-1970s was the way populist conservatives adopted the style of countercultural protest. Above, coal miners march in West Virginia against their schools' "dangerous" new textbooks, August 1974. Below, Louise Day Hicks (in dark glasses) leads South Boston's mothers in a march against school busing, September 1975.

As one of the quintessential Sun Belt success stories, Dallas was rarely out of the news. Above, almost eighty thousand youngsters gather in the Cotton Bowl to hear Billy Graham and Roger Staubach preach the gospel of Christ, June 1972. Below, the Cowboys' cheerleaders whip up fans before the players encounter the Pittsburgh Steelers in Super Bowl X, January 1976.

In 1976, almost nobody could have predicted what the poster above calls "The Miracle of Jimmy Carter" although these three men in his native Plains, Georgia, look mightily unimpressed. Below, the former governor chats to local townsfolk, while his brother, Billy, makes a defiant sartorial statement.

Ronald Reagan's speech was the undoubted highlight of the Republican convention in Kansas City in August 1976. Gerald Ford and Nelson Rockefeller seem genuinely delighted; Bob Dole looks a bit more quizzical. Meanwhile, Jimmy Carter was courting Hollywood, embodied here in the extravagantly collared form of Warren Beatty.

By the Carter years, the South Bronx had become a byword for everything that was wrong with the American city. Above, the predominantly Puerto Rican Savage Skulls discuss their next move. Below, Carter tours what looks like a war zone with New York's mayor Abraham Beame, October 1977.

Populist crusaders for conservative causes, both pictured in
June 1978: above, Phyllis Schlafly, the "sweetheart of the silent
majority," rallies opposition to the ERA in the Illinois State
Capitol; below, the chief author of California's Proposition 13,
Howard Jarvis, on polling day.

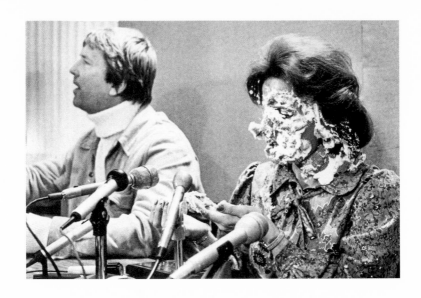

Voices of the moral majority: above, the antigay campaigner Anita Bryant wipes cream pie from her face during a press conference in Des Moines, October 1977; below, a remarkably relaxed Jerry Falwell studies the Bible beside his swimming pool in Lynchburg, Virginia, August 1980.

The Iranian revolution and the second oil shock were devastating blows to Carter's presidency. Above, a gas station owner in California enters into the spirit of the moment, May 1979. Below, the nation's commander in chief shows his mettle in the Catoctin Mountain Park race, September 1979.

By the end of 1979, anti-Iranian passions were running at fever pitch, and a canny Chicago firm sold hundreds of thousands of these Khomeini-target posters. Below, the ugly side of the new nationalism, as demonstrators in Beverly Hills corner an Iranian student, November 1979.

The central issue in 1980 was not so much ideology as leadership, and specifically Carter's lack of it. Above, Ronald Reagan promises economic regeneration outside the closed Campbell Works in Youngstown, Ohio, October 1980. Below, Carter and his future Democratic challenger Edward Kennedy put on a surprisingly convincing show of unity, June 1978.

On his final night in the White House, a sleepless Carter sat up with Hamilton Jordan and Walter Mondale, waiting for news about the hostages in Iran. Somehow, the president's rumpled cardigan and his aides' visible exhaustion speak volumes about the collapse of their ambitions. By contrast, Ronald and Nancy Reagan, pictured below with their family after his inauguration in January 1981, look like they have wandered in from the set of *Dallas* or *Dynasty*.

instance where I agree with the Republican platform . . . As far as foreign policy goes, Mr. Kissinger has been the president of this country."

This was all as anticipated, and the two men traded blows for the next half hour. Then Max Frankel of *The New York Times* asked about Helsinki, suggesting that it looked like "an agreement that the Russians have dominance in Eastern Europe." At that, Ford mentally reached for his prepared riposte. He began by reciting missile specs and grain sales, but then he turned to Helsinki. "I'm glad you raised it, Mr. Frankel," he said. "Now, what has been accomplished by the Helsinki agreement? Number one, we have an agreement where they notify us and we notify them of any military maneuvers that are to be undertaken. They have done it. In both cases where they've done so, there is no Soviet domination of Eastern Europe and there never will be under a Ford administration."

"Governor Carter?" asked the moderator, but Frankel broke in, evidently stunned by what he had just heard: "I'm sorry, I—could I just follow—did I understand you to say, sir, that the Russians are not using Eastern Europe as their own sphere of influence in occupying most of the countries there and in making sure with their troops that it's a Communist zone?" At that, Ford dug his hole a little deeper. "I don't believe, Mr. Frankel, that the Yugoslavians consider themselves dominated by the Soviet Union," he said sternly, while backstage his aides covered their mouths in horror. "I don't believe that the Rumanians consider themselves dominated by the Soviet Union. I don't believe that the Poles consider themselves dominated by the Soviet Union. Each of those countries is independent, autonomous: it has its own territorial integrity and the United States does not concede that those countries are under the domination of the Soviet Union."[20]

It was this second statement that really did the damage. What Ford meant to say was that his administration would never *concede* Soviet dominion over Eastern Europe. He was never the most articulate politician, and under pressure he had simply got confused. The follow-up, though, had made matters a lot worse: for the president to deny that "the Poles consider themselves dominated by the Soviet Union" was a hideous blunder. In the press gallery, remembered one reporter, "there was an audible intake of air. I kept thinking of the Alliance of Poles Hall in Cleveland, and how they might be throwing beer bottles at the screen." Backstage, Brent Scowcroft turned pale and muttered to Stuart Spencer: "You've got problems."[21]

The rest of the debate was essentially irrelevant: all the press talked about afterward was Eastern Europe. In the post-debate press conference, the first question for Ford's strategists was simply: "Are there Soviet troops in Poland?" "Yes," Scowcroft said wearily. Disastrously, though, the president refused to issue a quick retraction. And worse was to follow. "It has been alleged by some that I was not as precise as I should have been," he said at a businessmen's breakfast in the San Fernando Valley. But he had met some "courageous" people in Poland, "and they don't believe that they are going to be forever dominated, if they are, by the Soviet Union." His listeners could hardly believe their ears: *if they are!* It was "sheer stubbornness," said one White House aide, wearily shaking his head. "This is unbelievable," another reported to the press secretary, Ron Nessen. "The press is going wild! People are yelling and screaming, racing around filing bulletins and laughing!"[22]

At their next stop, Dick Cheney took Ford aside. The problem would not go away, Cheney explained, until Ford publicly admitted that he had made a mistake. Ford finally agreed, and as he was about to go out, Cheney asked how he was going to phrase it. Ford whirled around, his eyes blazing, jabbed a finger into Cheney's face, and shouted: "Poland is *not* dominated by the Soviet Union!" Cheney froze in panic—and then he saw Ford drop his arm, a grin spreading across the president's face. The president was still laughing when he reached the reporters and admitted that he "could have been more precise." "I recognize that there are, in Poland, Soviet divisions," he said, suddenly serious. "It is a tragedy."[23]

By delaying his apology, Ford ensured that his decent performance in the rest of the debate was completely overshadowed. Ethnic leaders were furious: the president of the Polish American Congress claimed that his members, who had been undecided, were now planning to vote for Carter. What's more, the fiasco played on Ford's biggest weakness, the perception that he was the stupid blunderer of *Saturday Night Live*. In the immediate aftermath of the debate, Teeter's focus group had crowned Ford the winner by eleven points. The next evening, the same group thought Carter had won by twelve points, then by twenty-seven points the next night, and finally by a whopping forty-five points. Ford had not just lost respect; he had lost time and momentum when he needed them most. His engines had stalled when they should have been on full throttle. It was a crucial turning point; George Gallup later called it the "decisive moment of the campaign."[24]

In the next two weeks, polls showed that Carter's slide was over. And as if trying to confirm that Republicans and debates just did not go well together, Ford's running mate, Bob Dole, promptly made his only notable contribution to the campaign during the first vice presidential debate in history. When Dole caustically described the two world wars, Korea, and Vietnam as "Democrat wars," and told the audience that the list of "killed and wounded in Democrat wars this century" would be "enough to fill the city of Detroit," most Republicans buried their heads in their hands. There was a sneering quality about Dole's performance, wrote Jules Witcover, that reminded him of Richard Nixon, the worst possible association in this campaign year.[25]

Even so, many voters still had doubts about Carter, and his aides were terrified that they would revert to the president at the last moment. On the eve of the third debate, a nonevent, Gallup had Carter at 47 percent and Ford at 41 percent, each a point down since early October. A further 10 percent were undecided, while 2 percent backed the former senator Eugene McCarthy, who was running an eccentric independent campaign to undo the Federal Election Campaign Act, restore the draft, cut the working week, and return to the strictest possible interpretation of the Constitution. McCarthy's candidacy, which nobody took very seriously, nevertheless seemed appropriate in such an extraordinarily unpredictable election year. And if the election was close, worried Carter's aides, then the maverick from Minnesota might attract enough voters to hand New York and Oregon to Ford.[26]

With internal polls showing the race tightening, Ford's campaign rallied for what Cheney called "the ten-day orgasm," a $10 million advertising blitz in the crucial battlegrounds. Some of these new ads were unashamedly negative, like the man-in-the-street spots in which voters explained why they were worried about Carter. "My friends here in Georgia don't understand when I tell them I'm going to vote for President Ford," one woman said. "It would be nice to have a president from Georgia—but not Carter." Others were more upbeat: in late October, the Ford team launched a new commercial drenched in patriotic imagery, cutting between images of farms, city skylines, the Statue of Liberty, and old shots of Ford on the football field, in high school and in college. "We're at peace with the world and at peace with ourselves," a voice-over said. "America is smiling again."[27]

Ford himself was now in the middle of a grueling seventeen-state swing. The day after the last debate, he campaigned in Virginia, North Carolina, South Carolina, and California; a few days later, he had breakfast in Wisconsin, lunch in Missouri, and dinner in Texas. Days melded into a blur of motorcades and sirens, cheering crowds and bobbing placards, the same speeches and the same questions. At every stop Ford poured scorn on the challenger. "Jimmy Carter will say anything to be President of the United States," ran one of his most familiar lines. "He wavers, he wanders, he wiggles and he waffles, and he shouldn't be President of the United States."[28]

More through sheer effort and his opponent's failings than any great virtues of his own, Ford somehow dragged himself back into contention. In Illinois, the *Chicago Sun-Times* reported that Carter's advantage had shrunk from ten points to just one point in a week. In New York, the *Daily News* showed Carter's lead slipping from nine points to six points. And when Carter's aides shook themselves awake on Saturday, October 30, for an exhausting journey from Tulsa to New Orleans to San Antonio and to Dallas, they heard that the latest Harris poll had Carter at 45 percent and Ford at 44 percent, with McCarthy at less than 1 percent.

At Carter headquarters in Atlanta, there was a real sense of panic now. Among independent voters and in the South he was bleeding support with every passing day. In states like Illinois, New Jersey, and Pennsylvania, he was desperately relying on the big-city mayors and labor bosses to turn out the blue-collar vote. Once Carter had boasted that he would never be the candidate of "the political bosses"; now he made a special trip to Philadelphia to implore Frank Rizzo, the grizzled incarnation of silent-majority politics, to get his people to the polls. On television Carter looked tired; from Atlanta there were reports of blazing rows among the staff. Jody Powell told friends that he had a "sick, knotted feeling." On the last Sunday night, shattered after flying from Fort Worth to San Francisco and on to Sacramento, Powell lay in his hotel room, unable to sleep. At four in the morning, he called his wife in Atlanta. "It was my low point," he said. "I was really thinking that Jimmy may well lose the election."[29]

In the Ford camp, the mood was one of barely suppressed optimism. Somehow, after being behind for so long, the president had drawn level. And Ford, never a natural campaigner, was living out his Harry Truman fantasy, hammering out his wooden speech at every stop with as much gusto as his hoarse voice could muster. Every night, too, he was on television answering easy questions from the baseball announcer Joe Garagiola, the quintessential "middle-aged, middle-America guy" who talked straight and used no fancy words. "Gosh, Mr. President, there sure are a lot of people worried about taxes, and just what are you going to do to help them out?" Joe would ask, furrowing his brow. "Gee, Mr. President, my hands used to get pretty sore playing baseball, but what happens to yours? They must get pretty banged up shaking all those hands!"

It cost $1 million to run six editions of the Joe and Jerry Show, and it made most reporters shudder with embarrassment, but Ford loved it. Watching him and Garagiola together, "manifestly and perfectly at ease with each other," wrote John Osborne in *The New Republic*, "one realized that Gerald Ford really is Archie Bunker, slightly modified, and that he was depending for election upon the nation's Bunkers in their numerous variations."[30]

Monday, November 1, the last day. In their final polls, Harris had Carter one point ahead, Gallup had him one point behind, effectively a dead heat. "Presidential Race Called Very Close on Eve of the Vote," read the headline in *The New York Times*.[31]

All the Democratic Party's big names were out on the streets for the last day of campaigning: Edward Kennedy in Boston, Abraham Beame in New York, Frank Rizzo in Philadelphia, Richard Daley in Chicago. Even Hubert Humphrey, just out of the hospital after cancer treatment, recorded an appeal that was rushed onto the radio in Pennsylvania. In Flint, Michigan, where unemployment had hit 8 percent, Jimmy Carter stood in the pouring rain and promised to put "our people back to work." And when it was all over, he showed his softer side to the press, joining them for a mock awards ceremony and singing "Amazing Grace" and "Auld Lang Syne" around a little electric piano as his plane flew south through the darkness toward home.[32]

Gerald Ford's schedule took him from an early morning airport rally in Akron to a midday speech on the steps of the statehouse in Columbus, Ohio, then to a shopping mall in Livonia, Michigan, and finally to a vast homecoming in Grand Rapids. His voice was now a desperate rasp, but there was no mistaking the sheer spirit as he climbed onto the platform, punching his fist to the Michigan fight song and croaking, "Let's go! Let's go! Let's go!" His aides were buoyant now, reveling in the greatest comeback in election history. Ron Nessen said that when it was all over, he would take Jody Powell on a tour of the White House, to show him what he was going to be missing.[33]

In Grand Rapids, beneath a banner that read, WELCOME JERRY AND BETTY, GR LOVES YOU, the emotion of the long campaign finally caught up with the president of the United States. Before one of the biggest crowds in the town's history, Gerald Ford joked about Betty's days at Fountain Street School and his memories of South High, and while the crowd roared, twice the president broke down, weeping tears of weariness and pride. And as he promised one final time that he would never let them down, the band struck up, and Ford, his arm around his wife, yelled into the microphone:

> Hail to the victors valiant
> Hail to the conqu'ring heroes
> Hail! Hail! to Michigan,
> The champions of the West![34]

· · ·

**Tuesday, November 2.** Election Day. "Ford and Carter Give Final Appeals in Race Still Viewed as Close," read the headline. Tom Wicker had called it "the most trivial and vituperative campaign in history." And yet there was still something indefinably special about Election Day, a sense of history in the making. It was a "beautiful, clear" morning, Elizabeth Drew recorded, "with an unexpected upbeat feel to it . . . We *are* free. We did get rid of a crooked, dangerous President, and we ended a wrong-headed war. Both took all too long to do, but acting as a free people, we did it. Election Day is something we share—it's the one communal act we have."[35]

In Plains, Georgia, Jimmy Carter left home to vote at 7:10 a.m., just four hours after he had returned from the longest campaign of his life. His son Chip was already waiting in the cold to vote at the concrete station, and Carter joined the line behind a group of black women, some of them toothless and wearing little more than rags. He was in the booth for five minutes, and when he emerged, he flashed his trademark toothy grin. Then he strolled over to the family warehouse for coffee with his brother, Billy, perching on the counter and showing the world his good-old-boy white socks. "You're gonna win, Jimmy," said one of Billy's friends. "I know," Carter said.[36]

Ford voted early too, in Grand Rapids, where it was even colder, and then he and Betty breakfasted on blueberry pancakes, just as they had when he was running for Congress. There was one last event before they flew back to the White House: the unveiling of a mural in Kent County Airport. It had been painted by a local artist, who had shown Ford as an Eagle Scout with his proud parents, as a high-school football player, behind the wheel of a Model T, and with Betty on their wedding day. Finally, there was a newspaper headline from 1974: "Ford Becomes President." And as Ford stood to thank the artist and the schoolchildren who had raised money for it, the memories flooded back, and he struggled to contain his tears. "It means so much to me because of the first Gerald R. Ford and his wife, Dorothy, my mother and father," he said, his voice shaking, beginning to sob. "I owe everything to them."[37]

It was at six thirty that evening, Washington time, that the television coverage started, and tens of millions of Americans gathered in front of their sets to watch Walter Cronkite on CBS, John Chancellor and David Brinkley on NBC, Barbara Walters and Howard K. Smith on ABC, those twentieth-century augurs revealing the will of the gods to men. In the West Wing of the White House, Gerald and Betty Ford were surrounded by an eclectic group of friends and supporters, among them the ubiquitous Joe Garagiola, who sat next to the president, chewing snacks and making supportive noises. The initial signs were not promising. As the coverage began, all three networks awarded Kentucky to Carter and Indiana to Ford. By eight thirty, NBC had added Florida, West Virginia, and South Carolina to Carter's column, and a few minutes later Walter Cronkite gave Texas to Carter. Ford suddenly felt "pretty lonesome," and then he felt a hand on his shoulder. "It's all right, Prez," Joe Garagiola said. "We got a long way to go."[38]

In Atlanta, Jimmy Carter and his family were ensconced in the Capitol Suite of the Omni International Hotel, a two-room apartment in fashionable tones of beige and brown. On one side stood a table with a huge, unsavory-looking yellow cake topped with a sugar map of Georgia. Carter was slumped a few feet away on a couch, his tie loosened, his feet on a coffee table, his eyes glued to three television sets. On the screen his brother, Billy, was sharing his wisdom with the nation. "Ninety percent of the reporters," he was saying, "can't read or write, and they'd be on welfare if they weren't reporters." How did he think the night was going? "I can't say what I think," Billy muttered thickly, "but I think terrible."[39]

Sweat and Scotch, cigarettes and coffee: the night went on, and now the big states were coming in. Ford was leading in New York and New Jersey; Carter was ahead in Pennsylvania, Illinois, and the president's home state of Michigan. Ford had already taken New Hampshire, Vermont, Kansas, Nebraska, Colorado, Utah, Idaho, Wyoming, Montana, and the Dakotas. But Carter was piling up votes across the South, a great arc of red on the NBC map from the Carolinas down through Georgia, Florida, Alabama, Louisiana, Arkansas, and Texas.* Unless the industrial states went for Ford, he was finished. In the White House, the president chewed hard on the stem of his pipe. In Atlanta, there were whoops of excitement on the fifteenth floor of the Omni International. Carter's suite was suddenly getting crowded, a sign that things were going his way. Daddy King and Coretta Scott King were there, shaking hands and grinning with delight; so too, bizarrely, was the actor George Peppard, posing for photographs with a bewildered Carter.[40]

Just before one in the morning, all three networks declared New York for Carter. Rosalynn gave a shriek of delight, jumping like a schoolgirl, while Carter grinned and reached to turn up the volume. The tide was with him, but it was not quite over yet. Michigan went at last to Ford; so too did New Jersey, Oklahoma, Arizona, and Iowa. Virginia was leaning

---

*This was the first time colored maps were used in television coverage: NBC, whose innovation it was, chose red for the Democrats and blue for the Republicans.

Ford's way, too. "Go, Big Blue," Garagiola was shouting at the screen in the White House. "We're gonna pull it out."

Two in the morning, and it was unbearably close now. Both NBC and CBS gave Carter 261 electoral votes, just 9 short of victory; ABC gave him 257. In the West Wing it was very quiet. Dick Cheney and Bob Teeter took Ford aside to look over the numbers, and the pollster murmured that although it looked bad, late returns might change everything. Ford's voice had gone now, and he looked dog tired. He had had enough. And as he walked down the corridor to bid farewell to his guests, he nearly bumped into Ron Nessen.

Ford did not know it, but Nessen was holding a piece of paper ripped from the UPI wire: "Flash: Washington—Carter Wins Presidency." "I'm going to bed," Ford said, squeezing his press secretary's arm reassuringly. "If I'm going to be worth a damn tomorrow, I'd better go to bed." Nessen nodded mutely; he did not show the president the wire. Moments later, the lights went out in the West Wing.[41]

At 3:28, CBS declared Hawaii for Carter. At 3:30, NBC's backroom boys projected Mississippi for Carter, but because the network had just cut to a local update, John Chancellor had to wait before making the historic announcement. It came a minute later, as Chancellor looked directly into the camera and said gravely: "NBC News projects James Earl Carter of the state of Georgia, elected President of the United States." As he spoke, the words "Carter Elected" flashed up on the screen.

In the Omni International, Carter's suite broke out into screams of delight. The candidate hugged his wife and children, grinning wider than ever, while around them their friends and aides and hangers-on went berserk with joy. "We did it! We did it!" Rosalynn was saying, over and over. Jody Powell hugged his wife, then walked across the room, looked Carter in the eye, and shook his hand. He tried to speak, but nothing came out. They embraced for thirty seconds, just holding each other, never saying a word.[42]

**Jimmy Carter won** the presidency with 40,831,881 votes, twenty-three states, and 297 electoral votes, while Gerald Ford won 39,148,634 votes, twenty-seven states, and 240 electoral votes. On the map, Carter's states formed a giant red crescent from Massachusetts and New York, down through Pennsylvania, Ohio, and the border states, and into the entire South, with the exception of Virginia. Ford's strength, by contrast, was concentrated in New England, the industrial Midwest, the entire Plains and Mountain states, and the West Coast. Turnout was dreadful: just

53 percent, down 10 percent since Kennedy's victory over Nixon, and a depressing indication of public discontent with the political process.[43]

An initial glance at the map suggests that Carter won because he managed to rebuild the New Deal coalition, winning votes from the South, blacks, the cities, and blue-collar workers. And yet, when analysts delved more deeply into the results, what was really striking was the fragility of his base. In southern and border states like Louisiana, Missouri, Florida, and Mississippi, the result was disturbingly close given that the election pitted a Southern Baptist against a stiff Republican from Michigan. Ominously for the Democrats, more white Southerners had voted for Ford than for Carter, especially in the booming new suburbs and cities, while Carter owed his regional sweep to blacks and rural whites. In the long run, the electoral map was misleading: never again would the Democrats do so well in the South.

There were other obvious weaknesses. Carter lost industrial states like Illinois, Michigan, and New Jersey, which were usually crucial to a Democratic victory. He lost the booming West Coast and performed poorly among Catholics. What had saved him was the very thing he had initially run against, the traditional Democratic machine. In the Northeast, Carter would probably have collapsed if it had not been for the AFL-CIO, which provided 120,000 volunteers, made over ten million calls, and handed out more than eighty million pieces of literature. No Democratic candidate in forty years had been less sympathetic to the labor unions, yet probably no candidate owed them more.[44]

As for Gerald Ford, he had managed one of the most unlikely comebacks in the history of presidential politics, and yet he had still fallen agonizingly short. His pollster Bob Teeter blamed the Eastern Europe gaffe, while Ford himself blamed Reagan's "divisive" challenge. The obvious factors, though, were his handling of the economy and his decision to pardon Nixon. In each case, Ford had gambled on putting the long-term national interest above short-term electoral calculation. In each case, he had lost.[45]

The effect of the pardon is often exaggerated. Carter rarely mentioned it on the campaign trail, and although Ford's polls found that 6 percent of voters named it as their reason for opposing him, there is no evidence that they would have voted for him anyway. The really significant factor, though, was Ford's refusal to pump prime the economy during the summer of 1976. His friend Jack Marsh remarked later that a late spending spree might have swung the election, especially in states like New York where unemployment was a major issue. "But it would have been totally inconsistent with the man," Marsh said, "with his integrity"—and of course it would have horrified the conservative wing of his party. The result was that Ford looked like just another uncaring Republican fat cat. Nixon would not have made the same mistake.[46]

When pollsters asked the public to list Ford's achievements at the end of his presidency, 24 percent said they did not know, and 24 percent said that he had no great achievements at all. But most commentators recognized that he had not done such a bad job. Above all, he was almost universally seen as a decent, uncomplicated man, a breath of fresh air after Nixon and Johnson. "Mr. Ford today enjoys the respect and affection of his fellow citizens," said *The New York Times* as he prepared to leave office. "Moreover, he leaves the country in better shape than he found it." But it was *The Washington Post*'s David Broder who put it best, calling Ford "a man of modesty, good character, honesty and openness." He could leave office confident, Broder said, that "history will record that he was, in truth, the President the country needed."[47]

**Ford heard the news** of his defeat soon after he had woken on Wednesday morning. He was too hoarse to say a word, but there was nothing to say. At ten o'clock he sat down with his closest aides to review the figures, and agreed that there was no point contesting the close results in Wisconsin and Ohio. An hour later he made the ritual concession call to Carter in Georgia, huskily whispering his congratulations down the line.

At midday, Ford stepped out into the press briefing room, his family by his side. Usually so healthy and cheerful, the president looked worn and haggard, his voice reduced to a ghastly undertone. After a few words, he asked Betty to read the text of his congratulatory telegram to Carter, and as she did so, Ford bit down hard on his lip. Beside him, his daughter, Susan, was crying silently. There was none of the sentimental mawkishness that had marked Nixon's departure just over two years before, though, just a sad and solemn dignity. At the end, in a nice gesture that spoke volumes, the Fords stepped down to thank the reporters who had followed them on the stump, some of whom were visibly moved themselves. It was hard for Ford to keep control, but somehow he did it. At the end, he turned back and whispered sadly: "I never was a good broken-field runner. I guess you all knew that."[48]

Fifteen minutes later, after Ford had regained the sanctuary of the Oval Office, he looked up and saw Joe Garagiola in the doorway. "We threw our arms around each other without saying a word," the president later recalled, "because nothing needed to be said. For as long as I live, I won't forget that scene. There we were, two has-been athletes, hugging each other in total silence." Then the mood broke, and the tears flowed. "Damn it," Garagiola sobbed, "we shoulda won. We shoulda won." Ford put an arm around his friend's shoulder. "Hey," he said, wiping his eyes, "there are more important things to worry about than what's going to happen to Jerry Ford."[49]

In Georgia the party was already under way. And as Jimmy Carter's car turned off into Plains, making for the green and white wooden depot that had served as his local headquarters, five hundred people came into view, hollering and waving for all they were worth. It was a special moment, one that he would never forget, as he made his way to the makeshift platform, his smile dazzlingly warm as his people pounded him on the back. "From now on," he said, laughing into the microphone, "you're going to have to call Billy 'Mr. Carter.'" Then he said softly and seriously: "I told you I didn't intend to lose."

And as Carter looked out from the platform and saw the friends and neighbors and familiar faces, the red and white bunting, and the debris from the previous night's party, he wept. "I came through twenty-two months and I didn't get choked up," he said, reaching for his wife, "until I turned that corner, and saw you standing here, and I said, 'People who are that foolish, we couldn't get beat.'" He laughed, and on the horizon the rising sun bathed the little storefronts in a golden glow. "The new sun is rising on a beautiful day," he said, "and there is a beautiful new spirit on this country, a beautiful new commitment to the future. I feel good about it, and I love every one of you."

Watching on television in the family quarters of the White House, Betty Ford turned to her daughter and said softly: "He doesn't know what he's gotten into."[50]

## Washington D.C., January 1977

**N**othing quite became Gerald Ford like the last days of his presidency. On his penultimate night in the White House, he whisked Betty off to Georgetown for a surprise dinner party before returning late for another surprise of his own. The Marine band had assembled for a farewell photograph, and as the bandsmen waited in the gloom by the grand staircase, Ford suggested a last dance to "Thanks for the Memory." As they were twirling around, other couples began gliding onto the floor from the darkened hallway: the Kissingers, the Harlows, the Lairds, and other friends from the administration. Betty had her back to the door; she only realized what was happening when someone tapped her on the shoulder, and tears sprang to her eyes. "Everyone crowded around, hugging and kissing her," Ford recalled. "Seeing her so happy was one of the greatest joys of my life."

The next evening, his last in the White House, Ford invited Nelson Rockefeller and his family to a farewell dinner, a discreet way to say sorry for dropping him from the ticket. There were no hard feelings, and Rockefeller was in great form, snapping away with his camera, the life and soul of the party. After reminiscing over a few bottles, the two men went up to the third floor and set up a practice driving range, whacking a golf ball down the hall. Rockefeller's son Nelson junior had a go too, twice taking violent swings with the club, and twice missing the ball entirely. "I wonder what President Ford thinks about me now," he said mournfully. Rockefeller grinned. "Don't worry," he said. "President Ford understands all about missing shots."[1]

When Ford awoke for his last breakfast in the White House, it was a clear, bitterly chilly day. It had been another dreadful winter, so cold there was even snow in Miami Beach. In Georgia, the president-elect's home state, eight out of ten schools were closed, while none of the state's industrial consumers could get any natural gas. But in his mansion bedroom across the street, Jimmy Carter did not feel the cold. He rose early, as usual, taking a five-thirty wake-up call from the Signal Corps, and then made some last-minute corrections to the most important speech of his life. Typically, he had read each of his predecessors' inaugural addresses and had spent weeks refining his own.[2]

Much of Carter's address was the standard patriotic fare: change, rebirth, and the American Dream. It was a shorter speech than most, read slowly in his Georgia drawl, and it adhered to the formula more closely than some had expected: a sign, perhaps, that the populist outsider had some conservative instincts. But it was the very first words that would echo in history. "For myself, and for our Nation," Carter said deliberately, "I want to thank my predecessor for all he has done to heal our land."

On the platform, as the crowd burst into surprised applause, Gerald Ford bit his lip. After a moment's hesitation, he reached across to clasp the new president's extended hand. It was an extraordinarily gracious moment, a wonderful way for Ford to end his term, and for Carter to begin. It showed Carter to be a generous and courteous winner, a man who had drawn a stark line under the bitterness and division of the past. If his presidency had ended at that moment, Jimmy Carter would have gone down as the greatest chief executive in the nation's history.[3]

There was one last populist touch before the day was done. Just moments after Carter's limousine had set off along the parade route to the White House, the car slowed to a halt, the doors opened, and to an excited buzz from the crowd the president and his wife got out and began to stride down the middle of the road, their three sons and their wives and little Amy joining them. Nothing like it had ever happened before, and Carter spotted supporters weeping as he walked past them. "It was one of those few perfect moments in life," he later recalled, "when everything seems absolutely right."

The feeling stayed with him as he reached the gates of the White House. Inside, he found it hard to shake a sense of awe as his Secret Service guards led him down the long corridors to the Oval Office and then discreetly withdrew to leave him alone with his emotions. He stood there in the empty silence, hesitating to break the mood, even to touch anything. The yellow carpet, he noticed, was new, and he felt a twinge of sympathy at the thought that Ford had chosen it with a second term in mind. Then he pulled aside the heavy window drapes, and the late afternoon sunlight flooded into the Oval Office.[4]

# Part Two

# Chapter Twelve    *Mr. Carter Goes to Washington*

I have never personally monitored who used or did not use
the White House tennis court.

—**JIMMY CARTER**, April 30, 1979

The first film that Jimmy Carter watched in the White House was *All the President's Men,* an appropriate choice for a moralistic outsider who hated Richard Nixon. He told the Marine band to stop playing "Hail to the Chief" whenever he walked into the room, and he made his senior assistants drive themselves to work instead of traveling in limousines. He sent his daughter to one of Washington's public schools; he stayed in voters' private homes when attending "town meetings" across the nation; he even took listeners' questions in a radio call-in show with the venerable anchorman Walter Cronkite. Occasionally, he held picnics for members of Congress on the South Lawn, showing up in jeans and a polo shirt.[1]

Behind the gimmicks, however, the Carter administration got off to an uneasy start. It was hard to change an organization built to win power into one designed to wield it, and persistent bickering had overshadowed the transition. Behind this lay a more serious problem, which was that Carter's team had absolutely no experience of Capitol Hill. This meant that when his cabinet finally emerged, it was staffed with members of the very establishment against which he had campaigned. The new secretary of state, Cyrus Vance, had been secretary of the Army during the 1960s; the new Pentagon chief, Harold Brown, had previously run the Air Force; and the new Treasury secretary, Michael Blumenthal, had worked for both Kennedy and Johnson. Even Gerald Ford's old antagonist James Schlesinger was back, in charge of energy. These were experienced men, but by no stretch of the imagination were they exciting appointments.

The key White House figures were Carter's old friends from Georgia: Hamilton Jordan as chief staff assistant, Jody Powell as press secretary, Stuart Eizenstat as head of domestic policy, Bert Lance as budget director. But Carter decided that he did not want a chief of staff, preferring a "spokes of the wheel" system. It was a bold decision, but a risky one. With no chief of staff, the danger was that Carter would have to spend time running the White House himself, supervising the mundane little things that Dick Cheney had handled so efficiently for Gerald Ford. Old Washington hands warned that the result would be chaos; time was to prove them right.[2]

Unlike his predecessor, Carter was lucky that his own party controlled both houses of Congress, as well as the balance of power on the Supreme Court. However, his inheritance was less rosy than it looked. With the old seniority system replaced by a proliferation of subcommittees, Congress was almost unmanageable. And as an outsider who had run against Washington and won only the narrowest of victories, Carter was in an unusually weak position. Liberal veterans joked that he was a "fluke," a "hick," or a "peanut farmer from some piddly-ass little gnat-hole in south Georgia," as Jody Powell colorfully put it.[3]

By far the most important man on the Hill was the new Speaker of the House, Tip O'Neill, an old-fashioned Boston pol who loved a large glass of whiskey, a fat cigar, and a good laugh. O'Neill was never going to be one of Carter's great soul mates, but their relationship got off to the worst possible start with a blazing row about tickets for the inaugural gala. Having ordered extra tickets for his family, O'Neill was furious to discover that they were seated at the very back of a balcony. When he called Hamilton Jordan to complain, the Georgian laughingly offered to give him his money back. "Don't be a wise guy," O'Neill snapped. "I'll ream your ass before I'm through." It was, he thought, a symbol of the Georgians' ignorance of Washington. "They were incompetent," he recalled. "They came with a chip on their shoulder against the entrenched politicians. Washington to them was evil. They were going to change everything and didn't understand the rudiments of it."[4]

If Carter had worked harder to get along with O'Neill, he might have enjoyed a happier term. But he could never bring himself to make the necessary gestures: almost unbelievably, he warned the Speaker that if Congress opposed him, he would appeal over their heads to the American people. For his part, O'Neill could not hide his distaste for the president's piety, keeping a mocking scorecard of the prayers at their weekly breakfasts. Even the breakfasts themselves were a source of tension, with congressional leaders appalled to be offered only coffee, juice, and rolls rather than the generous helpings of eggs, bacon, and sausages that Ford had given them. It was another small sign of the cultural gulf between the new president and the men he needed to turn his program into law.[5]

The truth was that for the relationship to work properly, Jimmy Carter would have had to have been somebody else. Even as governor of Georgia, he hated striking deals over whiskey and cigars. It was the old politics, he thought, the dirty politics of special interests. The engineer in him wanted comprehensive solutions to technical problems; compromise meant surrender. Time after time aides warned him to tread more carefully, but he took no notice. "It was just contrary to my nature," he admitted later. "Once I made a decision I was awfully stubborn about it." Walter Mondale, to whom compromise was the stuff of politics, remarked that "the worst thing you could say to Carter if you wanted to do something was that it was politically the best thing to do."[6]

Still, nobody could dispute that Carter worked extraordinarily hard. From six in the morning, he pored furiously over reams of paper, his eyes racing across reports behind the dark-rimmed glasses the public never saw. Everything had to be on paper, and he digested at least seventy documents a day, quite apart from writing memos of his own, holding meetings, and delivering speeches. It was an inhuman workload, and after a few days he realized that it was impossible. With characteristic self-discipline, however, he organized weekly speed-reading classes for himself, his wife, and their aides. Soon, he proudly recorded, his reading speed quadrupled. Nixon would have approved; Ford would have been appalled.[7]

Ironically, the president Carter most resembled was the one he most despised. Like Nixon, another self-made introvert, Carter was incapable of allowing his advisers to handle mundane matters. "Everybody has warned me not to take on too many projects so early in the administration," he wrote in his diary just eight days into his presidency, "but it's almost impossible for me to delay something that I see needs to be done." Like Nixon, he was obsessed with making every minute count, but spent far too much time meddling in guest lists and hospitality budgets. And like Nixon, he even had the gall to send his staff handwritten notes advising them to spend more time on "rest and a stable home life."[8]

One of the most common jokes about Carter was that he personally handled the bookings for the White House tennis court. Again, this invited parallels with Nixon, who had ordered that disloyal officials be banned from the courts. But Carter denied the story. "I have never personally monitored who used or did not use the White House tennis court," he earnestly explained at a press conference in April 1979. "I have let my secretary, Susan Clough, receive requests from members of the White House staff who wanted to use the tennis court at certain times, so that more than one person would not want to use the same tennis court simultaneously unless they were either on opposite sides of the net or engaged in a doubles contest."

The answer spoke volumes about the man and his style, but it was not strictly true. Carter's speechwriter James Fallows confirmed that he had to send the president's secretary a memo if he wanted to use the tennis court when Carter was in briefings or at Camp David. But he always added a space where the president could check yes or no. And sure enough, "Carter would make his decision and send the note back, initialed J."[9]

**At first, the American people** gave their new president the benefit of the doubt. More than most other chief executives, Carter had genuine novelty value, and two months into his presidency he was basking in one of the most prolonged honeymoons in history. At the end of March 1977, Gallup gave him an approval rating of 71 percent, while Harris put it even higher, at 75 percent. No president had enjoyed better ratings since Johnson in 1963. Tip O'Neill even said that Carter's first hundred days were the most successful since Roosevelt's first term. It could not last, and what ended it was water.[10]

During his campaign, Carter had promised to slash wasteful pork-barrel spending, and at the end of February he announced that he had a "hit list" of water projects that wasted taxpayers' money or threatened the environment. Carter knew perfectly well that these kinds of projects were sacrosanct on the Hill; a new dam could easily make a congressman's reputation in his home district. But he was determined to make an early stand, showing that an outsider from beyond the Beltway could bring much-needed financial discipline to Capitol Hill. Not only would it allow him to cement his populist image; it would prove that his promises of a cleaner, leaner government were more than campaign rhetoric.

At least that was the theory. Unfortunately, the Democratic power brokers were not impressed. In March the leaders of the Senate openly condemned the president's plan; shortly afterward the Senate voted by three to one to reinstate the endangered projects. Alarmed that Carter's majority was evaporating, Tip O'Neill brokered a deal that would eliminate only half the projects: a classic bit of political horse-trading, but disastrous for Carter's reputation as a reformer. It suggested either that Carter had picked a fight he could not win or that he simply lacked the guts for a scrap. And for those liberal congressmen who had risked the ire of their colleagues by backing him, it implied that he could not be trusted—and that deep down, he would always cave in to the establishment. "Signing this act was accurately interpreted as a sign of weakness on my part," Carter later admitted, "and I regretted it as much as any budget decision I made as president."[11]

Ironically, on the merits of the case Carter was completely right. To his critics, though, the water fiasco was a staggering example of arrogance, self-righteousness, and inexperience. The chairman of the Senate Finance Committee, Russell Long of Louisiana, was particularly angry: five of the projects were in his state, and by offending him, Carter lost a vitally important ally. "The concern around the Senate is that you are naïve or selfish or stubborn, perhaps all three," one aide wrote to Carter. "Most senators already see you as hard-nosed and they respect that, but they also see some signs which, to them, indicate that you are hard-headed and, even worse, high-handed."[12]

While the water controversy badly damaged Carter's image on Capitol Hill, he knew that the success of his presidency ultimately depended upon that perennial obsession, the economy. His own instincts were conservative: as governor of Georgia, he had been greatly impressed by the Club of Rome's apocalyptic report *The Limits to Growth*, but the modish emphasis on limits also chimed with Carter's puritanical temperament and enduring distrust of activist government. As always, however, his convictions were shrouded in a fog of ambiguity. Almost all of his economic advisers, such as his Council of Economic Advisers chief, Charles Schultze, were much more liberal than he was, holding fast to Keynesian principles that Carter did not share.[13]

During the 1976 campaign, Carter's priority had been to accelerate economic growth and put people back to work. By the end of his term, he promised, the economy would be growing at more than 5 percent a year, producing full employment, a balanced budget, and enough revenue to pay for energy conservation, health insurance, a higher minimum wage, and sweeping welfare reform. At the end of January 1977 his advisers unveiled the blueprint for the golden age: a stimulus package worth some $15 billion a year, including tax cuts, more than 400,000 new public service jobs, a public works program, investment in training and youth

schemes, and a $50 rebate for every taxpayer. There was no risk of infla-
tion, Schultze told Congress: it was "a prudent policy of economic stimulus that restores a steady and sustainable rate of economic recovery."[14]

Actually, it was nothing of the kind. What Carter's men did not realize was that inflationary pressures, from oil price rises to the expectations
of consumers, were simply too deep-seated to be controlled with the old
fiscal tools. Inflation might be in remission, but it had certainly not gone
away, and Carter's decision to spend his political capital on the stimulus
package was a bad blunder. "It was our biggest mistake," Stuart Eizenstat, his domestic policy chief, said ruefully, "misjudging the strength of
inflationary forces in early 1977 and having an economic policy which
over-stimulated the economy." The irony was that Carter had never really
liked the stimulus. His gut instincts were always more cautious, and he
had only gone along with it under pressure from his advisers—a decision
he would come to regret.[15]

At first, however, the biggest complaint was that Carter was too stingy.
Liberals and labor leaders complained that he should be spending even
more on public works, and a succession of big-city mayors, union bosses,
and even corporate executives trooped into the Oval Office and told
Carter to loosen the purse strings. They were even more annoyed when,
after the $50 tax rebate had already gone through the House, Carter can-
celed it, explaining that it would push up inflation. In fact this was a brave
and sensible decision. But again he looked like a man who could not
make up his mind and would sell legislators short even after they had
stuck their necks out to defend him.[16]

Meanwhile, Carter had begun to tackle the second defining domestic
issue of his presidency: energy. Despite the dreadful effects of the OPEC
oil shock and the great fuss about conservation and limits in the Nixon
years, it had been a complete nonissue in the 1976 election. Public interest in energy had evaporated: polls showed that most Americans thought
the oil shortages had been a trick by the oil companies to push up their
prices. Far from falling, energy consumption had continued to climb, and
the nation was even more reliant on foreign oil than before. It was a tribute to Carter's foresight, as well as his political courage, that he decided to
grasp the nettle so early in his administration.[17]

On the evening of February 2, just two weeks after Carter had taken the
oath of office, television viewers were startled to see their president sitting
beside a roaring White House fire, clad in that least inspiring of garments,
a beige cardigan. Carter had worn the cardigan at dinner with his family earlier that evening, and asked his advisers whether it might work on
television. They thought it was the perfect populist touch. Many viewers,

however, were astonished: for all its virtues, it was hard to imagine George Washington striding across the battlefield in a cardigan. "I don't like the president in a sweater," a Wall Street executive told *Time* magazine, while the *Chicago Tribune* proclaimed it "too folksy to be real." Somehow, the cardigan said more about Jimmy Carter than a thousand speeches; years later, when most Americans had forgotten what he had talked about, they still remembered the cardigan.[18]

What Carter had talked about was energy. The winter's natural gas shortages had convinced him that it was time for "a comprehensive long-range energy policy." There was no easy answer, he warned sternly, but he recommended "keeping our thermostats, for instance, at 65 degrees in the daytime and 55 degrees at night." Clearly that would not be enough, so at the end of April he returned to the television screens, this time without the cardigan, to present his much-advertised energy plan. "Some of the time he was Jimmy the evangelist, preaching to a nation living in energy sin," said *Newsweek*. "Then he was Jimmy the engineer, rattling off statistics and throwing around terms like retrofitting and cogeneration. And then he was Jimmy the leader, summoning the nation to fight the 'moral equivalent of war' and calling on everyone to sacrifice for the commonweal."[19]

The obvious problem was that Carter's plan was ludicrously complicated. Developed in secrecy by the supremely self-confident James Schlesinger, the National Energy Policy had 113 separate proposals, including new fuel-efficiency standards, a new gasoline tax, a tax on gas-guzzling cars, tax credits for solar power and home insulation, new nuclear power initiatives, a strategic petroleum reserve of one billion barrels, and extremely detailed schemes for the gradual decontrol of oil prices, which displeased Democrats who feared that higher prices would alienate their voters. The whole thing was so convoluted that when White House advisers went to brief congressional leaders, they ended up arguing among themselves about the details.[20]

One of Carter's greatest flaws was his habit of vastly inflating the importance of problems that were either very difficult to solve or simply beyond his direct control. Just as Lyndon Johnson had tightened his own noose by insisting that stalemate in Vietnam would be a disaster, so Carter recklessly declared that the fate of his energy plan would mean "either success or failure of my first year in office." In that case, his first year was a complete failure. The plan soon ran into trouble in the Senate, where, trapped in the bureaucratic maze of innumerable committees, it gradually lost its teeth. By October 1977, when the Senate finally approved a version of the plan, it was so far from the original that Senator Abraham

Ribicoff wondered "if the President shouldn't admit that his energy program is a shambles."

The real problem was that there was no domestic constituency for energy reform. Every section offended somebody, and Carter lacked the credibility, the clout, or the political skills to get what he wanted on Capitol Hill. The plan did pass eventually, but not until November 1978, and by this time it had lost most of the conservation measures, the gasoline tax, and much of the gas-guzzler tax. In the long run, it was a farsighted attempt to tackle the nation's gluttonous consumption of foreign oil; in the short term, it was another fiasco. Carter said afterward that he was "very proud" of it, but it took so long to pass that by the time he signed it into law, most people saw it as just another failure.[21]

In the meantime, Carter's administration had suffered a blow from which he never really recovered. In the summer of 1977, his budget director, Bert Lance, became embroiled in a hideously complex series of allegations that he had abused his position to benefit himself and the two Georgia banks he had run before the election. In fact, none of the charges was ever proved, despite investigators producing millions of pages of documents. But a report by the U.S. comptroller suggested that Lance had skirted close to the ethical edge, and fresh claims emerged that he had misused the banks' airplanes, allowed friends to run up vast overdrafts, and so on. By the beginning of September, reporters nostalgic for the good old days of Watergate were pestering for a special prosecutor. There could be only one result, and the longer Carter delayed, the worse the feeding frenzy became. Eventually, the president's closest allies told him that Lance had to go.[22]

A financial wizard whose shambling frame and boisterous style hid a sharp intellect, Lance had been a central figure in the Carter team. But he had also been Carter's closest friend in politics, a pious family man whose cheerful demeanor brought the best out of the serious-minded president. They had not only played tennis together; they prayed together at the White House almost every morning. "It is difficult for me to explain how close Bert was to me or how much I depended on him," Carter recalled. With Lance gone, Carter had lost a crucial confidant. Somehow, it is telling that after Lance left, Carter took up the solitary exercise of jogging, the ideal recreation for an increasingly isolated man.[23]

Lance's resignation brought the first stage of Carter's presidency to a miserable close. His pollster warned that the optimism surrounding the inauguration had vanished, but the president seemed ill equipped to restore it. Swamped in paperwork, often retiring to bed with three hundred pages of documents, he had visibly aged: his face was more lined, his eyes red rimmed, his sandy hair almost gray. Both Jordan and Powell begged him to slow down, while his old friend Peter Bourne recorded after one meeting: "Carter terribly tired and haggard—I was horrified and could not take my eyes off him." His appearance seemed somehow symbolic of a floundering administration with as much life and color as the president's cardigan. "If the Carter Administration were a television show," wrote the columnist Russell Baker as the year drew to a close, "it would have been canceled months ago."[24]

**In the first days** of 1978, as Washington shivered beneath a mantle of snow, Hubert Humphrey lost his long battle against cancer. As the liberal standard-bearer's body lay in state in the Capitol Rotunda, it was hard to shake the pervasive gloom. It must have been strange for Humphrey's friends to hear Jimmy Carter praising him as a voice for "the weak and the hungry and for the victims of discrimination and poverty." For as they saw it, Carter was a Georgia parvenu who had somehow stolen Humphrey's rightful office, and yet showed little interest in his liberal principles. Indeed, Carter apologized at the memorial service for "my own harsh words spoken under pressure" during the campaign, pointedly adding that Humphrey had been quick "to love and to forgive." But Humphrey's old comrades were less forgiving.

During the events to commemorate Humphrey's life, Carter was working on his first State of the Union address. But he still made time to attend a Senate reception before the memorial service, where the guests included Lady Bird Johnson and her daughter Lynda, Gerald Ford, Nelson Rockefeller, Henry Kissinger—and Richard Nixon. It was the first time Nixon had been back to Capitol Hill since his resignation. In the car on the way in, he stared in silence at the gray monuments across the Potomac, lost in thought. He had not slept well, racked with nerves. And when he walked into the reception, where Rockefeller and Kissinger were chatting away and the Fords had already started on the doughnuts, nobody noticed him at first. Nixon headed for the nearest corner and stood alone, staring miserably down at his shoes. A few of the guests noted that his pants, as usual, were too short.

It was Ford who broke the ice, striding cheerfully across the room, sticking out his hand, and asking Nixon how his golf game was going. The tension lifted, and Kissinger came across. "You as mean as ever, Henry?" asked Nixon. "Yes," his old confederate said solemnly. "But I don't have as much opportunity as before." They laughed, and then Rockefeller was among them, slapping backs and joking about the twists of fate that had brought them all together. At last Carter came across, forcing a stiff smile for a joint photograph. The others—even Nixon—were in their element. Oddly, it was the president who seemed the real outsider, aloof and awkward at the heart of his own capital.[25]

If Carter seemed preoccupied that morning, he had good reason. A strong State of the Union message was crucial to relaunch his administration, but his advisers could not agree on the tone he should strike. And although Carter's speech on January 19 included a moving tribute to Hubert Humphrey, the rest of the speech could hardly have sounded less like the Happy Warrior's beloved liberalism. "We need patience and good will," Carter said sternly, "but we really need to realize that there is a limit to the role and the function of government. Government cannot solve our problems, it can't set our goals, it cannot define our vision . . . Those of us who govern can sometimes inspire, and we can identify needs and marshal resources, but we simply cannot be the managers of everything and everybody."[26]

Carter's priorities were to fight inflation, slash government spending, and boost employment. But as so often, he struggled to free himself from the relentless grip of events. Business confidence was painfully low: in the last weeks of 1977, the Dow Jones index had fallen to its lowest level in two years, while only one in four voters approved of the president's handling of the economy and, curiously, more than half wrongly thought that the country was in recession. Nothing Carter did inspired much confidence: by February, the Dow Jones index was down to 753 points, its lowest level since the recession of Ford's first months.[27]

Above all, Carter's attempt to restart his administration was overshadowed by his disastrous handling of a coal strike that seemed likely to bring the entire industrial Midwest to a standstill. The strike had begun in December, when 165,000 members of the United Mine Workers walked out after rejecting a new contract offer. At first, nobody expected it to drag on, but by February the strike had lasted sixty days, longer even than the grueling strike of 1949. Coal production fell from nearly fifteen million tons to less than six million tons, and in the Midwest electricity companies begged their customers to cut down on their energy consumption— a vain hope, given that it was the middle of winter. In some areas, factories sent their workers home early and schools closed their doors.

Yet Carter seemed incapable of giving a lead. His efforts to stay out of the dispute only made him look weak, and when he finally stepped in, invoking the Taft-Hartley Act to declare a national emergency and force the miners back to work, most people thought he was much too late. By the end of March, when the miners finally agreed to a deal, his approval rating was down to just 40 percent, while two-thirds of Americans thought he had proved a weak leader. It was less a question of substance than one of style: while there was little Carter could have done to end the dispute, he had an unenviable knack of appearing a victim of events. If he could not handle the United Mine Workers, how would he deal with Leonid Brezhnev?[28]

Meanwhile, the economy continued to slide. Between January and April 1978, food and energy prices surged ahead, labor costs went up, the value of the dollar began to totter, and the wholesale price index jumped by the highest margin in more than three years. In April, Carter announced limits on wage deals for federal employees, setting "the example for labor and industry." But neither seemed at all impressed. The unions insisted that they had to protect their members' earnings in an age of inflation, while most business leaders were disappointed with the president's tooth-less proposals. Almost two out of three voters now told pollsters that inflation was their biggest concern, but approval of Carter's economic policy had collapsed to just 32 percent. The president's measures had been sim-ply "too vague," Charles Schultze admitted later. "We preached and pro-moted and jumped up and down, but with little effect."[29]

By the late spring of 1978, an administration that had begun with such high hopes was in serious trouble. Carter's tax and energy plans were becalmed, his foreign policy apparently confused, his inflation measures ineffectual. At the end of April an NBC poll gave Carter an approval rating of just 29 percent, an atrocious figure less than eighteen months into his administration. Even Gallup, which consistently recorded much higher ratings, recorded a drop from 75 to 40 percent in just a year. "Never before in the 43-year history of the Gallup Poll," said *The New York Times*, "has an incumbent President eligible for re-election stood lower in his party's esteem."[30]

For most Americans the summer of 1978 was the heyday of *Grease*, *Superman*, and the Bee Gees, of the *Bakke* case and California's Propo-sition 13. Carter later remembered it as the summer that led to Camp David, where in September he orchestrated a spectacular peace deal between Israel and Egypt. It was the greatest achievement of his presi-dency, the result of painstaking diplomacy, personal commitment, and sheer hard work. Yet although Camp David brought three decades of conflict between Egypt and Israel to an honorable end, it did little for Carter's domestic popularity, not least because the economic news was much less promising. With imports vastly outstripping American exports, the value of the dollar was steadily sinking, and Carter was coming under pressure from foreign leaders to do something about his nation's reliance on imported oil. In August 1978, a renewed spasm of currency instability saw the dollar's value drop still further. On the fifteenth, Carter's economic advisers warned that if it plunged any further, the results could be a stock market crash, the destruction of business confidence, and a global trade war.[31]

Hand in hand with the collapse of the dollar went the prospect of yet more price rises. By now inflation was deeply embedded in the world economy, and its causes—a rising sense of entitlement, declining productivity, rising international commodity prices, and, above all, the surging cost of oil—were clearly beyond any president's power to control. But Carter's weakness was fast becoming a national scandal, for since January 1978 food prices had gone up by a stinging 16 percent. "It is impossible to overestimate the importance of the inflation issue to your presidency," Jerry Rafshoon wrote to Carter. He recommended that Carter adopt the strongest possible measures, even if that risked a breach with labor and business leaders, for "it would be difficult to err on the side of too tough a program." Carter clearly agreed; he sent the memo back with a brief handwritten note: "Jerry OK."[32]

On October 24, Carter asked the networks for time to address the nation, yet again, on the threat of inflation. He could hardly have begun in a more fatalistic vein, admitting: "I do not have all the answers. Nobody does. Perhaps there is no complete and adequate answer." He did, however, have a series of "partial remedies," of which he gloomily remarked: "Some of them will help; others may not." These included new spending cuts, wage and price guidelines, the elimination of federal regulations, the loss of twenty thousand federal jobs, and a pledge to slash the budget deficit by the fiscal year 1980. Employers, he said, should hold their price increases to less than 6 percent a year, while workers should limit their pay demands to 7 percent, barely half the level of price rises. Yet even then, he admitted, he could not guarantee success. Times would be "difficult and unpleasant," and Americans "must face a time of national austerity."[33]

Carter's address could hardly have been gloomier if he had announced his intention to hurl himself into the Potomac. But it marked a sea change in government policy. Well into the 1980s, fighting inflation would be the single biggest domestic priority, with unemployment a very poor second. And to prove that he meant what he said, Carter immediately vetoed four spending bills and announced the appointment of Alfred Kahn, the nation's leading deregulation expert, as his new "inflation czar." Even Kahn, however, doubted that inflation could be beaten. It was "a profoundly social problem," he said later, "a sign of a society in some degree in dissolution, in which individuals and groups seek their self-interest and demand money compensation and government programs that simply add up to more than the economy is capable of supplying."[34]

Unfortunately, Carter's new offensive against inflation did not impress the markets. In the next few weeks the Dow Jones average fell by almost 10 percent, while the dollar slid further against other currencies. It was the same old story of too little, too late. And on the first day of November the Federal Reserve was forced to hike interest rates by a full percentage point, the highest rise since 1933, to a crippling 9.5 percent, desperately hoping to squeeze the uncertainty out of the economy.[35]

This was the economics of austerity, just as Carter had promised, but it appalled labor leaders who feared that high interest rates would throw thousands of loyal Democrats out of work. Most union bosses had never liked Carter, distrusting him as a southern conservative with no love for the workingman. To Carter, they seemed as alien as Soviet power-plant managers: when he invited the AFL-CIO leadership to lunch at the White House early in his term, he was horrified by their coarse language while he was saying grace. Now, when the union's president, George Meany, demanded a meeting to discuss the latest anti-inflation measures, Carter turned him down flat. "Right now, Meany looks like shit," he told his aides, "and we look good and he knows it."[36]

For a Democratic president to be so far out of step with the men who provided his party's money and muscle was simply extraordinary. It was supremely revealing that in March 1977, when the veterans of the New Deal held a dinner to celebrate Roosevelt's first inauguration, not a single representative of the administration bothered to attend. The gala was held just six blocks from the White House, but Carter did not even send ritual greetings. "Every time five Bessarabians get together in Waco, Texas, and request a presidential message, they get one," the liberal historian Arthur Schlesinger angrily wrote to Walter Mondale. "How in the world do you suppose a Democratic President, on the forty-fourth anniversary of the first inauguration of the greatest Democratic President of this century, could not manage a few words expressing his sense of the occasion?"[37]

The truth was that Carter had never been much interested in the traditions of the Democratic Party. Listening to reports of the 1936 campaign as a child, he had cheered for Landon, not Roosevelt. And while Mondale's ideal Democrat was a weary worker with cracked fingernails and oil on his overalls, Carter's was a southern small-business man, just like himself. "In many cases I feel more at home with the conservative Democratic and Republican members of Congress than I do with the others," he recorded one evening in January 1978. In later years, he laughingly remembered "the stricken expression on the faces of those Democratic leaders" when he talked about cutting spending. "All they knew about [economics]," he said, "was stimulus and Great Society programs."[38]

Even before Carter had taken office, Pat Caddell had warned him that his main opposition would come from "traditional Democrats" such as George McGovern and Edward Kennedy. Sure enough, it took just four months for McGovern to turn against Carter. And less than two years after Carter had walked to the White House to cheers and applause, a "Dump Carter" movement was forming on the liberal wing of the party. "He's a Republican," said Schlesinger. "He has the temperament of a small businessman who happened to become President." "We hate Carter," agreed a party leader from Wyoming. "After a while, even a dog knows the difference between being tripped over and being kicked."[39]

Liberals did not have to look far for the man who should be sitting in Carter's chair. By the late 1970s, his hair slate gray, his face thickening, Edward Moore Kennedy was comfortably the most recognizable man in the Senate, his name synonymous with the glamour and tragedy of a dynasty. He had suffered more than his fair share of heartbreak: quite apart from the murders of his brothers and his own terrible disgrace at Chappaquiddick, his son had been diagnosed with cancer, his marriage had fallen apart, and his wife had turned to drink. Georgetown gossips eagerly swapped stories about his nights on the town, but Kennedy remained enormously popular with ordinary Democrats. On tax reform and deregulation, he had moved ahead of the pack, but few senators worked harder to keep liberalism alive in an age of limits. In 1976, on the night Carter was nominated, just one delegate had broken ranks and voted for Kennedy, a Hungarian immigrant from Iowa who said simply: "I love him and believe he should have been the nominee." Deep down, millions of Democrats agreed—and Carter knew it.[40]

Behind the smiles for the cameras, Carter and Kennedy loathed each other. To Kennedy, it was simply inconceivable that this nonentity from Georgia sat in his brother's old office; to Carter and his aides, Kennedy was a "woman-killer" who had "inherited everything he had, from his political career to his bank account." And after months of uneasy collaboration, war was declared in the summer of 1978 when talks on a national health insurance program, a project close to Kennedy's heart, finally broke down. After one last meeting had failed to salvage the plan, Kennedy walked out of the White House and bluntly told reporters that the health-care prospects for millions of Americans had been destroyed by a "failure of leadership at the very top."[41]

At the beginning of December 1978, Carter flew to Memphis for the Democrats' midterm convention, an event designed to reignite support for the party after two hard years. But when he stood to address the delegates in the half-empty Cook Convention Center, they gave him a tepid welcome, applauding only when he delivered ritual attacks on Nixon and Ford. There was, said *Time*, "an undercurrent of feeling among many Democratic factions that Carter is not really their President." CBS even claimed that only six out of ten delegates would back Carter for renomination, a terrible embarrassment for the incumbent. But Carter showed no signs of wavering. The convention was not representative of the American people, he told his cabinet. It was stacked with liberals, and as Carter himself had put it during his campaign for the governorship of Georgia: "I was never a liberal. I am and have always been a conservative."[42]

It was Kennedy, not Carter, who captured the hearts of the Democrats in Memphis. The night after the president's speech had fallen flat, Kennedy took to the podium on the need for national health insurance. And as he neared the end, his face red with emotion, he abandoned his text, talking instead about the air crash that broke his back, his father's stroke, his son's cancer. "We were able to get the very best in terms of health care because we were able to afford it," he said. "But I want every delegate at this convention to understand that as long as I have a vote, and as long as I have a voice in the United States Senate, it's going to be for that Democratic platform plank that provides decent quality health care, North and South, East and West, for all Americans as a matter of right, not of privilege, for all."

The crowd was clapping, cheering now, and Kennedy pounded again on the lectern. They must not allow "drastic slashes in the federal budget at the expense of the elderly, the poor, the black, the sick, the cities, and the unemployed." Sometimes, he said, "a party must sail against the wind. We cannot afford to drift or lie at anchor. We cannot heed the call of those who say it is time to furl the sail."

It was wonderfully stirring stuff; as Kennedy stepped back to the speakers' table, the delegates were on their feet, roaring their approval. The chairman of the session, the young governor-elect of Arkansas, enthusiastically pounded Kennedy on the back; characteristically, Bill Clinton had spent the morning boning up on health care in his motel room. At the back of the hall, even some White House officials were cheering. A few feet away, Hamilton Jordan was standing beside Pat Caddell, his face clouded with tension. "That's it," Jordan said grimly. "He's running."[43]

# Interlude: Steeltown, U.S.A.

On Monday, September 19, 1977, Len Balluck was enjoying a day on the golf course with a group of friends. They played eighteen holes and sat chatting over coffee, and then Len began the short drive to his home in Youngstown, Ohio. It was a warm late summer's day, and life was good. He was forty-eight years old, happily married with two teenage children, a good job, and a "halfway decent" wage. He turned on the radio, and the news came on. "It said they were shutting down the Campbell Works and 5,000 jobs were going to be eliminated," he said later, recalling the terrible moment. "I didn't believe it. When I got home I sat there thinking, and all of a sudden the newspaper came and I saw the headlines. I felt a complete sense of shock. When [I saw] my wife, she said, 'Did you hear?' And I said, 'Yeah.' "[1]

For the people of Youngstown, the Campbell Works was not just a mill. It was a way of life. Youngstown was one of a number of towns—Clairton, Homestead, and Pittsburgh on the Monongahela River; Weirton and Steubenville on the Ohio; McDonald and Girard on the Mahoning—where the glow from the ovens and furnaces meant that the streets were never dark even at night, towns that epitomized the nation's industrial might. At its peak, it was a prosperous, thriving kind of place, with its own newspaper and department stores, busy downtown shops, impressive public parks, and attractive suburbs where the mill families lived. It was even the home of a national fast-food chain, Arby's, serving the kind of roast beef and chicken sandwiches that a red-blooded hard hat needed after work. It wore its nickname, Steeltown, U.S.A., as a badge of pride: only Pittsburgh produced more steel.[2]

Many local people traced the city's decline back to 1969, when Youngstown Sheet & Tube had been taken over by the Lykes Corporation, a real estate conglomerate that saw its new acquisition as little more than a source of cash. Steel was a declining business, and Lykes argued that environmental regulations made it impossible for Youngstown to compete with its Japanese rivals. By 1977, with Washington refusing to match the Japanese government's investment, the writing was on the wall.

Days after the company's announcement, the first workers to be laid off crossed the footbridge to the clock house, tossing their hard hats into the Mahoning in protest. A year later, Lykes announced plans to close Brier Hill, its other mill in the Mahoning Valley. At last, in November 1979, the guillotine fell, and U.S. Steel announced that it was closing all its facilities in the Youngstown area.[3]

Youngstown did not go down without a fight. At first, more than 100,000 Ohio and Pennsylvania steelworkers signed a petition calling on the government to provide emergency relief and import quotas to protect the local industry. Some declared they would do anything to keep the works open, even if it meant accepting pollution levels far higher than those stipulated by the government. Meanwhile, the United Steelworkers of America and the Catholic Church organized a campaign for the mills to be reopened under community ownership. Youngstown's Catholic bishop, James Malone, even issued a diocesan statement expressing "serious moral concern" at a cruel decision that would destroy "the lives of so many people as well as the future of Youngstown and the Mahoning Valley."[4]

At demonstrations and marches, steelworkers and their families sang a folk ballad written specially for the occasion, "Back to Work in Youngstown." "I'm going to own a little piece of a steel mill, / So will others in my neighborhood," they sang. "We'll all have a stake in what goes on, / And that sounds pretty damn good." But the song's optimism proved ill founded, for the idea never got off the ground. The federal government never advanced the necessary loans, while the steel companies showed no interest in playing along. "We're here to make money," U.S. Steel's chairman, David Roderick, said with disarmingly callous honesty. "You guys can't get that through your heads." Some historians see the workers' efforts as a sign that socialism was alive and well in Middle America. But the stark truth is that their campaign failed, the mills were demolished, and the local steel industry was destroyed.[5]

What happened to Youngstown could hardly have been a more powerful symbol of the vast economic forces sweeping away years of industrial history and blue-collar solidarity. Never had organized labor seemed so irrelevant in the face of irresistible global change. For even though their Democratic allies controlled both Congress and the White House, the unions' influence in Washington had reached its lowest point in living memory. In the media, there was a pervasive sense that they were sclerotic dinosaurs, marooned in a new age of deregulation, tax cuts, and cutthroat competition. And as the industrial heartland fell into apparently terminal decay, labor organizers and blue-collar workers slipped out of the headlines. Even the huge strikes of the 1970s, which involved millions of miners, autoworkers, and teamsters, failed to capture the national imagination. And even in New York City, once a temple to municipal unionism, labor was in retreat, losing battle after battle, howling with rage at the cuts in city services.[6]

"Along the Mahoning River, running through the heart of the city, stand remnants of a great empire," wrote *The Washington Post*'s Haynes Johnson in 1980. "Not so long ago they were symbols of American industrial might. Now, sitting gray and ghostlike, silent and deserted on this overcast October morning, they represent a dream that has died." A chill wind blew through Youngstown; litter rolled disconsolately past the shuttered gates of the Campbell Works. "I remember when the steel mills caused so much soot in this valley that the Mahoning River never froze over, and my father used to say to me, approvingly, 'See that silt on the windowsill? That's a sign of prosperity,' " said Bill Jones. His great-great-grandfather had been among the original founders of the town; his great-grandfather had helped to build the Ohio Canal system; his grandfather had sold merchandise to immigrant workers in the mills; his father had worked in the gravel industry used for the great furnaces along the river. "Now," he said sadly, "we have the cleanest valley around."

The Youngstown closures cost some ten thousand jobs, each one an individual and family tragedy. Len Balluck did not find another job for years. He was luckier than many; he had a pension, and his wife had a steady job as a schoolteacher. But three years on, as he stood outside the Campbell Works, he found it hard to control his feelings. "This used to be our parking lot," he said quietly. "It was always packed. You can see the grass growing in it now. Right in front of us is the main entrance. You can see how it's locked, and the rats are taking over—literally." He sighed as the wind blew past the padlocked gates. "I worked here for 23 years," he said. "We call it the graveyard."

From Buffalo and Johnstown to McKeesport and Aliquippa, from Pittsburgh and Gary to Cleveland and Warren, it was the same story: crippling losses, plant closures, job cuts, and unemployment; drugs, drink, divorce, and despair. Across the ravaged landscapes of the Rust Belt, wrote another reporter, "the dead steel mills [stood] as pathetic mausoleums to the decline of American industrial might that was once the envy of the world." They were the victims not of cruelty or miscalculation but of change, of history. But for people like Len Balluck and Bill Jones, who had known and loved these towns all their lives, it was like a death in the family. "I couldn't ride through there," Jones said of the desolate Campbell Works. "It would bring tears to my eyes. I would cry."[7]

# Chapter Thirteen    *Roots and Rights*

All I worry about is overcoming their barriers, and getting up
in the world. I have to live for me now.

**—WATTS STUDENT** on *Roots*, February 1977

In the late summer of 1977, five black teenagers went on trial in the
little town of Dawson, Georgia, charged with killing a white farmer in
a grocery-store robbery. The "Dawson Five," as they were called, had
become a cause célèbre for liberal activists and civil rights groups, and
there were whoops of delight when the prosecution fell apart and the five
men went free. But what stuck in many reporters' minds was an impression of an unrepentant corner of the Old South, stuck in its ways, obsessed
with the hatreds of the past.

The redbrick Terrell County Courthouse was air-conditioned, which
came as a blessed relief in the August heat, yet in other respects it felt a
long way from the shining towers of Atlanta. In 1960, "Terrible" Terrell
County had been the first jurisdiction sued by the Justice Department
for discriminating in voter registration. Since then, its officials, policemen, and ordinary white residents had been accused of arson, beatings,
shootings, and persistent harassment of black activists. Even in 1977, all
political and economic power remained in the hands of the white community, despite Terrell County being two-thirds black. In the heart of the
rural Black Belt, little seemed to have changed since the worst days of Jim
Crow.[1]

One black prisoner from the county farm told the court how he had been badly beaten by four policemen, losing his hearing in one ear, and then charged for assaulting an officer. A local civil rights worker told how in 1975 he had personally registered seventy black voters, only to find that officials had "lost" their records on Election Day. The black Baptist pastor told how his five-year-old daughter had been banned from using the toilet in a Dawson drugstore and ordered to go outside, behind a pile of boxes. Dawson, he said, suffered from "a racism so blatant the air is heavy with it." Its schools were still effectively segregated, its public officials were all white, and its black residents were "a hopeless, fear-ridden people because of the brutalities that have been perpetrated in this county."

Not even the hardest-hearted reporters could conceal their horror. "Even a day or so here, in the courtroom and roaming about Dawson and Terrell," wrote Tom Wicker, "puts in bitter perspective much facile journalism and more southern self-deception about the 'New South' and its racial development. Out beyond the booming cities with their proliferating high-rises and their plastic bands of fast-food shacks, there's a lot of old South still, a past that's never really passed, a life that's little changed."[2]

**A year after** the trial of the Dawson Five, the University of Chicago professor William Julius Wilson published a book called *The Declining Significance of Race*. It was a landmark in sociological scholarship, but it was also enormously controversial. There was no longer a "single or uniform black experience," Wilson argued, and the color of black Americans' skin was no longer the determining factor in their lives. Distracted by their unusual experience, middle-class intellectuals failed to realize that most poor blacks were crippled more by class than by race. "Economic dislocation," he concluded, "is more central to the plight of the black poor than is the problem of purely racial discrimination."[3]

To reviewers who put great store by the idea of a common black experience forged through slavery and discrimination, Wilson's book came as a shocking affront. The Association of Black Sociologists declared that it "obscures the problem of the persistent oppression of blacks" and that its members were "outraged over the misrepresentation of the black experience." Yet Wilson's emphasis on the diversity of the black experience, and on the social distinctions among blacks themselves, made a great deal of sense. For although the events in Dawson, Georgia, testified to the enduring racial prejudice and inequality in many corners of the nation, it was easy to paint a very different picture of black life in the 1970s.

Wilson was right, for example, to point to the emergence of the black middle class, which had gained ground over the previous two decades. This was a tremendously important development (and happened *before*, not after, the onset of affirmative action). In 1940, most black men had worked as laborers, sharecroppers, or domestic servants, while six out of ten women were servants, working long hours for little pay. By 1970, however, the picture was radically changing. More than one in five black men and one in three black women held white-collar jobs. By the mid-1970s it was perfectly normal, especially in the North, to see black schoolteachers, social workers, doctors, nurses, secretaries, salesmen, and small-business men. And almost every part of the country had what one writer called a "large, churchgoing, home-owning, childrearing, back-yard barbecuing, traffic-jam-cursing black middle class, remarkable only for the very ordinariness with which its members go about their classically American suburban affairs."[4]

The growth of this black middle class owed a great deal, of course, to the civil rights laws of the 1960s, but it arguably owed even more to education. Even without affirmative action, there would probably have been an unprecedented surge of black workers into professional and technical positions, simply because of the bigger pool of high-school and college graduates. Between 1960 and 1980, the proportion of black youngsters with four years of high school more than doubled, while the proportion attending college more than trebled. In 1963, George Wallace had made his notorious stand in the schoolhouse door against the admission of black students to the University of Alabama. Ten years later, the university was admitting six hundred black students a year, while Wallace himself, in a moment of supreme symbolism, was on hand to crown a black student as the school's homecoming queen.[5]

And this reflected a deeper change: the almost total disappearance, thanks to the civil rights movement, presidential leadership, and public education, of explicitly racist ideas from public life. By 1972, 97 percent of whites said that blacks should have equal opportunities to get a job, while 80 percent agreed that blacks were of equal intelligence, 84 percent favored integrated schools, and 85 percent said they would welcome black neighbors of their own social class. Even in the busing controversies of the early 1970s, very few conservatives voiced openly segregationist sentiments. While race continued to play a part in politics, blatantly racist politicians were virtually extinct by the end of the decade. By 1980, even in the South, unashamed white racists had been reduced to "a tiny remnant with no influence in any important sphere of American life."[6]

With the black middle class booming and racism apparently in retreat, it is not surprising that the mid-1970s were great years for black "firsts," from the first black Episcopalian bishop to the first black admiral in the U.S. Navy. But thanks to the Voting Rights Act of 1965, the most obvious examples were in the political arena. When Richard Hatcher and Carl Stokes won the mayoral elections in Gary and Cleveland in 1967, they became the first black mayors to run major industrial cities. Twelve years later there were 191 black mayors across the nation, controlling Los Angeles, Detroit, Atlanta, New Orleans, Newark, Richmond, and Birmingham. Across the board, the transformation was astonishing. In 1970, a total of 1,469 black officials held elected office around the nation, most of them at relatively low levels. By 1979, however, there were 4,607 black officials nationwide, with 2,768 in the old Confederacy. And perhaps most strikingly, no states had elected more black public servants than Louisiana and Mississippi, formerly the strongest pillars of segregation.[7]

All of this appears to add up to an extremely rosy picture, a panorama of black families making money, moving into the suburbs, sending their children to college, and voting for political representatives just like themselves. Yet some civil rights leaders protested that black progress was a complacent fiction, disguising the reality of enduring racial discrimination. "There may be a change in the atmosphere," John Lewis, formerly the chairman of the Student Nonviolent Coordinating Committee and later congressman from Georgia, explained in 1974, "but solid changes haven't occurred . . . When it got to hard things, and when the problem started to touch the North, the whites turned around." The National Urban Coalition's Carl Holman was even more pessimistic. "Racism comes much more naturally, and to a much broader spectrum of whites," he lamented, "than we could have imagined."[8]

After the heightened expectations of the 1960s, many activists found enduring inequalities hard to accept. "Blacks as a group are still behind whites," wrote the black historian Manning Marable in 1980; "no amount of statistical doubletalk will obscure this fundamental fact." Blacks made less money than whites, and while white household income slightly increased during the 1970s, black income remained stagnant. In 1980, median black household income was not much more than half that for whites, a ratio that had hardly changed for fifteen years. Even the figures for black life expectancy and infant mortality remained much worse than those for whites, with black children twice as likely to die in their first year and much more likely to fall ill. True, blacks were gaining ground, but they were starting from an appallingly low level.[9]

While middle-class blacks later remembered the 1970s as a time when they had taken their first steps up the ladder, poorer blacks remembered the decade as one in which the ladder had been kicked away. As factories

moved to the suburbs and the Sunbelt, and as automation and computers replaced manual labor, big-city blacks found themselves stranded by
the tides of economic change. Throughout the 1970s, the black unemployment rate remained more than twice that for whites, while for young
black men there were very few jobs at all. During the Carter years, unemployment among black men in their twenties stood at an estimated 25
percent, and in some cities, such as Detroit and New York, it was often far
higher.[10]

Without a job, a steady income, or a stake in society, all too many
young black men turned to crime. Official figures showed that not only
were young black men arrested for half of all violent crimes, but they
committed seven out of ten robberies. And they were by far the most likely
*victims* of crime, too, with an appallingly high proportion failing to reach
their middle years. According to the FBI, the chances of a black male
reaching the age of twenty-five in a major American city were no more
than three out of five; even more shockingly, the number one cause of
death for black men between twenty-five and thirty-four was murder. And
although black Americans accounted for barely a tenth of the total population, more than one in three prison inmates were black—and the proportion was going up.[11]

For all too many black families, life came depressingly close to the
bleak, violent pictures painted by Toni Morrison's searing first novel, *The
Bluest Eye* (1970), or Ntozake Shange's play *For Colored Girls Who Have
Considered Suicide When the Rainbow Is Enuf* (1975). Ten years before,
Daniel Patrick Moynihan had courted controversy with his report on the
"Negro family," which argued that ghetto life had become a "tangle of
pathology," marked by delinquency, school failure, and absent fathers. But
his words now seemed prophetic. In 1970 the illegitimacy rate for black
babies was already seven times higher than that for whites. By 1980, more
black children were born out of wedlock than within it, and less than half
lived with both their parents. By this stage, fully 40 percent of black families were headed by women, themselves often no more than teenagers. It
is hardly surprising that many women felt beleaguered, not only by white
racism and economic change, but by black men, too. The black woman,
wrote Michele Wallace in 1979, was "really the most vulnerable figure in
American society"—and, as she saw it, the culprits, obsessed with their
own virility, were black men.[12]

For thousands of black men and women growing up in the 1970s, life
could be hopelessly tough. Of course there were fabulous opportunities for a few: the young Condoleezza Rice, Oprah Winfrey, the teenage
Barack Obama. But in 1977, *Time* warned that the nation's inner cities

now housed "a large group of people who are more intractable, more socially alien and more hostile than almost anyone had imagined: the American underclass." It was "the great unmentioned problem of America today," Ted Kennedy told the NAACP a year later: the growth of "a group that threatens to become what America has never known—a permanent underclass in our society."[13]

Although the heavily black underclass is often seen as a product of the Reagan years, its roots went deeper. As factory employment dried up and the nuclear family fell apart, young men were drawn into the underworlds of prostitution, theft, mugging, and the drug trade. By 1980, half of Detroit's adult male population, now overwhelmingly black, worked only sporadically or not at all, while in the city's "high poverty" areas, where more than 110,000 people lived, fewer than three out of ten had jobs. In New York, almost half a million people, mostly black and Latino, were officially poor; in Philadelphia, 127,000; in Chicago, almost 200,000. In the nation as a whole, perhaps a third of young black men were unemployed in 1980.[14]

By this point, any visitor to an inner-city ghetto recognized the symptoms: dozens of young men hanging around on street corners, most of them high-school dropouts, most of them regular drug users, many of them inevitably sucked into the criminal underworld. As William Julius Wilson put it, they were the "truly disadvantaged," cut off emotionally from their fathers, educationally from the skills they needed, geographically from the jobs that might have given them a hand up. Wilson himself had been born to working-class parents in Pennsylvania: his academic success testified to the new opportunities for black Americans. But for every William Julius Wilson who made it, millions were left behind.[15]


**On Sunday, January 23, 1977,** three days after Jimmy Carter's inauguration, ABC broadcast the first episode of its new miniseries *Roots*. Based on Alex Haley's novel tracing his ancestors' journey from freedom in Africa to slavery in the antebellum South, it was something of a gamble on the part of the network. Since *Roots* had almost no sympathetic white characters and depicted a brutal world of rape and racism, some executives were afraid that viewers would be put off—which is why it was scheduled to run for eight consecutive nights in January, never a great time for network premieres, when an expensive failure would soon be forgotten.

But they need not have worried. The first episode of *Roots* was a sensational success, attracting the largest audience of the season. As the week went on, the ratings got better and better, and 100 million people watched the final episode, giving it a record-breaking 51.1 Nielsen rating and 71 percent audience share. By the end, it was estimated that more than half of the population had seen at least one episode, while sales of Alex Haley's book went through the roof, with 900,000 copies changing hands in a single month.[16]

There had never been a television hit like it. "My children and I just sat there, crying," a black public relations director from Nashville told *The New York Times*. "We couldn't talk. We just cried." The owner of Jock's, a popular Harlem bar, reported that people came in especially to watch the show; one night, they were so disgusted by the hero Kunta Kinte's treatment that they turned the jukebox off and sat around "to talk it out." Many others found it similarly upsetting: at a lunch counter elsewhere in Harlem, one woman said that she "had to cut the thing off about half way through and go to bed." In Watts, a teenager told journalists that it "should never have been shown," because at her high school "it only created more animosity between blacks and whites"; in San Francisco, black students reportedly chanted "Roots, Roots, Roots" at their white classmates. And more than a few black youngsters were struck by the parallels between the past and the present. One Kansas City senior said that the beatings and rapes "made me think of how many white people still think this way"; another Watts teenager, meanwhile, thought that "whites still hold us down."

Most viewers, however, found *Roots* genuinely inspirational. It "put some pride in me," one New Orleans teenager said, "that our ancestors were able to take all the things that happened to them and be able to say, 'look, we're free, we can be people.'" There were reports of booming enrollment in black studies and black history programs; parents named their children Kunta Kinte or Kizzy after the main characters; and travel agencies told of "a virtual explosion" in genealogical trips to Africa. White viewers, too, found the series intensely powerful. One Missouri high-school senior said that *Roots* had moved her to tears: "I never knew that such horrible things happened. I wasn't very proud of my ancestors. Since the movie I have felt sorry for our black population and whenever I see a black person I wonder if any of my ancestors tortured theirs."[17]

*Roots* was only one of many black cultural successes during the 1970s, from Michael Jackson and Donna Summer to Muhammad Ali and Larry Holmes, from *The Jeffersons* and *Diff'rent Strokes* to O. J. Simpson and Walter Payton. But it was also a milestone on the journey from assimilation to diversity. In the wake of Black Power, the "roots" motif was enormously popular, and even before Haley's novel reached the shelves, newspapers were reporting surging black interest in their African heritage—

a result, said a National Archives specialist, of "an emergence of black pride and an effort to trace a proud survival." Instead of wanting to be "full-fledged Americans, without regard to race, creed or color," wrote the radical black intellectual Harold Cruse, blacks should celebrate their own distinct identity, whether through dialect or dress, Afros or the arts. That way, they would build "Negro ethnic group consciousness" and turn Black Power into a cultural reality.[18]

The most sensational example of this new cultural assertiveness was the blaxploitation genre of the early 1970s, which ran the gamut from ghetto thrillers like *Shaft* (1971) and *Super Fly* (1972), with their shoot-outs, pimpmobiles, and funk sound tracks, to more lurid films such as *Blacula* (1972; "Warm young bodies will feed his hunger and hot, fresh blood his awful thirst!") and *Blackenstein* (1973; "To stop this mutha takes one bad brutha"). But blaxploitation was not the only sign of the simultaneous self-confidence and introspection of black culture in the 1970s. From the poems of Amiri Baraka and Maya Angelou to the extraordinary scenes of the Ali-Foreman "Rumble in the Jungle," from black models to Black Studies, African American culture was both more commercially successful and more deliberately inward looking than ever. "What we find," reported the southern regional director of the NAACP, "is [an] inward turn, blacks turning within their own community and their own institutions as a sort of defense."[19]

"Chocolate City," George Clinton called it in his funk album of 1975: an imagined world of black solidarity and self-rule, a vision of the nation's capital with Muhammad Ali as president, the Reverend Ike as Treasury secretary, Richard Pryor as minister of education, Stevie Wonder as secretary of fine arts, and Aretha Franklin as First Lady—and white faces confined to the "vanilla suburbs." While Chocolate City was, literally speaking, a metaphor for Washington, D.C., it was also, as the black poet Kenneth Carroll put it, a "metaphorical utopia . . . an assertion of self-consciousness, self-determination and self-confidence."[20]

Revealingly, however, it was a utopia with no place for the integrationist ideal, a fact that alarmed those who remembered the struggles of the past. At the 1976 Democratic convention, Barbara Jordan, the first black woman to deliver a keynote address, memorably warned delegates not to neglect the idea of the "common good." If they did, she said, "we will cease to be one nation and become instead a collection of interest groups: city against suburb, region against region, individual against individual, each seeking to satisfy private wants. If that happens, who then will speak for America? Who then will speak for the common good?" But it was already too late. In urban communities, reported *The New York Times* on the twenty-fifth anniversary of the *Brown* decision, spokesmen for integration were "increasingly lonely" figures. What mattered now was diversity: Chocolate City, not the melting pot.[21]


**Blacks were not** the nation's only minority citizens, and the decline of the integrationist ideal owed much to the fact that the nation's ethnic composition was changing rapidly. The oldest and poorest Americans of all, the Indians scattered on reservations from coast to coast, were more assertive in the 1970s than at any time in recent memory, occupying the sites of Alcatraz Island and Wounded Knee and vigorously protesting against the exploitation of their land. But now they competed for attention with millions of newcomers for whom the doors had been thrown open by the Immigration Act of 1965.[22]

By the beginning of the 1970s, more than 400,000 people were arriving every year, and by the end of the decade the annual influx had reached 800,000. These were not the Germans and Italians of previous immigration waves; they were Filipinos and Vietnamese, Chinese and Koreans, Jamaicans and Puerto Ricans, Mexicans and Cubans. In twenty years the nation's Asian population increased fivefold; by the mid-1980s there were fifty times as many Vietnamese, Korean, and Indian Americans as in 1965. In some New York City hospitals, Asian immigrants accounted for 80 percent of the medical staff, while parts of Los Angeles, like parts of Miami, were not so much bilingual as entirely Spanish speaking. The faces and voices of the nation were changing, and not everyone liked it. By 1990, warned one magazine, "California will become America's first Third World State"—not the wisest prediction ever made.[23]

While this new wave of immigration had an enormous impact on the cultural life of the nation, it coincided with another phenomenon that, in the long run, was to prove no less significant. What historians call the "rights revolution" was built on Titles VI and VII of the 1964 Civil Rights Act, which promised to protect workers from "discrimination on the basis of race, color, religion, sex, or national origin." The rights of disadvantaged groups, the argument ran, had been systematically abused for decades. Justice demanded that these rights be enshrined in law and protected by the long arm of the state. And with the economy booming and liberal optimism at its height, why limit rights to votes, jobs, homes, and education? Why not extend rights to freedom from risk, injury, fraud, exploitation, and pollution?[24]

The crucial impetus behind the rights revolution came not from Congress but from the courts and federal agencies, and its key figures were not politicians but judges, civil servants, lawyers, and lobbyists. It was the courts that struck down state rules and federal regulations if they did not meet the needs of the beneficiaries, or intervened to expand food stamps, educational aid, and Aid to Families with Dependent Children. It was the courts that extended new rights to elderly workers, non-English-speaking students, women, and the physically and mentally handicapped. And it was the courts that recognized welfare as a constitutional right, "more like 'property' than a 'gratuity,'" as Justice William Brennan wrote in *Goldberg v. Kelly* (1970). As a result, welfare entitlements were protected under the due process clause of the Constitution and could not be taken away without proper notice and an impartial hearing.[25]

There was a positive side to all this, of course: the rights revolution opened up American democracy, righted historical wrongs, and dispersed valuable benefits to vulnerable citizens. Yet relying on the courts and federal agencies meant that the rights revolution was never really exposed to a proper debate, and therefore never built up a genuinely national constituency. Above all, it fostered the impression that liberals were lofty elitists, handing down rulings from their judicial ivory towers, the benefits going to lobbyists, lawyers, and affluent professionals who knew how to work the system—the dreaded "special interests" of populist rhetoric. One historian calls them "social engineers of a new spoils system, without broad public discussion and consent."[26]

Yet, paradoxically, the fact that the rights revolution depended on the courts and the agencies explains why it survived the rise of conservatism in the 1970s and 1980s. It was in this supposedly conservative age, after all, that Americans gained the rights to "clean air and water; safe consumer products and workplaces; a social safety net including adequate food, medical care, and shelter; and freedom from public and private discrimination on the basis of race, sex, disability, and age." Meanwhile, women, racial minorities, gays and lesbians, illegal immigrants, migrant farmworkers, the poor, the handicapped, prisoners, the mentally retarded, and even atheists and pornographers all enjoyed new rights. And these liberal gains survived the Reagan and Bush years unscathed and even enhanced—all thanks to an unelected coalition of judges, lobbyists, bureaucrats, and social workers, quietly expanding their empires even as conservative politicians were proclaiming their hatred of government.[27]

If there was one element in the rights revolution that provoked more debate than any other, it was affirmative action. Curiously, although the origins of affirmative action can be traced back to Title VII of the 1964 Civil Rights Act, the bill's sponsors never anticipated its results. Hubert Humphrey, who steered the bill through the Senate, claimed that under no circumstances would it impose any kind of mandatory quotas. If anyone could find any evidence of quotas, he remarked, "I will start eating the pages one after another, because it is not in there."[28]

But affirmative action was to prove a good example of the way in which laws can have completely different effects from those anticipated. To cut a very long story short, by the early 1970s there had been a radical change in the ethos of the Equal Employment Opportunity Commission (EEOC), which was charged with enforcing the provisions of Title VII. At first, the commission came under pressure to push for outreach programs, but soon the EEOC decided that the problem was not individual prejudice but entrenched discrimination, and started judging cases not by the employer's intentions but by the end results. Even when the commission could not prove deliberate discrimination, it pushed for change, using hearings to embarrass companies into hiring more minority workers.[29]

Inevitably, this new strategy ended up in the courts. When black workers at the Duke Power Plant in North Carolina complained that none of them had been promoted to managerial positions, Duke retorted that as long as blacks had the appropriate school and college qualifications, they were eligible for promotion. But in *Griggs v. Duke Power Company* (1971), the Supreme Court decided otherwise. The point of the Civil Rights Act was to "achieve equality," said Chief Justice Warren Burger, and therefore the "consequences of employment practices" were crucially important. Duke's practices were "fair in form, but discriminatory in operation," and that was not good enough. After *Griggs*, any employment practice that resulted in imbalance was suspect. Businesses scrapped promotion requirements that stopped black workers getting ahead, while police and fire departments abolished height and weight requirements that held back female, Hispanic, and Asian applicants. Even the airlines abandoned their age limits for flight attendants.[30]

Meanwhile, the federal government had put its muscle behind affirmative action. In 1969 the Nixon administration launched a trial scheme in Philadelphia that required government contractors to meet goals for black employment. Nixon liked the idea, not least because it pitted two core Democratic groups—blacks and blue-collar unions—against each other. And by 1974 the "Philadelphia Plan" had been extended to cover all federal contractors, who had to devise "affirmative action compliance programs" to ensure the right proportions of black and women workers. The word "quotas" was never used; after all, Nixon had publicly called quotas "artificial and unfair." He preferred the word "goals." To their opponents, they were quotas all the same.[31]

Blacks were not the only beneficiaries of the Philadelphia Plan: in 1977 the Office of Management and Budget added American Indians, Spanish speakers, Asians, Eskimos, and Aleuts to the list of approved minorities. In the same year, the Public Works Employment Act enshrined quotas in law, stipulating that one in ten grants for public works should be "set aside" for minority contractors. Meanwhile, under a new generation of black mayors, cities began to set aside a share of their contracts, too, for minority-run businesses. In Atlanta, the new airport and downtown renewal projects were both set aside, and by 1978 black businesses enjoyed about 38 percent of the city's municipal contracts. And all the time the legacy of *Griggs* rolled on: by 1980 the Justice Department had filed suit against fifty-one city, county, and state governments, citing discrimination in the Philadelphia and Cincinnati police departments, the Atlanta, Boston, and Dallas fire departments, and *both* the police and the fire departments in Miami, Los Angeles, Chicago, and St. Louis.[32]

Ironically, affirmative action actually did very little to help the most vulnerable groups in society, such as the black men who desperately needed jobs to lift them out of the underclass, or black children in failing inner-city schools. Instead, the biggest beneficiaries were thriving minority businesses and middle-class women, who already had many of the skills for success and, to put it bluntly, knew how to work the system. Meanwhile, the costs were heavy, for few things did more to alienate white workers who felt they were losing out. By the end of the decade, fewer than one in five white voters believed that the government should give "special help" to blacks and minorities. "Those quotas and Philadelphia Plans made us angry," one unemployed Brooklyn carpenter remarked later. "They should create plans to help both sides. Create jobs, but don't take from one to give to the other and create bitterness."[33]

It was this fear of being supplanted that lay at the heart of white opposition to affirmative action. The cries of rage were loudest from those who most feared falling behind: the economically insecure children and grandchildren of Jewish, Italian, and Polish immigrants, alarmed by the disappearance of blue-collar jobs and terrified that they would have to pay the debts of history. Told that white workers had to "pay the price for those years of slavery," one Brooklyn antibusing leader demanded: "Who will pay the Jews for two thousand years of slavery? Who will compensate the Italians for all the ditches they dug?" One of his Jewish neighbors put it even more bluntly: "So you want to know how I became a bigot? I'll tell you. The blacks have options we don't. The Jews never had a civil rights movement. We fought for everything ourselves . . . And those giveaway programs. I'm not getting any!"

Perhaps if affirmative action had been tried in the 1950s and 1960s, with full employment and buoyant growth, it might have won greater support. But in conditions of stagflation, job cuts, and rising crime, it was bound to drive a wedge between liberal politicians and blacks, on the one hand, and white working-class Democrats, on the other. "I liked John Kennedy, and I liked the early civil rights movement," another Jewish man said. "I used to fight for the *schwartzes'* rights. I thought, all people have a right to public accommodation, to jobs according to ability. But if my kid has a ninety-nine average, why should he be deprived? He has one life to lead. What's fair is fair. The *schwartzes* want to get ahead. But not on my kid's back."[34]

**On the sweltering** morning of Wednesday, June 28, 1978, regular visitors to the Supreme Court noticed that Cecilia Marshall, Marjorie Brennan, Mary Ann Stewart, and Elizabeth Stevens had arrived in the crowded courtroom to support their husbands—always a sign that a major decision was coming. At ten o'clock, right on cue, Chief Justice Warren Burger and his eight black-robed colleagues filed into the court, looking "more solemn than usual." After two minor decisions, Burger turned to case 76-811, *Regents of the University of California v. Bakke*. An unnatural stillness hung over the courtroom as, peering through his thin spectacles, the frail figure of Lewis Powell began to read: "Perhaps no case in my memory has had so much media coverage. We speak today with a notable lack of unanimity. I will try to explain how we divided."

Allan Bakke was an exceedingly unlikely person to make legal history. Born in 1940 of Norwegian stock, he had originally studied engineering at the University of Minnesota, graduating with very respectable grades. Since he had paid for his studies by joining the naval reserve, he served four years in the Marine Corps and spent seven months in Vietnam, where he was promoted to captain. Afterward he took a NASA research position, but by this time he had already developed "an almost religious conviction" that his true vocation lay in medicine, and spent his spare time as an unpaid hospital volunteer.

Unfortunately for Bakke, moving into medicine was easier said than done. In 1972 he was rejected by both Northwestern and the University of Southern California, and a year later eleven more medical schools turned him down. The problem was that although he had two excellent degrees, he had been out of college for several years and was considered too old. However, he was clearly a very strong candidate, with much better grades than most applicants, extremely good MCAT scores, and a science test ranking that put him in the ninety-seventh percentile. At UC-Davis, his faculty interviewer reported that Bakke was "well qualified" on almost every conceivable ground, and therefore "a very desirable candidate." But Davis, like the other schools, turned him down.[35]

As Bakke was aware, Davis had an affirmative action program. Most major universities had quotas for black, Asian, or female applicants, and Davis, which had been extremely white until the beginning of the 1970s, was a typical example. Of 105 medical school places, five were reserved for the relatives of faculty members, local politicians, and important businessmen, while sixteen were set aside for "disadvantaged" students. No white student, however poor, ever got one of these sixteen places; instead, they usually went to blacks and Hispanics. Whether these groups needed a hand up, though, is dubious: minority students already won 27 percent of the places at the school, despite constituting only 11 percent of the total number of applicants. Finally, to add insult to Bakke's injury, the records of the successful minority students were greatly inferior to his own. His grade average was A minus; theirs was C plus. His MCAT score was in the top 10 percent; theirs were in the lowest third. By almost every standard except his skin color, he was a better applicant.[36]

In November 1973, Bakke formally complained that he had been a "victim of racial discrimination," and the following June he filed suit against the university. "My first concern is to be allowed to study medicine," he wrote. "Challenging the concept of racial quotas is secondary." Nevertheless, it was the issue of quotas that came to dominate the case. A record sixty-one amicus curiae briefs were filed, and while UC-Davis was backed up by civil rights groups, black organizations, and other universities, Bakke attracted support from the Order of the Sons of Italy in America, the Polish American Congress, the conservative Pacific Legal Foundation, Young Americans for Freedom, the U.S. Chamber of Commerce, and numerous Jewish groups, which were bitterly opposed to quotas because they had once been used to limit Jewish student numbers. Indeed, Bakke's lawyer Reynold Colvin was both president of San Francisco's biggest synagogue and president of the local American Jewish Committee.[37]

When Lewis Powell read the Court's decision, it was unclear at first who had won. Four justices—Burger, Stewart, Rehnquist, and Stevens—ruled that Bakke was a victim of discrimination and that Davis's racial considerations violated the Fourteenth Amendment. But another four justices— Brennan, White, Marshall, and Blackmun—took the opposite view. Harry Blackmun, a Nixon appointee who was gradually moving from right to left, put the liberal position most memorably. He looked forward, he said, to a time when affirmative action would no longer be necessary, but that was at least a decade away. "In order to get beyond racism, we must first take account of race. There is no other way. And in order to treat some persons equally, we must treat them differently."

It was Powell, another Nixon appointee, who played the crucial role. Confusingly, he sided with both sides and neither. On the question of Bakke's admission to Davis, he sided with the conservatives. The school's affirmative action plan, he wrote, was unconstitutional, because as "a classification based on race and ethnic background," it violated the Fourteenth Amendment. But on the wider principle of affirmative action, Powell sided with the liberals. While explicit quotas were unfair, he believed that a school could take race into account to ensure a "diverse student body" that would promote an atmosphere of "speculation, experiment and creation." The university should not use an "explicit racial classification," and racial diversity could be only one factor, but it was a factor nonetheless.[38]

Allan Bakke was naturally delighted. Throughout the long battle, he had studiously avoided publicity, even staying away from his California home and young family to escape the reporters. He was no political crusader; as his attorney put it, he was "a private man who felt that he'd been dealt with unfairly. He has stuck with it because it's his dream to become a doctor. He's a determined gentleman." When the press tracked him down after the ruling, he was picking apricots up a tree. "Great," he said laconically when his attorneys called with the good news. "You guys did it." "No," the lawyer said, "you did."[39]

Before the verdict, civil rights groups had issued dire warnings about the consequences of a Bakke victory, and the verdict was greeted with predictable outrage. "Bakke—We Lose," read the headline in New York's black *Amsterdam News*. The decision, said Vernon Jordan, head of the National Urban League, was part of a "national backlash against the movement toward economic and racial equality, a backlash fueled by selfish vindictiveness that threatens to fragment our society." It was a "devastating blow to our civil rights struggle," agreed the Reverend Jesse Jackson.[40]

Yet most observers recognized that the decision was rather more ambiguous. "Quotas: No / Race: Yes," read *Time*'s cover headline. As the Harvard law professor Alan Dershowitz put it, the decision "neither legitimized racial quotas nor put down affirmative action programs." So, for all the doom and gloom of the civil rights leaders, supporters of affirmative action were able to claim it as a victory. Carter's attorney general, Griffin Bell, even declared that for "the first time the Supreme Court has upheld affirmative action, and it has done it in about as strong a way as possible." The head of the EEOC, Eleanor Holmes Norton, predicted that the *Bakke* decision would make no difference to "hiring and promotion goals" in federal employment. "My reading of the decision," she said, "is that we are not compelled to do anything differently from the way we've done things in the past, and we're not going to."[41]

The really striking thing about the *Bakke* decision, in fact, was its limited impact. Allan Bakke went to medical school, but little else changed. Most university affirmative action plans survived, and many schools still had implicit quotas, confident that they could get around the Supreme Court's ruling by keeping them unwritten. And in June 1979 the Court gave affirmative action another fillip with its decision in *United Steelworkers of America v. Weber*. This time the protagonist was Brian Weber, a white technician at a chemical plant in Louisiana who had been overlooked for a training program that reserved half its places for black workers. Weber himself was no Allan Bakke: an outspoken blue-collar Cajun who liked to be photographed in his hard hat, he enjoyed the attention and looked forward to his place in history. But in June 1979 the Court voted by 5 to 2 to uphold affirmative action, as long as it was not imposed by the federal government. Civil rights leaders were delighted, and so were most employers. Before the ruling they felt trapped between a rock and a hard place. If they gave black workers a break, they were likely to face action from resentful whites; but if they did nothing, they risked losing their federal contracts. At last, said one report, they had firm "guidance on what they can and cannot do."[42]

By the end of 1979, the place of affirmative action in American life seemed unassailable. Although it did much less to promote black progress than its champions claimed, it had become one of the central pillars of a new liberal order, based on a philosophy of entitlements and apparently impervious to electoral fortune. And as the Harvard sociologist Daniel Bell had already warned, every group wanted its piece of the cake. "Women's groups believe *Weber* may help them expand their already considerable gains," reported *Time*. The head of the Mexican American Legal Defense and Educational Fund predicted that Hispanics would see the *Weber* ruling as "the means to open doors that have been closed for too long." Similar sentiments came from the executive director of the Polish American Congress. "If America's job opportunities and money are to be parceled out to groups," he said, "we are a definable group, and we want our share."

Disgruntled by his defeat, Weber himself predicted that the Supreme Court's decision would "have a negative effect on people all over the country toward blacks." But in the last months of the 1970s, there was plenty of evidence that Americans were beginning to leave the bitter legacy of places like Dawson, Georgia, far behind. There was still a long way to go, of course, and for those unlucky enough to be born into the growing underclass of the great cities, there was little light on the horizon. But at least there was hope, a commodity that had been in short supply in decades past. "I've done better than my parents ever dreamed," said James Nailor, a black electrician who was one of the first to be accepted into the Kaiser training program from which Brian Weber had been barred. "That's the American dream."[43]

# Chapter Fourteen  The Sweetheart of the Silent Majority

*I was for it at one time, but then I saw the women in Washington who were pushing it, and I said, "Hell, I don't want to be equal to them!"*

**—BARRY GOLDWATER, 1974**

R ain was falling in Houston as one of the longest torch relays in history reached its last leg after fourteen states, almost three thousand miles, and fifty-one days. Passed from hand to hand like the Olympic flame, the torch had been carried south from Seneca Falls, New York, by more than two thousand women, young and old, rich and poor, black and white. Some were famous athletes, but most were ordinary, unsung women, pounding the streets beside high-school and college running teams, cheered by hundreds of onlookers, their progress tracked by camera crews from local stations. Each had pledged to carry the torch for fifty miles, wearing an official "Women on the Move" T-shirt. And each had signed a Declaration of Sentiments drafted by the poet Maya Angelou in honor of the first women's rights declaration, more than a century before.

At noon on Friday, November 18, 1977, three young Houston runners, one white, one black, one Hispanic, carried the torch into the center of their city, a thousand women jogging at their heels. For the last mile, their pace slowed, and the well-known faces of Bella Abzug, Betty Friedan, and Billie Jean King bobbed alongside them on the tarmac. Outside the

Albert Thomas Convention Center, defying the drizzle, stood a crowd of delegates; as the tiny flame glinted in the distance, they let out a great roar of approval, and some began chanting, "ERA! ERA!" Up the runners went, up to the podium, where Susan B. Anthony, great-niece and namesake of the abolitionist and suffragist, was waiting. She took the torch, and then, to tumultuous applause, she repeated her ancestor's famous words: "Failure is impossible!"[1]

The idea for the National Women's Conference in Houston, Texas, had been born two years earlier, after a UN conference to mark International Women's Year in 1975. Meeting female delegates from all over the world and hearing about the commissions their governments had organized, the American representatives had been seized with enthusiasm to put on something similar at home. They successfully lobbied Congress for $5 million to fund a gathering in November 1977, "to promote equality between men and women." Thousands of delegates would be elected in fifty-six state and territorial conferences, and they would represent millions of American women in drawing up a national plan of action for the years to come.[2]

All in all, some twenty thousand people descended on Houston for the four-day national conference. It was a star-studded occasion: as well as Maya Angelou, Billie Jean King, and Betty Friedan, familiar faces included Rosalynn Carter, Betty Ford, and Lady Bird Johnson. According to the official report, the delegates were of "all colors, cultures, and heritages," among them "secretaries, teachers, nuns, nurses, lawyers, doctors, ministers, factory workers, farmers, waitresses, students, scientists, migrant workers, Members of Congress, mayors, business owners, and at least one astrologer." Yet many were already activists of one kind or another: more than one in four belonged to the National Organization for Women, one in three to the League of Women Voters, and one in five to some other women's association. The general atmosphere was unquestionably somewhere to the left of center, reflecting the views of the typical American feminist, as opposed to the typical American woman.[3]

While few women could seriously have objected to the discussions about employment, insurance, or rural affairs, other areas were rather more controversial, such as the plank on reproductive freedom, which called for universal sex education and private insurance provision for abortion. The most contentious plank of all, however, was that on sexual preference, which overtly endorsed lesbian rights, much to the displeasure of older activists such as Betty Friedan. Yet when Friedan took the stage to discuss the plank, her words astonished the audience. "As someone who has grown up in Middle America," she admitted, she had the reputation of being "violently opposed to the lesbian issue." But "now my priority is in passing the ERA. And because there is nothing in it that will give any protection to homosexuals, I believe we must help the women who are lesbians." As she finished, there were great roars of delight from the galleries. Minutes later, the plank passed with a handsome majority. On television, viewers saw "hundreds of young women hugging, cheering, and raising clenched fists," and from the balconies descended hundreds of pink and yellow balloons with the slogan "We Are Everywhere."[4]

For feminism's fiercest critics, however, the conference's emphasis on abortion and lesbians was a gift. Those who claimed that "a vote for equal rights is a vote for lesbian quotas on school faculties, junior-high abortion clinics, compulsory round-the-clock day care, and the overthrow of capitalism . . . didn't have to make it up," remarked the *Washington Star*, because the Houston delegates had "put the package together." The delegates, said the intemperate California congressman Robert Dornan, were "sick, anti-God, pro-lesbian and unpatriotic." They were "anti-family, anti-God, and anti-America," agreed the Reverend Jerry Falwell, who thought the conference "full of women who live in disobedience to God's laws."[5]

From the beginning, conservatives had been deeply disturbed by the prospect of the Houston conference. It would be a "front for radicals and lesbians," warned Phyllis Schlafly, the nation's most vocal opponent of the Equal Rights Amendment, who organized a campaign urging Christian women to make their presence felt at the state conventions. Few feminists saw this coming, and in states such as Utah and Mississippi they were astonished to find themselves sitting beside hundreds of women deeply opposed to abortion, the ERA, sex education, and gay rights. In Missouri, where fewer than four hundred people had registered for the workshops, the organizers were taken aback when a further five hundred men and women registered on the door, voted for anti-ERA candidates, and then went straight home to St. Louis. The same trick worked in Oklahoma: a church group arrived en masse, elected a conservative slate, passed a resolution commending homemaking as "the most vital and rewarding career for women," and promptly went home. It was brilliant in its way, although for the organizers it must have been heartbreaking.[6]

In total, the antifeminist forces elected a majority of delegates in a dozen states, concentrated in the South and the West. Although many of these delegates approved of issues like rape prevention measures and federal programs to help victims of child abuse, they were overwhelmingly opposed to abortion, lesbianism, and the ERA. At the Houston conference, however, they were almost invisible, largely because experienced liberal organizers like Bella Abzug refused to give them a hearing. One conservative delegate, a nurse from Virginia who worshipped at Jerry Falwell's Baptist church, enjoyed the "broadening experience" of seeing socialists and lesbians marching through the streets, but found herself ostracized when she admitted her opposition to abortion and the ERA. And of course the hostility flowed both ways. The feminists were "very unhappy women," full of "self-pity" and "man-hating," said a conservative delegate from New Jersey. "The women-libbers are trying to dress up abortion," said a third delegate from Washington, "but no matter how you dress it up, it comes down to killing a baby."[7]

For the conservative delegates, Houston had an alternative attraction. While the main conference was discussing the problems of disabled women and the ERA, fifteen thousand people headed across town to the Astro Arena for a three-hour national pro-family rally. Most were "white and well dressed" couples with small children; their name tags suggested that most were from Texas, Alabama, Oklahoma, and Utah, and many carried placards bearing messages such as "God Made Adam and Eve, Not Adam and Steve" and "Not Gay, but Happy People—Happy, Texas." Groups such as Stop ERA, the National Right to Life Movement, and the John Birch Society were much in evidence, and the general mood was summed up by a Tennessee housewife whose "God's Way" button, she said, denoted that "homosexuality is a sin, that God meant for a woman to take care of the family, and that every child that was conceived was a life that could not be taken." But the real star of the show was Clay Smothers, an outspoken black Texas state representative. "I have had enough civil rights to choke a hungry goat," he thundered to rousing cheers. "I ask for victory over the perverts in this country. I want the right to segregate my family from these misfits and perverts."[8]

The curious thing about the Houston conference was that both feminists and conservatives left town buoyed with optimism. As feminist delegates assembled for the closing ceremony on Monday morning, the atmosphere was heavy with emotion. "I think we accomplished more in this meeting than we could possibly have hoped for," Bella Abzug told the audience. Many women held hands and sang along with Margie Adam, a California singer-songwriter. Others, said the official conference report, "shed unashamed tears at the final moments of sisterhood that had touched them so much . . . As the great hall emptied out, the last sounds were the voices of stragglers singing 'We Shall Go Forth' and 'We Shall Overcome.' It was a life-changing and history-changing event. Neither individual women nor the country would ever be quite the same again."[9]

And yet, in their euphoria, many failed to take heed of what had happened just five miles away in the Astro Arena, or to mark the lessons of those turbulent state conventions. For while Houston represented the crest of the feminist wave, in the long run the conference was a failure. One anti-ERA activist turned the pamphlets she collected from lesbian and Marxist groups into an exhibit shown in thirty states. Another conservative called it "the best recruiting tool I ever had" and said she merely needed to "spend twenty minutes reading the Houston resolutions" to wavering audiences.

"The Women's Lib movement," Phyllis Schlafly wrote afterward, "has sealed its own doom by deliberately hanging around its own neck the albatross of abortion, lesbianism, pornography and Federal control." In her long battle against the ERA, she later reflected, Houston was her Midway: a decisive turning point that opened the way to victory.[10]

**The last tobacco commercial** on American television, broadcast just before midnight on New Year's Day 1971, was for Virginia Slims cigarettes. Launched three years earlier, the long, narrow Slims were designed to appeal to affluent young women, counteracting the bad publicity about the health risks of smoking. They were marketed as glamorous, attractive, and independent: advertisements showed them being smoked by languid models, and television commercials drew a lighthearted contrast with the oppressed women of former generations, who supposedly could not smoke without their husbands' consent. At the end of every commercial, a choir triumphantly intoned the familiar Slims slogan: "You've come a long way, baby."[11]

Women had indeed come a long way. At the beginning of the 1960s, a married woman could not even borrow money in her own name. Women and men were paid at different rates for the same work; employers could advertise for men only; union contracts had separate seniority lists for men and women; and graduate schools often imposed a strict cap on women students. Some states barred women from jury duty; some bars refused to serve them. Women did not run big corporations, universities, or federal departments; they did not govern states; they did not sit on the Supreme Court; they did not fight fires, or arrest criminals, or serve in the Army, or repair cars, or drive trucks.[12]

Ten years later, however, their expectations had undergone an astonishing transformation. Thanks to the expansion of education, the rise of white-collar services, the transformation of industry, and the rise of birth control, they enjoyed unprecedented social, cultural, and financial independence. Between 1970 and 1980 the proportion of American women in the workforce rose from 43 percent to just over 51 percent, while the female proportion of law graduates leaped from 5 percent to almost 30 percent, and of medical students from 8 to 23 percent. Even in the newspapers, readers encountered women not merely as brides and mothers but also as "gas station attendants, traveling salesmen, doormen, welders, truck drivers, steelworkers, members of a road gang, and pest exterminators." There were female highway patrolmen, female police officers, female roustabouts, even female miners in the coalfields of Kentucky. In theory, anything was possible.[13]

Underlying all this was what one historian calls "a modest revolution in public policy." Its cornerstone was Title VII of the 1964 Civil Rights Act, which outlawed discrimination on grounds of "race, color, religion, sex, or national origin." Behind this, however, lay a bizarre history. The word "sex" was not in the original bill, but was added by a conservative congressman from Virginia, "Judge" Howard Smith. Legend has it that Smith only added "sex" as a facetious attempt to cripple the bill. In fact, he was a long-running supporter of the Equal Rights Amendment, so his addition may have been seriously meant. In any case, it had a lasting impact. "Hearings, votes, and legislative victories came with breathtaking speed," one feminist wrote later, "and Congress passed more legislation on behalf of women's rights than it had considered seriously for decades."[14]

The balance sheet for 1972 alone makes impressive reading: not only did Congress pass Title IX to prohibit discrimination in education; it also approved the Equal Rights Amendment, extended the Equal Pay Act to cover administrative and professional positions, and passed the Equal Employment Opportunity Act. Two years later, the Equal Credit Opportunity Act allowed women to apply for credit without their husbands' permission. Meanwhile, the Supreme Court guaranteed women's right to terminate their pregnancies, entitled them to the same legal age of majority, welfare payments, pension plans, and Social Security benefits as men, and insisted that they participate fully on juries. "No longer is the female destined solely for the home and the rearing of the family," wrote Justice Harry Blackmun, "and the male for the marketplace and the world of ideas." All in all, women's rights had never been better protected. "We put sex discrimination provisions into everything," recalled the flamboyant liberal Democrat Bella Abzug. "There was no opposition. Who'd be against equal rights for women?"[15]

For Abzug, however, there was one crucial step left. Born amid the high-minded suffragist feminism of the early 1920s, the Equal Rights Amendment had been introduced in every session of Congress between 1923 and 1970. For all its simplicity—"Equality of rights under the law shall not be denied or abridged by the United States or by any State on account of sex"—it had never come close to succeeding. But by the end of the 1960s, thanks to feminist pressure, the involvement of women in the workforce, and the rights revolution, the ground had shifted. By 1970, not only had the American Association of University Women, the League of Women Voters, the ACLU, and the ADA all joined the campaign, but so had the United Auto Workers and the Department of Labor. After pressure from his wife and daughters, even Richard Nixon threw his weight behind it, as did Barry Goldwater and Strom Thurmond. "I am in full support of the Equal Rights Amendment," wrote Ronald Reagan to a women's group, "and will be pleased if you are able to find a use for my name in attracting additional support."[16]

At first, the ERA seemed unstoppable. Congress approved it by a crushing margin in March 1972; within a year it had been ratified by thirty states, and by 1975 only four more were needed. Public support remained high, peaking at 74 percent in 1974, while opposition never exceeded 34 percent. Support among senior politicians was virtually unanimous, while mainstream magazines like *Good Housekeeping, Family Circle, Cosmopolitan,* and even *Playgirl* ran a concerted campaign in the ERA's favor. On top of all that, the pro-ERA effort spent millions of dollars on advertising and lobbying, and it could count on the intellectual momentum of the feminist movement, the organizational muscle of the labor unions, and the enthusiasm of a great variety of celebrities, from Alan Alda, Ann Landers, and Lily Tomlin to Jean Stapleton, Garry Trudeau, and Henry Winkler.[17]

From the outset, however, the ERA faced grassroots opposition. Oklahoma rejected it in the spring of 1972, and that fall Illinois, Ohio, Nevada, and Louisiana also turned it down. By 1974, it was obvious that the ERA had serious problems in the South and the West, where seventeen state legislatures had considered and rejected it. In January 1975, North Dakota became the last state to ratify the amendment, but by this stage Tennessee had already rescinded its approval. As if to deflate any feminist optimism after the North Dakota victory, seven Sunbelt states promptly rejected it once again. There was even talk that other states—perhaps Idaho, perhaps Kentucky—might rescind their approvals.[18]

The key figure in the campaign to stop the ERA was a conservative activist from Missouri whose pious Catholicism masked the fact that she was a woman ahead of her time, showing great independence and bare-knuckle spirit. Born in 1924, Phyllis Schlafly worked for the American Enterprise Institute, where she became a fierce advocate for free-market capitalism, before getting married and becoming a housewife. However, she remained heavily active in politics, joining her local Federation of Republican Women, and in 1952 she won the Republican congressional primary in her Illinois district, although she lost in the general election. A delegate at both the 1956 and the 1960 Republican conventions, Schlafly was a great admirer of Barry Goldwater, and her book *A Choice Not an Echo*, a withering denunciation of the moderate Republican establishment, sold an estimated three million copies in 1964.

In the short term, however, the book did her no good. In 1967, party bosses made sure Schlafly was overlooked for the presidency of the National Federation of Republican Women, which provoked her into a rare outburst against sexist discrimination. It was unfair, she said, "to keep the women doing the menial work, while the selection of candidates and the policy decisions are taken care of by the men." As a result, she began to build an independent network, sending her *Phyllis Schlafly Report* to the women who had backed her. Her goals, she said, were "morality in government, constitutional government, a strong national defense, and free enterprise," and her newsletter kept alive the Goldwater flame, rejecting compromise with liberalism and denouncing détente overseas. Soon she had five thousand readers, and her reputation spread. In June 1972 she was even invited to testify before the Senate Foreign Relations Committee, where she fiercely attacked Henry Kissinger and the SALT treaty.[19]

In many ways Schlafly was everything that feminists despised. A mother of six who kicked off her speeches by thanking her husband for letting her out of the house, she dressed in trim pastel suits, wore her hair in an old-fashioned bouffant, and was the incarnation of suburban Republican propriety. "I'd like to burn you at the stake!" Betty Friedan snapped during a public debate. But as Schlafly's biographer Donald Critchlow remarks, the similarities between them were extraordinary, from their middle-class Midwestern upbringing to their impatience with the complacency of the Eisenhower years and their combination of motherhood and activism. Both wrote national best sellers in the early 1960s; both saw themselves as rebels taking on the status quo; both became champions for broader social movements. Friedan told Schlafly she thought her "a traitor to your sex, an Aunt Tom." But she was more like her great antagonist than she cared to admit.

Schlafly's real interest was always foreign policy, and she came upon the ERA issue almost by chance when invited to discuss it at a conservative forum. "What's wrong with 'equal rights' for women?" she asked in the February 1972 issue of her newsletter. The answer was that it threatened the family, "the basic unit of society, which is ingrained in the laws and customs of our Judeo-Christian civilization." Schlafly agreed that better job opportunities and equal pay were fine ideas, but thought the feminist agenda was "anti-family, anti-children and pro-abortion." The ERA would not only "abolish a woman's right to child support and alimony"; it would "absolutely and positively make women subject to the draft." All in all, she said, "the women's libbers view the home as a prison, and the wife and mother as a slave" (which in some cases was indeed true). They did not understand "that most women want to be a wife, mother and homemaker—and are happy in that role."

The reaction to Schlafly's article was so enthusiastic that by September 1972 she had put together the bare bones of a national organization, Stop ERA. Like so many conservative groups in the 1970s, it succeeded because it was simultaneously narrow, being limited to the single issue of the ERA, and broad, welcoming women of all faiths, classes, and backgrounds. Crucially, it appealed to hundreds of women who had not previously been involved in politics: young evangelical Christians, burning with righteous anger about the nation's decline into godlessness, promiscuity, and homosexuality. Schlafly herself was a Catholic, but like Jerry Falwell after her, she knew better than to let doctrinal differences get in the way of good politics, and the muscle of the evangelical churches, as well as the support of anti-abortion groups and donations from insurance companies, proved vital to her campaign.[20]

Feminism had been seen as fair game for criticism ever since its revival in the late 1960s. Since few leading feminists were renowned for their sense of humor, it was easy to caricature them as overearnest bluestockings trying to compensate for their sexual frustrations. Hugh Hefner, that self-proclaimed expert on the fairer sex, denounced the "highly irrational, emotional, kookie trend that feminism has taken" and in a leaked internal memo ordered *Playboy*'s writers to "do a really expert, personal demolition job on the subject." But he was not the only man who mourned the passing of the days when men were men and women wore aprons. In "Are the Good Times Really Over," Merle Haggard mourned the end of an era "before microwave ovens, when a girl could still cook, and still would." And the novelist Norman Mailer became virtually a professional critic of women's liberation. In his fifty-five-thousand-word *Harper's* essay "The Prisoner of Sex," he denounced feminists as man-hating harpies, and he famously debated Germaine Greer in a highbrow version of the Billie Jean King–Bobby Riggs "Battle of the Sexes" with, many observers thought, a similar outcome.[21]

Plenty of people saw feminism as a new front in the long struggle between Christian values and godless secularism. Jerry Falwell argued that Christians believed not in equal rights but in "superior rights" for women, "in opening the door for our women, helping them with their coats, providing them with their living, and protecting them from their enemies." The ERA, he said, "degrades womanhood, and may one day cause our women to use unisex toilets and fight in the trenches on the battlefield, where men belong." (The dangers of unisex toilets were a common refrain in anti-ERA meetings.) In the rhetoric of the New Right, feminists were second only to homosexuals in the list of villains threatening the American family. Feminists were "hard-faced and hard-hearted women," wrote a spokeswoman for the Heritage Foundation. They were self-pitying narcissists, coldhearted career women, uncaring mothers who put self-indulgence before family values and were bringing up a generation of delinquents.[22]

The most scathing denunciation of feminism, though, came from the pen of George Gilder, an intense young journalist who had moved from liberal Republicanism to the New Right and now strove to knit together different strands of the conservative movement by arguing that supply-side economics was part of the Christian moral tradition. Unusually, he was also a great believer in extrasensory perception. "ESP is important to me," he said, explaining that he had once had a neighbor with psychic powers. "It absolutely exists."[23]

Gilder first came to prominence, however, not as a champion of the paranormal but as "America's number one antifeminist." In the early 1970s he caused a minor controversy by defending Nixon's veto of a congressional day-care bill, whereupon he was fired from his post at the liberal Ripon Society and invited to debate the issue on national television. As Gilder reflected, "It was clear I'd reached pay dirt." The result was *Sexual Suicide* (1973), in which he argued that when women denied their biological difference from men, they rejected "the deepest sources of identity and love." Feminism, he went on, "usually consists of taking jobs and money away from men, while granting in return such uncoveted benefits as the right to cry." Neglected by their selfish mothers, youngsters would inevitably fall into the indoctrinating clutches of the federal government, "a generation of kinless children to serve as the Red Guards of a totalitarian state." "Women's place," he concluded, "*is* in the home."[24]

Gilder's book earned him the title of NOW's Male Chauvinist Pig of the Year, succeeding Norman Mailer. But to reduce the issue to one of male chauvinist pigs versus outspoken feminist women would be completely inaccurate, because many women, too, shared Gilder's views. The Miami beautician Marabel Morgan made a fortune telling women how she had turned her marriage around by subordinating herself to her husband's desires. After six years, she explained, their relationship had turned stale. He hated women's liberation, while she was always challenging his opinions. But after reading the Bible, she changed course completely, becoming the very model of a Stepford wife. Soon she was hosting "Total Woman" seminars across the nation and appearing on *The Phil Donahue Show.* The trick was for a wife to "listen attentively to her husband, to admire his every trait, to pander to his every whim." Among other things, she recommended greeting him at the door clad only in Saran Wrap. "It is only when a woman surrenders her life to her husband, reveres and worships him and is willing to serve him, that she becomes really beautiful to him," she wrote. "She becomes a priceless jewel, the glory of femininity, his queen."[25]

Given that *The Total Woman* became the nation's bestselling nonfiction title of 1974, it is clear that not all American women were suffused with feminist enthusiasm. *Time* suggested that most of Morgan's readers were white churchgoers from the Sunbelt, but unease with women's liberation transcended regional or religious boundaries. When the magazine *Redbook* sent a reporter to gauge the mood of American women in the winter of 1972, she was astonished by the hostility toward feminism among housewives and workingwomen alike. "This whole Women's Liberation thing is a crock of you-know-what," remarked a female worker at a General Electric plant in Ohio. "I suppose you're going to start opening car doors for them . . . Before I know it, it'll be my turn to pay."

And to the reporter's amazement, most housewives seemed happy with their lot and horrified by the thought of working. "I *like* what I'm doing," insisted one. "I don't want to go out and do what my husband is doing," protested another. An Illinois farmer's wife in her thirties said that the very thought of women's liberation made her laugh. "Today's women have all the freedom they please," she said. "I think the trouble with these women who complain about their lives is that they're disorganized. With a washer and a dryer, I don't see how any woman can get behind."[26]

The usual feminist explanation was that these women were prisoners of "false consciousness," having been brainwashed into accepting their own subjugation. This was obviously a rather self-serving argument, allowing feminists to cast themselves as enlightened and everyone else as deluded. A more obvious explanation was that many women, particularly those who had settled down as wives and mothers in the 1950s and 1960s, were offended by the argument that they had wasted their lives as domestic slaves. As the sociologist Kristin Luker pointed out, conservative women had often made early decisions to get married and have a family. It is hardly surprising that feminism infuriated them; not only did it strike at their values, but it made a mockery of their life choices. "Feminists say,

'You're a servant, you're the house slave of the man,'" complained one Brooklyn housewife. "That's why a lot of women I know in Canarsie went against the ERA."[27]

Feminism also alienated millions of women because, rightly or wrongly, its exponents were seen as spoiled middle-class radicals who sneered at the values of ordinary people. In Boston, for example, Alice McGoff had brought up her children alone after her husband's death, working as a hat-check attendant and salad chef. She came from a family of strong-minded women, union activists, and even suffragists. But while she agreed with the principle of equality, "this kooky new movement" did not appeal to her at all. It was led, she thought, "by a bunch of college girls and chichi women from the suburbs who stewed over such burning issues as whether a girl could join an all-male soccer team or whether ads for cosmetics and designer jeans were 'demeaning' to women." And its leaders seemed completely "oblivious to her needs."[28]

As in so many populist movements of the day, this class element was central to the Stop ERA campaign. "We are a group of wives, mothers, and working women," began one mimeographed letter to Ohio legislators. "Those women lawyers, women legislators, and women executives promoting ERA have plenty of education and talent to get whatever they want in the business, political and academic world. We, the wives and working women, need you, dear Senators and Representatives, to protect us. We think this is the man's responsibility, and we are dearly hoping you will vote NO on ERA."[29]

The reaction of women against the ERA was not, as is sometimes claimed, a "status revolt" of economic losers. In North Carolina, for instance, more than half of the women who mobilized against the ERA were college-educated, affluent people, often with steady jobs. As the journalist Andrew Kopkind noted in 1977, the women who opposed the amendment were "as diverse a lot as those in favor," from "the jeans-clad young mothers of the suburban New Right" to "the blue-haired Republican ladies of the old." In South Dakota, the Stop ERA chairman was an Austrian immigrant who had fled from the Nazis. In North Dakota, the chairman was one of twelve children born to Hispanic parents. In Vermont, he was a former McGovern voter in his twenties.[30]

What these people had in common was a shared body of values. The great majority of Stop ERA activists were highly religious; as they saw it, gender roles were God-given, and the family was the centerpiece of Christian society. One of the group's key figures in Illinois, Dorothy Waldvogel, was a farmer's wife and a keen churchgoer, opposed to abortion and uneasy with homosexuality. But she was not some reactionary dinosaur;

indeed, she wore "men's shoes, white socks, blue jeans, a plain shirt—and hair as loose and long as Peter Frampton's." "I've been divorced," she said. "I know all about unequal credit laws. I couldn't get the water company to put the bill in my name. I needed that law against sex discrimination. But I don't know what these women libbers are trying to do with this country except get us stirred up."[31]

Although women like Dorothy Waldvogel were amateurs with little political experience, their campaign was a brilliant example of citizens' activism. They baked pies and cakes, they presented legislators with flowers, they took their daughters to state capitals with signs reading, PLEASE DON'T DRAFT ME, and they generally presented an unthreatening, even sentimental image to the world. Legislators who voted against the ERA often received thank-you cards decorated with interlinked hearts and drawings of adoring women. Inside, the caption read: "For recognizing the difference, you are terrific, fantastic, and marvelous."[32]

By contrast, the pro-ERA campaign, which was much better funded, was tactically inept, relying on outdated, divisive protest techniques. Many activists remembered the civil rights and antiwar movements and thought they simply needed to re-create the rallies and marches of their youth. In Florida, for instance, activists demonstrated outside legislators' homes at seven in the morning, painted slogans on a state senator's driveway, and even daubed the state capitol with feminist catchphrases. Similarly counterproductive plans included an economic boycott of states that had not ratified the ERA, the distribution of Phyllis Schlafly voodoo dolls, and, most bizarre of all, a "witch's curse," which called on "the Goddesses of all beginnings Ea, Astare, Ishtar, Lilith" to "witness our rites in the name of the righteousness for wimmin!" None of this, needless to say, did any good.[33]

What was fatal for the ERA was its association with the deeply divisive issues of abortion and lesbianism, a result not only of Schlafly's propaganda but of the images sent out from the Houston conference. Even though the ERA had almost nothing to do with either *Roe v. Wade* or the gay rights movement, the amendment became a symbol of secularism and sexual liberation. Rosalynn Carter, for one, was disturbed "that some of the more controversial issues have been mistakenly identified with the amendment." The Democratic governor of Missouri, who had supported the amendment before the Houston conference, backed away from it afterward. "I was for equal pay for equal work," he said, "but after they went down to Houston and got all tangled up with all those lesbians, I can tell you, Missouri will never ratify ERA."[34]

In the three months after Houston, the ERA was rejected in Georgia,

Alabama, South Carolina, and Florida. With time running out, Congress approved an extension until 1982, but momentum continued to dribble away. In 1979, South Dakota rescinded its assent; in 1980 a renewed attempt to win assent in Illinois failed; and in 1982 the Florida Senate also rejected the amendment. Some feminists tried more radical tactics, including hunger strikes and demonstrations outside the national Republican headquarters, but it was no good. As late as June 1982, polls showed that the public still backed the ERA by 56 percent to 34 percent, but on the last day of the month the deadline expired. It was, gushed Schlafly at a press conference on Capitol Hill, "the most remarkable political victory of the twentieth century."[35]

One of the ironies of the ERA battle was that, ultimately, the amendment had been beaten not by men but by women, and by an independent, ambitious, articulate woman at that. Another was that its defeat did not really matter. By the end of the 1970s, equal rights were enshrined in a host of legislative reforms and judicial decisions, which meant that women were treated equally by federal programs, could expect equal Social Security payments, had equal access to jobs, credit, and the housing market, and were even admitted to military academies—just as Schlafly had feared.

But the battle over the ERA did have one major consequence. It turned Phyllis Schlafly into a household name and made her a symbol of the new politics of moral populism. In some ways she was the heir to a long tradition: devout, enterprising women had long been seen as guardians of republican virtue. But through the Stop ERA campaign she helped to pioneer a new kind of right-wing politics: media savvy, steeped in cultural anxiety, directed against liberal secularism, populist rather than patrician. In mobilizing a new generation of women to work for the conservative movement, and in feeding the flames of cultural controversy, she left a deep imprint on American politics. As an admirer put it the day after the final defeat of the ERA, she was the "sweetheart of the silent majority," and a herald of things to come.[36]

**If Congress had approved** the ERA sooner, it might have escaped the conservative backlash. But feminism was a latecomer to the Great Society party, and after a brief shining moment at the beginning of the decade it fell victim to the economic frustrations, limited horizons, and increasingly sour public mood of the mid-1970s. In an era of stagflation, any movement hoping to redistribute power and opportunities faced an uphill struggle. Many feminist radicals, suffering the inevitable letdown after their countercultural summers, turned inward. The issues seemed more complicated, the obstacles harder to overcome. "This seems to be where we are, 10 years or so into the second wave of feminism," wrote Gloria Steinem in 1978. "Raised hopes, a hunger for change, and years of hard work are running head-on into a frustrating realization that each battle must be fought over and over again at different depths, and that one inevitable result of winning the majority to some changed consciousness is a backlash from those forces whose power depended on the old one."[37]

By the midpoint of the Carter administration, feminism's collective momentum had disappeared. Instead of coming together, women seemed to be moving apart, forming splinter groups, from the National Chicana Conference to the National Black Feminist Organization, from the Women of All Red Nations to the Third World Lesbian and Gay Conference. For many of these groups, what really mattered was the personal, not the collective. Older or more conservative activists felt alienated by the new vogue for "political lesbianism": as a Kansas City feminist wrote in 1974, she "felt uncomfortable with lesbians," because they treated her as "inadequate, inferior, backsliding, not feminist enough." At a national women's studies meeting, the historian Ruth Rosen "sat stunned as every group created a caucus, and every caucus demanded to be heard." She watched "Jewish, Islamic, Christian, Chicana, African-American, disabled, fat, and anorexic women, along with white lesbian feminists and Third World lesbian feminists, fight each other for visibility." Difference, she concluded, had become "more seductive than solidarity"; sadly, "women rather than men were becoming the new enemy."[38]

The paradox was that, in some ways, feminists had good cause for celebration, from the unprecedented visibility of female judges and athletes to rising female admissions at law and medical schools. Yet there was a palpable sense of disappointment that in an age of diminished expectations, feminists would be forced to settle for much less than they had hoped for. Robin Morgan wrote of a sense of "impatience and despair"; other activists wrote position papers asking, "Will the women's movement survive?" or threw themselves more deeply into cultural separatism.[39]

Meanwhile, most women still worked in what *Ms.* called the "pink-collar ghetto" of sales, secretarial, and catering jobs, with few opportunities to progress to senior levels. At the end of the decade women's incomes still amounted to just 57 percent of men's. Even more disturbing, though, was what sociologists called the "feminization" of poverty: by the dawn of the 1980s, thanks to low pay, fewer jobs, divorce, and child-care responsibilities, women accounted for two out of three poor Americans, with 100,000 mothers falling beneath the poverty line every year. In different circumstances, this would surely have been the ultimate feminist issue. Unfortunately, many activists seemed more concerned with university hiring policies and the iniquity of the word "chairman."[40]

Feminism's fall from grace at the end of the 1970s was reflected in the changing attitude of Jimmy Carter. In 1976, Carter had run as a strong supporter of the ERA: when asked where he stood on the issue, he would flash his trademark grin and say, "I can answer that in three words. I'm for it." In office, he appointed more women to senior posts than any of his predecessors. His wife, Rosalynn, was the most influential First Lady since Eleanor Roosevelt, attending cabinet meetings beginning in February 1978. Yet it was never enough. Carter worked hard for the ERA, and Rosalynn was reputed to have made crucial calls to sway Indiana legislators toward voting yes in 1977. Yet some feminists, who seemed to have a very tenuous grasp on political reality, insisted that Carter had let them down.[41]

Their mutual resentment finally came to a head in January 1979, when Carter's own National Advisory Committee for Women, co-chaired by the irrepressible Bella Abzug, published a report critical of the president's economic record. In their next White House meeting, Abzug lectured Carter on his failings in front of about forty people. A few moments later, after she had boasted to the press of her triumph, Hamilton Jordan told her that she had been fired. Carter had had enough: his relationship with the feminist movement was over. NOW's executive board even announced it would oppose Carter in 1980 no matter who ran against him, an extraordinarily myopic decision. "It was as though every woman in this country was fired," Abzug complained afterward with prodigious vanity. "Right now women have no power. We are on the fringes of democracy looking in."[42]

If Bella Abzug seriously thought that a new president would mark an improvement in the fortunes of the women's movement, she was very much mistaken. For in the coming decade, many feminists would find themselves drifting, their spirits depressed, their movement directionless. One day, when the torch lit amid such excitement in Seneca Falls and carried on a wave of hope all the way to Houston had almost been forgotten, they would look back on the lost possibilities of the 1970s and wonder what might have been.[43]

## Chapter Fifteen    *Whatever Happened to California?*

California to Liberal Government: Drop Dead

—*Newsweek*, June 19, 1978

Perhaps nothing captures the melancholic self-absorption of the mid-1970s better than the record that dominated the album charts during the early months of the Carter presidency, selling sixteen million copies in all: the Eagles' bestselling album *Hotel California*. What the lyrics meant was anybody's guess; what mattered was the dreamy effect, the languid rhythms that seemed to capture so perfectly the laid-back, druggy atmosphere of Los Angeles in the Carter years. The band's singer and co-writer Don Henley claimed that it was supposed to be a "little bicentennial statement using California as a microcosm of the whole United States, or the whole world, if you will." While the album's themes included such contemporary favorites as divorce, drugs, and the disintegration of the American Dream, the overall subject, he said, was "how the West was lost."[1]

Like so many of their generation, the Eagles had been drawn west by a dream of a better life, a coastal paradise of progress and enlightenment beneath eternally blue skies. During the 1960s teenagers across the world had sung along to "California Girls" and "California Dreamin,' " imagining new lives in the parks of San Francisco and on the beaches of

Southern California. The Golden State was the land of "the surfing boys and leggy girls, the hikers and farmers and futurists, the kooks and the activists," said *Time* in 1969. It was the home of "the hippie movement, the pop-drug culture, widespread sexual permissiveness, campus revolt and . . . virulent ghetto riots." It was the greatest trendsetter in the nation: a state of twenty million people, with the world's sixth-biggest economy, growing faster than countries like Israel or Japan. Where California led, others followed. And despite the persistence of poverty in the ghettos and the fields, the average Californian, with his high wages and ranch house, his credit card and color television, was materially better off than anyone else on the planet.[2]

Yet while the media drooled over beads and bangles, drugs and divorces, swingers and communes, many missed the far more significant story unfolding in California's suburbs and small towns. It was in prosperous Orange County, where Mickey Mouse delighted the tourists at Disneyland and Richard Nixon brooded in his San Clemente hideaway, that it was most visible. Formerly a quiet backwater of orange groves and trading townships, Orange County had been transformed by defense spending and light industry, its population ballooning to 1.5 million in 1970 and hitting 2 million ten years later. The newcomers were engineers, businessmen, lawyers, and doctors, upwardly mobile but desperately keen to preserve their gains. They lived in neat suburban enclaves, unimpeachably modern in design, but fiercely nostalgic in their ethos. Like most Southern Californians, they had been born in the conservative states of the South and the Midwest. And they brought with them not only the popular culture and musical tastes of their childhoods but also evangelical Protestantism, individualism, and a deep antipathy to big government.[3]

As a shifting society of winners and losers, migrants and dreamers, twentieth-century California had thrown up more than its fair share of political eccentrics. Few of them, however, were quite as strange as the man who in November 1974 won the contest to succeed Ronald Reagan. Edmund G. "Jerry" Brown Jr., the son of the man Reagan had defeated back in 1966, could hardly have been less like his gregarious, glad-handing father. Tall, pale, severely ascetic, he had spent four years in a Jesuit seminary and relaxed on the campaign trail by reading Zen manuals and Sufi parables, listening to mournful singer-songwriters, and making deadpan jokes in Latin. Nobody knew what to make of him, but it was the year of the Democratic Watergate landslide, so they elected him anyway.

Brown's gnomic pronouncements left most observers baffled: was he a liberal or a conservative? "I take a somewhat jaundiced view of the ability of government to perform," he told one reporter. He was against progressive education and in favor of law and order; he believed in "activism in government," but was tired of "the kind of '60s liberalism that involves pushing money after every problem." His favorite theme was the importance of limits. Delivering his inaugural address in January 1975, Brown reminded his listeners of "the rising cost of energy, the depletion of our resources, the threat to the environment, the uncertainty of our economy and the monetary system, the lack of faith in government, the drift in political and moral leadership." Three years later, he declared that Americans needed "more discipline and a leaner life-style." "You don't have to *do* things," he said. "Maybe by avoiding doing things you accomplish quite a lot."[4]

Although Brown's message anticipated the green politics of the early twenty-first century, it was widely mocked at the time, not least in the *Doonesbury* comic strip. The governor's peculiar personality, a mixture of Jesuit austerity and New Age psychobabble, meant that he was rarely out of the gossip columns, whether he was recommending that California launch its own space missions or dating the country-rock singer Linda Ronstadt. He practiced what he preached, shunning the governor's mansion for a bare bachelor apartment and driving himself to work in a modest Plymouth sedan. But when he was asked what kind of leadership he offered, his answer confirmed the "Governor Moonbeam" stereotypes. "Bold leadership," Brown said. "Big thinking. Thinking for the year 2000. Where does America fit in? Where does the planet, where do we as a species, fit into the whole flow of things?"[5]

"Big thinking" struck a chord with California voters in the mid-1970s. As a society of migrants brought together by their pursuit of wealth and happiness, Californians had long seemed peculiarly prone to cultural anxiety. Paradise could easily turn sour, transforming dreamers into drifters and strivers into malcontents, and it was this fear of failure that drove so many into the cults and communes of the 1970s. Every day five hundred people moved out of the state, their dreams of worldly success shattered. On their way out they passed hundreds coming in, bent on the pursuit of paradise, yet doomed to disappointment in their turn.[6]

Beneath the superficial glamour of California life, the undercurrent of anxiety had rarely run harder and faster than in the mid-1970s. With the economy in recession, jobless rates stood at almost 10 percent, and the state was coming under growing pressure to raise taxes and slash services. Factories and employers were heading south, think tanks and theaters were closing, and people were increasingly moving out of the big cities. Even the Golden State's blue skies had lost much of their luster: over Los Angeles there glowered a permanent cloud of smog, topped up every day by five million cars pouring out exhaust fumes. San Francisco, San Diego, and even Palm Springs had some of the most polluted skies in the nation; rivers and lakes were besmirched by garbage and excrement; along the coastline, otters and pelicans struggled to survive in a sea of pesticides.

"Whatever happened to California?" asked *Time* magazine in 1977, noting that Ronald Reagan's grand governor's mansion, just ten years old, now stood empty while his frugal successor lived downtown in a $275-a-month apartment. "Today this monument to the California dream stands cold and mute, an incongruous reminder of an era that no longer exists . . . California has clearly lost the magic it once had."[7]

**The decline of** the California dream made an appropriate metaphor for the fortunes of the ideology that, under Jerry Brown's father, had defined the state's political life in the 1950s and 1960s. Unlike his son, Pat Brown had been an irrepressibly optimistic liberal of the old school, never leaving home without a big new water program or highway scheme in his back pocket. Like other liberals of the day, he had total confidence in economic growth to solve the nation's problems. And like other liberals, he was a faithful disciple of the creed handed down from the British economist John Maynard Keynes, which held that government had a duty to intervene in the economy to keep demand high and unemployment down. Even though Keynes, who died in 1946, had mocked politicians who became "the slaves of some defunct economist," his ideas had become the blueprint for the age of affluence. With their promise of endless growth, they allowed governments to satisfy voters without raising taxes, and with their tacit approval of government activism they gave the nod to expensive welfare programs. At its peak in the 1960s, Keynesian liberalism was more than an economic school: it was a religious faith.[8]

Keynesianism always had its critics, from old-fashioned Republican conservatives to Sunbelt libertarians like Barry Goldwater. Conservatives often argued that it undermined competition and free enterprise, rewarded sloth and failure, and had set the nation on the road to serfdom. During the good times, as Goldwater discovered in 1964, few people were willing to listen. But ten years later, everything had changed. The Nixon years had shattered voters' trust in politicians, their faith in government, and their confidence in the American economy. The combination of recession and inflation was something Keynes had never anticipated and for which his disciples had no solution. To put it bluntly, Keynesianism was no longer delivering the goods.

Meanwhile, step-by-step, conservative economists were beginning to demolish the walls of certainty surrounding Keynes's ideas. At the University of Virginia, the "public choice" theorists James M. Buchanan and Gordon Tullock argued that there was no such thing as the public interest, as liberals claimed. Instead, there was merely the aggregation of decisions made by private actors for their own ends, with politics as a marketplace for the pursuit of self-interest. Then there was the "rational expectations" school, associated with the University of Chicago's Robert Lucas, who suggested that government intervention was bound to be counterproductive because the people it set out to influence—businessmen, say—had already predicted what it might do and made their plans accordingly. Forecasting what specific policies would do was useless, Lucas thought, since the rules of the game were always changing. At the time, this seemed a hugely exciting and influential insight. Rational expectations, Franco Modigliani, the liberal president of the American Economic Association, announced in 1976, had delivered "the death blow to the already battered Keynesian position."[9]

Then there was the challenge of small-government libertarianism. There had always been libertarians, of course, such as the economist Friedrich von Hayek and the eccentric novelist Ayn Rand, but they were long regarded as reactionary crackpots. By the early 1970s, however, libertarianism had become unexpectedly fashionable, thanks to the rebellious spirit of the youthful counterculture and the backlash against the Vietnam War. Weedy pacifists who marched against "the machine" might seem a long way from Ayn Rand's muscular mavericks, but their disdain for authority meant that they were, if not bedfellows, then at least propping up the same late-night bar. Meanwhile, libertarianism not only had unprecedented academic credibility, thanks to the Harvard philosopher Robert Nozick, whose book *Anarchy, State, and Utopia* (1974) called for a limited "night watchman" state and won a National Book Award; it also had serious money behind it. By the mid-1970s, the oil tycoon Charles Koch was spending millions on the Cato Institute in Washington, the Institute for Humane Studies in California, the magazines *Inquiry* and *Libertarian Review*, the Council for a Competitive Economy, and Students for a Libertarian Society. The Libertarian Party itself remained electorally insignificant. But the rise of libertarian ideas dealt a heavy blow to the intellectual foundations of Keynesian liberalism, and struck a chord with millions who resented high taxes and distrusted big government.[10]

The most effective champion of the antiliberal cause, however, was a brilliant, aggressive little man who stood just five feet three inches tall in his socks, had been born to poor Jewish immigrants in Brooklyn, and had turned himself into the most influential economist in the world. When

Milton Friedman won the Nobel Prize in Economics for 1976, it was a sign of his notoriety that demonstrators protested outside the Stockholm ceremony, while the liberal economist Melville Ulmer told *The New Republic* that the award was "as incongruous as a peace prize for Idi Amin, or a literature prize for Spiro Agnew." Yet most American economists, whether of the left or the right, conceded that Friedman's scholarship set him apart. He was "the *architect* of much that is best in our conservative tradition," wrote the liberal economist and Nobel laureate Paul Samuelson, "and not just the *expositor* of that viewpoint." "One doesn't have to agree with Friedman's right-wing laissez-faire philosophy," remarked *The Washington Post*'s economics writer Hobart Rowen, "to acknowledge a great brain and teacher, and the man's determination, audacity, and shock value."[11]

Friedman had been raining down blows on liberalism's reputation since the early 1960s, when his defense of the free market, *Capitalism and Freedom* (1962), sold half a million copies and ensured his appointment as an economic adviser to Barry Goldwater. In 1966 he began writing a regular column for *Newsweek,* and a year later he was elected president of the American Economic Association, delivering a famous presidential address that demolished the cherished notion of the Phillips curve, which held that if governments let inflation gently rise and fall, they could virtually eradicate the threat of unemployment. As the architect of monetarism, Friedman argued that liberal tax-and-spend policies to boost consumer demand were a terrible mistake. The result of liberal policies, he explained in his Nobel lecture in 1976, was simply "larger and larger doses of inflation to keep down the level of unemployment." Instead, the government ought to accept a "natural" level of joblessness and concentrate on regulating the money supply to keep inflation low. If inflation got out of control, as in the 1970s, the only remedy was to slash the money supply, irrespective of the human cost in failing business and disappearing jobs. For Friedman, unemployment was unfortunate, but inflation was fatal.[12]

It was a sign of how far the pendulum had swung since Pat Brown's heyday that by the time his son became governor of California, Friedman was easily the most famous economist in the Western world. His intellect was unquestionable, his output prolific, his energy unstinting, and thanks partly to his efforts, for the first time in years it was fashionable to be conservative. At the end of the decade, he was even given his own PBS series, *Free to Choose,* which he used to denounce the threat posed by government to personal freedom and to promote the importance of restoring free-market values. For Friedman, however, the battle was far from won. Too many people, he later lamented, still thought that "government was the answer to every problem." And it was to puncture that illusion—as he saw it—that in the summer of 1978 he answered a call for help from another conservative, aggressive little man from the Golden State. "Don't let politicians fool you," Milton Friedman told the voters of California a few days later. "Proposition 13 will work."[13]


**The man responsible** for the greatest tax revolt in modern history was a very implausible character indeed, with a life story that, as one writer once remarked, sounded "like something from a page of Horatio Alger with an assist from Mel Brooks' Two-Thousand-Year-Old-Man." Born in Utah in 1903, Howard Jarvis had led a bizarrely full-blooded life, starting out in semipro baseball, sparring with the boxer Jack Dempsey, and running a chain of struggling newspapers. After moving to Los Angeles, he dabbled in real estate, manufactured a string of gadgets, and finally opened a chain of household-appliance factories. Meanwhile, he drank with Gary Cooper and Clark Gable and began to make a name for himself in conservative circles, supporting Richard Nixon and campaigning for Dwight Eisenhower.

Although Jarvis had long entertained political ambitions, three bids for office, including a campaign for mayor of Los Angeles, all ended in tears. Many local Republicans did not trust him, remembering how he had set up an unauthorized fund-raising committee for Barry Goldwater, only to pocket all the money in "fees" without giving the candidate a single cent. In 1976 he pulled the same stunt again, chairing the "Friends of [Samuel] Hayakawa" to raise funds for the Republican politician's Senate campaign. Again, the candidate never saw a penny, and Hayakawa eventually went to court to close Jarvis's operation down. "Nobody here takes Jarvis seriously," wrote a local civil liberties campaigner. "He hasn't even succeeded in getting acceptance among the right-wing organizations."[14]

But Jarvis did have one great asset: his obsessive loathing of tax. He sometimes told audiences that all taxes were "grand theft" and called the income tax "un-American and illegal," but the one that most offended him was the state property tax. Few taxes were less popular: to the typical California homeowner in a new development called Sunny Hills or Hacienda Heights, the idea of being dragged beneath the poverty line by a tax on his beloved house was deeply frightening. In a society of strivers, nothing scared people more than the thought of losing their homes and their social status. Across Southern California tax-resistance groups proliferated, giving Jarvis the perfect forum to air his militant message. Cutting the property tax was his mission in life. "I'm going to stay in this tax thing," he announced, "until I win or die."[15]

Public fury about property taxes had been growing since the mid-1960s, when the state legislature had passed reforms that unwittingly sent many homeowners' bills soaring. Previously, crooked assessors had kept taxes down in exchange for campaign donations. But with suburbs spreading across the state, even quiet farms and rural backwaters had rocketed in value—and so did their taxes. Jarvis did his best to capitalize, rushing from one meeting to the next, tearing across the Southern California valleys to harangue school boards and supervisors. He became a fixture at Los Angeles's civic auditorium, where officials would wearily turn off his microphone to silence his tirades. But even when Governor Reagan backed a complicated tax-reduction plan in 1973, the issue never really caught fire. The economic outlook was still fairly bright, and the Democrats in Sacramento were quick to offer generous exemptions for residential taxpayers. Jarvis could count on only a few hundred core supporters, most of them anxious retirees and landlords. Often he found himself speaking to just six people in a suburban living room.[16]

And yet the tide was flowing in Jarvis's favor. Complaints about high taxes reflected the genuine reality of a burden becoming heavier by the year. In the mid-1950s, a typical married father of two paid around 5.5 percent of his income in federal income taxes and 2 percent in Social Security contributions. Despite Kennedy's tax cut in the early 1960s, however, exemptions did not keep pace with surging income, and by the late 1970s Mr. Average paid more than 11 percent of his wage in federal income taxes and more than 6 percent in Social Security. Blue-collar Americans did not even have the consolation of knowing that the burden fell most heavily on the wealthy. In the Eisenhower era an average family was taxed at around 12 percent, while a family four times wealthier was taxed at more than 20 percent. But by the Carter years the gap had narrowed: the average family was now taxed at 23 percent and the rich one at 30 percent.[17]

Behind this lay the problem of "bracket creep," which seriously threatened many families' living standards. Thanks to inflation, middle-class households found themselves pushed into steeply rising marginal tax rates originally intended for the very rich. On top of that, between 1964 and 1980 Social Security payroll taxes had grown by almost 800 percent. The inevitable losers were the very people the taxes were supposed to benefit: low-income, hardworking Democratic loyalists. It was not even as though they were noticeably more prosperous: inflation and taxes meant that real family income fell by 2 percent every year from 1973 to 1981. By the end of the decade, the average worker's spending power was at its lowest level since the Kennedy years.[18]

Not surprisingly, many ordinary voters felt unfairly treated. In 1977, nine out of ten Americans agreed that "the big tax burden falls on the little man in this country." A year later, eight out of ten said that taxes were "unreasonable." Not all politicians were blind to the problem: Jimmy Carter memorably called the tax system "a disgrace to the human race." But his reform plan got nowhere, and when he did cut taxes in 1978, the main beneficiaries were the rich. Many liberals never grasped that anti-tax resentment posed a terrible threat to their political ambitions. "My husband works hard, and the taxes keep going up," said one Brooklyn housewife. "The taxes go to the poor, not to us. And the rich have their tax accountants. The middle-income people are carrying the cost of liberal social programs on their backs."[19]

When Jarvis announced a new drive to put tax reduction on the California state ballot in May 1977, he was pushing at an unbolted door. With the stock market stagnant, investors had poured their money into West Coast real estate, and house prices were soaring by absurd margins. Between April 1974 and April 1978, the value of an ordinary family home in Los Angeles leaped from $37,800 to $83,200. And since rising property values meant rising tax bills, families faced bills that had doubled or even quadrupled in just four years. Their homes had become millstones around their necks. "I had hoped that by age 65 the house would be paid for and I would have a place to live," one woman wrote desperately to Jerry Brown. "But I now see that all the planning is in vain because our government will not allow this to happen."[20]

Jarvis's proposal—Proposition 13—was enticingly simple. First, property values would be rolled back to their 1975 levels and could be raised by no more than 2 percent a year for inflation. Only when the property changed hands would its value be reassessed. Second, the tax rate would be limited to 1 percent per property, with the returns shared out among the various local jurisdictions. For the first time, therefore, homeowners would know exactly what they had to pay—and it was a lot less than before. Under the 1977 rates a typical Los Angeles homeowner paid about $2,200 on his $70,000 home. If Proposition 13 passed, however, his taxes would be frozen at $700 a year. And there was no reason to worry about taxes going back up again. Under Proposition 13, no new taxes could be raised unless they were approved by two-thirds of the electorate—about as likely as Farrah Fawcett running for the presidency.[21]

In the past, Sacramento had regularly appeased public anger with tax relief. But this time the Democratic majority left it far too late, and on the last day of the session a relief bill fell short. The one man who could have provided the necessary leadership was the governor. But Jerry Brown was far too busy with his alternative-energy projects and space missions to bother with the grubby business of coalition building. In any case, with an election looming he was unwilling to antagonize the suburbs or the business community. Tax relief, he later confessed, needed "more time than I had attention span to deal with," as well as hard choices between "business and residential taxpayers . . . and I didn't have the stomach for it."[22]

Meanwhile, the seventy-five-year-old Howard Jarvis was in ebullient form, charging relentlessly from homeowners' meetings to radio talk shows, while his activists set up tables in shopping malls, urging passersby: "Sign this—it will help lower your taxes." Although Jarvis received handsome support from small-business men and landlords, this was not really a business-funded conspiracy or a "revolt of the haves," as one journalist famously called it. In fact, the campaign's records showed that most contributions came from ordinary retirees, real estate agents, farmers, doctors, teachers, and housewives: people who felt that their small slice of the American Dream was threatened by inflation, taxes, and profligate government, and who often gave less than $100 each. There were so many of them that by the time Jarvis turned in his signatures, he had more than a million names, twice as many as he needed to get Proposition 13 on the ballot.[23]

Perhaps surprisingly, it was the campaign *against* Proposition 13 that attracted five-figure donations from major corporations, such as Southern California Edison, Bank of America, Pacific Mutual Insurance, Standard Oil, and Southern Pacific Railroad. Their executives were worried that if Jarvis won, the state would recoup its losses in higher business taxes, and so they threw their support behind the No campaign. And they were not alone. The governor's office, the state legislature, the Chamber of Commerce, the League of Women Voters, the Teachers' Association, the AFL-CIO, and even the California Taxpayers' Association campaigned against Proposition 13, arguing that it was much too reckless. It was not difficult, therefore, for Jarvis to pose as the champion of the people against the powerful. "You are the people," he told his supporters, "and you will have to take control of the government again or else it is going to control you."[24]

Twenty years earlier Jarvis would have been derided as a crank, but in an age of anxiety his attacks on taxes and spending struck a powerful chord. To ordinary homeowners he seemed a scourge of the establishment, and like other populists—such as the eccentric doctor Francis Townsend, whose insurance plan had aroused enormous enthusiasm in California during the Depression—he struck a chord with lower-middle-class homeowners with something to lose. His campaign consultants, recognizing that "he was somebody ordinary taxpayers could identify with," built their entire effort around "this one guy and his struggles," giving it a more human focus. One reporter likened him to an angry Muppet. Yet the more irate Jarvis became, the more it confirmed his cantankerous authenticity.[25]

Even so, Jarvis's campaign seemed so radical that in other circumstances it might well have failed. In May 1978, with only a month to go before Californians voted, polls gave it a narrow margin of just 3 percent, with 19 percent undecided and the No campaign picking up momentum. But then, quite unexpectedly, he enjoyed a stroke of good fortune when the new assessor for Los Angeles County, Alexander Pope, yielded to public pressure and brought forward the release of the new property-tax assessments, which had been scheduled for after the election. Thanks to inflation, many Angelenos found that their property taxes had doubled or even trebled, and every night television bulletins showed horrified citizens in floods of tears. "I don't know if I can walk to the car," gasped one housewife, reeling from the news that her tax had jumped from $2,000 to more than $5,500. Even Pope himself found that his liability had soared from $535 to more than $3,000. Howard Jarvis could hardly have asked for better publicity.[26]

The Los Angeles assessments decisively altered the course of the campaign. On June 6, 1978, seven out of ten registered voters—unheard of outside a presidential year—made their way to their local polling stations, where two out of three cast their ballots in favor of Proposition 13. It was a revolt not just of the haves but also of the have-nots. While its most ardent supporters were elderly white homeowners, most other groups supported it too: rich and poor, young and old, conservatives and moderates. The teachers' unions had waged a four-month campaign against Proposition 13, yet their members voted overwhelmingly for it. Most Californians, it turned out, were more worried about their homes and their pocketbooks than about public services and the state budget. "I'm for it," a sixty-year-old Los Angeles school janitor told reporters. "Even if they lay me off, because they were taxing me out of my home. I've been paying on it for 27 or 28 years. Where am I going to get another home? I'd rather go out and find a new job."[27]

**With Proposition 13 approved,** millions of homeowners saw their tax bills slashed at a stroke. According to the California Taxpayers' Association, taxpayers saved a staggering $228 billion over the next ten years. But the biggest winners were the major corporations that owned much of the property in the state. The Pacific Telephone and Telegraph Company saved an estimated $130 million in tax liabilities, Pacific Gas and Electric saved $90 million, and Southern California Edison $53.5 million. In Los Angeles alone, Lockheed saved almost $10 million, and IBM got a tax cut of more than $6 million. "People everywhere," said a delighted Richard Nixon, "want to reduce government spending, the burden of taxes, and the spiral [of] inflation which is the cruelest tax of all." But despite its populist overtones, Proposition 13 was a "striking bonanza for the haves." Thanks to Howard Jarvis, Nixon himself had saved $27,500 in taxes on his $2 million home.[28]

But Proposition 13 came at a heavy cost. It eliminated around 27 percent of all city revenues, 40 percent of county revenues, 50 percent of school district revenues, and up to 90 percent for some fire districts. By 1980, Los Angeles had closed four libraries, two health centers, and three neighborhood service centers, while San Francisco laid off a thousand teachers, doubled transit fares, and made deep cuts in its libraries, parks, and public works budgets. These cuts had visible consequences: empty library shelves, scruffy parks, mental patients wandering the streets. But they fell most heavily on schools. In the town of Little Lake, after-school sports were canceled, class sizes rocketed, and there was a freeze on book purchases. In Modesto, there were no new textbooks, crayons, paper supplies, or even cleaning rags. The school newspaper was abolished; the custodian came only once a week; wastebaskets overflowed with litter; walls were still daubed with the previous year's graffiti. There was no such thing as a free lunch.[29]

Of course California still had much to celebrate: as early as 1971, the press had christened the southern San Francisco Bay Area "Silicon Valley," and even as Howard Jarvis was pounding the streets, two college dropouts, Steve Wozniak and Steve Jobs, were working on their first computers. But even years later, long after Silicon Valley had become a byword for staggering technological innovation and Apple had become one of the best-known brands in the world, the impact of Proposition 13 could still be felt.* With revenues slashed, California could no longer maintain its progressive reputation, and the gap between rich and poor widened further than anywhere else in the nation. Schools remained underfunded and overcrowded; parks grew shabby; the urban infrastructure, the cleanliness of the environment, and the quality of the air all deteriorated. Proposition

---

*In the long run, historians will probably judge that the technological breakthroughs made on the West Coast were by far the most important legacy of the 1970s. But their social and cultural potential was not really evident until the Reagan years.

13 was not solely to blame. But as Peter Schrag writes, it marked the tipping point from an age of optimism to an era of neglect.[30]

It also heralded a new era in California politics. Having campaigned against Proposition 13, Jerry Brown now declared himself a "born-again tax cutter," promising to "limit the public sector" and "curb spending," and even making toe-curling joint appearances alongside the triumphant Howard Jarvis. Meanwhile, plebiscitary politics was all the rage. After June 1978, the initiative became a central part of California politics, dressed up with populist rhetoric and accompanied by vast advertising and media interest. The Golden State found itself trapped in "a condition of permanent neopopulism," reaching its apogee in 2003, when, just a year after having been reelected, Governor Gray Davis was recalled by the voters and replaced with an Austrian bodybuilder. Voters were furious about spiraling energy bills, the governor's failure to provide adequate relief, and a pervasive sense that they were being cheated by the energy companies. Those with long memories could hardly miss the parallels.[31]

Even at the time, many commentators recognized that Proposition 13 was a watershed. In *Newsweek*, Meg Greenfield wrote that "the Great Tax Revolt of 1978" would "herald a conservative reaction" just as surely as the New Deal had "launched Big Government." Indeed, most conservatives were ecstatic. A second American Revolution was on the way, said California's former governor Ronald Reagan, for Proposition 13 was "a little bit like dumping those cases of tea off the boat in Boston harbor." By contrast, most liberals were aghast. In the White House, Pat Caddell warned President Carter that this was not "just a tax revolt. It's a revolution against government." And at the ADA national convention, George McGovern declared that thanks to its criticisms of welfare, the Proposition 13 campaign had "undertones of racism"—a good example of liberals' growing eagerness to blame racism for every conceivable conservative advance.[32]

In the short term, Proposition 13 made Howard Jarvis a national celebrity. He made the cover of *Time* and the national talk shows; he went to Europe to meet Margaret Thatcher and Jacques Chirac; and in the fall of 1978, his American Tax Reduction Movement wrote to all the major party candidates for Congress, asking them to support a $100 billion cut in federal spending and a $50 billion cut in taxes. Everywhere, activists clamored to follow California's example; everywhere, local politicians rushed to appease public resentment. By 1979, tax-reduction measures were on the ballot in seventeen states, and twelve voted to approve them. From Maine and Massachusetts to Nevada and New Mexico, spending limits, property-tax ceilings, and income tax cuts were all the rage. In just over a year, thirty-seven states cut their property taxes, while twenty-eight slashed income taxes. Even in states like Idaho and Nevada, where taxes were relatively low, voters chose to limit property taxes to just 1 percent of assessed value.[33]

Crucially, Proposition 13 also played into the hands of a new intellectual movement regarded with utter scorn by many economists, but nonetheless increasingly popular on the Republican right. For almost four years *The Wall Street Journal*'s iconoclastic young columnist Jude Wanniski had been telling readers that only massive tax cuts could jolt the economy out of the cycle of stagflation. "The national economy is being choked by taxes—asphyxiated," he wrote in December 1974. "It is simply absurd to argue that increasing unemployment will stop inflation. To stop inflation you need more goods, not less." What became known as supply-side theory, Wanniski claimed, offered a simple answer to the nation's ills. Since the key to the economy was not demand but supply, the quickest route to prosperity was for the government to cut high marginal tax rates. This would increase the incentives for individuals to save and invest, ensuring high levels of production and output. Not only would low taxes raise output; they might encourage such incredible growth that government revenues would actually go up. Everyone would come out ahead; all you had to do was slash taxes.[34]

Wanniski had picked up the rudiments of supply-side theory from his friend Arthur Laffer, formerly a junior professor at the University of Chicago and a controversial budget forecaster in the Nixon administration. Laffer, meanwhile, had got his ideas from the eccentric Canadian economist Robert Mundell, a former Chicago and Columbia professor who was now holed up in a ruined Italian villa, from which he issued increasingly heretical opinions about the road to prosperity. But while Wanniski claimed that supply-side was nothing less than a "Copernican revolution in economic policy," most orthodox economists thought it was nonsense. The supply-siders, said the liberal Princeton economist Alan Blinder, were armed "with neither theory nor evidence, just boldfaced assertions." And if anything, conservative economists were even more scathing. Herbert Stein, chairman of the Council of Economic Advisers under Nixon and Ford, thought that Laffer's predictions were "extreme to the point of bizarre," while economists had recognized the importance of supply "since the first parrot had gotten a Ph.D. in economics for learning to say 'supply and demand.'" "I'm for cutting taxes," agreed Alan Greenspan, "but not for Laffer's reasons. I don't know anyone who seriously believes his argument."[35]

The supply-siders, however, had two things in their favor. First, anything that justified tax cuts was bound to appeal to conservative politicians. Reagan's first budget director, David Stockman, for example, admitted that he embraced the new theory as "a Trojan horse," providing "new clothes for the unpopular doctrine of the old Republican orthodoxy." It was, he admitted, the perfect cover for old-fashioned trickle-down theory. "It's kind of hard to sell 'trickle down,' " he said, "so the supply-side formula was the only way to get a tax policy that was really 'trickle down.' "[36]

Perhaps more important, though, supply-side was relentlessly optimistic. Like evangelical Protestantism, observed the journalist Sidney Blumenthal, supply-side "promised hope and opportunity; it discounted sacrifice and complexity." For while liberals donned their hair shirts and pondered the age of limits, and while Milton Friedman talked of high interest rates and natural rates of unemployment, Laffer and Wanniski promised a golden future of endless growth. Unlike orthodox economics, supply-side promised not gruel today and jam tomorrow but jam today, tomorrow, and always. It had no room for doubters; it was an object lesson in the power of positive thinking.[37]

Even before Howard Jarvis celebrated victory in California, supply-side was making inroads on Capitol Hill. At the end of 1976, Wanniski had found the perfect congressional cheerleader: Jack Kemp, the former Buffalo Bills quarterback and AFL Most Valuable Player, who had been elected to Congress from New York's Erie County and was widely seen as a rising star of the Republican Party. Crucially, Kemp was a moderate, independent-minded figure, a self-described "bleeding-heart conservative" and "civil-rights Republican" who supported the ERA and disdained what he called the politics of "fear" and "resentment." Nobody could dismiss him as an old-fashioned reactionary, for Kemp was almost evangelical in his optimism. Cutting taxes, he claimed, would mean regeneration for his beloved Buffalo, jobs for the Bills' blue-collar fans, progress for New York's blacks, and opportunities for all. "Opportunity, the chance to make it and to improve your life, that's what the American Dream was and is all about," he wrote in 1979. "What poisons that dream is when government stands in the way, throwing up roadblocks that are really unnecessary."[38]

Kemp had already proposed one tax-reduction bill even before he met Wanniski, but now he decided to go further. In July 1977, in tandem with Delaware's Republican senator, William Roth, he introduced the Kemp-Roth tax reduction bill, an extraordinarily bold bid to slash personal income taxes by 30 percent over three years. The highest rate would fall from 70 to 50 percent, and the lowest from 14 to 8 percent, while federal revenues would fall by an estimated $124 billion. Kemp's colleagues rallied to the cause, and the party leadership in the House and the Republican National Committee endorsed the bill. By the end of the year, Kemp-Roth was the hottest issue on Capitol Hill.[39]

Kemp-Roth ignited a firestorm of academic debate. Liberals lined up to denounce the bill: MIT's Franco Modigliani warned that such radical tax cuts would "do irreparable damage" to the American economy, while Gardner Ackley, who had chaired Lyndon Johnson's Council of Economic Advisers, called it "the most irresponsible policy proposal—seriously advanced by people who should know better"—since the 1930s. Many balanced-budget conservatives, too, were appalled by what appeared a wildly reckless measure. Yet many Republicans recognized that here was the perfect pretext to force the government to rein in spending. Even Milton Friedman, no admirer of supply-side, told *Newsweek*'s readers that he backed Kemp-Roth, because "the only effective way to restrain government spending is by limiting government's explicit tax revenue—just as a limited income is the only effective restraint on any individual's or family's spending."[40]

With the American people, Kemp-Roth was an immediate hit. Squeezed by rising prices and bracket creep, ordinary householders were gasping for breath, their liabilities mounting, even though their incomes had stagnated. Polls showed support running at two to one, and when California approved Proposition 13, Kemp seemed to be tapping a rich vein of public sentiment. With the 1978 midterms looming, the Republican Party organized a seven-city "Tax Clipper" tour to publicize the bill. And although Kemp-Roth remained in limbo by the time of the next presidential election, it had become a major political asset for the Republican right. As the historian Robert Collins puts it, "Kemp and his allies had succeeded wildly in seizing control of the debate about the future shape of the economy and direction of policy."[41]

**It is hard** to exaggerate the importance of tax reduction to the rise of the New Right in the late 1970s. Proposition 13 had extraordinary resonance, partly because the nation had been born in a gigantic tax revolt, and partly because nobody, anywhere, likes paying taxes. While the economic merits of supply-side theory remained very dubious, it made a vital contribution to the revival of conservatism, offering Republican politicians a new set of ideas, a new vocabulary, and a new faith with which to address the nation's woes. After years of being mocked for their dour negativity, conservatives now campaigned as the champions of growth, of boundless possibilities, of patriotic optimism. Theirs was the perfect populist message for the times, for in the supply-side universe everyone was a winner. "There is a tidal wave coming, equivalent to the one that hit in 1932," predicted Jack Kemp. "It's going to happen again, and we'll find millions upon millions of Americans surprising themselves by voting Republican . . . because they see in the GOP a better shot at the American Dream."[42]

By contrast, it was as though the stuffing had been knocked out of American liberalism. Against the background of soaring crime, closing factories, and nationwide tax revolts, the traditional gospel of confident, interventionist government, which had underpinned Pat Brown's stewardship of California and the presidencies of Kennedy and Johnson, seemed to have lost its relevance. In Washington, Jimmy Carter promised a radical reform of the tax structure, but nothing happened. Further to the left, Edward Kennedy argued for a more progressive tax system, but he struggled to be heard above the cacophony of conservative voices. Some Democrats still called for full employment or demanded an interventionist "industrial policy"; others pinned their hopes on technology and deregulation; still others, like Jerry Brown, tried to reinvent themselves as tax cutters. But there was no sense of coherence, no direction. With Keynesianism out of fashion, they were like medieval monks who had lost their faith: confused, fractious, forlorn in a world deprived of the comforts of certainty.[43]

Compared with the spread of evangelicalism, the backlash against crime, or the rise of the neoconservatives, the tax revolt was a singularly unglamorous phenomenon. Yet Proposition 13 was a landmark in postwar history, for few issues did more to promote the conservative cause. Crucially, it tapped a rich vein of populist resentment—against elites and establishments, against doctors and teachers, against welfare spending and affirmative action—that was fast becoming the most dynamic force in American politics. It brought conservatism new recruits, new funds, and a new sense of momentum. It dragged traditional Democratic voters away from their old loyalties; it fostered a growing antigovernment ethos; and it offered a deceptively simple remedy for the complicated mess in which many ordinary Americans found themselves. "Proposition 13," said the National Urban League's president, Vernon Jordan, "has become the new spirit of America." As so often, California had offered a taste of the future.[44]

# Chapter Sixteen  *Apocalypse Now*

The past two weeks will be remembered as the period when President Carter packed it in, put the finishing touches on a failed presidency.

—*The New Republic*, August 4, 1979

**A**s the sun rose over Tehran on the first day of February 1979, it revealed a city nursing its wounds. Along the wide avenues of the Iranian capital, haggard men were already forming in line for emergency paraffin supplies. Around them, the spectacle of looted storefronts, burned-out cars, and shattered glass testified to the anarchy that had governed the streets for weeks. Clouds of thick black smoke still rose from bonfires of tires and trash, while charred scraps of newspaper drifted along the sidewalks. In the deserted gardens of the royal palace, leaves tumbled along the grass, and the trees shivered in the wind.

Shortly before nine that morning, a chartered Air France 747 appeared as a distant speck in the skies above Tehran. It circled the airport for twenty minutes, the captain waiting nervously for clearance. Finally, at 9:30 a.m., the plane skidded to a halt on the same tarmac from which Iran's ruler, the Shah, had left seventeen days before. Below, a mob of reporters, cameramen, and airport workers waited. Then the door opened, and a French flight officer stepped down the stairs, supporting with his left hand a tall figure dressed entirely in black, his gaunt features utterly impassive: Ayatollah Ruhollah Khomeini, back in his native land for the first time in almost fifteen years.

The pandemonium that followed was like nothing even experienced foreign correspondents had ever seen before. Inside the terminal more than a thousand clerics had packed into the glass building, roaring with excitement; yet as they chanted his name, the ayatollah stood impassive and motionless. THE FLAG OF THE REVOLUTION IS IN YOUR HANDS, read a banner draped across the arrivals hall. YOU ARE OUR RELIGIOUS, POLITICAL, MILITARY, ECONOMIC, AND SOCIAL LEADER. And the ayatollah did not disappoint. "Our final victory," he told the crowd in his hypnotic monotone, "will come when all foreigners are out of the country. I beg God to cut off the hands of all evil foreigners and all their helpers."

On the other side of the airport was a scene of extraordinary, almost biblical chaos. Along the streets between the airport and the city center were gathered hundreds, thousands, millions of people, people peering from windows and from rooftops, people packed onto building sites and into flats, people hanging off cranes and onto ledges, people running madly beside the ayatollah's Mercedes van, people screaming and shouting with ecstasy: a sea, an ocean of humanity, roaring its approval in the warm air. *Le Monde* thought ten million were there, others slightly fewer, but it was almost certainly the biggest gathering in human history. There were so many people that cameramen struggled for a view through the clouds of dust, and dozens were trampled underfoot in the chaos. One young woman interviewed by an American reporter burst into tears when he asked what it all meant. "I can't explain," she said simply. "It's just the point of victory for our people. It means it is the wish of God that he is here."[1]

**The Iranian Revolution** was not only a severe setback for American foreign policy and a profound humiliation for Jimmy Carter; it was one of the pivotal moments of the twentieth century. It toppled a corrupt, repressive monarchy, unleashed a crippling oil shock and global economic crisis, pioneered a new brand of religious fundamentalism, and bequeathed an autocratic regime that, for all its corruption and stagnation, still endures today. Nobody knew it at the time, but the ayatollah's return from exile was a turning point in the history of relations between the West and the Middle East, and between the United States and the Islamic world.

With its vast oil reserves and strategic location on the crossroads between the Middle East and central Asia, Iran had long been the cornerstone of American policy in the region. Its despotic ruler, Shah Mohammad Reza Pahlavi, was corrupt, decadent, vain, and weak. But he owed his survival to the CIA, which had orchestrated a coup in 1953 to stop Iran from falling to anticolonial nationalism, and for decades he had been one of the West's most reliable allies. Richard Nixon had told him to consider himself Washington's policeman in the Persian Gulf; Henry Kissinger had ordered his staff to let the Shah buy whatever American arms and equipment he wanted. And since the Shah was wallowing in money after the OPEC oil shock, that meant an awful lot of guns. By 1978 he had blown $12 billion on American jet fighters, destroyers, submarines, and missiles: an arsenal, he thought, worthy of the ancient Persians.[2]

Given the corruption of the Shah's rule, as well as the brutality of his American-trained secret police—who regularly beat their prisoners' feet, ripped out their nails, sodomized them with cattle prods, hung weights from their testicles, and raped them in front of their spouses—Jimmy Carter might have been expected to keep him at arm's length. For all his fine words about human rights, however, Carter had no intention of losing such an oil-rich ally. Briefing his new ambassador, William Sullivan, Carter explained that the Shah was "a close friend and a trusted ally" and that Iran was a "force for stability and security in the Persian Gulf region." When Sullivan reminded him of the secret police's appalling record, Carter insisted that Iran's friendship "was of such importance that we should continue the collaboration between our two intelligence agencies."[3]

Carter did not meet the Shah until November 1977, when he welcomed him to the White House amid clouds of tear gas fired by police to dispel Iranian protesters. Photographs showed the two men with tears running down their cheeks, yet Carter's men were struck by the Shah's dignity. To Hamilton Jordan, he was "easily the most impressive" foreign leader they had yet received. Carter, too, was smitten. A few weeks later, during a whistle-stop world tour, he arranged to spend New Year's Eve in Tehran, where he paid the Shah a startlingly effusive tribute. "Iran, because of the great leadership of the Shah, is an island of stability in one of the more troubled areas of the world," Carter said in an impromptu toast. "We have no other nation on Earth who is closer to us in planning for our mutual military security. We have no other nation with whom we have closer consultation on regional problems that concern us both. And there is no leader with whom I have a deeper sense of personal gratitude and personal friendship."[4]

Carter's extraordinary words made it all the more embarrassing when, just weeks later, the Shah's regime began to disintegrate. Resentment had been growing for years: prices were out of control, the cities' high-rise apartment buildings were overcrowded with rural migrants, and religious leaders were stoking the flames of anti-Western feeling. Astonishingly, however, American intelligence seemed blind to the signals. When William Sullivan arrived as ambassador in the summer of 1977, he was appalled to find that few of his staff "spoke Farsi or knew the culture of the country," while they had almost no contact with liberal or Islamic opposition leaders. So when rumors spread that the Shah was seriously ill, the embassy claimed that "the Russians in fact are spreading the stories" and that "the Shah is fine." In fact, he was already dying from cancer. And yet as late as September 1978, when law and order had long since broken down, the Defense Intelligence Agency reported that he was "expected to remain actively in power over the next ten years"—a prediction not even the Shah himself would have endorsed.[5]

In many ways, Carter's policy toward Iran reflected the broader weaknesses of his foreign policy. After promising a new approach based on human rights, he had found himself supporting a corrupt and cruel regime based on increasingly shaky foundations. As the Shah's government began to totter, American policy seemed stuck in a bog of feckless ambiguity. While Sullivan insisted that the Shah was doomed, Carter's hawkish national security adviser, Zbigniew Brzezinski, refused to hear a word against the Iranian monarch. As a result, instead of having a clear line on Iran, Carter's officials were confronted with a bewildering variety of instructions: "The Shah should hang tough, the Shah should abdicate, military force should be used, human rights must be observed, the military should stage a coup, the military should stand aside, a regency should be established." As one later remarked, they should simply have "flipped a coin and then stuck to a policy." Instead, they dithered until it was too late.[6]

When the Shah fled Iran, therefore, Carter looked extremely foolish. But the damage went beyond hurt pride. Some observers saw the revolution as a catastrophe to rank alongside the loss of China and the fall of South Vietnam: Henry Kissinger, for instance, called it "a major setback for American security." But many American businessmen, too, saw the revolution as a disaster. General Motors, DuPont, General Tire, Warner-Lambert, Gillette, Pfizer, Pepsi, Colgate-Palmolive, Coca-Cola, and Johnson & Johnson all had major Iranian interests, and if the ayatollahs turned against the West, they stood to lose millions. But this was as nothing compared with the prospect of yet another oil shock. Iran boasted the world's second-largest reserves of natural gas and third-largest oil fields, which had been shut down by strikes against the Shah. By Christmas Day 1978, most American oil workers had been evacuated, and Iranian petroleum exports had come to a complete halt. In Tehran, gasoline was rationed; in Europe, oil prices surged by 20 percent.[7]

Although other OPEC members increased their output to make up for the shortfall, global oil production at the beginning of 1979 was two million barrels a day lower than in the last quarter of 1978. There was talk of a worldwide Islamic upheaval, of global depression, of conflict between the West and the rest. And as nervous buyers rushed to build inventories, prices soared from $13 a barrel to a whopping $34—this compared with just $2 a barrel in 1972. It was as though Iran had been shaken by a giant earthquake, writes Daniel Yergin, from which "a giant tidal wave surged around the world. All were swept up in it; nothing and no one escaped. When the wave finally spent its fury two years later, the survivors would look around and find themselves beached on a totally new terrain."[8]

**At the end of 1978,** Jimmy Carter had committed himself to a new offensive against inflation, the curse of American life since the beginning of the decade. But he had never anticipated a second oil shock. As oil prices went up, so did the cost of other commodities. Food prices went up by almost 5 percent in just four weeks, the shock reverberating in every household in the nation. Although Carter's advisers employed a vast range of weapons to bring inflation down—wage and price guidelines, spending cuts, federal job cuts, high interest rates, credit controls, deregulation measures—nothing seemed to work. By March 1979 the inflation rate was out of control. "The news is grim indeed," the president's chief forecaster reported, warning that if surging consumer prices were sustained, the result would be an annual inflation rate of 15 percent.[9]

By now, inflation had become what *The Washington Post*'s William Greider called "a permanent fixture of American life." As prices went up, even "daily chores as routine as grocery shopping induced a sense of running on a treadmill that was moving faster and faster." There was a "contagion of fear," wrote Theodore White: everyday conversations were "drenched and stained in money." At cocktail parties, rich New Yorkers lamented the soaring costs of beach houses on Long Island, Broadway tickets, and college fees. As always, though, the impact was even greater for the poor—the old lady struggling to afford a box of Quaker Oats that once cost ten cents and now cost seventy-nine; the lonely widower weighing the apples to find the heaviest; the harassed mother reaching to the back of the shelf, hoping to find a rogue bottle of aspirin with last year's price. "The inflation makes you feel you're shoveling shit against the tide," was how a Brooklyn plumber aptly put it.[10]

Inflation turned Americans from savers into spendthrifts, for, as Greider pointed out, "even with higher interest rates, a loan made today to purchase an automobile or television set would be paid back tomorrow in dollars that were worth less." So why not borrow? Why not spend? In the ten years after 1973, when Visa pioneered the computerized authorization system, credit card spending escalated from $3.5 billion a year to $66 billion. Total consumer debt, meanwhile, surged from $15 billion in 1975 to an astonishing $315 billion in 1979. With the deregulation of the New York Stock Exchange and the rise of discount brokerages, cash management accounts, and money market mutual funds, the casino of speculative capitalism had been thrown open to more people than ever before. "You can't afford not to buy," a young Paine Webber economist told *The New York Times*. "Get your money out of the bank and spend it!"[11]

To Carter, such sentiments were anathema. By the time he delivered his budget message to Congress in January 1979, it was clear that spending cuts and small government were the order of the day, while in his second State of the Union address he promised to "reduce government interference" in the economy and to weed out "wasteful or unnecessary" programs. Once again, liberal critics were outraged. For Jesse Jackson, Carter's budget was the economic equivalent of the neutron bomb, killing the people but leaving the buildings intact. If Carter had been elected in 1932, said Arthur Schlesinger, "we still would be in the Great Depression." Even Tip O'Neill, usually publicly loyal, made his objections quite clear: "I'm not going to let people go to bed hungry for an austerity program."[12]

Meanwhile, as oil prices continued to rise, Carter contemplated the prospect of severe shortages. On April 5, tight-lipped as ever, he appeared on television again. "Our nation's energy problem is serious," he began gloomily, "and it's getting worse." His solution horrified liberal Democrats: all price controls would be lifted by September 1981, giving the oil companies additional revenue for exploration and development. At the same time, he asked Congress for a windfall tax of 50 percent on extra oil revenue, to be spent on mass transit, alternative-energy sources, and relief for poor families. Decontrol, he admitted, was "a painful step, and I'll give it to you straight: Each of us will have to use less oil and pay more for it." But as so often, he wanted the public to embrace the spirit of sacrifice: "I ask you to drive 15 miles a week fewer than you do now. At least once a week take the bus [to work], go by carpool or, if you work close enough to home, walk."[13]

*Newsweek* called it a "prime-time TV summons to the Age of Limits," while Carter's policy chief, Stuart Eizenstat, thought it "one of his most courageous and most important decisions." But most liberals were appalled. The plan was "seriously flawed" and "a self-inflicted wound," declared Ted Kennedy, accusing Carter of putting the oil companies above the ordinary consumers of the industrial states. Even though polls showed that the public approved of Carter's plan, his talk of thrift and sacrifice seemed politically poisonous. Gallup found that his approval rating had tumbled into the low 30s; one NBC poll put it as low as 29 percent. Meanwhile, according to a *Los Angeles Times* poll, the president was already twenty-three points behind Edward Kennedy in the race for the Democratic nomination and a staggering fifty-one points behind in New Hampshire.[14]

It was at this point that Carter's speechwriter James Fallows published a cover story in *The Atlantic Monthly* that was one of the most withering indictments of a sitting president ever written by his own staff. Having worked for Carter since 1976, Fallows was now completely disillusioned. Carter, he wrote, was a good man, but he had no sense of direction, no ideology, no vision. Unlike, say, Roosevelt, he did not surround himself with people who made him think. He boasted of having seen the entire world on the main street of Plains; he was so sure of his own virtue that he never bothered to learn the lessons of the past. He was happy to learn Spanish or to improve his jogging, but he "stubbornly, complacently resists attempts to challenge his natural style." For Fallows, the explanation lay not merely in Carter's southern populism but also in the "combination of arrogance, complacency, and—dread thought—insecurity at the core of his mind and soul."[15]

Coming from someone who had been so close to Carter, this was extraordinary stuff, and it cut so deep precisely because it rang so true. When the story broke in the middle of April, the media lapped it up, particularly Fallows's revelation about Carter and the tennis court bookings. To make matters worse, days later the news broke that Bert Lance had been indicted on twenty-two felony counts. The general reaction, though, was worse than shock or horror: it was pity. At home, Carter struggled to deal with ridicule and bickering; abroad, he seemed powerless to cope with the aftermath of the Iranian Revolution. "The poor guy," one of Carter's aides said when he heard the news about Lance. "He's really getting it from all sides this week." "Poor Jimmy Carter," echoed the *Post*'s Meg Greenfield, "the ironies and indignities and injustices never seem to end."[16]

·  ·  ·

**On March 16, 1979,** Columbia Pictures released the film *The China Syndrome,* a classic 1970s conspiracy thriller in which a reporter played by Jane Fonda uncovers a terrible cover-up at a nuclear power plant. Twelve days later, at a nuclear power station near Harrisburg, Pennsylvania, fact came terrifyingly close to emulating fiction. When a pump failed at Three Mile Island, emergency crews frantically scrambled to shut down the plant before its overheated core went into meltdown. It was the nearest the nation ever came to an American Chernobyl. Some 100,000 local residents fled their homes while the engineers were trying to shut down the plant, and the backlash against nuclear power was swift and unforgiving, with marches and sit-ins across the nation. "The world has never known a day like today," Walter Cronkite told viewers on the third evening of the crisis. "It faced the considerable uncertainties and dangers of the worst nuclear power plant accident of the atomic age—and the horror tonight is that it could get much worse."[17]

Three Mile Island came at the worst possible time for Jimmy Carter. With gasoline prices up by 55 percent since the beginning of the year, rumors began to circulate that the nation's supplies would soon run out. By May, prices in California had reached a dollar a gallon, and lines outside the pumps stretched for fifty, a hundred, even five hundred cars. Worried gas station owners reported that motorists were queuing from five in the morning; some began rationing their daily sales so that they would last the month, closing as early as 10:00 a.m. to avoid running out. There were reports of fistfights at the busiest stations; one Los Angeles owner was taken to the hospital after being attacked; and a local man was arrested after assaulting a pregnant woman who had pushed ahead of him. As always, though, there were winners as well as losers. In one line in the San Fernando Valley, a college student studied his textbook as he waited in the sun, his eyes devouring a young female driver who had lowered the straps of her blouse to top up her tan. A few yards away through the noonday haze, the owner of the nearby liquor store rubbed his hands with glee. Business, he said, had never been better.[18]

At first it fell to Jerry Brown to deal with the crisis, introducing fines for dealers who sold more than twenty gallons at a time or topped up any tank more than half full. At the same time, he revived a device from the 1973 shock, ordering drivers of cars with even-numbered license plates to buy gasoline only on even-numbered days, and the rest on odd-numbered days. Yet the crisis spread: by mid-May there were reports of gas stations running dry in New York, New Jersey, and Pennsylvania. In Washington, Carter insisted that his decontrol plan would provide a long-term solution. But like most drivers, the president was running out of patience.

The crisis was not his fault, he told the press, and it was wrong to look for "scapegoats." It was just a shame, he added, that "the American people refuse to face the inevitable prospect of fuel shortages."[19]

Carter was simply being realistic, but now motorists began to panic. Watching the lengthening gas line, older observers remembered the run on the banks at the beginning of the Depression. And as before, government action seemed only to make matters worse. With the federal government using an allocation system that observed strict geographical patterns, major urban areas began to run dry while rural counties had plenty of gas. Some states limited motorists to just $5 of gasoline, which only meant that drivers came back to stations much more often. Even the gas lines themselves contributed to the gas lines, since an ordinary car consumed seven-tenths of a gallon every hour it waited in line. According to one estimate, American motorists wasted a staggering 150,000 barrels of oil a day just by waiting in line.[20]

By the middle of June, California's gas lines had become a national crisis of unprecedented proportions. In Levittown, Pennsylvania, irate truckers blockaded the expressways and launched the nation's first "energy riot," with two nights of fighting leaving a hundred people injured. In North Carolina, the governor mobilized the National Guard to defend gas stations in Greensboro and Charlotte. Not surprisingly, anger at the gas lines blurred into frustrated, xenophobic rage against the oil producers of the Middle East. One popular poster showed a grinning American G.I. standing over a dying Arab, a mushroom cloud looming in the background. "How much is the gas now?" read the caption. And John Updike's fictional hero Harry Angstrom spoke for millions of Americans when he looked forward to the days of solar power, when "we can tell those Arabs to take their fucking oil and grease their camels with it." "Jesus, those Arabs," remarked one of his golfing buddies. "Wouldn't it be bliss just to nuke 'em all?"[21]

For many people, the gas lines were yet another example of the machinations of the corporate establishment. With its cast of New York bankers, Washington bureaucrats, Texas oilmen, and Arab sheiks, this was a crisis made for the populist imagination. Polls found that only 14 percent of the public believed there was a "real" energy shortage, while almost eight out of ten people agreed that it had been "deliberately brought about by oil companies." Exxon's chairman, Clifton Garvin, went on *The Phil Donahue Show* to address their suspicions, but whenever he tried to explain the complications of oil inventories, he was cut off. One day, he found himself at the back of a gas line in his hometown of Greenwich, Connecticut. Recognizing the chairman of Exxon, the local dealer offered to let him drive to the front of the line. "How are you going to explain that to everyone else?" asked Garvin. "I'll tell them who you are," the dealer replied. Garvin shuddered. "I'm sitting right here," he said.[22]

It was on the weekend of June 23 and 24 that the crisis reached its nadir. On Saturday, an American Automobile Association survey found that less than half of the nation's gas stations were open. An independent truckers' strike, now three weeks old, had turned vicious: on the Long Island Expressway, a hundred truckers blocked rush-hour traffic, with lines stretching for thirty miles. In Trenton, New Jersey, a disc jockey nailed himself into his booth and played the same country single for hours as a protest against the shortages. In Bridgeport, Connecticut, dozens of gas stations were vandalized, the pumps smashed in an orgy of frustration. And Sunday was even worse. Across New York's metropolitan area, more than 95 percent of gasoline stations were closed, mass-transit lines were impossibly crowded, and transportation officials insisted that the situation was "critical." For thousands of motorists, whether stranded in lines or trapped at home, the car, the symbol of freedom and opportunity, had become a prison.[23]

A few days later, on his way to work, Stuart Eizenstat pulled over at his local Amoco station on Connecticut Avenue. The line was already so long that it took him forty-five minutes, and by the time he got to the White House, Carter's domestic adviser was seething. For the first time, it struck him that Jimmy Carter simply did not understand the plight ordinary Americans were facing. Still angry, he set down his thoughts on paper and sent them to the president. The energy crisis, he acknowledged, had come at the worst possible time, since inflation was out of control and a recession looked inevitable. But "nothing else has so frustrated, confused, angered the American people—or so targeted their distress at you personally."[24]

Carter was on the other side of the world, having flown to Tokyo for a bitter, fractious G7 meeting with other Western leaders. But when the president received Eizenstat's apocalyptic memorandum the next day, he decided enough was enough. Canceling a planned vacation in Hawaii, Carter flew straight back to Washington, and on the way he began work on yet another televised address to the nation, scheduled for the evening of Thursday, July 5. His aides briefed the press that this would be the defining speech of his presidency; but then, on the morning of the big day, the White House abruptly announced that it had been canceled. Rumors in Washington suggested that Carter's aides had been arguing furiously about what he was to say. In the Energy Department, officials were in shock. "We just don't know what it means," one said. "We had worked all last night to put the thing together."[25]

Carter's decision to cancel the speech struck observers as the strangest twist yet in a presidency notable for its unpredictability. In fact, it reflected deep divisions within the White House about the way forward. Eizenstat and Vice President Mondale wanted Carter to strike an assertive note, blaming OPEC for the oil crisis, while Jerry Rafshoon and Pat Caddell advised him to adopt a more introspective, even pessimistic tone. Carter himself was conscious that he had "already made four speeches to the nation on energy and that they had been increasingly ignored" and that he was desperate "to do something to get the attention of the news media and the public." Accordingly, he had decided to take a few days at Camp David to invite people "whom we trusted to give me advice on where we should go from here." His vice president thought this was an absurd idea. But Carter rarely suffered from self-doubt. "I felt a remarkable sense of relief and renewed confidence," he recorded in his diary.[26]

To his deep unease, Mondale discovered that the president had been listening to his personal pollster, Pat Caddell. Forever armed with the latest data, obsessed with keeping abreast of cultural trends, the shaggy-haired young pollster cut an incongruous figure among the backslapping Georgians who usually had the president's ear. Crucially, however, both Jimmy and Rosalynn Carter were impressed by Caddell's interest in spiritual issues. As early as 1975, he had talked of a "crisis of confidence in the political process and the future of the nation." In place of the old optimism, Caddell said, had come a "pervasive pessimism . . . and the result of this pessimism is alienation." In April 1979 he spent hours persuading Rosalynn that the president must do something drastic to reverse the slide. She suggested that Caddell put his thoughts on paper, and the seventy-five-page result, sent to Carter under the title "Of Crisis and Opportunity," became one of the most infamous documents in presidential history. Skeptical aides called it the "Apocalypse Now" memorandum.[27]

Caddell told the president that ordinary Americans were suffering from a psychological "malaise," a "crisis of confidence marked by a dwindling faith in the future." Borrowing from the cultural critics Christopher Lasch, Daniel Bell, and Robert Bellah, he argued that Americans had "turned increasingly inward," with spending and selfishness having replaced sacrifice and service. John Maynard Keynes had once said that meeting the challenge of affluence required a return to the "certain principles of religion and traditional virtue." That, Caddell thought, was Jimmy Carter's mission now. The president must reach a new covenant with the American people; if he failed, "the spiritual bonds will weaken, and invisibly, the country will become intangibly but inexorably only a shadow of its former self."[28]

To a hardheaded political veteran like Walter Mondale, Caddell's memo was nonsense. But the idea that the nation was suffering from a deep-seated religious crisis naturally appealed to a born-again Baptist. If nothing else, Jimmy Carter had always fancied himself as the moral guide of the American people. So when he canceled his big energy speech, he naturally turned to Caddell for inspiration. Energy policy, the pollster advised, must be the vehicle to bring national spiritual rebirth: the president should emphasize "value restoration, national unity, and national purpose." Carter was delighted. Caddell's analysis, he wrote in a handwritten letter of thanks, was "a masterpiece."[29]

Meanwhile, media speculation had reached fever pitch. Some said that Carter had suffered a nervous breakdown; others, that he was about to produce a dramatic new initiative to break the political deadlock. "What Are You Up to, Mr. President?" asked the *New York Post*. But as news began to emerge, public bewilderment only increased. Over the next eight days more than 130 people were invited to meet the president, a bizarre selection of people described by *The New Republic* as a "tableau from *Who's Who*," from economists, intellectuals, and civil rights leaders to state governors and even a Greek Orthodox archbishop. This was not a brainstorming session on energy policy; it was something much stranger, an informal seminar about the psychological health of the nation. As guests arrived, Hamilton Jordan handed out copies of Christopher Lasch's book *The Culture of Narcissism* (1979). Sessions in the rustic lodges lasted well into the night, with Carter listening earnestly, propped cross-legged against a cushion and making extensive notes. Like some medieval hermit addicted to self-mortification, he seemed to relish his guests' outspoken criticism. "I learned a lot," he wrote later, "and so did the people who visited with me."[30]

What was really extraordinary about this exercise in presidential therapy, though, was the list of people Carter did not invite. Hardly any of his guests knew anything about energy policy, and he did not bother to consult his cabinet or most congressional power brokers. The result was precisely what he wanted, a "national prayer meeting" of the woolliest, most self-flagellating kind. But it also confirmed that Carter was remarkably uninterested in the traditions and resources of the Democratic Party. Roosevelt or Johnson would have been appalled, while Mondale was so disillusioned that he seriously considered resigning. After a long talk with

Carter, he decided to stay. But he still thought the president's ideas were madness.[31]

**On the evening** of Sunday, July 15, Carter prepared to address the nation. After such a long delay, nobody quite knew what to expect. "Jimmy Carter is coming down from the mountaintop," reported *The New York Times*, "to address the country tonight in airtime that was originally slotted by one national network for 'Moses the Lawgiver.'" Behind the scenes, Carter's aides were still fighting over the speech, and the result was a weird hybrid, one-third Caddell and two-thirds Eizenstat, one-third moral jeremiad and two-thirds facts and figures. But Carter was happy with it, and in the last hours before the speech he worked with Jerry Rafshoon on keeping his face unsmiling, flashing his eyes, and clenching his fist to emphasize just how tough he was. Then it was ten o'clock, and it was time.[32]

More than sixty-five million Americans were watching as the gray-haired president appeared on their screens, his face grim and set. "Good evening," Carter said. "This is a special night for me. Exactly three years ago, on July 15, 1976, I accepted the nomination of my party to run for President of the United States." He acknowledged the problems of the last three years, but explained that "the true problems of our nation are much deeper—deeper than gasoline lines or energy shortages, deeper even than inflation or recession. And I realize more than ever that as President I need your help."

He wanted to talk first, he said, about "a subject even more serious than energy or inflation. I want to talk to you right now about a fundamental threat to American democracy." Then he came to the words that would define his presidency:

> The threat is nearly invisible in ordinary ways. It is a crisis of confidence. It is a crisis that strikes at the very heart and soul and spirit of our national will. We can see this crisis in the growing doubt about the meaning of our own lives and in the loss of a unity of purpose for our nation.
>
> The erosion of our confidence in the future is threatening to destroy the social and the political fabric of America.

Americans, he said, had "always had a faith that the days of our children would be better than our own." In recent years they had lost their way, defining themselves by "owning things and consuming things," and coming to worship "self-indulgence and consumption." But "piling up material goods," Carter said sternly, could not "fill the emptiness of lives which have no confidence or purpose." Instead, he urged his listeners to have "faith in each other, faith in our ability to govern ourselves, and faith in the future of this nation." For "restoring that faith and that confidence to America," Carter said sternly, "is now the most important task we face."

Then he came to the Eizenstat section of the speech, and his tone abruptly changed. Energy, he said, would be the "standard around which we can rally." There followed the usual laundry list of import quotas, alternative-energy programs, a conservation scheme, and an "Energy Mobilization Board" to help fight the moral equivalent of war. Carter asked his listeners to embrace the spirit of sacrifice, "to take no unnecessary trips, to use carpools or public transportation whenever you can, to park your car one extra day per week, to obey the speed limit, and to set your thermostats to save fuel." "Whenever you have a chance," he added, "say something good about our country."[33]

Originally titled "Energy and the Crisis of Confidence," Carter's speech was an extraordinary rhetorical gamble. No modern president had ever attacked his countrymen's love of "self-indulgence and consumption," criticized their obsession with "owning" and "consuming," or told them that "piling up material goods" was not a route to happiness. Even more striking was his intense pessimism: when Carter talked of a "crisis of the American spirit," he was giving his listeners something they had never heard from their chief executive. Presidents usually tell the American people that they are a nation chosen by God, capable of overcoming any challenge. But perhaps only a born-again Baptist could have embraced with such vigor the classic evangelical tropes of the retreat to Camp David, the confession of sin, the commitment to recovery, and the promise of rebirth for himself and for the nation.[34]

It is a myth that Carter diagnosed a "malaise" of the American spirit: he never even used the word.* And it is also a myth that the speech was an immediate disaster. At first, analysts praised the president for speaking clearly and decisively, and giving an impressive and patriotic lead. Letters and telegrams were overwhelmingly supportive, editorial reaction was generally favorable, and a CBS/*New York Times* poll taken the next evening found that Carter's approval rating had jumped from 26 percent to 37 percent, which was still low but a much better basis for recovery. The gamble, it seemed, had paid off.[35]

---

*In an episode of *The Simpsons* broadcast fourteen years later, a statue of Jimmy Carter, "history's greatest monster," carries the inscription "Malaise Forever."

It was what Carter did next, though, that sealed his fate. In probably the biggest single blunder of his administration, he asked all senior officials to submit their resignations, explaining that he would decide overnight which to accept. This was a move straight from Richard Nixon's playbook, inspired by Jerry Rafshoon, who told Carter that it would be "a clear signal that you mean to get tough and do business differently." By the Thursday following the speech, he had effectively fired five cabinet members: Mike Blumenthal (Treasury), Joe Califano (Health, Education, and Welfare), Griffin Bell (attorney general), Brock Adams (Transportation), and James Schlesinger (Energy). In each case he had good reason. Blumenthal had fallen out with the president's other economic advisers, Califano was in open revolt against the anti-inflation policy, Bell wanted to leave anyway, and both Adams and Schlesinger had proved insubordinate. But the combination of all five gave the impression that Carter's administration had fallen apart. *Time* called it the most "puzzling purge in the history of the U.S. presidency." On the exchange markets, the value of the dollar plummeted. So did Carter's approval rating, down to a dismal 23 percent—even lower than before the speech.[36]

Now the gloves came off. Looking again at the speech, many commentators accused Carter of blaming the public for his own mistakes. The *Los Angeles Times* charged him with posing as a "pastor with a profligate flock," while in a stinging essay for *Time*, Lance Morrow wrote that Carter stood exposed as an "inadequate and dispiriting figure," the speech "an implicit confession of his own failures as a leader." It was "pop sociology stew," agreed *The New Republic*. Even Hugh Sidey, usually so quick to praise the man in the Oval Office, recorded his "deep sadness" at the spectacle of "a disorganized and sometimes insensitive Jimmy Carter, overreacting to demands for leadership in an effort to save himself" and "trying to show how tough he is."[37]


**The era of growth** is over and the era of limits is upon us," wrote the economist Robert Lekachman in the fall of 1979. Millions of Americans agreed: in August, a record 84 percent told Gallup's researchers that the country was on the wrong track, while 67 percent thought it was in "deep and serious trouble." According to another survey, more than five out of ten Americans thought that "next year will be worse than this year," while seven out of ten agreed that "the land of plenty is becoming the land of want." It was not merely a question of blaming the federal government or the eastern establishment; to many observers, pessimism had seeped into the American soul. As Updike's hero Harry Angstrom puts it while contemplating the gas lines outside his car showroom: "The great American ride is ending."[38]

Carter was right: this was a genuine crisis of confidence. But the president seemed powerless to reverse it; indeed, he had become a symbol of failure, "Jimmy Hoover." In many ways it was an apt comparison. Both Hoover and Carter were former engineers who had vaulted over the party stalwarts to claim the presidency. Both had been deeply shaped by their rural Protestant backgrounds; both saw themselves as above ideology and believed that technocratic efficiency could solve the nation's problems. But both struggled to work with their party's leaders in Congress, and both ran into trouble when their policies offended the old guard. Above all, both were much more similar to their successors than is usually realized: just as Hoover's Reconstruction Finance Corporation paved the way for the New Deal, so Carter's fiscal conservatism and Cold War revivalism anticipated Reagan. But that was not, of course, what Carter's critics meant. They meant merely that he was a failure.[39]

Carter's public reputation was now about as bad as could be imagined. In an attempt to relaunch his administration, he had appointed Hamilton Jordan as his chief of staff, but Jordan's own image could hardly have been worse. The newspapers reported that at a Washington party he had groped the Egyptian ambassador's buxom wife with the words "I've always wanted to see the pyramids," while another woman claimed that after she had rebuffed his drunken advances, Jordan had spat amaretto and cream down her dress. Worse was to come: just weeks after Jordan's promotion, the owners of New York's Studio 54 nightclub claimed they had seen him snorting cocaine. Jordan had indeed visited the club in the summer of 1978, but vehemently denied the charges. The matter was eventually dropped, but many who had seen Jordan on the campaign trail wondered if the story contained a grain of truth. Not for nothing was his Georgetown apartment nicknamed the "Animal House."[40]

In the media, contempt for the Georgians had reached unprecedented levels. "If the President had been set upon by a pack of wild dogs," remarked Jody Powell, "a good portion of the press would have sided with the dogs and declared that he had provoked the attack." Indeed, when a mysterious aquatic rabbit attacked him while he was vacationing in Plains that summer, "hissing menacingly, its teeth flashing and nostrils flared," many journalists could hardly contain their amusement. Hilariously, Carter denied initial reports that he had beaten off the assailant with a paddle. He had merely "splashed water toward" it, he said—which some thought a pretty good metaphor for his foreign policy. But by now he could do nothing right. *The New Republic*, always very critical of the president, was particularly scathing. "It's over for Jimmy Carter," the magazine said bluntly. "He needed a new image, so he took the advice of his pollster, his ad man, and his wife and wound up immobilizing his own government, imperiling the American dollar on the international market, and looking more than ever like a crude, erratic, unstable amateur . . . The Carter administration has simply imploded, collapsed completely under the weight of its own incompetence."[41]

On September 15, the president took part in a ten-kilometer run in Catoctin Mountain Park, near Camp David. He had been jogging for months, pushing himself to improve his time, and with the number 39 on his chest and a garish yellow headband on his brow, he was confident of beating his personal best. But as he neared the top, Carter began to wheeze. Given the punishing heat, other runners would have slowed down, but Carter staggered on, gasping to his bodyguards: "I've got to keep trying." Seconds later he crumpled into their arms. Photographs showed an ashen-faced, rubber-legged, gray-haired man, pushing himself too hard, sweating profusely, and finally collapsing in an undignified heap. Ironically, Carter was one of the fittest presidents in modern history. But his countrymen would never have known it from the pictures.[42]

# Chapter Seventeen    Nuke the Ayatollah!

How would you like it if the U.S. mission in Teheran were taken
hostage and held in return for the Shah?

**—ANONYMOUS GOVERNMENT OFFICIAL,** quoted in
*Newsweek,* June 4, 1979

**B**arry Rosen was typing out a routine report when he heard the shouting outside the American embassy. After a few moments, he got up
and joined his secretary at the window. The crowd outside seemed
larger than normal, but it was the usual mixture of angry young men,
women in their jet-black chadors, and shabby old men with white beards,
pumping their fists in the air as they brandished posters of Ayatollah Khomeini and chanted the usual anti-American slogans. As press attaché at
the American embassy, Rosen had been in Iran for almost a year, and he
had seen it all before. Then, before his astonished eyes, the men started
clambering over the embassy gates.

Rosen moved quickly, locking the outer door and rushing back into
his inner office to find and destroy the most sensitive papers. This was the
second time people had broken into the embassy; it was tiresome, but not
particularly frightening, and his biggest worry was that Washington might
order him home. But while all these thoughts were going through his
head, and before he had had a chance to find the papers, he heard a clatter as his secretary, evidently frightened by the intruders' threats, took the
bar off the outer door. Before he knew it, they were inside. "Get out!" he

shouted in fluent Farsi, more angry than afraid, hardly able to take these nervous young men and women seriously. But they did not move. "Leave this room immediately or you will be hurt," one of them said. "We're now in control of this place. You are flouting the will of the Iranian people." Rosen started to protest, but then he saw the club in his face. It was pointless to argue with this bunch of frightened kids, he thought. Anyway, it would soon be over, just like the last time.

It was ten o'clock in the morning of Sunday, November 4, 1979, and Barry Rosen had no idea how wrong he was. Across the wooded grounds of the embassy compound, three hundred young men and women were swarming toward the office buildings. In the chancery, staff retreated to the second floor, while beneath them young Iranians flooded into the building, pulling out files and drawers in their excitement. Twelve Americans took refuge inside the communications vault, where they hurriedly fed documents into the incinerator. But when they heard the invaders shouting that they would begin shooting prisoners if they did not open the door, their resistance evaporated.

One by one they were led outside into the drizzle, their hands tied behind their backs and strips of white cloth across their eyes—an image that would soon be seared into the memories of every man and woman in the United States. Inside the abandoned embassy, there were no Americans left, just packs of Iranian students, roaming in search of documents and booty. All around them it looked like Saigon all over again. Desks lay smashed and ransacked, files were strewn all over the corridors, and framed photos of Jimmy Carter and Cyrus Vance lay broken on the floor, their faces smiling up through a veil of shattered glass.[1]

**Perhaps the most** extraordinary thing about the occupation of the American embassy in Tehran was that so many people had seen it coming. After all, the embassy had been attacked twice already during the early months of 1979, while Iranian army units, Islamic militants, and revolutionary groups were fighting for control of the streets. On the second occasion, Ayatollah Khomeini himself had sent apologies to Ambassador William Sullivan and promised help if it ever happened again. But while Sullivan argued that the Carter administration ought to reach out to the Islamic clerics, other officials took a very different view. The national security adviser, Zbigniew Brzezinski, urged Carter to back a right-wing coup, insisting that only the army could save Iran from Communism. The president himself was unimpressed by suggestions that he build bridges with the ayatollahs. On the same day that he rejected Sullivan's plan, Carter read an interview Khomeini had given to *Le Monde*, translated by the NSC staff. He sent it back with one word handwritten at the top: "Nutty."[2]

While Carter refused to reach out to Iran's new leader, he also seemed markedly reluctant to rekindle his romance with the old one. Before the Shah had fled Iran, Sullivan had arranged a new home for him at Walter Annenberg's desert estate in Palm Springs—the very place that had sheltered Richard Nixon after his own flight from power. But the Shah had dallied in Egypt and Morocco, soaking up the winter sun, a sick, gaunt, unhappy figure preparing for a life of American exile. By the time he was ready to move on, Sullivan had got cold feet, reporting to Washington that the Shah's arrival in California would be bound to provoke another attack on the embassy. The NSC staff, too, predicted that it would mean "mass arrests of Americans in Tehran," and "almost certainly . . . still another attack on the embassy." Brzezinski, however, thought it would be "repugnant" to break their word to an old friend. But when he raised the issue with Carter, the president—who had made such a fuss about his affection for the Shah—snapped that he "did not want the shah in the United States playing tennis while Americans in Tehran were kidnapped or killed." That effectively ended the discussion.[3]

By the summer of 1979 the Shah had become the world's most celebrated refugee. Increasingly frail but still determined to keep his cancer a secret, he moved first to the Bahamas and then to Mexico, destinations arranged by his old friend Henry Kissinger. Not only was Kissinger appalled by Carter's treatment of one of their closest allies, he was working at the behest of David Rockefeller, president of the Chase Manhattan Bank and younger brother of Kissinger's old patron. A great friend of the Shah's, Nelson Rockefeller had inconveniently dropped dead of a heart attack in January 1979 while "working on a book about his art collection" (in fact, he had been entwined with a female aide, a hobby he shared with the Shah). David—whose bank had considerable holdings in Iran— promised that he would look after the Shah's interests in the United States and sent his staff to sort out his affairs in Mexico.[4]

At first, Carter tried to ignore the Kissinger-Rockefeller campaign. "Fuck the Shah," he snapped at Zbigniew Brzezinski. "I'm not going to welcome him when he has other places where he'll be safe." But the Shah's deteriorating health changed everything, especially when Rockefeller's people confirmed to the State Department that he had cancer. At the weekly foreign policy breakfast on October 19, Cyrus Vance insisted that "common decency and humanity" meant they must admit the Shah for treatment in New York. If Carter let him die in Mexico, Hamilton Jordan added, Kissinger would tell the world "that first you caused the

Shah's downfall and now you've killed him." Carter gave in, but only after a fight. As the meeting was breaking up, he asked: "Does somebody have an answer as to what we would do if the diplomats in our Embassy are taken hostage?" Nobody spoke. "I gather not," Carter said calmly. "On that day we will all sit here with long, drawn, white faces and realize we have been had."[5]

Three days later, the Shah, his wife, and their dogs boarded a private jet to New York. At first the Iranian reaction was more muted than many people had expected. In Tehran, Bruce Laingen, acting ambassador after Sullivan's recall, breathed a sigh of relief. "The reaction to the shah's travel here by the Iranian Government and public has been mild," read a report sent to Jimmy Carter on the night after the Shah's arrival in New York, "and the situation in Tehran is calm."[6]

It was at about this time that Ibrahim Asgharzadeh, a twenty-two-year-old engineering student, met some friends for tea in the village of Sherman, on the northern outskirts of Iran's capital. There they came up with a plan to show the world their fury at the Shah and his Western friends. On November 2 they called a secret meeting at Tehran's Polytechnic University. The mood was tense—they feared an American-backed coup at any moment—but they were determined to take matters into their own hands. "If we don't act rapidly, if we show weakness," one said, "then a superpower like the United States will be able to meddle in the internal affairs of any nation in the world." In two days' time, they would make history.[7]

**For the sixty** American hostages held in the embassy compound, the first days of their captivity were a terrifying experience. They were not always badly treated; there were sandwiches and cigarettes as well as threats and blows, and some of their captors were almost friendly. It was the sheer unpredictability of their situation that made it frightening. One of the hostages, a CIA communications expert, had been evacuated from the embassy roof in Saigon, and he was much more scared this time. The hostage takers were anxious young men and women, riding high on adrenaline, capable of anything. What if they lost interest and turned the hostages over to the crowds on the streets? What if they lost patience and started shooting? What if the Iranian government made a rescue attempt, and the hostages were trapped, blind and helpless, in the cross fire?[8]

Yet in Washington, there was no immediate panic. The State Department, NSC, and CIA all believed that Khomeini would soon intervene, as did many of the students, who had brought enough food for only three days. Rescuing the hostages was dismissed as impossible, given their location in the heart of a landlocked city in the center of Iran. Instead, everyone agreed that quiet diplomacy would do the trick, especially as Iran had billions of dollars' worth of assets in American banks.[9]

Only Jimmy Carter was not so sanguine. Early in the morning he would walk alone in the White House gardens, thinking of the hostages; late at night he would stare at the ceiling, mulling over "steps I could take to gain their freedom without sacrificing the honor and security of our nation." This was not just self-serving rhetoric; his aides thought he had an unusually personal stake in the hostages' fate. Whether he was attending a prayer service in the National Cathedral or comforting their families a few days after their capture, anxiety was written on his face in thin gray lines. Meeting the families was a gesture nobody expected, but it spoke volumes about his commitment. The hostages' safety, he told congressional leaders, was "constantly a burden on my mind, no matter what I am thinking about. If I am worrying about an announcement that I am going to be a candidate for president or if I am worrying about the windfall profits tax or if I am worrying about anything else, I am always concerned about the hostages."[10]

It would be no exaggeration to say that Carter became genuinely obsessed with the hostage crisis. His adviser Hedley Donovan recalled that Carter "discussed their plight with literally thousands of people in briefings and meetings in the White House," as well as praying for them every night and receiving delegations from their families. Rather more cynically, Hamilton Jordan calculated that if Carter kept the hostage crisis on the front pages, it would drive off not only the bad economic news but the threat of Edward Kennedy's presidential challenge. Just four days after the kidnapping he persuaded the president to cancel a visit to Canada, and from that point onward the hostages came before any other issue.[11]

In the long run, this so-called Rose Garden strategy became a serious political handicap. Associating himself with the hostage issue would only reap dividends for Carter when they were liberated. If the crisis dragged on, it would do him no good to be associated with yet another failure. What is more, he had turned himself into a prisoner in the White House. He was a "trapped man," wrote Elizabeth Drew a few weeks later, "his fate, like that of the Americans held in Tehran, hostage to the unpredictable, conflicting, confusing voices from Iran."[12]

What made handling the crisis even more difficult was the fact that nobody knew whether Khomeini was really running affairs in Tehran, or what he wanted. Even the CIA could provide no useful intelligence about his motives. At first he was astonished by the students' audacity, and even told his men to "kick them out." But as crowds poured onto the streets of Iran celebrating their achievement, he realized that the crisis could be a powerful political tool. "We keep the hostages, finish our internal work, then release them," he explained to one of his allies. "This has united our people. Our opponents dare not act against us. We can put the [new Islamic] constitution to the people's vote without difficulty, and carry out the presidential and parliamentary elections. When we have finished all these jobs, we can let the hostages go."[13]

It was the hostage crisis that turned Khomeini into the unlikeliest of television stars. The students, he told Mike Wallace on 60 *Minutes*, had merely arrested "a bunch of spies," while Carter had broken international law by refusing to hand back the Shah for trial. Indeed, one of the most compelling subplots of the drama was the personal struggle between these two deeply religious men. "Why should we be afraid?" Khomeini jeered. "Carter is beating an empty drum. Carter does not have the guts to engage in a military action." When Carter announced a package of sanctions, the old cleric returned to the attack. "This 'humanitarian' thinks he can mobilize the whole world into starving us," he said scornfully. "Unfortunately for Mr. Carter, his secretary of state went round but nobody took any notice of him." No less an expert than Richard Nixon complimented the ayatollah on his communications strategy. "If he's crazy," Nixon remarked in his first live interview since 1974, "he's crazy like a fox in one respect. He knows how to manipulate the media."[14]

With a story rich in suspense, sympathetic American heroes, fanatical foreign villains, and plenty of political conspiracy and military action, the hostage crisis might have been scripted for television. For the networks, it was terrific news: after the ordeal of Vietnam, here was a story in which there were no shades of gray, just black and white. Every night they had new pictures of Iranian mobs shaking their fists, denouncing the Great Satan, and setting light to the American flag. "Nowhere was the gulf between the Iranian and the American worlds more angrily felt," said the head of the State Department's working group on the hostage crisis, "than in the American living room, with fanatical Iranian faces daily screaming hatred from TV screens."[15]

If the crisis belonged to anyone, then it belonged to ABC, which had managed to get a television crew to Tehran before the Iranians closed the airport. At 11:30 every night the network ran a special broadcast, initially titled *The Iran Crisis: America Held Hostage*, turning Ted Koppel into a national star and eventually evolving into *Nightline*. The very first show began with an image of a blindfolded, terrified Barry Rosen, and from then on viewers were hooked. Despite the late hour, some twelve million people watched every night, and audiences for late-night television in general went up by four million. Much to the discomfort of the White House, the show reminded viewers how long the hostages had been imprisoned—"Day 57," "Day 74," "Day 312"—hammering home Carter's failure to get them out. On CBS, Walter Cronkite's evening bulletins ended with a similar formula. "And that's the way it is," he would say, "on January 16, the fiftieth day of the hostages' captivity."[16]

There were those, their voices often barely audible beneath the patriotic fervor, who saw the crisis as an opportunity to attack the alleged imperialism of American foreign policy. At Christmas, the Iranians allowed the hostages to be visited by a delegation of radical clergymen, led by William Sloane Coffin, the former CIA agent, Yale chaplain, and peace activist. Coffin had already told the press that while "we scream about the hostages, few Americans heard the screams of tortured Iranians." Now, to the hostages' amazement, Coffin advised them against "self-pity." He was envious of them, he confided, for having "an extended period of quiet" to rest and think.

Other radical visitors to Tehran were even more insensitive. In January 1980 the American Indian activist John Thomas encouraged the students to put the hostages on trial and even led crowds outside the embassy in a chant of "Death to Carter." A month later, another delegation of peace activists showed up in Tehran, led by the veteran protester and University of Kansas professor Norman Forer, who praised the Iranian students for their "bold and courageous effort" and condemned "the wanton exploitation of the hostage situation by the [American] warmongers and moneychangers." With friends like these, the hostages needed no enemies.[17]

The vast majority of Americans, however, felt nothing but sympathy for the captives. "When I watch TV, the news, and I see what they do to that flag, it gets me in the heart," one man explained in one of the first *America Held Hostage* broadcasts. Even when some hostages appeared on television, reading statements condemning the Shah and defending their captors, it did not dent the public pity for their plight. At Washington's National Cathedral, bells tolled every day at noon, once for each day of their captivity, while in Lawrence, Massachusetts, churches rang their bells fifty times a day in sympathy. Manhattan's ten thousand cabdrivers drove with their lights blazing in the daytime to express their solidarity, and hundreds of thousands of letters flooded into the Iranian embassy. Not for years had there been such a surge of open, unashamed patriotism; it was as though the clouds of Vietnam and Watergate had suddenly opened, allowing the light of national pride to shine through.[18]

But there was a belligerent side to this outpouring of emotion. An Iran-

Air flight had to be diverted to Montreal when workers at JFK Airport refused to service the plane, and ships were turned away after longshoremen refused to unload vessels flying the Iranian flag. Meanwhile, when small groups of Iranian students organized protests calling for Carter to hand over the Shah, the president ordered the Justice Department to check the visas of all Iranian students and deport those with irregularities. "I may have to sit here and bite my lip and show restraint and look impotent, but I am not going to have those bastards humiliating our country in front of the White House!" Carter told Hamilton Jordan. "And let me tell you something else, Ham, if I wasn't President, I'd be out on the streets myself and I'd probably take a swing at any Khomeini demonstrator I could get my hands on."[19]

In this respect, the president was undoubtedly in tune with the mood of the nation. In Beverly Hills, local youths attacked Iranian students with baseball bats, putting some of them in the hospital. In Riverside, California, an Iranian student was found shot to death in what the police called an "execution." In Houston, protesters burned the Iranian flag in front of the country's consulate; at St. Louis University, security guards had to disarm a man toting a shotgun and asking where he could find the Iranian students. "No more Iranian students will be permitted on these premises until the hostages are released," read a sign at the Mustang Ranch, a brothel near Reno, suggesting that not all Iranians shared their beloved ayatollah's asceticism.[20]

Meanwhile, the born-again country singer Pat Boone recorded "The Hostage Prayer," while disc jockeys played titles like "Go to Hell Ayatollah!" and "Take Your Oil and Shove It," or a song to the tune of "Barbara Ann": "Bomb, bomb, bomb / bomb, bomb, Iran." At Ohio State, students chanted, "Nagasaki, Hiroshima, why not Iran?" At Princeton, students hung a bedsheet from their dormitory with the slogan "Nuke the Ayatollah." In El Paso, a shooting range invited visitors to spend all day firing at a target of the ayatollah. And in New York, Christmas shoppers looking for that special gift could pick up an ayatollah doll. "Make him your prisoner," advised the marketing blurb. "Act now—get rope, pins, other torture equipment. Fabulous gift item."[21]

At the beginning of December, *The Washington Post* ran a moving interview with Penne Laingen, wife of the imprisoned acting ambassador. "I've hung a Christmas wreath on the door and have taken out our Advent candles," she said, "and as we've always done, I'm lighting one every Sunday. I know that it's what Bruce expects me to be doing." She drew comfort from candlelight vigils around the country and was touched by the public support. Her greatest solace, though, came from ringing the bells in her local Episcopal church in Chevy Chase, Maryland. She hoped that others might do the same, for there was "something about the sound of bells that conveys hope and joy and optimism." Finally, she told the paper that she had "tied a yellow ribbon round the old oak tree" in her yard, a gesture inspired by Tony Orlando and Dawn's number one hit of 1973, which itself drew on stories of women wearing yellow ribbons to remember their sweethearts in the U.S. Cavalry. "One of these days Bruce is going to untie that yellow ribbon," she said. "It's going to be out there until he does."[22]

That Christmas, yellow ribbons were everywhere: around trees and lampposts, pinned to lapels and fluttering from flagpoles, even pasted to cars in the form of bumper stickers. When the Pittsburgh Steelers beat the Los Angeles Rams in the Super Bowl, there was a gigantic yellow ribbon tied around the Pasadena Rose Bowl. It was a gesture endorsed by President Carter, who had made the hostage crisis the centerpiece of his holiday. Dedicating the White House Christmas tree on national television, he asked his audience to join him in a silent prayer for "fifty Americans who don't have freedom, who don't have joy, and who don't have warmth, who don't have their families with them."

When Amy threw the switch to turn on the lights, the national tree remained dark except for the star on the top. It was "a star of hope," her father explained. "We will turn on the other lights on the tree when the American hostages come home. Merry Christmas, everybody."[23]

**Carter spent Christmas Day** alone at Camp David with Rosalynn and Amy. It was the first time in twenty-six years that he had not spent Christmas in Georgia with his extended family, but he thought the hostage crisis was too serious to warrant a break in the South. It was, he gloomily noted in his diary, a "relatively lonely" day, the highlights being the phone calls to his family in Plains and Amy's excitement at her presents, which she insisted on opening at five thirty in the morning. In the evening, the three of them watched the film *The Black Stallion*; then, quietly, they went to bed.[24]

Only afterward did Carter learn that even as his family was enjoying Christmas Day, huge transport planes were landing at Kabul International Airport, airlifting Soviet troops into the landlocked capital of Afghanistan. Meanwhile, on the Amu Darya River that marked the Soviet Union's southern border, pontoon bridges were creaking beneath the weight of the 108th Motorized Rifle Division. Two days later, KGB commandos stormed the Afghan presidential palace, killing President Hafi-zullah Amin and installing his Communist rival Babrak Karmal as the country's new leader under Soviet protection. On December 28, Radio Kabul announced that Afghanistan's Revolutionary Council had issued an invitation to the Soviet Union for further military assistance and that the Kremlin had accepted.[25]

One of the baffling things about Carter's reaction to the Soviet occupa-tion was that he seemed so surprised. Yet there had been Soviet military advisers in Afghanistan since the early 1970s, and Kabul's Communist rul-ers had been begging the Kremlin to intervene against their tribal oppo-nents since April 1978. Far from rushing to invade, the Soviet leaders had been reluctant to get involved, only changing their minds in December 1979. But they never expected a fierce response from the United States. Since Afghanistan was a Communist country bordering their southern republics and had long been part of their sphere of influence, the Soviet leaders assumed that Washington would accept their need for a buffer against the turmoil in Iran. From their point of view, moving troops south was merely a necessary step to ensure their own security.[26]

Yet Carter seemed personally horrified by the Christmas occupation. "The invasion of Afghanistan was direct aggression by the Soviet armed forces against a freedom-loving people," he recalled in his memoirs; worse, it was a clear "threat to the rich oil fields of the Persian Gulf" and a dramatic step toward the Kremlin's goal of world domination. At Camp David, he immediately broke off his vacation, flying back to Washington that morning. From there, he sent Brezhnev a message on the hotline warning that it could mark "a fundamental and long-lasting turning point in our relations." "This is the most serious international development that has occurred since I have been President," he wrote in his diary at the beginning of January.[27]

Coming so soon after the Tehran embassy takeover, the Soviet occu-pation of Afghanistan was also a terrible blow to Carter's credibility. Although his admirers could point to notable successes abroad—the Pan-ama Canal treaties, the resumption of relations with China, and, most spectacularly, the Camp David Accords between Egypt and Israel—there was a growing sense that the United States was losing the Cold War. In Ethiopia, the Russians were airlifting vast quantities of arms to the Marxist dictator Colonel Mengistu. In Angola, Cuban troops had joined Russian advisers to prop up the new Marxist regime. In Zaire, Cuban mercenar-ies had stirred up unrest in the vital copper and cobalt belt. And as early as 1978, analysts were talking of an "arc of crisis" stretching from Angola through Mozambique, Zaire, Ethiopia, South Yemen, Iran, Afghanistan, Pakistan, Vietnam, and Cambodia, all either war-torn or deeply unstable, and either allied with the Communist bloc or veering toward it.[28]

Even in its Central American backyard the administration seemed powerless to control events. When Carter withdrew support for Nicaragua's brutal strongman Anastasio Somoza, the result was a peasant revolution led by the Cuban-backed Sandinistas. To the president's critics it was yet another humiliating defeat, the shock exacerbated when Somoza's troops murdered an American reporter during the last days of the regime. His death was shown on television to millions of Americans, yet another illustration of the nation's apparent impotence in the face of a disintegrating world. It was little wonder that the cover of *BusinessWeek* showed the Statue of Liberty with a tear trickling down her cheek, above the damning headline: "The Decline of U.S. Power."[29]

Like Ford and Kissinger before him, Carter struggled to dispel the impression that he was Neville Chamberlain with a southern drawl. The neoconservatives had never liked him, and by the summer of 1979 the knives had come out. Carter was guilty of "appeasement in its purest form," said Henry Jackson, "ominously reminiscent of Great Britain in the 1930s." This was a familiar neoconservative theme, reflecting the sense that the United States was in a kind of Weimar phase, its morals degraded by permissiveness, its economy crippled by inflation, its social structures eroded by decadence and apathy. In the writings of Norman Podhoretz, for example, contempt for moral dissipation and horror at Carter's diplomacy were inseparably entwined. Always the most outspoken of the neoconservatives, Podhoretz was "struck very forcibly" by parallels with Chamberlain's Britain, blaming a culture of self-hatred in "the universities, certain sections of the media, in the publishing industry," which were always "harping on the danger of confrontation and nuclear war." This apparently owed a great deal to the "homosexual ethos," which had discredited the old martial virtues, destroyed the ideal of the family, and undermined national self-confidence. The real blame for Soviet expansion, Podhoretz concluded, went to the heart of the "American homosexual literary world."[30]

In fact, the Soviet position was much weaker than it looked, and the economic rot that would bring down the Communist empire had already set in. But few Western observers realized that at the time; even Carter's secretary of defense, Harold Brown, told Congress that there was a serious "disparity in defense spending between the United States and Soviet Union." In the words of Eugene Rostow, a member of the Committee on the Present Danger, the threat was "worse than it has ever been." The growth of Soviet power, he explained in 1978, was "without parallel in modern history," thanks to an arms budget that left the West "behind in almost every relevant category of military power." For Rostow, "the point is obvious and by now beyond dispute. The Soviet Union *is* engaged in a policy of imperial expansion all over the world."[31]

All of this could hardly fail to influence a politician as keen to appear "tough" as Jimmy Carter. A common myth is that for three years he pursued a well-meaning but weak foreign policy, naively hoping to build bridges with the Communists even as they were plotting to take over the world. True, in his early days he talked airily about a new foreign policy based on "justice, equity, and human rights," free from the "inordinate fear of communism." But this did not last long. More and more Carter listened not to his patrician secretary of state, Cyrus Vance, the insider's insider and champion of détente, but to his intense, hatchet-faced national security adviser, Zbigniew Brzezinski, who despised the State Department and believed in raw power. Meanwhile, although arms negotiations had finally produced a second SALT treaty, ferocious criticism from neoconservative hawks ("appeasement," "global retreat") made congressional approval highly unlikely. Even détente's original architects were now reinventing themselves as hawks. "We are at war," Richard Nixon told readers in *The Real War* (1980), calling it "a titanic struggle in which the fates of nations are being decided." Under Carter, complained Henry Kissinger, "there is no penalty for opposing the United States and no reward for friendship to the United States." He was "sick and tired," he said, "of seeing Americans pushed around."[32]

Not surprisingly, public opinion had decisively shifted. By 1980, one in two Americans thought the nation was falling behind the Soviet Union, while 60 percent agreed that "too little" was spent on defense. Even television joined the crusade. In ABC's science fiction series *Battlestar Galactica* (1978–79), the Twelve Colonies have been at war with the robotic Cylons for a thousand years. When the Cylons suggest a galactic SALT conference, the well-meaning human president, surrounded by anemic liberal advisers, agrees to attend. "Forgive me, Mr. President, but they hate us with every fiber of their existence," says his military commander. "We love freedom. We love independence—to feel, to question, to resist oppression. To them, it's an alien way of existing they will never accept." But the president ignores his advice and walks straight into a trap. Even then the politicians—flabby lovers of luxury—argue for détente, telling the military to throw down their arms. Only a second Cylon trap makes them realize the importance of military readiness and the folly of détente.[33]

Carter was well aware of the changing mood. In September 1979,

Brzezinski warned that his administration was seen as "the most timid since World War II." What "the country craves, and our national security needs" was "both a more assertive tone and a more assertive substance to our foreign policy." In short, Brzezinski wrote, "I believe that for international reasons as well as domestic political reasons you ought to *deliberately toughen both the tone and substance of our foreign policy.* The country associates assertiveness with leadership, and the world at large expects American leadership."[34]

Afghanistan gave Carter the perfect opportunity to show his mettle. If he raised the stakes, he calculated, then he would be seen as the patriotic hero who had stood up to Soviet aggression, the national leader leading a new moral crusade. "I want to go to the maximum degree," he recorded in his diary. Meeting his advisers a few days later, he demanded a grain embargo, a sweeping sanctions package, and even an American boycott of the Moscow Olympics that summer. Some of his proposals—curtailing Soviet fishing privileges, cutting cultural exchange programs, staying away from the Olympics—struck his aides as petty and absurd. But when Carter was in full flow, burning with self-righteous passion, it was hard to stop him.[35]

The overreaction was contagious. Addressing the members of the nation's Olympic committee, who were supposed to be deciding independently whether to go to Moscow, Mondale told them that the occupation of Afghanistan was akin to "the story of Hitler's rise." "History holds its breath," he said solemnly, "for what is at stake is no less than the future security of the civilized world." The committee duly voted for a boycott, which had no discernible effect; indeed, Soviet forces remained in Afghanistan for another nine years. Still, it did have one major consequence: a British sprinter won the men's hundred meters for the first time since 1924. For this, if nothing else, it was worth it.[36]

Carter's reaction marked a turning point in American foreign policy. Not only did he demand compulsory draft registration for men reaching the age of nineteen; he also asked Congress for a major defense spending increase of 5 percent per year, in real terms, over the next five years. In both of these measures, as well as in his belligerent rhetoric and his decision to send massive aid to Pakistan and the Afghan tribal insurgents, he was laying the foundations for the policies of the 1980s. And in Presidential Directive 59, which he signed in July and deliberately leaked in order to advertise his toughness, the administration committed itself to winning a protracted nuclear war. For the first time in ten years, the United States was talking not of cutting arms and lessening tension but of massive new programs to fight and win a third world war.[37]

Yet there was an anxious, febrile quality to this new militarism. It was inspired not by victory but by humiliation, by a succession of crises that played on all the anxieties of the decade, from oil prices and gas lines to embattled families and embassies under siege. And what Brzezinski called the crescent of crisis, stretching from the Horn of Africa up into Iran, Afghanistan, and Pakistan, was a bleeding wound in the nation's sense of impregnability. In Saudi Arabia, hundreds of pilgrims were slaughtered in a militant attack on the Grand Mosque in Mecca. In Pakistan, a mob burned the American embassy to the ground. A week later, the embassy in Libya suffered the same fate. "Already the flames of anti-Western fanaticism that Khomeini fanned in Iran threaten to spread through the volatile Soviet Union, from the Indian subcontinent to Turkey and southward through the Arabian Peninsula to the Horn of Africa," *Time* told its readers, crowning the ayatollah its Man of the Year for 1979. "Not only was 1979 his year; the forces of disintegration that he let loose in one country could threaten many others in the years ahead."[38]

While the nation's Olympic hockey team restored some pride with its extraordinary victory over the much-vaunted Soviet Union at Lake Placid in February, the orgy of flag-waving excitement was itself a symptom of the growing international tension. What gave the Miracle on Ice such resonance, in fact, was that it came against the background of apparently unending chaos and humiliation. A joke circulating in Washington that spring said it all. President Carter receives an unexpected visit from the ghost of Theodore Roosevelt, who asks how the world has changed since his day.

"The Soviets have invaded Afghanistan," Carter says. "Are you retaliating with conventional forces or with nuclear weapons?" asks the former Rough Rider. "Uh, neither," says Carter. "We're boycotting the Olympics in Moscow." "What else?" asks Roosevelt. "Iranians have taken over an embassy in Tehran and they're holding fifty-three of our diplomats hostage," Carter says miserably. "How many bombers have you sent over?" asks TR. "How many divisions have you committed?" "None," Carter replies. "We're using diplomatic restraint."

There is a stunned pause, and then Roosevelt bursts out laughing. "I get it, you're joking!" he says, chuckling. "Next you're gonna tell me you gave away the Panama Canal!"[39]

# Interlude: America's Team

I n the spring of 1979, after the Dallas Cowboys had lost Super Bowl XIII to the Pittsburgh Steelers, Bob Ryan of NFL Films was deputed to put together the Cowboys' annual highlights film, as he did with every other franchise in the National Football League. Looking for a title, Ryan called the Cowboys' public relations director and suggested *Champions Die Hard.* "I don't like that," the Dallas man said. "We're not dead or dying." Ryan thought for a second and then asked: "How about something that projects the Cowboys as a national team?" He had noticed that when the Cowboys played on the road, a surprising proportion of the fans cheered for Dallas, so what about something like *America's Team?* "I like that," the public relations man said. "That sounds good."[1]

The Cowboys' emblematic coach, Tom Landry, hated the nickname America's Team. To Landry, it seemed an arrogant gesture that would inspire other teams to play even harder against them. But the Cowboys' marketing men loved it, and the name captured the team's genuine nationwide appeal. Apart from a one-year dip in 1974, Landry's boys made it to the play-offs every season between 1966 and 1983, a record unrivaled in the league. They had a reputation for innovative tactics, fast and disciplined play, and a sense of style that no rivals could match. By 1977, Cowboys merchandise accounted for almost a third of all NFL-branded sales. They had 225 radio stations across the country, while the Cowboys newspaper sold 100,000 copies, half of them outside Texas. And on television they reigned supreme. Three of the four most watched sports events in American history involved the Cowboys, while they held the highest ranking for Sunday, Monday, Thursday, and Saturday games. The Pittsburgh Steelers might have won more Super Bowls, but in terms of nationwide appeal nobody came close to America's Team.[2]

By the early 1970s, professional football had overtaken baseball to become the nation's most popular sport. *Monday Night Football,* which began on September 21, 1970, and made national figures of Howard Cosell, Frank Gifford, and Don Meredith, was watched in sixty million homes, while the Super Bowl had become an unofficial national holiday.

More people watched the Kansas City Chiefs win the decade's first Super Bowl than had seen Neil Armstrong walk on the moon six months earlier. It was "the Great American Time Out, a three-hour pause on a Sunday afternoon in January that is—as sheer, unadorned spectacle—an interval unique," gushed a *Time* cover story on the eleventh Super Bowl in 1977. "Work goes undone, play ceases too; telephones stop ringing, crime disappears, romance is delayed and, in all the land, there is just one traffic jam worthy of the title—on highways leading to the Super Bowl site."[3]

No team better encapsulated football's new status than the Cowboys. Transformed by oil, finance, and federal spending, Dallas was a classic Sunbelt success story, the center of a vast empire of suburbs, highways, churches, and malls, sprawling over eleven counties and encompassing two and a half million people. It was "a city of wealth," said *Time*, "wrought with sharp pencils and calculating minds." And among its most celebrated additions was Texas Stadium, completed in 1971 at a cost of $300 million: a model of modernity located close to the freeways, complete with capacious hospitality suites for the city's businessmen. The atmosphere was "like a country club," one of the Cowboys' players, Cornell Green, said later. "People started wearing minks to the game."[4]

In the Cowboys, Landry and his innovative general manager, Tex Schramm, built a franchise to match the city. The players' uniforms combined metallic silver-blue helmets and pants with clean white jerseys, conjuring up images of astronauts and spaceships. Soon after Schramm began working for the Cowboys, he called in the Service Bureau Corporation, a subsidiary of IBM, to help him use computers to organize scouting information. Their groundbreaking computer system meant that throughout the 1970s, no franchise scouted or drafted better. To the Cowboys' critics, though, it was a symbol of their corporate arrogance, epitomized by the icily self-controlled figure stalking the sidelines. Tom Landry's players, remarked the journalist B. J. Phillips in 1978, had been assembled "with a loan officer's eye for the sure, steady return and an actuary's fetish for minutiae." They were "too computerized, too efficient, too heartless"; their presence on the field was "as chilling as a ranch-house visit from a cold-eyed Dallas banker holding an overdue mortgage."[5]

Landry apart, nobody epitomized the Cowboys more than their quarterback Roger Staubach, "Captain America." A devout Midwestern Catholic who had served for three years in Vietnam, Staubach never smoked or drank and spent all his free time with his wife and children. "I like sex as much as Joe Namath does," he told *NFL Today*. "I just have it with one woman." Selected for six Pro Bowls, he recorded the league's best passing rating in 1971, 1973, 1978, and 1979 while building a reputation as a spokesman for the Fellowship of Christian Athletes. "I believe in Christian principles, being faithful to my wife," he declared on winning the Super Bowl MVP award in 1972. "But if that's square, that's my life. I enjoy my Christian ideals. I believe there's something greater than what we're here for." It was no surprise that he campaigned for Ronald Reagan in 1980, or that Texas Republicans approached him to run for the Senate. The only surprise was that he turned them down.[6]

As many observers remarked, Staubach's values were remarkably similar to those of his coach. They were "men cut from the same competitive cloth," said *The New York Times*, "with family, church and football the priorities." A small-town, born-again Texan who had flown bombing missions over Europe and read from the Bible in the locker room, Tom Landry made no secret of his conservative values. "In our country," he once told the Fellowship of Christian Athletes, "we are destroying man's competitive spirit in so many ways." It had become "fashionable to expect the government to guarantee almost anything," but modern society, with its "murder, rioting and looting," was "sick." Football was "the last place where we have discipline," Landry said, urging his audience to "stand up" for Christ.[7]

Like many Southerners of his generation, Landry was appalled by the cultural changes of the 1970s. In 1977, he told reporters that the nation was "organized no differently from a football team. It is built on competition, discipline and paying the price. Take away those things and you have chaos, weakness and immorality." His words struck a chord with many local fans, for Dallas was a deeply conservative town in the 1970s, its culture dominated by the Baptist and Methodist churches and its politics by oil, business, and the Republican Party. Most fans cared more about their coach's record than his politics. Even so, one of the reasons Landry became such a hero in the town was that, as one sportswriter put it, "for many of the Dallas fans, [he] represented exactly what they had been raised to believe in: God, hard work, and faith."[8]

By the 1977 season, which ended with the Cowboys crushing the Denver Broncos to win their second Super Bowl, it had become a truism that football represented distinctly conservative values. In an age of retreat abroad and alleged decadence at home, it seemed a throwback to a bygone era of simple heroism, reasserting traditional American manliness at a time when the headlines were full of American impotence. Even the teams' names—the Cowboys, the Steelers, the Giants, the Vikings—were redolent of martial values that seemed to be dying out elsewhere. Football, wrote William Phillips in *Commentary*, had made "respectable the most primitive feelings about violence, patriotism, manhood," and perhaps that was why it was more popular than ever. Its audience, another essayist noted, was "Middle America in the raw, the Silent Majority at its noisiest, relieving its frustrations in the visual excitement of the nation's most popular sport."

No team captured Middle America's imagination more successfully than the Cowboys. As Art Spander of the *San Francisco Examiner* pointed out, they had come to represent values that seemed increasingly precious during the Carter years. "These are difficult, complex times in America," Spander wrote. "Inflation, court-ordered busing, oil crises, lack of leadership. People seek a simpler life, a hero. That would be the cowboy—small *c*—and the Old West." It would also be "with a capital *C*," the Cowboys. "Our best cars are from Europe," he lamented. "Our best electronic equipment and cameras are from Japan. What happened to the Great American Dream of working harder, producing better? It's alive and living in Texas Stadium."[9]

# Chapter Eighteen  Conservatives for Change

When they ask, "Well, why are you a Conservative?" I tell them,
"I'm a Conservative because I'm for change."

**—SENATOR ROGER JEPSEN,** March 1979

A fter Gerald Ford's defeat in the presidential election of 1976, many observers thought that the game was up for the Republican Party. Humiliated by the Watergate scandal, hammered in the 1974 midterms, and bleeding from the long battle between Ford and Reagan, the party of Lincoln seemed to be staggering toward oblivion. In *The New York Times*, Warren Weaver wrote that the Republican Party was "perhaps closer to extinction than ever before in its 122-year history." The Republicans had "lost their grip on the American establishment," agreed the distinguished political scientist Everett Carll Ladd, while the elections expert Gerald Pomper forecast "the decline of the Republicans to a permanent minority or even their replacement by a new party." Even the conservative columnist Robert Novak predicted "the long descent of the Republican Party into irrelevance, defeat, and perhaps eventual disappearance."[1]

What all of these experts underestimated, of course, was the rising appeal of conservatism. But then, underestimating conservatism was nothing new; during the 1950s, a generation of "consensus historians" had effectively suggested that there had never been any such thing as

American conservatism at all. Yet conservatism had both a rich history and an extremely promising future. Its themes—belief in private property and free enterprise; opposition to Communism, socialism, and New Deal liberalism; a strong sense of American nationalism and manifest destiny; commitment to traditional moral and cultural standards—were deeply rooted in the nation's past. And almost beneath the surface of political events, a new conservative generation had reached maturity: the generation of Pat Buchanan and George Will, the tens of thousands of college students who had joined Young Americans for Freedom, the 100,000 subscribers who read William F. Buckley's *National Review*, the twenty-seven million who had voted for Barry Goldwater, the thirty-nine million who had voted for Gerald Ford.[2]

Despite the accusations of its opponents, the new conservatism of the postwar decades was not a business-funded conspiracy any more than it was an elite-driven enterprise directed from William F. Buckley's Connecticut estate. It was, above all, a grassroots movement, born in the mundane coffee mornings, study groups, and educational campaigns of innumerable local activists. In many places, suburban anti-Communist groups laid the foundations; in others, the motivating themes might be revulsion at cultural change or anger at high taxes. As early as 1960, observed the British reporter Godfrey Hodgson, there was "a whole structure of crusades, campaigns, radio stations, newsletters, storefronts, action groups, committees, lecture bureaus, lobbies, and assorted voluntary organizations of every kind."[3]

One of the biggest mistakes liberals ever made was to underestimate their adversaries as kooks, eccentrics, losers, blindly lashing out against progress and modernity. Even academic scholars, like the experts who contributed essays to Daniel Bell's collection *The New American Right* (1955), regarded conservatives as glorified psychiatric patients. Conservative beliefs, wrote the political scientist Herbert McClosky, appealed to "the uninformed, the poorly educated and . . . the less intelligent," to people "bewildered" by the modern world. And when Barry Goldwater won the Republican nomination, most scholars dismissed his success as an embarrassing fluke. His ideas, wrote Richard Hofstadter, were "so bizarre, so archaic, so self-confounding, so remote from the basic American consensus" that it was a miracle he had made it so far. His campaign was essentially "a kind of vocational therapy, without which [his supporters] might have to be committed."[4]

This was a complete misreading of the kinds of people whose efforts gave the New Right its momentum. The activists who attended coffee mornings, stuffed envelopes, and wrote letters to local newspapers tended to be affluent, middle-class people, heading up the social ladder. They held managerial or professional positions associated with new industries like aerospace and computing, lived in pleasant suburban communities, and were personally happy and successful. They saw themselves as perfectly reasonable, modern people, and to them conservatism simply made sense. They liked its emphasis on hard work, which seemed to have brought them so many rewards. They liked its libertarian, individualistic themes, which matched their love of suburban privacy and self-improvement. They liked its strict Christian piety, which reminded them of the moral values they had learned as children. And they liked its sense of "coherence, community, and commitment," which they found in their suburban churches and volunteer groups.

They were not cranks or losers; they were ordinary homeowners, parents, and taxpayers. As one of their great champions, who first ran for political office in 1974, remarked of his suburban Atlanta constituents, they lived in "a sort of Norman Rockwell world with fiber-optic computers and jet airplanes." It was a world that would later be named after him: Newtland.[5]

**Whenever Richard Viguerie** took a pause for reflection during a busy day in his windowless, air-conditioned, high-security office building in Falls Church, Virginia, he usually thought about lists. A rumpled, amiable character in his mid-forties, a pious Catholic, and a devoted family man, Viguerie had none of William F. Buckley's patrician hauteur. It was once said that he looked like a used-car salesman. But he had something much more important than Yankee style. He had lots of lists.

The son of a Texas oilman and a long-standing admirer of Douglas MacArthur and Joe McCarthy, Viguerie had become executive secretary of Young Americans for Freedom in 1961, when he was just twenty-eight. Since the organization was badly in debt, he devoted his energies to raising funds. A shy man, he "didn't like asking people for money," so he wrote them letters instead. That seemed to work, so he hired more secretaries, bought a mimeograph machine, and sent out more letters. More money came in; more letters went out. Viguerie had found his calling. At the beginning of 1965, he set up his own company, RAVCO, dedicated to raising money for conservative causes through the pioneering method of direct mail.[6]

Viguerie's first list contained the names of seventy-five hundred people who had given money to Barry Goldwater. As he collected more names, RAVCO went from strength to strength. In 1968 he helped George Wallace break new records for raising money from small contributors, and four years later he turned down an approach from George McGovern. In 1976, Viguerie worked for Wallace again, but by this stage he was already doing good business with the Republican Party. That fall, political action committees retaining his services raised more money than the Republican National Committee and its House and Senate campaign committees put together. By the end of the decade, his Falls Church offices were sending a hundred million pieces of mail a year to some twenty-five million voters. Even at night, two huge computers hummed away, while printing presses thundered out letter after letter. From Citizens for Decent Literature to Conservative Books for Christian Leaders, from No Amnesty for Deserters to the Committee for Responsible Youth Politics, no conservative group could do without Richard Viguerie's lists.[7]

The odd thing about direct mail was that it was an incredibly expensive way for politicians to raise money. In 1974, RAVCO raised $198,568 for Americans for Effective Law Enforcement, but 90 percent of it was swallowed up in Viguerie's fees. Two years later, Viguerie helped the Committee for the Survival of a Free Congress raise $1.7 million, yet only sixteen cents in every dollar actually reached the candidates. But Viguerie insisted that direct mail was "only partly fundraising; it's mostly advertising." By encouraging ordinary citizens to think about the issues, he argued, direct mail allowed conservatives to "bypass the monopoly the left has in the media, and let us go directly to the people." Indeed the ethos of direct mail was fervently populist, even apocalyptic in tone, warning recipients of the terrible threat of "militant gays," "liberal educators," "cruel atheists," "big union bosses," "baby killers," and "Godless politicians." The whole point, said Terry Dolan of the National Conservative PAC, was to "make them angry." "We are trying to be divisive," he admitted. "The shriller you are, the better it is to raise money."[8]

Viguerie was just one of the ideological entrepreneurs who made up the central command of the New Right in the 1970s. It would be going too far to call them a conspiracy, but, as *Harper's* remarked, "any diagram of [its] organization looks like an octopus shaking hands with itself, so completely interlocked are the directorates of its various components." Other prominent figures included Terry Dolan and Howard Phillips of the Conservative Caucus. But perhaps the most important was Paul Weyrich, a sleek, baby-faced political organizer from Wisconsin.[9]

Weyrich had become involved with conservative politics as a student during the Goldwater campaign, and by the late 1960s he had moved to Capitol Hill as press secretary to Colorado's Republican senator Gordon Allott. Still only in his mid-twenties, he was amazed by the sheer disorganization of life on the Hill, not least the failure of conservative senators to talk to lobby groups or even one another. But there was not much he could do about it—until he met his fairy godmother, the Colorado brewing magnate Joseph Coors. Weyrich persuaded him to invest in the Analysis Research Corporation, which was supposed to coordinate research for conservative congressmen, but it soon fell apart. So in 1973, Coors put up another $250,000 for Weyrich to set up an entirely new organization, the Heritage Foundation.[10]

The story of the Heritage Foundation is an excellent example of the way in which the New Right, when closely examined, turns out to be rather less new after all. As a millionaire businessman with German roots, Coors was the kind of person who had been financing conservative causes for decades. But Weyrich, too, was firmly rooted in the Old Right. His father, a conservative German Catholic, had idolized the Midwestern isolationist Robert Taft, and young Paul claimed to have "read everything he wrote." Weyrich also acknowledged his debt to the Catholic "radio priest" Father Coughlin, another isolationist who had fiercely denounced Franklin D. Roosevelt and the East Coast elite. He equally admired a third conservative champion, Joe McCarthy, the darling of many Midwestern Germans and another master of scaremongering populism. There was nothing very new, in other words, about Weyrich's brand of Catholic conservatism.[11]

Of course some institutions predated the appearance of Weyrich and Coors on the national scene, the classic example being the American Enterprise Institute (AEI), the grandame of the free-market world since 1943. But while the AEI was a kind of Brooks Brothers Brookings, the Heritage Foundation was the "feisty kid on the conservative block," as Ronald Reagan put it. By 1980 it employed dozens of full-time staff, had a budget of well over $5 million, and was pouring out hundreds of papers on everything from economics and welfare to immigration and national defense. It organized seminars for congressmen, sponsored Capitol Hill internships for students, and boasted a huge "resource bank" of facts and ideas. As one reporter put it, Heritage was the perfect "ideological filtration system" for the new conservative politics.[12]

Yet Weyrich's vision went well beyond think tanks and lobby groups. He dreamed of a vast conservative coalition reaching across sectarian boundaries, welcoming West Coast libertarians and big-city Catholics, evangelical Christians and self-made tycoons. For all the success of single-issue groups like the National Rifle Association and Focus on the Family, Weyrich was not satisfied. Instead, he encouraged broad-based organizations—the Heritage Foundation, the Committee for the Survival of a Free Congress, the Conservative Caucus—to advise a wide range of local activists on fund-raising, lobbying, and protesting, to print their newsletters, to explain how to qualify initiatives for state ballots. Behind many of the populist campaigns of the decade, from the Kanawha County textbook protests to Anita Bryant's anti-gay-rights campaign, were the advisers and accountants of organizations like the Heritage Foundation.[13]

Above all, Weyrich insisted that conservatives talk to one another. "Organization is our bag," he said. "We preach and teach nothing but organization." At lunches and dinners, at informal Capitol Hill receptions, and at weekly planning meetings, he gathered a shifting cast of activists and politicians, from Jesse Helms and Phyllis Schlafly to Richard Viguerie and Terry Dolan. By 1978, it was hard to tell where one group ended and another began. In dozens of newsletters and magazines—*National Review, Human Events, Conservative Digest, Washington Weekly, The American Spectator*, even *The Wall Street Journal*—their ideas percolated through to a wider public. Thanks to Weyrich, Viguerie, and their allies, the New Right became "an institutionalized, disciplined, well-organized, and well-financed movement of loosely knit affiliates."[14]

Despite their corporate backing, Weyrich and Viguerie saw themselves as outsiders challenging an entrenched liberal elite. In the words of Roger Jepsen, running for the Senate in Iowa on a fierce anti-abortion platform, they were "conservatives for change," standing for ordinary people fed up with stagflation, moral decadence, and national decline. Their adversaries were the classic foes of the populist imagination: professors and planners, bureaucrats and politicians, journalists and broadcasters, people that George Wallace had called "pointy heads," that Spiro Agnew had called "an effete corps of impudent snobs," and that the former LAPD chief Ed Davis, the darling of law-and-order groups, called "Beverly Hills and Bel-Air swimming pool Communists."[15]

No two words better summed up their adversaries, though, than the dreaded phrase "eastern establishment."* It was not an expression that people used to describe themselves; it was the ultimate term of populist opprobrium, dripping with contempt for sissified Ivy League liberals, the heirs to the Wall Street millionaires and Jewish bankers against whom populists had inveighed decades before. For conservatives, the very term "East Coast" was loaded with meaning: the East Coast that had sold out to sex and socialism, the East Coast awash with drugs and rolling in money,

---

*The phrase "the Establishment" is generally attributed to the British journalist Henry Fairlie, who used it in print in 1955. Writing in *The New Yorker* thirteen years later, Fairlie claimed that he had got it from Emerson. In any case, it was in common use on both sides of the Atlantic by the turn of the 1970s.

the East Coast that looked down on the plain folk of the South and the West. The worst of it was that the liberals had the gall to revel in their own decadence. No self-respecting conservative, noted the journalist Alan Crawford, could contemplate without a shudder the diabolical "cocktail parties" at which Easterners, crazed with marijuana, cocaine, and their own academic achievements, hatched their infernal "plots against the republic."[16]

Anti-eastern sentiment drew on genuine bitterness at federal environmental policies that supposedly threatened the economic development of states like Wyoming and Arizona. But it also tapped into a long-standing tradition: the entrepreneurial, lower-middle-class, anti-establishment populism associated with such diverse figures as William Jennings Bryan, Huey Long, and Joe McCarthy. Kevin Phillips even claimed that the New Right's true father was Andrew Jackson, who, by using the franking privilege to solicit contributions, had invented direct mail to bypass "the elitist, pro-Adams media." And Weyrich remained a keen admirer of Father Coughlin, whose fiery radio sermons, dripping with anti-eastern resentment and overt anti-Semitism, had delighted so many Midwesterners during the 1930s. As the neoconservative Jeane Kirkpatrick astutely put it, the New Right was "not really new at all, but . . . a strain of nativist populism whose roots are deep in American history."[17]

**Like any political movement,** populist conservatism was doomed to failure unless it could get its hands on some serious money. Even liberalism, despite its opponents' belief that it was nothing more than socialism in disguise, had long maintained surprisingly close links with big business. For decades, corporations such as General Electric, IBM, Pan Am, Standard Oil, and Bank of America had been sympathetic to liberalism because they liked its emphasis on free trade and economic growth. The Kennedy and Johnson administrations were full of corporate veterans such as Robert McNamara and Dean Rusk, and even Jimmy Carter's presidential campaign drew strong support from multinational executives. The chairman of Coca-Cola took time off to promote his candidacy, Henry Ford II publicly backed him, and Carter appointed twenty-eight members of the internationalist, free-trade Trilateral Commission to positions in his administration. Antagonizing big business was never on his agenda.[18]

But the relationship between big business and the Democratic Party was heading for trouble. Once, even the most conservative executive could console himself by glancing at his profit sheets. But the long recession of the Ford years had a searing impact on a generation of executives, and the enduring threat of inflation meant that confidence never really recovered. Domestic demand remained sluggish, foreign rivals were making inroads into global markets, and high interest rates made it prohibitively expensive to invest in new technology. Corporate profits collapsed, with gross margins tumbling from just under 16 percent during the 1960s to barely 10 percent in the 1970s. After-tax profits were even more alarming, falling by half during the same period.[19]

For businessmen used to boundless growth, the challenge of stagflation came as a dreadful shock. Capitalism was "beset by crisis," said *Time* in 1975, pointing to Britain's rampant inflation and collapsing pound, the soaring prices in Canada and Australia, the terrible recessions in Italy and France. Intellectuals and students had turned against the capitalist system, losing faith in its ability to build a just society; meanwhile, the "free market is being steadily hemmed in by the power of omnipresent government regulators, mass unions and giant corporations." Milton Friedman offered a suitably gloomy conclusion. Capitalist democracy, he warned, might well prove "an accident" in the long sweep of history; perhaps humanity was destined to sink back into "tyranny and misery."[20]

While executives hardly expected tears of sympathy from their fellow citizens, they at least hoped for a little understanding. But thanks to the popular reaction against corruption and pollution, the revulsion against authority, and anger at the plight of the economy, the image of business seemed irredeemably tarnished. By 1979, eight out of ten people agreed that "there is too much power concentrated in the hands of a few large companies," while six out of ten supported the idea of federal limits on business profits. In films of the era, businessmen are almost always conspiratorial villains, from *Chinatown*'s Noah Cross to *Superman*'s Lex Luthor. And businessmen on television—Boss Hogg in *The Dukes of Hazzard*, JR in *Dallas*—were even worse. As aficionados of detective shows knew, the man in the pin-striped suit usually did it. "On almost every episode of *Columbo*," protested the conservative journalist Ben Stein, "a rich businessman has killed someone and seeks to bully Columbo into leaving him alone because of his high status . . . Not even the smallest of businessmen is exempt from the mark of Cain."[21]

With even mainstream Democrats like Henry Jackson and Frank Church denouncing oil companies and multinational corporations, corporate boardrooms began to fall out of love with liberalism. Keynesianism had manifestly failed to stave off inflation and recession, while younger executives were eager to fight back against the crippling taxes, pettifogging rules, and suffocating regulations that, they claimed, made it impossible to compete in an age of globalization. "What we were doing wasn't working," reflected John Harper, chairman of the aluminum giant Alcoa. "All the polls showed business in disfavor. We didn't think people understood how the economic system works. We were getting short shrift from Congress. I thought we were powerless in spite of the stories about how we could manipulate everything." So in 1972, Harper set up the Business Roundtable, bringing together leading chief executives to fight back against "government's growing involvement in the day-to-day conduct of business." The Business Roundtable did not endorse individual candidates. But its values—leaner government, lower taxes, lighter regulations—were unarguably closer to conservatism than to New Deal liberalism.[22]

Harper's ambitions would reach spectacular fulfillment by the end of the 1970s. With the breakup of the old congressional hierarchy, lobbying was one of the great growth industries of the decade. Not only did conservative institutions like the Scaife and Olin foundations pour money into think tanks, law firms, and advocacy groups, but hundreds of corporations employed bright young things to fight for their interests in the corridors of power. By the middle of the decade, the leading 500 firms had already spent more than $400 million on "advocacy advertising," employed 8,000 lobbyists on Capitol Hill, and funded around a hundred political action committees (PACs) to support sympathetic candidates. By 1980 they employed 15,000 lobbyists and supported almost 1,500 PACs, favoring Republican candidates over Democrats by a ratio of two to one—at a cost of more than $1 billion.[23]

For many executives, the first priority was to reverse the tide of government regulation. Under pressure from the environmentalist and consumer movements, Congress had passed more than twenty-five major consumer protection laws between 1967 and 1973, while federal spending on economic regulations ballooned from $166 million to $428 million. The expansion of "social" regulatory agencies in the same period, such as the Environmental Protection Agency and the Occupational Safety and Health Administration, meant that spending on social regulations rocketed from $1.4 billion to $4.3 billion. Banks, credit agencies, food, drugs, cosmetics, manufactured goods, automobiles, advertising, packaging, even water and air: nothing, it seemed, escaped the purview of the federal government.[24]

The anti-regulation movement was heavily funded by industries threatened by global competition and extremely vulnerable to the new wave of social regulations. Many corporations paid for academic studies downplaying the environmental impact of their factories, while the Scaife, Smith Richardson, and Olin foundations, funded by petrochemicals, pharmaceuticals, and chemicals, respectively, spent millions on research and lobbying to discredit the regulatory state. A classic example was Consumer Alert, founded by the conservative activist Barbara Keating in 1977. Keating argued that regulations hurt ordinary citizens by pushing up prices and stifling growth. Her party trick was to tell audiences that the ordinary hamburger was now subject to 41,000 regulations, 200 legal statutes, and 111,000 judicial decisions. Of course nobody bothered to check. As so often in politics, it was the symbolism, not the accuracy, that really mattered.[25]

Meanwhile, deregulation was picking up intellectual momentum, backed by academic papers from Cornell, the University of Chicago, and the Brookings Institution. Even liberals came out in favor: for Ted Kennedy, for instance, deregulation seemed the ideal way to bring lower prices and economic recovery, while it immediately appealed to Jimmy Carter's small-business instincts. By 1978, Carter's Regulatory Analysis Review Group was considering market-based alternatives to federal agencies, and in the same year he pushed through airline deregulation, masterminded by the Cornell economist Alfred Kahn. Trucking, railroads, and financial institutions followed within two years. In the long run, the British ambassador to Washington predicted, the Carter administration would be remembered "for the bringing of a profound and quiet revolution: the deregulation of huge tracts of American industry and commerce."[26]

It was a sign of how far and how quickly the center of gravity had shifted that during his reelection campaign, Carter spoke of deregulation as one of his greatest achievements. "We believe that we ought to get the Government's nose out of the private enterprise of this country," he told a Democratic gala dinner in New Jersey in October 1980. "We've deregulated rail, deregulated trucking, deregulated airlines, deregulated financial institutions, working on communications, to make sure that we have a free enterprise system that's competitive . . . so that the customers get a better deal and the business community gets a better deal as well." His Republican opponent must have been proud of him.[27]

**In the old days,** populist movements had run out of steam because they failed to translate grassroots anger into electoral momentum. But with Viguerie poring over his lists and Weyrich dashing from meeting to meeting, the New Right was determined not to make the same mistake. The challenge was to find the right vehicle for winning and wielding power, and at first many doubted that the Republican Party, which they associated with Nixon, Rockefeller, and Wall Street, was at all suitable. Viguerie, who conducted a long flirtation with Wallace's old American Independent organization, thought it would never be possible "successfully to market the word 'Republican,' " such was the damage of Watergate. "You could as easily sell Edsel or Typhoid Mary," he said.[28]

In fact, talk of a third party was unnecessary, for the Republican Party was in the throes of rapid change. Under Nixon, its center of gravity had moved steadily toward the South and the West, while the party's small liberal wing was in deep decline. By the mid-1970s it was almost impossible to be picked as a Republican candidate without voicing strong support for low taxes, tough sentences, and Christian values. Even some conservatives worried that the party was lurching too far to the right. Barry Goldwater, who had backed Ford over Reagan in 1976, was horrified by the New Right's intolerant views on abortion and homosexuality. Religious issues, he declared, had "little or nothing" to do with conservatism, and he vowed to "fight them every step of the way if they try to dictate their moral convictions to all Americans in the name of conservatism." But by this point even Goldwater had been left behind: no longer a hero to younger Republicans, he was now dismissed in conservative publications as "lazy" and "soft."[29]

The first test for the New Right came in the 1978 congressional elections, but its task was made much easier by the new rules of the game. In the aftermath of Watergate, new election laws had imposed strict limits on campaign donations. An individual could give no more than $1,000, while PACs were limited to $5,000. But with the number of corporate PACs ballooning from eighty-nine in 1974 to more than eight hundred in 1980, elections were soon awash with money. In 1978, Republican candidates picked up $9 million from corporate PACs, $11 million from trade-association PACs, and $3 million from other pro-business PACs, while the labor unions gave the Democrats just $9 million. For an ambitious candidate, the obvious lesson was to take antilabor and pro-business positions. These new donations were "not just numbers," remarked Senator Adlai Stevenson III of Illinois: they were "a revolutionary element in American politics."[30]

The other great innovation was the New Right's emphasis on cultural issues, which had never in living memory played such a key role in congressional elections. A year earlier, a lobbyist reported that mail to Democratic congressmen was running "ten-to-one, a hundred-to-one, against bussing, abortion, gay rights." It was not only Democrats who had something to fear. Moderate Republicans such as Edward Brooke and Charles Percy faced debilitating primary challenges from conservatives attacking their records on abortion, busing, and the ERA. In Illinois conservatives made a determined effort to oust the moderate Republican congressman John Anderson, an outspoken defender of abortion rights, gun control, and the Panama treaties. His Republican opponent, a minister in the evangelical Open Bible Church, enjoyed support from the Committee for the Survival of a Free Congress and the National Conservative PAC, while Richard Viguerie organized a direct-mail drive on his behalf. It was not enough to drive Anderson out, but conservatives pledged they would get him eventually. A year later he announced that he would give up the seat.[31]

Elsewhere the New Right was rather more effective. Although news of the Camp David Accords blunted the impact of their campaign, the Republicans still picked up fifteen House seats, seven governorships, and three hundred state legislature seats. In the Senate, the New Right helped to elect three populist conservatives, Gordon Humphrey (New Hampshire), Roger Jepsen (Iowa), and William Armstrong (Colorado), while in the House, Weyrich now commanded the attention of about forty representatives, both Republicans and Democrats. Even in hitherto liberal states, conservatism was on the march. In Minnesota, the state of Hubert Humphrey and Eugene McCarthy, the Republicans took both Senate seats and the statehouse; in Massachusetts, Michael Dukakis was kicked out of the governor's mansion after raising taxes.[32]

By playing on Panama, taxes, and abortion, the Republicans had made significant inroads into the white evangelical and small-town votes. And Kemp-Roth proved a powerful weapon: while twelve states approved tax-reduction measures, eight out of ten voters agreed that government was "spending too much." "The real message of the election returns," said *Newsweek*, was a new "consensus on inflation as the priority target and tax-and-spend government as the primary villain." The real measure of conservatism's momentum was that even liberal Democrats now had to "talk like Republicans to survive."[33]

What all this meant was that as conservatives looked forward to the next presidential election, they felt a palpable quickening of the blood, a sense that if they picked the right candidate and events fell in their favor, they might see a true believer in the White House. Crucially, the very image of conservatism had changed: once fusty and eccentric, it now seemed young, confident, and aggressive, the creed of the Sunbelt and the suburbs, the wave of the future. The Grand Old Party had become a "party of ideas," said Daniel Patrick Moynihan, "a party of the People arrayed against a Democratic Party of the State."[34]

· · ·

**Many conservatives found** it hard to be enthusiastic about the obvious front-runner for the Republican nomination in 1980. Although polls had Ronald Reagan streets ahead of the other contenders, he was widely thought to be past his best. "I think a man approaching seventy is going to have a hard time giving a new speech when he's given the same speech two hundred nights for twenty years," said the political consultant John Deardourff. Reagan was "a man of the Sixties," agreed *National Review*'s conservative columnist John Coyne. It was "difficult for one who has been a long-time Reagan admirer" to admit, but he was "obsolete," a "middle-aged anachronism." Meanwhile, White House aides made no secret of their eagerness to face Reagan. "There's so much to work with," Pat Caddell remarked in December 1979, "when you look at the data you just salivate." Hamilton Jordan could hardly contain his glee at the thought of Reagan's nomination. "The American people," he said, "are not going to elect a seventy-year-old, right-wing, ex–movie actor to be president."[35]

But Reagan had been keeping busy. His campaign organization had been recycled into a pressure group, Citizens for the Republic, run by his old press secretary Lyn Nofziger, while Reagan himself maintained a high profile. By 1979 he had given more than a thousand daily radio broadcasts carried on 286 stations, most of which he wrote unassisted, while his column ran in 226 newspapers. According to his own estimate, he reached two million people a week, discussing everything from defense spending to tax cuts. Perhaps his favorite topic, though, was the issue that had almost won him the nomination: the Panama Canal.[36]

By the summer of 1977, Carter had negotiated two treaties to hand over the canal by the end of the century. Most political observers thought it a good deal, and he won applause from the Catholic Church, the Chamber of Commerce, and major banks, shipping companies, and multinational corporations, as well as "old" conservatives like Barry Goldwater and William F. Buckley. Public opinion, however, remained unswervingly hostile: almost eight out of ten people told one poll that they opposed the treaties. It was a "sexy" and "populist" issue, explained Richard Viguerie, arousing passion out of all proportion with its importance. "There is no Panama Canal, there is an American canal at Panama," declared the American Conservative Union, spending almost $400,000 on a documentary film distributed to 270 stations and sponsoring a "Truth Squad" of Republican congressmen to carry the message from coast to coast.[37]

What lay behind the Panama issue, of course, was Vietnam. Not only were memories of the conflict still raw, but at the very moment when the treaties came up for ratification, films like *Coming Home* and *The Deer Hunter* were reminding the American public of the shame of defeat. The Panama treaties, said the deeply conservative Utah senator Orrin Hatch, were "the culmination of a pattern of appeasement and surrender that has cost us so much around the world." This was not just xenophobic nationalism, David McCullough, the author of a bestselling history of the canal, told the president. It was a lament for lost greatness, with the canal as the physical embodiment of the nation's disappearing "confidence and energy, youth and sense of purpose."[38]

Panama was the perfect subject for a patriotic populist. It "could never have become a nation without the canal," Reagan told a radio audience in 1978; before then, it was "a disease-ridden, jungle swamp." Even many admirers thought this was going too far. William F. Buckley challenged him to a public debate, while John Wayne sent a string of intemperate open letters: "I'll show you point by God damn point where you are misinforming the people. This is not my point of view against your point of view. These are facts." Yet while public opinion ran heavily in Reagan's favor, the Senate approved both treaties in April 1978, an increasingly rare victory for the so-called establishment against the tide of populism. The Senate vote, Reagan told reporters, was "a very extreme case of ignoring the sentiment of the people of our country."[39]

Despite its defeat, the Panama battle was vitally important for the New Right. It allowed conservatives to drape themselves in the Stars and Stripes, to paint the "liberal establishment" as apologists for retreat, and to make inroads into the hearts and minds of floating voters. Viguerie estimated that the affair added 400,000 names to his mailing lists and helped him to bring down twenty liberal congressmen in the next few years. But it was a crucial fight for Reagan, too, cementing his place as the darling of the grassroots right. When the Republican National Committee sent out an anti-treaty appeal under his signature, it made $700,000 within a matter of days. With support like that, he would be almost impossible to stop.[40]

Behind the headlines, however, Reagan was quietly moderating his rhetoric so that he would appeal to voters outside his conservative base. His old aides like Michael Deaver and Lyn Nofziger, who preferred a Sunbelt strategy, found themselves sidelined; instead, Reagan paid attention to his Machiavellian campaign director, John Sears, who wanted him to become the candidate of party unity. He needed to get rid of his old image as a "saber-rattler" and to stop "scaring the hell out of people," explained his foreign policy adviser Richard Allen in the summer of 1978. Although

Allen knew Reagan hated to be "fuzzy, indefinite and 'political-sounding' on issues on which you feel strongly," there nevertheless must be "a deliberate attempt to soften the delivery of your message."[41]

If Reagan had been a conservative zealot, he would have ignored Allen's advice. But he listened, and his evolution in the late 1970s is one of the least recognized elements of his rise to power. "I know I'm supposed to be a terrible right-wing person," he told *The Wall Street Journal*, "but I just wish people who think that would look at my record in California." There, he said, he had introduced conjugal visits for convicted felons, made the income tax "more progressive," and increased welfare payments to the "truly needy." Meanwhile, he deliberately accepted speaking engagements in the Northeast and the Midwest and ostentatiously refused to support the antigay Briggs Initiative in California. "Gone is the would-be charismatic insurgent of several years ago," wrote an incredulous Kevin Phillips. "Now we have in his place a 67-year-old party regular preaching unity while aides hint he'd serve only one term."[42]

For the partisans of the New Right, all this was deeply disturbing. Both Weyrich and Viguerie feared, quite correctly, that Reagan was an instinctive compromiser surrounded by political professionals rather than keepers of the right-wing faith. Weyrich even warned activists that they could expect "no input in [a Reagan] administration." On the other hand, Reagan had more credibility among the disciples of Milton Friedman, who admired his commitment to free-market principles and was willing to accept a little flexibility. "You want a principled man, which Reagan is," Friedman said once. "But he is not a rigidly principled man, which you don't want."[43]

Reagan's flexibility went down less well with that rather less eminent economics salesman, Jude Wanniski. When they first met to discuss supply-side theory, Wanniski found Reagan "shallow" and his jokes "irrelevant." Yet one of Reagan's closest advisers, Martin Anderson, was already a true believer, and in "Policy Memorandum No. 1," the blueprint for Reaganomics, he sketched out a supply-side approach to the economy, including massive cuts in income taxes, capital gains taxes, and corporate taxes. In fact it was no surprise that Reagan embraced supply-side theory. Not only did tax cuts hold great appeal for potential donors, but the success of Proposition 13 suggested they would help to win over former Democrats, one of his main goals in 1980. Above all, though, they were the perfect vehicle for Reagan's irrepressible optimism, allowing him to draw a stark contrast with the miserable Jimmy Carter. The American people, Reagan said, faced a choice between "their government of pessimism, fear, and limits, [and] ours of hope, confidence, and growth." Who would choose fear and limits ahead of hope and growth?[44]

**If Reagan was** to face Carter, he needed first to banish the specter of Gerald Ford. Although the former president had a strong following among Republican stalwarts, he was enjoying his retirement in Palm Springs and Vail, Colorado, and preferred the rigors of the golf course to the privations of the campaign trail. Instead, Ford's admirers found their candidate in the upright, hail-fellow-well-met figure of George Bush. With a stunning résumé, taking in the House of Representatives, the United Nations, the Republican National Committee, China, and the CIA, Bush had a vast list of contacts. His campaign staff was full of moderate Republicans from his New England stomping ground, while he boasted early support from Yankee grandees such as Henry Cabot Lodge and Elliot Richardson. Journalists joked that his staff "looked as if they'd been picked from the Harvard and Yale crew rosters of the past twenty years." But he was honest, prudent, and hardworking: in 1978 alone he traveled 96,000 miles to hobnob with local Republican activists, and a year later he chalked up another 246,000 miles. Few people loved him, but almost nobody disliked him.[45]

Since Bush supported the ERA, opposed a constitutional ban on abortion, and had once backed gun registration, many people thought him far too moderate for the Republicans in 1980. One commentator joked that his politics were "slightly to the center of center," while his nephew remarked that he had "no political ideology." But even Bush recognized that the days of Rockefeller Republicanism were over, and his platform called for welfare cuts, increased defense spending, and the dismissal of "McGovern-type regulators." Although he famously called Reagan's supply-side plan "voodoo economics," he too promised to slash taxes. He was "the Tweed Reagan," quipped *National Review*, while John Anderson nicknamed him "Ronald Reagan in Brooks Brother suits." Still, this was no trivial distinction: it was a long time since the Republicans had nominated a country-club patrician. "We have the Schlitz drinkers; Bush has the sherry drinkers," quipped one Reagan aide. Very few sherry drinkers voted in the Republican primaries.[46]

But while Bush hit the ground running in Iowa, learning the lessons of Carter's early successes in 1976, Reagan kicked off his campaign in staggeringly complacent fashion. It was a sign of his overconfidence that he was in Bel Air, watching a preview of *Kramer vs. Kramer* with Hollywood friends, when the news came through that Bush had won Iowa by two thousand votes. Reagan, said one friend, looked "like a man who had been knocked down by a car but was too stunned to realize what had happened to him." But for all the talk about Bush's "Big Mo," the shock was exactly what Reagan needed. The morning after his humiliation, his campaign chairman, Paul Laxalt, reached for another football metaphor, reminding him of the previous week's Super Bowl in Pasadena, where the Pittsburgh Steelers had hauled back a fourth-quarter deficit to beat Reagan's beloved Los Angeles Rams. "The Steelers wouldn't have won," Laxalt said, "if Terry Bradshaw had been sitting on his ass for three quarters, and you were sitting on your ass in Iowa."[47]

Reagan got the message. By the time he returned to New Hampshire, the complacent favorite who had lost in Iowa had disappeared. In his place was a hard-hitting outsider who spent three weeks bashing abortion, government spending, and the Soviet Union and tirelessly reminding voters of Bush's moderate record. Meanwhile, Bush seemed to freeze under pressure, as though afraid of saying anything controversial. He performed atrociously at the first Republican debate in Manchester on February 20, and three days later his fate was sealed in farcical fashion at a debate sponsored by the *Nashua Telegraph* and paid for by the Reagan campaign. Originally, the debate was supposed to be a two-man affair, but at the last minute Reagan agreed to open it up to the other candidates. Amid general chaos, Reagan and the "Nashua Four" stormed the stage while Bush sat sulking "like a small boy who has been dropped off at the wrong birthday party." When the *Telegraph*'s editor Jon Breen ordered that his microphone be turned off, Reagan snapped: "I am paying for this microphone, Mr. Green!" It was hardly one of the great witticisms of the century, but it captured the difference between the confident cowboy from California and the prim patrician from New England. "Reagan is winning this primary right now," one reporter muttered amid the bedlam. Three days later, he took New Hampshire by almost 30 percent.[48]

With a victory under his belt, Reagan never looked back. On the day of the New Hampshire primary he fired John Sears as his campaign manager, appointing in his stead the former SEC chairman William Casey and eventually bringing back California veterans such as Ed Meese and Michael Deaver. Surrounded by old friends, he felt more at ease; his campaign was his own again. And as Bush's ship slowly disappeared beneath the waterline, Reagan turned the primary contest into a coronation. By mid-May, he had prevailed in all but four of the thirty-three primaries they contested, with Bush winning only his New England heartland of Massachusetts and Vermont and the industrial states of Pennsylvania and

Michigan. On May 26, after Reagan's victory in Oregon put him over the top, Bush formally pulled out of the race, and it was over.[49]

With more than 60 percent of the primary votes, Reagan was the nominee of the Republican Party. Many party insiders were still worried that he was too extreme: no less a figure than Gerald Ford told *The New York Times* that wherever he went, he heard the "sentiment that Governor Reagan cannot win," because everyone knew that "a very conservative Republican can't win in a national election." Many Democrats, however, could hardly contain their glee. Reagan had won the nomination despite having the worst press of any candidate in the race, and people were bound to remember Bush's line about "voodoo economics." The consensus, wrote James Reston, was that Reagan was "too old, too ideological and too narrowly based on the conservative wing of the minority Republican Party to appeal to the independent voters and threaten Carter's domination of the center." Carter's men were reportedly "jubilant"; indeed, they could not "quite believe their good luck." If so, they were in for a shock.[50]

# Chapter Nineteen  Soldiers of God

The paranoid spokesman sees the fate of conspiracy in apocalyptic
terms—he traffics in the birth and death of whole worlds, whole political
orders, whole systems of human values. He is always manning the
barricades of civilization. He constantly lives at a turning point.

—**RICHARD HOFSTADTER**, "The Paranoid Style
in American Politics" (1964)

Three years after the tall ships had sailed out of New York Harbor,
one of the nation's most celebrated preachers decided it was time
to revive the bicentennial spirit. During the nation's birthday celebrations, the Reverend Jerry Falwell had held "I Love America" rallies
on the steps of state capitols up and down the country. Now, faced with
thousands of unsold bicentennial Bibles, he announced a new tour of
every statehouse in the Union, packed into a few short months. It was a
punishing schedule, but it was worth it: the rallies were big, brassy events,
and thousands turned up to watch. The platforms were decked out with
American flags; there was always a band playing patriotic hymns; and
Falwell usually brought a thirty-three-member student choir, "scrubbed
to a sparkle," from Liberty Baptist College, his educational institution in
Lynchburg, Virginia.

In Richmond, where the tour kicked off, Falwell was in expansive form,
smart and commanding in his dark business suit. God loved the United
States of America, he reminded his audience; but the American people

were giving heaven a hard time. The federal government was encouraging socialism, the public schools were spreading humanism, and the liberals in Hollywood, the "infidels and in-for-hells," were peddling smut and subversion. To cries of "Amen" from the crowd, he held up a Bible. "If a man stands by this book, vote for him," he said. "If he doesn't, don't."

He ended with a verse from the second book of Chronicles: "If my people which are called by my name shall humble themselves and pray, and seek my face and turn from their wicked ways; then will I hear from heaven and will forgive their sin, and will heal their land." Then he retired for a long lunch, to which local pastors were invited, free of charge. There he told them about his plans for a new kind of religious organization, one that combined traditional morality with pragmatic political influence. It was called the Moral Majority.[1]

**In his influential book** *Culture Wars* (1991), the sociologist James Davison Hunter argues that the major cultural cleavage in American society divides the "progressives" from the "orthodox." Progressives are not necessarily atheists or even liberals, but they base their moral views on the individual conscience and rational inquiry. By contrast, the orthodox, whether Protestant, Catholic, or Jewish, look to "an external, definable, and transcendent authority" for their traditional moral views. Each camp takes an inflexible view of contemporary cultural issues; each believes that defeat would send American society into a new dark age. There can be no compromise, because there is too much at stake. It is a "struggle over national identity," writes Hunter, "*over the meaning of America*, who we have been in the past, who we are now, and perhaps most important, who we, as a nation, will aspire to become."[2]

In an age when television beamed the moral corruption of the modern American city into even the most remote rural outpost of pious Protestantism, the political mobilization of evangelical Christians was probably inevitable. But it would surely not have occurred so quickly if they had not been so offended by the advance of "secular humanism." For many evangelicals, the chief villains were the members of the Warren Court, responsible for judgments from *Roth v. United States* (1957), the first of many decisions relaxing the obscenity laws, to *Engel v. Vitale* (1962), the landmark decision outlawing public prayers in schools. Indeed, as the sociologist Nathan Glazer noted a few years later, it was the very success of liberalism that gave the religious right its influence. The religious backlash was a "defensive offensive," he remarked: a vain attempt to roll back the tide of secularism, born not of strength but of weakness.[3]

The iconic example of the clash between progressivism and orthodoxy, to use Hunter's terms, was abortion. In the first full year after *Roe v. Wade* (1973), almost a million women chose to terminate their pregnancies, and by 1976 there were 676 abortions in New York for every thousand births, while in Washington, D.C., there were actually as many abortions as there were babies born. Yet *Roe v. Wade* initially provoked surprisingly little comment from evangelical preachers, largely because abortion was considered a Catholic issue. Even in the early 1970s there was little love lost between Catholics and evangelical Protestants, and so the anti-abortion campaign was initially dominated by the Catholic Church, which sponsored a "Pastoral Plan for Pro-Life Activities" as well as the National Committee for a Human Life Amendment. By contrast, Jerry Falwell did not even mention abortion in his sermons until 1978.[4]

This is not to say, of course, that evangelicals looked on abortion with cheerful equanimity. Immediately after the *Roe* decision, Billy Graham's *Christianity Today* warned that "the American state no longer supports, in any meaningful sense, the laws of God." As the abortion rate soared, unease turned into fury. In 1976 the brilliant pediatric surgeon C. Everett Koop, who had saved the lives of thousands of babies, published *The Right to Live, the Right to Die*, setting out the moral case against abortion and euthanasia. On Graham's advice, Koop then took part in a four-hour documentary, *Whatever Happened to the Human Race?* which was exhibited in churches across the nation. "Nothing has had an impact across the board that compares to [that] series," said Harold Brown, one of the first Protestant pastors to devote himself to the anti-abortion cause. "Today, you won't find many who call themselves evangelicals who don't hold a very strong 'pro-life' position."[5]

Although Falwell and other evangelical preachers were surprisingly slow to throw themselves into the campaign against abortion, the pro-life movement of the mid-1970s played a key role in the mobilization of Christian conservatives and the backlash against the ERA. Like other populist campaigns, it appealed to particular kinds of people: a study of California activists found that eight out of ten were women, most of whom were married, and only 14 percent of whom worked outside the home. They were not only less affluent than activists in the pro-choice movement; they were also much more religious: more than two-thirds said their faith was "very important" in their lives. Although a minority already belonged to anti-ERA or anti-sex-education groups, most had never been involved in political campaigns before. "I'm a housewife and the mother of three children. That's my bag. That's what I do. I take care of my children, my husband," explained one woman from New Jersey. "But when this issue of abortion surfaced in this country, that was the dividing line for me from a society that I didn't want to live in. I just could not exist in a society that could legalize the killing of unborn children."[6]

Like other populist campaigns, the pro-life movement traded in extraordinarily fierce rhetoric. "STOP THE BABY KILLERS," began a typical fund-raising letter, warning that abortionists were "killing a living baby, a tiny human being with a beating heart and tiny fingers." Falwell even told his congregation that abortion had "annihilated more children than Pharaoh murdered in Egypt, than Herod slaughtered when seeking the Christ child, than the Nazis slaughtered of the Jews in World War II." And in some ways this rhetoric paid off: as early as 1976 the Hyde Amendment restricted the use of Medicare funds for abortions, while many states demanded mandatory waiting periods and the consent of husbands and parents or limited the number of abortion clinics. Yet public opinion remained remarkably consistent. In 1980, only 7 percent of a nationwide sample opposed abortion in all cases. Meanwhile, more than 80 percent supported it if a mother's life was threatened or in cases of rape or congenital health defects, and 50 percent backed it in cases of illegitimacy, poverty, or unwanted pregnancy. Opposition undoubtedly grew during the next few decades; even so, despite all the commercials and campaigns, despite the rhetoric, the marches, and the violence, polls thirty years later found that support still outweighed opposition by roughly 80 percent to 20 percent.[7]

While the anti-abortion movement failed to overthrow *Roe v. Wade*, it had a profound impact on American conservatism. First, it provided a rallying point for traditionalists of all denominations, bringing Catholics and Protestants together in one movement and paving the way for the Moral Majority. Beyond that, it became a symbol for the apparent disintegration of sexual order and the collapse of the American family. Abortion was only one of several threats: one survey concluded that "divorce, infidelity, casual sexual relationships, women pursuing careers that take them away from husbands and young children—the stuff of television soap operas—are [all] regarded as symptoms of a decadent moral order." All were supposedly orchestrated by the same liberal-secular-humanist conspiracy. "We as Christians have to unite against the evil that's taking over this country," an activist explained in 1977. "It's evil to allow murder of little babies under our Constitution. It's evil to allow homosexuals to marry and be adoptive parents. It's evil to have federally funded day-care centers . . . It's evil to bus your children across the city when you live across the street from a perfectly good school."[8]

What this amounted to, therefore, was a crisis that threatened the very survival of the nation. Visiting Falwell's church, the journalist Frances FitzGerald found that many of his congregation believed the nation was "now in the most serious crisis in its history," beleaguered by "pornography, abortion, divorce, militant homosexuality, drugs, crime, and atheistic humanism," which were paving the way for Communist victory. "America, like the Roman Empire, is in decline," she wrote, paraphrasing the views of her contacts. "Christians must act now, for civilization itself is at stake. America is the last launching pad for world evangelism, and if it falls to Communism—as a result of its own decay—that will mean the end of Christianity."[9]

This built, of course, on a long tradition of apocalyptic rhetoric. Although evangelicals argued that judicial liberalism, sexual promiscuity, and the decline of the nuclear family had plunged the nation into an unprecedented crisis, in a sense they were living in a familiar mental world—a world of impending disaster and terrible threats, only with pornographers, liberated women, and homosexuals replacing the Catholics and Communists that had terrified their predecessors. Still, none of this meant that their anxiety and anger were any less intense. "At stake, as [evangelicals] see it," wrote the conservative journalist Alan Crawford in 1979, "is nothing less than the future of society itself." Defeat would mean the end of all that they loved; this was a battle they simply had to win.[10]

**If there was** one threat that particularly disturbed evangelical preachers, it was homosexuality. Infidelity, adultery, and fornication were normal and understandable temptations, from which not even the godliest pastor was immune. But homosexuality was utterly incomprehensible. It was not just a lapse or a weakness, writes the historian William Martin, but "a perversion of nature, an abomination in the sight of God, an act deserving of imprisonment and perhaps even death."[11]

To the horror of many preachers, however, homosexuality seemed to be on the march. Although two out of three people told a Harris poll in 1970 that homosexuals were "harmful to society," attitudes were changing. When Lance Loud put on makeup and jewelry in the PBS documentary series *An American Family* three years later, he was not shunned or ostracized. Quite the reverse: he found himself a national icon, singing on *The Dick Cavett Show*, writing columns for gay magazines, and touring the nation with his band, the Mumps. His newfound celebrity reflected a climate of increasing tolerance, both in law and, more grudgingly, in the public mind. Between 1971 and 1980, twenty-two states repealed their laws forbidding sodomy, forty cities banned antigay discrimination, and more than a hundred corporations adopted equal employment policies covering homosexuals. And in December 1973 the American Psychiatric Association removed homosexuality from its list of mental illnesses so that, as one writer puts it, "several million people defined as sick became well."[12]

To those who fondly recalled the moral climate of the 1950s, the unprecedented assertiveness of gay life after the Stonewall riots of June 1969 seemed a shocking challenge. "Gays on the March," proclaimed a *Time* cover story in 1975, reporting on the "gay studies classes in 50 colleges, gay dances in churches, gay synagogues, gay Alcoholics Anonymous groups, a lesbian credit union, even a gay Nazi Party and a Jewish lesbian group formed to fight it." In areas like the Castro in San Francisco, noted Frances FitzGerald, "you could walk for blocks and see only young men," lounging in the doorways in their tight jeans and leather jackets, strolling down the sidewalks with their arms draped lazily around each other's shoulders, their newfound political power reflected in the success of the charismatic Harvey Milk. In New York, wrote the gay journalist Andrew Kopkind, men could "eat in gay restaurants, shop on gay avenues in gay boutiques, listen to gay-oriented music, share gay living quarters, dance in gay discos, vacation in gay garden spots, worship in gay churches, read gay magazines and gay novels, snack on gay pizza and gay burgers, . . . sail on gay cruises, get high on gay drugs pushed by gay dealers, and spend all their social hours with gay friends."[13]

After years of oppression, it was not surprising that some homosexuals tried to turn their backs on the straight world. The National Gay Task Force's Ronald Gold boasted that he could "get my windows washed by a gay person, get my television repaired, do anything and never see a straight person again." Yet the barriers between straight and gay culture remained extremely permeable; indeed, by the end of the decade it was debatable whether they even existed at all. After all, by far the most popular musical phenomenon of the late 1970s, disco, had been born in Manhattan's gay subculture during the Nixon years. The clubs where disco originated—the bacchanalian Sanctuary in Hell's Kitchen and the mellow Loft down on Broadway—appealed overwhelmingly to gay men. Disco, wrote Andrew Kopkind, was above all the sound track "for the shops, the bars, the restaurants and the offices where gays go about their business."[14]

By the beginning of 1977 disco had become distinctly respectable: even Jimmy Carter's inaugural celebrations boasted the "Portable Peach" mobile disco from Atlanta, featuring the terrifying spectacle of "disco dancers in peanut costumes dancing to the music of the Bicentennial Disco Mix." But it never quite lost its original associations. The essence of disco, said one producer in 1979, remained its "gayness," which broke with the "white, straight, male, young and middle-class ethos" of 1960s rock music. And of course this was why so many white, straight, male, young, and middle-class rock fans hated it. Even the most diluted, mainstream forms of disco replaced the snarling growl of the rock star with the affected falsetto of the Bee Gees, making a mockery of the exaggerated masculinity that had long been so important to teenage fans. The shock jock Steve Dahl, who famously blew up ten thousand records during the shambolic "Disco Demolition Derby" at Chicago's Comiskey Park, had previously taken advice from a consulting firm, Burkhart/Abrams Associates, which reported that many white teenage boys thought disco "superficial, boring, repetitive and 'short on balls.' " What they meant, explained *The Village Voice*, was that it was "music for gay people"—the kind of music that summed up everything wrong with American society under Jimmy Carter.[15]

The most controversial attack on gay self-assertion, however, was led not by a Chicago shock jock or even by a fire-and-brimstone fundamentalist, but by a woman most Americans associated with something distinctly sweeter—orange juice. Born in 1940 and raised by pious Baptist grandparents, Anita Bryant was crowned Miss Oklahoma at eighteen, married a Miami disc jockey, and became a minor chart star of the early 1960s. As her pop career was drawing to a close, the Florida Citrus Commission hired her as its public face, and her jingle "Come to the Florida Sunshine Tree" became a familiar sound from coast to coast. "People connect orange juice, Florida and Anita Bryant so much," joked the state's governor, Reubin Askew, "that it becomes difficult to decide which to visit, which to listen to and which to squeeze." For millions of people she was a reassuring figure, proud of her faith and keen to entertain American troops in Vietnam, a war she strongly supported. Her public standing was such that she sang at both Democratic and Republican conventions and performed the national anthem at Super Bowl III, while in January 1973 she sang "The Battle Hymn of the Republic" at Lyndon Johnson's funeral.[16]

The shock was all the greater, therefore, when in January 1977 Bryant launched a "crusade" to repeal a gay rights ordinance in Dade County, Florida, which included Miami and Miami Beach. The latter had a large gay community, drawn by the sunshine and the libertarian atmosphere: hence the ease with which Dade County had put through the antidiscrimination ordinance in the first place. But there was also a general sense of flux and anxiety. Miami was in the throes of rapid demographic change: segregation had been demolished, white families were moving out, and thousands of Cuban immigrants were moving in. Older voters worried that Dade County was being submerged by immigrants and homosexuals, and saw the ordinance as a disgraceful provocation. All they needed was a champion, and with her Baptist convictions and picture-perfect looks, Anita Bryant fit the bill.[17]

Bryant argued that since the Bible condemned homosexuality as "an abomination against the laws of God and man," gay rights represented "an insidious attack on God." What was more, the Dade County ordinance was actually a "recruitment plan," by which "militant homosexuals" ("highly financed" and "highly organized," like all good conspiracies) intended to corrupt the children of the "straight-thinking normal majority." Her movement's official title was Save Our Children, and it made an extraordinary series of allegations against Miami's gay community, using headlines from recent newspapers: "Teacher Accused of Sex Acts with Boy Students," "Homosexuals Used Scout Troop," "Ex-teachers Indicted for Lewd Acts with Boys," and so on. *"I don't hate the homosexuals!"* Bryant explained in one of her letters. "But as a mother I must protect my children from their evil influence . . . Do you realize what they want? *They want to recruit our school children under the protection of the laws of our land."*[18]

Although Bryant presented herself as an ordinary wife and mother, she had powerful allies. The crucial organizational figure in Save Our Children was actually Mike Thompson, a Miami public relations expert who had produced conservative documentaries attacking the Panama Canal treaties and SALT II. Senator Jesse Helms offered valuable advice; so did Phyllis Schlafly and senior figures in the anti-ERA campaign. Finally, the battle gave the Reverend Jerry Falwell an early taste of the political limelight. A ferocious critic of homosexuality, he invited Bryant onto his *Old-Time Gospel Hour* and staged a huge antigay rally in the Miami convention center. "So-called gay folks," he told one meeting, "would just as soon kill you as look at you." In a nice irony, however, his chief ghostwriter, the evangelical pastor Mel White, later came out himself.[19]

On June 7, 1977, Dade County gave Anita Bryant a handsome victory, overturning the gay rights ordinance by 69 to 31 percent. "The normal majority," she exclaimed delightedly, "have said, 'Enough! Enough! Enough!' " What she did not anticipate, however, was the sheer rage of gay communities across the nation. In New York, several thousand assembled outside the Stonewall Inn chanting, "Gay rights now!" while in San Francisco, Harvey Milk led four thousand men on a protest march through the center of town. Smaller demonstrations in other cities—Chicago, Los Angeles, Houston, New Orleans—testified to the new visibility and self-confidence of gay Americans.[20]

For some historians, the real significance of the Bryant campaign was what it revealed about the strength of the nation's gay communities. A year later, Milk helped to defeat California's controversial Briggs Initiative, which threatened any schoolteacher suspected of promoting homosexuality with summary dismissal. Its author, John Briggs, was a Republican state senator from Orange County and a born-again Christian, and his supporters included Anita Bryant and Jerry Falwell, who addressed thousands of hymn-singing supporters at revivalist rallies up and down the coast. Yet many local conservatives opposed Briggs's measure, among them Ronald Reagan, who warned that it would "infringe on basic rights of privacy and perhaps even constitutional rights." What would happen, Reagan asked, "if an overwrought youngster, disappointed by bad grades, imagined it was the teacher's fault and struck out by accusing the teacher of advocating homosexuality? Innocent lives could be ruined." When the initiative lost by more than a million votes, Reagan deserved a share of the credit—though it was not an achievement his conservative disciples usually remembered.[21]

Outside California, however, gay Americans had good reason for alarm at the passions Anita Bryant had unleashed. For three consecutive years readers of *Good Housekeeping* voted her their Most Admired Woman, while Save Our Children attracted financial support and adherents in almost every state in the Union. When the people of Dade County were asked to vote on a new gay rights ordinance a few weeks after the first ballot, they rejected it by the same margin as before. In April 1978, voters in St. Paul, Minnesota, followed their example by repealing a gay rights ordinance by two to one, and the people of Wichita, Kansas, and Eugene, Oregon, followed suit a few weeks later. In each case, Protect America's Children, an offshoot of Bryant's organization, played a vital role in raising money and mobilizing voters.[22]

For evangelical conservatives, however, these were mere skirmishes in a wider campaign. "We are losing the war against homosexuals," warned one piece of direct mail sent to thousands of Christian families a couple of years later. The latest outrage was that "gays were recently given permission to lay a wreath on the Tomb of the Unknown Soldier at Arlington Cemetery to honor any sexual deviants who served in the military. That's right—the gays were allowed to turn our Tomb of the Unknown Soldier into: THE TOMB OF THE UNKNOWN SODOMITE!"

It was classic scaremongering: apocalyptic, outrageous, and undeniably effective. Its author was the same man who had cut his teeth helping Anita Bryant win the battle of Dade County, a man who was making the issues of homosexuality and national decline his own, a man who had worked his way up from small-town obscurity to become one of the most controversial religious figures in the nation—the Reverend Jerry Falwell.[23]

**Jerry Falwell was** born in 1933 in the mill town of Lynchburg, Virginia. A bright and assertive boy, he was captain of the football team and class valedictorian, but he was not at all pious. His father, a hard-drinking entrepreneur, never set foot in a church service, while Jerry went only because it was "the thing to do" and would often slip out to read comics. However, soon after enrolling at Lynchburg College to study engineering, he suddenly transferred to Baptist Bible College in Missouri. Precisely why this happened remains unclear. Falwell had rarely been exposed to evangelical religion, none of his family was religious, and he had undergone no great spiritual crisis. His own story was that he had seen the light after accompanying a friend to a local Baptist church one Sunday. Others, however, claimed that he had only gone that day to meet girls—a story with some credibility, since not only did Falwell marry the pianist, but his friend married the organist.

As a Bible student, Falwell remained driven, ebullient, and self-confident, a prankster who drove a motorbike through the boys' dorm and used a garden hose to fill a friend's room with water. After graduating in 1956, he returned home and founded his own church in an empty building that had just been vacated by the Donald Duck Bottling Company. He was only twenty-two years old, but he was full of ambition. Within weeks he was giving Sunday sermons for a local radio company and hosting worship shows for a television station, while on weekdays he worked his way through every house in Lynchburg, introducing his new church. The hard work paid off: within a year, his Thomas Road congregation had swelled from 35 to 864 people.[24]

Falwell later described his parishioners as "grassroots, typical Southern people, blue-collar—few exceptions—sincere, honest, God-fearing people." But Lynchburg was changing. When Falwell was growing up, it had been a sleepy mill town with a poor rural hinterland. By the late 1950s, however, it was caught up in the great transformation that turned the Old South into the Sunbelt. New highways brought new investment; in came corporations from Europe and the North, along with shopping malls and office buildings, corporate bosses and young white-collar professionals. When Frances FitzGerald visited Lynchburg in 1979, she found a sprawling town of shopping plazas, gasoline stations, and fast-food outlets. It was a "clean city," she wrote, "full of quiet streets and shade trees [and] windowless buildings with landscaped lawns." There was little crime or delinquency, the medical services were good, and the schools were well equipped and racially integrated. "If there is a single public nuisance for the young in this town," she thought, "it is surely boredom."[25]

By the 1970s, Falwell's pews were full of people who had worked their way up from poverty to affluence: secretaries, skilled factory workers, technicians, and small-business men. They were not bitter refugees from some trailer-park wilderness but cheerful, successful Americans. The men wore double-knit shirts and heavy brass rings; the women wore "demure print dresses" and had their hair "coiffed and lacquered." Boys wore white shirts and had close-cropped hair; teenage girls wore low-cut floral dresses, high heels, and their hair long and loose, "flipped and curled in *Charlie's Angels* style." All looked "fresh-faced and extraordinarily clean," the very picture of middle-class respectability—as did Falwell himself in his dark business suit.

Falwell looked like a successful businessman because at a basic level that was exactly what he was. He was not an old-fashioned fire-and-brimstone man or a charismatic healer; he was an entrepreneur. Local businessmen commented that he was "a born leader and the best salesman they had ever seen." He had his own thousand-seat auditorium and color cameras, while a Massachusetts computer firm prepared direct mailings on everything from Bible studies to the dangers of homosexuality. Meanwhile, his weekly *Old-Time Gospel Hour*, broadcast on 325 different television stations, allowed him to reach a market of 1.5 million people. Fund-raising pitches included an offer of inspirational literature and "Jesus First" pin for just $9.95, or a regular color magazine for $10 a month, or more "Jesus First" pins and a Crusader's Passport for $15 a month. By 1977, *Gospel Hour* revenue topped $35 million—much of which actually paid for the fund-raising itself.[26]

By the late 1970s, Thomas Road was easily the biggest church in Lynchburg, packed with four thousand people every Sunday. It was a genuinely impressive institution, employing sixty pastors, who were helped by about a thousand volunteers. On Sundays, the church held three general services and Sunday-school classes for every age-group; on Wednesdays there was a general prayer meeting. There were separate ministries for children, teenagers, adults, the elderly, the mentally handicapped, the deaf, the unmarried, the divorced, and convicted felons, and each ministry offered weekly activities, from Bible classes and self-help lectures to sports outings and picnics. The organization was so big, wrote FitzGerald, "that any Thomas Road member, old or young, could spend all his or her time in church or in church-related activities."

In his early years, Falwell disdained political involvement and preached the classic fundamentalist doctrine of separation from the sinful world. Preachers were not called to "reform externals," he told his flock in 1965, adding that his mission was to "regenerate the inside," not "clean up the outside." Indeed, Falwell said, "believing the Bible as I do, I would find it impossible to stop preaching the pure saving gospel of Jesus Christ, and begin doing anything else—including fighting Communism, or participating in civil-rights reforms." By 1976, however, he had changed his mind: it turned out that reforming externals was part of his mission after all. By this time he had launched his "I Love America" statehouse tours, and he must have realized that there was an enormous market for a mixture of evangelical Christianity, militant nationalism, and political showmanship. "The idea that religion and politics don't mix," he explained in a bicentennial sermon, "was invented by the Devil to keep Christians from running their own country."[27]

But Falwell's politics went well beyond moral jeremiads about abortion and homosexuality. Like most southern churches, Thomas Road was initially segregated, and Falwell did not baptize a black worshipper until 1971. Fiercely anti-union, he opposed almost all government action on behalf of the poor, including food stamps and welfare for all but the sick and the old. "The free enterprise system," he explained, "is clearly outlined in the Book of Proverbs." On other issues, too, he was extremely conservative: in his book *America Can Be Saved!* (1979) he cheerfully described himself as "to the right of wherever you are. I thought Goldwater was too liberal!" Often his statements were so inflammatory that it was hard to tell the preacher from the prankster: pondering the issue of American Communists, for example, he suggested that "not only should we register them but we should stamp it on their foreheads and send them back to Russia."[28]

The Presbyterian fundamentalist Carl McIntire, himself a fierce anti-Communist, once wrote that righteousness required "violent attacks" on people outside the Church. Falwell, too, liked fighting talk. The Church was "an organized army equipped for battle," he said, while the members of his congregation were "Marines who have been called of God to move in past the shelling, the bombing and the foxholes and, with bayonet in hand, encounter the enemy face-to-face and one-on-one bring them under submission to the Gospel of Christ." These words were shrewdly chosen, for Virginia had a strong military tradition, and the counties around Lynchburg had sent thousands of young men to Korea and Vietnam. They were fighting a war, Falwell told them, "between those who love Jesus Christ and those who hate Him." And they could hardly ask for a better commander. Christ "wasn't effeminate," Falwell reminded them. "The man who lived on this earth was a man with muscles . . . Christ was a he-man!"[29]

**In August 1978,** the Internal Revenue Service announced its intention to revoke the tax-exempt status of private schools with an "insignificant number of minority students." At first glance, there were extremely good grounds for its decision. During the 1960s, white evangelical churches had set up hundreds of so-called segregation academies, appealing to white parents who were determined to escape racial integration. Some were unashamedly discriminatory, such as Bob Jones University, which refused to admit black students until 1971. For years the IRS had been determined to move against Bob Jones: at last, in January 1976, it announced that the university's tax exemption had been revoked retroactively. Two years later, under pressure from civil rights groups, it extended its ruling to cover schools across the nation.

Although civil rights activists applauded the IRS decision, it proved enormously controversial. Not all private schools were segregation academies; many had been founded for other reasons, attracting parents who disliked the rise of sex education, the teaching of evolution, or the use of challenging new textbooks. The schools themselves were often labors of love, staffed by teachers who were paid less than if they had remained in the public sector, and relying on help from parents. Yet their pupils did just as well in standardized tests as children from public schools, and most were happy, orderly, and reasonably competent institutions. This was clearly a winning formula: during the 1970s, a new Christian school was founded somewhere every day.[30]

The IRS decision, therefore, provoked outrage from schools that were innocent of racial discrimination. When Paul Weyrich and his friend Robert Billings, a Bob Jones graduate and Baptist missionary, established Christian School Action to fight the decision, they found an enormous pool of support. Within a few weeks, the White House, members of Congress, and the IRS itself had received more than 500,000 letters denouncing the new regulations, while Jerry Falwell complained that "in some states it's easier to open a massage parlor than to open a Christian school." A series of hearings followed before the IRS reluctantly suspended the plan. Just to make sure, however, Senator Jesse Helms sponsored an amendment to stop the federal government investigating tax violations by Christian schools.[31]

It is hard to overestimate the importance of the IRS decision in the mobilization of the religious right. What galvanized the Christian community, Paul Weyrich said, "was not abortion, school prayer, or the ERA. I am living witness to that because I was trying to get those people interested in those issues and I utterly failed." But the IRS decision was "interference from government, and suddenly it dawned on them that they were not going to be able to be left alone to teach their children as they pleased." It was the moment when "conservatives made the linkage between their opposition to government interference and the interests of the evangelical movement."[32]

New Right activists had been aware of the potential for Christian mobilization for years. "The next real major area of growth for the conservative ideology and philosophy is among evangelical people," Richard Viguerie told an interviewer in 1976. But the key figure in bringing religion and politics together was Paul Weyrich. It had long been his ambition to unite working-class Catholics and evangelicals, and by 1979 he had strong links with all the major Christian conservative groups, including the Conservative Caucus, Christian Voice, and Ed McAteer's Religious Roundtable, which appealed to Southern Baptists. What he lacked, however, was a showman: a man who would appeal to independent Baptist groups and fundamentalist churches, a man who could take Christian conservatism on the road, a big, ebullient front man. What he needed, in other words, was Jerry Falwell.[33]

Falwell hardly needed an invitation to take up the challenge. One night, he later recalled, he was flying back to Lynchburg from a speaking engagement when, in the darkness, he heard God's call to bring "the good people of America" together to fight decadence, permissiveness, and secularism. A few weeks later, at a rally on Capitol Hill, he called on Christians to unite against "pornography, obscenity, vulgarity, [and] profanity." Not long afterward, he sent his private plane to bring Paul Weyrich down to Lynchburg for talks on a new organization. "Out there is what you might call a moral majority," Weyrich told him. "If we could get these people active in politics there is no limit to what we could do." Falwell's eyes widened. "What did you say?" he asked. When Weyrich repeated his words, Falwell almost burst with excitement. "That's it!" he exclaimed. "That's the phrase I've been looking for!"[34]

The great attraction of the name Moral Majority was that it was utterly nondenominational; indeed, the organization was not even exclusively Christian, with Falwell describing it simply as "pro-life, pro-family, pro-moral, and pro-American." This set it apart from other organizations, and perhaps only Falwell could have carried it off. Although he was often caricatured as rigid and intolerant, he never went in for the sectarian bickering that obsessed other preachers. This ecumenical approach did not go down well with his rivals: the fiercely anti-Catholic Bob Jones called him "the most dangerous man in America" and considered the Moral Majority "the work of Satan." Still, although Falwell knew that many evangelicals "shuddered to think of sitting at the same table with a Roman Catholic or a Jew or, God forbid, a Mormon," he insisted that it was perfectly godly to "work with people who don't agree with you theologically, if in so doing you improve your country."[35]

The Moral Majority was the perfect vehicle for Falwell's brand of spiritual showmanship. Beginning in the summer of 1979, he spent most of his time on the road, lecturing at churches, prayer breakfasts, rallies, and press conferences and shaking the hands of thousands of Americans. It was an impressive feat of stamina, worthy of the most dedicated presidential candidate. And the result was a stunning overnight success, knitting together populist reaction, fundamentalist protest, and moralistic outrage. It was built on the foundations of existing religious groups, especially those formed to fight the IRS decision, but its ambitions were much greater. The Moral Majority would register millions of evangelical voters, Falwell hoped; it would mobilize conservatives to speak in a "clear and effective voice"; it would lobby for a "Family Protection Agency"; finally, it would help local communities "to fight pornography, homosexuality [and] the advocacy of immorality in school textbooks."[36]

Some prominent evangelicals refused to join the Moral Majority, chief among them Billy Graham, who thought that clergymen had no right to "speak with authority on the Panama Canal or superiority of armaments." But by 1981, Falwell's group had four million names on its mailing list and, at a conservative estimate, about 400,000 committed members: far fewer than his exaggerated claims, but impressive nonetheless. Of course it was never a "majority": while Falwell claimed that the religious right had some fifty million supporters, most scholarly estimates put the true figure at perhaps seven million. But it was still a striking figure and, as one historian puts it, "a historic breakthrough."[37]

**The Moral Majority** was always meant to have a strong influence on the Republican platform in 1980, and Falwell followed the presidential primaries with keen interest. The nominee, however, was not an obvious candidate for evangelical support. Not only was Ronald Reagan divorced; he had spent many years in Hollywood, dating nubile starlets and picking up an impressive stock of raunchy anecdotes. Above all, as governor of California, Reagan had been no great friend to the religious right and had signed the most liberal abortion bill in the nation, paving the way for well over a million California abortions by 1980. He was not even a regular churchgoer.[38]

But Reagan was a master at persuading people to listen to what he said rather than watch what he did. Like most fundamentalists, he was a fervent patriot who believed that the American people were a chosen people inhabiting a city on a hill. And he was extremely skillful at telling evangelicals what they wanted to hear, even if he only vaguely believed it himself. Always keen on a good story, he was fascinated by prophecies of the end of the world. In 1971 he astonished friends by announcing that "everything is in place for the battle of Armageddon and the second coming of Christ." During his battle with Gerald Ford, he claimed that he had "developed a new relationship with God [and] had an experience that could be described as 'born again' "—something that, on the evidence of his unchanged personality, continued fondness for dirty jokes, and reluctance to go to church, seems to have been utterly untrue.[39]

In the election year of 1980, Reagan's flirtation with the religious right reached its climax. At the Republican convention in July, he ended his acceptance speech on a famously religious note:

> I have thought of something that's not a part of my speech and worried over whether I should do it.
> Can we doubt that only a Divine Providence placed this land, this island of freedom, here as a refuge for all those people in the world who yearn to breathe free—Jews and Christians enduring persecution behind the Iron Curtain, the boat people of Southeast Asia, of Cuba and of Haiti, the victims of drought and famine in Africa, the freedom fighters in Afghanistan, and our own countrymen held in savage captivity?

What came next was brilliant political theater, a master craftsman at work. "I'll confess that I've been a little afraid to suggest what I'm going to suggest," Reagan said quietly, his voice apparently choked with emotion. "I'm more afraid not to. Can we begin our crusade joined together in a moment of silent prayer?" He paused, and the silence was charged with exquisite anticipation. Then, after a few moments, his words echoing around the hushed convention hall, he said simply and solemnly: "God bless America."[40]

A few weeks later, with the polls deadlocked, Reagan arrived in Dallas for a conference organized by the Religious Roundtable. Major speeches were scheduled for the city's new Reunion Arena, whose seventeen thousand seats were filled to capacity by local Christians. Jerry Falwell was on the bill; so were Pat Robertson, Jesse Helms, Phyllis Schlafly, and Paul Weyrich. But Reagan's speech was easily the most anticipated of the conference. In a press conference beforehand, he had already signaled his intentions by questioning the theory of evolution, deploring abortion, and denouncing the Supreme Court. And when he stood up to speak, the atmosphere was heavy with excitement.

That day, August 22, 1980, would always be remembered for his opening words—words that not only captured Reagan's rhetorical mastery but also showed just how far evangelical politics had come. "I know you can't endorse me," he said calmly. "But I want you to know that I endorse you and what you are doing." There was a moment's pause and then, as cries of "Amen!" rolled around the hall, a thunderous ovation. The soldiers of God had found their general.[41]

# Chapter Twenty  *To Sail Against the Wind*

> I get sick of the news. This country is sad,
> everybody can push us around.
>
> —**JOHN UPDIKE**, *Rabbit Is Rich (1981)*

On a breezy Saturday in late October 1979, seven thousand people gathered on Columbia Point, Boston, for the dedication of the John F. Kennedy Library, a gleaming white monument to Camelot's vanished optimism. When Jimmy and Rosalynn Carter arrived on the promontory, Edward Kennedy did his best to be welcoming, awkwardly showing them around the cavernous library. But Carter was left in no doubt what the Kennedys thought of him. As he sat on the stage overlooking the dazzling waters of Dorchester Bay, he listened impassively as Robert Kennedy's son Joseph launched a bitter attack on the Federal Reserve and the oil companies. When the president leaned forward to kiss Jacqueline Kennedy Onassis, she ostentatiously grimaced with disgust, a painfully symbolic moment analyzed by every political commentator in the land.

Both Carter and Kennedy were at their rhetorical best that day by the harbor. The senator's speech was gentler than usual, striking a personal note as he remembered his brother, but there was a political edge to it, too. John Kennedy had been a champion of compassion, his brother said, who taught him "to sail against the wind" and "made America the apostle of peace and strength in a troubled and divided world." In his "brief unfinished journey, he made us believe once more in the great historic purpose of this land. He filled America with pride and made the nation young again."

For once, though, it was Carter who carried off the honors. He had never met President Kennedy, but on hearing of his death, he had "wept openly, for the first time in more than ten years, for the first time since the day my own father died." Kennedy's vision still moved him, but his predecessor had been "a man of his own time" who had once remarked that "change is the law of life":

> The carved desk in the Oval Office which I use is the same as when John F. Kennedy sat behind it, but the problems that land on that desk are quite different.
>
> President Kennedy was right: Change is the law of life. The world of 1980 is as different from what it was in 1960 as the world of 1960 was from that of 1940. Our means of improving the world must also be different . . .
>
> We have a keener appreciation of limits now—the limits of government, limits on the use of military power abroad, the limits of manipulating, without harm to ourselves, a delicate and a balanced natural environment.

The issues were different, Carter said. So were the solutions, but "President Kennedy's message—the appeal for unselfish dedication to the common good—is more urgent than it ever was."[1]

Carter's appearance was generally considered a great success. Some critics shook their heads at his impulsive decision to squeeze Joan Kennedy's hand while her husband was talking, an odd gesture probably born of embarrassment—although there were those who recalled that Jimmy Carter was a man with lust in his heart. But it was perhaps the only time that Carter really captured the spirit of the party he led, the only time he successfully blended the rhetoric of limits with the egalitarian values of the liberal tradition. Whether he could hang on to the Democratic nomination, however, was another matter. On the first day of November, his Gallup rating fell to a miserable 29 percent, and among Democratic voters he trailed Kennedy by two to one. "He hasn't a single friend up here," one Democratic senator told the reporter Haynes Johnson. "Not one soul."[2]

. . .

**Through all the travails** of the 1970s, true believers had consoled themselves that the last of the Kennedys would eventually lead them to a new golden age of progressive liberalism. As the Carter administration ran aground and disaster followed disaster, Edward Kennedy's coronation seemed increasingly inevitable. In April 1979, even before the gasoline crisis, he led Carter among Democrats by 58 to 35 percent. By July, after the malaise speech fiasco, the margin was 66 to 30 percent. Almost every week brought more pressure for him to throw his hat into the ring: a full-page advertisement in the *Los Angeles Times*, a write-in campaign in New Hampshire, draft-Kennedy movements in Iowa, Illinois, and Florida. Even the intellectual inspirations behind the crisis-of-confidence speech, Christopher Lasch and Robert Bellah, thought that Kennedy ought to run.[3]

Never the most thick-skinned of men, Carter took the news of these draft-Kennedy efforts very badly. At a White House dinner in June, he told several congressmen that if Kennedy ran, "I'll whip his ass." Embarrassed by the spectacle of a high-school nerd trying to pass himself off as a street-corner bully, his guests tried to ignore him, so the president loudly repeated the phrase. Afterward, Carter's aides asked his guests to confirm the story if any reporters asked about it. The aides then passed out the guests' unlisted home phone numbers to make sure that reporters did. It was an old Nixon trick, and as false and embarrassing as ever. Carter, said the *Washington Monthly*, "had the manner of a certified accountant trying to be one of the boys."[4]

If Carter had hoped that he would intimidate his rival into backing down, he was greatly mistaken. Like his brothers, Ted Kennedy liked to think of himself as a fighter. Quite apart from his experience and glamour, he also had a strong following in the labor unions, liberal organizations, and public-interest lobbies, and among blacks, feminists, and gay rights groups. In the fall of 1979, it was by no means obvious that this ultraliberal coalition was dead. While Keynesian economics had fallen from fashion, in other respects liberalism remained surprisingly healthy. The emblematic programs of the Great Society had now been in place for ten years and were widely accepted. The controversial decisions of the Warren Court, too, were becoming an accepted part of the nation's legal fabric. Thanks to the rights revolution, women, homosexuals, blacks, the elderly, and the disabled had entitlements most had never thought possible, while the *Bakke* and *Weber* cases had confirmed the legality of affirmative action.

In universities and the arts, in Hollywood and the publishing industry, liberal assumptions seemed firmly entrenched. For all the efforts of the religious right and for all the talk of a backlash against the legacy of the 1960s, the fact remains that in moral and cultural terms, American society became steadily more permissive. More marriages broke up, more pregnancies were terminated, more children were born out of wedlock, more gays and lesbians came out. In this respect at least, liberalism not only survived the 1970s but emerged triumphant.[5]

Kennedy's advisers could also take heart from the fact that, for all the talk of a right turn, many Americans still held liberal views. Although voters increasingly disapproved of welfare payments to poor and unemployed blacks, their support for Social Security, Medicare, and other programs remained extremely strong. As Ronald Reagan's pollster Richard Wirthlin argued, it was "very difficult" to make the case that Americans were "moving in a more conservative direction." True, cutting taxes and spending more on defense won more support than "five or ten years ago." But the trends did not present "a nice, neat picture." On specific issues such as food stamps and health insurance, Wirthlin noted, Americans "frequently opt for the liberal choice." They did "want to take care of the needy, and they are clearly more liberal on the life-style issues, like the use of drugs, the ERA, abortion, gay rights, and their attitudes toward marriage." Gerald Ford's old pollster Bob Teeter agreed. While the public clearly held more conservative views on tax, crime, and welfare, he said, "when the problems are fair housing and getting black kids an education, those same people look more liberal."[6]

If Kennedy was to win the nomination, he needed to tap this residual affection for old-fashioned liberalism, to present a compelling strategy for defeating inflation, and to convince voters that he was a better leader than Jimmy Carter. But with the seizure of the American embassy in Tehran, the entire picture changed. It was the miracle Jimmy Carter needed, and the overnight transformation in his personal standing was truly astonishing. In just four weeks, despite the fact that the hostages remained in Iran, Carter's approval rating shot up from 30 percent to 61 percent, eclipsing even the Roosevelt boom after Pearl Harbor. It was a "stunning" comeback, said George Gallup: "the largest increase in presidential popularity in the four decades of the Gallup Poll."[7]

At a stroke, the hostage crisis pushed the economy off the front pages, allowed Carter to present himself as the patriotic candidate, and gave him the chance to follow a classic presidential incumbent's Rose Garden strategy. Announcing his candidacy in a brief televised statement at the beginning of December, Carter explained that he would forgo campaigning in order to "lead our response to an ever-changing situation of the greatest security, sensitivity and importance." It was clever politics, playing to the advantages of his incumbency. By mid-December the reversal of fortunes was complete. Carter led Kennedy by 48 to 40 percent, outstripping him among every age-group, in every part of the country, and even among self-described liberals. In trial heats, he even led Ronald Reagan by 14 percent.[8]

But Kennedy's misery was also self-inflicted. He never recovered from an abysmal performance in two interviews broadcast by CBS on the evening of November 4, just hours after the hostages were taken. The interviewer, Roger Mudd, knew the senator socially, and there was nothing unusual about his questions. But Kennedy's answers were so incoherent as to be embarrassing. Perhaps it was understandable that on Chappaquiddick he faltered badly: "Oh there's, the problem is, from that night, I, I found the conduct, the behavior almost beyond belief myself. I mean that's why it's been, but I think that's the way it was . . ." But when Mudd asked why Kennedy wanted to be president, a high-school debater would have given a better answer. "Well, I'm, were I to, to make the announcement, and, to run, the reasons that I would run is because I have a great belief in this country, that it is, has more natural resources than any nation of the world," he began, before veering off into rambling platitudes about the "greatest educated population in the world." He ended with a weak promise to build a better yesterday: "It just seems to me that this nation can cope and deal with its problems in a way that it has in the past."[9]

Behind the Mudd interview lay a deeper issue. In retrospect, it is staggering that Kennedy's aides never grasped that his involvement in the death of a young woman, Mary Jo Kopechne, was a major problem. Astoundingly, when Tip O'Neill mentioned it to Kennedy, the senator said, "Yeah, my pollsters tell me it's a three- to five-percent moral issue." "Let me tell you something," O'Neill replied. "You can't measure morals." He was right. At the very least, the stain of Chappaquiddick made it impossible for Kennedy to pose as a moral leader or a plain-talking fellow the voters could trust. By contrast, Carter's television spots introduced the president as a loyal husband and doting father, a family man, and a good man, inevitably raising an implicit contrast with his rival.[10]

Even without Chappaquiddick, Kennedy was in an extremely difficult position. Not only had the hostage crisis relegated his campaign to the inside pages, but his key issues had been eclipsed by the crisis in the Middle East. After Kennedy's formal announcement in December, it was another two weeks before he appeared on the evening news. On top of all that, he was criticizing an incumbent president who was holed up in the Oval Office negotiating for the hostages' release. The risk was that Kennedy would look unpatriotic, which is precisely what happened when he told a San Francisco television station that the administration should abandon the Shah. Kennedy was undermining Carter's attempts to get the hostages out, his critics claimed. More than half of voters thought he had "hurt America" by speaking out against the Shah, while the newspapers had a field day. "Teddy: The Toast of Tehran," roared the front page of the *New York Post*.[11]

Announcing his candidacy in November, Kennedy had explained that the two themes of his campaign would be presidential leadership and malaise, which he considered an excuse for Carter's incompetence and lack of vision. While soaring rhetoric came naturally, what was more elusive was a coherent program for economic recovery. Like many liberals, Kennedy remained stubbornly attached to the old-time religion of the 1960s, promising new money for welfare and a massive health insurance plan, with inflation curbed by gasoline rationing and wage controls. To most commentators, however, it all seemed painfully unrealistic. Carter claimed that Kennedy's was the "old philosophy of pouring out new programs and new money," in contrast with his own "fiscal prudence." In many ways there was something admirable about Kennedy's refusal to abandon the social commitments of the Great Society. But as David Broder put it, his "essential appeal was a nostalgic wish to recapture a vanished past, rather than deal with the hard choices facing America in the future."[12]

While Kennedy's unimaginative program came as a deep disappointment, it was as nothing compared with his performance on the stump. He seemed anxious and stiff, either stumbling over his words or reading mechanically from a prepared script. This was not unusual for a candidate mounting his first presidential campaign; the difference, though, was that expectations were so great. "His voice is strained, his timing is off," wrote Ellen Goodman in *The Boston Globe*. "Everything is wrong." As the perception grew that Kennedy was in trouble, the money began to dry up. Unlike his brothers, he could not dip into the family coffers, because the new campaign finance laws had put strict limits on individual contributions. "Before long," one aide confided even before the first votes had been cast, "the Kennedy campaign could collapse."[13]

The campaign did not collapse, but as their candidate limped from defeat to defeat, Kennedy's admirers might have preferred that it had. On the night of January 21, as the people of Iowa trudged home through the snow, the caucus results were worse than any of his supporters could have imagined. He had not merely lost; he had lost by a margin of almost two to one. Worse was to follow. A month later, in a New Hampshire primary that he had once been a runaway favorite to win, Kennedy finished 10 percent behind the president. It was a collapse of extraordinary dimensions. In the Granite State, which borders his home state of Massachusetts, Kennedy had once been thirty-five points clear. Now the question was not whether he would win, but when he would pull out.[14]

Kennedy fought on, stubbornly and bravely, but the glorious coronation had turned into an exercise in self-mortification. The biggest humiliation came in Illinois, whose industrial towns, unionized workers, and big-city Catholics should have been easy pickings. Unfortunately for Kennedy, Chappaquiddick had destroyed his popularity among Chicago's conservative Catholics. As he walked through the sleet in the city's St. Patrick's Day parade, jeers drowned out the applause. "When are you going to learn to drive?" one heckler shouted. "Where's Mary Jo?" a drunk yelled in his face. When a youth threw firecrackers into his path, Kennedy almost buckled with shock. It took the support of the Secret Service to keep him marching on, his face fixed in a rigid grin. The next day, Carter won Illinois by a crushing thirty-five points. Even Kennedy's delegate hunters now thought the president's lead was insurmountable.[15]

At the end of March, Kennedy at last caught a break, winning New York and Connecticut as voters punished Carter for stringent budget cuts and a muddle at the UN over American opposition to Israeli settlements. If the challenger could pull off another upset in Wisconsin a week later, then perhaps his delegate hunters might be wrong after all. But on April 1, as Wisconsin's voters were brewing their first coffees of the day, the networks broke into their breakfast shows with live coverage from the Oval Office. Standing behind his desk was the grinning figure of the president of the United States. There had been a "positive development" in the hostage negotiations, he said: the captives were about to be handed over by the radical students to the care of the Iranian authorities. "Do you know when they'll be actually released, I mean, brought home?" one of the reporters asked. Carter smiled. "I presume that we will know more about that as the circumstances develop," he said. "We do not know the exact time schedule at this moment."[16]

Carter's aides always denied there had been any political motivation in scheduling such a dramatic announcement in the middle of the breakfast shows on primary day. It guaranteed victory in Wisconsin, choking off Kennedy's momentum, but in the long run it backfired horribly. Carter had spoken too soon: the hostages were not handed over to the Iranian government, and remained no closer to coming home. The episode came to haunt his campaign; until the very last day, his opponents accused him of using the hostages for political gain, warning of a last-minute diplomatic surprise to swing the election. Kennedy's biographer comments that Carter was probably "taking political advantage of an exaggerated hope, blearily measured when the cables came into the White House Situation Room before dawn." But if Carter had not been unforgivably cynical, then he had been embarrassingly gullible. Appropriately, as Kennedy's spokesman pointed out, it was April Fools' Day.[17]

**Throughout the opening months** of 1980, Carter had deliberately adopted a relatively soft line toward Iran. Optimistic that the Soviet occupation of Afghanistan would push the ayatollahs into the arms of the West, he had sent Hamilton Jordan to hold a series of increasingly bizarre secret meetings with Iranian representatives, even getting the CIA to lend him a wig and false mustache. All the time, however, public patience was wearing dangerously thin. "Iran: Enough," declared a hard-hitting *Washington Post* editorial five days after Wisconsin. The United States, the *Post* said, was "increasingly seen as a country that shrinks from asserting what even its enemies recognize as a legitimate interest in protecting its diplomats from a mob." Even Hamilton Jordan's twelve-year-old nephew asked him: "Why doesn't the President do something?" "Like what?" Jordan asked. "Bomb Iran and wipe 'em out," the boy shot back. "A lot of my friends at school say that Jimmy Carter doesn't have the guts to do anything."[18]

It is to Carter's credit than instead of lobbing missiles into Iran, he had the patience to wait until every diplomatic route had been exhausted. That all the hostages made it out alive owed much to his restraint. But it did not endear him to Americans who, after the shame of Vietnam and the shock of the energy crisis, were sick of being humiliated on the world stage. Even the physical contrast between the glaring ayatollah and the sad-eyed Carter seemed to reflect his weakness. As one account puts it, "the very folds of the president's face and the hang of his heavy lips seemed a mask of disappointment. The leader of the free world looked whipped." When *The Boston Globe*'s editorial writer frivolously titled one column "Mush from the Wimp," it was a sign of how far Carter's stock had fallen that nobody realized it was a joke for the copy editor rather than a serious headline. More than 160,000 copies of the paper were distributed before the headline was changed to the distinctly Carter-esque "All Must Share the Burden."[19]

Even Carter's patience, however, was not inexhaustible. On March 22, he summoned his national security team to Camp David and announced that it was time to consider more drastic options. At his invitation, General David Jones, chairman of the Joint Chiefs of Staff, outlined a new proposal to the group. This was the brainchild of Colonel Charlie Beckwith, a former Georgia all-state footballer, Special Forces commander, and founder of Delta Force, an elite counterterrorism unit specializing in hostage rescue operations. Beckwith's plan required eight Marine helicopters to fly from an aircraft carrier in the Indian Ocean to a remote desert location in central Iran. At this point, code-named Desert One, they would be met by six C-130 Hercules transports carrying more fuel, equipment, and the Delta Force team. The refueled helicopters would then drop the team outside Tehran, from where they would make their way into the city, rescue the hostages, and escort them to a soccer stadium across the street. Next, the helicopters would take them to an airstrip outside the city, which would have been captured in the meantime by a force of Rangers. Finally they would be picked up by C-141 transport planes and flown to safety with a fighter escort.[20]

Even in a James Bond film, this scheme would have sounded ludicrously complicated. Something was bound to go wrong, and the list of what-ifs was enormous. Yet, while Cyrus Vance thought the plan was madness, both Carter and Brzezinski were tempted. On April 7, Carter broke off diplomatic relations with Iran. Two days later, Brzezinski sent him a memorandum on the case for action. "In my view," it concluded, "a carefully planned and boldly executed rescue operation represents the only realistic prospect that the hostages—any of them—will be freed in the foreseeable future. Our policy of restraint has won us well-deserved understanding throughout the world, but it has run out. It is time for us to act. Now."[21]

The very next day, Carter convened an urgent meeting of the National Security Council. It was a crucial moment: Vance was away in Florida, and his lugubrious deputy, Warren Christopher, sat silently as, one by one, Carter's defense chiefs voiced their support for the mission. When Vance returned a few days later, the momentum seemed unstoppable. At a stormy NSC meeting on April 15, the secretary of state repeated that the mission was wildly far-fetched and was bound to trigger outrage across the Islamic world. But nobody was listening. "There was an awkward silence as Vance scanned the room," noted Hamilton Jordan, "looking from Zbig, to Mondale, to Harold Brown, to Jody, and finally to me, his eyes begging for support." After a long pause, Carter rehearsed the arguments in favor. There was another long silence, and Vance lowered his eyes to his legal pad. Then Carter turned to General Jones with questions about the operation.[22]

The next evening, Carter's military chiefs met in the White House

Situation Room. Many dressed informally to throw reporters off the scent, and Charlie Beckwith was stunned to see Walter Mondale in a jogging suit and Hamilton Jordan in well-worn Levi's. But Beckwith, who had never thought much of Jimmy Carter, was very impressed with the president's no-nonsense manner, and the admiration was mutual. As Beckwith outlined his plans, Carter's certainty grew. The mission would go ahead, he said finally, and the military would run it with no interference from the White House. "I was full of wonderment," Beckwith wrote later. "I was proud to be an American and to have a president do what he'd just done." But Carter had a last word for the man who had created Delta Force. "I want you, before you leave for Iran, to assemble all your force and when you think it's appropriate to give them a message from me," the president said. "Tell them that in the event this operation fails, for whatever reason, the fault will not be theirs, it will be mine." It was a generous thing to say. "God bless you, Mr. President," Beckwith burst out as Carter left the room.[23]

At dawn on the morning of Thursday, April 24, Beckwith's men gathered in their Egyptian base for a final inspection in their scruffy jeans and black field jackets. Almost all of them had written "death letters" for their wives if the mission went wrong. In one of the empty hangars, Major Jerry Boykin stood in front of a blown-up photograph of their imprisoned countrymen and read aloud a passage from the first book of Samuel: "And David put his hand in a bag, and took thence a stone, and slang it, and smote the Philistine in the forehead, that the stone sunk into his forehead; and he fell on his face to the earth. So David prevailed over the Philistine with a stone and a sling." When he had finished, they prayed in silence. Then, spontaneously, they began singing "God Bless America," many with tears in their eyes, as though in homage to the final scene in *The Deer Hunter*.[24]

In Washington, the president's men forced themselves to go through the usual routine as if nothing were happening, all the time knowing that the first helicopters should be at Desert One by midday. "I could hardly hide my excitement," recalled Jordan, whose secretary asked if he was feeling all right. At lunchtime, he joined Carter in the Oval Office for sandwiches. Harold Brown reported that there was already some bad news. Flying into the desert from the Indian Ocean, the eight helicopters had unexpectedly run into a dust storm. One went down and had to be abandoned; a second, lost and in danger of crashing into a mountain, had turned back. Still, with six working helicopters the mission could still go ahead—just as long as nothing else went wrong.[25]

Later that afternoon, Jordan was going through the motions of a campaign strategy meeting when the phone rang. "Come to the Oval Office at once," Carter said. When Jordan reached the study, Carter said bluntly: "I had to abort the rescue mission." Stunned silence: Jordan thought that his boss looked "devastated," his hopes crushed by a stupid technical fault. "At least there were no American casualties and no innocent Iranians hurt," Carter said quietly. There was a long pause, and then the red phone began to ring. Carter picked it up and said: "Yes, Dave?" Then he closed his eyes, and his advisers knew at once that something dreadful had happened.

"Are there any dead?" Carter asked, swallowing hard. There was another pause, and then he said softly: "I understand." The president hung up. "No one said a word," Jordan recalled. Finally, Cyrus Vance, who had handed in his resignation a few days earlier, broke the silence. "Mr. President," he said gently, "I'm very, very sorry."[26]


**Carter had always known** that Operation Eagle Claw was a long shot: in a secret report, the CIA had predicted that more than half of the hostages would lose their lives. But the Delta Force team never even got to Tehran. At Desert One, a third helicopter had developed a fault, and in the confusion as the team tried to get away, a collision between two aircraft sparked a conflagration that killed eight American servicemen. By any standards it was an utter debacle, made worse by the fact that the survivors left behind their mission documents in their haste to escape. And the press was predictably unforgiving. "Debacle in the Desert," screamed the cover of *Time* over a picture of a miserable gray president, calling it "a military, diplomatic and political fiasco." Once so impressive, the nation's military machine was now "incapable of keeping its aircraft aloft even when no enemy knew they were there, and even incapable of keeping them from crashing into each other."[27]

In Tehran, ecstatic crowds gathered as news of the disaster spread into the streets. At a ghoulish press conference the Americans' charred remains were exhibited to general applause, including a blackened forearm, still wearing a military-style watch. Meanwhile, the hostages were taken from the American embassy, split up, and hidden in locations across the country. There could be no rescue now. Indeed, although the yellow ribbons continued to flutter, many Americans seemed to lose hope that their countrymen would ever be home. The media had lost interest, remarked the journalist Jonathan Schell at the end of May, and the captives "seemed to disappear from the face of the earth": no more interviews with friends and relatives, no more well-meaning missionaries visiting Tehran, no more headlines about possible breakthroughs. A couple of months later, the hostage crisis had almost disappeared, save for Walter Cronkite's reminders as he signed off every night.[28]

As for Jimmy Carter, the debacle only bore out what people already suspected: that he was a loser, a miserable man who specialized in announcing bad news. It confirmed his "image as inept," said *Time*, while Joseph Kraft wrote in *The Washington Post* that he was "unfit to be President at a time of crisis." His public standing now seemed almost beyond repair; by now, just 18 percent of the public thought Carter a "very strong leader," while seven out of ten people agreed it was time for a change in the Oval Office. Even his family was now fair game. Once seen as a comic southern character, Billy Carter had been in and out of an alcohol addiction clinic in California, while revelations that he had taken money to act as Libya's unregistered "foreign agent" appalled many commentators and seriously embarrassed his brother.[29]

But it was not merely for Carter that 1980 marked a low point. For the American people in general, it was a year of deep anxiety and retrenchment, of factory layoffs and conspiracy theories, of humiliation abroad and turmoil at home. In Santa Fe, New Mexico, dozens died in a horrific prison riot. In Fort Chaffee, Arkansas, rioting greeted the influx of thousands of Cubans who had fled in the Mariel boat lift. In Atlanta, dozens of black children and teenagers were found murdered, apparently by a single serial killer. And in Miami, the worst race riot in a decade left eighteen dead and $100 million worth of property in flames.[30]

The American Dream, said *The New York Times*, was over. It had given way to the "dismay and confusion that accumulate when inflation and recession change the value of money and all that money means, culturally and psychologically; when the assumptions of several generations about America's expertise and leadership and this country's pre-eminent place in the world are jumbled and wounded; when values are distorted and called into question by economic conditions that affect, in different ways, every class in society." In the old days, a suburban school librarian told the paper, "it seemed possible to look forward to a time when things would be O.K." But now, she said, "I feel it's always going to be like this. The whole situation is frightening and I don't know where it will end."[31]

What worried Carter's advisers more than anything was the wretched state of the economy. Inflation was now totally out of control: In January 1980, wholesale prices climbed at what would be an annual rate of 21 percent. A month later, on the day of the New Hampshire primary, the consumer price index showed that inflation was running at an annual rate of 18.2 percent, the highest in modern American history—which meant that every pension or fixed salary would lose half its value in just five years. Even Carter conceded that inflation had now reached the "crisis stage," while *BusinessWeek,* the voice of Wall Street conservatism, warned that "the U.S. is in danger of becoming another Brazil, with an intolerably high rate of inflation institutionalized. The result will be an end to the democratic system."[32]

In January, Carter unveiled his latest budget, printed in green and white campaign colors. Defense spending was up, and there were moderate increases in some health and education programs. But there was no relief for taxpayers, as many Democrats had hoped. On the left, Carter's critics were furious; on Wall Street, however, the consensus was that he had been nowhere near tough enough. Bond prices continued to fall, and when the American Bankers Association met at the end of February, Salomon Brothers' chief economist called for a "national state of emergency," triggering yet another stock market slide. A month later, Carter released an even more stringent budget to appease the markets. This time, spending on cherished liberal programs such as food stamps and child-health assistance was slashed by $3 billion in 1980 and by $17 billion in 1981, with strict controls on consumer credit and a ten-cents-per-gallon gasoline levy. Almost overnight, consumer borrowing dried up.[33]

By this time, Carter had acquired a powerful ally in the battle against inflation. In the reshuffle following his crisis-of-confidence speech, he had chosen a new man to run the Federal Reserve Board: Paul Volcker, a six-foot-seven Princeton graduate who had been director of planning for Chase Manhattan and president of the New York Federal Reserve. Bright, conservative, and intensely strong willed, Volcker was seen as Wall Street's candidate for the post, and in his first meeting with Carter he emphasized "the need for tighter money." It was the most important appointment Carter ever made. Almost unwittingly, he had handed over not only control of the Federal Reserve but also the future of the economy to a man who would pay any price to bring down inflation.[34]

In October 1979, Volcker took the decision that would define his time at the Federal Reserve, raising the discount interest rate and announcing that the Fed would stick to strict monetary targets, based on a combination of reserves and money in circulation. This was a simple but radical step, giving him tighter control over the money supply, dramatizing his determination to bring down inflation, and protecting him from political pressure when the higher rates began to hurt. In public, Carter supported the decision. In private, he winced as the Fed squeezed the breath out of the economy. But conservatives were delighted by what *Newsweek* called "radical shock treatment." It was "the most important change in monetary policy in a generation," said Alan Greenspan.[35]

By January 1980, interest rates had reached their highest level since World War II. Two months later, most banks increased their lending rates to 17 percent, and by the beginning of April rates had broken through the dreaded 20 percent ceiling, violating usury laws in some states. This was not just unpleasant medicine; it was economic chemotherapy of the most painful kind.[36]

The inevitable result was recession. There was no point denying it; everyone knew it was coming. As Carter's economic chief, Charles Schultze, explained to the president in April, a builder starting work on a new house now had to pay more than 20 percent on a construction loan and then find a buyer willing "both to pay the extra price and to assume a 15 to 16 percent mortgage," while a "typical business firm" was paying as much as 20 percent interest to meet its capital needs. Not surprisingly, housing starts were down by 42 percent in a year, while car sales were down 24 percent, throwing thousands of Detroit workers onto the unemployment lines. Between April and June, corporate profits fell by more than 18 percent, the third-biggest decline in history. Already struggling in the harsh winds of global competition, many industries seemed in terminal decline: U.S. Steel, for example, lost a staggering $561 million in just three months, its woes summed up by the closure of the iconic Youngstown and Homestead plants.[37]

If Gerald Ford had not refused to pump prime the economy for electoral gain, then Carter might never have won the presidency in the first place. The irony was that now that he faced a similar dilemma, he made exactly the same choice, preferring unpopular long-term discipline to a crowd-pleasing bonanza. In many ways this was a testament to Carter's sense of responsibility. But the result was a nightmare for his reelection team. By May, after the sharpest rise in more than thirty years, unemployment had reached 7.8 percent, meaning that more than eight million Americans were out of work. These were not just figures; these were shattered lives, defeated expectations, broken homes. In rusting Baltimore, twenty-six thousand people lined up for just seventy-seven openings in the Social Security Administration, while in the streets of Boston, Wichita, and Miami frustration boiled over into racial violence. If all the unemployed people in the nation stood in line, remarked Ronald Reagan, it would reach all the way from New York to Los Angeles. Even for those still working, there was nothing to celebrate. In 1979 and 1980, average gross weekly earnings fell from $189 to $172, while median family income fell by almost $1,500. The promise of the affluent society had withered away. Tomorrow was not better than today, it was worse.[38]

Carter's critics could not have hoped for a better gift. Kennedy hammered again and again at the issue of unemployment, insisting that the president had deserted blue-collar Americans and echoing Ronald Reagan's insistence that only tax cuts could restart the motor of affluence. While Kennedy and Reagan promised a return to the days of growth, Carter sounded like the voice of doom. In May, Stuart Eizenstat warned that his policy was "viewed solely as one of austerity, pain and sacrifice" and that no president "had been re-elected during a serious recession for which he could be blamed." But Carter refused to throw traditional Democrats a bone or two. "The team came down, unanimous in asking me to approve a tax reduction and a moderate spending program to assuage Kennedy and to stimulate the economy," he noted in his diary. "I was adamantly against it and, after considerable discussion, prevailed."[39]

Carter's insistence on holding the line against inflation, even if it meant handing the tax-cut issue to his opponents, was admirably principled. If nothing else, the markets would have been horrified if he had abandoned his commitment to a balanced budget, while most voters agreed that beating inflation must be the priority. But his fiscal conservatism undermined one of the central pillars of the Democratic coalition. How could the party live up to the promise of Roosevelt and Kennedy when its president cut programs rather than created them? How could he sustain his populist image when he failed to protect the blue-collar workers of the industrial North? How could he win reelection when he abandoned millions of ordinary Americans to unemployment and poverty?

The recession came too late to save Kennedy's campaign. Although he reeled off a string of late victories, including Pennsylvania, California, and New Jersey, he never came close to toppling the incumbent. On the other hand, Carter had little to celebrate. Having made such a strong start, he had staggered to the finish line in a manner reminiscent of his jogging fiasco. Every day he had been forced to rebut Kennedy's allegations of incompetence and indecision, and with every defeat his presidential authority had taken a heavy knock. "Every extra week and month we were forced to campaign against Kennedy sapped our strength and made the chances of winning the general election more difficult," reflected Hamilton Jordan. Carter's advertising guru, Jerry Rafshoon, even thought that Kennedy paved the way for Ronald Reagan, hammering home the message that the Republicans would use to woo blue-collar workers in the fall.[40]

On June 25, both Jordan and Pat Caddell sent reports to Carter. The

Kennedy challenge, Jordan wrote bleakly, had "hurt us very badly, not only within the Democratic Party but with the electorate as a whole." Not only had Kennedy's attacks severely damaged Carter's image, but the president's attempts to portray himself as the "tougher" of the two had only made him look like a "manipulative politician bent on re-election at all costs." Caddell's report, meanwhile, made even more depressing reading. "The issues structures could not be worse," he wrote. "After a long period of runaway inflation . . . we face what could be a worse *political* problem—unemployment . . . The public is anxious, confused, hostile, and sour . . . *More to the point, the American people do not want Jimmy Carter as their President . . . By and large the American people do not like Jimmy Carter.* Indeed a large segment could be said to loathe the President."[41]

It was an astoundingly downbeat way to prepare for the rigors of a general election campaign. Yet as the economy continued to slide and the public contemplated humiliation in Iran, Caddell was not exaggerating. It was about this time that a reporter, interviewing the president of the International Association of Machinists, asked if there was any way Carter could redeem himself with the public. The union man thought for a second. Then he said simply: "Die."[42]

**In August 1980** the Democrats returned to Madison Square Garden. Originally, Carter's aides had wanted to hold their convention in the South, but party rules prohibited the convention being held in any state that had not ratified the ERA. Rarely had the Democrats gathered with such little enthusiasm. As the convention opened, the latest Gallup poll gave Carter an approval rating of just 21 percent, the lowest in history. In an ABC-Harris poll, meanwhile, 77 percent disapproved of his performance, another all-time record. Nationwide, he was almost thirty points behind Ronald Reagan, and in California he was running third behind Reagan and the independent John Anderson. Not even Herbert Hoover had run for reelection from a more wretched position.[43]

Four years before, Carter's men had been the kings of Manhattan. Now the mood was very different. The streets were too crowded, the security too tight, the atmosphere too hot, the prices too high. Four years before, delegates had queued outside the Garden to buy hot dogs at forty-five cents each; now they cost sixty cents. Hotel rooms and Broadway tickets cost twice as much as in 1976, while gasoline cost $1.40 a gallon, a painful reminder of the administration's troubles. But the difference was a question more of mood than of money. "Some say it is simply that the streets are dirtier and the prices higher," wrote one reporter. "But others think that between then and now there has been a dissipation of the spirit of 1976 . . . Most say they still love New York, but some admit they are a bit more likely to notice the overflowing trash bins and the sleeping derelicts on street corners because the high drama that colored their vision last time has gone."[44]

On the convention's first day, Kennedy formally conceded defeat. But on Tuesday night he came to the Garden and gave one of the great rhetorical performances in Democratic history, a stirring defense of liberalism in the age of limits. His tone was somber as he began, and the packed convention was deathly quiet. Elizabeth Drew wrote that she had never known a floor "so still."

He came, he said, "not to argue as a candidate" but to affirm "the cause of the common man and the common woman." He repeated his commitment to liberal economics, condemning "unemployment, high interest rates, and human misery as false weapons against inflation" and urging his fellow Democrats to provide "jobs for all who are out of work." It was "surely correct that we cannot solve problems by throwing money at them," he admitted, "but it is also correct that we dare not throw out our national problems onto a scrap heap of inattention and indifference." After thanking his family and offering perfunctory congratulations to the president, he reached his rousing conclusion:

> Someday, long after this convention, long after the signs come down, and the crowds stop cheering, and the bands stop playing, may it be said of our campaign that we kept the faith. May it be said of our Party in 1980 that we found our faith again.
>
> And may it be said of us, both in dark passages and in bright days, in the words of Tennyson that my brothers quoted and loved, and that have special meaning for me now:
>
> *I am a part of all that I have met . . .*
> *Tho' much is taken, much abides . . .*
> *That which we are, we are—*
> *One equal temper of heroic hearts . . . strong in will*
> *To strive, to seek, to find, and not to yield.*

Madison Square Garden was still, the air burning with emotion— mourning for Kennedy's brothers, pride at his words, regret at his rejection. "For me, a few hours ago, this campaign came to an end," Kennedy said, his voice richer and more passionate than ever. "For all those whose cares have been our concern, the work goes on, the cause endures, the hope still lives, and the dream shall never die."[45]

"For several eerie seconds," remembered Hamilton Jordan, "the convention hall was silent—as if everyone, friend or foe, knew that great words had been uttered." Then the crowd let out a roar of approval, and the chanting—"We want Ted! We want Ted!"—started up, raw in its need. Tip O'Neill made a feeble effort to restore order, but on the floor many delegates were weeping, others hollering themselves hoarse. In the Carter campaign trailers around the hall, nobody said a word. "Great speech," the president's fund-raiser Robert Strauss murmured at last. "Great speech."[46]

The following evening, Jimmy Carter came before the convention. Standing there at the podium, he looked a slight, wan figure compared with four years before, his hair completely gray, his face lined and tired. He tried to reach the rhetorical high notes, his voice straining more than usual, much of his speech a litany of attacks on Ronald Reagan. He talked of his experience, of the "complex and difficult" decisions he had made in the Oval Office, of the "hard reality" that faced the American people. "I don't claim that every decision that we have made has been right or popular," he said at one point. "We've made mistakes, and we've learned from them." Indeed, he even made a dreadful gaffe in the speech itself, paying tribute to "Hubert Horatio *Hornblower*" rather than Hubert Humphrey. Liberal critics who suspected that Carter cared nothing for the party's traditions now had all the proof they needed. Although the audience applauded at the end, one reporter noted, "[It] is cheerless. Carter just does not give a lift to occasions; he does not seem to know how to."[47]

At last, to compound the general air of incompetence and defeatism, Edward Kennedy arrived onstage several minutes late and conspicuously refused to raise Carter's hand in the air in the traditional gesture of reconciliation. While an obviously frustrated president wore a fixed grin of embarrassment, Kennedy merely wandered around the stage waving at the delegates. It "looked worse than hell," thought Robert Strauss. Watching in California, Ronald Reagan was highly entertained. "If that's the best they can do in unity, they have a long way to go," he said delightedly.[48]

**Carter had not yet** given up hope. On August 18, Rosalynn's birthday, he gave her a present only he could have chosen: a little picture frame, inside which he had written a verse from Ecclesiastes 9:9—"Live happily with the woman you love through the fleeting days of life, for the wife God gives you is your best reward down here for all your earthly toil"— translated into Spanish. But there was also a present from the "people of the country": a new poll showing that for all its mishaps, the convention had slashed Reagan's lead to just seven points. It never occurred to Carter that he would not claw back the advantage. Between himself and Reagan, he noted in his diary, were "perhaps the sharpest divisions" of any two candidates in his lifetime. "We're on the right side," he wrote, "and if we can present our case clearly to the American people, we will win overwhelmingly in November."[49]

Others, however, were not so sanguine. It was about this time that Paul Volcker began telling a joke that summed up better than any commentary Carter's desperate predicament. When Gerald Ford left the White House, the joke ran, he handed his successor three envelopes and told him to open them one at a time if his problems became too much. After his first year, Carter opens the first envelope. The paper inside reads: "Attack Jerry Ford."

Carter does precisely that, but things still get worse. So, a year later, he opens the second envelope. The note reads: "Attack the Federal Reserve." Again, Carter does as instructed; again, things only get worse. At last, overwhelmed by the pressure of the revolution in Iran, the hostage crisis, the gas lines, the invasion of Afghanistan, inflation, and recession, Carter rips open the third envelope. The note inside reads simply: "Prepare three envelopes."[50]

# Chapter Twenty-one  *Rendezvous with Destiny*

Reagan doesn't have that presidential look.

**—UNITED ARTISTS EXECUTIVE,** rejecting him for a part in
*The Best Man* (1964)

D etroit, July: the Republicans in town, the atmosphere hot and heavy with the expectation of victory. Ronald Reagan was reportedly unhappy about the location; he would have preferred a Sunbelt boomtown, not a decaying Rust Belt metropolis. Even as the delegates arrived, there was a sense of disconnection between the city and the convention. Many were staying at the new Renaissance Center, a gigantic hotel complex designed like a fortress, protected by a thirty-foot concrete wall, and referred to as the "city within a city." Downtown businessmen, many of them black, complained that delegates seemed frightened to visit their stores, while reporters cheekily asked city spokesmen to help them compile a list of "mugging spots" for delegates to avoid.

Yet Detroit was the perfect location for a Republican candidate keen to reach out to blue-collar Democrats. No city in the nation was a better symbol of urban decay, rampant crime, and racial division. By 1980, six out of ten residents were black; almost 100,000 of them lived below the poverty line, while 300,000 were eligible for food stamps. Unemployment figures were appalling: at least 20 percent across the city, and perhaps

60 percent among young black men. The Motor City had become the Murder City, with one of the highest crime rates in the nation. The streets were run-down urban prairies, their walls covered with graffiti, their inhabitants in thrall to dope and heroin. Days before the Republicans arrived, sanitation workers walked out, leaving piles of garbage to fester on the sidewalks. Pointing to a yawning budget deficit, the city's mayor, Coleman Young, said there was nothing he could do: "I ain't got no more goddamn money."[1]

What underlay all Detroit's troubles was the plight of the car industry. It was the supreme irony: the innovation that had made the Motor City great, that had been such a symbol of American affluence, had now become an emblem of decline. After losing an eye-watering $700 million in the first nine months of 1979, Chrysler had been forced to beg for a government bailout that apparently defied all the rules of the free enterprise system. As Michigan's congressmen were the first to point out, half a million jobs depended on the government's generosity, and not even Jimmy Carter could ignore the stakes. In return, the United Auto Workers agreed to wage cuts and layoffs. The bad news did not end there: a year later, General Motors lost $763 million and Ford more than $1 billion. Across the board, from steel to machine tools, American manufacturing was in deep trouble. In June 1980, a special issue of *BusinessWeek* described the nation's competitive decline as "nothing short of an economic disaster."[2]

Although Reagan agreed to meet unemployed autoworkers on the convention's second day, the mood inside the Joe Louis Arena could hardly have been more different from the misery on the streets of Detroit. To the traditional pageantry, Reagan's men had added a veneer of showbiz glitz. Pat Boone was there to pledge allegiance to the flag, Glen Campbell and Tanya Tucker to sing the national anthem, Jimmy Stewart, Ginger Rogers, and the Osmonds to lend their support. And behind the glitter there was political substance to gladden the hearts of the true believers. The Republican platform called for the complete decontrol of oil prices and more nuclear power, it promised to slash taxes by a third in three years, and it was committed to "military superiority" over the Soviet Union. It promised the restoration of capital punishment, and it urged the return of prayer in public schools. It represented "a rightward move," said its proud author, the Texas senator John Tower.[3]

The only real question concerned Reagan's running mate. The obvious candidate was George Bush, but Reagan had his doubts about Bush's "spunk" and had a surprise in mind for the delegates. In June, visiting Gerald Ford to patch up their differences, Reagan had casually mentioned the vice presidency, and by the time Ford arrived in Detroit, he was seriously tempted. Most of Ford's friends urged him to go for it; only Dick Cheney, who thought that the vice presidency was a "really rotten, stinking job," argued otherwise. When it came to the crunch, however, Ford could not face the prospect of making official visits to Equatorial Guinea and handing out medals to the Wichita State cheerleading squad. If he was coming back to Washington, he wanted real power: a "co-presidency," as Walter Cronkite put it. That was too much for Reagan, whose advisers were relieved when Ford eventually withdrew his hat from the ring—which meant that the second spot went to George Bush after all.[4]

On the final night of the convention, Reagan was in fine form, a born communicator at ease with his party. Much of his address was familiar to anyone who had followed his career: ferocious denunciations of waste, taxes, and inflation; promises of radical tax cuts; a hard line in foreign affairs. Yet Reagan's relentless optimism was a long way from the strident negativity of Goldwater's address sixteen years before, or from the gloomy realism of Carter's malaise speech. "They say that the United States has had its day in the sun; that our nation has passed its zenith," Reagan said of his opponents. "They expect you to tell your children that the American people no longer have the will to cope with their problems; that the future will be one of sacrifice and few opportunities. My fellow citizens, I utterly reject that view. The American people, the most generous on earth, who created the highest standard of living, are not going to accept the notion that we can only make a better world for others by moving backwards ourselves. Those who believe we can have no business leading the nation."

It was his climax that got the most attention, and said most about the man. In his speech for Goldwater in 1964, Reagan had echoed Franklin D. Roosevelt's summons to a "rendezvous with destiny." And now, in his closing words, sending a message to millions of Democrats watching on television, he pulled off one of the rhetorical robberies of the century:

> The time is now to redeem promises once made to the American people by another candidate, in another time and another place. He said, "For three long years I have been going up and down this country preaching that government—federal, state, and local—costs too much. I shall not stop that preaching. As an immediate program of action, we must abolish useless offices. We must eliminate unnecessary functions of government . . . and, like the private citizen, give up luxuries which we can no longer afford. I propose to you, my friends, and through you that government of all kinds, big and little be made solvent and that the example be set by the President of the United States and his Cabi-

net." So said Franklin Delano Roosevelt in his acceptance speech to the Democratic National Convention in July 1932.

Perhaps only Reagan, the man who had voted for Roosevelt and still idolized him decades later, could have done it.[5]

**Coming out of** the convention, Reagan was in an effervescent mood, buoyed by a palpable sense of momentum. His advisers told reporters that his key themes were leadership, restoration, and rebirth; they were keen to reach white evangelical voters, as well as blue-collar workers hit by inflation, high interest rates, and unemployment. The trick was to emphasize family values without sounding too censorious, to promise prosperity without sounding too naive, to offer tax cuts without sounding too profligate, to champion strong national defense without sounding too belligerent. Since Reagan had already done it in California, there seemed no reason why he might not pull it off again.[6]

Unfortunately for Reagan, however, his fall campaign could hardly have got off to a worse start. On August 3, en route to address the National Urban League in New York, he made a brief stop in Philadelphia, Mississippi, for the Neshoba County Fair. Philadelphia was not just any small town in Mississippi: it was the site of one of the most famous crimes of the 1960s, the murder of three civil rights activists with the complicity of the local police. Reagan's pollster Richard Wirthlin begged him not to go. But Reagan had given his word to the local congressman, Trent Lott—and so it was that in front of ten thousand hollering fairgoers, he stood up and declared: "I believe in states' rights."

In the white South the event was a triumph. Everywhere else it was a disaster, reawakening all the old fears of Reagan's extremism. Patricia Harris, the first black woman appointed to the cabinet, claimed that whenever Reagan spoke, blacks "will see the specter of a white sheet behind him." Coretta Scott King wondered whether a Reagan victory would mean that "we are going to see more of the Ku Klux Klan and a resurgence of the Nazi Party." White liberals were no less alarmed. "Reagan croons, in love accents, his permission to indulge a functional hatred of poor people and blacks," the commentator Garry Wills told the readers of *Esquire*.[7]

But the Neshoba affair was a textbook example of Reagan's extraordinary ambiguity. At one level, it was a simple case of a conservative candidate using racially charged code words to appeal to white Southerners. On the other hand, Reagan hardly needed to sell himself to white voters in Mississippi, and his handlers were furious with him. The fuss completely overshadowed his speech to the National Urban League later that day, in which the candidate denied that he was "anti-black and anti-disadvantaged," and it undermined his efforts to paint himself as a reasonable man. What Reagan really needed to do was to win over floating voters in industrial states, and Wirthlin's polls showed that the Neshoba episode hurt him among moderate white voters in Illinois, Ohio, and Pennsylvania, who had no desire to vote for another George Wallace.

Finally, there is no evidence that Reagan had an ounce of prejudice in his body. He was consistently blind to racial nuances, but he never showed the slightest personal intolerance. As a sports announcer he had opposed the segregation of professional baseball; as an actor he resigned from a country club that excluded Jews; as governor of California he appointed more black officials than all his predecessors put together. In this context, the Neshoba episode looks less like a cynical masterstroke and more like a thoughtless blunder by a candidate who did not understand the signifi-cance of his words and their setting.[8]

Neshoba set the stage for an extraordinary succession of gaffes. Some grew out of the tension between Reagan's conservative instincts and the need to fight a more centrist campaign, such as when he told the Veterans of Foreign Wars that Vietnam had been "a noble cause." Then there was his penchant for exaggeration, such as his claim that the New Deal had been inspired by fascism, which contained a tiny grain of truth (since there were slight similarities with corporatist experiments in Europe) but was a reckless thing to say publicly. Worse was his remark at the Michigan State Fair, where, tired after trudging through the sweltering fairground, he lashed out at Carter for opening his campaign in Tuscumbia, Alabama, "the city that gave birth to and is the parent body of the Ku Klux Klan." Not only was this factually wrong; it was a terrible error of judgment. "I blew it," Reagan told his aides afterward. "I should never have said what I said."[9]

His most famous gaffe, though, came in Ohio, where his eagerness to impress local steelworkers carried him into the realms of fantasy. After denouncing environmental regulations, Reagan insisted that trees caused more pollution than cars and factories. "Decaying vegetation," he said, released "93 percent of the oxides of nitrogen" in the atmosphere: true enough, but he had mixed up nitrous oxide, given off by plants, with nitro-gen dioxide, a toxic compound produced by car engines and power sta-tions. Finally, he rounded off a memorable performance by claiming that winds blowing across the Santa Barbara oil slicks had "purified the air and prevented the spread of infectious diseases," an incredible remark from a man who had been California's governor at the time of the terrible oil spill.

Not surprisingly, his comments caused great amusement among the press corps. "Mr. Reagan v. Nature," read the title of an editorial in *The Washington Post*. "Smog, smog," demonstrators chanted at him for days afterward, while at one campaign stop a tree displayed the sign: CHOP ME DOWN BEFORE I KILL AGAIN. Even his own staff could not resist joking at his expense: as Reagan's plane flew over a forest fire a few days later, his speechwriter Ken Khachigian looked out and said solemnly: "Killer trees."[10]

Eventually, Reagan got his act together. His aides banned him from making unscripted asides and kept reporters as far away from the candidate as possible. Crucially, Nancy Reagan asked Stuart Spencer, who had run his campaigns in California, to come aboard, and he impressed on Reagan the virtue of self-discipline. But his lead had evaporated: on September 14 a *Washington Post* poll showed Reagan and Carter in a dead heat. A week later, *The New York Times* gave Carter a three-point lead, and a foregone conclusion had turned into a nail-biter. "I have this terrible feeling," a Reagan aide told *The Wall Street Journal*, "we're about to snatch defeat from the jaws of victory."[11]

Reagan's gaffes were so damaging because they played on his existing weaknesses. As Wirthlin had already warned, he was bound "to be pictured as a simplistic and untried lightweight (Dumb), a person who consciously misuses facts to overblow his own record (Deceptive), and, if president, one who would be too anxious to engage our country in a nuclear holocaust (Dangerous)." Yet he never seemed to take it personally; indeed, reporters were surprised by his good spirits. On the plane, he found it easy to unwind, cuddling up with his wife, relaxing with his beloved comics, always ready with a funny story. Even skeptical newspapermen found it hard to dislike him. He was "a nice guy, a happy secure person who likes himself and most other people," concluded a *Washington Post* profile. "He radiates traditional American values," agreed the editor of the liberal *Nation*. "He is not a hater. He likes people. He appears to feel there is good in almost everyone. He is a very secure man; what you see is what he is."[12]

While Reagan saw himself as the quintessential Hollywood hero, the cowboy riding in to sort out the town, Jimmy Carter could have played the personification of Gloom in some bleak Scandinavian film. Reagan offered "the kind of leadership that makes Americans feel good about their country," remarked Nixon's old friend Len Garment, while "Carter conveys a sense of self-flagellation, of guilt about our power and our past." The physical contrast seemed to say it all. Carter was "puny" and "weak"; Reagan was "strong" and "manly." Carter had allowed American hus-bands and fathers to be taken prisoner by Iranian fanatics; Reagan was the traditional father who would restore masculine authority. That Carter was a devoted husband, strict father, and Christian family man, and that Reagan was a non-churchgoing Hollywood divorcé, whose own children complained about his lack of paternal care, were neither here nor there.[13]

The other great benefit of Reagan's style was that it allowed him to say things that would otherwise have sounded terrifying. Even when he turned his guns on "welfare queens," his personal affability meant that he escaped serious criticism. And all the time he pounded relentlessly at Jimmy Carter's record, the softest target of all. In this respect, the cam-paign looked like a replay of 1932, when Hoover's economic record had been so dismal that few noticed the inconsistencies of Roosevelt's rem-edies. "A recession is when your neighbor loses his job," Reagan joked at a Labor Day picnic in Jersey City. "A depression is when you lose yours. And recovery is when Jimmy Carter loses his!"[14]

Yet Carter was nothing if not a fighter, and he was not prepared to take the criticism lying down. From the beginning of the campaign, his advis-ers had recognized that he could hardly run on his record, so Hamilton Jordan devised a campaign that would "make Reagan the issue." Since almost half of all voters feared that Reagan would get the country into a third world war, it was a good idea. The problem, though, was that Carter was apt to go just a little too far. Four years before, he had got away with low jabs at Scoop Jackson and Hubert Humphrey, but as president he was held to higher standards. Even the DNC executive director implored Hamilton Jordan to stop the president crossing the line, warning that he was hearing "more and more about Jimmy Carter having a 'mean streak' behind his smile."[15]

Yet Carter did not listen, perhaps because he was desperate to land a blow on the challenger, or simply because negative campaigning had worked so well for him in the past. On September 16 he spoke to a black congregation in Atlanta, criticizing Reagan for opposing the 1964 Civil Rights Act (which Carter himself had not publicly supported) and warn-ing darkly of "the stirrings of hate and the rebirth of code words like 'states' rights.' " On October 6, speaking at a fund-raiser in Chicago, he warned that Reagan would drive the nation into an undeclared civil war. "You'll determine whether or not this America will be unified," Carter told his audience, "or, if I lose the election, whether Americans might be separated, black from white, Jew from Christian, North from South, rural from urban." Partisan listeners applauded; among the press, however, there were gasps of disbelief. When Jody Powell came out afterward to talk to reporters, he looked "thunderstruck."[16]

"I can't be angry," Reagan told reporters the next day, wearing his best wounded-but-magnanimous look. "I'm saddened that anyone, particularly someone who has held that position, could intimate such a thing." A few days later, a television ad showed Nancy fighting back tears as she condemned Carter's "cruel" attack. The press coverage, which drew the inevitable contrast with Carter's old promises about love and compassion, was unanimous. His statements, said *The New Republic*, were "frightful distortions, bordering on outright lies." One *Boston Globe* columnist joked that Carter's "darker side" emerged in election years as surely as "the werewolf grows long fangs" during a full moon. Most biting of all, however, was the verdict of *The Washington Post*, which remarked that Carter had a "miserable record of personally savaging political opponents (Hubert Humphrey, Edward Kennedy) whenever the going got rough." The president evidently had "few limits," said the *Post*, "beyond which he will not go in the abuse of opponents and reconstruction of history."[17]

For voters unimpressed by Reagan's gaffes and Carter's rhetoric, there was a third choice: John Anderson, the retiring Republican congressman from Illinois, who had finished well behind Reagan in the primaries and decided to run as an independent. Although his sober suits and thick glasses made him look more like a bank manager than a leader of men, Anderson was an appealingly independent-minded politician. Liberal Rockefeller Republicans had been an increasingly rare breed since the late 1960s, either dying off or defecting to the Democrats as the Grand Old Party's center of gravity shifted to the conservative South and West. But unlike some of his colleagues, Anderson refused to swim with the tide. Instead of making a secret of his moderation, he turned it into his raison d'être, standing on a platform of urban regeneration, mass transit, gun restrictions, and a hike on gasoline taxes. He was also an evangelical Protestant, but to the horror of religious conservatives he not only backed the ERA but argued that the federal government should finance abortion for the poor. His economic agenda, meanwhile, included a balanced budget and no tax cuts—the latter a sign of his independence in a year when tax cuts were all the rage.[18]

With his cerebral style, dry wit, and unconventional platform, Anderson appealed to the "brie-and-Chablis" set, the kinds of people who lived in college towns and leafy suburbs in Massachusetts, Minnesota, and Washington state, the forerunners of the Birkenstock liberals of the first decade of the twenty-first century. "She drives a Volvo," Jack Germond and Jules Witcover wrote in a satirical portrait of the "typical" Anderson supporter. "When she attends a League of Women Voters coffee, she selects a prune Danish on purpose. She thinks wine-and-cheese parties are 'great fun.' " A few days later, they had a letter from a female Anderson fan who lived in a Portland suburb, drove a Volvo, was president of the local League of Women Voters, and had eaten a Danish at a league meeting the day before, although not a prune one. "Do you know me?" she asked in wonder.[19]

When Anderson announced his candidacy in May, his poll standing was over 25 percent. On campuses his name was everywhere. Feminists liked him, *The New Republic* endorsed him, and the *Doonesbury* cartoonist, Garry Trudeau, affectionately teased his shoestring campaign. But as the race tightened, his support fell away, leaving a rump of former Democrats and liberal true believers, the kinds of people who had been madly for Adlai and clean for Gene. In the end, Anderson won just six million votes and 7 percent of the total and did not carry a single precinct. Paul Newman, Kurt Vonnegut, Gore Vidal, Norman Lear, and Arthur Schlesinger voted for him, as did Jacqueline Onassis. At least he could console himself that he had attracted a glamorous crowd.[20]

**With the hostages** still in Tehran, the newspapers full of economic gloom, and Reagan aiming at his own feet, the election seemed impossible to call. Most observers agreed that if the hostages came home, Carter would make it; on the other hand, would Anderson take more votes from the president or the challenger? When the League of Women Voters arranged a debate for September 21 and invited Anderson to join the two major candidates, Carter refused to turn up. Fifty million Americans watched Reagan and Anderson discussing their differences amid a lot of jokes at the absent president's expense. But Carter's position seemed vindicated when Anderson's support continued to fall, and in the middle of October the president began to pull clear.[21]

On October 14, Wirthlin's polls put Carter ahead by two points. In the Reagan camp, all was consternation. "I'm going to have to debate that guy," Reagan told Stuart Spencer. Having a one-on-one debate so close to polling day was an enormous gamble: if Reagan made one of his gaffes, he could blow the election. But he was losing momentum; unless he debated, it might be all over anyway. Of course there was always the possibility that Carter would refuse the challenge. But he had already said that he would take Reagan on, and his pride would not let him back down. Besides, most of Carter's aides were confident that he would wipe the floor with "an elderly former actor," as Jordan put it. It was their biggest mistake of the campaign.[22]

The debate was scheduled for Tuesday, October 28, seven days before the nation voted. Never had there been a later meeting of the two main candidates; never had so much been riding on one confrontation. Yet during Reagan's dress rehearsal, with Carter played by the intense young congressman David Stockman, the governor fell apart. His performance was "miserable," Stockman recalled. "I was shocked. He couldn't fill up the time. His answers weren't long enough. And what time he could fill, he filled with woolly platitudes." Driving home, a depressed Stockman could hardly believe it. On economic matters, Reagan "had only the foggiest idea of what supply-side was all about," while none of his aides "had any more idea." But it was too late now; the showdown was at hand.[23]

An estimated hundred million people, the largest audience for a political event in history, were watching on television as Jimmy Carter and Ronald Reagan faced each other in Cleveland's historic Music Hall. This was the big one, a clash of philosophies tipped to be the most decisive debate in presidential history. "It has become the world heavyweight championship and the Super Bowl combined," wrote Elizabeth Drew; "the only thing missing is Howard Cosell." Before the cameras were switched on, the two contenders took their positions behind their lecterns. The president seemed stiff, nervous, his eyes puffy, his face taut with tension. The challenger, as always, looked younger than his sixty-nine years: tall, handsome, determined. Before they started, he strode across to Carter and held out his hand, a gesture that clearly took the president by surprise, and that brought home the difference in stature, and in confidence, between them.[24]

From the outset, Reagan went out of his way to play down his supposed extremism. "I'm only here to tell you that I believe with all my heart that our first priority must be world peace," he said in his very first answer. While Carter talked about arms control, nuclear proliferation, and relations with the Soviet Union, Reagan stuck to his theme. "I have seen four wars in my lifetime. I'm a father of sons; I have a grandson," he said calmly. "I don't ever want to see another generation of young Americans bleed their lives into sandy beachheads in the Pacific, or rice paddies and jungles in Asia, or the muddy battlefields of Europe."[25]

As time went on, Reagan's emphasis on peace—a trick from Nixon's playbook—clearly frustrated his opponent. Carter repeatedly mentioned his experience and moderation, using the words "Oval Office" and calling Reagan's policies "disturbing," but he never landed a telling blow. Perhaps this was why, after an exchange about the SALT treaty, he tried a new line of attack. "I had a discussion with my daughter, Amy, the other day, before I came here, to ask her what the most important issue was," he said earnestly. "She said she thought nuclear weaponry—and the control of nuclear arms." It sounded like a shameless bid for public sympathy—assuming, that is, that Amy did not really determine her father's nuclear policy—and Carter's aides were horrified. "Oh my God, not that!" exclaimed Jerry Rafshoon. "It's so bad that it's funny."[26]

Reagan, meanwhile, was visibly gaining in confidence. When the president accused him of having opposed Medicare, Reagan merely shook his head and said, half-laughing, half-sorrowful: "There you go again." Actually, Carter had made a perfectly good point. But in his affable way, Reagan had neatly demonstrated the temperamental gulf between them. After Carter had closed with some earnest remarks about his experience, Reagan ended with a peroration that would live long in political legend. When voters stood in the polling booth, he said, they should ask themselves five simple questions:

> Are you better off than you were four years ago? Is it easier for you to go and buy things in the stores than it was four years ago? Is there more or less unemployment in the country than there was four years ago? Is America as respected throughout the world as it was? Do you feel that our security is as safe, that we're as strong as we were four years ago?

It was the work of his speechwriter David Gergen, and it was unanswerable. It turned the election into a referendum on Carter's record, a vote that the president could never win. And Carter's aides knew it. "He's a goddamn actor," someone muttered backstage. "And a good one," Jordan said quietly.[27]

In the next day's papers, many analysts suggested that Carter's command of detail had carried the day. But this missed the point of the debate, which was less about substance than about style. By standing toe-to-toe with the president and coming across as serious and reasonable, Reagan had done exactly what he needed to do. *Newsweek* crowned him the winner by 34 percent to 26 percent, and Harris gave him the victory by 44 percent to 26 percent. Plausibility and charm, as so often, mattered more than intensity and detail.[28]

What the effect would be, however, nobody could tell. The polls remained extraordinarily tight. Gallup had Reagan three points clear; Harris gave him a five-point lead; *Newsweek* and *The Washington Post* had Carter ahead by one point. Among "likely" voters, however, Gallup had the president six points clear, while Caddell's polls suggested that

Democrats were "coming home" to Carter. "Never in the forty-five-year history of presidential election surveys," declared George Gallup, "has the Gallup poll found such volatility and uncertainty."[29]

Reagan seemed in uncommonly good form during the final weekend, rolling oranges down the aisle of his plane every time they took off and bantering with reporters about the number of times they photographed him in the act. When they pointed out that one day he might have to autograph the pictures for well-wishers, he joked that he would have plenty of time. "You know," he said with a grin, "after you've canceled Social Security and started the war, what else is there for you to do?" There was good reason for his high spirits. Unknown to the press, Wirthlin's polls now showed Reagan with a lead of between nine and eleven points. It was far too early to be celebrating, but if nothing changed, he was going to win.[30]

If nothing changed. That was the Reagan camp's greatest fear, that just before the election Carter would appear on television, grinning behind the Oval Office desk, with the news that the hostages were coming home. Ever since the convention, Reagan's campaign manager, William Casey, had been muttering about an "October Surprise" that would throw the election to the Democrats. "We were really scared to death, because we didn't know how it would play," Lyn Nofziger said later. In fact, Wirthlin's projections suggested that if the hostages came home, the result would be a ten-point bounce, handing Carter the election. The euphoria "would have rolled over the land like a tidal wave," thought Michael Deaver. "Carter would have been a hero, and many of the complaints against him forgotten. He would have won."[31]

A popular conspiracy theory holds that the Reagan campaign struck a secret deal with the ayatollahs, encouraging them to hold on to the hostages until after Election Day, while Reagan promised to sell them arms through Israel. It is hard, though, to see why the Iranians would do business with the hawkish Reagan. In any case, they tried to interest Carter in a complicated new deal on the last weekend of the campaign; why would they bother, if they had already reached an agreement with the Republicans? Not surprisingly, a Senate investigation found no evidence of a plot; neither did a hugely detailed House report, the chairman concluding that most of the "witnesses" were "wholesale fabricators." Independent investigations in *Newsweek*, *The New Republic*, and the *Village Voice*, meanwhile, came to the same conclusion. That the Iranians held on to the hostages suggests not some dastardly conspiracy but their sheer contempt for the man who had once called himself the Shah's great friend.[32]

Meanwhile, Carter still hoped for a last-gasp breakthrough. The morning of Saturday, November 1, found him in Houston, where he rose at six and went for a three-mile run with his Secret Service agents. Always pushing himself, always running, he flew from Houston to Brownsville, Abilene, San Antonio, and Fort Worth, and then on to Milwaukee, and finally to Chicago. Even after he had retired to his suite at the airport Hyatt, his mind was racing. Thousands of miles to the east, the Iranian parliament was meeting to discuss the terms of a hostage deal. Carter had already given instructions that if there was any major news, he wanted to fly back to Washington immediately. Now he sat in his suite and waited. Just before four, the phone rang. The Iranians had issued their terms. An hour later, while Chicago was sleeping, Carter's motorcade swept out of the Hyatt toward the military gate at O'Hare Airport.[33]

"I will never forget the flight back to Washington," Carter recalled later, "heading eastward into the rising sun." As Air Force One streaked toward the dawn, he went into the cockpit to admire "one of the most beautiful sunrises I have ever seen." In a quiet moment alone he prayed, asking that "the Iranian nightmare would soon be over, and that my judgment and my decisions might be wise ones"; then he joined Powell and Jordan for eggs and bacon. The Republicans, said Powell gleefully, "won't know how to handle a November surprise." Carter shook his head and allowed himself a moment of wonder that the election might be decided "not in Michigan or Pennsylvania or New York—but in Iran."[34]

And then—disappointment. As Carter stepped out onto the South Lawn, Brzezinski was waiting with the news that there had been no breakthrough after all. The Iranians were offering nothing new: they wanted him to cancel all American claims against Iran, release their frozen assets, hand back the Shah's millions, and promise never to interfere in Iranian affairs. When the networks broke into their football coverage later that day, Carter looked "somber and weary." The Iranian decision, he told the nation, was a "significant development," but there was no chance of the hostages being released immediately. "I wish that I could predict when the hostages will return," he said gloomily. "I cannot."[35]


**Monday, November 3:** the last day before the polls opened and the American people decided. It was almost exactly a year since the Iranian students had stormed the American embassy in Tehran. In a coincidence too perfect for fiction, Election Day would be the first anniversary of the embassy takeover.

For Jimmy Carter, there was one last effort. He left Washington early that morning, flying to Akron, Ohio, to shore up his blue-collar vote, then down to St. Louis and across the Mississippi for a speech in Granite City, Illinois. Then Springfield, Missouri; then Detroit; then west to Portland and Seattle; then back to the place it had all begun, Plains, Georgia, to cast his vote on Election Day. Nobody could ever accuse him of not working hard, and on this last day he pushed himself further than ever, his voice hoarse, his eyes red with exhaustion. To his aides, he seemed quietly confident. That morning, Caddell had reported that Saturday night's polls had him tied with Reagan, perhaps even slightly ahead. Now, Caddell said, he needed to win back blue-collar Democrats tempted by Reagan's promise of new leadership. "I think you should make a plea this last day," Caddell said, "for Democrats to come home."[36]

Jimmy Carter had never sounded more like a Democrat than he did on that last day. No man who opposed Social Security had the right to quote Franklin D. Roosevelt, he said; no man who criticized the minimum wage had the right to quote Harry Truman; no man who opposed arms control had the right to quote John Kennedy; "and no man who campaigned around this nation against Medicare and called it socialism has any right to quote Lyndon Baines Johnson."

"I come here to you as a Democrat, a man proud to be a Democrat," he said. "I believe in the heritage and the mission of the Democratic Party, the heritage and the mission of Franklin Delano Roosevelt, the heritage and the mission of Harry S. Truman, the heritage and the mission of John Fitzgerald Kennedy, the heritage and the mission of Lyndon Baines Johnson. Think back in your own lives what these men have meant to you." He ended with Robert Kennedy's words in Los Angeles on the day he was killed: "I ask you to recognize the hard and difficult road to a better America. The people must decide this election. I ask you to vote for yourselves. For your sake, and for the sake of your children, vote."[37]

As Carter's plane streaked west through the darkening sky, the networks were showing the two main candidates' final appeals to the American people. Carter's speech, recorded a week before, was a classic incumbent's appeal based on his experience of making tough decisions, ending with another attempt to reclaim Roosevelt's legacy. But Reagan's address, taped earlier that day in Peoria, Illinois, was something more: a defiant rejection of the idea of limits, and a stirring evocation of the American Dream. He talked with misty eyes about the first settlers who set out to build a city on a hill, about the astronauts killed in the conquest of space, about the Chicago Cubs outfielder who grabbed an American flag from demonstrators at Dodger Stadium, prompting the crowd to rise and sing "God Bless America."

He recalled Arthur Fiedler and the Boston Pops playing their bicentennial concert on that memorable Fourth of July night, when the nation had come together to celebrate its birthday. And he asked:

Does history still have a place for America, for her people, for her great ideals? There are some who answer, "No," that our energy is spent, our days of greatness at an end, that a great national malaise is upon us. I find no national malaise. I find nothing wrong with the American people . . .

Last year I lost a friend who was more than a symbol of the Hollywood dream industry. To millions he was a symbol of the country itself. Duke Wayne did not believe our country was ready for the dustbin of history. Just before his death he said in his blunt way, "Just give the American people a good cause and there's nothing they can't lick."

"Let us resolve tonight," Reagan concluded, gazing earnestly into the camera, that "they will say of our day and of our generation, we did keep faith with our God, that we did act worthy of ourselves, that we did protect and pass on lovingly that shining city on a hill. Thank you, and goodnight."[38]

**When the phone rang,** Hamilton Jordan's first thought was "Hostages." It was two in the morning, eastern time. As he shook himself awake, he realized that it was Pat Caddell. "Ham!" the voice said excitedly, and Jordan's heart leaped. And then the voice said, "Ham, it's all over—it's gone!" and reality came crashing down.

"The sky has fallen in," Caddell gabbled. "We are getting murdered . . . I've never seen anything like it in polling. Here we are neck and neck with Reagan up until the very end and everything breaks against us." "What do you mean, breaks against us?" Jordan asked. "It's going to be a big Reagan victory, Ham," Caddell said, "in the range of eight to ten points." Jordan said nothing, for there was nothing to say. It had all gone, everything they had worked for—broken, smashed, vanished in an instant.

An hour later, the phone rang on Air Force One, where Jody Powell was waiting for the president to finish his Seattle speech. "Jody, brace yourself," the voice began. When Powell put down the phone, he poured himself a stiff drink. Then he walked into the hangar, where the president was still speaking. "There's not a single person listening to my voice that can't contact at least 50 or 100 people between now and the time the polls close tomorrow," Carter was saying, to huge applause. At the end, one of his advance men put on a tape of his old campaign song, "Why Not the

Best?" and it looked to some people as though Carter had a tear in his eye. Rarely had he seemed so charged with emotion. In the background, Powell stepped into the night rain and lit a cigarette.

It was not until Carter had returned to the plane, where he found Powell back on the phone to Caddell, that he heard the news. Before his press secretary could explain, Carter had taken the phone and said cheerfully: "What's happening, Patrick?" Caddell took a deep breath. "Mr. President," he said, "I'm afraid it's gone." There was a long silence. "It was like the air went out of the whole conversation," Caddell said later. They should probably work out something to tell the crowd in Plains, he added nervously. "You all talk to Jody and work something out," Carter said, his voice suddenly totally devoid of emotion. "I'm going to try and get some sleep."[39]

Air Force One landed in Georgia just before seven, in the thick fog of a November morning. Election Day had come at last. When Jimmy Carter climbed out of his limousine outside Plains High School, his face matched the weather: gray, gloomy, his eyes red and tired, his smile thin. Talking to reporters, he said only that he hoped to win; when one of them reminded him that he had not yet come out with his trademark preelection phrase, he said flatly: "Okay, I don't expect to lose. Right on."

At the old railroad depot, the scene of his victory celebrations four years before, Carter seemed too exhausted even for emotion. The same crowd of friends and neighbors was waiting excitedly for their favorite son; this time, however, he seemed on automatic pilot, giving them his routine stump speech. Only at the end did his eyes fill with tears as he thanked all those who had "gone all over the nation to speak for me and shake hands with people in other states, to tell them that you have confidence in me and that I would not disappoint them if I became president." His voice broke for a moment, and he lowered his eyes to the ground. "God bless you. Thank you," he said. "Don't forget to vote."[40]

It was a cold, overcast day on the East Coast. In Brooklyn, once a Democratic stronghold, the sociologist Jonathan Rieder found only three people in the first hour of voting who were willing to admit supporting the president. "I just don't trust Carter," said an Italian who had just voted for Ronald Reagan. "I voted last time on trust, and look where it got me." He shook his head. "Carter is not aggressive enough. The whole world shits on the United States, and we do nothing about it. We need to get our prestige back."

As millions of people made their way to their local polling stations, the rain grew heavier. In the West, it was a lovely clear day; in the East, rain pounded down as the afternoon dark drew in. At the local Democratic clubhouse, Rieder found that the mood was as black as the skies, volunteers reporting that their voters were simply not turning out. But in Beverly Hills, the Reagan team was already preparing to celebrate. The day before, Wirthlin's computers had issued their last prediction: a ten-point victory for the challenger. At eleven the next morning, he told Reagan's men to draft his victory speech. But the candidate was not declaring victory just yet. Casting his vote in the sunshine of Pacific Palisades, Reagan joked that he had voted for Nancy.[41]

This time there would be no agonizing wait. In the past, networks had waited until the votes had partially been counted before projecting a winner, but NBC's executives were so confident in their exit polls that they were ready to project immediately. So at one minute past seven on the East Coast, even as people were still voting in forty-four states, John Chancellor announced that Ronald Reagan was heading for "a very substantial victory" and called Indiana, Mississippi, and Florida for the challenger. Half an hour later, Chancellor added Alabama, Virginia, Ohio, and Kentucky to the Republican column. The show had been on the air for just half an hour, and it was all over already. By eight o'clock, Reagan had picked up Connecticut, New Jersey, Pennsylvania, Michigan, Illinois, North Dakota, South Dakota, Kansas, Missouri, Tennessee, Oklahoma, and Texas, a sea of blue on the NBC map surrounding a forlorn island of red in Carter's home state. "This isn't an election," wrote Elizabeth Drew, her eyes glued to the television in disbelief, "it's an earthquake."

Incredibly, Reagan already had 261 electoral votes, just 9 short of victory. "Well, the time has come," Chancellor said. "NBC News now makes its projection for the presidency." It was just 8:15 p.m., and millions of Americans, in the afternoon sunshine of the West Coast, were still waiting to vote. The screen turned blue, the words "REAGAN ELECTED" flashing in white. "Ronald Wilson Reagan, of California, a sports announcer, a film actor, governor of California, is our projected winner at 8:15 Eastern Standard Time on this election night."[42]

In Pacific Palisades, where the afternoon air was still warm and the sky clear and bright, the polls would not close for another two hours. Ronald Reagan was in the shower when, through the steam, he saw Nancy coming into the bathroom. Swathed in towels, she shouted that there was someone on the telephone. "It's Jimmy Carter," she said. Reagan turned off the shower, shook water from his hair, and reached for a towel. Then he picked up the extension, while Nancy stood by his side, her eyes fixed on her husband. Reagan said nothing, just listened. Finally, he said, "Thank you, Mr. President," and hung up. He turned to his wife and said simply: "He conceded."

"Standing in my bathroom with a towel wrapped around me, my hair dripping with water," Reagan wrote later, "I had just learned I was going to be the fortieth president of the United States."[43]

**Ronald Reagan won** forty-four states and 489 electoral votes, leaving Carter and Mondale with only six states and the District of Columbia. In Congress, the Republicans made astonishing inroads, picking up thirty-three seats in the House, their biggest gain in fourteen years, and winning a Senate majority for the first time since 1954. Among the casualties were some of liberalism's most familiar and respected names: Birch Bayh in Indiana, Gaylord Nelson in Wisconsin, Frank Church in Idaho, and George McGovern in South Dakota, hammered by the National Conservative PAC and the Moral Majority for his positions on abortion, defense, and the Panama Canal. The heart had been ripped out of the Democratic Party.

For Democrats, the election returns made for appalling reading. Reagan had won half the blue-collar vote and a plurality of white union members. He won the Catholic vote, the Irish vote, the Italian vote, the Polish and Slavic votes. He won the independent vote and the moderate vote; he won every demographic group except for black Americans, the very youngest, the very poorest, and the least educated. Even in the South, he picked up 61 percent of the vote, a landmark in the region's political history and a shocking humiliation for his Georgian opponent. While some analysts pointed to a growing gender gap, with Reagan winning 54 percent of the male vote and only 46 percent of the female vote, he still won more women's votes than Jimmy Carter—a stunning reversal for a president who had worked so hard for the ERA.[44]

In the South, as elsewhere, many observers thought that cultural issues had won the day for Reagan. Jerry Falwell claimed that his troops had given Reagan his two-to-one margin of victory among white evangelicals and had therefore "elected" the president. But even if born-again Christians had stuck with Carter, the Republican candidate would still have won. In any case, evangelicals had been voting for Republican candidates for years, since many were white Southerners drawn to the Grand Old Party for economic reasons. If the Moral Majority had never existed, they probably would have voted for Reagan anyway.[45]

But the Moral Majority did have an impact. Studies suggested that it had helped to boost registration and turnout in evangelical areas, while *The New York Times* noted that "thousands of fundamentalist Protestant churches" had become "political centers for Mr. Reagan and other Republican candidates." And then, of course, there was money. In 1979–80, the Republican National Committee raised around $40 million to the Democrats' $4 million. With independent New Right groups spending millions more, the Democrats always faced an uphill battle. The National Conservative PAC spent almost $1 million on negative advertising; according to one estimate, its targets typically faced two hundred television ads a week, often on subjects such as abortion, homosexuality, and family values. With liberal candidates having relatively limited funds to run ads of their own, it was hardly surprising that they found it so difficult to fight back.[46]

But behind all the talk of Reagan Democrats and the Moral Majority, of culture wars and electoral realignment, one fact attracted rather less attention. With almost one in two eligible voters refusing to cast a ballot, turnout was simply atrocious.* For all the talk of a Reagan landslide, it is worth remembering that barely one in four Americans actually voted for him. The fact that so many people preferred to stay at home, even at a time of economic crisis and international tension, spoke volumes about the pervasive disillusionment of the 1970s. Perhaps this was the ultimate verdict on the decade, the fact that more Americans voted for nobody at all than voted for the winner. The political scientist Walter Dean Burnham called it "the largest mass movement of our time"—a movement of people who, when asked to pronounce between Reagan, Carter, and Anderson, simply refused to choose.[47]

**"At Last!"** read a banner headline in the conservative journal *Human Events* the week after the election. November 1980, it explained, marked the end of a chapter in American history. "Basically, the New Deal died yesterday," agreed Paul Tsongas, the young Democratic senator from Massachusetts. To have any chance of surviving, "liberalism must extricate itself from the 1960s" and "find a new rationale." If it failed, he said, "then the last meeting of liberals will inevitably be held in an old people's home."[48]

Was liberalism finished? In some ways it certainly seemed like it. Having put their faith in economic growth for so long, liberals had never come up with coherent answers to the stagflation of the 1970s, which pitted class against class, put a brake on rising living standards, and drastically curtailed government's ability to tax and spend. Polls showed that

---

*It is worth noting, though, that turnout has been consistently wretched ever since. Whatever else Ronald Reagan accomplished in office, he did not manage to persuade more Americans to become involved in politics.

68 percent of voters thought their taxes were too high, while half agreed that the power of government was too strong. Inflation, unemployment, crime, taxes, delinquency, abortion, homosexuality, feminism, Vietnam, and Iran all seemed to be pushing the electorate into the arms of the Republicans. In places like industrial Macomb County, outside Detroit, union members had defected in overwhelming numbers to Reagan's banner, many blaming taxes, crime, and busing. Abroad, too, the center-left seemed in disarray. In Britain, Margaret Thatcher's conservative revolution had been under way for more than a year, while in Canada and West Germany, Brian Mulroney and Helmut Kohl were on the brink of power. "Everywhere we look in the world," Reagan told his British soul mate, "the cult of the state is dying."[49]

Yet it is surely wrong to think of 1980 as a conservative realignment when fewer than one in three voters described themselves as "conservative" and when only one in ten Reagan voters said they had been swayed by the candidate's ideology. Polls showed that most Americans still believed in activist government. The vast majority still supported Social Security and Medicare; most still supported abortion and the Equal Rights Amendment; and most were moving toward more liberal positions on race, homosexuality, and women's rights. Indeed, for all the talk of a "Reagan revolution," only 22 percent of Americans supported a federal tax cut, only 36 percent supported cuts in domestic spending, and only 19 percent opposed a new arms deal with the Soviet Union. Most people remained smack in the middle of the ideological spectrum. "There was no party realignment in 1980," said Reagan's pollster Richard Wirthlin, who knew what he was talking about.[50]

Conservative writers often treat Reagan's victory as the inevitable culmination of years of hard work. George Will, for example, quipped that Barry Goldwater won the 1964 election, but it took sixteen years to count the votes. But the reality is more complicated. There was no natural progression from Joseph McCarthy and Barry Goldwater to Ronald Reagan and George W. Bush. Conservatism suffered more than its fair share of false starts, and Reagan's rise to power was smoothed by one unlikely contingency after another: the fall of Richard Nixon, the self-destruction of Edward Kennedy, the primary victories of Gerald Ford, the blunders of Jimmy Carter, the Iranian hostage crisis, the botched rescue mission. If things had worked out differently, then Reagan could easily have spent the 1980s in retirement in Los Angeles. Indeed, given the economic circumstances, it is striking that the election remained so close until the end. Although the map made it look like a landslide, Reagan won only

51 percent of the vote. If just two in every hundred voters had changed their minds, Carter would have won eleven more states and 124 more electoral votes.[51]

The real story of 1980 was not Reagan's victory but Carter's defeat. In a *Time* magazine poll, two out of three voters agreed that the election was "mostly a rejection of President Carter." And the single most important issue was not abortion, crime, or even Iran but the economy—which is why Reagan's "Are you better off than you were four years ago?" refrain struck such a chord. No incumbent had ever won reelection with such a terrible economic record. "We never had a chance of winning that campaign," Hamilton Jordan admitted many years later. "It was only ultimately a nagging doubt about Ronald Reagan that kept that race close up until the final days."[52]

Every president has his successes, and Carter's admirers later pointed to the Camp David Accords as evidence of his leadership skills. To hold him solely responsible for the soaring inflation and interest rates of the late 1970s, meanwhile, is ridiculous. He could no more keep down world prices than he could turn back the clock to a lost pre-globalization age of American trade supremacy, or keep a lid on the turbulent passions in revolutionary Iran. And in truth, many of his instincts were correct. He was right to emphasize fighting inflation, right to coax the economy toward gradual deregulation, right to urge Americans toward energy conservation, and right to see that global security depended upon a peaceful compromise in the Middle East.[53]

In some ways, Carter's problem was that he was ahead of his time, his blend of fiscal conservatism and southern populism anticipating Bill Clinton's appeal a decade later. But there was also more continuity with Ronald Reagan than is usually realized. It was Carter who insisted that big-government liberalism be consigned to history, launched the great wave of deregulation, and began cutting welfare budgets. It was Carter who lectured the Soviet leaders about human rights, began sending aid to the insurgents in Afghanistan, and asked for more defense spending to meet the challenge of a renewed Cold War. If, by some fluke, Carter had won in 1980, he would probably have taken the election as a mandate for confrontation abroad and conservatism at home. His reelection would not have been a victory of liberalism over Reaganism; it would have been the victory of Reaganism lite.[54]

The biggest difference would have been the man at the top. After all the debris had been cleared away, what was left was Jimmy Carter's utter failure as a national leader. It is a feeble excuse to say that he was undone by events beyond his control. All presidents have to cope with the pressure of events: the greatest Democratic hero of all, Franklin D. Roosevelt, showed that even the bleakest economic inheritance and most terrifying international challenges need not be obstacles to political success. But Carter was no Franklin Roosevelt. A stirring speaker who roused public passion, a shrewd operator who worked well with Congress, a dynamic administrator who set and stuck to clear goals, might have survived the tempest. Jimmy Carter was not that man.

Perhaps the most appropriate verdict came a year after Carter's defeat, from a labor leader who ranked him alongside Calvin Coolidge. "I consider his abilities mediocre, his actions pusillanimous, and his Administration a calamity for America's working people," he said. "Since an obelisk soaring 555 feet into the air symbolizes the nation's admiration and respect for George Washington, it would seem the only fitting memorial for Jimmy Carter would be a bottomless pit."[55]

# Washington, D.C., January 1981

We can and will resolve the problems which now confront us . . .
We are Americans.

**—RONALD REAGAN,** January 20, 1981

Jimmy Carter spent his last day in the White House slumped on an Oval Office sofa, waiting impatiently for news from Tehran. In the early hours of the morning, his officials had concluded a deal for the release of the hostages, handing over $8 billion in Iranian assets in return. His dearest hope was to have time to fly to West Germany, where the hostages would be housed in an American military hospital, before the inauguration. But his luck had run out long before. In the cruelest of twists, the Iranians rejected one of the crucial bank documents, and the transfer of funds had to begin all over again. Morning turned into afternoon, and his last chance disappeared.[1]

That night, his last in the White House, Carter sat hunched behind his desk, staring wordlessly at the ticking grandfather clock, his face haggard with tension. Occasionally he curled up on a couch, a blue blanket wrapped around his worn beige cardigan, his eyes fixed on the clock. Meticulous to the last, he made notes in a little pad at his side: the details of conversations, facts and figures from the bankers, or merely the time as his presidency drained away. He had rarely seemed more alone, bent over his pad, his tired eyes staring into the distance, his introverted figure uncannily reminiscent of another departing president almost six and a half years before.

At 6:35 a.m., Deputy Secretary of State Warren Christopher called to report that the transfer of funds had gone ahead. "That's great," Carter said quietly, his voice thick with fatigue, and called his wife to tell her the good news. As he waited, his photographer captured the scene for posterity: the president, bent forward on the Oval Office couch, his head resting on his hand, a picture of sleepless exhaustion; to his right, the shaggy-haired Hamilton Jordan, a study in disappointment and dejection; to his left, Lloyd Cutler, the White House counsel, tired but quizzical; finally, slumped in the corner chair, Vice President Mondale, his tie loosened, his suit rumpled, his face ravaged with weariness. It was no way to end a presidency, yet there was something cruelly appropriate about it.[2]

At seven, Carter asked an aide to call the president-elect, who was staying across the street at Blair House. A few moments later the aide reported that Reagan had asked not to be disturbed. "You're kidding," Carter said, rubbing his sore eyes in disbelief. It was true: Reagan was fast asleep, having told his aide Michael Deaver not to come over till eight. When Deaver arrived, Nancy was having her hair done. "Where's the governor?" Deaver asked. Without moving her head, she replied: "I guess he's still in bed." Chuckling, Deaver looked into the bedroom, where he could vaguely make out Reagan, wrapped up in blankets in the middle of the bed. "It's eight o'clock," Deaver said. "You're going to be inaugurated as President in a few hours." From the bundle of blankets, a sleepy voice came back: "Do I have to?"[3]

Reagan returned Carter's call at half past eight, and they talked for six or seven minutes. Afterward, Carter's aides asked: "What did he say?" "He mostly listened," Carter said, deadpan. "But when I finished, he said, 'What hostages?'" They all laughed, but it was not really a time for jokes. By now they had got confirmation that the hostages had been moved to the Tehran airport. But then: nothing. Even at 10:45, with only fifteen minutes until the Reagans arrived for coffee, Carter was still bent over his desk, unwashed and unshaven. Only after Rosalynn begged him to change did he rush over to the family quarters and throw on his formal morning suit. As he stared at his haggard face in the bathroom mirror, he wondered "if I had aged so much as President or whether I was just exhausted."[4]

As the limousine swept Carter and Reagan down Pennsylvania Avenue toward the Capitol, Carter could think of nothing but the hostages. Reagan was not unsympathetic; before leaving, he had instructed Deaver that if there was any news, he wanted to be told at once so that he could allow Carter to take the applause. But as they sat in the car, there was only a long, excruciating silence. Finally, Reagan began telling a couple of his favorite stories about the good old days in Hollywood under Jack Warner. While Reagan chuckled at his own punch lines, Carter struggled to raise a ghastly smile. "He kept talking about Jack Warner," he said afterward, despairing at the memory. "Who's Jack Warner?"[5]

Just before noon the two men walked out of the Capitol and onto the inaugural platform at the West Front. It was one of the warmest Inauguration Days in history, and the location deliberately broke with tradition, symbolizing a new direction under a man from the West. Reagan looked confident and cheerful in his $1,000 morning suit; Carter seemed uncomfortable and unhappy, shattered with disappointment. Just moments before, he had called Jordan one last time, but there was still no news. Now Jordan was following the ceremony on television. He watched as Reagan raised his right hand and intoned: "I, Ronald Reagan, do solemnly swear . . ." The picture cut to Carter, his eyes closed. "I wondered if he was sleeping or praying," Jordan recalled. "He looked pale, wrinkled, and very tired."[6]

As the new president began to deliver his inaugural address, Jordan's secretary hissed: "You've got to get out of here. The Reagans will be on their way." As he pounded up the stairs, Jordan realized that everything had changed. Already the pictures of Jimmy, Rosalynn, and Amy Carter were gone; in their places were images of Ronald and Nancy Reagan on horseback, grinning in the California sunshine. In the Oval Office, Reagan's men were stripping the bookcases of Carter's beloved biographies. With the boom of the cannon echoing around the deserted corridors, the White House curator poked his head around the door. "Oh, I see you've rearranged the furniture," he said. "I'm glad. I didn't like the president's—that is, the past arrangement. This is much better." He glanced at the busts of Washington, Franklin, and Truman. "If you don't like Mr. Truman," he added, "you can move Mr. Truman out." Then he walked over to the Cabinet Room, where aides were hoisting portraits of Coolidge and Eisenhower in place of Jefferson and Truman. "We're just putting it all back the way it was when Nixon and Ford were here," one of them explained.[7]

At the Capitol, the sun had broken through the clouds. Much of what Reagan was saying went back to his General Electric days: "Government is not the solution to our problem, government is the problem." But then his gaze turned to Arlington National Cemetery, with its rows of white markers, each a sign of "the price that has been paid for our freedom."

Under one such marker, he said, lay "a young man, Martin Treptow, who left his job in a small town barbershop in 1917 to go to France with the famed Rainbow Division."

When Treptow was killed, his comrades found a diary on his body. "On the flyleaf under the heading 'My Pledge,'" Reagan went on, "he had written these words: 'America must win this war. Therefore I will work, I will save, I will sacrifice, I will endure, I will fight cheerfully and do my utmost, as if the issue of the whole struggle depended on me alone.'" With the crowd listening in rapt attention, the new president drew the inevitable lesson, asking them to "believe in our capacity to perform great deeds, to believe that together with God's help we can and will resolve the problems which now confront us. And after all, why shouldn't we believe that? We are Americans."

Only later did reporters realize that Martin Treptow was not buried at Arlington at all. In reality, he lay beneath a granite slab in his hometown of Bloomer, Wisconsin. Reagan's speechwriter Ken Khachigian cheerfully took the blame. Not until many years later did he admit that he had always wanted to cut the story, only for Reagan to insist that it stay in. To Reagan, the moral symbolism was what mattered, not the factual truth.[8]

Jimmy Carter had slipped quietly away at the end of his successor's speech, already yesterday's man. A few hours later, a cold rain was falling as his helicopter landed at the Plains baseball field. On the platform erected in his honor, the red, white, and blue bunting hung limp and sodden, while bedraggled high-school bands played tunes of welcome. From the platform he thanked the crowd, and then, his voice almost breaking, he announced that "the aircraft carrying the fifty-two American hostages has cleared Iranian airspace." There were cheers of delight and a respectful silence as he remembered the men who had lost their lives in the rescue attempt. Finally, he thanked the American people, his family, and the people of Plains. "You've honored us," he said, "beyond anything imaginable as I walked the streets of this town to sell raw peanuts to the merchants in the stores here."[9]

But his journey was not quite over. The next morning, as rain continued to fall, Carter and his closest aides left for West Germany to greet the returned hostages. Carter looked old, Jordan thought, "as old and tired as I had ever seen him." They slept a little on the plane, but Carter spent most of the time studying photos of the prisoners and learning their names. There were real fears that the hostages might not want to see him, but when he walked into the Wiesbaden hospital room, the fifty-two gaunt men and women began to applaud. As he circled the room, most embraced him; almost all were crying.

Yet Jordan noticed that not all of them smiled when Carter addressed them. He had called them heroes, but few felt heroic, and some felt an indefinable sense of shame at their suffering and powerlessness. "Heroes? We're not heroes," one of the hostages, Charles Jones, told the press. "We're survivors. That's all. Just survivors."[10]

**Ronald Reagan announced** the hostages' release in the palatial surroundings of the Capitol Rotunda, the setting for his inauguration luncheon. "Each table had a bouquet of California roses, freesias and anemones, with crystal ware from the House and china from the Senate," reported *Time*. "For the ladies, there were small silver-plated boxes filled with jelly beans." But all thoughts of luxury were forgotten as the president rose to his feet for the ritual toast. "With thanks to Almighty God, I have been given a tag line, the get-off line everyone wants at the end of a toast or speech," he said. "Some thirty minutes ago, the planes bearing our prisoners left Iranian airspace and are now free of Iran. We can all drink to this one."[11]

The inaugural festivities had been in full swing since the weekend, and already the austerity of the Carter White House seemed a distant memory. In 1976, all the events had been open to the public, and most had been free. Now a simple ball ticket cost $100, while a box at Frank Sinatra's Monday night gala cost $10,000. Never had there been such an air of naked commercialism. Pepsi and American Express paid more than $3 million for commercial time at the gala, while celebrities like Sinatra, Donny Osmond, and Ed McMahon urged their fellow citizens to buy souvenir medals, scarves, ties, and tote bags.

Four years before, Rosalynn Carter had worn an old blue chiffon dress to the inaugural balls. On her husband's first night, Nancy Reagan wore a hand-beaded James Galanos gown, part of an outfit that cost an estimated $25,000. "When Nancy Reagan came glittering down the staircase to the bejeweled, waiting throng," *The New York Times* commented, "it was almost as if a signal had been given to the assembled partisans that a new era of style had begun." Designers were delighted. "She's going to have a great influence on fashion," said Mollie Parnis, who had made clothes for every First Lady since the 1950s. "I don't think people care what Mrs. Reagan pays for something as long as she looks pretty."[12]

Washington had never seen such glamour. Overnight, Plains on the Potomac had become Hollywood's East Coast franchise, the tarmac at Washington National Airport so crowded with private jets that some had to be turned away. Johnny Carson captured the tone when he quipped that Reagan's was "the first administration to have a premiere." In the best Hollywood style, the demand for limousines was so great that reinforcements were summoned from New York. They were backed up outside every museum, gallery, hotel, and restaurant in the city, waiting outside Georgetown parties and five-star dining rooms while their passengers dined on lobster, veal, shrimp, and steak and knocked back gallons of chardonnay from Reagan's home state. Under the new president, explained *The New York Times*, "fine American wines," like limousines and private jets, were set to become "an important part of daily life."[13]

Never can an inauguration have offered a more accurate preview of the years to come. The presidential couple looked magnificent, Reagan cutting a handsome figure as he shook hands and slapped backs, his First Lady a picture of expensive elegance. Yet it later emerged that the great party had been an enormous fraud, funded not by private contributions but by ordinary Americans' tax dollars and staffed by employees illegally borrowed from the Pentagon. It also cost a lot more than Reagan's people had claimed: not $8 million, or even $10 million, as some reporters suspected, but a staggering $16 million, five times what the hated Georgians had spent in 1976. But by the time the General Accounting Office (GAO) revealed the damning figures, it was already 1983. Most people had lost interest, and Reagan got away with it—as he always did.[14]

But the Reagans' self-indulgence did not escape criticism. For dedicated conservatives who had come to Washington to restore the virtues of thrift and self-discipline, it was a shock to see the First Lady in a dress that cost enough to keep fifty people in food stamps for a year. The cost of Nancy Reagan's outfit was "outrageous," said the vice chairman of the Republican Women's Task Force, "when there are people out there who are eaten up by inflation." "The thing that offended me most," said a Republican civic leader from Houston, "was the great extravagance at a time when we're supposed to be cutting the budget and showing restraint on all unnecessary frills." Even modern conservatism's founding father was unimpressed. "When you've got to pay $2,000 for a limousine for four days, $7 to park and $2.50 to check your coat, at a time when most people in this country just can't hack it," complained Barry Goldwater, "that's ostentatious."[15]

There were those, of course, who dismissed the critics as whining killjoys. *Time*'s veteran correspondent Hugh Sidey remarked that it was nice to "have some class this time around," while *Vogue*'s Leo Lerman wrote that even the poorest people enjoyed seeing conspicuous excess because it gave them "a sense of security." The Californians who had come to

Washington to celebrate their victory had no doubts. "This," said an entrepreneur from Culver City, gazing across the throng of revelers in their tuxedos and mink coats, "is what America's all about."[16]

At Union Station, where organizers had arranged to distribute expensive gala tickets, tables were piled high with gourmet food prepared by the finest French chefs: stuffed clams and raw oysters, lobsters and scallops, éclairs and brioches, carpaccio and chardonnay. But beneath the glitz, the station was in a desperate condition. Once the neoclassical gateway to the capital and a monument to the golden age of the railroads, it had fallen into horrendous disrepair. In 1976 it had been badly renovated and used as a markedly unsuccessful bicentennial visitor center, and two years later the GAO reported that the structure was in danger of collapse. Even as Reagan's guests circulated around the gourmet tables, some noticed mold in the ceiling and cigarette burns in the carpet.

As they swallowed their expensive cakes and pastries, they tried to ignore the shabby drunks and derelicts, a small army of the capital's homeless, gathering outside the doors, drawn by the aroma of the food. First one, then another slipped past security and made for the tables, and for a few glorious moments the forgotten Americans found themselves shoulder to shoulder with the rich and famous. But it was only for a minute or two; then the guards were on them, and the illusion was broken, and they were back outside, shivering with cold as Washington toasted the new era.[17]

# *Acknowledgments*

Historians in the 1970s had not yet succumbed to the mania for writing ever longer and more elaborately ingratiating acknowledgments of a kind that would shame even the most self-indulgent Oscar winner. When Peter Carroll published the first historical account of the decade, the fine *It Seemed Like Nothing Happened*, in 1982, his acknowledgments were five sentences long and thanked just twelve people. Although the acknowledgments to Arthur Schlesinger's huge biography of Robert Kennedy (one of the biggest nonfiction best sellers of the decade and a book that sparked my love of American history) ran for several pages, they were little more than a list of libraries, archives, and interviewees. In his disinclination to acknowledge his college roommates, the man who cut his hair, or the people who ran the coffee shop on the corner, Schlesinger remains a model.

By far my biggest scholarly debt, reflected in the notes and bibliography, is to the historians who have already written about this period. I am also grateful to the staff of the Library of Congress, the National Archives at College Park, the Kennedy, Ford, and Carter presidential libraries, the New York and Boston public libraries, and the Vere Harmsworth Library at the Rothermere American Institute, Oxford, where I was fortunate to spend two years as a senior fellow. To the staff of the Rothermere Institute, to the visiting fellows and speakers who read or listened to my early thoughts, and to the American historians at the universities of Cambridge, Sheffield, and Oxford, I am much indebted. I am especially grateful to Gareth Davies, whose pioneering work on rights-based liberalism changed the way I thought about recent American politics; to Stephen Tuck, both for his thoughts on African American history and for his devotion to the Molineux cause; and to Joe Merton, whose research on ethnic politics of the 1970s makes him the Steve Walsh of young historians.

Although I did not begin work on this book in earnest until 2004, I had been thinking about it for years, inspired first by Steve Spackman and Tony Badger, and later by Robert Cook and Hugh Wilford. I was very fortunate to be asked to present some early thoughts at two international conferences, Tony Badger's joint Cambridge University—Boston University conference on the politics of the 1970s in March 2007, and Iwan Morgan and Robert Mason's conference on the Republican Party in the 1970s at the University of London two years later. In both cases I learned far more from my fellow participants than they learned from me. My friends Simon Hall and Martin O'Neill offered valuable advice, and I am especially grateful to Andrew Preston for making the supreme sacrifice, putting aside his three-thousandth trip to a theological archive so that he could read my chapters in draft. At the Wylie Agency, Andrew Wylie and Scott Moyers more than lived up to their elevated reputations. And at Knopf, Andrew Miller and his team showed extraordinary patience, tact, and skill in dealing with an author who not only delivered years late but handed in a first draft more than half a million words long.

But my biggest personal debt is to my family: my parents, Rhys and Hilary Sandbrook; my brother Alex; and above all my beloved wife, Catherine Morley, whom I met while working on this book in Oxford, and who put up with it with such good grace for so long. With the self-control of Pat Nixon, the guts of Betty Ford, the drive of Rosalynn Carter, and the glamour of Nancy Reagan, she deserves a lot better than to be married to a man with the memory of Ronald Reagan, the humility of Jimmy Carter, the wit of Gerald Ford, and the charm of Richard Nixon. It is my good fortune, however, that fate has dealt her such a poor hand.

# Notes

## PREFACE

1. Schulman, *Seventies*, pp. 50–51.
2. Merry, *Taking On the World*, p. 525; *New York Times*, July 20, 1975; *Time*, December 25, 1978.

## WASHINGTON, D.C., AUGUST 1974

1. Nixon, *RN*, pp. 1080–84; Woodward and Bernstein, *Final Days*, pp. 474–93.
2. Nixon, *RN*, p. 1086; Woodward and Bernstein, *Final Days*, p. 493.
3. Woodward and Bernstein, *Final Days*, p. 496; Nixon, *RN*, pp. 1087–88.
4. Nixon, *RN*, p. 1088; Haig, *Inner Circles*, p. 505; Werth, *31 Days*, p. 10; Kissinger, *Years of Upheaval*, p. 1213.
5. Woodward and Bernstein, *Final Days*, pp. 498–99; Anson, *Exile*, pp. 16–20.
6. Anson, *Exile*, p. 16.
7. Gerald R. Ford, *Time to Heal*, p. 26, and see pp. 40–41.
8. Anson, *Exile*, pp. 17–18, 22, 26–27, 30.
9. Reeves, *A Ford, Not a Lincoln*, pp. 65–66; Anson, *Exile*, p. 24; Werth, *31 Days*, pp. 13–15.

## CHAPTER ONE: CONSPIRACY THEORY

1. *Time*, August 19, 1974; McCarthy, *Mask of State*, p. 3; Carroll, *It Seemed Like Nothing Happened*, p. 156; Mieczkowski, *Gerald Ford and the Challenges of the 1970s*, p. 21.
2. *New York Times*, February 25, 1974; Frum, *How We Got Here*, p. 29.
3. Frum, *How We Got Here*, pp. 30, 61; Bok, *Lying*, p. 258.
4. Bok, *Lying*, p. xviii; Chafe, *Unfinished Journey*, pp. 457–59; see also Frum, *How We Got Here*, p. 282; James T. Patterson, *Restless Giant*, p. 89.
5. Gillon, *Boomer Nation*, p. 189; Pater and Pater, *What They Said in 1974*, p. 39.
6. Samuelson, *Good Life and Its Discontents*, p. 41; Steigerwald, *The Sixties and the*

*End of Modern America*, pp. 243–45; Schulman, *Seventies*, p. xv; Broder, *Changing of the Guard*, pp. 425–27; *New York Times*, May 14 and 20, 1975; W. E. Upjohn Institute for Employment Research, *Work in America*, p. 49.

7. Hofstadter, "Paranoid Style in American Politics," pp. 77–86; Killen, *1973 Nervous Breakdown*, pp. 242–49; *Time*, March 5, 1973; Pynchon, *Gravity's Rainbow*; Kirkpatrick Sale, "The World Behind Watergate," *New York Review of Books*, May 3, 1973; Jenkins, *Decade of Nightmares*, pp. 53–54.

8. *New York Times*, December 22, 1974; Andrew, *For the President's Eyes Only*, pp. 397–424; Weiner, *Legacy of Ashes*, pp. 327–29, 335–39. The Family Jewels report is online at www.gwu.edu/~nsarchiv/NSAEBB/NSAEBB222/index.htm.

9. Andrew, *For the President's Eyes Only*, pp. 411–15.

10. *New York Times*, September 25, 1975.

11. See Sutherland, *Bestsellers*, pp. 38–46; Biskind, *Easy Riders, Raging Bulls*, pp. 160–61, 163–64; Lev, *American Films of the 70s*, pp. 58–59; Ryan Gilbey, *It Don't Worry Me*, pp. 9–23; Feeney, *Nixon at the Movies*, pp. 267–69.

12. See Lev, *American Films of the 70s*, pp. 49–54; Feeney, *Nixon at the Movies*, p. 320.

13. *New York Times*, August 13, 1974; *Time*, August 19, 1974.

14. *Time*, August 19, 1974; Betty Ford, *Times of My Life*; James Cannon, *Time and Chance*, pp. 74, 88–89; Troy, *Affairs of State*, pp. 208, 213, 215–19; *Washington Star*, August 10, 1974; *New York Times*, August 18, 1974.

15. *Time*, August 19, 1974; Mieczkowski, *Gerald Ford and the Challenges of the 1970s*, pp. 28–29; Gerald R. Ford, *Time to Heal*, p. 127; Werth, *31 Days*, p. 137.

16. *Esquire*, January 1976; *Time*, June 9, 1975, January 13, 1975; Mieczkowski, *Gerald Ford and the Challenges of the 1970s*, p. 25.

17. Schlesinger, *Imperial Presidency*, pp. x, 376; John Robert Greene, *Presidency of Gerald R. Ford*, pp. 54, 101; Mieczkowski, *Gerald Ford and the Challenges of the 1970s*, p. 66; Berkowitz, *Something Happened*, pp. 96–98; *Newsweek*, October 18, 1976.

18. Hodgson, *All Things to All Men*, pp. 140–43; Berkowitz, *Something Happened*, pp. 91–92; Broder, *Changing of the Guard*, pp. 35–36.

19. See Berkowitz, *Something Happened*, p. 89.

20. Hodgson, *All Things to All Men*, p. 135; Mieczkowski, *Gerald Ford and the Challenges of the 1970s*, p. 67; Berkowitz, *Something Happened*, pp. 94–99.

21. Hodgson, *All Things to All Men*, pp. 158, 179; James T. Patterson, *Restless Giant*, p. 88.

22. *Washington Post*, May 23, 1976.

23. *New York Times*, December 15, 1975; *Time*, December 29, 1975; on Kennedy's changing image, see Alan Brinkley, *Liberalism and Its Discontents*, pp. 210–21.

24. Werth, *31 Days*, pp. 302–3; Schulman, *Seventies*, p. 104; *Rolling Stone*, November 7, 1974; *Time*, September 23, 1974.

25. Gerald R. Ford, *Time to Heal*, pp. 176–78.

26. Anson, *Exile*, pp. 57, 59–60; Ambrose, *Nixon: Ruin and Recovery*, p. 464.

27. Gerald R. Ford, *Time to Heal*, p. 178.

28. Ibid., pp. 175–76; James Cannon, *Time and Chance*, p. 383; Thomas P. O'Neill, *Man of the House*, p. 268; Werth, *31 Days*, pp. 47, 318; *American Heritage*, December 1996; Anson, *Exile*, p. 59; Kutler, *Wars of Watergate*, p. 564; Mieczkowski, *Gerald Ford and the Challenges of the 1970s*, pp. 30–32; *New York Times*, September 9, 1974; *Time*, September 23, 1974; John Robert Greene, *Presidency of Gerald R. Ford*, p. 55.

29. Gerald R. Ford, *Time to Heal*, pp. 3–13, 197–99; John Robert Greene, *Presidency of Gerald R. Ford*, pp. 42–45.
30. John Robert Greene, *Presidency of Gerald R. Ford*, pp. 45–46; Werth, *31 Days*, pp. 212–14.
31. Gerald R. Ford, *Time to Heal*, pp. 158, 166–67; Jaworski, *The Right and the Power*, p. 292; Kutler, *Wars of Watergate*, pp. 559–60, 568; John Robert Greene, *Presidency of Gerald R. Ford*, pp. 46, 51–52.
32. Gerald R. Ford, *Time to Heal*, pp. 161–62; Robert T. Hartmann, *Palace Politics*, pp. 257–61; Anson, *Exile*, pp. 46–48; James Cannon, *Time and Chance*, pp. 373–75; Kutler, *Wars of Watergate*, pp. 567–68, 571.
33. James Cannon, *Time and Chance*, p. 376; Kutler, *Wars of Watergate*, p. 567; John Robert Greene, *Presidency of Gerald R. Ford*, pp. 64–66; Mieczkowski, *Gerald Ford and the Challenges of the 1970s*, p. 34.
34. Greenberg, *Nixon's Shadow*, p. 215; *American Heritage*, December 1996; Woodward, "Gerald R. Ford"; *Christian Science Monitor*, May 29, 2001.
35. Gerald R. Ford, *Time to Heal*, pp. 191–92; Robert T. Hartmann, *Palace Politics*, pp. 294–95.
36. Mieczkowski, *Gerald Ford and the Challenges of the 1970s*, p. 1; Nessen, *It Sure Looks Different from the Inside*, p. xiv.
37. *New Republic*, November 2, 1974; John Robert Greene, *Presidency of Gerald R. Ford*, pp. 55–56; Mieczkowski, *Gerald Ford and the Challenges of the 1970s*, p. 61; Barone, *Our Country*, pp. 533–34; *Newsweek*, March 24, 1975; Mason, *Richard Nixon and the Quest for a New Majority*, p. 212.
38. Mieczkowski, *Gerald Ford and the Challenges of the 1970s*, pp. 22–23; Reeves, *A Ford, Not a Lincoln*, pp. 191–92.
39. See Mieczkowski, *Gerald Ford and the Challenges of the 1970s*, pp. 48–49.
40. Ibid., p. 50; John Robert Greene, *Presidency of Gerald R. Ford*, p. 62; *New Republic*, January 3, 1976, January 4, 1975.

### CHAPTER TWO: IF HE'S SO DUMB, HOW COME HE'S PRESIDENT?

1. *New York Times*, December 31, 1974, January 1, 1975.
2. Gerald R. Ford, *Time to Heal*, p. 227; Barone, *Our Country*, pp. 535–36; *Washington Post*, December 31, 1974.
3. Gerald R. Ford, *Time to Heal*, pp. 232–33; Mieczkowski, *Gerald Ford and the Challenges of the 1970s*, pp. 158–61.
4. *New York Times*, January 16, 1975; *Washington Post*, January 16, 1975.
5. James Cannon, *Time and Chance*, pp. 15–16; Samuelson, *Good Life and Its Discontents*, pp. 69–70, 163; Cohen, *Consumers' Republic*, pp. 7–9; Leuchtenberg, *Troubled Feast*, p. 55.
6. Samuelson, *Good Life and Its Discontents*, pp. 9, 34–39, 41; Iwan W. Morgan, *Beyond the Liberal Consensus*, pp. 3–5; Broder, *Changing of the Guard*, pp. 40, 69–70; Collins, *More*, p. 163; and see U.S. Bureau of the Census, *Statistical Abstract of the United States, 1976* (Washington, D.C., 1976), table 689, p. 424.
7. *Washington Post*, November 6, 1975.
8. *New York Times*, August 20, 25, and 18, 1974; James T. Patterson, *Restless Giant*, p. 7.
9. Carroll, *It Seemed Like Nothing Happened*, pp. 131–32; Ehrlichman, *Witness to Power*, p. 254; Iwan W. Morgan, *Beyond the Liberal Consensus*, pp. 37–38,

102–3; Samuelson, *Good Life and Its Discontents*, pp. 96–97; Collins, *More*, pp. 72, 108–28.

10. Frum, *How We Got Here*, p. 291; *New York Times*, March 31, 1973. For accounts of the boycott, see Carroll, *It Seemed Like Nothing Happened*, pp. 130–31; Cohen, *Consumers' Republic*, pp. 368–69.

11. *New York Times*, April 2, 5, and 30, 1973.

12. Edsall, *Chain Reaction*, p. 105; *Newsweek*, March 4, 1974; Carroll, *It Seemed Like Nothing Happened*, p. 131.

13. U.S. Bureau of the Census, *Statistical Abstract of the United States*, 1976, table 714, p. 443.

14. See Kuttner, *Revolt of the Haves*, pp. 201–2; Horowitz, *Anxieties of Affluence*, p. 204; Berkowitz, *Something Happened*, p. 55; Rieder, *Canarsie*, p. 98.

15. Lichtenstein, *State of the Union*, pp. 194–95; *Washington Post*, November 21 and 29, 1974.

16. *Washington Post*, April 30, 1975, May 25, 1975, February 2, 1977.

17. *BusinessWeek*, September 26, 1970; *Time*, November 9, 1970, February 7, 1972, October 30, 1972; Cowie, "Vigorously Left, Right, and Center," pp. 75–76, 78–79; Joshua B. Freeman, *Working-Class New York*, pp. 209–14, 251; Zaretsky, *No Direction Home*, pp. 104–7, 114.

18. Iwan W. Morgan, *Beyond the Liberal Consensus*, pp. 88–90; James T. Patterson, *Restless Giant*, p. 62; Berkowitz, *Something Happened*, pp. 66–67; Hodgson, *World Turned Right Side Up*, p. 190.

19. Ferguson and Rogers, *Right Turn*, pp. 81–82; Frum, *How We Got Here*, p. 25; Collins, *More*, p. 130; Rieder, *Canarsie*, p. 250. For a broader discussion of the "Europeanization" of American culture, see Pells, *Not Like Us*, pp. 278–324.

20. Yergin, *Prize*, pp. 541–42, 549; Mieczkowski, *Gerald Ford and the Challenges of the 1970s*, pp. 198–99; Reichley, *Conservatives in an Age of Change*, pp. 358–59.

21. *Public Papers of the Presidents of the United States: Richard Nixon, 1973* (Washington, D.C., 1975), pp. 301–19, 623–30; Yergin, *Prize*, pp. 567, 590–91; Carroll, *It Seemed Like Nothing Happened*, p. 119; Reichley, *Conservatives in an Age of Change*, p. 361; Small, *Presidency of Richard Nixon*, pp. 201–2; Mieczkowski, *Gerald Ford and the Challenges of the 1970s*, p. 200.

22. *New York Times*, May 20, 1973, July 8, 1973, September 4 and 23, 1973, October 16, 17, and 19, 1973, November 5, 1973; *Washington Post*, July 6 and 11, 1973, October 17, 1973; Kissinger, *Years of Upheaval*, pp. 499–522, 534–37, 545–52; Isaacson, *Kissinger*, p. 514; Yergin, *Prize*, pp. 595–96, 598–99, 601, 605–8, 614–15, 625.

23. *Public Papers of the Presidents of the United States: Richard Nixon, 1973*, pp. 916–22; *New York Times*, November 9, 1973; Nixon, *RN*, p. 985; Small, *Presidency of Richard Nixon*, p. 202; Mieczkowski, *Gerald Ford and the Challenges of the 1970s*, p. 211; Carroll, *It Seemed Like Nothing Happened*, p. 118.

24. Simon, *Time for Truth*, pp. 50–55; Mieczkowski, *Gerald Ford and the Challenges of the 1970s*, pp. 201–10; *New York Times*, December 3, 1973; and see Yergin, *Prize*, pp. 616–17.

25. Carroll, *It Seemed Like Nothing Happened*, p. 118; Frum, *How We Got Here*, pp. 318–20; Mieczkowski, *Gerald Ford and the Challenges of the 1970s*, pp. 206–7.

26. Mieczkowski, *Gerald Ford and the Challenges of the 1970s*, pp. 105–7; Nixon, *RN*, p. 985; *New York Times*, May 31, 1974, October 26, 1975; Jenkins, *Decade of Nightmares*, pp. 71–73; *Time*, February 10, 1975.

27. Ehrlich, *Population Bomb*, pp. 5–6, 44; Robert Gottlieb, *Forcing the Spring*, pp. 256–57; Whitaker, *Striking a Balance*, p. 264; Collins, *More*, pp. 132–39; Horowitz, *Anxieties of Affluence*, p. 200; Mitchell, "From Conservation to Environmental Movement"; Zaretsky, *No Direction Home*, p. 92; *Time*, December 10, 1973.

28. Kutler, *Wars of Watergate*, p. 78; Small, *Presidency of Richard Nixon*, pp. 196–99; *Public Papers of the Presidents of the United States: Richard Nixon*, 1970 (Washington, D.C., 1971), pp. 8–16; Robert Gottlieb, *Forcing the Spring*, pp. 105–14, 125; Schumacher, *Small Is Beautiful*, pp. 21, 57; Shi, *Simple Life*, pp. 269–70.

29. *New Republic*, March 7, 1970; Hayward, *Age of Reagan*, pp. 251, 253; Carroll, *It Seemed Like Nothing Happened*, p. 312; Frum, *How We Got Here*, pp. 123, 173–76; *New York*, May 29, 1978; Schulman, *Seventies*, p. 90.

30. *New York Times*, January 1 and 6, 1974.

31. *Washington Post*, August 9, 1974; Mieczkowski, *Gerald Ford and the Challenges of the 1970s*, p. 107; *New York Times*, August 29, 1974.

32. Collins, *More*, pp. 153–54; Mieczkowski, *Gerald Ford and the Challenges of the 1970s*, pp. 114–15.

33. John Robert Greene, *Presidency of Gerald R. Ford*, p. 68; Mieczkowski, *Gerald Ford and the Challenges of the 1970s*, pp. 74–76, 78–80; *Washington Post*, June 23, 1976.

34. *Washington Post*, October 9, 1974; Mieczkowski, *Gerald Ford and the Challenges of the 1970s*, pp. 95, 132–36.

35. Frum, *How We Got Here*, pp. 300–301; Mieczkowski, *Gerald Ford and the Challenges of the 1970s*, pp. 136–38.

36. Mieczkowski, *Gerald Ford and the Challenges of the 1970s*, pp. 139–43.

37. Reichley, *Conservatives in an Age of Change*, p. 391; *Time*, October 28, 1974; Mieczkowski, *Gerald Ford and the Challenges of the 1970s*, pp. 126–27, 148, 151–52.

38. *Economist*, August 31, 1974; Mieczkowski, *Gerald Ford and the Challenges of the 1970s*, pp. 154–55; Nessen, *It Sure Looks Different from the Inside*, pp. 76–77.

39. *New York Times*, July 25, 1975; Collins, *More*, p. 155; Mieczkowski, *Gerald Ford and the Challenges of the 1970s*, pp. 77, 129–30, 155; *New York Times*, August 8, 1975; *Washington Post*, December 8, 1974.

40. *New York Times*, October 1, 1976; Reichley, *Conservatives in an Age of Change*, pp. 359–81; John Robert Greene, *Presidency of Gerald R. Ford*, pp. 76–77; Mieczkowski, *Gerald Ford and the Challenges of the 1970s*, pp. 83–89, 171–73, 215–70.

41. *New York Times*, September 7 and 26, 1975; Gerald R. Ford, *Time to Heal*, pp. 311–12; Allen, *Side Effects*, p. 89.

42. Mieczkowski, *Gerald Ford and the Challenges of the 1970s*, pp. 38, 49, 53.

43. *New York Times*, September 15, 1975; Gerald R. Ford, *Time to Heal*, pp. 313–14, 338–39; John Robert Greene, *Presidency of Gerald R. Ford*, pp. 79–81; Mieczkowski, *Gerald Ford and the Challenges of the 1970s*, pp. 175–83.

44. Gerald R. Ford, *Time to Heal*, pp. 350–51; Mieczkowski, *Gerald Ford and the Challenges of the 1970s*, pp. 187–88; Shirley, *Reagan's Revolution*, pp. 111–12.

45. Mieczkowski, *Gerald Ford and the Challenges of the 1970s*, p. 189; Collins, *More*, pp. 167–69.

46. Gerald R. Ford, *Time to Heal*, pp. 428–29; Collins, *More*, p. 156; Mieczkowski, *Gerald Ford and the Challenges of the 1970s*, pp. 190–93.

47. Gerald R. Ford, *Time to Heal*, p. 333.

## CHAPTER THREE: ARCHIE'S GUYS

1. Transcript of Oval Office conversation, May 13, 1971, reprinted in *Harper's*, February 2000.
2. See *New York Times*, January 12 and 24, 1971, February 21, 1971, March 12, 1972; David Gunzerath, "All in the Family," in the online Encyclopedia of Television, www.museum.tv/archives/etv/A/htmlA/allinthefa/allinthefa.htm; Adler, "*All in the Family*"; Carroll, *It Seemed Like Nothing Happened*, pp. 61–63; Berkowitz, *Something Happened*, pp. 206–7.
3. Ozersky, *Archie Bunker's America*, p. 6; Adler, "*All in the Family*," pp. 87, 236, 240.
4. David Wild, "Changing the Channel," in Kahn, George-Warren, and Dahl, *Rolling Stone*, p. 28.
5. Sugrue, *Origins of the Urban Crisis*.
6. *Saturday Evening Post*, April 20, 1968.
7. Scammon and Wattenberg, *Real Majority*, p. 57; *Washington Post*, January 6, 1970.
8. *Harper's*, August 1969; *Newsweek*, October 6, 1969; Pete Hamill, "Revolt of the White Lower-Middle Class," *New York*, April 14, 1969, reprinted in Howe, *White Majority*, pp. 10–22. On the history of the "Middle Americans" idea, see Mason, *Richard Nixon and the Quest for a New Majority*, pp. 43–47.
9. *Time*, January 5, 1970.
10. Mason, *Richard Nixon and the Quest for a New Majority*, p. 20.
11. See the table of FBI figures in Edsall, *Chain Reaction*, p. 112. For alternative, though no less chilling, figures drawn from the Bureau of the Census, see Thernstrom and Thernstrom, *America in Black and White*, p. 262.
12. James Q. Wilson, *Thinking About Crime*, pp. 235–36.
13. James T. Patterson, *Restless Giant*, pp. 41–43; Rieder, *Canarsie*, pp. 75–76.
14. Edsall, *Chain Reaction*, p. 45; Moynihan, *Maximum Feasible Misunderstanding*, pp. xii–xiii; Janowitz, *Last Half Century*, p. 377; Rieder, *Canarsie*, p. 180.
15. See Lev, *American Films of the 70s*, pp. 30–34.
16. *New Yorker*, January 15, 1972; Lev, *American Films of the 70s*, p. 36; Feeney, *Nixon at the Movies*, p. 280; Edsall, *Chain Reaction*, p. 113; Lukas, *Common Ground*, pp. 412, 304.
17. Rieder, *Canarsie*, pp. 68, 78, 26.
18. Glazer, *Affirmative Discrimination*, pp. 177–95; Rieder, *Canarsie*, p. 97. See also Furstenberg, "Public Reaction to Crime in the Streets"; Sugrue, *Origins of the Urban Crisis*, p. 267; Dan T. Carter, *Politics of Rage*, p. 349; Lassiter, *Silent Majority*, p. 7.
19. James T. Patterson, *Grand Expectations*, p. 672; Gillon, *That's Not What We Meant to Do*, p. 68; Rieder, *Canarsie*, p. 102.
20. Witcover, *Marathon*, pp. 293–94.
21. *New York*, August 1, 1977; *New York Times*, July 14 and 15, 1977, August 15, 1977; *New York Post*, July 15, 1977; Goodman, *Blackout*, p. 151.
22. *Washington Post*, July 16, 1977; Mahler, *Ladies and Gentlemen, the Bronx Is Burning*, pp. 230–31; James Goodman, *Blackout*, p. 219.
23. *New York Times*, July 17 and 23, 1977.
24. Rieder, *Canarsie*, p. 6; Joshua B. Freeman, *Working-Class New York*, p. 237; Stossel, *Sarge*, p. 596.
25. Rieder, *Canarsie*, p. 200.

26. Dan T. Carter, *Politics of Rage*, p. 378; *New York Times*, June 17, 1970; Kazin, *Populist Persuasion*, p. 221.

27. *Harper's*, August 1969; Pettigrew, Riley, and Vanneman, "George Wallace's Constituents."

28. Dan T. Carter, *Politics of Rage*, p. 394; Carlson, *George C. Wallace and the Politics of Powerlessness*, p. 6.

29. Dan T. Carter, *Politics of Rage*, p. 314; Steigerwald, *The Sixties and the End of Modern America*, pp. 238–39.

30. See Shafer and Johnston, *End of Southern Exceptionalism*, pp. 168–71; Edsall, *Chain Reaction*, pp. 10, 78–79; Dan T. Carter, *Politics of Rage*, pp. 472–74.

31. Edsall, *Chain Reaction*, p. 85; Patrick Buchanan and Ken Khachigian, "Assault Strategy," June 8, 1972, reprinted in Oudes, *From: The President*, pp. 463–74; Cowie, "Vigorously Left, Right, and Center," pp. 89–90; Leuchtenberg, *Troubled Feast*, p. 220.

32. *Congressional Quarterly Weekly Report*, March 11, 1972, p. 534; Phillips, *Emerging Republican Majority*, pp. 32, 172; Cowie, "Nixon's Class Struggle," p. 280; Mason, *Richard Nixon and the Quest for a New Majority*, pp. 98–99, 169; *New York Times*, September 27, 1972; *Time*, May 12, 1975. My thanks to Dr. Joe Merton for advice on this section.

33. W. E. Upjohn Institute for Employment Research, *Work in America*, p. 36; Skrentny, *Minority Rights Revolution*, pp. 277–328; Jacobson, *Roots Too*, pp. 18–20.

34. Novak, *Rise of the Unmeltable Ethnics*, pp. 82, 206; *New York Times*, June 17, 1970, November 27, 1970.

35. *New York Times*, February 27, 1977; Jacobson, *Roots Too*, pp. 30–31, 39–41, 131; Vecoli, "Resurgence of American Immigration History."

36. Thomson and Christie, *Scorsese on Scorsese*, p. 48; Jacobson, *Roots Too*, pp. 53, 73–74; *New York Times*, June 29, 1971.

37. *Sight and Sound* (Autumn 1972); Feeney, *Nixon at the Movies*, pp. 299–300.

38. *New York Times*, June 29, 1971; Jacobson, *Roots Too*, pp. 17–18, 48–53, 244; Gans, "Symbolic Ethnicity."

39. Jacobson, *Roots Too*, p. 7; Novak, *Rise of the Unmeltable Ethnics*, pp. 71, 5, 35.

40. Novak, *Rise of the Unmeltable Ethnics*, p. 336; Schulman, *Seventies*, pp. 70–71.

41. Quoted in Schulman, *Seventies*, p. 76.

42. *New York Times*, September 10, 1977; Mahler, *Ladies and Gentlemen, the Bronx Is Burning*, pp. 300–301.

43. Edsall, *Chain Reaction*, pp. 111–12; Jenkins, *Decade of Nightmares*, p. 139; Mahler, *Ladies and Gentlemen, the Bronx Is Burning*, pp. 135, 233, 295.

44. Barone, *Our Country*, p. 567. For a scathing verdict on Koch's stewardship of New York City, see Joshua B. Freeman, *Working-Class New York*, pp. 290–305.

## CHAPTER FOUR: THE PORNO PLAGUE

1. *Charleston Gazette*, September 13, 1974; James Moffett, *Storm in the Mountains*, pp. 16–20.

2. See William Martin, *With God on Our Side*, pp. 117–18.

3. *Charleston Gazette*, October 12, 1993; William Martin, *With God on Our Side*, pp. 118–22.

4. William Martin, *With God on Our Side*, pp. 125–26. On earlier protests, see

McGirr, *Suburban Warriors*, pp. 227–31; William Martin, *With God on Our Side*, pp. 100–116.

5. Crawford, *Thunder on the Right*, p. 37; William Martin, *With God on Our Side*, pp. 130, 132–35.

6. James Moffett, *Storm in the Mountains*, pp. 19, 22–24.

7. Ibid., p. 188; William Martin, *With God on Our Side*, pp. 139–40; Zimmerman, *Whose America?* pp. 160–85, 207–11.

8. James Moffett, *Storm in the Mountains*, p. 54; *Human Events*, July 29, 1978; William Martin, *With God on Our Side*, p. 132.

9. FitzGerald, *Cities on a Hill*, p. 412; Kremen, *Dateline: America*, p. 156.

10. Elaine Tyler May, *Homeward Bound*; Zaretsky, *No Direction Home*, pp. 5–7; Klatch, *Women of the New Right*, pp. 23–25.

11. *New York Times*, February 15, 1973; Ruoff, *American Family*, pp. 3–52, 97; Killen, *1973 Nervous Breakdown*, pp. 55–59.

12. See *Newsweek*, January 15, 1973; Killen, *1973 Nervous Breakdown*, pp. 67–70; *New York Times Magazine*, February 18, 1973.

13. Wandersee, *On the Move*, pp. 130–31; Allyn, *Make Love, Not War*, pp. 256–58; James T. Patterson, *Restless Giant*, p. 50; *Newsweek*, March 12, 1973.

14. Gettleman and Markowitz, *Courage to Divorce*, p. 45; Sheehy, *Passages*, p. 208.

15. *New York*, May 22, 1972.

16. Zaretsky, *No Direction Home*, pp. 15–17; Evans, *Tidal Wave*, p. 55.

17. Zaretsky, *No Direction Home*, pp. 10, 13; *Washington Post*, January 2, 1977.

18. Roof, *Generation of Seekers*, p. 50; Bahr, "Changes in Family Life in Middletown, 1924–77," p. 47; Carroll, *It Seemed Like Nothing Happened*, pp. 281–82; Frum, *How We Got Here*, p. 92.

19. Carroll, *It Seemed Like Nothing Happened*, p. 280; Wandersee, *On the Move*, p. 133; *Newsweek*, July 16, 1973; Watson, *Defining Visions*, pp. 4, 65.

20. Mayer, *Changing American Mind*, pp. 36–38, 158–61, 180–84; Yankelovich, *New Rules*, p. 99; Kassorla, *Nice Girls Do*.

21. Laumann, Gagnon, Michael, and Michaels, *Social Organization of Sexuality*, p. 201; Carroll, *It Seemed Like Nothing Happened*, p. 265; James T. Patterson, *Restless Giant*, pp. 48–49.

22. Allyn, *Make Love, Not War*, p. 100; Leuchtenberg, *Troubled Feast*, p. 190.

23. *New York Times*, May 10, 1971.

24. *Rolling Stone*, May 6, 1976; *Time*, January 16, 1978; *Washington Post*, February 23, 1978; Allyn, *Make Love, Not War*, pp. 207–10, 213–14, 225–27, 236–38; Shapiro, *Turn the Beat Around*, p. 51.

25. *Report of the Commission on Obscenity and Pornography*, pp. 121–35, 262.

26. Ibid., pp. 157–59; *New York Times*, January 24, 1971.

27. Braunstein, " 'Adults Only,' " pp. 132–35; *Newsweek*, January 15, 1973; *Time*, January 15, 1973; *New York Times*, January 21, 1973.

28. Braunstein, " 'Adults Only,' " pp. 130, 133–34, 140; Mahler, *Ladies and Gentlemen, the Bronx Is Burning*, pp. 124–25; *New York Times*, August 15, 1973.

29. *New York Times*, November 15, 1976, March 25 and 26, 1977.

30. *Time*, April 5, 1976.

31. Robin Morgan, "Theory and Practice: Pornography and Rape," in *Going Too Far*, pp. 163–70; Rosen, *World Split Open*, pp. 191–92; Allyn, *Make Love, Not War*, pp. 287–89.

32. Rieder, *Canarsie*, pp. 133, 137–38.

33. Ibid., pp. 142–43.
34. See William Martin, *With God on Our Side*, pp. 341–43.

## INTERLUDE: BORN TO RUN

1. *Crawdaddy*, March 1973; Knobler and Mitchell, *Very Seventies*, pp. 102–12.
2. *New York Times*, January 21, 1973; *Real Paper*, May 22, 1974.
3. *New York Times*, August 15, 1975.
4. *New York Times*, December 16, 1973; Robert Santelli, "Working-Class Hero," in Kahn, George-Warren, and Dahl, *Rolling Stone*, pp. 74–77.
5. *Time*, October 27, 1975; *Newsweek*, October 27, 1975; Sounes, *Seventies*, pp. 248–50.
6. See *New York Times*, August 29, 1975, October 5, 1975; *Rolling Stone*, October 9, 1975; *Village Voice*, January 26, 1976.
7. *Time*, May 3, 1971; Carroll, *It Seemed Like Nothing Happened*, pp. 71, 297–300; Sutherland, *Bestsellers*, pp. 76–77; *New York Times*, January 17, 1974; Marcus, *Happy Days and Wonder Years*, pp. 24–29.
8. *Time*, October 27, 1975.

## CHAPTER FIVE: LET'S LOOK FEROCIOUS

1. *Chicago Daily News*, May 6, 1975; Butler, *Fall of Saigon*, pp. 483–88; oral history of Major Jim Kean in Engelmann, *Tears Before the Rain*, pp. 133–36.
2. *Rolling Stone*, June 5, 1975; *Chicago Daily News*, May 6, 1975.
3. *New York Times*, May 12, 1975.
4. Frank Snepp, "Toothpaste," *Granta* 15 (Spring 1985), p. 121; oral history of Thomas Polgar in Engelmann, *Tears Before the Rain*, p. 74.
5. *Real Paper*, July 2, 1975.
6. *New York Times*, May 1 and 2, 1975.
7. *Washington Post*, May 3, 1975; *New York Times*, May 2, 1975.
8. Gerald R. Ford, *Time to Heal*, pp. 256–57; Mieczkowski, *Gerald Ford and the Challenges of the 1970s*, p. 294.
9. Isaacson, *Kissinger*, p. 647; Kissinger, *Years of Renewal*, p. 471; Kissinger to Ford, c. May 12, 1975, "Vietnam (23)," box 20, National Security Adviser, Presidential Country Files for East Asia and the Pacific, Ford Library.
10. See Isaacson, *Kissinger*, pp. 647–48; Hanhimäki, *Flawed Architect*, pp. 388–89, 477.
11. John Robert Greene, *Presidency of Gerald R. Ford*, pp. 143–44.
12. NSC minutes, May 13, 1975 (first meeting), and May 12, 1975, box 1, NSC Meeting Minutes, National Security Adviser, Ford Library; Gerald R. Ford, *Time to Heal*, p. 276.
13. NSC minutes, May 13, 1975 (second meeting), box 1, NSC Meeting Minutes, National Security Adviser, Ford Library; Isaacson, *Kissinger*, pp. 649–50.
14. NSC minutes, May 14, 1975, box 1, NSC Meeting Minutes, National Security Adviser, Ford Library; John Robert Greene, *Presidency of Gerald R. Ford*, pp. 148–50; Gerald R. Ford, *Time to Heal*, p. 282; Isaacson, *Kissinger*, pp. 650–51; Kissinger, *Years of Renewal*, pp. 566–72.
15. John Robert Greene, *Presidency of Gerald R. Ford*, p. 149; *Time*, May 26, 1975.
16. John Robert Greene, *Presidency of Gerald R. Ford*, pp. 149–51; Isaacson, *Kissinger*, p. 651; *Washington Post*, May 15, 1975; Gerald R. Ford, *Time to Heal*, p. 284; *Time*, May 26, 1975; *Newsweek*, May 26, 1975; Shawcross, *Sideshow*, p. 434.

17. Engelhardt, *End of Victory Culture*, p. 254; Baskir and Strauss, *Chance and Circumstance*, p. 6.

18. Karnow, *Vietnam*, p. 670; Gillon, *Boomer Nation*, p. 58; Kovic, *Born on the Fourth of July*, p. 39; *Life*, May 22, 1970.

19. Gillon, *Boomer Nation*, pp. 169–70, 171; Carroll, *It Seemed Like Nothing Happened*, p. 98; and see Scott, *Politics of Readjustment*.

20. Engelhardt, *End of Victory Culture*, pp. 177–78, 180.

21. *Time*, February 26, 1973; *New York Times*, March 3, 1973, June 2, 4, 9, and 10, 1973, February 10, 1974; Zaretsky, *No Direction Home*, pp. 57–58; Howes, *Voices of the Vietnam POWs*, p. 145.

22. *Time*, February 26, 1973; Zaretsky, *No Direction Home*, pp. 55–56; Roth, *My Life as a Man*, pp. 20, 172, 230, 299.

23. Warren Farrell, *Liberated Man*; Fasteau, *Male Machine*, p. 198; Schulman, *Seventies*, pp. 177–81.

24. Garthoff, *Détente and Confrontation*, pp. 8–14, 1148; Kissinger, *Years of Upheaval*, pp. 238, 981; LaFeber, *America, Russia, and the Cold War*, pp. 266–97; Gaddis, *Strategies of Containment*, pp. 274–309; Gaddis, *Cold War*, pp. 181–82; White House Background Press Briefing, December 18, 1969, transcript online at the State Department Web site, www.state.gov/r/pa/ho/frus/nixon/i/20702.htm.

25. Gerald R. Ford, *Time to Heal*, pp. 209–17; Kissinger, *Years of Renewal*, pp. 298–300; *Washington Post*, December 6, 1974; *New York Times*, November 29, 1974; Robert G. Kaufman, *Henry M. Jackson*, p. 288.

26. *Reader's Digest*, July 1975; Isaacson, *Kissinger*, pp. 653–57, 610; Iwan W. Morgan, *Beyond the Liberal Consensus*, p. 72.

27. Zumwalt, *On Watch*, p. 319; Isaacson, *Kissinger*, p. 697; *National Review*, February 6, 1976; *New York Times*, October 13, 1974.

28. Kissinger, *Years of Upheaval*, p. 984; Blumenthal, *Rise of the Counter-establishment*, p. 128; Wills, *Lead Time*, p. 120; Isaacson, *Kissinger*, pp. 611–12; Robert G. Kaufman, *Henry M. Jackson*, pp. 248–51.

29. Isaacson, *Kissinger*, pp. 657–58.

30. *New York Times*, July 4, 1975; *Wall Street Journal*, July 18, 1975; Hayward, *Age of Reagan*, p. 439; Robert G. Kaufman, *Henry M. Jackson*, p. 292.

31. *Time*, July 14, 1975; *National Review*, August 29, 1975.

32. *Time*, July 28, 1975; Conference on Security and Cooperation in Europe, "Final Act," August 1, 1975, www.osce.org/documents/html/pdftohtml/4044_en.pdf.html; Garthoff, *Détente and Confrontation*, pp. 527–28; Isaacson, *Kissinger*, pp. 660–63; Hanhimäki, *Flawed Architect*, pp. 436–37; Dobrynin, *In Confidence*, p. 274; Kissinger, *Years of Renewal*, p. 663.

33. *New York Times*, July 25 and 21, 1975; *Wall Street Journal*, July 23, 1975; *Time*, August 4, 1975; Gerald R. Ford, *Time to Heal*, p. 300; Kissinger, *Years of Renewal*, pp. 864–65; Mieczkowski, *Gerald Ford and the Challenges of the 1970s*, p. 298.

34. Kissinger, *Years of Renewal*, pp. 304–8; Garthoff, *Détente and Confrontation*, pp. 347–48, 505–16; Robert G. Kaufman, *Henry M. Jackson*, pp. 266–68, 272–81; Hanhimäki, *Flawed Architect*, pp. 366–68, 379–80.

35. *New Republic*, June 14, 1975; Isaacson, *Kissinger*, p. 605; John Robert Greene, *Presidency of Gerald R. Ford*, p. 66.

36. *New York Times*, November 11 and 24, 1975; *Washington Post*, November 5, 1976; Kissinger, *Years of Renewal*, pp. 836–37; Gerald R. Ford, *Time to Heal*, pp. 326, 329–31; John Robert Greene, *Presidency of Gerald R. Ford*, pp. 161–62.

37. Robert Teeter and Stuart Spencer to Richard Cheney, "Analysis of Early Research," November 12, 1975, box 63, Robert M. Teeter Papers, Ford Library; Teeter to Cheney, December 24, 1975, "Memoranda and Polling Data: Teeter (3)," box 4, Foster Chanock Files, Ford Library; Kissinger, *Years of Renewal*, pp. 850–51, 860–61; Mann, *Rise of the Vulcans*, pp. 69–71.

38. Bayard Rustin and Carl Gershman, "Africa, Soviet Imperialism, and the Retreat of American Power," *Commentary*, March 1977, pp. 57–58; Isaacson, *Kissinger*, p. 682.

39. Garthoff, *Détente and Confrontation*, pp. 732–57, 1125–35, 1161; Robert Tucker, "Beyond Détente," *Commentary*, March 1977, p. 45; Edward N. Luttwak, "Defense Reconsidered," *Commentary*, March 1977, pp. 57–58; Reichley, *Conservatives in an Age of Change*, pp. 349, 352–53.

40. Cahn, "Team B"; Cahn, *Killing Détente*; Robert G. Kaufman, *Henry M. Jackson*, p. 296; *Boston Globe*, November 2, 2003; *Washington Post*, January 2, 1977; *Time*, October 14, 1991; Cahn interviewed on the BBC documentary *The Power of Nightmares*, January 18, 2005; and see Garthoff, *Détente and Confrontation*, pp. 607–8.

41. Intelligence Community Experiment in Competitive Analysis, "Soviet Strategic Objectives: An Alternative View," Report of Team B, National Intelligence Estimates Files, Records of the Central Intelligence Agency, RG 263, National Archives, pp. 2–3, 5, 42. Italics in original.

42. Garthoff, *Détente and Confrontation*, p. 604; "Common Sense and the Common Danger," in Tyroler and Kampelman, *Alerting America*, pp. ix–xi, 4–6; Ehrman, *Rise of Neoconservatism*, p. 112; Hodgson, *World Turned Right Side Up*, pp. 236–37; Robert G. Kaufman, *Henry M. Jackson*, p. 296.

43. *U.S. News and World Report*, April 7, 1975; Mieczkowski, *Gerald Ford and the Challenges of the 1970s*, p. 289; *Washington Post*, May 1, 1975; *Economist*, April 5, 1975; Gerald R. Ford, *Time to Heal*, p. 275.

44. Guenter Lewy, *America in Vietnam* (New York, 1978), p. vi; *New York Times*, December 17, 1978; Sylvia Shin Huey Chang, "Restaging the War," p. 91.

45. *New York Times*, March 25, 1979, April 6, 1979; *Time*, April 23, 1979; *New Yorker*, December 18, 1978; Michael Dempsey et al., "Four Shots at *The Deer Hunter*," *Film Quarterly* 32, no. 4 (Summer 1979), pp. 10–22; *Nation*, May 12, 1979.

46. *New York Times*, April 26, 1979, March 25, 1979, April 6, 1979; *Time*, April 23, 1979.

47. *Rolling Stone*, August 25, 1977, November 5, 1987.

48. Hodgson, *World Turned Right Side Up*, pp. 223–24; Sutherland, *Bestsellers*, p. 92; Engelhardt, *End of Victory Culture*, p. 266; *Time*, May 30, 1977. On the conservatism of *Star Wars*, see Lev, *American Films of the 70s*, pp. 167–75; Biskind, *Easy Riders, Raging Bulls*, pp. 343–44.

## CHAPTER SIX: SOUTHIE WON'T GO

1. *Boston Globe*, April 6, 7, and 9, 1976; Lukas, *Common Ground*, pp. 323–24.

2. *Boston Globe*, April 9 and 10, 1976; and see Louis Masur, *The Soiling of Old Glory: The Story of a Photograph That Shocked America* (New York, 2008).

3. *Boston Globe*, April 7, 8, and 9, 1976.

4. Edsall, *Chain Reaction*, p. 88; Thernstrom and Thernstrom, *America in Black and White*, pp. 322–23.

5. Schuman, Steeh, and Bobo, *Racial Attitudes in America*, pp. 144–47; Thernstrom and Thernstrom, *America in Black and White*, p. 331; Hochschild, *New American Dilemma*, pp. 191, 180.

6. Lassiter, *Silent Majority*, p. 16; Lukas, *Common Ground*, p. 61; Formisano, *Boston Against Busing*, pp. 25, 226. As the notes below indicate, my account of the Boston busing crisis leans heavily on these superb (and definitive) works.

7. Andrew Kopkind, "Boston's Bitter Bicentennial," *New York Times*, July 23, 1976; Alan Lupo, quoted in Hampton and Fayer, *Voices of Freedom*, p. 594.

8. Lukas, *Common Ground*, pp. 122–24, 132, 235–36; Formisano, *Boston Against Busing*, pp. 10–11, 35–36, 45–46.

9. *Boston Globe*, June 22, 1974; Lukas, *Common Ground*, pp. 222–31, 238–39; Formisano, *Boston Against Busing*, pp. 67–69.

10. Lukas, *Common Ground*, pp. 239–40; Formisano, *Boston Against Busing*, pp. 69–70; Malloy, *Southie Won't Go*, p. 6.

11. Malloy, *Southie Won't Go*, p. 4.

12. Formisano, *Boston Against Busing*, pp. 118–20.

13. Ibid., p. 70; Lukas, *Common Ground*, p. 240; see also the highly critical account in Thernstrom and Thernstrom, *America in Black and White*, pp. 331–32.

14. *Boston Globe*, April 4, 1974; Lukas, *Common Ground*, pp. 219–20; Formisano, *Boston Against Busing*, pp. 8, 58–63.

15. Lukas, *Common Ground*, pp. 137–38; Formisano, *Boston Against Busing*, pp. 55–57, 179–83.

16. Peggy Lamson, "The White Northerner's Choice: Mrs. Hicks of Boston," *Atlantic Monthly*, June 1966, pp. 58–62; Formisano, *Boston Against Busing*, p. 39; Lukas, *Common Ground*, pp. 129–30, 134–35.

17. *Newsweek*, November 16, 1967; Lukas, *Common Ground*, pp. 116, 136.

18. Formisano, *Boston Against Busing*, p. 71.

19. Ibid., pp. 4, 138–40; Terry H. Anderson, *The Movement and the Sixties*, p. 406.

20. *Boston Globe*, May 14, 1974, September 1, 1974; Formisano, *Boston Against Busing*, pp. 63, 73–75, 83–84.

21. *Boston Globe*, September 8, 1974.

22. *Boston Globe*, September 10, 1974; Lukas, *Common Ground*, pp. 261–62; Clymer, *Edward M. Kennedy*, pp. 223–24.

23. *Boston Globe*, September 13 and 30, 1974, October 7 and 8, 1974; *New York Times*, October 5, 1974; and see the excellent summary in Formisano, *Boston Against Busing*, pp. 77–81.

24. Formisano, *Boston Against Busing*, pp. xii–xiii; Malloy, *Southie Won't Go*.

25. *New York Times*, December 12, 1974.

26. *Boston Globe*, May 5 and 7, 1975; Lukas, *Common Ground*, pp. 244–45, 251.

27. Lukas, *Common Ground*, p. 153; Formisano, *Boston Against Busing*, pp. 120–21; *Christian Science Monitor*, September 2, 1975.

28. Lukas, *Common Ground*, pp. 280–81.

29. Frum, *How We Got Here*, pp. 260–61; Formisano, *Boston Against Busing*, pp. 117, 212.

30. See Formisano, *Boston Against Busing*, pp. 214–15.

31. Lukas, *Common Ground*, p. 128.

32. Ibid., pp. 451–52; Formisano, *Boston Against Busing*, p. 39; *Boston Globe*, May 7, 1975.

33. Bullard and Stoia, *Hardest Lesson*, pp. 64–71; Formisano, *Boston Against Busing*, p. xiii.

34. Malloy, *Southie Won't Go*, p. 60; *Boston Sunday Globe Magazine*, December 7, 1975.

35. Crawford, *Thunder on the Right*, p. 261.
36. *Boston Globe*, September 11, 1975, September 4, 1985, March 25, 1976; Lukas, *Common Ground*, p. 133; *Boston Globe*, September 11, 1975; Formisano, *Boston Against Busing*, p. 177.
37. *Boston Sunday Globe*, April 13, 1975; Formisano, *Boston Against Busing*, p. 178.
38. *Boston Globe*, April 10, 1975; Lukas, *Common Ground*, pp. 474–75; Formisano, *Boston Against Busing*, pp. 3, 172–202.
39. *Time*, September 8, 1975; *U.S. News and World Report*, May 14, 1979; Frum, *How We Got Here*, pp. 253–54.
40. Lassiter, *Silent Majority*, pp. 277–78, 316–17.
41. Ibid., pp. 176, 194–95, 208–12.
42. Thernstrom and Thernstrom, *America in Black and White*, p. 329; Lassiter, *Silent Majority*, pp. 310–15.
43. *Milliken v. Bradley*, 418 U.S. 717 (1974); Lawrence M. Friedman, *American Law in the 20th Century*, p. 296; Frum, *How We Got Here*, p. 255.
44. *San Francisco Chronicle*, September 7, 1980; Hodgson, *More Equal Than Others*, p. 177; Lassiter, *Silent Majority*, pp. 298–300; Lawrence M. Friedman, *American Law in the 20th Century*, p. 296.
45. See Formisano, *Boston Against Busing*, pp. 197–200.
46. Lukas, *Common Ground*, p. 649; Thernstrom and Thernstrom, *America in Black and White*, pp. 333–34; Formisano, *Boston Against Busing*, p. 211.
47. *Boston Globe*, December 31, 2006, January 27, 2004.
48. *Boston Globe*, May 11, 2007.

## CHAPTER SEVEN: REDNECK CHIC

1. *Time*, May 31, 1971.
2. Schulman, *Seventies*, p. xiii; Lyndon B. Johnson, *Vantage Point*, p. 95.
3. *Time*, May 31, 1971; Phillips, *Emerging Republican Majority*, p. 437; and see Mason, *Richard Nixon and the Quest for a New Majority*, pp. 47–50.
4. *New York Times*, May 10, 1970.
5. *New York Times*, January 9, 1977; and see Cobb, *Industrialization and Southern Society*; Schulman, *From Cotton Belt to Sun Belt*. The statistics are from Shafer and Johnston, *End of Southern Exceptionalism*, pp. 11–12.
6. Schulman, *From Cotton Belt to Sun Belt*, pp. 112–73; Faulkner is quoted in Schulman, *Seventies*, p. 113.
7. *New York Times*, February 9, 1976.
8. *Fortune*, June 1977; Schulman, *Seventies*, pp. 110–11.
9. Arsenault, "End of the Long Hot Summer," pp. 598, 611, 613, 619–20.
10. Frum, *How We Got Here*, p. 325; Broder, *Changing of the Guard*, pp. 338–39; *New York Times*, January 9, 1977.
11. *Time*, September 6, 1976.
12. Jenkins, *Decade of Nightmares*, p. 145; Mahler, *Ladies and Gentlemen, the Bronx Is Burning*, pp. 245–64.
13. *New York Times*, November 10, 1974, July 29, 1977, August 5, 1977; Mahler, *Ladies and Gentlemen, the Bronx Is Burning*, pp. 7–8.
14. Kenneth Jackson, *Crabgrass Frontier*, pp. 272–80; Joshua B. Freeman, *Working-Class New York*, pp. 273–74; James T. Patterson, *Restless Giant*, pp. 37–38.

15. *Time*, October 20, 1975; Hargreaves, *Superpower*, pp. 13–16; *New York Times*, September 1, 1974; Cannato, *Ungovernable City*, pp. 549–51; Joshua B. Freeman, *Working-Class New York*, pp. 209–14, 251–55, 258–70; Mahler, *Ladies and Gentlemen, the Bronx Is Burning*, p. 224; John Robert Greene, *Presidency of Gerald R. Ford*, pp. 90–95.

16. *New York Times*, May 29, 1975, July 2, 1975; Joshua B. Freeman, *Working-Class New York*, pp. 261–67; Mahler, *Ladies and Gentlemen, the Bronx Is Burning*, pp. 8–9.

17. *New York Times*, December 28, 1972; Cannato, *Ungovernable City*, p. 526; Mahler, *Ladies and Gentlemen, the Bronx Is Burning*, p. 233.

18. Mahler, *Ladies and Gentlemen, the Bronx Is Burning*, p. vii; *New York Times*, June 3, 1969.

19. *New York Times*, January 15 and 18, 1973; Mahler, *Ladies and Gentlemen, the Bronx Is Burning*, pp. 330–31.

20. *New York Times*, May 24, 1975, February 11 and 14, 1976, January 9, 1977, July 29, 1977; Schulman, *Seventies*, p. 106; Ferretti, *Year the Big Apple Went Bust*, p. 181; *Washington Post*, July 16, 1977.

21. FitzGerald, *Cities on a Hill*, p. 17; *San Diego Union*, September 13, 1981; Lassiter, *Silent Majority*, pp. 123–24; Arsenault, "End of the Long Hot Summer," pp. 620–21.

22. *New York Times*, February 9, 1976, February 10, 1978, January 9, 1977.

23. Lassiter, *Silent Majority*, pp. 11–12, 47–54, 111.

24. *Time*, May 31, 1971; *New York Times*, July 5, 1979; see also Lassiter, *Silent Majority*, pp. 109–12.

25. *Time*, June 21, 1971; *Atlanta Constitution*, March 23, 1975; Lassiter, *Silent Majority*, p. 114; *New York Times*, December 16, 1977.

26. Lassiter, *Silent Majority*, pp. 213–14; *New York Times*, April 5, 1975, February 12, 1976.

27. Bass and De Vries, *Transformation of Southern Politics*, p. 499; Lassiter, *Silent Majority*, p. 13.

28. *Time*, March 15, 1971.

29. Black and Black, *Rise of Southern Republicans*, pp. 3, 40, 59.

30. Dan T. Carter, *Politics of Rage*, p. 12; Shafer and Johnston, *End of Southern Exceptionalism*, pp. 168–71.

31. Louis Harris, *Is There a Republican Majority?* p. 69; Black and Black, *Rise of Southern Republicans*, pp. 24, 61–62, 257; Shafer and Johnston, *End of Southern Exceptionalism*, pp. 2, 16, 27, 31, 86.

32. Black and Black, *Rise of Southern Republicans*, pp. 103–5; Lassiter, *Silent Majority*, pp. 121–22.

33. *Washington Post*, November 7, 1970; Lassiter, *Silent Majority*, p. 249; Thernstrom and Thernstrom, *America in Black and White*, p. 500.

34. Black and Black, *Rise of Southern Republicans*, pp. 115–16; see also Timothy Noah, "The Legend of Strom's Remorse," *Slate*, December 16, 2002, www.slate.com/id/2075453/; Dan T. Carter, *Politics of Rage*, pp. 457, 461–63.

35. Broder, *Changing of the Guard*, pp. 364–65, 381; Shafer and Johnston, *End of Southern Exceptionalism*, pp. 81–91; *Time*, May 31, 1971; Black and Black, *Rise of Southern Republicans*, pp. 141–43, 173; Lassiter, *Silent Majority*, pp. 269, 274–75.

36. Egerton, *Americanization of Dixie*, pp. 20, xxi.

37. Sale, *Power Shift*; *New York Review of Books*, May 3, 1973; Schulman, *Seventies*, pp. 108–9, 256.

38. Schulman, *Seventies*, pp. 103, 115–17.

39. *New York Times*, July 19, 1971; *Time*, May 6, 1974; Schulman, *Seventies*, pp. xiv, 116.

40. Egerton, *Americanization of Dixie*, p. 203; see also Ben Marsh, "A Rose Colored Map," *Harper's*, July 1977; DiMaggio and Peterson, "From Region to Class"; Cobb, "From Muskogee to Luckenbach."

41. *Time*, May 6, 1974; Nixon, *RN*, p. 539; Schulman, *Seventies*, pp. 39, 115–16.

42. Cohen, *Consumers' Republic*, p. 339; Dan T. Carter, *Politics of Rage*, pp. 316, 381.

43. Blake, "*The Dukes of Hazzard*, Television's Simple South, and Resurrecting the Outlaw Hero"; Schulman, *Seventies*, pp. 116–17; John Shelton Reed, "The Banner That Won't Stay Furled," *Southern Cultures* 8, no. 1 (Spring 2002), pp. 97–99.

44. Bourne, *Jimmy Carter*, p. 251.

45. *Time*, January 3, 1977.

## CHAPTER EIGHT: THE MAN OF A THOUSAND FACES

1. The clip can be seen at www.youtube.com/watch?v=w5OW2hl3eQQ.

2. Morris, *Jimmy Carter*, p. 20; Stroud, *How Jimmy Won*, p. 31.

3. Wooten, *Dasher*, pp. 94, 126–28; Morris, *Jimmy Carter*, pp. 30–37, 41–49, 65, 75, 81–87, 94–95, 100–101; Bourne, *Jimmy Carter*, pp. 25–27, 33–36, 40, 45–50.

4. Stroud, *How Jimmy Won*, pp. 91–93, 102–6; Troy, *Affairs of State*, pp. 239–41.

5. Stroud, *How Jimmy Won*, pp. 131–33; Morris, *Jimmy Carter*, pp. 106–7, 121.

6. Bourne, *Jimmy Carter*, pp. 80–97, 119–43, 148; Wooten, *Dasher*, pp. 223–38; Morris, *Jimmy Carter*, pp. 119, 143.

7. Morris, *Jimmy Carter*, pp. 145–46; Bourne, *Jimmy Carter*, pp. 153, 157.

8. Stroud, *How Jimmy Won*, p. 152; Morris, *Jimmy Carter*, p. 157; Wooten, *Dasher*, pp. 279–81; Bourne, *Jimmy Carter*, p. 168.

9. Wooten, *Dasher*, p. 280; Schram, *Running for President*, pp. 93–94; Morris, *Jimmy Carter*, pp. 156–58.

10. Stroud, *How Jimmy Won*, pp. 181–89 (Jordan), 217–27 (Powell), 199–208 (the others); Bourne, *Jimmy Carter*, pp. 185–86; Morris, *Jimmy Carter*, p. 172.

11. Wooten, *Dasher*, pp. 287, 290–91; Morris, *Jimmy Carter*, p. 185.

12. Morris, *Jimmy Carter*, pp. 178–79, 183–84; Bourne, *Jimmy Carter*, pp. 189–90.

13. Wooten, *Dasher*, pp. 288–89, 292–95; Bourne, *Jimmy Carter*, pp. 192–93; Morris, *Jimmy Carter*, pp. 186–87; *Washington Post*, October 10, 1972.

14. *Time*, May 31, 1971; Wooten, *Dasher*, pp. 326–29; Bourne, *Jimmy Carter*, pp. 200–220.

15. Jordan to Carter, November 4, 1976, reprinted in part in Schram, *Running for President*, pp. 52–54; Bourne, *Jimmy Carter*, pp. 225–33.

16. Schram, *Running for President*, pp. 61–62, 72; Bourne, *Jimmy Carter*, pp. 240, 246, 250–69.

17. Witcover, *Marathon*, p. 111; Morris, *Jimmy Carter*, pp. 194, 212–14, 217–19.

18. *New York Times*, September 24, 1974, November 22, 1974; Clymer, *Edward M. Kennedy*, pp. 209, 225–26; Gillon, *Democrats' Dilemma*, pp. 151–53.

19. *Time*, February 17, 1975; *New York Times*, April 8, 1976; Witcover, *Marathon*, p. 157; Robert G. Kaufman, *Henry M. Jackson*, pp. 302–5, 311–13, 322.

20. *Wall Street Journal*, December 7, 1972; *New York Times*, March 16, 1975; Reichley, *Conservatives in an Age of Change*, p. 320; Leuchtenberg, "Jimmy Carter and the Post–New Deal Presidency," p. 18.

21. Stossel, *Sarge*, pp. 628–30; Witcover, *Marathon*, pp. 127–28, 144–45, 147, 152–54.
22. Stroud, *How Jimmy Won*, p. 256; Witcover, *Marathon*, p. 139; Drew, *American Journal*, p. 43; Schram, *Running for President*, pp. 13, 29–30; Carson and Johnson, *Mo*, pp. 151, 154, 156–59, 171.
23. *New York Times*, October 27, 1975; Bourne, *Jimmy Carter*, p. 278; *New York Times Magazine*, December 14, 1975.
24. *New York Times*, January 19, 20, and 21, 1976; Witcover, *Marathon*, pp. 213–14.
25. Schram, *Running for President*, p. 18; Greenfield, *Real Campaign*, pp. 18–19.
26. *Washington Star*, January 21, 1976; *New York Times*, January 21, 1976; Witcover, *Marathon*, p. 207; Schram, *Running for President*, pp. 7, 11; Stossel, *Sarge*, pp. 633–36.
27. Schram, *Running for President*, pp. 22–23; *Newsweek*, February 2, 1976; Stroud, *How Jimmy Won*, pp. 427–28; Bourne, *Jimmy Carter*, pp. 288–89.
28. *New York Times*, February 27 and 28, 1976; Witcover, *Marathon*, p. 235; Schram, *Running for President*, pp. 19–20; Carson and Johnson, *Mo*, pp. 161–62; Bourne, *Jimmy Carter*, p. 291.
29. Broder, *Changing of the Guard*, p. 14; *Harper's*, March 1976; oral history interview with Stuart Eizenstat, January 29–30, 1982, p. 10, Miller Center, University of Virginia.
30. Morris, *Jimmy Carter*, p. 53; Wooten, *Dasher*, p. 25; Drew, *American Journal*, pp. 145, 348.
31. Jimmy Carter, *Keeping Faith*, p. 74; Stroud, *How Jimmy Won*, p. 15; Drew, *American Journal*, pp. 92–93, 190; Hayward, *Age of Reagan*, pp. 490–91; *New York Times*, August 12, 1976.
32. Hargrove, *Jimmy Carter as President*, p. 7; Wooten, *Dasher*, p. 38; and see Skowronek, *The Politics Presidents Make*, pp. 362–64.
33. Wooten, *Dasher*, pp. 348–49.
34. Barone, *Our Country*, p. 551; Wooten, *Dasher*, pp. 32, 38, 352–53; Shogan, *Promises to Keep*, p. 43.
35. Witcover, *Marathon*, p. 259.
36. Stroud, *How Jimmy Won*, p. 261; Witcover, *Marathon*, p. 165; Dan T. Carter, *Politics of Rage*, pp. 457–58.
37. Drew, *American Journal*, pp. 124, 127.
38. *Washington Post*, March 7, 1976; Witcover, *Marathon*, pp. 257–58; Stroud, *How Jimmy Won*, pp. 170–72; *Nation*, April 3, 1976; *Washington Post*, October 10, 1976.
39. *New York Times*, March 11, 1976; Stroud, *How Jimmy Won*, pp. 267–69; Bourne, *Jimmy Carter*, pp. 299–300.
40. *Time*, April 5, 1976.
41. *New York Times*, March 26, 1976, April 2, 4, and 7, 1976; Drew, *American Journal*, pp. 132–34, 146–53; Robert G. Kaufman, *Henry M. Jackson*, pp. 328–30; Witcover, *Marathon*, pp. 284–86; Carson and Johnson, *Mo*, p. 165.
42. *New York Times*, March 28, 1976, April 7 and 8, 1976; Drew, *American Journal*, pp. 68–72, 79–80, 139; Witcover, *Marathon*, pp. 297–99; Stroud, *How Jimmy Won*, pp. 279–81, 286.
43. *New York Times*, May 3 and 4, 1976; *Washington Post*, May 3 and 6, 1976; Schram, *Running for President*, pp. 134–36; Witcover, *Marathon*, pp. 321–26.
44. Patrick Anderson, *Electing Jimmy Carter*, pp. 2, 164, 168; Wooten, *Dasher*, p. 216; Witcover, *Marathon*, p. 211; Drew, *American Journal*, pp. 98, 90; Stroud, *How Jimmy Won*, p. 137.

45. Witcover, *Marathon*, p. 343; Stroud, *How Jimmy Won*, pp. 305–6.
46. Schram, *Running for President*, pp. 198, 219–20; and see Morris, *Jimmy Carter*, pp. 226–28; Dionne, *Why Americans Hate Politics*, pp. 126–27.
47. Drew, *American Journal*, pp. 290–91.
48. *Washington Post*, July 14, 1976; Stroud, *How Jimmy Won*, pp. 319–20; Patrick Anderson, *Electing Jimmy Carter*, p. 55.
49. Gerald M. Pomper, "The Nominating Contests and Conventions," in Pomper et al., *Election of 1976*, pp. 30–31; Terry H. Anderson, *The Movement and the Sixties*, p. 412.
50. Bourne, *Jimmy Carter*, p. 332; Stroud, *How Jimmy Won*, p. 328; Drew, *American Journal*, pp. 296, 288.
51. Stroud, *How Jimmy Won*, p. 321; Drew, *American Journal*, p. 307.
52. *New York Times*, July 16, 1976; *Washington Post*, July 16, 1976; Witcover, *Marathon*, p. 368.
53. Patrick Anderson, *Electing Jimmy Carter*, pp. 49–63; *Time*, October 4, 1976; *New York Times*, July 16, 1976.
54. Drew, *American Journal*, p. 317.
55. Schram, *Running for President*, p. 218; Patrick Anderson, *Electing Jimmy Carter*, p. 65.

## INTERLUDE: TV'S SUPER WOMEN

1. *Time*, November 22, 1976.
2. *New York Times*, October 17, 1976, March 7, 1977; *Time*, November 22, 1976; Watson, *Defining Visions*, pp. 192–93.
3. Watson, *Defining Visions*, p. 113; *Time*, November 22, 1976; *New York Times*, November 21, 1976, September 11, 1977; the Rand interview is on YouTube.

## CHAPTER NINE: THE WEIRDO FACTOR

1. Stroud, *How Jimmy Won*, pp. 166–69.
2. Witcover, *Marathon*, p. 272; William Martin, *With God on Our Side*, p. 149; *Boston Globe*, April 5, 1976.
3. Bourne, *Jimmy Carter*, pp. 305–7; William Martin, *With God on Our Side*, pp. 148–51; Schram, *Running for President*, p. 113.
4. *Washington Post*, March 28, 1976; *Newsweek*, October 26, 1976; *Christianity Today*, July 1976; *New Republic*, May 8, 1976; William Martin, *With God on Our Side*, pp. 151, 153–54.
5. Hunter, *Culture Wars*, p. 367; U.S. Bureau of the Census, *Statistical Abstract of the United States, 1981* (Washington, D.C., 1983), tables 79, 80, and 81, pp. 52–54; Hodgson, *World Turned Right Side Up*, pp. 165–66; Formisano, *Boston Against Busing*, p. 164.
6. Wuthnow, *Restructuring of American Religion*, pp. 153–72; Roof, *Generation of Seekers*, p. 52; James T. Patterson, *Restless Giant*, p. 144; and see Greeley, *Religious Change in America*.
7. Martin E. Marty, "The Spirit's Holy Errand: The Search for a Spiritual Style in Secular America," *Daedalus* 96, no. 1 (Winter 1967), pp. 97–115; Rossinow, *Politics of Authenticity*, esp. pp. 53–84; *Time*, June 21, 1971; *Life*, June 30, 1972; Terry H. Anderson, *The Movement and the Sixties*, pp. 381–83.

8. *Time*, December 26, 1977; Balmer, *Mine Eyes Have Seen the Glory*, pp. 13–31; McGirr, *Suburban Warriors*, pp. 243–46.

9. *Ramparts*, July 1973; Lou Cannon, *Governor Reagan*, p. 172; *New York Times*, February 15, 1970; Frum, *How We Got Here*, pp. 133–34.

10. Jenkins, *Decade of Nightmares*, pp. 38–39, 129–33.

11. Roof, *Generation of Seekers*, pp. 14–15, 22–23.

12. See ibid., pp. 194–200, 255–61.

13. Bellah et al., *Habits of the Heart*; Inglehart, *Silent Revolution*; Inglehart, *Modernization and Postmodernization*; Collins, *Transforming America*, pp. 151–57; Richard Bach, *Jonathan Livingston Seagull*.

14. *Time*, November 13, 1972; *New York Times*, August 23, 1972; Schulman, *Seventies*, pp. 78–79.

15. Bradford Martin, "Cultural Politics and the Singer/Songwriters of the 1970s"; on Roth, see Morley, *Quest for Epic in Contemporary American Fiction*, pp. 84–118.

16. Morley, *Quest for Epic in Modern American Fiction*; Yankelovich, *New Rules*, pp. 4–5.

17. Rogow, *Psychiatrists*, p. 15; Hale, *Rise and Crisis of Psychoanalysis in the United States*, pp. 276–99, 302; Greenberg, *Nixon's Shadow*, pp. 236–39; Frum, *How We Got Here*, pp. 100–102.

18. See Shepard, *Fritz*, pp. 57–63, 159.

19. *New York Times*, May 2, 1976; *Washington Post*, December 9, 1993; Pressman, *Outrageous Betrayal*; Frum, *How We Got Here*, p. 135.

20. Peter Marin, "The New Narcissism," *Harper's*, October 1975, pp. 45–56.

21. *Time*, September 20, 1976; Hendin, *Age of Sensation*; Battan, "The 'New Narcissism' in 20th-Century America"; Zaretsky, *No Direction Home*, pp. 187–92.

22. Tom Wolfe, "The 'Me' Decade and the Third Great Awakening," *New York*, August 23, 1976, pp. 26–40.

23. Christopher Lasch, "The Narcissist Society," *New York Review of Books*, September 30, 1976; Lasch, *Culture of Narcissism*. For analysis, see Horowitz, *Anxieties of Affluence*, pp. 211–17; Zaretsky, *No Direction Home*, 200–214.

24. See Imogen Tyler, "From 'The Me Decade' to 'The Me Millennium' "; Zaretsky, *No Direction Home*, pp. 185–87, 194.

25. *Time*, October 4, 1976.

26. William Martin, *With God on Our Side*, pp. 2–4, 150; Gillon, *Boomer Nation*, p. 109.

27. Alan Brinkley, "Passions of Oral Roberts"; William Martin, *With God on Our Side*, pp. 16–18, 258–59.

28. Boyer, "Evangelical Resurgence in 1970s American Protestantism," pp. 29–30; Marsden, *Fundamentalism and American Culture*, pp. 176–98; William Martin, *With God on Our Side*, pp. 39–48.

29. Egerton, *Americanization of Dixie*, p. 198; *Time*, December 26, 1977.

30. Hodgson, *World Turned Right Side Up*, p. 166; Boyer, *When Time Shall Be No More*, p. 3.

31. Alan Brinkley, "Problem of American Conservatism"; Roof, *Generation of Seekers*, pp. 11–12, 13–15.

32. FitzGerald, *Cities on a Hill*, p. 190; Roof, *Generation of Seekers*, p. 15; McGirr, *Suburban Warriors*, pp. 49–50.

33. Roof, *Generation of Seekers*, p. 91; Hodgson, *World Turned Right Side Up*, p. 270; McGirr, *Suburban Warriors*, pp. 94, 248, 256–57, 261.

34. *Time*, July 21, 1975, February 4, 1980; Hadden and Swann, *Prime Time Preachers*, pp. 34–37, 73–83; Joel A. Carpenter, "From Fundamentalism to the New Evangelical Coalition," in Marsden, *Evangelicalism and Modern America*, pp. 8, 11; William Martin, *With God on Our Side*, p. 18; FitzGerald, *Cities on a Hill*, pp. 126–27.

35. Hadden and Swann, *Prime Time Preachers*, pp. 34–37.

36. William Martin, "The Birth of a Media Myth," *Atlantic Monthly*, June 1981, pp. 7, 10–11; Hadden and Swann, *Prime Time Preachers*, pp. 6–7, 51–52, 55, 60–62, 178–79; and see Diamond, *Not by Politics Alone*, pp. 63–67.

37. *Time*, December 27, 1977; *New Republic*, September 29, 1986; Alan Brinkley, "Passions of Oral Roberts"; Hadden and Swann, *Prime Time Preachers*, pp. 12–13, 22–24, 101–2; McGirr, *Suburban Warriors*, pp. 252–54.

38. Hadden and Swann, *Prime Time Preachers*, pp. 29–30; McGirr, *Suburban Warriors*, pp. 249–53.

39. *New York Times*, May 15, 1980; *Time*, May 26, 1980, February 7, 1983, March 18, 1985; Hadden and Swann, *Prime Time Preachers*, p. 29; McGirr, *Suburban Warriors*, pp. 250–51.

40. Wuthnow, "Political Rebirth of American Evangelicals," pp. 167–68; William Martin, *With God on Our Side*, pp. 11–13.

41. Dan T. Carter, *Politics of Rage*, pp. 298–99, 346, 460–61.

42. William Martin, *With God on Our Side*, pp. 97–98.

43. Frady, *Billy Graham*, pp. 235–37; *Charlotte Observer*, October 15, 1971; William Martin, *With God on Our Side*, pp. 25–46, 95–98.

44. *New York Times*, October 10, 1976; *Time*, January 2, 2007; Troy, *Affairs of State*, pp. 230, 232–33.

## CHAPTER TEN: REAGAN COUNTRY

1. *Time*, July 19, 1976; Remarks of the President at Valley Forge State Park, Remarks of the President at Independence Hall, July 4, 1976, Fourth of July Weekend, box 190, ARBA Records, NARA II.

2. *Time*, July 19, 1976; *New York Times*, July 5 and 6, 1976; Lukas, *Common Ground*, pp. 528–30.

3. *Bicentennial Times*, April 1976, June 1976, July 1976, December 1976, box 157, ARBA Records, NARA II; *Time*, September 29, 1975; *Chicago Tribune*, November 11, 1975; *Washington Star*, January 19, 1976; *Philadelphia Evening Bulletin*, February 2, 1976; *Washington Post*, July 7, 1976; *Chicago Tribune*, July 7, 1976.

4. *Time*, July 19, 1976; John Robert Greene, *Presidency of Gerald R. Ford*, p. 190.

5. Reichley, *Conservatives in an Age of Change*, p. 319; *Conservative Digest*, September 1975, June 1975; Crawford, *Thunder on the Right*, p. 234; Blumenthal, *Rise of the Counter-establishment*, p. 35; Kutler, *Wars of Watergate*, p. 577.

6. *New York Times*, October 4, 1974, November 8, 1975; *Los Angeles Times*, February 18, 1975; Betty Ford, *Times of My Life*, pp. 168, 194; Troy, *Affairs of State*, pp. 209–13, 220–22; Critchlow, *Phyllis Schlafly and Grassroots Conservatism*, pp. 233–34.

7. *New York Daily News*, December 20, 1975; Witcover, *Marathon*, p. 58; Troy, *Affairs of State*, pp. 223–25.

8. Brennan, *Turning Right*, pp. 52–53; Rusher, *Rise of the Right*, p. 264; Mason, *Richard Nixon and the Quest for a New Majority*, p. 215; Howard Callaway to President Ford, "Weekly Report Number One," July 15, 1975, box 14, Richard B. Cheney Files, Ford Library; *Washington Post*, July 24 and 25, 1975; Gerald R. Ford, *Time to*

*Heal*, p. 328; and see John Robert Greene, *Presidency of Gerald R. Ford*, pp. 159–61; Douglas Brinkley, *Gerald R. Ford*, pp. 115, 118.

9. Lou Cannon, *President Reagan*, pp. 17–18.

10. Wills, *Reagan's America*, pp. 1–2; Lou Cannon, *Governor Reagan*, pp. 17–18; Diggins, *Ronald Reagan*, pp. 58–60.

11. Lou Cannon, *Governor Reagan*, pp. 11–15, 18, 21, 79–80; Collins, *Transforming America*, pp. 31–32; Haynes Johnson, *Sleepwalking Through History*, pp. 42–43; Noonan, *What I Saw at the Revolution*, p. 150.

12. Lou Cannon, *President Reagan*, pp. 22–23; Wills, *Reagan's America*, pp. 178–79.

13. Leuchtenberg, *In the Shadow of FDR*, p. 211; Wills, *Reagan's America*, pp. 215–58; Dallek, *Right Moment*, p. 33; Lou Cannon, *Governor Reagan*, pp. 82–102.

14. Dallek, *Right Moment*, pp. 33–34; Collins, *Transforming America*, p. 35; Lou Cannon, *Governor Reagan*, pp. 93, 101.

15. Hamby, *Liberalism and Its Challengers*, p. 346; Wills, *Reagan's America*, pp. 282–83; Lou Cannon, *Governor Reagan*, pp. 108–9, 122–25; Dallek, *Right Moment*, pp. 67–68.

16. Dallek, *Right Moment*, pp. 72–76.

17. *New Republic*, July 2, 1966; *New York Times*, June 1 and 6, 1966; Lou Cannon, *Governor Reagan*, pp. 116–17, 139; Lou Cannon, *President Reagan*, p. 25; Ehrman, *Eighties*, pp. 21–22; Reeves, *President Reagan*, pp. xii–xiii; Collins, *Transforming America*, p. 51.

18. James Q. Wilson, "A Guide to Reagan Country," *Commentary*, May 1967, p. 37; Lou Cannon, *Governor Reagan*, pp. 118–21, 174; Diggins, *Ronald Reagan*, pp. xvii, 40–41, 51.

19. Dallek, *Ronald Reagan*, pp. 38–39; Lou Cannon, *Governor Reagan*, pp. 171–389, esp. pp. 227–28; Wills, *Reagan's America*, pp. 312–13.

20. Dallek, *Ronald Reagan*, pp. 42–43, 47; Crawford, *Thunder on the Right*, p. 121; Lou Cannon, *Governor Reagan*, pp. 297–321, 359, 213–14; Wills, *Reagan's America*, p. 315.

21. Witcover, *Marathon*, pp. 65–66; Shirley, *Reagan's Revolution*, pp. 22–23; Lou Cannon, *Governor Reagan*, pp. 395–99; Hayward, *Age of Reagan*, pp. 388–89.

22. Mason, *Richard Nixon and the Quest for a New Majority*, pp. 216–18; Shirley, *Reagan's Revolution*, pp. 34–38.

23. *New York Times*, November 20 and 21, 1975; Shirley, *Reagan's Revolution*, pp. 91–92; Hayward, *Age of Reagan*, pp. 459–60; *Boston Globe*, January 30, 1976.

24. *Christian Science Monitor*, June 3, 1976; Drew, *American Journal*, pp. 51–52; Witcover, *Marathon*, pp. 388–89.

25. Drew, *American Journal*, p. 49; *Chicago Daily News*, November 21, 1975; *Time*, November 24, 1975; *New Republic*, January 3, 1976; *New York Times*, November 19, 1975; *Harper's*, February 1976.

26. Shirley, *Reagan's Revolution*, pp. 80–85; Witcover, *Marathon*, pp. 374, 380–83; *Time*, January 19, 1976.

27. Drew, *American Journal*, pp. 28–29, 31–32.

28. *Time*, March 8, 1976; *New Republic*, January 24, 1976; Witcover, *Marathon*, pp. 393–94; Lou Cannon, *Governor Reagan*, pp. 412–13.

29. Witcover, *Marathon*, p. 394; Lou Cannon, *Governor Reagan*, pp. 414–15.

30. Stroud, *How Jimmy Won*, p. 248; Witcover, *Marathon*, p. 395; Lou Cannon, *Governor Reagan*, p. 416; Shirley, *Reagan's Revolution*, pp. 128–29.

31. Witcover, *Marathon*, p. 398.

32. Ibid., pp. 400, 403; Lou Cannon, *Governor Reagan*, p. 420.

33. *New York Times*, March 5, 1976.

34. Witcover, *Marathon*, pp. 401–2.

35. Shirley, *Reagan's Revolution*, pp. 158, 160, 167; Witcover, *Marathon*, pp. 408–13; *New Republic*, April 10, 1976; *New York Times*, March 22, 1976; Lou Cannon, *Governor Reagan*, p. 425.

36. Shirley, *Reagan's Revolution*, pp. 174–76; Lou Cannon, *Governor Reagan*, pp. 432–34.

37. Drew, *American Journal*, p. 237; *New York Times*, March 31, 1976, April 1, 1976; Witcover, *Marathon*, p. 417; Shirley, *Reagan's Revolution*, pp. 185–86.

38. "An Explanation of the Reagan Victories in Texas and the Caucus States," c. May 1976, "Reagan, Ronald (2)," box 25, Jerry Jones Files, Ford Library; *Washington Post*, April 21, 1976.

39. *Washington Star*, May 5, 1976; *New Republic*, May 15, 1976.

40. Witcover, *Marathon*, pp. 422, 425–29, 433; *New York Times*, May 22, 1976; Gerald R. Ford, *Time to Heal*, p. 388; *Washington Post*, May 27, 1976; *Time*, July 19, 1976.

41. *Time*, August 16, 1976.

42. Witcover, *Marathon*, p. 475.

43. *New York Times*, July 20, 1976; *Washington Post*, July 21, 1976; Lou Cannon, *Governor Reagan*, pp. 427–28; *Washington Post*, July 19, 1976.

44. Witcover, *Marathon*, pp. 456, 458–61; Lou Cannon, *Governor Reagan*, pp. 429–30; Shirley, *Reagan's Revolution*, pp. 272–75.

45. *Washington Post*, July 27 and 28, 1976; *New York Times*, July 28, 1976; Witcover, *Marathon*, p. 463; Shirley, *Reagan's Revolution*, pp. 275, 277–78, 280; Gerald R. Ford, *Time to Heal*, p. 394.

46. Drew, *American Journal*, p. 395; Gerald R. Ford, *Time to Heal*, p. 399.

47. Gerald R. Ford, *Time to Heal*, pp. 400–404.

48. *New York Times*, August 20, 1976; *New York Review of Books*, September 16, 1976; Drew, *American Journal*, pp. 365, 383–85, 392; Nessen, *It Sure Looks Different from the Inside*, pp. 229–31; Mann, *Rise of the Vulcans*, pp. 72–73; Republican Party platform, August 18, 1976, www.presidency.ucsb.edu/ws/index.php?pid=25843.

49. *New York Times*, August 20, 1976; *Washington Post*, August 20, 1976; Lou Cannon, *Governor Reagan*, pp. 432–33.

50. *New York Times*, August 20, 1976; Drew, *American Journal*, pp. 407–9.

51. The transcript is at www.reaganfoundation.org/reagan/speeches/convention.asp; see also *Washington Post*, August 21, 1976; Martin Anderson, *Revolution*, pp. 64–72.

## CHAPTER ELEVEN: THE JIMMY AND JERRY SHOW

1. Schram, *Running for President*, pp. 273–75; Stroud, *How Jimmy Won*, p. 344; Witcover, *Marathon*, pp. 545–46; Patrick Anderson, *Electing Jimmy Carter*, pp. 101–2.

2. Schram, *Running for President*, pp. 120–21, 219–21.

3. Witcover, *Marathon*, p. 517; Schram, *Running for President*, pp. 239–50 (which reprints the Jordan "blueprint" for victory); Hayward, *Age of Reagan*, p. 499; Drew, *American Journal*, p. 418; Skowronek, *The Politics Presidents Make*, pp. 376–79.

4. Gerald R. Ford, *Time to Heal*, pp. 377–78, 414; Witcover, *Marathon*, p. 530.

5. Schram, *Running for President*, pp. 287, 309.

6. See Pomper et al., *Election of 1976*, pp. 36–40, 44; Iwan W. Morgan, *Beyond the Liberal Consensus*, pp. 106–8.

7. Mason, *Richard Nixon and the Quest for a New Majority*, p. 227; Jamieson, *Packaging the Presidency*, pp. 347–49, 374.

8. Patrick Anderson, *Electing Jimmy Carter*, pp. 67–68, 162; Drew, *American Journal*, pp. 310, 416; *Atlantic Monthly*, June 1976; Stroud, *How Jimmy Won*, pp. 179, 184, 218, 223, 336, 347; Witcover, *Marathon*, p. 524; Bourne, *Jimmy Carter*, pp. 315–16, 337.

9. Schram, *Running for President*, p. 301.

10. *Playboy*, November 1976.

11. Patrick Anderson, *Electing Jimmy Carter*, p. 112; William Martin, *With God on Our Side*, p. 158; Jamieson, *Packaging the Presidency*, p. 363.

12. Witcover, *Marathon*, pp. 570, 589–90; Stroud, *How Jimmy Won*, pp. 356–57.

13. Schram, *Running for President*, p. 304; *National Review*, October 1, 1976; Patrick Anderson, *Electing Jimmy Carter*, pp. 115–16.

14. *Newsweek*, October 4, 1976; Gerald R. Ford, *Time to Heal*, pp. 414–15; Nessen, *It Sure Looks Different from the Inside*, pp. 258, 263; Witcover, *Marathon*, pp. 573–74.

15. Transcript of the first presidential debate, September 23, 1976, www.debates.org/pages/trans76a.html; Stroud, *How Jimmy Won*, pp. 363–66; Drew, *American Journal*, pp. 438–39.

16. Stroud, *How Jimmy Won*, pp. 368, 371; *New York Times*, September 27, 1976.

17. Witcover, *Marathon*, pp. 585–87, 590–92; *New York Times*, October 1 and 5, 1976.

18. Jimmy Carter, *Why Not the Best?* p. 141; *New York Times*, March 16, 1976, June 24, 1976.

19. NSC briefing book, folder 1, box 2, White House Special Files, Ford Library; "The Foreign Policy Debate," October 3, 1976, box 2, White House Special Files, Ford Library; John Robert Greene, *Presidency of Gerald R. Ford*, p. 184; Isaacson, *Kissinger*, p. 701.

20. Stroud, *How Jimmy Won*, p. 374; transcript of the second presidential debate, October 6, 1976, www.debates.org/pages/trans76b.html.

21. Witcover, *Marathon*, p. 598; John Robert Greene, *Presidency of Gerald R. Ford*, p. 185.

22. Gerald R. Ford, *Time to Heal*, pp. 423–25; Witcover, *Marathon*, pp. 600, 602–3; Robert T. Hartmann, *Palace Politics*, p. 413.

23. Schram, *Running for President*, p. 322.

24. Witcover, *Marathon*, pp. 603, 607; *New Republic*, October 23, 1976; Isaacson, *Kissinger*, p. 703.

25. Witcover, *Marathon*, pp. 614–15.

26. See Sandbrook, *Eugene McCarthy*, pp. 262–74.

27. Mieczkowski, *Gerald Ford and the Challenges of the 1970s*, p. 336; Witcover, *Marathon*, p. 617; Drew, *American Journal*, p. 494. Ford's campaign commercials are online at www.4president.tv and livingroomcandidate.movingimage.us/index.php.

28. Gerald R. Ford, *Time to Heal*, pp. 428, 430–31; Witcover, *Marathon*, p. 619.

29. Witcover, *Marathon*, p. 629; Drew, *American Journal*, pp. 488–89, 508–9, 518, 521; Stroud, *How Jimmy Won*, pp. 383–98; Schram, *Running for President*, pp. 348–49.

30. *New Republic*, November 6, 1976; Witcover, *Marathon*, pp. 625, 628; Stroud, *How Jimmy Won*, p. 392; Schram, *Running for President*, p. 343.

31. *New York Times*, November 1, 1976.

32. *New York Times*, November 2, 1976; Drew, *American Journal*, p. 526; Stroud, *Why Jimmy Won*, p. 403; Schram, *Running for President*, pp. 349–50.

33. *Chicago Tribune*, November 1, 1976; Witcover, *Marathon*, pp. 630–31.

34. Gerald R. Ford, *Time to Heal*, p. 432; *New Republic*, November 13, 1976; Schram, *Running for President*, p. 359.

35. *New York Times*, November 2, 1976; Carroll, *It Seemed Like Nothing Happened*, p. 204; Drew, *American Journal*, p. 529.

36. Stroud, *How Jimmy Won*, pp. 407–8.

37. Gerald R. Ford, *Time to Heal*, p. 433.

38. Ibid.; Witcover, *Marathon*, p. 3.

39. Stroud, *How Jimmy Won*, pp. 410–11; Schram, *Running for President*, p. 352.

40. Witcover, *Marathon*, pp. 4, 7–9; Schram, *Running for President*, p. 354.

41. Gerald R. Ford, *Time to Heal*, p. 434; Witcover, *Marathon*, pp. 12–13.

42. Witcover, *Marathon*, p. 12; Schram, *Running for President*, p. 355; Stroud, *How Jimmy Won*, p. 411.

43. For these and other statistics, see Pomper et al., *Election of 1976*, esp. pp. 54–83.

44. See ibid., pp. 62–63; Barone, *Our Country*, pp. 556–58; Dionne, *Why Americans Hate Politics*, pp. 128–31; Burton I. Kaufman, *Presidency of James Earl Carter, Jr.*, pp. 19–20; Stroud, *Why Jimmy Won*, p. 432.

45. James Cannon, *Time and Chance*, p. 414; Schram, *Running for President*, p. 367; Lou Cannon, *Governor Reagan*, p. 434; Douglas Brinkley, *Gerald R. Ford*, pp. 139–40.

46. Reichley, *Conservatives in an Age of Change*, pp. 401–3; Mieczkowski, *Gerald Ford and the Challenges of the 1970s*, pp. 193, 340.

47. Mieczkowski, *Gerald Ford and the Challenges of the 1970s*, pp. 46–47; *New York Times*, January 13, 1977; Thomas P. O'Neill, *Man of the House*, p. 271; *Washington Post*, January 16, 1977.

48. Gerald R. Ford, *Time to Heal*, pp. 434–35; Betty Ford, *Times of My Life*, pp. 272–73; *New Republic*, November 13, 1976; Schram, *Running for President*, p. 359.

49. Gerald R. Ford, *Time to Heal*, p. 435.

50. Drew, *American Journal*, p. 543; Stroud, *How Jimmy Won*, pp. 413–14; Schram, *Running for President*, p. 357.

## WASHINGTON, D.C., JANUARY 1977

1. Gerald R. Ford, *Time to Heal*, pp. 440–41.

2. *Time*, January 24, 1976; Jimmy Carter, *Keeping Faith*, p. 19.

3. *Washington Post*, January 21, 1977; Wooten, *Dasher*, pp. 53–54; Jimmy Carter, *Keeping Faith*, pp. 19–21.

4. Jimmy Carter, *Keeping Faith*, pp. 17, 23–24.

## CHAPTER TWELVE: MR. CARTER GOES TO WASHINGTON

1. Wooten, *Dasher*, pp. 373–74.

2. Burton I. Kaufman, *Presidency of James Earl Carter, Jr.*, pp. 25–27; Bourne, *Jimmy Carter*, pp. 357–64.

3. Oral history interview with Hamilton Jordan, November 6, 1981, pp. 3–16, Miller Center, University of Virginia; Leuchtenberg, "Jimmy Carter and the Post–New Deal Presidency," p. 10; Powell, *Other Side of the Story*, p. 207.

4. Thomas P. O'Neill, *Man of the House*, pp. 310–11; John A. Farrell, *Tip O'Neill and the Democratic Century*, pp. 450–52.

5. Thomas P. O'Neill, *Man of the House*, pp. 302, 315–16; Morris, *Jimmy Carter*, pp. 243–44.

6. Oral history interview with Jimmy Carter, November 29, 1982, p. 69, Miller Center; James T. Patterson, *Restless Giant*, p. 112.

7. Wooten, *Dasher*, pp. 305–6; Jordan, *Crisis*, p. 34; Jimmy Carter, *Keeping Faith*, pp. 56–57.

8. Jimmy Carter, *Keeping Faith*, p. 65; Troy, *Affairs of State*, p. 260; *Washington Post*, February 4, 1977.

9. *Public Papers of the Presidents of the United States: Jimmy Carter, 1979* (Washington, D.C., 1980), bk. 1, p. 751; *Atlantic Monthly*, May 1979.

10. Burton I. Kaufman, *Presidency of James Earl Carter, Jr.*, p. 31; Morris, *Jimmy Carter*, p. 242; Jimmy Carter, *Keeping Faith*, p. 73.

11. John A. Farrell, *Tip O'Neill and the Democratic Century*, pp. 461–62; Jimmy Carter, *Keeping Faith*, p. 79.

12. Biven, *Jimmy Carter's Economy*, p. 80; Skowronek, *The Politics Presidents Make*, pp. 386–87; John A. Farrell, *Tip O'Neill and the Democratic Century*, p. 458.

13. Biven, *Jimmy Carter's Economy*, pp. 27, 46, 59, 258; Collins, *More*, pp. 157–58.

14. Biven, *Jimmy Carter's Economy*, pp. 36, 70; Hargrove, *Jimmy Carter as President*, pp. 88–89; *Public Papers of the Presidents of the United States: Jimmy Carter, 1977* (Washington, D.C., 1978), bk. 1, pp. 47–55, 349–50; Melvin Dubofsky, "Jimmy Carter and the End of the Politics of Productivity," in Fink and Graham, *Carter Presidency*, p. 100.

15. Hargrove, *Jimmy Carter as President*, pp. 106, 90–91; Biven, *Jimmy Carter's Economy*, pp. 125, 206.

16. Hargrove, *Jimmy Carter as President*, p. 90; Biven, *Jimmy Carter's Economy*, pp. 72, 75–78; *Time*, January 24, 1977; Schulman, "Slouching Toward the Supply Side," p. 55.

17. Barrow, "Age of Limits," p. 160; Morris, *Jimmy Carter*, p. 256.

18. *Time*, February 14, 1977.

19. *Public Papers of the Presidents of the United States: Jimmy Carter, 1977*, bk. 1, pp. 71, 656–63; *Newsweek*, May 2, 1977.

20. Barrow, "Age of Limits," pp. 162–66; Hargrove, *Jimmy Carter as President*, pp. 47–51; Burton I. Kaufman, *Presidency of James Earl Carter, Jr.*, pp. 33–34.

21. *Time*, October 31, 1977; *Congressional Quarterly Weekly Report*, October 8, 1977; Barrow, "Age of Limits," pp. 166–67; Jimmy Carter, *Keeping Faith*, p. 107.

22. Jimmy Carter, *Keeping Faith*, pp. 129–33; Burton I. Kaufman, *Presidency of James Earl Carter, Jr.*, pp. 60–62.

23. Skowronek, *The Politics Presidents Make*, pp. 387–89; *New York Review of Books*, September 29, 1977; *Atlantic Monthly*, May 1979; Carter oral history interview, pp. 10–11; Jimmy Carter, *Keeping Faith*, pp. 127–28; Bourne, *Jimmy Carter*, p. 415.

24. Patrick Caddell, "Summary of Issue Concerns of the American People," August 31 to September 12, 1977, box 33, Staff Office Files, Chief of Staff—Jordan, Carter Library; *Newsweek*, May 2, 1977; Bourne, *Jimmy Carter*, p. 524 (note to p. 422); *New York Times*, December 18, 1977.

25. *Washington Post*, January 16, 1978; Time, January 30, 1978; Anson, *Exile*, pp. 183–85; Solberg, *Hubert Humphrey*, pp. 455–56.

26. *Washington Post*, January 20, 1978.

27. Burton I. Kaufman, *Presidency of James Earl Carter, Jr.*, pp. 73, 76.

28. *New York Times*, March 7, 1978; Burton I. Kaufman, *Presidency of James Earl Carter, Jr.*, pp. 78–79; Morris, *Jimmy Carter*, pp. 257–59.

29. Burton I. Kaufman, *Presidency of James Earl Carter, Jr.*, pp. 80–81; Schulman, "Slouching Toward the Supply Side," p. 58; Biven, *Jimmy Carter's Economy*, pp. 136–39; Hargrove and Morley, *The President and the Council of Economic Advisers*, p. 488.

30. Burton I. Kaufman, *Presidency of James Earl Carter, Jr.*, pp. 81–82; *New York Times*, May 7, 1978.

31. Biven, *Jimmy Carter's Economy*, pp. 114–15, 168–70.

32. Hargrove, *Jimmy Carter as President*, pp. 95–96, 98; Biven, *Jimmy Carter's Economy*, pp. 134–35; Jerry Rafshoon to President Carter, September 1, 1978, box 145, "Domestic Policy Staff—Eizenstat," Carter Library; Schulman, "Slouching Toward the Supply Side," p. 58.

33. *Public Papers of the Presidents of the United States: Jimmy Carter, 1978* (Washington, D.C., 1979), bk. 2, pp. 1839–45.

34. Oral history interview with Alfred Kahn, December 10–11, 1981, pp. 2–6, Miller Center; exit interview with Alfred Kahn, tape 1, Carter Library, quoted in Schulman, "Slouching Toward the Supply Side," pp. 59–60.

35. Biven, *Jimmy Carter's Economy*, pp. 169–71.

36. Oral history interview with Stuart Eizenstat, January 29–30, 1982, p. 102, Miller Center; Dubofsky, "Jimmy Carter and the End of the Politics of Productivity," p. 97; Burton I. Kaufman, *Presidency of James Earl Carter, Jr.*, pp. 101, 115.

37. *Washington Post*, March 9, 1977; Leuchtenberg, "Jimmy Carter and the Post–New Deal Presidency," p. 15.

38. Gillon, *Democrats' Dilemma*, p. 171; Jimmy Carter, *Keeping Faith*, p. 102; Carter oral history interview, p. 66.

39. Caddell to Carter, "Initial Paper on Political Strategy," November 1976, box 4, Jody Powell Papers, Carter Library; *Washington Post*, May 11, 1977; *New York Times*, February 24, 1979; Hayward, *Age of Reagan*, p. 514; *Washington Post*, September 2, 1978.

40. Clymer, *Edward M. Kennedy*, pp. 245–48, 252.

41. *New York Times*, July 29, 1978; Burton I. Kaufman, *Presidency of James Earl Carter, Jr.*, pp. 104–5; Patrick Anderson, *Electing Jimmy Carter*, p. 72; Powell, *Other Side of the Story*, p. 185; Clymer, *Edward M. Kennedy*, pp. 247, 253–54, 281; Theodore H. White, *America in Search of Itself*, pp. 274–75.

42. *New York Times*, December 9, 10, and 11, 1978; *Time*, December 18, 1978; *Washington Post*, September 2, 1978.

43. *New York Times*, December 10, 1978; Clymer, *Edward M. Kennedy*, pp. 276–77.

## INTERLUDE: STEELTOWN, U.S.A.

1. *Washington Post*, October 26, 1980.

2. *New York Times Magazine*, June 6, 1982; Berkowitz, *Something Happened*, pp. 121–22.

3. Lynd, *Fight Against Shutdowns*, pp. 22–23; Lynd, "Community Right to Industrial Property," pp. 930–31.

4. See Lynd, *Fight Against Shutdowns*, pp. 926–58; Lynd, "Community Right to Industrial Property," pp. 931–35; Berkowitz, *Something Happened*, p. 122.

5. Tom Hunter, "Back to Work in Youngstown," Youngstown Save Steel Jobs Rally Materials, Gerald Dickey Collection, Youngstown Historical Center of Industry and Labor, omp.ohiolink.edu/OMP/YourScrapbook?user=yhc2003; Lynd, "Community Right to Industrial Property," p. 935.

6. Cowie, "Vigorously Left, Right, and Center," p. 101; Lichtenstein, *State of the Union*, pp. 185–90, 212–34; Joshua B. Freeman, *Working-Class New York*, pp. 272, 280–81.

7. *Washington Post*, October 26, 1980; Lynd, *Fight Against Shutdowns*, pp. 6–9; Cowie, "Vigorously Left, Right, and Center," p. 96.

## CHAPTER THIRTEEN: ROOTS AND RIGHTS

1. Chaney, "Political Changes in Terrible Terrell."

2. *New York Times*, August 16, 1977.

3. *New York Times*, February 28, 1978; William Julius Wilson, *Declining Significance of Race*, pp. 22, 182.

4. Pinkney, *Myth of Black Progress*, p. 15; Thernstrom and Thernstrom, *America in Black and White*, pp. 184–87; Garreau, *Edge City*, p. 146.

5. Edsall, *Chain Reaction*, pp. 116–17; Thernstrom and Thernstrom, *America in Black and White*, pp. 190, 192; Schulman, *Seventies*, p. 54.

6. Edsall, *Chain Reaction*, p. 13; Lassiter, *Silent Majority*, p. 169; Schuman, Steeh, and Bobo, *Racial Attitudes in America*, pp. 75, 107, 118; Thernstrom and Thernstrom, *America in Black and White*, p. 500.

7. *New York Times*, December 30, 1979; Broder, *Changing of the Guard*, p. 309; Thernstrom and Thernstrom, *America in Black and White*, p. 289.

8. *New York Times*, May 12, 1974.

9. Marable, *From the Grassroots*, p. 212; *New York Times*, December 30, 1979; James T. Patterson, *Restless Giant*, p. 18.

10. Thernstrom and Thernstrom, *America in Black and White*, p. 234; Fairclough, *Better Day Coming*, p. 298; George, *Post-soul Nation*, p. 12.

11. *New York Times*, December 30, 1979, May 16, 1982; George, *Post-soul Nation*, p. 12; see also Edsall, *Chain Reaction*, p. 16; Department of Justice, *Bureau of Justice Statistics Bulletin: Prisoners in 2005* (Washington, D.C., 2006).

12. U.S. Department of Labor, "The Negro Family: The Case for National Action" (1965), www.dol.gov/oasam/programs/history/webid-meynihan.htm; Edsall, *Chain Reaction*, p. 107; Thernstrom and Thernstrom, *America in Black and White*, pp. 237–38, 240; U.S. Bureau of the Census, *Statistical Abstract of the United States, 2002* (Washington, D.C., 2002), p. 59; Wandersee, *On the Move*, p. 136; Gillon, *That's Not What We Meant to Do*, pp. 74–76; Kelley and Lewis, *To Make Our World Anew*, pp. 551–52; *New York Times*, January 12, 1979; Wallace, *Black Macho and the Myth of the Superwoman.*

13. *Time*, August 29, 1977; Auletta, *Underclass*, p. 26.

14. Sugrue, *Origins of the Urban Crisis*, pp. 261–62, 269; Christopher Jencks, "Is the American Underclass Growing?" in Jencks and Peterson, *Urban Underclass*, pp. 55–56.

15. See William Julius Wilson, *Truly Disadvantaged.*

16. *New York Times*, January 26, 1977; *Time*, February 7, 1977.

17. *New York Times*, January 28, 1977, February 20, 1977, March 19, 1977.

18. *New York Times*, October 11, 1976, February 21, 1977; Jacobson, *Roots Too*, p. 312;

Cruse, *Crisis of the Negro Intellectual*, pp. 8–9; Cruse, *Plural but Equal*, p. 346; Van Deburg, *New Day in Babylon*, p. 171; and see Street, *Culture War in the Civil Rights Movement*.

19. Nelson George, "Fools, Suckas, and Baadasssss Brothers," in Kahn, George-Warren, and Dahl, *Rolling Stone*, pp. 58–61; Guerrero, *Framing Blackness*, pp. 69–74; Lev, *American Films of the 70s*, pp. 127–33; *New York Times*, December 20, 1979.

20. *Washington Post*, February 1, 1998; Schulman, *Seventies*, pp. 60–63.

21. Democratic Party platform, July 12, 1976, www.presidency.ucsb.edu/ws/index. php?pid=29606; *New York Times*, July 15, 1976, May 17, 1979.

22. Carroll, *It Seemed Like Nothing Happened*, pp. 104–9, 252–56.

23. Gillon, *That's Not What We Meant to Do*, pp. 176–83; Schrag, *Paradise Lost*, p. 57; Broder, *Changing of the Guard*, p. 280.

24. See Kalman, *Strange Career of Legal Liberalism*; Sandel, *Democracy's Discontent*; Samuel Walker, *Rights Revolution*; Lawrence M. Friedman, *American Law in the 20th Century*; Skrentny, *Minority Rights Revolution*.

25. Sunstein, *After the Rights Revolution*, pp. 12–30; Davies, *See Government Grow*, pp. 277–88; Melnick, *Between the Lines*, p. 45; Samuelson, *Good Life and Its Discontents*, p. 184; James T. Patterson, *Restless Giant*, p. 24; *Goldberg v. Kelly*, 397 U.S. 254 (1970); see also Davies, *From Opportunity to Entitlement*, a superb study.

26. Skocpol, *Diminished Democracy*, pp. 127–74, 199–228; James T. Patterson, *Restless Giant*, pp. 27, 86–90; Otis L. Graham Jr., "Liberalism After the Sixties: A Reconnaissance," in William H. Chafe (ed.) *The Achievement of American Liberalism* (New York, 2003) p. 309.

27. Sunstein, *After the Rights Revolution*, pp. 12–30; Graham, "Liberalism After the Sixties," pp. 309–10; Edsall, *Chain Reaction*, p. 45; Hodgson, *More Equal Than Others*, p. 10; Davies, *See Government Grow*, pp. 1–8.

28. *Congressional Record*, April 9, 1964, p. 7420.

29. Graham, *Civil Rights Era*, pp. 106–9; Thernstrom and Thernstrom, *America in Black and White*, pp. 424–29; Gillon, *That's Not What We Meant to Do*, pp. 120–41.

30. *Griggs v. Duke Power Co.*, 401 U.S. 424 (1971); Gillon, *That's Not What We Meant to Do*, pp. 148–51.

31. Kotlowski, *Nixon's Civil Rights*, pp. 99–115; Gillon, *That's Not What We Meant to Do*, pp. 142–48.

32. Terry H. Anderson, *In Pursuit of Fairness*, pp. 155–57; Jacoby, *Someone Else's House*, pp. 434–35; Edsall, *Chain Reaction*, p. 124.

33. Heidi Hartmann, "Who Has Benefited from Affirmative Action in Employment?"; James T. Patterson, *Restless Giant*, p. 27; Eric Porter, "Affirming and Disaffirming Actions: Remaking Race in the 1970s," in Bailey and Farber, *America in the 70s*, p. 58; Lichtenstein, *State of the Union*, p. 207; Schuman, Steeh, and Bobo, *Racial Attitudes in America*, pp. 74–75; Rieder, *Canarsie*, p. 118.

34. Edsall, *Chain Reaction*, pp. 143–44; Rieder, *Canarsie*, pp. 109–10, 112.

35. *Time*, July 10, 1978; Sindler, *"Bakke," "DeFunis," and Minority Admissions*, pp. 55–67; Timothy J. O'Neill, *"Bakke" and the Politics of Equality*, pp. 20–26.

36. Orlando Patterson, *Ordeal of Integration*, pp. 9–11; Sindler, *"Bakke," "DeFunis," and Minority Admissions*, p. 55; Thernstrom and Thernstrom, *America in Black and White*, pp. 413–14.

37. Hodgson, *World Turned Right Side Up*, p. 154.

38. *Regents of the University of California v. Bakke*, 438 U.S. 265 (1978).

39. *Time*, July 10, 1978.

40. *U.S. News and World Report,* July 10, 1978; *Time,* July 10, 1978; *Newsweek,* August 14, 1978; Schwartz, *Behind "Bakke,"* p. 148.

41. *New York Times,* June 29, 1978; *Time,* July 10, 1978.

42. Thernstrom and Thernstrom, *America in Black and White,* p. 418; *United Steelworkers of America v. Weber,* 443 U.S. 193 (1979); *Time,* December 25, 1978, April 9, 1979, July 9, 1979; Lichtenstein, *State of the Union,* p. 205.

43. Bell, *Cultural Contradictions of Capitalism,* pp. 23, 233; *Time,* July 9, 1979.

## CHAPTER FOURTEEN: THE SWEETHEART OF THE SILENT MAJORITY

1. National Commission on the Observance of International Women's Year, *The Spirit of Houston: The First National Women's Conference* (Washington, D.C., 1977), pp. 193–203, 128–29.

2. Ibid., pp. 117–20, 251–52; Wandersee, *On the Move,* pp. 186–88.

3. *New York Times,* November 19, 1977; *Spirit of Houston,* pp. 119–21; Wandersee, *On the Move,* pp. 192, 194.

4. *Spirit of Houston,* pp. 165–66; *Time,* December 5, 1977; Wandersee, *On the Move,* pp. 194–95.

5. Felsenthal, *Sweetheart of the Silent Majority,* p. 291; Melich, *Republican War Against Women,* pp. 87–88; Falwell, *Listen, America!* p. 155; Robison, *Attack on the Family,* p. 672.

6. Critchlow, *Phyllis Schlafly and Grassroots Conservatism,* pp. 244–45; *New York Times,* July 25, 1977; *Spirit of Houston,* pp. 104–5, 109–11, 227–28; Wandersee, *On the Move,* pp. 189–90.

7. *Ms.,* November 1977; *Time,* December 5, 1977; Susan M. Hartmann, *From Margin to Mainstream,* p. 147; Critchlow, *Phyllis Schlafly and Grassroots Conservatism,* p. 245; William Martin, *With God on Our Side,* pp. 163–64; Broder, *Changing of the Guard,* p. 274; *New York Times,* November 20, 1977.

8. *New York Times,* November 20, 1977; *Time,* December 5, 1977; William Martin, *With God on Our Side,* pp. 161, 165–66.

9. *Spirit of Houston,* p. 170.

10. Brown, *For a "Christian America,"* pp. 117, 119; Critchlow, *Phyllis Schlafly and Grassroots Conservatism,* pp. 247–48.

11. The commercials can be viewed online at UC–San Francisco's Tobacco Industry Archive, www.archive.org/details/tobaccoarchives.

12. Rosen, *World Split Open,* pp. xi, 19; Evans, *Tidal Wave,* pp. 1, 18–20.

13. Chafe, *American Woman,* p. 18; U.S. Bureau of the Census, *Statistical Abstract of the United States, 1981* (Washington, D.C., 1981), tables 635, 636, and 637, pp. 380–81; Wandersee, *On the Move,* pp. 128–29; Randour, "Research Report"; Hodgson, *More Equal Than Others,* pp. 150–52; Rosen, *World Split Open,* pp. 303, 308.

14. Susan M. Hartmann, *From Margin to Mainstream,* p. 127; Brauer, "Women Activists, Southern Conservatives"; *New York Times,* August 21, 1965; *Wall Street Journal,* June 22, 1965; Rosen, *World Split Open,* pp. 71–73; Evans, *Tidal Wave,* pp. 62–63.

15. *Stanton v. Stanton,* 421 U.S. 7 (1975); Susan M. Hartmann, *From Margin to Mainstream,* pp. 108–13; Evans, *Tidal Wave,* pp. 67, 70.

16. Becker, *Origins of the Equal Rights Amendment;* Jo Freeman, *Politics of Women's Liberation,* pp. 209–21; Critchlow, *Phyllis Schlafly and Grassroots Conservatism,*

pp. 213–14; Susan M. Hartmann, *From Margin to Mainstream*, pp. 66–67; Troy, *Affairs of State*, p. 192; Hayward, *Age of Reagan*, p. 309.

17. *Washington Post*, March 22, 23, and 24, 1972; *Ms.*, July 1972; Wandersee, *On the Move*, pp. 177–78; Susan M. Hartmann, *From Margin to Mainstream*, p. 138; Critchlow, *Phyllis Schlafly and Grassroots Conservatism*, pp. 217, 230–32.

18. See Critchlow, *Phyllis Schlafly and Grassroots Conservatism*, pp. 218–19, 235.

19. See Felsenthal, *Sweetheart of the Silent Majority*, pp. 9–269; Critchlow, *Phyllis Schlafly and Grassroots Conservatism*, pp. 12–211; the quotation is from the latter, p. 161.

20. Critchlow, *Phyllis Schlafly and Grassroots Conservatism*, pp. 12, 217–20, 226, 230–31, 236.

21. Bailey, "She 'Can Bring Home the Bacon,' " pp. 113–16; Russell Miller, *Bunny*, p. 193; Rosen, *World Split Open*, p. 302.

22. *Time*, February 26, 1979; William Martin, *With God on Our Side*, p. 163; Marshner, *New Traditional Woman*, p. 3; Zaretsky, *No Direction Home*, pp. 186–99.

23. *Washington Post*, February 13, 1981.

24. Faludi, *Backlash*, p. 285; Gilder, *Sexual Suicide*, pp. 43, 13, 262, 238, 248.

25. Marabel Morgan, *Total Woman*, pp. 61, 97; *Time*, March 14, 1977.

26. *Redbook*, February 1972; Bailey, "She 'Can Bring Home the Bacon,' " pp. 114–15.

27. Luker, *Abortion and the Politics of Motherhood*, pp. 199–200; Rieder, *Canarsie*, p. 150.

28. Lukas, *Common Ground*, p. 271.

29. Critchlow, *Phyllis Schlafly and Grassroots Conservatism*, p. 224.

30. Crawford, *Thunder on the Right*, p. 148; Tedin, Brady, Buxton, Gorman, and Thompson, "Social Background and Political Differences Between Pro- and Anti-ERA Activists"; Arrington and Kyle, "Equal Rights Activists in North Carolina"; Burris, "Who Opposed the ERA?"; *New Times*, September 30, 1977; Critchlow, *Phyllis Schlafly and Grassroots Conservatism*, pp. 221–22.

31. *Birmingham News*, February 5, 1975; Susan M. Hartmann, *From Margin to Mainstream*, pp. 133–34; Critchlow, *Phyllis Schlafly and Grassroots Conservatism*, pp. 222–24; *New Times*, September 30, 1977.

32. Susan M. Hartmann, *From Margin to Mainstream*, pp. 136–37; Critchlow, *Phyllis Schlafly and Grassroots Conservatism*, p. 223.

33. William Martin, *With God on Our Side*, p. 162; Susan M. Hartmann, *From Margin to Mainstream*, p. 138; Critchlow, *Phyllis Schlafly and Grassroots Conservatism*, pp. 213, 227–28, 278.

34. *Time*, December 5, 1977; William Martin, *With God on Our Side*, p. 165.

35. *New York Times*, July 1, 1982.

36. Ibid.; see also Critchlow, *Phyllis Schlafly and Grassroots Conservatism*, pp. 8, 18, 267–68, 302.

37. *Ms.*, July 1978; Evans, *Tidal Wave*, pp. 111, 174–75.

38. Jacobson, *Roots Too*, p. 366; Evans, *Tidal Wave*, pp. 102–3, 142–43; Koedt, *Radical Feminism*, pp. 240–46; Johnston, *Lesbian Nation*, p. 276; Robin Morgan, *Going Too Far*, p. 178; Wandersee, *On the Move*, pp. 49–52; Rosen, *World Split Open*, pp. 170–74, 239.

39. Rosen, *World Split Open*, p. 263.

40. Stallard, Ehrenreich, and Sklar, *Poverty in the American Dream*, pp. 1–16.

41. Patrick Anderson, *Electing Jimmy Carter*, p. 10; Susan M. Hartmann, "Feminism,

Public Policy, and the Carter Administration"; Troy, *Affairs of State*, pp. 252–54; Susan M. Hartmann, *From Margin to Mainstream*, p. 150.

42. Susan M. Hartmann, "Feminism, Public Policy, and the Carter Administration," pp. 228–29; *New York Times*, January 13, 1979, December 11, 1979; Critchlow, *Phyllis Schlafly and Grassroots Conservatism*, pp. 254–55.

43. The label "post-feminist" was coined in *The New York Times Magazine*, October 17, 1982.

## CHAPTER FIFTEEN: WHATEVER HAPPENED TO CALIFORNIA?

1. See Hoskyns, *Hotel California*, pp. 248–55.

2. *Time*, November 7, 1969, July 18, 1977; Kirse Granat May, *Golden State, Golden Youth*.

3. McGirr, *Suburban Warriors*, pp. 28, 46–47, 86, 92.

4. *Time*, October 21, 1974; *Los Angeles Times*, January 7, 1975; Broder, *Changing of the Guard*, p. 22; Rapoport, *California Dreaming*, p. 156.

5. Broder, *Changing of the Guard*, pp. 21–22.

6. *Time*, November 7, 1969.

7. *Time*, July 18, 1977.

8. *Time*, December 31, 1965. On Keynesianism, see Skidelsky, "Fall of Keynesianism"; Clark, "Keynesian Consensus." The best discussion of Keynes's economic ideas is Skidelsky, *John Maynard Keynes*, pp. 537–624.

9. See Buchanan and Tullock, *Calculus of Consent*, online at www.econlib.org/library/Buchanan/buchCv3c20.html, ch. 20; Lucas, "Expectations and the Neutrality of Money"; Lucas, "Econometric Policy Evaluation: A Critique"; Krugman, *Peddling Prosperity*, pp. 8, 48–52; Modigliani, "Monetarist Controversy."

10. Nash, *Conservative Intellectual Movement in America*, pp. 146–47, 158–71; Nozick, *Anarchy, State, and Utopia*, pp. ix, 30–31; Dionne, *Why Americans Hate Politics*, pp. 272–73, 276, 281.

11. *New Republic*, November 6, 1976; *New York Times*, December 14, 1976; Hayward, *Age of Reagan*, p. 524; *Washington Post*, October 21, 1976.

12. The Nobel lecture is reprinted in Leube, *Essence of Friedman*; see also Milton Friedman, "Quantity Theory of Money"; Milton Friedman, "Role of Monetary Policy"; Friedman and Schwartz, *Monetary History of the United States*. For summaries of Friedman's thought in a wider political context, see Blumenthal, *Rise of the Counter-establishment*, pp. 87–111; Hodgson, *World Turned Right Side Up*, pp. 196–203.

13. On *Free to Choose*, see *New York Times*, January 6, 1980; *Time*, March 10, 1980; *Washington Post*, May 15, 1980; on Friedman and Proposition 13, see www.foxandhoundsdaily.com/blog/joel-fox/proposition-13-and-milton-friedman.

14. *Washington Post*, August 29, 1978; Kuttner, *Revolt of the Haves*, pp. 39–41; Schrag, *Paradise Lost*, pp. 129–31; Crawford, *Thunder on the Right*, pp. 101–2. For a rather less objective account, see Jarvis, *I'm Mad as Hell*.

15. Kuttner, *Revolt of the Haves*, p. 39; Schrag, *Paradise Lost*, p. 131; McGirr, *Suburban Warriors*, p. 238.

16. Kuttner, *Revolt of the Haves*, pp. 29–44; Lo, *Small Property Versus Big Government*, pp. 77, 112–15; Lou Cannon, *Governor Reagan*, pp. 324, 364–67; Schulman, *Seventies*, pp. 205–6.

17. Figures from Edsall, *Chain Reaction*, pp. 105–6; Steuerle, *Tax Decade*, pp. 214–17.

18. Edsall, *Chain Reaction*, p. 106; Iwan W. Morgan, *Beyond the Liberal Consensus*, p. 92.

19. Ferguson and Rogers, *Right Turn*, pp. 100–101; Biven, *Jimmy Carter's Economy*, pp. 199–200; Rieder, *Canarsie*, p. 106.

20. *Los Angeles Times*, November 19, 1978; Kuttner, *Revolt of the Haves*, p. 51; Schrag, *Paradise Lost*, p. 133; Schulman, *Seventies*, p. 210.

21. See Kuttner, *Revolt of the Haves*, pp. 65–67; Schrag, *Paradise Lost*, pp. 139–41.

22. Kuttner, *Revolt of the Haves*, p. 64; Schrag, *Paradise Lost*, p. 144.

23. Jarvis, *I'm Mad as Hell*, p. 48; Schrag, *Paradise Lost*, p. 142.

24. *Los Angeles Times*, May 3, 1978; Kuttner, *Revolt of the Haves*, p. 70; Schrag, *Paradise Lost*, pp. 145–47; Carroll, *It Seemed Like Nothing Happened*, p. 324. On business and Proposition 13, see also Ferguson and Rogers, *Right Turn*, p. 102; Daniel A. Smith, *Tax Crusaders and the Politics of Direct Democracy*, pp. 71–80; Edsall, *Chain Reaction*, pp. 130–31.

25. *Los Angeles Times*, June 7, 1970; Kuttner, *Revolt of the Haves*, pp. 10, 77–78; Schulman, *Seventies*, pp. 207–9.

26. *Los Angeles Times*, May 18, 25, and 26, 1978; Kuttner, *Revolt of the Haves*, pp. 70–71, 73–76; Schrag, *Paradise Lost*, pp. 146–47, 149.

27. *Los Angeles Times*, June 11, 1978; Sears and Citrin, *Tax Revolt*, pp. 98–101; Kuttner, *Revolt of the Haves*, p. 97; *Washington Post*, June 16, 1978.

28. Schrag, *Paradise Lost*, pp. 151–52; Kuttner, *Revolt of the Haves*, p. 20; Jarvis, *I'm Mad as Hell*, p. 119; *New York Times*, September 24, 1978.

29. Kuttner, *Revolt of the Haves*, pp. 85–89; Schrag, *Paradise Lost*, pp. 154–55.

30. See Schrag, *Paradise Lost*, pp. 167–68, 174, 114–15, 10.

31. *Washington Post*, November 1, 1978; Hayward, *Age of Reagan*, p. 528; Kuttner, *Revolt of the Haves*, pp. 59, 304–6; Schrag, *Paradise Lost*, pp. 9, 194.

32. *Newsweek*, June 19, 1978; *Washington Post*, June 18, 1978; *New York Times*, September 24, 1978.

33. *Washington Post*, December 13, 1978; Kuttner, *Revolt of the Haves*, pp. 325–27; Schrag, *Paradise Lost*, p. 158; *National Review*, July 20, 1979; *Newsweek*, September 24, 1979; Schulman, *Seventies*, pp. 212–15.

34. *Wall Street Journal*, December 11, 1974; Blumenthal, *Rise of the Counter-establishment*, pp. 180–82. On the origins of supply-side, see Wanniski, "Mundell-Laffer Hypothesis"; Canto, Joines, and Laffer, *Foundations of Supply-Side Economics*, p. xv; Blumenthal, *Rise of the Counter-establishment*, pp. 178–79; Krugman, *Peddling Prosperity*, p. 88. For a balanced summary, see Collins, *More*, pp. 182–84.

35. Broder, *Changing of the Guard*, p. 165; *Washington Times*, May 28, 1986; Blumenthal, *Rise of the Counter-establishment*, pp. 173–78; Martin Anderson, *Revolution*, p. 146; Wanniski, "Mundell-Laffer Hypothesis"; Collins, *More*, pp. 185–86; Blinder, *Hard Heads, Soft Hearts*, p. 87; *Wall Street Journal*, March 19, 1980, October 14, 1981.

36. Krugman, *Peddling Prosperity*, pp. 89–92; Greider, "Education of David Stockman."

37. *Wall Street Journal*, November 9, 1981; Blumenthal, *Rise of the Counter-establishment*, pp. 169–70, 196; Hodgson, *World Turned Right Side Up*, p. 213; Dionne, *Why Americans Hate Politics*, pp. 249–52, 255.

38. Blumenthal, *Rise of the Counter-establishment*, pp. 185–86; Broder, *Changing of the Guard*, p. 166; *New York Times*, August 11, 1996; Kemp, *American Renaissance*, p. 2; Blumenthal, *Rise of the Counter-establishment*, p. 203. On Kemp and supply-side, see also Collins, *More*, pp. 174–75.

39. Roberts, *Supply-Side Revolution*, pp. 30–31; Blumenthal, *Rise of the Counter-establishment*, pp. 78–82; Collins, *More*, pp. 176–77.

40. See Collins, *More*, pp. 177–78, the best discussion of the Kemp-Roth debate.

41. *Washington Post*, September 21, 1978; Kemp, *American Renaissance*, p. 10; Crawford, *Thunder on the Right*, p. 242; Collins, *More*, pp. 178–79.

42. Kemp, *American Renaissance*, p. 13.

43. See Collins, *More*, pp. 188–89; Hodgson, *World Turned Right Side Up*, pp. 206–9.

44. *New York Times*, December 30, 1979.

## CHAPTER SIXTEEN: APOCALYPSE NOW

1. BBC television news report, February 1, 1979, news.bbc.co.uk/onthisday/hi/dates/stories/february/1/newsid_2521000/2521003.stm; *New York Times*, February 2, 1979.

2. Kissinger to William Rogers, "Follow-Up on the President's Talk with the Shah of Iran," July 25, 1972, www.gwu.edu/~nsarchiv/NSAEBB/NSAEBB21/03–01.htm; *Washington Post*, March 2, 1974; Gary Sick, *All Fall Down*, pp. 5–17; Shawcross, *Shah's Last Ride*, pp. 38–41, 47, 56–60, 72, 91, 162–63, 165–66, 168, 179; Bill, *The Eagle and the Lion*, pp. 183–85; David Harris, *Crisis*, pp. 12–13, 111–12.

3. Sullivan, *Mission to Iran*, pp. 21–22.

4. Sick, *All Fall Down*, pp. 25–30, 344 n. 7; Jordan, *Crisis*, pp. 88–89; Sullivan, *Mission to Iran*, p. 134; Gaddis Smith, *Morality, Reason, and Power*, pp. 185–86; Shawcross, *Shah's Last Ride*, p. 130.

5. Sullivan, *Mission to Iran*, p. 40; Yergin, *Prize*, p. 677; Brzezinski, *Power and Principle*, p. 67; Sick, *All Fall Down*, pp. 46, 60–61, 90; Jimmy Carter, *Keeping Faith*, p. 438; Shawcross, *Shah's Last Ride*, pp. 230–38; David Harris, *Crisis*, p. 21.

6. David Harris, *Crisis*, p. 97; Yergin, *Prize*, p. 67.

7. *New York Times*, January 1, 5, and 17, 1979; Farber, *Taken Hostage*, pp. 94, 112; Yergin, *Prize*, p. 681.

8. *Time*, February 5, 1979; Yergin, *Prize*, pp. 684–87.

9. Blinder, "Anatomy of Double-Digit Inflation in the 1970s"; Burton I. Kaufman, *Presidency of James Earl Carter, Jr.*, pp. 114, 135–36; Hargrove, *Jimmy Carter as President*, p. 107; Biven, *Jimmy Carter's Economy*, pp. 164, 197, 206.

10. Greider, *Secrets of the Temple*, pp. 16–17; Theodore H. White, *America in Search of Itself*, pp. 155–57; Rieder, *Canarsie*, p. 252.

11. *Newsweek*, May 29, 1978; Greider, *Secrets of the Temple*, p. 17; *New York Times*, May 13, 1979; Nocera, *Piece of the Action*, pp. 89–186; Schulman, *Seventies*, pp. 135–39.

12. *New York Times*, January 24, 1979; *New Republic*, April 12, 1980; *U.S. News and World Report*, January 22, 1979; *Washington Post*, January 25, 1979; and see Gillon, *Democrats' Dilemma*, pp. 251–52.

13. *Public Papers of the Presidents of the United States: Jimmy Carter*, 1979 (Washington, D.C., 1980), bk. 1, pp. 609–14.

14. *Newsweek*, April 16, 1979; Biven, *Jimmy Carter's Economy*, p. 177; oral history interview with Stuart Eizenstat, January 29–30, 1982, pp. 71, 112–13, Miller Center, University of Virginia; *Time*, April 16, 1979; *U.S. News and World Report*, April 16, 1979; Burton I. Kaufman, *Presidency of James Earl Carter, Jr.*, pp. 132, 135.

15. James Fallows, "The Passionless Presidency," *Atlantic Monthly*, May 1979, pp. 33–48.

16. *New York Times*, April 26, 1979; *Washington Post*, May 24, 27, and 30, 1979.

17. Stephens, *Three Mile Island*, p. 4; Carroll, *It Seemed Like Nothing Happened*, pp. 218–19, 321–22; Robert Gottlieb, *Forcing the Spring*, pp. 177–84; Yergin, *Prize*, pp. 601–3; and see J. Samuel Walker, *Three Mile Island*.

18. Yergin, *Prize*, pp. 691–92; *New York Times*, May 5, 1979.

19. *New York Times*, May 5, 9, and 16, 1979.

20. Yergin, *Prize*, p. 692; Berkowitz, *Something Happened*, pp. 130–31.

21. Updike, *Rabbit Is Rich*, pp. 224, 171; Jenkins, *Decade of Nightmares*, p. 155.

22. Morris, *Jimmy Carter*, p. 261; Yergin, *Prize*, pp. 692–93.

23. *New York Times*, June 23, 24, and 25, 1979; Yergin, *Prize*, p. 694.

24. Eizenstat to Carter, June 28, 1979, "Trip to Japan and Korea," box 137, Presidential Handwriting File, Staff Secretary's File, Carter Library.

25. *New York Times*, July 4 and 5, 1979; Jimmy Carter, *Keeping Faith*, pp. 111–14; Burton I. Kaufman, *Presidency of James Earl Carter, Jr.*, pp. 152, 185.

26. Jimmy Carter, *Keeping Faith*, pp. 115–16.

27. *New Yorker*, August 27, 1979; Morris, *Jimmy Carter*, pp. 3–4, 12; Broder, *Changing of the Guard*, pp. 409–11, 402; Horowitz, *Anxieties of Affluence*, p. 227.

28. Patrick Caddell, "Of Crisis and Opportunity," April 23, 1979, "Memoranda: President Carter 1/10/79–4/23/79," box 40, Jody Powell, Press Office Files, Carter Library.

29. Morris, *Jimmy Carter*, pp. 3–4; Horowitz, *Anxieties of Affluence*, pp. 229–30; Zaretsky, *No Direction Home*, pp. 216–17; *New Yorker*, August 27, 1979; Carter to Caddell, July 16, 1979, box 139, Presidential Handwriting File, Staff Secretary's File, Carter Library.

30. *New York Times*, July 15, 1979; Hayward, *Age of Reagan*, pp. 574–75; *New Republic*, August 4, 1979; Horowitz, *Anxieties of Affluence*, p. 236; Jimmy Carter, *Keeping Faith*, pp. 116–20.

31. Hodgson, *World Turned Right Side Up*, p. 218; *New Yorker*, August 27, 1979; Gillon, *Democrats' Dilemma*, pp. 260–62.

32. *Washington Post*, July 14, 1979; *New York Times*, July 15, 1979; Horowitz, *Anxieties of Affluence*, pp. 234–37.

33. *Public Papers of the Presidents of the United States: Jimmy Carter*, 1979, bk. 2, pp. 1235–40.

34. See Hahn, "Flailing the Profligate"; Ribuffo, " 'Malaise' Revisited"; Horowitz, *Anxieties of Affluence*, pp. 238–39.

35. *New York Times*, July 17 and 18, 1979; Burton I. Kaufman, *Presidency of James Earl Carter, Jr.*, p. 145; Morris, *Jimmy Carter*, pp. 6–7.

36. Gillon, *Democrats' Dilemma*, pp. 264–65; Burton I. Kaufman, *Presidency of James Earl Carter, Jr.*, pp. 145–47.

37. Morris, *Jimmy Carter*, pp. 261–62; Horowitz, *Anxieties of Affluence*, pp. 239–41; *Time*, July 30, 1979, August 6, 1979; *New Republic*, August 4, 1979.

38. *New York Times*, November 1, 1979; Hayward, *Age of Reagan*, p. 609; Yankelovich, *New Rules*, pp. 25, 182–83; Updike, *Rabbit Is Rich*, p. 3.

39. *New York Times*, February 7, 1979, March 31, 1979; Skowronek, *The Politics Presidents Make*, pp. 363–71.

40. *Washington Post*, February 12 and 19, 1978; Jordan, *Crisis*, pp. 172–73; Powell, *Other Side of the Story*, pp. 109–17, 126–56.

41. Powell, *Other Side of the Story*, pp. 104–8, 123–24; *Washington Post*, August 30 and 31, 1979, September 1, 1979; *New York Times*, August 31, 1979, September 1, 4, and 5, 1979; *New Republic*, August 4, 1979.

42. *Time*, October 1, 1979.

## CHAPTER SEVENTEEN: NUKE THE AYATOLLAH!

1. My account follows Bowden, *Guests of the Ayatollah*, the best narrative account of the hostage crisis, esp. pp. 32–33, 62–65, 82–84, 91–93, 151–53; see also *New York Times*, November 5 and 6, 1979; Wells, *444 Days*, pp. 55–83; Ebtekar, *Takeover in Tehran*, pp. 69–70; David Harris, *Crisis*, pp. 204–7; Farber, *Taken Hostage*, pp. 131–36.

2. Sullivan, *Mission to Iran*, pp. 216–19, 257–68; Sick, *All Fall Down*, pp. 114–22, 132–37; Moens, "President Carter's Advisers and the Fall of the Shah," pp. 226–27; David Harris, *Crisis*, pp. 134–41; Farber, *Taken Hostage*, p. 101.

3. Sick, *All Fall Down*, pp. 138, 177–78; Shawcross, *Shah's Last Ride*, pp. 89–90, 101–3, 121–26; Brzezinski, *Power and Principle*, p. 472.

4. Shawcross, *Shah's Last Ride*, pp. 140–41, 151–55, 220–27, 238–40; Jimmy Carter, *Keeping Faith*, pp. 452–53; *New York Times*, April 23, 1979; Farber, *Taken Hostage*, p. 124.

5. *New York Times Magazine*, May 17, 1981; Vance, *Hard Choices*, p. 371; Jordan, *Crisis*, p. 24; Gillon, *Democrats' Dilemma*, p. 271.

6. Sick, *All Fall Down*, pp. 181, 184–85; David Harris, *Crisis*, p. 196; Bowden, *Guests of the Ayatollah*, p. 19.

7. There are conflicting accounts of the plan's origins: see Ebtekar, *Takeover in Tehran*, pp. 51–53; Bowden, *Guests of the Ayatollah*, pp. 8–10.

8. David Harris, *Crisis*, p. 218; Bowden, *Guests of the Ayatollah*, pp. 76, 86–101, 129.

9. Jordan, *Crisis*, p. 19; Farber, *Taken Hostage*, pp. 139–40.

10. Jimmy Carter, *Keeping Faith*, p. 459; David Harris, *Crisis*, p. 213; transcript of the President's Meeting with Select Members of Congress, December 5, 1979, pp. 4–5, 10, box 61, Jody Powell Papers, Carter Library.

11. Jimmy Carter, *Keeping Faith*, p. 594; Donovan, *Roosevelt to Reagan*, p. 181; Jordan, *Crisis*, pp. 41–44.

12. See Jimmy Carter, *Keeping Faith*, pp. 14, 594; Drew, *Portrait of an Election*, p. 48.

13. Andrew, *For the President's Eyes Only*, pp. 440, 442; Theodore H. White, *America in Search of Itself*, pp. 15–16; Moin, *Khomeini*, pp. 227–28; and see Bowden, *Guests of the Ayatollah*, pp. 93–94, 140–41, 249.

14. Kapuściński, *Shah of Shahs*, p. 121; Bowden, *Guests of the Ayatollah*, pp. 160–61, 200, 246, 253; Jordan, *Crisis*, p. 63; *New York Times*, November 28, 1979.

15. Harold H. Saunders, "The Crisis Begins," in Kreisberg, *American Hostages in Iran*, p. 47.

16. Donovan and Scherer, *Unsilent Revolution*, pp. 140–41, 144–47.

17. *Time*, January 7, 1980; Bowden, *Guests of the Ayatollah*, pp. 274–78, 330, 356–59.

18. Farber, *Taken Hostage*, p. 139; Bowden, *Guests of the Ayatollah*, pp. 191, 243, 416–29, 477–80.

19. Jordan, *Crisis*, p. 40.

20. Farber, *Taken Hostage*, p. 151; Bowden, *Guests of the Ayatollah*, pp. 210–11; *Time*, November 26, 1979.

21. Frum, *How We Got Here*, p. 344; Bowden, *Guests of the Ayatollah*, p. 243; Donovan and Scherer, *Unsilent Revolution*, p. 142; Leuchtenberg, *Troubled Feast*, p. 280.

22. *Washington Post*, December 10, 1979.

23. *Washington Post*, December 14, 1979; *Public Papers of the Presidents of the United States: Jimmy Carter*, 1979 (Washington, D.C., 1980), bk. 2, p. 2245.

24. Jimmy Carter, *Keeping Faith*, p. 470.

25. *New York Times*, December 27, 1979; Garthoff, *Détente and Confrontation*, pp. 1018–19; and see especially Lyakhovskiy, "Inside the Soviet Invasion of Afghanistan."

26. Garthoff, *Détente and Confrontation*, pp. 1017, 1023–46; Lyakhovskiy, "Inside the Soviet Invasion of Afghanistan," pp. 8–34.

27. Jimmy Carter, *Keeping Faith*, pp. 471–73.

28. Andrew, *For the President's Eyes Only*, p. 436; Garthoff, *Détente and Confrontation*, pp. 727–28.

29. Gaddis Smith, *Morality, Reason, and Power*, pp. 118–22; *BusinessWeek*, March 12, 1979.

30. *Washington Post*, June 13, 1979; *Congressional Record*, August 13, 1978, p. 9981; *New York Times*, November 26, 1979; Norman Podhoretz, "The Culture of Appeasement," *Harper's*, October 1977, pp. 25–32; for a discussion of all this, see Blumenthal, *Rise of the Counter-establishment*, pp. 142–44; Zaretsky, *No Direction Home*, pp. 178–81.

31. Garthoff, *Détente and Confrontation*, pp. 732–57, 875–77, 964–68, 1134–35, 1143, 1161; Rostow is quoted in Skinner, Anderson, and Anderson, *Reagan in His Own Hand*, pp. 93–95.

32. *Public Papers of the Presidents of the United States: Jimmy Carter, 1978* (Washington, D.C., 1979), bk. 1, pp. 531, 955–62, 1056–57; *New York Times*, March 20, 1978, June 9, 1978, November 26, 1979; *Washington Post*, June 8, 1978; Robert G. Kaufman, *Henry M. Jackson*, pp. 382–88; Ehrman, *Rise of Neoconservatism*, pp. 113–14; Kissinger, *For the Record*, pp. 191–230; Nixon, *Real War*, p. 253; and see also Brzezinski, *Power and Principle*, pp. 42–43, 319–20; Garthoff, *Détente and Confrontation*, pp. 624–25, 655–64; Gaddis Smith, *Morality, Reason, and Power*, pp. 35–38; Vance, *Hard Choices*, pp. 26–28.

33. Frum, *How We Got Here*, p. 344; Hayward, *Age of Reagan*, p. 596; Sutherland, *Bestsellers*, p. 95.

34. Brzezinski to Carter, NSC Weekly Report 109, September 13, 1979, box 42, Zbigniew Brzezinski Papers, Carter Library.

35. *New York Times*, January 1 and 2, 1980; Brzezinski, *Power and Principle*, p. 566; Gaddis Smith, *Morality, Reason, and Power*, pp. 9, 48, 222–24, 245; Jimmy Carter, *Keeping Faith*, pp. 475–76; Garthoff, *Détente and Confrontation*, pp. 817–18, 1060–63, 1065–67, 1070–71.

36. *New York Times*, April 13, 1980; Gaddis Smith, *Morality, Reason, and Power*, p. 227.

37. Garthoff, *Détente and Confrontation*, pp. 1064, 1078; Gaddis Smith, *Morality, Reason, and Power*, p. 236; Brzezinski, *Power and Principle*, pp. 454–59; *Washington Post*, February 15, 1980; *New York Times*, July 21, 1980, August 23, 1980. On the CIA, the mujahideen, and the Taliban, see Rashid, *Taliban*, pp. 25–29; Weiner, *Legacy of Ashes*, pp. 336–37; and especially Coll, *Ghost Wars*, pp. 42–46.

38. *New York Times*, November 25, 1979; *Time*, January 7, 1980.

39. Bowden, *Guests of the Ayatollah*, p. 398.

## INTERLUDE: AMERICA'S TEAM

1. Golenbock, *Landry's Boys*, p. 384.

2. St. John, *Landry*, p. 345; MacCambridge, *America's Game*, pp. 323–24.

3. MacCambridge, *America's Game*, pp. 275–78; *Time*, January 10, 1977.

4. *Time*, January 16, 1978; Golenbock, *Landry's Boys*, pp. 273–74; MacCambridge, *America's Game*, pp. 304–5.

5. St. John, *Landry*, pp. 336–37; Golenbock, *Landry's Boys*, pp. 341–45; MacCambridge, *America's Game*, pp. 205–6, 213–14, 324; *New York Times*, January 9, 1978; *Time*, January 16, 1978.

6. Golenbock, *Landry's Boys*, pp. 235–38; MacCambridge, *America's Game*, p. 324; *New York Times*, January 18, 1972, September 22, 1980.

7. *New York Times*, January 9, 1978; St. John, *Landry*, pp. 44–45, 200–205, 253–59; Golenbock, *Landry's Boys*, pp. 71–72.

8. St. John, *Landry*, p. 350; Golenbock, *Landry's Boys*, p. 154.

9. MacCambridge, *America's Game*, pp. 231, 324–25; *Commentary*, July 1969; *Time*, October 9, 1971; *San Francisco Examiner*, September 9, 1979.

## CHAPTER EIGHTEEN: CONSERVATIVES FOR CHANGE

1. *New York Times*, November 24, 1976; Ladd, *Transformations of the American Party System*, pp. 258–59; Gerald M. Pomper, "The Presidential Election," in Pomper et al., *Election of 1976*, p. 82; *Time*, August 23, 1976.

2. Nash, *Conservative Intellectual Movement in America*, pp. 134–71, 321–24; and see Judis, *William F. Buckley, Jr.*

3. Hodgson, *World Turned Right Side Up*, p. 62; Critchlow, *Phyllis Schlafly and Grassroots Conservatism*, p. 6.

4. Bell, *New American Right*; McClosky, "Conservatism and Personality"; *Saturday Evening Post*, September 29, 1964; Perlstein, *Before the Storm*, p. xiii; *New York Review of Books*, October 8, 1964.

5. McGirr, *Suburban Warriors*, pp. 83, 94, 8–9; Lassiter, *Silent Majority*, pp. 7–8; Appleborne, *Dixie Rising*, pp. 27, 44–45.

6. Crawford, *Thunder on the Right*, p. 43; Dionne, *Why Americans Hate Politics*, p. 229; Broder, *Changing of the Guard*, p. 183; Perlstein, *Before the Storm*, pp. 162–63.

7. William Martin, *With God on Our Side*, p. 88; Crawford, *Thunder on the Right*, pp. 47–49; Broder, *Changing of the Guard*, p. 185; Dan T. Carter, *Politics of Rage*, pp. 338, 456.

8. *U.S. News and World Report*, March 3, 1979; Crawford, *Thunder on the Right*, pp. 51–53, 70–75, 146, 272.

9. L. J. Davis, "Conservatism in America," *Harper's*, October 1980, p. 21.

10. *Washington Post*, May 4, 6, and 7, 1975; Broder, *Changing of the Guard*, pp. 179–80; Bellant, *Coors Connection*, pp. 1–14.

11. Crawford, *Thunder on the Right*, p. 270; Bellant, *Coors Connection*, pp. xiii–xv, 2.

12. Broder, *Changing of the Guard*, pp. 95–96, 180; Blumenthal, *Rise of the Counter-establishment*, pp. 32–45.

13. Viguerie, *New Right*, pp. 78–98; Nash, *Conservative Intellectual Movement in America*, p. 332; Hodgson, *More Equal Than Others*, p. 14.

14. Crawford, *Thunder on the Right*, pp. 3, 40, 30–31, 5–6.

15. Ibid., p. 275; *Time*, September 8, 1975; *Newsweek*, August 29, 1977.

16. Crawford, *Thunder on the Right*, pp. 81–83.

17. Alan Brinkley, "Problem of American Conservatism," pp. 418–19; Kazin, *Populist Persuasion*, p. 1 and passim; Crawford, *Thunder on the Right*, pp. xiii, 294, 307, and see pp. 290–310 generally.

18. Ferguson and Rogers, *Right Turn*, pp. 46–52, 105–6.

19. Ibid., pp. 78–113; Samuelson, *Good Life and Its Discontents*, pp. 114–15

20. *Time*, July 14, 1975.

21. Polls quoted in Ferguson and Rogers, *Right Turn*, p. 14; Irving Kristol, "On Corporate Capitalism in America," in Glazer and Kristol, *American Commonwealth, 1976*, p. 126; Watson, *Defining Visions*, pp. 148–49.

22. *New York Times*, December 3, 1974, July 28, 1985; Yergin, *Prize*, pp. 655–57; Ferguson and Rogers, *Right Turn*, pp. 88–90; Blumenthal, *Rise of the Counter-establishment*, pp. 69–70, 77–78.

23. See Herman, *Corporate Control, Corporate Power*, pp. 384–85 n. 77.

24. See Sunstein, *After the Rights Revolution*, pp. 12–30; Cohen, *Consumers' Republic*, pp. 346, 357–58.

25. *Congressional Record*, November 14, 1979, pp. 757–58; Schaller, *Right Turn*, p. 34; Ferguson and Rogers, *Right Turn*, p. 86; Crawford, *Thunder on the Right*, p. 27.

26. Alfred Kahn, *Economics of Regulation*, p. 325; Derthick and Quick, *Politics of Deregulation*, pp. 45–50; Cohen, *Consumers' Republic*, p. 391; Ferguson and Rogers, *Right Turn*, pp. 106–7; Biven, *Jimmy Carter's Economy*, pp. 217–28.

27. *Public Papers of the Presidents of the United States: Jimmy Carter, 1980* (Washington, D.C., 1981), p. 2532.

28. Crawford, *Thunder on the Right*, pp. 236–37.

29. *Congressional Record*, September 16, 1981; Crawford, *Thunder on the Right*, pp. 113–17.

30. Kutler, *Wars of Watergate*, pp. 580–81; *Time*, December 18, 1978; Gillon, *That's Not What We Meant to Do*, pp. 212–14; Crawford, *Thunder on the Right*, p. 45; Broder, *Changing of the Guard*, p. 202.

31. *New Times*, September 30, 1977; *Washington Post*, November 3, 6, and 12, 1978; *New York Times*, March 23, 1978; Crawford, *Thunder on the Right*, pp. 279–81, 286–87.

32. Crawford, *Thunder on the Right*, pp. 267–68, 277; Barone, *Our Country*, p. 576.

33. *Newsweek*, November 20, 1978; see also Kuttner, *Revolt of the Haves*, p. 24; Edsall, *Chain Reaction*, p. 134; Critchlow, *Phyllis Schlafly and Grassroots Conservatism*, p. 263.

34. *New York Times*, July 7, 1980.

35. *National Review*, April 16, 1976; Crawford, *Thunder on the Right*, pp. x–xi, 120; Germond and Witcover, *Blue Smoke and Mirrors*, pp. 102–3; Busch, *Reagan's Victory*, pp. 55, 45, 131; Hayward, *Age of Reagan*, pp. 607–8; Lou Cannon, *Governor Reagan*, pp. 455, 451.

36. Lou Cannon, *Governor Reagan*, pp. 433, 440; Crawford, *Thunder on the Right*, pp. 17, 21, 60; Skinner, Anderson, and Anderson, *Reagan in His Own Hand*, pp. xv, 221.

37. Hodgson, *World Turned Right Side Up*, p. 228; Critchlow, *Phyllis Schlafly and Grassroots Conservatism*, pp. 256–57; Crawford, *Thunder on the Right*, p. 107.

38. Iwan W. Morgan, *Beyond the Liberal Consensus*, p. 143; George D. Moffett, *Limits of Victory*, p. 134.

39. Skinner, Anderson and Anderson, *Reagan in His Own Hand*, p. 208; Wills, *Reagan's America*, p. 335; Hayward, *Age of Reagan*, p. 548.

40. Hodgson, *World Turned Right Side Up*, pp. 229–30; Critchlow, *Phyllis Schlafly and Grassroots Conservatism*, pp. 257–59.

41. Lou Cannon, *Governor Reagan*, pp. 442–49; Hayward, *Age of Reagan*, pp. 614, 597.

42. *Wall Street Journal*, July 19, 1978; Crawford, *Thunder on the Right*, p. 120.

43. Crawford, *Thunder on the Right*, p. 118; *Fortune*, May 19, 1980; Blumenthal, *Rise of the Counter-establishment*, pp. 118–21.

44. Hayward, *Age of Reagan*, p. 619; Blumenthal, *Rise of the Counter-establishment*,

pp. 166–67, 199–201; Stockman, *Triumph of Politics*, pp. 47–49; Martin Anderson, *Revolution*, pp. 111–21; Hodgson, *World Turned Right Side Up*, pp. 210–13; Collins, *More*, pp. 194–97.

45. Theodore H. White, *America in Search of Itself*, pp. 238, 302; Busch, *Reagan's Victory*, pp. 46–47.

46. Theodore H. White, *America in Search of Itself*, p. 238; Schweizer and Schweizer, *Bushes*, p. 279; *National Review*, February 22, 1980; Germond and Witcover, *Blue Smoke and Mirrors*, pp. 117–18; Hayward, *Age of Reagan*, p. 625; Parmet, *George Bush*, p. 226.

47. Hayward, *Age of Reagan*, pp. 615, 628, 630, 636; Lou Cannon, *Governor Reagan*, pp. 456–58; Busch, *Reagan's Victory*, p. 65; Van der Linden, *Real Reagan*, p. 172; Germond and Witcover, *Blue Smoke and Mirrors*, p. 119.

48. *New York Times*, February 21, 24, 29, and 28, 1980; Germond and Witcover, *Blue Smoke and Mirrors*, pp. 123–24, 128–29; Hayward, *Age of Reagan*, pp. 638–39, 641; Lou Cannon, *Governor Reagan*, pp. 458–63.

49. Lou Cannon, *Governor Reagan*, pp. 463, 465–69.

50. *New York Times*, February 29, 1980, March 2, 1980; Lou Cannon, *Governor Reagan*, pp. 468–69; Busch, *Reagan's Victory*, pp. 73, 96.

## CHAPTER NINETEEN: SOLDIERS OF GOD

1. *Time*, October 1, 1979; Hadden and Swann, *Prime Time Preachers*, pp. 135–36; William Martin, *With God on Our Side*, p. 203.

2. Hunter, *Culture Wars*, pp. 44–50.

3. Hodgson, *World Turned Right Side Up*, pp. 162, 167–68; Glazer, "Fundamentalists," p. 250.

4. *New York Times*, January 16 and 20, 2003; James T. Patterson, *Restless Giant*, p. 52; William Martin, *With God on Our Side*, p. 193; Susan M. Hartmann, *From Margin to Mainstream*, p. 142; Lader, *Politics, Power, and the Church*, pp. 57–58.

5. *Christianity Today*, February 16, 1973; William Martin, *With God on Our Side*, pp. 194–95.

6. James T. Patterson, *Restless Giant*, pp. 138–39; Luker, *Abortion and the Politics of Motherhood*, pp. 194–97.

7. Letter c. 1979 reprinted in Crawford, *Thunder on the Right*, pp. 53–54; Carroll, *It Seemed Like Nothing Happened*, pp. 269–70; Susan M. Hartmann, *From Margin to Mainstream*, p. 120.

8. Zaretsky, *No Direction Home*, pp. 2–4, 19; Roof, *Generation of Seekers*, p. 96; *New York Times*, September 30, 1977.

9. FitzGerald, *Cities on a Hill*, pp. 181–82.

10. Crawford, *Thunder on the Right*, p. 145; and see FitzGerald, *Cities on a Hill*, pp. 184–85; McGirr, *Suburban Warriors*, pp. 240–43.

11. William Martin, *With God on Our Side*, pp. 100–101.

12. *New York Times*, August 24, 1970, December 16, 1973; Ruoff, *American Family*, pp. 104, 127; Broder, *Changing of the Guard*, p. 146; Killen, *1973 Nervous Breakdown*, pp. 47–48.

13. *Time*, September 8, 1975; Randy Shilts, *The Mayor of Castro Street: The Life and Times of Harvey Milk* (New York, 1982), pp. 61–64; FitzGerald, *Cities on a Hill*, pp. 11–12, 34, 44–46, 54–55; Shapiro, *Turn the Beat Around*, pp. 57–58; *Village Voice*, June 25, 1979.

14. *New York Times*, October 25, 1977; Braunstein, " 'Adults Only,' " pp. 142–43; Lawrence, *Love Saves the Day*, pp. 12–27, 33–39; Mahler, *Ladies and Gentlemen, the Bronx Is Burning*, pp. 156–57; Shapiro, *Turn the Beat Around*, pp. 16–18, 22–23; *Village Voice*, February 12, 1979.

15. *Billboard*, January 22, 1977; Shapiro, *Turn the Beat Around*, pp. 100–1, 177, 189, 227–32; *Village Voice*, February 12, 1979; on Disco Demolition, see www.whitesox interactive.com/History&Glory/DiscoDemolition.htm.

16. Bryant, *Anita Bryant Story*; Bryant and Green, *At Any Cost*; *St. Petersburg Times*, April 28, 2002.

17. *New York Times*, January 19, 1977; Jenkins, *Decade of Nightmares*, p. 120; and see Stepick, Grenier, Castro, and Dunn, *This Land Is Our Land*.

18. *New York Times*, May 10, 1977; Bryant, *Anita Bryant Story*, pp. 42–43, 90, 16; Crawford, *Thunder on the Right*, p. 52.

19. Crawford, *Thunder on the Right*, pp. 37, 153; William Martin, *With God on Our Side*, pp. 197–98; Mel White, *Stranger at the Gate*.

20. *New York Times*, June 8, 9, 17, and 27, 1977; *Time*, June 20, 1977; FitzGerald, *Cities on a Hill*, p. 51; Rich, *On Lies, Secrets, and Silence*, pp. 223–24.

21. *Los Angeles Times*, September 23, 1978, October 6 and 31, 1978, November 9, 1978; *San Francisco Chronicle*, September 24, 1978; FitzGerald, *Cities on a Hill*, p. 67; Crawford, *Thunder on the Right*, pp. 313–14; McGirr, *Suburban Warriors*, p. 258.

22. Crawford, *Thunder on the Right*, pp. 37, 152, 313–14.

23. William Martin, *With God on Our Side*, p. 205.

24. Falwell and Towns, *Church Aflame*; Falwell, *Strength for the Journey*; FitzGerald, *Cities on a Hill*, pp. 143–49; William Martin, *With God on Our Side*, pp. 55–58.

25. William Martin, *With God on Our Side*, p. 56; FitzGerald, *Cities on a Hill*, pp. 133–34.

26. Crawford, *Thunder on the Right*, p. 160; FitzGerald, *Cities on a Hill*, pp. 13, 128–29, 135–37, 149–53.

27. Jerry Falwell, "Ministers and Marchers," March 21, 1965, reprinted in Young, *God's Bullies*, pp. 310–11; Speer, *New Christian Politics*, pp. 19–20; Dan T. Carter, *Politics of Rage*, pp. 460–61; FitzGerald, *Cities on a Hill*, pp. 177–79.

28. William Martin, *With God on Our Side*, pp. 57–58; Schaller, *Right Turn*, p. 33; FitzGerald, *Cities on a Hill*, p. 173; Sherry, *In the Shadow of War*, p. 353.

29. FitzGerald, *Cities on a Hill*, pp. 164, 166.

30. Hodgson, *World Turned Right Side Up*, pp. 176–77; William Martin, *With God on Our Side*, pp. 168–69.

31. Falwell, *Listen, America!* p. 220; Freedman, "The Religious Right and the Carter Administration"; William Martin, *With God on Our Side*, p. 172.

32. Edsall, *Chain Reaction*, p. 132; William Martin, *With God on Our Side*, p. 173.

33. *New York Times*, August 1, 1976; Hodgson, *World Turned Right Side Up*, p. 180; William Martin, *With God on Our Side*, pp. 170–71, 199–200.

34. Falwell, *Listen, America!* p. 6; Hodgson, *World Turned Right Side Up*, pp. 180–81; for a very similar version, see William Martin, *With God on Our Side*, p. 200.

35. Falwell, *Listen, America!* pp. 257–58; *Boston Globe*, May 16, 2007; *Washington Post*, May 16, 2007; FitzGerald, *Cities on a Hill*, p. 410; William Martin, *With God on Our Side*, p. 204.

36. Falwell, *Listen, America!* pp. 257–63.

37. Liebman, "Mobilizing the Moral Majority in the New Christian Right"; Brudney

and Copeland, "Evangelicals as a Political Force," p. 1079; James T. Patterson, *Restless Giant*, p. 139. On Billy Graham, see Denton Lotz, "Billy Graham: An Appreciation," *Baptist History and Heritage*, June 22, 2006.

38. See Diggins, *Ronald Reagan*, pp. 22, 33, 37.

39. Lou Cannon, *President Reagan*, pp. 247–48; *Christianity Today*, July 2, 1976; *New York Review of Books*, August 5, 1976.

40. Ronald Reagan, "Time to Recapture Our Destiny," July 17, 1980, www.reaganfoundation.org/reagan/speeches/speech.asp?spid=18>.

41. *New York Times*, August 23 and 24, 1980; Hadden and Swann, *Prime Time Preachers*, pp. 130–33; William Martin, *With God on Our Side*, pp. 215–18.

## CHAPTER TWENTY: TO SAIL AGAINST THE WIND

1. *New York Times*, October 21, 1979. The texts of both speeches are online at www.jfk-library.org/JFK+Library+and+Museum/Kennedy+Library+Foundation/History/.

2. Germond and Witcover, *Blue Smoke and Mirrors*, p. 55; Haynes Johnson, *Sleepwalking Through History*, p. 35; *National Review*, October 26, 1979.

3. Barone, *Our Country*, p. 581; Burton I. Kaufman, *Presidency of James Earl Carter, Jr.*, p. 140; Busch, *Reagan's Victory*, pp. 37–38; Horowitz, *Anxieties of Affluence*, p. 242.

4. Germond and Witcover, *Blue Smoke and Mirrors*, p. 52; Clymer, *Edward M. Kennedy*, pp. 280–81; *Washington Monthly*, September 1979.

5. See Samuel Walker, *Rights Revolution*, pp. 180–83; James T. Patterson, *Restless Giant*, pp. 67, 80, 85; Ehrman, *Eighties*, pp. 108–9, 172–81, 185.

6. Ferguson and Rogers, *Right Turn*, pp. 14–15, 18–19; Edsall, *Chain Reaction*, p. 152; Schaller, *Right Turn*, p. 41; Broder, *Changing of the Guard*, pp. 411–12.

7. Bowden, *Guests of the Ayatollah*, p. 211; *Newsweek*, December 17, 1979; Germond and Witcover, *Blue Smoke and Mirrors*, p. 86.

8. Burton I. Kaufman, *Presidency of James Earl Carter, Jr.*, pp. 161–62.

9. *New York Times*, November 5, 1979; *Washington Post*, November 5, 1979; Germond and Witcover, *Blue Smoke and Mirrors*, pp. 48–78, esp. pp. 61–70; Clymer, *Edward M. Kennedy*, pp. 259, 286–87.

10. Jamieson, *Packaging the Presidency*, p. 380; Germond and Witcover, *Blue Smoke and Mirrors*, pp. 66–67; Jordan, *Crisis*, p. 22; *Boston Globe*, November 5, 1979; Clymer, *Edward M. Kennedy*, pp. 285, 296–97; Drew, *Portrait of an Election*, p. 54.

11. *New York Times*, December 4, 1979; *Washington Post*, December 4, 1979; Germond and Witcover, *Blue Smoke and Mirrors*, pp. 87–88; Hayward, *Age of Reagan*, p. 649; Clymer, *Edward M. Kennedy*, pp. 294–95.

12. *Washington Post*, November 8, 1979; *New York Times*, January 29, 1980; Germond and Witcover, *Blue Smoke and Mirrors*, p. 78; Drew, *Portrait of an Election*, pp. 33–35, 57–58; Clymer, *Edward M. Kennedy*, pp. 302–3; *Public Papers of the Presidents of the United States: Jimmy Carter, 1979* (Washington, D.C., 1980), bk. 2, p. 1,982; Broder, *Changing of the Guard*, p. 78.

13. Clymer, *Edward M. Kennedy*, p. 293; Theodore H. White, *America in Search of Itself*, p. 278; Drew, *Portrait of an Election*, pp. 40, 49, 53, 62; Hayward, *Age of Reagan*, p. 649.

14. The figures are from Theodore H. White, *America in Search of Itself*, p. 16.

15. *Chicago Tribune*, March 18 and 19, 1980; *New York Times*, March 20, 1980; Clymer, *Edward M. Kennedy*, pp. 304–5.

16. *New York Times*, March 26 and 27, 1980; Clymer, *Edward M. Kennedy*, pp. 305–7; *Public Papers of the Presidents of the United States: Jimmy Carter, 1980–1981* (Washington, D.C., 1982), bk. 1, p. 576.

17. Germond and Witcover, *Blue Smoke and Mirrors*, p. 157; Powell, *Other Side of the Story*, pp. 217–19; Clymer, *Edward M. Kennedy*, p. 308.

18. Jordan, *Crisis*, pp. 69–70, 160–68 and passim; *Washington Post*, April 6, 1980; Bowden, *Guests of the Ayatollah*, p. 408.

19. Bowden, *Guests of the Ayatollah*, p. 192; *Boston Globe*, March 15, 1980; *New York Times*, July 29, 1992.

20. Sick, *All Fall Down*, pp. 233–35, 283–85; David Harris, *Crisis*, pp. 243–44, 328–29; Beckwith, *Delta Force*; Bowden, *Guests of the Ayatollah*, pp. 112–13, 413.

21. Beckwith, *Delta Force*, pp. 226–29; Ryan, *Iranian Rescue Mission*, ch. 2; Andrew, *For the President's Eyes Only*, pp. 449–52; Bowden, *Guests of the Ayatollah*, pp. 223–33, 409; Sick, *All Fall Down*, p. 290.

22. Sick, *All Fall Down*, p. 292; Jimmy Carter, *Keeping Faith*, pp. 506–7; Jordan, *Crisis*, pp. 250–54.

23. Beckwith, *Delta Force*, pp. 4–10.

24. Ibid., p. 294; Jordan, *Crisis*, pp. 278–79; Bowden, *Guests of the Ayatollah*, pp. 433–34.

25. Jordan, *Crisis*, pp. 270–71.

26. My account of the debacle follows Jimmy Carter, *Keeping Faith*, pp. 514–18; Jordan, *Crisis*, pp. 271–75; David Harris, *Crisis*, pp. 355–61; Bowden, *Guests of the Ayatollah*, pp. 435–68 (probably the best narrative account).

27. Andrew, *For the President's Eyes Only*, p. 454; David Harris, *Crisis*, p. 351; *Newsweek*, May 5, 1980; *New Republic*, May 10, 1980; *Time*, May 5, 1980.

28. Farber, *Taken Hostage*, p. 175; Bowden, *Guests of the Ayatollah*, p. 479; *New Yorker*, June 2, 1980.

29. *Washington Post*, April 29, 1980; Bowden, *Guests of the Ayatollah*, pp. 480–82; Burton I. Kaufman, *Presidency of James Earl Carter, Jr.*, pp. 172, 189–91.

30. *Washington Post*, May 21 and 22, 1980; Porter and Dunn, *Miami Riot of 1980*.

31. *New York Times Magazine*, July 13, 1980.

32. Biven, *Jimmy Carter's Economy*, pp. 4–5; Burton I. Kaufman, *Presidency of James Earl Carter, Jr.*, pp. 167–68; Theodore H. White, *America in Search of Itself*, p. 22; Frum, *How We Got Here*, p. 292.

33. Biven, *Jimmy Carter's Economy*, pp. 7, 203–6; Hargrove, *Jimmy Carter as President*, pp. 102–4; Schulman, "Slouching Toward the Supply Side," pp. 61–62.

34. Greider, *Secrets of the Temple*, pp. 46–47; Volcker and Gyohten, *Changing Fortunes*, p. 16.

35. *Newsweek*, October 22, 1979; Biven, *Jimmy Carter's Economy*, pp. 240–46, 249–51.

36. Biven, *Jimmy Carter's Economy*, pp. 6–7; Burton I. Kaufman, *Presidency of James Earl Carter, Jr.*, p. 168; *Wall Street Journal*, February 21, 1980.

37. Biven, *Jimmy Carter's Economy*, p. 6; Burton I. Kaufman, *Presidency of James Earl Carter, Jr.*, pp. 169, 178, 183; Jenkins, *Decade of Nightmares*, pp. 181–82.

38. Hayward, *Age of Reagan*, p. 684; Edsall, *Chain Reaction*, pp. 134–35.

39. Eizenstat to Carter, May 24, 1980, box BE-13, White House Central Files—Subject File, Carter Library; Jimmy Carter, *Keeping Faith*, p. 541.

40. Burton I. Kaufman, *Presidency of James Earl Carter, Jr.*, pp. 181–83; Busch, *Reagan's Victory*, pp. 77–78; Jordan, *Crisis*, p. 58; Jamieson, *Packaging the Presidency*, pp. 388–90.

41. Jordan to Carter, June 25, 1980, reprinted in Jordan, *Crisis*, pp. 305–9; Theodore H. White, *America in Search of Itself*, p. 379.

42. Wills, *Reagan's America*, p. 463 n. 3.

43. Burton I. Kaufman, *The Presidency of James Earl Carter, Jr.*, p. 193; Jordan, *Crisis*, p. 313; Drew, *Portrait of an Election*, p. 222.

44. Powell, *Other Side of the Story*, p. 241; Jordan, *Crisis*, pp. 320–21; Drew, *Portrait of an Election*, p. 252; *New York Times*, August 14, 1980.

45. Edward M. Kennedy, "Address to the Democratic National Convention," August 12, 1980, www.jfklibrary.org/Historical+Resources/Archives/Reference+Desk/Speeches/EMK/Address+to+the+Democratic+National+Convention.htm; Drew, *Portrait of an Election*, pp. 249–51; Germond and Witcover, *Blue Smoke and Mirrors*, pp. 202–3.

46. Jordan, *Crisis*, pp. 326–27.

47. *Public Papers of the Presidents of the United States: Jimmy Carter, 1980–1981* (Washington, D.C., 1982), bk. 2, pp. 1532–40; Drew, *Portrait of an Election*, p. 259; Jordan, *Crisis*, p. 332.

48. *New York Times*, August 15 and 16, 1980; Germond and Witcover, *Blue Smoke and Mirrors*, pp. 207, 192–93; Clymer, *Edward M. Kennedy*, pp. 192–93.

49. Jimmy Carter, *Keeping Faith*, pp. 554, 549.

50. Wills, *Reagan's America*, p. 362.

## CHAPTER TWENTY-ONE: RENDEZVOUS WITH DESTINY

1. *Los Angeles Times*, July 13 and 17, 1980; *Time*, July 21, 1980; Theodore H. White, *America in Search of Itself*, pp. 312–13.

2. *Newsweek*, August 13, 1979, October 29, 1979; Lichtenstein, *State of the Union*, p. 233; Barone, *Our Country*, pp. 599–600; Collins, *Transforming America*, pp. 9, 113; *BusinessWeek*, June 30, 1980.

3. *Time*, July 21, 1980.

4. *Washington Post*, July 18, 1980; Germond and Witcover, *Blue Smoke and Mirrors*, pp. 167–72, 174–83, 187–88; Lou Cannon, *Governor Reagan*, pp. 472–75; Hayward, *Age of Reagan*, pp. 666–68.

5. *New York Times*, July 18, 1980; *Time*, July 28, 1980.

6. *Time*, July 21, 1980.

7. *Washington Post*, August 11, 1980; *National Review*, August 22, 1980; Black and Black, *Rise of Southern Republicans*, pp. 215–16; Hayward, *Age of Reagan*, pp. 696–97.

8. Lou Cannon, *Governor Reagan*, p. 478; Diggins, *Ronald Reagan*, p. 57; and see Cannon's piece in *The New York Times*, November 18, 2007.

9. *Los Angeles Times*, August 27, 1980; *Washington Post*, September 2 and 3, 1980; Lou Cannon, *Governor Reagan*, pp. 479–82; Busch, *Reagan's Victory*, pp. 108–11.

10. *Washington Post*, October 9, 10, and 15, 1980; Lou Cannon, *Governor Reagan*, pp. 495–98; Hayward, *Age of Reagan*, pp. 694–95.

11. Lou Cannon, *Governor Reagan*, pp. 483–86; *Washington Post*, September 14, 1980; Hayward, *Age of Reagan*, p. 676.

12. Reeves, *President Reagan*, p. 3; Martin Anderson, *Revolution*, pp. 53, 286, 293; Haynes Johnson, *Sleepwalking Through History*, pp. 46, 55–56; *Washington Post*, October 22, 1980; Troy, *Morning in America*, p. 36.

13. *Time*, July 21, 1980; Jenkins, *Decade of Nightmares*, pp. 20, 155, 161.

14. Busch, *Reagan's Victory*, p. 101; Hayward, *Age of Reagan*, pp. 459–60, 685–87; Diggins, *Ronald Reagan*, p. 329; *Washington Post*, September 2, 1980.

15. Patrick Caddell to Carter, August 18, 1980, box 77, Chief of Staff Files, Carter Library; Burton I. Kaufman, *Presidency of James Earl Carter, Jr.*, pp. 197–98; Germond and Witcover, *Blue Smoke and Mirrors*, p. 249.

16. Lou Cannon, *Governor Reagan*, pp. 489, 492; Busch, *Reagan's Victory*, p. 99; Germond and Witcover, *Blue Smoke and Mirrors*, pp. 244–45, 256.

17. Lou Cannon, *Governor Reagan*, pp. 488–89, 492; Troy, *Affairs of State*, p. 282; Burton I. Kaufman, *Presidency of James Earl Carter, Jr.*, p. 201; *New Republic*, September 27, 1980; Hayward, *Age of Reagan*, p. 698; *Washington Post*, September 18, 1980.

18. *New York Times*, June 9, 1980; Germond and Witcover, *Blue Smoke and Mirrors*, pp. 229–30; Busch, *Reagan's Victory*, pp. 43, 103; and for a more detailed (and sympathetic) account, see Bisnow, *Diary of a Dark Horse*.

19. Germond and Witcover, *Blue Smoke and Mirrors*, pp. 234–35, 239.

20. On Anderson's political lineage, see Sandbrook, *Eugene McCarthy*, pp. 221–23; on his electoral impact, or lack of it, see Busch, *Reagan's Victory*, pp. 132–40.

21. *New York Times*, September 22, 1980; Busch, *Reagan's Victory*, p. 112.

22. Germond and Witcover, *Blue Smoke and Mirrors*, pp. 267–70; Jordan, *Crisis*, pp. 352–53.

23. There are slightly different accounts of the Stockman-Reagan sessions; in some, Stockman was playing Anderson, in others, Carter. In fact, he prepared Reagan for both debates, although he only mentions Anderson in his book. See Stockman, *Triumph of Politics*, pp. 44–47; Blumenthal, *Rise of the Counter-establishment*, p. 224.

24. Drew, *Portrait of an Election*, pp. 321–22; Germond and Witcover, *Blue Smoke and Mirrors*, p. 278.

25. Transcript of the presidential debate, October 28, 1980, www.debates.org/pages/trans80b.html.

26. Germond and Witcover, *Blue Smoke and Mirrors*, p. 280; Jordan, *Crisis*, pp. 355–56.

27. Transcript of the presidential debate, October 28, 1980, www.debates.org/pages/trans80b.html; Germond and Witcover, *Blue Smoke and Mirrors*, p. 281; Jordan, *Crisis*, p. 357.

28. *New Republic*, November 8, 1980; Burton I. Kaufman, *Presidency of James Earl Carter, Jr.*, p. 205; Hayward, *Age of Reagan*, p. 707; Busch, *Reagan's Victory*, pp. 119–20.

29. Hayward, *Age of Reagan*, p. 708; Morris, *Jimmy Carter*, p. 286; Busch, *Reagan's Victory*, p. 120; *Washington Post*, November 3, 1980.

30. Germond and Witcover, *Blue Smoke and Mirrors*, pp. 8, 290–91; Lou Cannon, *Governor Reagan*, p. 506.

31. Germond and Witcover, *Blue Smoke and Mirrors*, pp. 8–9; David Harris, *Crisis*, pp. 381–82; Deaver, *Behind the Scenes*, p. 99.

32. The most coherent statement of the October Surprise theory is Sick, *October Surprise*; see also Sick's piece in the *New York Times*, April 15, 1991. For rebuttals, see U.S. Senate Committee on Foreign Relations, *The "October Surprise" Allegations and the Circumstances Surrounding the Release of the American Hostages Held in Iran* (Washington, D.C., 1992); U.S. House Committee on Foreign Affairs, *Joint Report of the Task Force to Investigate Certain Allegations Concerning the Hold-*

*ing of American Hostages by Iran in 1980* (Washington, D.C., 1993); *Newsweek*, November 11, 1991; *New Republic*, November 18, 1991; *Village Voice*, February 25, 1992. See also the sensible discussions in Busch, *Reagan's Victory*, pp. 122–24; Bowden, *Guests of the Ayatollah*, pp. 628–29.

33. Germond and Witcover, *Blue Smoke and Mirrors*, pp. 1–2, 11–13.

34. Jimmy Carter, *Keeping Faith*, p. 566; Jordan, *Crisis*, pp. 361–62.

35. *New York Times*, November 3, 1980; Germond and Witcover, *Blue Smoke and Mirrors*, p. 18.

36. *New York Times*, November 4, 1980; Germond and Witcover, *Blue Smoke and Mirrors*, pp. 6, 293; Drew, *Portrait of an Election*, pp. 333–34; Jordan, *Crisis*, p. 363.

37. *Public Papers of the Presidents of the United States: Jimmy Carter, 1980–1981* (Washington, D.C., 1982), bk. 2, pp. 2665–66.

38. *New York Times*, November 4, 1980; Jamieson, *Packaging the Presidency*, pp. 414–15, 444–45; Lou Cannon, *Governor Reagan*, pp. 509–10.

39. Jordan, *Crisis*, pp. 365–69; Germond and Witcover, *Blue Smoke and Mirrors*, pp. 299–304.

40. *New York Times*, November 5, 1980; *Washington Post*, November 5, 1980; Germond and Witcover, *Blue Smoke and Mirrors*, pp. 304–6.

41. *New York Times*, November 5, 1980; Rieder, *Canarsie*, pp. 258–59; Lou Cannon, *Governor Reagan*, p. 510.

42. Drew, *Portrait of an Election*, pp. 337–38; Hayward, *Age of Reagan*, pp. 711–12; clips of NBC's coverage can be seen on YouTube.

43. Jordan, *Crisis*, pp. 371–73; Reagan, *American Life*, p. 222.

44. *Washington Post*, November 4, 1980; Black and Black, *Rise of Southern Republicans*, pp. 211–19; Busch, *Reagan's Victory*, pp. 1, 105–6, 126–29, 153–54, 161.

45. Dionne, *Why Americans Hate Politics*, pp. 234–36.

46. *Washington Post*, October 28, 1980; *New York Times*, November 6, 1980; Busch, *Reagan's Victory*, pp. 102, 147; Critchlow, *Phyllis Schlafly and Grassroots Conservatism*, pp. 262, 264–66.

47. Iwan W. Morgan, *Beyond the Liberal Consensus*, pp. 166–67; Burnham, *Current Crisis in American Politics*.

48. Hayward, *Age of Reagan*, p. 714; *Washington Post*, November 6, 1980; Broder, *Changing of the Guard*, p. 6.

49. Edsall, *Chain Reaction*, pp. 3–5, 101–3, 152, 181; Dionne, *Why Americans Hate Politics*, p. 136; Busch, *Reagan's Victory*, p. 143; Schulman, *Seventies*, p. 310 n. 69.

50. Dionne, *Why Americans Hate Politics*, p. 136; Troy, *Morning in America*, p. 49; Ehrman, *Eighties*, pp. 47–48; *Time*, February 2, 1981; Broder, *Changing of the Guard*, p. 2.

51. See Hayward, *Age of Reagan*, p. xii; Critchlow, *Phyllis Schlafly and Grassroots Conservatism*, pp. 4–5; Lou Cannon, *Governor Reagan*, p. 393; Busch, *Reagan's Victory*, p. 126.

52. *Time*, February 2, 1981; Biven, *Jimmy Carter's Economy*, pp. 3, 13; Burton I. Kaufman, *Presidency of James Earl Carter, Jr.*, p. 206; Morris, *Jimmy Carter*, p. 287.

53. See Skowronek, *The Politics Presidents Make*, p. 381; Burton I. Kaufman, *Presidency of James Earl Carter, Jr.*, pp. 2–3; Morris, *Jimmy Carter*, pp. 280–81; Schulman, "Slouching Toward the Supply Side," pp. 62–63.

54. Biven, *Jimmy Carter's Economy*, p. 259. On the Carter-Reagan parallels, see Schulman, "Slouching Toward the Supply Side," pp. 62–67; Jenkins, *Decade of Nightmares*, pp. 175–77; Skowronek, *The Politics Presidents Make*, pp. 405–6.

55. Burton I. Kaufman, *Presidency of James Earl Carter, Jr.*, pp. 3, 210; Leuchtenberg, "Jimmy Carter and the Post–New Deal Presidency," p. 17.

## WASHINGTON, D.C., JANUARY 1981

1. *New York Times*, January 19 and 20, 1981; Sick, *All Fall Down*, pp. 318–38.
2. Jordan, *Crisis*, pp. 395–97; Jimmy Carter, *Keeping Faith*, pp. 3, 9–11; the photograph is on p. 6.
3. Jordan, *Crisis*, p. 397; Deaver, *Behind the Scenes*, pp. 98–99; Reeves, *President Reagan*, p. 1.
4. Jordan, *Crisis*, p. 397; Jimmy Carter, *Keeping Faith*, p. 13.
5. Jordan, *Crisis*, p. 404; Lou Cannon, *President Reagan*, p. 80; Reeves, *President Reagan*, p. 2.
6. Jordan, *Crisis*, p. 17; Reeves, *President Reagan*, p. 3.
7. *Washington Post*, January 21, 1981.
8. *New York Times*, January 21, 1981; *Time*, February 2, 1981; Lou Cannon, *President Reagan*, pp. 73–77; Reeves, *President Reagan*, pp. 4–7.
9. *New York Times*, January 21, 1981; Jordan, *Crisis*, pp. 405–6; Bourne, *Jimmy Carter*, p. 474.
10. Jordan, *Crisis*, pp. 406–14; Bowden, *Guests of the Ayatollah*, p. 587; Wells, *444 Days*, p. 435.
11. *Time*, February 2, 1981.
12. *New York Times*, January 18, 21, and 22, 1981.
13. *New York Times*, January 18, 19, and 20, 1981; *Washington Post*, January 19, 20, and 21, 1981.
14. Haynes Johnson, *Sleepwalking Through History*, p. 22.
15. Leamer, *Make-Believe*, p. 3; *New York Times*, January 21, 1981; *Time*, February 2, 1981.
16. *Newsweek*, February 2, 1981; *Washington Post*, January 20, 1981.
17. *Washington Post*, January 22, 1981, February 1, 1981.

## Sources and Further Reading

Writing about the 1970s is a task made immeasurably easier because, after years of neglect, historians are now beginning to investigate almost every conceivable aspect of the period, from the fall of Saigon to the rise of air-conditioning. Without this outpouring of scholarship, this book not only would have taken longer to write but also would have been far poorer as a result. And like anyone writing a broad history, I have run up large debts to those scholars who have trodden these paths before, as acknowledged in the notes and bibliography. Perhaps my biggest debt is to those who have already written histories of the 1970s: Peter Carroll, David Frum, Philip Jenkins, and especially Bruce Schulman. And of course I have done a fair bit of digging of my own, with the aim of producing a book that says something new about this pivotal but underappreciated moment in the nation's history.

Perhaps the most illuminating sources for the history of the 1970s are the daily newspapers and weekly magazines. As recently as ten years ago, searching the pages of a newspaper usually meant weeks hunched over an antediluvian microfilm reader, but the advent of digitized collections has changed everything. In general, I relied heavily on *The New York Times, The Washington Post*, the *Los Angeles Times*, and *The Wall Street Journal*, while for the chapter on busing I used the microfilmed *Boston Globe* at the Boston Public Library. Periodicals such as *Time, Commentary, The Atlantic Monthly, National Review, The Nation, The Economist*, and *The New York Review of Books* all have online archives. And no historian can ignore the invaluable data of the *Statistical Abstract of the United States* series, produced every year by the Bureau of the Census. I made most use of the editions for 1970, 1974, 1976, and 1981—once again, a task made much easier because they can be downloaded as PDFs from www.census .gov/prod/www/abs/statab1951-1994.htm.

On political matters, I made extensive use of the *Public Papers of the Presidents of the United States* series, which carries the transcripts of everything that Richard Nixon, Gerald Ford, and Jimmy Carter said in public after they had taken the oath of office, from speeches to press conferences. These, too, are now online at the outstanding Web site run by John Woolley and Gerhard Peters at the University of California at Santa Barbara, www.presidency.ucsb.edu/, which also carries the texts of convention speeches and the national platforms of the two major parties. Thousands of documents and transcripts relating to foreign policy and the Cold War, meanwhile, can be downloaded from the National Security Archive at the George Washington University, www.gwu.edu/~nsarchiv/. Presidential campaign commercials can be viewed online at the Museum of the Moving Image's Living Room Candidate Web site, www .livingroomcandidate.org/, and some other speeches and clips are on YouTube, including the priceless appearances of Ford, Carter, and Reagan on *What's My Line?* Transcripts and videos of the formal presidential debates, meanwhile, are at the Web site of the Commission on Presidential Debates, www.debates.org.

The National Archives (NARA) system remains an extraordinary resource for the historian. At the National Archives at College Park, Maryland, I made occasional sorties into the collections of the Richard Nixon Presidential Materials Project, while my account of the bicentennial draws on the records of the American Revolution Bicentennial Administration (ARBA). For my chapters on the Ford administration, I relied on the works of historians such as A. James Reichley, John Robert Greene, and Yanek Mieczkowski, but I also dipped into the holdings of the splendid Gerald R. Ford Presidential Library at Ann Arbor, Michigan. The Ford Library deserves particular praise for scanning many crucial documents and putting them online, including full sets of national security study and decision memoranda and the minutes of cabinet and National Security Council meetings, as well as selected documents relating to the end of the Vietnam War and the 1976 campaign. The Jimmy Carter Library in Atlanta, Georgia, has fewer online documents, but it does carry the transcripts of several oral history interviews. More oral histories of the Carter presidency, meanwhile, are online at the Web site of the Miller Center of Public Affairs at the University of Virginia, www.millercenter .org/scripps/digitalarchive/oralhistories/carter. And the Reagan Library in Simi Valley is gradually putting selected speeches for Reagan's pre-presidential career online, at www .reagan.utexas.edu/archives/speeches/.

## SELECTED BOOKS AND ARTICLES

Ackerman, John A. "The Impact of the Coal Strike of 1977–1978." *Industrial and Labor Relations Review* 32, no. 2 (January 1979), pp. 175–88.

Adler, Richard P. *"All in the Family": A Critical Appraisal.* New York, 1979.

Agnew, Spiro T. *Go Quietly . . . or Else.* New York, 1980.

Akins, James. "The Oil Crisis: This Time the Wolf Is Here." *Foreign Affairs,* April 1973, pp. 462–90.

Allen, Woody. *Side Effects.* New York, 1980.

Allyn, David. *Make Love, Not War: The Sexual Revolution: An Unfettered History.* Boston, 2000.

Ambrose, Stephen E. *Nixon: Ruin and Recovery, 1973–1990.* New York, 1991.

——— . *Nixon: The Triumph of a Politician, 1962–1972.* New York, 1989.

Anderson, Martin. *Revolution.* New York, 1988.

Anderson, Patrick. *Electing Jimmy Carter: The Campaign of 1976.* Baton Rouge, La., 1994.

Anderson, Terry H. *In Pursuit of Fairness: A History of Affirmative Action.* New York, 2004.

——— . *The Movement and the Sixties: Protest in America from Greensboro to Wounded Knee.* New York, 1995.

Andrew, Christopher. *For the President's Eyes Only: Secret Intelligence and the American Presidency from Washington to Bush.* New York, 1995.

Andrews, Nigel. *Jaws.* London, 2000.

Andriote, John-Manuel. *Victory Deferred: How AIDS Changed Gay Life in America.* Chicago, 1999.

Anson, Robert Sam. *Exile: The Unquiet Oblivion of Richard M. Nixon.* New York, 1984.

Appleborne, Peter. *Dixie Rising: How the South Is Shaping American Values, Politics, and Culture.* New York, 1996.

Arrington, Theodore S., and Patricia A. Kyle. "Equal Rights Activists in North Carolina." *Signs* 3, no. 3 (Spring 1978), pp. 666–80.

Arsenault, Raymond. "The End of the Long Hot Summer: The Air Conditioner and Southern Culture." *Journal of Southern History* 50, no. 4 (November 1984), pp. 597–628.

Auletta, Ken. *The Underclass.* New York, 1982.

Bach, Richard. *Jonathan Livingston Seagull.* New York, 1970.

Bach, Steven. *Final Cut: Dreams and Disaster in the Making of "Heaven's Gate."* London, 1985.

Bahr, Howard M. "Changes in Family Life in Middletown, 1924–77." *Public Opinion Quarterly* 44, no.1 (Spring 1980), pp. 35–52.

Bailey, Beth. "She 'Can Bring Home the Bacon': Negotiating Gender in the 1970s." In Bailey and Farber, *America in the 70s,* pp. 107–28.

Bailey, Beth, and David Farber, eds. *America in the 70s.* Lawrence, Kans., 2004.

Baker, Carrie N. "The Emergence of Organized Feminist Resistance to Sexual Harassment in the 1970s." *Journal of Women's History* 19, no. 3 (Fall 2007), pp. 161–84.

Balmer, Randall. *Mine Eyes Have Seen the Glory: A Journey into the Evangelical Subculture in America.* New York, 2000.

Barnouw, Erika. *Tube of Plenty: The Evolution of American Television.* New York, 1990.

Barone, Michael. *Our Country: The Shaping of America from Roosevelt to Reagan.* New York, 1990.

Barrow, John C. "An Age of Limits: Jimmy Carter and the Quest for a National Energy Policy." In Fink and Graham, *Carter Presidency,* pp. 158–78.

Baskir, Lawrence M., and William A. Strauss. *Chance and Circumstance: The Draft, the War, and the Vietnam Generation.* New York, 1978.

Bass, Jack, and Walter De Vries. *The Transformation of Southern Politics: Social Change and Political Consequence Since 1945.* New York, 1976.

Battan, Jesse F. "The 'New Narcissism' in 20th-Century America: The Shadow and Substance of Social Change." *Journal of Social History* 17, no. 2 (Winter 1983), pp. 199–220.

Baxter, John. *George Lucas: A Biography.* London, 2000.

Becker, Susan T. *The Origins of the Equal Rights Amendment: Feminism Between the Wars.* Westport, Conn., 1981.

Beckwith, Charlie, with Donald Knox. *Delta Force.* New York, 1983.

Bell, Daniel. *The Cultural Contradictions of Capitalism.* New York, 1976.

———, ed. *The New American Right.* New York, 1955.

Bellah, Robert A., et al. *Habits of the Heart: Individualism and Commitment in American Life.* New York, 1985.

Bellant, Russ. *The Coors Connection.* Cambridge, Mass., 1991.

Benchley, Peter. *Jaws.* London, 1975.

Berkowitz, Edward D. *Something Happened: A Political and Cultural Overview of the Seventies.* New York, 2006.

Berman, Larry. *No Peace, No Honor: Nixon, Kissinger, and Betrayal in Vietnam.* New York, 2001.

Bill, James A. *The Eagle and the Lion: The Tragedy of American-Iranian Relations.* New Haven, Conn., 1988.

Biskind, Peter. *Easy Riders, Raging Bulls: How the Sex 'n' Drugs 'n' Rock 'n' Roll Generation Saved Hollywood.* London, 1998.

Bisnow, Mark. *Diary of a Dark Horse: The 1980 Anderson Presidential Campaign.* Carbondale, Ill., 1983.

Biven, W. Carl. *Jimmy Carter's Economy: Policy in an Age of Limits.* Chapel Hill, N.C., 2002.

Black, Conrad. *Richard Milhous Nixon: The Invincible Quest.* London, 2007.

Black, Earl, and Merle Black. *The Rise of Southern Republicans.* Cambridge, Mass., 2002.

Blake, Ted. "*The Dukes of Hazzard,* Television's Simple South, and Resurrecting the Outlaw Hero." *storySouth* (Summer 2002), www.storysouth.com/summer2002/dukeshazzard.html.

Blinder, Alan S. "The Anatomy of Double-Digit Inflation in the 1970s." In Robert E. Hall, ed., *Inflation: Causes and Effects,* pp. 261–82. Chicago, 1982.

———. *Hard Heads, Soft Hearts: Tough-Minded Economics for a Just Society.* New York, 1987.

———. "The Rise and Fall of Keynesian Economics." *Economic Record* (December 1988), pp. 278–94.

Blumenthal, Sidney. *The Rise of the Counter-Establishment: From Conservative Ideology to Political Power.* New York, 1986.

Bok, Sissela. *Lying: Moral Choice in Public and Private Life.* New York, 1978.

Boston Women's Health Book Collective. *Our Bodies, Ourselves.* New York, 1973.

Bourne, Peter G. *Jimmy Carter: A Comprehensive Biography from Plains to Post-presidency.* New York, 1997.

Bowden, Mark. *Guests of the Ayatollah: The First Battle in the West's War with Militant Islam.* London, 2006.

Boyer, Paul S. "The Evangelical Resurgence in 1970s American Protestantism." In Schulman and Zelizer, *Rightward Bound,* pp. 29–51.

———. *When Time Shall Be No More: Prophecy Belief in Modern American Culture.* Cambridge, Mass., 1992.

Brauer, Carl M. "Women Activists, Southern Conservatives, and the Prohibition of Sex Discrimination in Title VII of the 1964 Civil Rights Act." *Journal of Southern History* 49, no. 1 (February 1983), pp. 37–56.

Braunstein, Peter. " 'Adults Only': The Construction of an Erotic City in New York During the 1970s." In Bailey and Farber, *America in the 70s,* pp. 129–56.

Brennan, Mary C. *Turning Right: The Conservative Capture of the GOP.* Chapel Hill, N.C., 1995.

Brinkley, Alan. *Liberalism and Its Discontents.* Cambridge, Mass., 1998.

———. "The Passions of Oral Roberts." In Brinkley, *Liberalism and Its Discontents,* pp. 266–76.

———. "The Problem of American Conservatism." *American Historical Review* 99, no. 2 (April 1994), pp. 409–29.

Brinkley, Douglas. *Gerald R. Ford.* New York, 2007.

Broder, David S. *Changing of the Guard: Power and Leadership in America.* New York, 1981.

Brown, Ruth Murray. *For a "Christian America": A History of the Religious Right.* Amherst, N.Y., 2002.

Brownmiller, Susan. *Against Our Will: Men, Women, and Rape*. New York, 1975.

Brudney, Jeffrey, and Gary Copeland. "Evangelicals as a Political Force: Reagan and the 1980 Religious Vote." *Social Science Quarterly* 65 (December 1984), pp. 1072–79.

Bryant, Anita. *The Anita Bryant Story*. Old Tappan, N.J., 1977.

Bryant, Anita, and Bob Green. *At Any Cost*. Old Tappan, N.J., 1978.

Brzezinski, Zbigniew. *Power and Principle: Memoirs of the National Security Adviser, 1977–1981*. New York, 1983.

Buchanan, James M., and Gordon Tullock. *The Calculus of Consent: Logical Foundations of Constitutional Democracy*. Ann Arbor, Mich., 1962.

Bullard, Pamela, and Judith Stoia. *The Hardest Lesson: Personal Accounts of a School Desegregation Crisis*. Boston, 1980.

Burnham, Walter Dean. *The Current Crisis in American Politics*. New York, 1983.

Burr, William, ed. *The Kissinger Transcripts: The Top Secret Talks with Beijing and Moscow*. New York, 1999.

Burris, Val. "Who Opposed the ERA? An Analysis of Judicial Support for Gender-Based Claims." *Social Science Quarterly* 64, no. 2 (June 1983), pp. 305–17.

Busch, Andrew. *Reagan's Victory: The Presidential Election of 1980 and the Rise of the Right*. Lawrence, Kans., 2005.

Butler, David. *The Fall of Saigon*. London, 1986.

Cahn, Anne Hessing. *Killing Détente: The Right Attacks the CIA*. University Park, Pa., 1998.

———. "Team B: The Trillion-Dollar Experiment." *Bulletin of the Atomic Scientists* 49, no. 3 (April 1993), pp. 20–27.

Cannato, Vincent J. *The Ungovernable City: John Lindsay and His Struggle to Save New York*. New York, 2001.

Cannon, James. *Time and Chance: Gerald Ford's Appointment with History*. Ann Arbor, Mich., 1998.

Cannon, Lou. *Governor Reagan: His Rise to Power*. New York, 2003.

———. *President Reagan: The Role of a Lifetime*. New York, 2000.

Canto, Victor A., Douglas H. Joines, and Arthur B. Laffer. *Foundations of Supply-Side Economics: Theory and Evidence*. New York, 1983.

Capozzola, Christopher. " 'It Makes You Want to Believe in the Country': Celebrating the Bicentennial in an Age of Limits." In Bailey and Farber, *America in the 70s*, pp. 29–49.

Caputo, Philip. *A Rumor of War*. New York, 1977.

Carlson, Jody. *George C. Wallace and the Politics of Powerlessness*. New Brunswick, N.J., 1981.

Carroll, Peter N. *It Seemed Like Nothing Happened: America in the 1970s*. New Brunswick, N.J., 1990.

Carson, Donald W., and James W. Johnson. *Mo: The Life and Times of Morris K. Udall*. Tucson, Ariz., 2001.

Carson, Rachel. *Silent Spring*. Greenwich, Conn., 1964.

Carter, Dan T. *The Politics of Rage: George Wallace, the Origins of the New Conservatism, and the Transformation of American Politics*. Baton Rouge, La., 1995.

Carter, Jimmy. *Keeping Faith: Memoirs of a President*. London, 1982.

———. *Why Not the Best?* New York, 1975.

Chafe, William H. *The American Woman: Her Changing Social, Economic, and Political Roles, 1920–1970*. New York, 1972.

———. *The Unfinished Journey: America Since World War II*. New York, 2003.

Chaney, Betty. "Political Changes in Terrible Terrell." *Southern Changes* 2, no. 7 (1980), pp. 7–10.

Chang, Jeff. *Can't Stop, Won't Stop: A History of the Hip-Hop Generation.* New York, 2005.

Chang, Sylvia Shin Huey. "Restaging the War: *The Deer Hunter* and the Primal Scene of Violence." *Cinema Journal* 44, no. 2 (Winter 2005), pp. 89–106.

Chester, Lewis, Bruce Page, and Godfrey Hodgson. *An American Melodrama: The Presidential Campaign of 1968.* New York, 1969.

Clark, Peter. "The Keynesian Consensus." In David Marquand and Anthony Seldon, eds., *The Ideas That Shaped Post-war Britain*, pp. 67–87. London, 1996.

Clymer, Adam. *Edward M. Kennedy: A Biography.* New York, 1999.

Cobb, James C. "From Muskogee to Luckenbach: Country Music and the 'Southernization' of America." *Journal of Popular Culture* 16, no. 3 (Winter 1982), pp. 81–91.

——. *Industrialization and Southern Society, 1877–1984.* Lexington, Ky., 1984.

Cohen, Lizabeth. *A Consumers' Republic: The Politics of Mass Consumption in Postwar America.* New York, 2003.

Coll, Steve. *Ghost Wars: The Secret History of the CIA, Afghanistan, and Bin Laden, from the Soviet Invasion to September 10, 2001.* New York, 2004.

Collins, Robert M. *More: The Politics of Economic Growth in Postwar America.* Oxford, 2000.

——. *Transforming America: Politics and Culture During the Reagan Years.* New York, 2007.

Comfort, Alex. *The Joy of Sex: A Cordon Bleu Guide to Lovemaking.* New York, 1972.

Commoner, Barry. *The Closing Circle: Nature, Man, and Technology.* New York, 1971.

Cowie, Jefferson. "Nixon's Class Struggle: Romancing the New Right Worker, 1969–1973." *Labor History* 43, no. 3 (Summer 2002), pp. 257–83.

——. " 'A One-Sided Class War': Rethinking Doug Fraser's 1978 Resignation from the Labor-Management Group." *Labor History* 44, no. 3 (2003), pp. 307–14.

——. "Vigorously Left, Right, and Center: The Crosscurrents of Working-Class America in the 1970s." In Bailey and Farber, *America in the 70s*, pp. 75–106.

Crawford, Alan. *Thunder on the Right: The "New Right" and the Politics of Resentment.* New York, 1980.

Critchlow, Donald T. *Phyllis Schlafly and Grassroots Conservatism.* Princeton, N.J., 2005.

Cruse, Harold. *The Crisis of the Negro Intellectual.* New York, 1967.

——. *Plural but Equal: Blacks and Minorities in America's Plural Society.* New York, 1988.

Curry, George E., ed. *The Affirmative Action Debate.* Cambridge, Mass., 1996.

Curvin, Robert, and Bruce Porter. *Blackout Looting! New York City, July 13, 1977.* New York, 1979.

Dallek, Matthew. *The Right Moment: Ronald Reagan's First Victory and the Decisive Turning Point in American Politics.* Oxford, 2004.

Daughen, Joseph R., and Peter Binzen. *The Cop Who Would Be King: Mayor Frank Rizzo.* Boston, 1977.

Davies, Gareth. *From Opportunity to Entitlement: The Transformation and Decline of Great Society Liberalism.* Lawrence, Kans., 1999.

——. "The Great Society After Johnson: The Case of Bilingual Education." *Journal of American History* 88, no. 4 (March 2002), pp. 1,405–29.

———. *See Government Grow: Education Politics from Johnson to Reagan*. Lawrence, Kans., 2007.

Deaver, Michael K., with Mickey Hershowitz. *Behind the Scenes*. New York, 1987.

Derthick, Martha, and Paul J. Quick. *The Politics of Deregulation*. Washington, D.C., 1985.

Diamond, Sara. *Not by Politics Alone: The Enduring Influence of the Religious Right*. New York, 1998.

Diggins, John Patrick. *Ronald Reagan: Fate, Freedom, and the Making of History*. New York, 2007.

DiMaggio, Paul, and Richard A. Peterson. "From Region to Class: The Changing Locus of Country Music." *Social Forces* 53, no. 3 (March 1975), pp. 497–506.

DiMaggio, Paul, Richard A. Peterson, and Jack Esco Jr. "Country Music: Ballad of the Silent Majority." In R. Serge Denisoff and Richard A. Peterson, eds., *The Sounds of Social Change*, pp. 31–56. Chicago, 1972.

Dionne, E. J., Jr. *Why Americans Hate Politics*. New York, 1992.

Dobrynin, Anatoly. *In Confidence: Moscow's Ambassador to America's Six Cold War Presidents*. New York, 1995.

Donovan, Hedley. *Roosevelt to Reagan: A Reporter's Encounters with Nine Presidents*. New York, 1985.

Donovan, Robert J., and Ray Scherer. *Unsilent Revolution: Television News and American Public Life*. Cambridge, U.K., 1992.

Dorrien, Gary J. *The Neoconservative Mind: Politics, Culture, and the War of Ideology*. Philadelphia, 1993.

Dougan, Clark, David Fulgham, et al. *The Vietnam Experience: The Fall of the South*. Boston, 1985.

Douglas, Susan. *Where the Girls Are: Growing Up Female with the Mass Media*. New York, 1994.

Drew, Elizabeth. *American Journal: The Events of 1976*. New York, 1977.

———. *Portrait of an Election: The 1980 Presidential Campaign*. New York, 1981.

Dubovsky, Melvyn. "Jimmy Carter and the End of the Politics of Productivity." In Fink and Graham, *Carter Presidency*, pp. 95–116.

Ebtekar, Massoumeh, with Fred A. Reed, *Takeover in Tehran: The Inside Story of the 1979 U.S. Embassy Capture*. Vancouver, 2000.

Edsall, Thomas Byrne, with Mary D. Edsall. *Chain Reaction: The Impact of Race, Rights, and Taxes on American Politics*. New York, 1992.

Egerton, John. *The Americanization of Dixie, the Southernization of America*. New York, 1974.

Ehrlich, Paul R. *The Population Bomb*. New York, 1971.

Ehrlich, Paul R., and Anne H. Ehrlich. *The End of Affluence: A Blueprint for Your Future*. New York, 1974.

Ehrlichman, John. *Witness to Power: The Nixon Years*. New York, 1982.

Ehrman, John. *The Eighties: America in the Age of Reagan*. New Haven, Conn., 2005.

———. *The Rise of Neoconservatism: Intellectuals and Foreign Affairs, 1945–1994*. New Haven, Conn., 1995.

Eizenstat, Stuart E. "President Carter, the Democrats, and the Making of Domestic Policy." In Rosenbaum and Ugrinksy, *Presidency and Domestic Policies of Jimmy Carter*, pp. 3–16.

Engelhardt, Tom. *The End of Victory Culture: Cold War America and the Disillusioning of a Generation*. New York, 1995.

Engelmann, Larry. *Tears Before the Rain: An Oral History of the Fall of South Vietnam.* New York, 1990.

Evans, Sara M. *Personal Politics.* New York, 1979.

———. *Tidal Wave: How Women Changed America at Century's End.* New York, 2003.

Fairclough, Adam. *Better Day Coming: Blacks and Equality, 1890–2000.* New York, 2002.

Faludi, Susan. *Backlash: The Undeclared War Against American Women.* New York, 1991.

Falwell, Jerry. *Listen, America!* Garden City, N.Y., 1980.

———. *Strength for the Journey.* New York, 1987.

Falwell, Jerry, and Elmer Towns. *Church Aflame.* Nashville, 1971.

Farber, David. *Taken Hostage: The Iran Hostage Crisis and America's First Encounter with Radical Islam.* Princeton, N.J., 2004.

Farrell, Amy. *Yours in Sisterhood: "Ms. Magazine" and the Promise of Popular Feminism.* Chapel Hill, N.C., 1998.

Farrell, John A. *Tip O'Neill and the Democratic Century.* Boston, 2001.

Farrell, Warren. *The Liberated Man.* New York, 1974.

Fasteau, Marc F. *The Male Machine.* New York, 1974.

Feeney, Mark. *Nixon at the Movies.* Chicago, 2004.

Feldstein, Martin, ed. *The American Economy in Transition.* Chicago, 1980.

Felsenthal, Carol. *Sweetheart of the Silent Majority: The Biography of Phyllis Schlafly.* Garden City, N.Y., 1981.

Fenton, James. "The Fall of Saigon." *Granta* 15 (Spring 1985), pp. 27–116.

Ferguson, Thomas, and Joel Rogers. *Right Turn: The Decline of the Democrats and the Future of American Politics.* New York, 1986.

Ferretti, Fred. *The Year the Big Apple Went Bust.* New York, 1976.

Fink, Gary M., and Hugh Davis Graham, eds. *The Carter Presidency: Policy Choices in the Post–New Deal Era.* Lawrence, Kans., 1998.

Firestone, Shulamith. *The Dialectic of Sex: A Case for Feminist Revolution.* New York, 1970.

FitzGerald, Frances. *Cities on a Hill: A Journey Through Contemporary American Cultures.* New York, 1986.

Foner, Eric. *Reconstruction: America's Unfinished Revolution, 1863–1877.* New York, 1989.

Ford, Betty, with Chris Chase. *The Times of My Life.* New York, 1978.

Ford, Gerald R. *A Time to Heal.* New York, 1979.

Formisano, Ronald P. *Boston Against Busing: Race, Class, and Ethnicity in the 1960s and 1970s.* Chapel Hill, N.C., 2004.

Frady, Marshall. *Billy Graham: A Parable of American Righteousness.* Boston, 1979.

Franklin, H. Bruce. *M.I.A., or Mythmaking in America.* Brooklyn, 1992.

Freedman, Robert. "The Religious Right and the Carter Administration." *Historical Journal* 48, no. 1 (March 2005), pp. 231–60.

Freeman, Jo. *The Politics of Women's Liberation: A Case Study of an Emerging Social Movement and Its Relation to the Policy Process.* New York, 1975.

Freeman, Joshua B. *Working-Class New York: Life and Labor Since World War II.* New York, 2000.

Freeman, Richard B. *The Overeducated American.* New York, 1976.

French, Marilyn. *The Women's Room.* New York, 1977.

Friedan, Betty. *The Feminine Mystique.* New York, 1963.

——. *It Changed My Life: Writings on the Women's Movement.* New York, 1976.

Friedman, Lawrence M. *American Law in the 20th Century.* New Haven, Conn., 2002.

Friedman, Milton. *Capitalism and Freedom.* Chicago, 1982.

——. "The Quantity Theory of Money: A Restatement." In Milton Friedman, ed., *Studies in the Quantity Theory of Money,* pp. 3–21. Chicago, 1956.

——. "The Role of Monetary Policy." *American Economic Review* 58, no. 1 (March 1968), pp. 1–17.

Friedman, Milton, and Anna Schwartz. *A Monetary History of the United States, 1867–1960.* Princeton, N.J., 1963.

Frum, David. *How We Got Here: The 70's, the Decade That Brought You Modern Life (for Better or Worse).* New York, 2000.

Furstenberg, Frank F. "Public Reaction to Crime in the Streets." *American Scholar* 40, no. 4 (Autumn 1971), pp. 601–10.

Gaddis, John Lewis. *The Cold War.* London, 2006.

——. *Strategies of Containment: A Critical Appraisal of Postwar American National Security.* New York, 1982.

Gans, Herbert J. "Symbolic Ethnicity: The Future of Ethnic Groups and Cultures in America." *Ethnic and Racial Studies* 2, no. 1 (1979), pp. 1–20.

Garreau, Joel. *Edge City: Life on the New Frontier.* New York, 1991.

Garthoff, Raymond. *Détente and Confrontation: American-Soviet Relations from Nixon to Reagan.* Washington, D.C., 1994.

George, Nelson. *Post-Soul Nation: The Explosive, Contradictory, Triumphant, and Tragic 1980s as Experienced by African Americans.* New York, 2004.

Germond, Jack W., and Jules Witcover. *Blue Smoke and Mirrors: How Reagan Won and Why Carter Lost the Election of 1980.* New York, 1981.

Gettleman, Susan, and Janet Markowitz. *The Courage to Divorce.* New York, 1974.

Gilbey, Ryan. *It Don't Worry Me: "Nashville," "Jaws," "Star Wars," and Beyond.* London, 2003.

Gilder, George F. *Sexual Suicide.* New York, 1973.

Gillon, Steven M. *Boomer Nation: The Largest and Richest Generation Ever and How It Changed America.* New York, 2004.

——. *The Democrats' Dilemma: Walter F. Mondale and the Liberal Legacy.* New York, 1992.

——. *That's Not What We Meant to Do: Reform and Its Unintended Consequences in the Twentieth Century.* New York, 2000.

Gitlin, Todd. *The Sixties: Years of Hope, Days of Rage.* New York, 1993.

Glad, Betty. *Jimmy Carter: In Search of the Great White House.* New York, 1980.

Glazer, Nathan. *Affirmative Discrimination: Ethnic Inequality and Public Policy.* New York, 1975.

——. "Fundamentalists: A Defensive Offensive." In Neuhaus and Cromartie, *Piety and Politics,* pp. 245–58.

Glazer, Nathan, and Irving Kristol, eds. *The American Commonwealth, 1976.* New York, 1976.

Goldberg, Robert A. *Barry Goldwater.* New Haven, Conn., 1995.

Goldman, Albert. *Disco.* New York, 1978.

Golenbock, Peter. *Landry's Boys: An Oral History of a Team and an Era.* Chicago, 2005.

Goodman, James. *Blackout.* New York, 2003.

Gordon, Robert J. "Postwar Macroeconomics: The Evolution of Events and Ideas." In Feldstein, *American Economy in Transition,* pp. 101–82.

Gottlieb, Carl. *The "Jaws" Log: 25th Anniversary Edition.* New York, 2001.

Gottlieb, Robert. *Forcing the Spring: The Transformation of the American Environmental Movement.* Washington, D.C., 1993.

Graham, Hugh Davis. *Civil Rights and the Presidency: Race and Gender in American Politics, 1960–1972.* Oxford, 1992.

———. *The Civil Rights Era: Origins and Development of National Policy, 1960–1972.* New York, 1990.

Grant, Amy. *Mosaic: Pieces of My Life So Far.* New York, 2007.

Greeley, Andrew. *Religious Change in America.* Cambridge, Mass., 1989.

Greenberg, David. *Nixon's Shadow: The History of an Image.* New York, 2003.

Greene, Gayle. *Changing the Story: Feminist Fiction and the Tradition.* Bloomington, Ind., 1991.

Greene, John Robert. *The Presidency of Gerald R. Ford.* Lawrence, Kans., 1995.

Greenfield, Jeff. *The Real Campaign: How the Media Missed the Story of the 1980 Campaign.* New York, 1982.

Greider, William. "The Education of David Stockman." *Atlantic Monthly,* December 1981, pp. 27–54.

———. *Secrets of the Temple: How the Federal Reserve Runs the Country.* New York, 1987.

Guerrero, Ed. *Framing Blackness: The African-American Image in Film.* Philadelphia, 1993.

Hacker, Andrew. *The End of the American Era.* New York, 1970.

Hadden, Jeffrey K., and Charles E. Swann. *Prime Time Preachers: The Rising Power of Televangelism.* Reading, Mass., 1981.

Hahn, Dan F. "Flailing the Profligate: Carter's Energy Sermon of 1979." *Presidential Studies Quarterly* 10 (Fall 1980), pp. 583–87.

Haig, Alexander. *Inner Circles: How America Changed the World: A Memoir.* New York, 1992.

Haldeman, H. R. *The Haldeman Diaries: Inside the Nixon White House.* New York, 1995.

Hale, Nathan G., Jr. *The Rise and Crisis of Psychoanalysis in the United States: Freud and the Americans, 1917–1985.* New York, 1995.

Hamby, Alonzo L. *Liberalism and Its Challengers: From FDR to Bush.* Oxford, 1992.

Hampton, Henry, and Steve Fayer, eds. *Voices of Freedom: An Oral History of the Civil Rights Movement from the 1950s Through the 1980s.* New York, 1990.

Hanhimäki, Jussi. *The Flawed Architect: Henry Kissinger and American Foreign Policy.* Oxford, 2004.

Hargreaves, Robert. *Superpower: A Portrait of America in the 70s.* New York, 1973.

Hargrove, Erwin C. *Jimmy Carter as President: Leadership and the Politics of the Public Good.* Baton Rouge, La., 1988.

Hargrove, Erwin C., and Samuel A. Morley, eds. *The President and the Council of Economic Advisers.* Boulder, Colo., 1984.

Harrington, Michael. "The Welfare State and Its Neoconservative Critics." *Dissent* (Fall 1973), pp. 435–54.

Harris, David. *The Crisis: The President, the Prophet, and the Shah—1979 and the Coming of Militant Islam.* New York, 2004.

Harris, Louis. *Is There a Republican Majority?* New York, 1954.

Hartmann, Heidi. "Who Has Benefited from Affirmative Action in Employment?" In Curry, *Affirmative Action Debate,* pp. 77–96.

Hartmann, Robert T. *Palace Politics: An Insider's Account of the Ford Years*. New York, 1980.

Hartmann, Susan M. "Feminism, Public Policy, and the Carter Administration." In Fink and Graham, *Carter Presidency*, pp. 224–39.

——. *From Margin to Mainstream: American Women and Politics Since 1960*. New York, 1989.

Hayward, Steven F. *The Age of Reagan: The Fall of the Old Liberal Order, 1964–1980*. Roseville, Calif., 2001.

Heilbrun, Carolyn G. *The Education of a Woman: The Life of Gloria Steinem*. New York, 1995.

Hendin, Herbert. *The Age of Sensation*. New York, 1975.

Herman, Edward S. *Corporate Control, Corporate Power*. New York, 1981.

Herring, George C. *America's Longest War: The United States and Vietnam, 1950–1975*. New York, 1986.

Heylin, Clinton. *Bob Dylan: Behind the Shades Revisited*. New York, 2003.

Hochschild, Jennifer L. *The New American Dilemma: Liberal Democracy and School Desegregation*. New Haven, Conn., 1984.

Hodgson, Godfrey. *All Things to All Men: The False Promise of the Modern American Presidency*. London, 1980.

——. *More Equal Than Others: America from Nixon to the New Century*. Princeton, N.J., 2005.

——. *The World Turned Right Side Up: A History of the Conservative Ascendancy in America*. Boston, 1996.

Hoff, Joan. *Nixon Reconsidered*. New York, 1994.

Hofstadter, Richard. "The Paranoid Style in American Politics." *Harper's*, November 1964, pp. 77–86.

Horowitz, Daniel. *The Anxieties of Affluence: Critiques of American Consumer Culture, 1939–79*. Amherst, Mass., 2004.

——. *Betty Friedan and the Making of "The Feminine Mystique": The American Left, the Cold War, and Modern Feminism*. Amherst, Mass., 1998.

Hoskyns, Barney. *Hotel California: The True-Life Adventures of Crosby, Stills, Nash, Young, Mitchell, Taylor, Browne, Ronstadt, Geffen, the Eagles, and Their Many Friends*. Hoboken, N.J., 2006.

Howe, Louise Kapp, ed. *The White Majority*. New York, 1970.

Howes, Craig. *Voices of the Vietnam POWs: Witnesses to Their Fight*. New York, 1993.

Hudson, Cheryl, and Gareth Davies, eds. *Ronald Reagan and the 1980s*. New York, 2008.

Hughes, Robert. *American Visions: The Epic History of Art in America*. London, 1997.

Hung, Nguyen Tien, and Jerrold Schecter. *The Palace File*. New York, 1986.

Hunter, James Davison. *Culture Wars: The Struggle to Define America*. New York, 1992.

Inglehart, Ronald. *Modernization and Postmodernization: Cultural, Economic, and Political Change in 43 Societies*. Princeton, N.J., 1997.

——. *The Silent Revolution: Changing Values and Political Styles Among Western Publics*. Princeton, N.J., 1977.

Isaacs, Arnold R. *Without Honor: Defeat in Vietnam and Cambodia*. New York, 1984.

Isaacson, Walter. *Kissinger: A Biography*. New York, 1992.

Jackson, Kenneth T. *Crabgrass Frontier: The Suburbanization of the United States*. New York, 1985.

Jackson, Kevin, ed. *Schrader on Schrader*. London, 1990.

Jacobson, Matthew Frye. *Roots Too: White Ethnic Revival in Post–Civil Rights America.* Cambridge, Mass., 2006.

Jacoby, Tamar. *Someone Else's House: America's Unfinished Struggle for Integration.* New York, 2000.

Jaffa, Harry V. *How to Think About the American Revolution: A Bicentennial Cerebration.* Durham, N.C., 1978.

Jamieson, Kathleen Hall. *Packaging the Presidency: A History and Criticism of Presidential Campaign Advertising.* New York, 1984.

Janowitz, Morris. *The Last Half Century: Societal Change and Politics in America.* Chicago, 1978.

Jarman, Derek. *The Last of England.* London, 1987.

Jarvis, Howard, with Robert Pack. *I'm Mad as Hell.* New York, 1979.

Jaworski, Leon. *The Right and the Power.* New York, 1977.

Jencks, Christopher, and Paul E. Peterson, eds. *The Urban Underclass.* Washington, D.C., 1991.

Jenkins, Philip. *Decade of Nightmares: The End of the Sixties and the Making of Eighties America.* Oxford, 2006.

Joe, Radcliffe A. *This Business of Disco.* New York, 1980.

Johnson, Haynes. *Sleepwalking Through History: America in the Reagan Years.* New York, 1992.

Johnson, Lyndon B. *The Vantage Point: Perspectives of the Presidency.* New York, 1971.

Johnston, Jill. *Lesbian Nation: The Feminist Solution.* New York, 1973.

Jones, Howard Mumford. *The Age of Energy: Varieties of American Experience, 1865–1915.* New York, 1970.

Jones, Landon Y. *Great Expectations: America and the Baby Boom Generation.* New York, 1980.

Jong, Erica. *Fear of Flying.* New York, 1973.

Jordan, Hamilton. *Crisis: The Last Year of the Carter Presidency.* New York, 1982.

Judis, John B. *William F. Buckley, Jr.: Patron Saint of the Conservatives.* New York, 1988.

Kahn, Alfred. *The Economics of Regulation: Volume II: Institutional Issues.* Cambridge, Mass., 1988.

Kahn, Ashley, Holly George-Warren, and Shawn Dahl, eds. *Rolling Stone: The Seventies.* New York, 1998.

Kalman, Laura. *The Strange Career of Legal Liberalism.* New Haven, Conn., 1996.

Kapuściński, Ryszard. *Shah of Shahs.* London, 1982.

Karnow, Stanley. *Vietnam: A History.* London, 1994.

Kassorla, Irene. *Nice Girls Do—and Now You Can Too!* New York, 1980.

Kaufman, Burton I. *The Presidency of James Earl Carter, Jr.* Lawrence, Kans., 1993.

Kaufman, Robert G. *Henry M. Jackson: A Life in Politics.* Seattle, 2000.

Kazin, Michael. *The Populist Persuasion.* New York, 1995.

Kelley, Robin D. G., and Earl Lewis, eds. *To Make Our World Anew: A History of African Americans.* New York, 2001.

Kemp, Jack. *An American Renaissance: A Strategy for the 1980s.* New York, 1979.

Keyssar, Helene. *Robert Altman's America.* New York, 1991.

Killen, Andreas. *1973 Nervous Breakdown: Watergate, Warhol, and the Birth of Post-Sixties America.* New York, 2006.

King, Billie Jean. *Billie Jean.* New York, 1974.

Kissinger, Henry. *American Foreign Policy.* New York, 1977.

———. *Diplomacy.* New York, 1994.

——. *For the Record: Selected Statements, 1977–1980*. Boston, 1981.

——. *White House Years*. London, 2000.

——. *Years of Renewal*. London, 2000.

——. *Years of Upheaval*. London, 2000.

Klatch, Rebecca E. *Women of the New Right*. Philadelphia, 1987.

Knobler, Peter, and Greg Mitchell, eds. *Very Seventies: A Cultural History of the 1970s from the Pages of "Crawdaddy" Magazine*. New York, 1995.

Koedt, Anne. *Radical Feminism*. New York, 1973.

Kotlowski, Dean J. *Nixon's Civil Rights: Politics, Principle, and Policy*. Cambridge, Mass., 2001.

Kovic, Ron. *Born on the Fourth of July*. New York, 1976.

Kreisberg, Paul H., ed. *American Hostages in Iran: The Conduct of a Crisis*. New Haven, Conn., 1985.

Kremen, Bennett. *Dateline: America: Dispatch from an Altering Nation*. New York, 1974.

Kristol, Irving. *On the Democratic Idea in America*. New York, 1972.

——. *Reflections of a Neoconservative*. New York, 1983.

Krugman, Paul. *Peddling Prosperity: Economic Sense and Nonsense in the Age of Diminished Expectations*. New York, 1994.

Kutler, Stanley I. *The Wars of Watergate: The Last Crisis of Richard Nixon*. New York, 1990.

——, ed. *Abuse of Power: The New Nixon Tapes*. New York, 1997.

Kuttner, Robert. *Revolt of the Haves: Tax Rebellions and Hard Times*. New York, 1980.

Ladd, Everett Carll, Jr. *Transformations of the American Party System*. New York, 1978.

Lader, Lawrence. *Politics, Power, and the Church: The Catholic Crisis and Its Challenge to American Pluralism*. New York, 1987.

LaFeber, Walter. *America, Russia, and the Cold War, 1945–2000*. New York, 2001.

Laqueur, Walter. *Thursday's Child Has Far to Go: A Memoir of the Journeying Years*. New York, 1993.

Lasch, Christopher. *The Culture of Narcissism: American Life in an Age of Diminishing Expectations*. New York, 1979.

Lassiter, Matthew D. *The Silent Majority: Suburban Politics in the Sunbelt South*. Princeton, N.J., 2005.

Laumann, Edward O., John H. Gagnon, Robert T. Michael, and Stuart Michaels. *The Social Organization of Sexuality: Sexual Practices in the United States*. Chicago, 1994.

Lawrence, Tim. *Love Saves the Day: A History of American Dance Music Culture, 1970–1979*. Chapel Hill, N.C., 2003.

Leamer, Laurence. *Make-Believe: The Story of Nancy and Ronald Reagan*. New York, 1983.

Leube, Kurt R., ed. *The Essence of Friedman*. Stanford, Calif., 1987.

Leuchtenberg, William E. *In the Shadow of FDR: From Harry Truman to Ronald Reagan*. Ithaca, N.Y., 1985.

——. "Jimmy Carter and the Post–New Deal Presidency." In Fink and Graham, *Carter Presidency*, pp. 7–28.

——. *A Troubled Feast: American Society Since 1945*. Glenview, Ill., 1983.

Lev, Peter. *American Films of the 70s: Conflicting Visions*. Austin, Tex., 2000.

Levison, Andrew. *The Working-Class Majority*. New York, 1974.

Levy, Mark, and Michael Kramer. *The Ethnic Factor*. New York, 1973.

Lichstenstein, Nelson. *The Most Dangerous Man in Detroit: Walter Reuther and the Fate of American Labor.* New York, 1995.

——. *State of the Union: A Century of American Labor.* Princeton, N.J., 2002.

Liebman, Robert C. "Mobilizing the Moral Majority in the New Christian Right." In Liebman and Wuthnow, *New Christian Right,* pp. 54–59.

Liebman, Robert C., and Robert Wuthnow, eds. *The New Christian Right: Mobilization and Legitimation.* New York, 1983.

Lindsey, Hal. *The Late, Great Planet Earth.* New York, 1973.

Lo, Clarence Y. H. *Small Property Versus Big Government.* Berkeley, Calif., 1990.

Logevall, Fredrik, and Andrew Preston, eds. *Nixon in the World: American Foreign Relations, 1969–1977.* New York, 2008.

Lucas, Robert E., Jr. "Econometric Policy Evaluation: A Critique." *Carnegie-Rochester Conference Series on Public Policy* 1 (1976), pp. 19–46.

——. "Expectations and the Neutrality of Money." *Journal of Economic Theory* 4 (April 1972), pp. 103–24.

Lukas, J. Anthony. *Common Ground: A Turbulent Decade in the Lives of Three American Families.* New York, 1985.

Luker, Kristin. *Abortion and the Politics of Motherhood.* Berkeley, Calif., 1985.

Lyakhovskiy, Aleksandr Antonovich. "Inside the Soviet Invasion of Afghanistan and the Seizure of Kabul, December 1979." *Cold War International History Project Working Paper No. 51,* www.wilsoncenter.org/.

Lynd, Staughton. *The Fight Against Shutdowns: Youngstown's Steel Mill Closings.* San Pedro, Calif., 1982.

——. "The Genesis of the Idea of a Community Right to Industrial Property in Youngstown and Pittsburgh, 1977–1987." *Journal of American History* 74, no. 3 (December 1987), pp. 926–58.

MacCambridge, Michael. *America's Game: The Epic Story of How Pro Football Captured a Nation.* New York, 2005.

MacKinnon, Catharine A. *Sexual Harassment of Working Women: A Case of Sex Discrimination.* New Haven, Conn., 1979.

Mahler, Jonathan. *Ladies and Gentlemen, the Bronx Is Burning: 1977, Baseball, Politics, and the Battle for the Soul of a City.* New York, 2005.

Malloy, Ione. *Southie Won't Go: A Teacher's Diary of the Desegregation of South Boston High School.* Urbana, Ill., 1986.

Mann, James. *Rise of the Vulcans: The History of Bush's War Cabinet.* New York, 2004.

Marable, Manning. *From the Grassroots: Essays Toward Afro-American Liberation.* Boston, 1980.

Marcus, Daniel. *Happy Days and Wonder Years: The Fifties and the Sixties in Contemporary Cultural Politics.* New Brunswick, N.J., 2004.

Marsden, George. *Fundamentalism and American Culture.* New York, 1980.

——, ed. *Evangelicalism and Modern America.* Grand Rapids, 1984.

Marshner, Connaught C. *The New Traditional Woman.* Washington, D.C., 1982.

Martin, Bradford. "Cultural Politics and the Singer/Songwriters of the 1970s." In Schulman and Zelizer, *Rightward Bound,* pp. 128–47.

Martin, William. *With God on Our Side: The Rise of the Religious Right in America.* New York, 2005.

Mason, Robert. *Richard Nixon and the Quest for a New Majority.* Chapel Hill, N.C., 2004.

May, Elaine Tyler. *Homeward Bound: American Families in the Cold War Era*. New York, 1988.

May, Kirse Granat. *Golden State, Golden Youth: The California Image in Popular Culture, 1955–1966*. Chapel Hill, N.C., 2002.

Mayer, William G. *The Changing American Mind: How and Why American Public Opinion Changed Between 1960 and 1988*. Ann Arbor, Mich., 1992.

McCarthy, Mary. *The Mask of State: Watergate Portraits*. New York, 1974.

McClosky, Herbert. "Conservatism and Personality." *American Political Science Review* 52 (March 1958), pp. 27–45.

McGilligan, Patrick. *Robert Altman: Jumping off the Cliff*. New York, 1989.

McGirr, Lisa. *Suburban Warriors: The Origins of the New American Right*. Princeton, N.J., 2001.

Meadows, Donella, et al. *The Limits to Growth: A Report for the Club of Rome's Project on the Predicament of Mankind*. New York, 1974.

Melich, Tanya. *The Republican War Against Women: An Insider's Report from Behind the Lines*. New York, 1996.

Melnick, R. Shep. *Between the Lines: Interpreting Welfare Rights*. Washington, D.C., 1994.

Merry, Robert W. *Taking On the World: Joseph and Stewart Alsop—Guardians of the American Century*. New York, 1996.

Mieczkowski, Yanek. *Gerald Ford and the Challenges of the 1970s*. Lexington, Ky., 2005.

Milkman, Ruth. *Farewell to the Factory: Auto Workers in the Late Twentieth Century*. Berkeley, Calif., 1997.

Miller, Russell. *Bunny: The Real Story of "Playboy."* New York, 1984.

Miller, Stephen Paul. *Seventies Now: Culture as Surveillance*. Durham, N.C., 1999.

Millett, Kate. *Sexual Politics*. New York, 1970.

Mitchell, Robert Cameron. "From Conservation to Environmental Movement: The Development of the Modern Environmental Lobbies." In Michael Lacey, ed., *Government and Environmental Politics: Essays on Historical Development Since World War Two*, pp. 81–113. Washington, D.C., 1989.

Modigliani, Franco. "The Monetarist Controversy; or, Should We Forsake Stabilization Policies?" *American Economic Review* 67 (March 1977), pp. 1–19.

Moens, Alexander. "President Carter's Advisers and the Fall of the Shah." *Political Science Quarterly* 106, no. 2 (Summer 1991), pp. 211–37.

Moffett, George D. *The Limits of Victory: The Ratification of the Panama Canal Treaties*. Ithaca, N.Y., 1985.

Moffett, James. *Storm in the Mountains: A Case Study of Censorship, Conflict, and Consciousness*. Carbondale, Ill., 1988.

Moin, Baqer. *Khomeini: Life of the Ayatollah*. New York, 2000.

Morgan, Iwan W. *Beyond the Liberal Consensus: A Political History of the United States Since 1965*. London, 1994.

Morgan, Marabel. *The Total Woman*. New York, 1973.

Morgan, Robin. *Going Too Far: The Personal Chronicle of a Feminist*. New York, 1978.

———, comp. *Sisterhood Is Powerful: An Anthology of Writings from the Women's Liberation Movement*. New York, 1970.

Morley, Catherine. *The Quest for Epic in Contemporary American Fiction: John Updike, Philip Roth, and Don DeLillo*. New York, 2008.

Morris, Kenneth E. *Jimmy Carter: American Moralist*. Athens, Ga., 1996.

Moynihan, Daniel Patrick. *Maximum Feasible Misunderstanding: Community Action in the War on Poverty.* New York, 1969.

Moynihan, Daniel Patrick, with Suzanne Weaver. *A Dangerous Place.* New York, 1978.

Mumford, Lewis. *The Myth of the Machine: Technics and Human Development.* New York, 1967.

Nash, George H. *The Conservative Intellectual Movement in America Since 1945.* Wilmington, Del., 1996.

National Commission on the Observance of International Women's Year. *The Spirit of Houston: The First National Women's Conference.* Washington, D.C., 1977.

Nessen, Ron. *It Sure Looks Different from the Inside.* Chicago, 1978.

Neuhaus, Richard John, and Michael Cromartie, eds. *Piety and Politics: Evangelicals and Fundamentalists Confront the World.* Washington, D.C., 1987.

Nixon, Richard M. *The Real War.* New York, 1980.

——. *RN: The Memoirs of Richard Nixon.* London, 1978.

Nocera, Joseph. *A Piece of the Action: How the Middle Class Joined the Money Class.* New York, 1995.

Noonan, Peggy. *What I Saw at the Revolution.* New York, 1990.

Novak, Michael. *The Rise of the Unmeltable Ethnics.* New York, 1971.

Nozick, Robert. *Anarchy, State, and Utopia.* New York, 1974.

O'Neill, Nena. *The Marriage Premise.* New York, 1977.

O'Neill, Thomas P., with William Novak. *Man of the House: The Life and Political Memoirs of Speaker Tip O'Neill.* New York, 1987.

O'Neill, Timothy J. *"Bakke" and the Politics of Equality.* Middletown, Conn., 1985.

Osborne, John. *White House Watch: The Ford Years.* Washington, D.C., 1977.

Oudes, Bruce, ed. *From: The President: Richard Nixon's Secret Files.* London, 1989.

Ozersky, Josh. *Archie Bunker's America: TV in an Era of Change, 1968–1978.* Carbondale, Ill., 2003.

Parmet, Herbert S. *George Bush: The Life of a Lone-Star Yankee.* New York, 1997.

——. *Richard Nixon and His America.* Boston, 1990.

Pater, Alan, and James Pater, eds. *What They Said in 1974: The Yearbook of Spoken Opinion.* Beverly Hills, Calif., 1975.

Patterson, James T. *Grand Expectations: The United States, 1945–1974.* New York, 1997.

——. *Restless Giant: The United States from Watergate to "Bush v. Gore."* New York, 2005.

Patterson, Orlando. *The Ordeal of Integration: Progress and Resentment in America's "Racial" Crisis.* Washington, D.C., 1997.

Pells, Richard. *Not Like Us: How Europeans Have Loved, Hated, and Transformed America Since World War II.* New York, 1997.

Perlstein, Rick. *Before the Storm: Barry Goldwater and the Unmaking of the American Consensus.* New York, 2001.

Pettigrew, Thomas F., Robert T. Riley, and Reeve D. Vanneman. "George Wallace's Constituents." *Psychology Today,* February 1972, pp. 47–49.

Phillips, Kevin. *The Emerging Republican Majority.* New York, 1970.

Pinkney, Alphonso. *The Myth of Black Progress.* New York, 1984.

Pirsig, Robert M. *Zen and the Art of Motorcycle Maintenance.* New York, 1974.

Podhoretz, Norman. *Breaking Ranks.* New York, 1979.

——. *Making It.* New York, 1967.

——. *The Norman Podhoretz Reader.* New York, 2004.

Pollock, Dale. *Skywalking: The Life and Films of George Lucas.* Cambridge, Mass., 1999.

Pomper, Gerald M., et al. *The Election of 1976*. New York, 1977.

Porter, Bruce, and Marvin Dunn. *The Miami Riot of 1980*. Lexington, Mass., 1984.

Powell, Jody. *The Other Side of the Story*. New York, 1984.

Pressman, Steven. *Outrageous Betrayal: The Real Story of Werner Erhard from Est to Exile*. New York, 1993.

Price, Richard. *Bloodbrothers*. New York, 1976.

Pynchon, Thomas. *Gravity's Rainbow*. New York, 1973.

Randour, Mary Lou. "Research Report: Women in Higher Education: Trends in Enrollment and Degrees Earned." *Harvard Educational Review* 52 (May 1982), pp. 191–201.

Rapoport, Roger. *California Dreaming: The Political Odyssey of Pat & Jerry Brown*. Berkeley, Calif., 1982.

Rashid, Ahmed. *Taliban: Militant Islam, Oil, and Fundamentalism in Central Asia*. New Haven, Conn., 2000.

Reagan, Ronald. *An American Life*. New York, 1999.

Reagan, Ronald, with Richard G. Hubler. *Where's the Rest of Me?* New York, 1965.

Reeves, Richard. *A Ford, Not a Lincoln*. New York, 1975.

———. *President Reagan: The Triumph of Imagination*. New York, 2005.

Reich, Charles. *The Greening of America*. New York, 1970.

Reichley, A. James. *Conservatives in an Age of Change: The Nixon and Ford Administrations*. Washington, D.C., 1981.

*Reporting Vietnam: Part Two: American Journalism, 1969–1975*. New York, 1998.

*Report of the Commission on Obscenity and Pornography*. New York, 1970.

Reston, James. *The Innocence of Joan Little*. New York, 1977.

Ribuffo, Leo. " 'Malaise' Revisited: Jimmy Carter and the Crisis of Confidence." In John Patrick Diggins, ed., *The Liberal Persuasion: Arthur Schlesinger, Jr., and the Challenge of the American Past*, pp. 164–84. Princeton, N.J., 1997.

Rich, Adrienne. *On Lies, Secrets, and Silence*. New York, 1979.

Rieder, Jonathan. *Canarsie: The Jews and Italians of Brooklyn Against Liberalism*. Cambridge, Mass., 1985.

Ringer, Robert J. *Looking Out for Number One*. New York, 1977.

Roberts, Paul Craig. *The Supply-Side Revolution: An Insider's Account of Policymaking in Washington*. Cambridge, Mass., 1984.

Robison, James. *Attack on the Family*. Wheaton, Ill., 1980.

Rogow, Arnold A. *The Psychiatrists*. New York, 1970.

Roof, Wade Clark. *A Generation of Seekers: The Spiritual Journeys of the Baby-Boom Generation*. New York, 1993.

———. *Spiritual Marketplace: Baby Boomers and the Remaking of American Religion*. Princeton, N.J., 1999.

Rosen, Ruth. *The World Split Open: How the Modern Women's Movement Changed America*. New York, 2001.

Rosenbaum, Hebert D., and Alexej Ugrinsky, eds. *The Presidency and Domestic Policies of Jimmy Carter*. Westport, Conn., 1994.

Rossinow, Doug. *The Politics of Authenticity: Liberalism, Christianity, and the New Left in America*. New York, 1998.

Roth, Philip. *My Life as a Man*. New York, 1974.

Rowen, Hobart. *Self-Inflicted Wounds: From LBJ's Guns and Butter to Reagan's Voodoo Economics*. New York, 1994.

Ruoff, Jeffrey. *An American Family: A Televised Life*. Minneapolis, 2002.

Rusher, William A. *The Rise of the Right*. New York, 1984.

Ryan, Paul B. *The Iranian Rescue Mission: Why It Failed*. Annapolis, Md., 1985.

Sadat, Jehan. *A Woman of Egypt*. New York, 1987.

St. John, Bob. *Landry: The Legend and the Legacy*. Nashville, 2000.

Sale, Kirkpatrick. *Power Shift: The Rise of the Southern Rim and Its Challenge to the Eastern Establishment*. New York, 1975.

Salter, Kenneth W., ed. *The Trial of Inez Garcia*. Berkeley, Calif., 1976.

Samuelson, Robert J. *The Good Life and Its Discontents: The American Dream in the Age of Entitlement, 1945–1995*. New York, 1995.

Sandbrook, Dominic. "The Baptist and the Messiah: Ronald Reagan and Margaret Thatcher." In Hudson and Davies, *Ronald Reagan and the 1980s*, pp. 175–90.

——. *Eugene McCarthy and the Rise and Fall of Postwar American Liberalism*. New York, 2004.

——. "Salesmanship and Substance: The Influence of Domestic Politics and Watergate." In Logevall and Preston, *Nixon in the World*, pp. 85–103.

Sandel, Michael J. *Democracy's Discontent: America in Search of a Public Philosophy*. Cambridge, Mass., 1996.

Sansweet, Stephen J. *Star Wars: From Concept to Screen to Collectible*. San Francisco, 1992.

Sawhill, Ray. "A Movie Called *Nashville*." Salon.com, June 27, 2000, archive.salon.com/ent/movies/feature/2000/06/27/nashville/index.html.

Scammon, Richard, and Ben Wattenberg. *The Real Majority: An Extraordinary Examination of the American Electorate*. New York, 1970.

Schaller, Michael. *Right Turn: American Life in the Reagan-Bush Era, 1980–1992*. Oxford, 2007.

Schecter, Susan. *Women and Male Violence: The Visions and Struggles of the Battered Women's Movement*. Boston, 1982.

Schlesinger, Arthur M., Jr. *The Imperial Presidency*. London, 1974.

Schrag, Peter. *Paradise Lost: California's Experience, America's Future*. Berkeley, Calif., 1999.

Schram, Martin. *Running for President, 1976: The Carter Campaign*. New York, 1977.

Schulman, Bruce J. *From Cotton Belt to Sun Belt: Federal Policy, Economic Development, and the Transformation of the South, 1938–1980*. Oxford, 1991.

——. *The Seventies: The Great Shift in American Culture, Society, and Politics*. New York, 2001.

——. "Slouching Toward the Supply Side: Jimmy Carter and the New American Political Economy." In Fink and Graham, *Carter Presidency*, pp. 51–71.

Schulman, Bruce J., and Julian E. Zelizer, eds. *Rightward Bound: Making America Conservative in the 1970s*. Cambridge, Mass., 2008.

Schulzinger, Robert D. *A Time for War: The United States and Vietnam, 1941–1975*. New York, 1997.

Schumacher, E. F. *Small Is Beautiful: Economics as Though People Mattered*. New York, 1973.

Schuman, Howard, Charlotte Steeh, and Lawrence Bobo. *Racial Attitudes in America: Trends and Interpretations*. Cambridge, Mass., 1985.

Schwartz, Bernard. *Behind "Bakke": Affirmative Action and the Supreme Court*. New York, 1988.

Schweizer, Peter, and Rochelle Schweizer. *The Bushes: Portrait of a Dynasty*. New York, 2004.

Scott, Wilbur J. *The Politics of Readjustment: Vietnam Veterans Since the War.* New York, 1993.

Sears, David O., and Jack Citrin. *Tax Revolt: Something for Nothing in California.* Cambridge, Mass., 1985.

Shafer, Byron E., and Richard Johnston. *The End of Southern Exceptionalism: Class, Race, and Partisan Change in the Postwar South.* Cambridge, Mass., 2006.

Shapiro, Peter. *Turn the Beat Around: The Secret History of Disco.* London, 2005.

Shawcross, William. *Murdoch: The Making of a Media Empire.* New York, 1997.

———. *The Shah's Last Ride: The Fate of an Ally.* New York, 1988.

———. *Sideshow: Kissinger, Nixon, and the Destruction of Cambodia.* London, 1980.

Sheehan, Neil. *A Bright Shining Lie: John Paul Vann and America in Vietnam.* New York, 1989.

Sheehy, Gail. *Passages: Predictable Crises of Adult Life.* New York, 1976.

Shepard, Martin. *Fritz: An Intimate Portrait of Fritz Perls and Gestalt Therapy.* New York, 1975.

Sherry, Michael. *In the Shadow of War: The United States Since the 1930s.* New Haven, Conn., 1996.

Shi, David. *The Simple Life: Plain Living and High Thinking in American Culture.* New York, 1985.

Shilts, Randy. *And the Band Played On: Politics, People, and the AIDS Epidemic.* New York, 2000.

Shirley, Craig. *Reagan's Revolution: The Untold Story of the Campaign That Started It All.* Nashville, 2005.

Shogan, Robert. *Promises to Keep: Carter's First Hundred Days.* New York, 1977.

Shone, Tom. *Blockbuster: How the "Jaws" and Jedi Generation Turned Hollywood into a Boom-Town.* London, 2005.

Short, Philip. *Pol Pot: The History of a Nightmare.* London, 2004.

Sick, Gary. *All Fall Down: America's Fateful Encounter with Iran.* London, 1985.

———. *October Surprise: America's Hostages in Iran and the Election of Ronald Reagan.* New York, 1991.

Silberman, Charles E. *Criminal Violence, Criminal Justice.* New York, 1987.

Simon, William E. *A Time for Truth.* New York, 1978.

Sindler, Allan P. *"Bakke," "DeFunis," and Minority Admissions: The Quest for Equal Opportunity.* New York, 1978.

Skidelsky, Robert. "The Fall of Keynesianism." In David Marquand and Anthony Seldon, eds., *The Ideas That Shaped Post-war Britain*, pp. 41–66, London, 1996.

———. *John Maynard Keynes: The Economist as Saviour, 1920–1937.* London, 1992.

Skinner, Kiron K., Annelise Anderson, and Martin Anderson, eds. *Reagan in His Own Hand: The Writings of Ronald Reagan That Reveal His Revolutionary Vision for America.* New York, 2001.

Skocpol, Theda. *Diminished Democracy: From Membership to Management in American Civic Life.* Norman, Okla., 2003.

Skowronek, Stephen. *The Politics Presidents Make: Leadership from John Adams to George Bush.* Cambridge, Mass., 1993.

Skrentny, John D. *The Minority Rights Revolution.* Cambridge, Mass., 2002.

Slater, Philip. *The Pursuit of Loneliness.* Boston, 1970.

Small, Melvin. *The Presidency of Richard Nixon.* Lawrence, Kans., 1999.

Smith, Daniel A. *Tax Crusaders and the Politics of Direct Democracy.* New York, 1988.

Smith, Gaddis. *Morality, Reason, and Power: American Diplomacy in the Carter Years.* New York, 1986.

Solberg, Carl. *Hubert Humphrey: A Biography.* New York, 1984.

Sorokin, Pitirim. *The American Sex Revolution.* Boston, 1956.

Sounes, Howard. *Down the Highway: The Life of Bob Dylan.* New York, 2001.

———. *Seventies: The Sights, Sounds, and Ideas of a Brilliant Decade.* London, 2006.

Speer, James A. *New Christian Politics.* Macon, Ga., 1984.

Stallard, Karin, Barbara Ehrenreich, and Holly Sklar. *Poverty in the American Dream: Women and Children First.* New York, 1983.

Steigerwald, David. *The Sixties and the End of Modern America.* New York, 1995.

Steinfels, Peter. *The Neoconservatives.* New York, 1979.

Stephens, Mark. *Three Mile Island.* New York, 1980.

Stepick, Alex, Guillermo Grenier, Max Castro, and Marvin Dunn. *This Land Is Our Land: Immigrants and Power in Miami.* Berkeley, Calif., 2003.

Steuerle, C. Eugene. *The Tax Decade: How Taxes Came to Dominate the Public Agenda.* Lanham, Md., 1992.

Stockman, David A. *The Triumph of Politics: Why the Reagan Revolution Failed.* New York, 1986.

Stossel, Scott. *Sarge: The Life and Times of Sargent Shriver.* Washington, D.C., 2004.

Street, Joe. *The Culture War in the Civil Rights Movement.* Gainesville, Fla., 2007.

Stroud, Kandy. *How Jimmy Won: The Victory Campaign from Plains to the White House.* New York, 1977.

Stuart, Jan. *The "Nashville" Chronicles: The Making of Robert Altman's Masterpiece.* New York, 2000.

Sugrue, Thomas J. *The Origins of the Urban Crisis: Race and Inequality in Postwar Detroit.* Princeton, N.J., 2005.

Sullivan, William H. *Mission to Iran: The Last U.S. Ambassador.* New York, 1981.

Sunstein, Cass R. *After the Rights Revolution: Reconceiving the Regulatory State.* Cambridge, Mass., 2000.

Sutherland, John. *Bestsellers: Popular Fiction of the 1970s.* London, 1981.

Tedin, Kent L., David W. Brady, Mary E. Buxton, Barbara M. Gorman, and July L. Thompson. "Social Background and Political Differences Between Pro- and Anti-ERA Activists." *American Politics Quarterly* 5, no. 3 (July 1977), pp. 395–404.

Terkel, Studs. *Working.* New York, 1972.

Tewkesbury, Joan. *Nashville: An Original Screenplay.* New York, 1976.

Thernstrom, Stephan, and Abigail Thernstrom. *America in Black and White: One Nation, Indivisible.* New York, 1999.

Thom, Mary. *Inside "Ms.": 25 Years of the Magazine and the Feminist Movement.* New York, 1997.

———, ed. *Letters to "Ms.," 1972–1987.* New York, 1987.

Thomson, David, and Ian Christie, eds. *Scorsese on Scorsese.* London, 1989.

Todd, Olivier. *Cruel April: The Fall of Saigon.* New York, 1990.

Toffler, Alvin. *The Third Wave.* New York, 1980.

Torgoff, Martin. *Can't Find My Way Home: America in the Great Stoned Age, 1945–2000.* New York, 2004.

Troy, Gil. *Affairs of State: The Rise and Rejection of the Presidential Couple Since World War II.* New York, 1997.

———. *Morning in America: How Ronald Reagan Invented the 1980s.* Princeton, N.J., 2005.

Turner, Frederick Jackson. "The Significance of the Frontier in American History." *Report of the American Historical Association* (1893), pp. 199–227.

Tyler, Imogen. "From 'The Me Decade' to 'The Me Millennium': The Cultural History of Narcissism." *International Journal of Cultural Studies* 10, no. 3 (2007), pp. 343–63.

Tyroler, Charles, and Max Kampelman, eds. *Alerting America: The Papers of the Committee on the Present Danger*. Washington, D.C., 1984.

Updike, John. *Rabbit Is Rich*. New York, 1981.

Vance, Cyrus R. *Hard Choices: Critical Years in America's Foreign Policy*. New York, 1983.

Van Deburg, William L. *New Day in Babylon: The Black Power Movement and American Culture, 1965–1975*. Chicago, 1993.

Van der Linden, Frank. *The Real Reagan*. New York, 1981.

Vecoli, Rudolph. "The Resurgence of American Immigration History." *American Studies International* 17 (Winter 1979), pp. 46–66.

Viguerie, Richard. *The New Right: We're Ready to Lead*. Falls Church, Va., 1981.

Vogel, Ezra F. *Japan as Number One: Lessons for America*. Cambridge, Mass., 1979.

Volcker, Paul, and Toyoo Gyohten. *Changing Fortunes: The World's Money and the Threat to American Leadership*. New York, 1992.

Walker, J. Samuel. *Three Mile Island: A Nuclear Crisis in Historical Perspective*. Berkeley, Calif., 2004.

Walker, Samuel. *The Rights Revolution: Rights and Community in Modern America*. New York, 1998.

Wallace, Michele. *Black Macho and the Myth of the Superwoman*. New York, 1979.

Wandersee, Winifred D. *On the Move: American Women in the 1970s*. Boston, 1988.

Wanniski, Jude. "The Mundell-Laffer Hypothesis—a New View of the World Economy." *Public Interest* 39 (Spring 1975), pp. 31–52.

———. *The Way the World Works*. New York, 1978.

Watson, Mary Ann. *Defining Visions: Television and the American Experience Since 1945*. Fort Worth, Tex., 1998.

Weiner, Tim. *Legacy of Ashes: The History of the CIA*. London, 2007.

Wells, Tim. *444 Days: The Hostages Remember*. New York, 1985.

Werth, Barry. *31 Days: The Crisis That Gave Us the Government We Have Today*. New York, 2006.

Wetterhahn, Ralph. *The Last Battle: The Mayaguez Incident and the End of the Vietnam War*. New York, 2001.

W. E. Upjohn Institute for Employment Research. *Work in America*. Cambridge, Mass., 1973.

Whitaker, John C. *Striking a Balance: Environment and Natural Resources in the Nixon-Ford Years*. Washington, D.C., 1976.

White, Mel. *Stranger at the Gate: To Be Gay and Christian in America*. New York, 1995.

White, Theodore H. *America in Search of Itself: The Making of the President, 1956–1980*. New York, 1982.

———. *The Making of the President, 1972*. New York, 1973.

Will, George F. *The Pursuit of Happiness and Other Sobering Thoughts*. New York, 1978.

Wills, Garry. *Lead Time: A Journalist's Education*. Garden City, N.Y., 1983.

———. *Reagan's America: Innocents at Home*. London, 1988.

Wilson, James Q. *Thinking About Crime*. New York, 1975.

Wilson, William Julius. *The Declining Significance of Race*. Chicago, 1980.

——. *The Truly Disadvantaged: The Inner City, the Underclass, and Public Policy*. Chicago, 1987.

Witcover, Jules. *Marathon: The Pursuit of the Presidency, 1974–1976*. New York, 1977.

——. *Very Strange Bedfellows: The Short and Unhappy Marriage of Richard Nixon and Spiro Agnew*. New York, 2007.

Woodward, Bob. "Gerald R. Ford." In Caroline Kennedy, ed., *Profiles in Courage for Our Time*, pp. 295–315. New York, 2002.

Woodward, Bob, and Carl Bernstein. *The Final Days*. London, 1977.

Wooten, James. *Dasher: The Roots and the Rising of Jimmy Carter*. London, 1978.

Wozniak, Steve. *iWoz*. New York, 2006.

Wuthnow, Robert. "The Political Rebirth of American Evangelicals." In Liebman and Wuthnow, *New Christian Right*, pp. 167–87.

——. *The Restructuring of American Religion: Society and Faith Since World War II*. Princeton, N.J., 1988.

Yankelovich, Daniel. *New Rules: Searching for Self-Fulfillment in a World Turned Upside Down*. New York, 1981.

Yergin, Daniel. *The Prize: The Epic Quest for Oil, Money, and Power*. New York, 1992.

Young, Perry Deane. *God's Bullies: Power Politics and Religious Tyranny*. New York, 1982.

Zaretsky, Natasha. *No Direction Home: The American Family and the Fear of National Decline, 1968–1980*. Chapel Hill, N.C., 2007.

Zimmerman, Jonathan. *Whose America? Culture Wars in the Public Schools*. Cambridge, Mass., 2002.

Zumwalt, Elmo. *On Watch: A Memoir*. New York, 1976.

## ILLUSTRATION CREDITS

**A NOTE ABOUT THE AUTHOR**

Born in Shropshire, England, in 1974, Dominic Sandbrook was educated at Oxford, St. Andrews, and Cambridge. He taught American history at the University of Sheffield and is a former senior fellow of the Rothermere American Institute, Oxford. He is the author of *Eugene McCarthy: The Rise and Fall of Postwar American Liberalism*, as well as three best-selling books on modern British history, *Never Had It So Good*, *White Heat*, and *State of Emergency*. He is also a journalist and critic, writing regularly for the London *Daily Telegraph*, *Daily Mail*, and *Sunday Times*, and a columnist for the *New Statesman* and *BBC History*.

## A NOTE ON THE TYPE

The text of this book was set in Electra, a typeface designed by W. A. Dwiggins (1880–1956). This face cannot be classified as either modern or old style. It is not based on any historical model, nor does it echo any particular period or style. It avoids the extreme contrasts between thick and thin elements that mark most modern faces, and it attempts to give a feeling of fluidity, power, and speed.

**COMPOSED BY** *North Market Street Graphics, Lancaster, Pennsylvania*

**PRINTED AND BOUND BY** *Berryville Graphics, Berryville, Virginia*

**DESIGNED BY** *Iris Weinstein*